ESSAYS ON ARISTOTLE'S ETHICS

MAJOR THINKERS SERIES

General Editor

Amélie Oksenberg Rorty

ESSAYS ON
ARISTOTLE'S ETHICS

Edited by Amélie Oksenberg Rorty

UNIVERSITY OF CALIFORNIA PRESS
Berkeley   Los Angeles   London

University of California Press
Berkeley and Los Angeles, California

University of California Press, Ltd.
London, England

Library of Congress Cataloging in Publication Data
Main entry under title:

Essays on Aristotle's ethics.

    (Major thinkers series : 2)
    1. Aristoteles. Ethica—Addresses, essays, lectures.
2. Ethics—Addresses, essays, lectures. I. Rorty,
Amélie. II. Series
B430.A5R66   171'.3   78-62858

Printed in the United States of America

1 2 3 4 5 6 7 8 9

Contents

Acknowledgments

Thomas Nagel, "Aristotle on *Eudaimonia*" originally appeared in *Phronesis* 17 (1972), 252-259.

J. L. Ackrill, "Aristotle on *Eudaimonia*" originally appeared in the *Proceedings of the British Academy* 60 (1974), 339-359.

David J. Furley, "Self-Movers" originally appeared in *Aristotle on Mind and the Senses: Proceedings of the Seventh Symposium Aristotelicum*, ed. G. E. R. Lloyd and G. E. L. Owen (Cambridge: At the University Press, 1978), pp. 165-179.

J. L. Ackrill, "Aristotle on Action" originally appeared in *Mind* 87 (1978), 595-601.

J. O. Urmson, "Aristotle's Doctrine of the Mean" originally appeared in the *American Philosophical Quarterly* 10 (1973), 223-230.

Richard Sorabji, "Aristotle on the Role of Intellect in Virtue" originally appeared in the *Proceedings of the Aristotelian Society*, n.s. 74 (1973-74), 107-129.

David Wiggins, "Deliberation and Practical Reason" originally appeared in a different form in the *Proceedings of the Aristotelian Society*, n.s. 76 (1975-76), 29-51.

David Wiggins, "Weakness of Will, Commensurability, and the Objects of Deliberation and Desire" originally appeared in the *Proceedings of the Aristotelian Society*, n.s. 79 (1978-79), 251-277.

John M. Cooper, "Aristotle on Friendship" originally appeared as "Friendship and the Good" in *The Philosophical Review* 86 (1977),

290-315, and as "Aristotle on the Forms of Friendship" in *The Review of Metaphysics* 30 (1976-77), 619-648.

Kathleen V. Wilkes, "The Good Man and the Good for Man in Aristotle's Ethics" originally appeared in *Mind* 87 (1978), 553-571.

John McDowell, "The Role of *Eudaimonia* in Aristotle's Ethics" originally appeared in *The Proceedings of the African Classical Association* 15 (1980).

Amélie Oksenberg Rorty, "The Place of Contemplation in Aristotle's *Nicomachean Ethics*" originally appeared in a different form in *Mind* 87 (1978), 343-358.

The Editor gratefully acknowledges permission to reprint these papers.

Introduction

Philosophers and classicists have recently turned their attentions to Aristotle's ethics, particularly to the *Nicomachean Ethics*. While they have been at great pains to reconstruct the historical Aristotle rather than to mine him for insights he might not have recognized as his, the interest that classical philosophers have in these issues is not merely historical or antiquarian.

Some of the impetus for the return to Aristotelian scholarship in ethics has come from a sense of the impoverishment of recent moral philosophy. In the wake of the influence of emotivism in ethics, moral philosophers concentrated on meta-ethical issues, on methodological problems in moral reasoning. They were concerned to analyze the meanings of moral terms or concepts and to map the relations among them (e.g., do judgments about what is *right* presuppose those about what is *good*?); they also examined the logical status of moral imperatives, the rules for valid arguments in ethics (e.g., must conclusions about obligations rest on arguments that are not empirical?). The primary battles were between naturalists, who thought that ethical assertions and imperatives could be supported by empirical arguments, and those who thought that moral imperatives ultimately require a ground of obligation that no factual considerations could provide.

But not all recent moral philosophy is methodological in character. Moral philosophers in the Kantian tradition attempt to establish the necessary a priori principles to which moral reasoning must conform and by

1

which moral reasoning must be (freely) motivated. They want to determine the conditions for rational moral agency. When they deal with specific moral issues, their question is: what does *rationality* require? The question whether human beings are rational in the required sense, whether rational moral motivation can provide a model of characteristic psychological motivation, is covered, on the philosophical side, by the dictum that "ought implies can." The actual investigation of the connections between rational and psychological motivation is delegated to the empirical sciences, whose results were thought to be in principle irrelevant to the analysis of the necessary conditions for morality.

In contrast, utilitarians do not draw sharp distinctions between philosophical and empirical investigations. They take the evaluation of actions or practices, rather than of motivating principles, to be the proper domain of ethics. The task of the moral philosopher is primarily to determine the principles by which to guide policy decisions and secondarily to evaluate such policies. But utilitarians discovered unexpected difficulties in applying the principle of utility to generate specific policy decisions. Some of these problems—problems about constructing a calculus to measure happiness (or utiles)—were regarded as technical difficulties in the theory. How are the various measures of happiness—intensity, complexity, duration, range—to be weighted? How are interpersonal comparisons of utility to be measured? Other problems that utilitarians now face are moral rather than technical. It has been argued that the consistent application of act utilitarianism generates moral decisions that violate common moral sensibility. On the utilitarian principle it would be right to punish the innocent if doing so could promote the greatest happiness of the greatest number. The only thing wrong with such a policy would be that adopting it might generate more harm than benefits: in itself it could not be wrong.

Aristotle's perspective on the issues of moral philosophy is entirely different from the perspective of either Kantians or utilitarians. He writes the *Nicomachean Ethics* for those who have the traits, constitutions, and some of the habits that would enable them to become virtuous, for those capable of responsible action, and particularly for those who might be statesmen. His emphasis is on character and its proper development rather than on the rules for the propriety of rational motives or for the evaluation of the consequences of actions. Ethics appears firmly within psychology, and it moves to political theory. Since ethics is practical, issuing in particular actions, it requires a dialectical, rather than a scientifically demonstrative, approach. We cannot deduce moral truths from universal necessary premises. Nevertheless, general truths established by reasoned investigations into common beliefs and common practices, along with an understanding of the general constitutions and character of the species, can give a solid, though not a certain, basis for generalization in ethics.

But the recent return to a study of Aristotle is no more motivated by the attractions of naive and patchwork eclecticism than it is by the delights of antiquarian researches. We cannot use Aristotle to solve problems within the Kantian and utilitarian systems. The problems of those systems do not arise, and can barely even be formulated, within Aristotle's ethics; much less can they find their proper solution there. By the same token one could not show that Aristotle was free of those problems. What attracts contemporary classical philosophers to Aristotle's ethics is rather the investigation of a self-contained, enormously illuminating theory, rich in practical consequences as well as in theoretical insights.

Characteristically, Aristotle canvasses previous opinions on a large range of subjects: What is happiness? What are the conditions for responsible and voluntary action? How does a person become virtuous? In what does virtue consist, and how are the virtues to be characterized? What is the contribution of intellectual knowledge to the moral practical life? What is pleasure? What are the respective claims of the practical political life and the contemplative life? Aristotle's own account is constructed by attempting to do justice to the varieties of previous opinions.

The articles in this collection are arranged to form a continuous commentary on the *Nicomachean Ethics* following the organization and sequence of discussions and arguments of that book. There is considerable scholarly debate about whether the *Nicomachean Ethics* forms a continuous whole: there is some evidence that the central "common" books—Books 5-7—really belong to the *Eudemian Ethics*; and there is a consensus that the *NE* is a compendium of lecture notes. But tracing the pattern of the present organization of the book is quite independent of determining whether that organization was imposed by an editor (or by Aristotle himself), who took material from different strata of Aristotle's writing, incorporating earlier material into much later work. Even if the book is a thing composed of threads and patches, the organization of those threads and patches composes a perfectly coherent pattern.

The *Ethics* begins with the question "What is the good for man?" After a dialectical survey of opinion on the subject, it presents the claim that *eudaimonia*—happiness, or, as it has sometimes been translated, human flourishing—is the good for man. Happiness is then defined as an activity of the soul in accordance with rationality and virtue, with human excellence. But since there are several types of excellence, the question arises: Which is the best and most complete? Does happiness consist in an active and comprehensive practical life or in the exercise of man's highest and best faculties, those for contemplation? The papers by Thomas Nagel and J. L. Ackrill pose this question.

What are the metaphysical and psychological presuppositions that guide and inform Aristotle's discussions in the *Ethics*? How do the final causes of a species define the excellences of that species? What metaphysical views about the actualization of potentialities stand behind the arguments in the *Ethics*? David J. Furley's "Self-Movers" and T. H. Irwin's "The Metaphysical and Psychological Basis of Aristotle's Ethics" investigate these questions.

The definition of virtue is offered in Book 2: Virtue is a dispositional characteristic, a *hexis* concerning actions and reactions (*pathe*) involving choice; it consists in acting in a mean relative to us, a mean that is defined by a rational principle of the sort followed by a person of practical wisdom. The substance of Books 2-6 consists of an analysis of the components and consequences of this definition.

Virtue is a hexis: The development of proper habits, especially habits concerning pleasures, is the key to the moral life. The article by M. F. Burnyeat gives an account of Aristotle's views about how to become good and how a person's ends, his actions, and his thoughts are developed through practice.

Virtue is a hexis concerning actions: Aristotle turns in Book 3 to an account of voluntary action. Ackrill's "Aristotle on Action" is an analysis of Aristotle's account of how action is distinguished from behavior and how actions are identified by the agent's intentions.

Virtue is a hexis concerning actions and pathe: L. A. Kosman analyzes the much-neglected function of (proper) reactions and emotions in moral life. He discusses the relations between *pathos* and *praxis*, asking whether habits of pathe can be developed in the same way as habits of praxeis.

Virtue is a hexis... involving choice: In Book 3 Aristotle gives an analysis of the conditions for voluntary and for deliberate action. For an action to be voluntary, it is necessary that the agent could have done otherwise, that he knew what he was doing, that he was not compelled. In "Reason and Responsibility in Aristotle," Irwin gives a detailed account of the presuppositions and consequences of Aristotle's discussion of the conditions of responsible action.

Virtue... consists in acting in a mean relative to us: Aristotle next turns, in Book 4, to an analysis of the mean, and how it is to be found in a range of particular virtues. J. O. Urmson gives an account of what it is to act "in a mean relative to us": he defends Aristotle against charges of recommending mediocre moderation. Books 3-5 give an account of the range of traditional virtues, showing how they involve acting in the mean. David Pears takes one of the most difficult of these—courage—

and discusses Aristotle's attempt to construe it as involving action within the mean. Bernard Williams analyzes Aristotle's treatment of justice, arguing that there is an ambiguity in the discussion: Aristotle wavers between defining justice as a character trait and defining it by a set of rules.

Virtue . . . consists in acting in a mean defined by a rational principle: In Book 6 Aristotle gives an account of the intellectual activities and their contributions to practical life. Richard Sorabji's "Aristotle on the Role of Intellect in Virtue" gives an account of the various intellectual virtues and their practical applications.

Virtue . . . consists in acting in a mean defined by a rational principle such as would be used by a person of wisdom: The article by David Wiggins examines the relation between the ends of the *phronimos* and his practical reasoning. He discusses the way in which those ends become ingredient in and constitutive of actions. In his paper on the weakness of the will, Wiggins shows how, on Aristotle's account, an agent's desires and patterns of deliberation are formed by, and express, his ends. He explores the ways in which this view of the relation between character and action leaves room for the phenomena of weakness of will.

Since Book 6 leaves us with a strong identification between virtue and practical wisdom, the question arises whether Aristotle has returned to Socratic intellectualism and whether he must treat all forms of wrongdoing as involuntary ignorance. Amélie O. Rorty examines the distinctions among the varieties of wrongdoing—vice, *akrasia*, and self-indulgence—resting on the distinctions among the intellectual virtues which are drawn in Book 6. She argues that the discussion of pleasure in Book 7 is meant to continue the discussion of akrasia: it provides an explanation of why the *akrates* forgets what he knows.

John M. Cooper analyzes Books 8 and 9, the extended discussion of friendship and its function in developing and exercising the self-reflective traits of the virtuous.

Because Aristotle still needs to establish that the virtuous life *is* happy and that it brings the goods and satisfactions traditionally associated with eudaimonia, he returns to a discussion of pleasure in Book 10. Julia Annas analyzes Aristotle's treatment of pleasure, discussing the relation between his theory and earlier, traditional theories.

After the discussion of pleasure, Aristotle returns to an examination of eudaimonia. John McDowell argues that eudaimonia is the end for the sake of which all action is taken, rather than the end for the sake of which it ought to be undertaken. His analysis leads him to a discussion of the proper domain of praxeis as the subjects of *prohairesis*; of the proper significance of the *ergon* argument; of the appropriate reading of Aristotle's explanation of akrasia; and of the proper scope of Aristotle's notion of "the moral," in contrast with modern notions.

There are still some questions to be settled: the claims of the theoretical life as the most virtuous, happy life. The papers by Kathleen V. Wilkes and Rorty evaluate the respective claims of the practical and the theoretical life: they attempt to answer the questions posed by Nagel and Ackrill.

Book 10 ends with a transition to the tasks of the statesman, the tasks of constructing the sort of polity in which the citizens can lead virtuous lives. Martha Craven Nussbaum analyzes the ideals of self-realization and self-respect that guide Plato and Aristotle, contrasting their views on the relation between the political and the moral life.

Because there is an excellent bibliography of work on Aristotle's ethics in the recently published and easily available *Articles on Aristotle: Ethics and Politics,* edited by Jonathan Barnes, Malcolm Schofield, and Richard Sorabji (London: Duckworth, 1977; New York: St. Martin's Press, 1978), pp. 219-233, I have decided not to include a bibliography. Instead readers are urged to consult the Barnes, Schofield, and Sorabji volume. Malcolm Schofield and Richard Sorabji kindly encouraged the publication of this book as a sequel to theirs. They made numerous helpful suggestions, as did J. L. Ackrill, M. F. Burnyeat, and David Wiggins.

We are also grateful to Gregory Vlastos, who despite his suspicions of what he regards as Aristotle's pernicious moral and political elitism, has influenced many of the contributors to this volume. Vlastos's work as a scholar, as a teacher and colleague, and as a man of practical wisdom in the academy has been responsible for some of the remarkable vitality of classical philosophy in recent years.

1

Aristotle on Eudaimonia[1]

Thomas Nagel

The *Nicomachean Ethics* exhibits indecision between two accounts of *eudaimonia*—a comprehensive and an intellectualist account. According to the intellectualist account, stated in Book 10, chapter 7, eudaimonia is realized in the activity of the most divine part of man, functioning in accordance with its proper excellence. This is the activity of theoretical contemplation. According to the comprehensive account (described as "secondary" at 1178a9), eudaimonia essentially involves not just the activity of the theoretical intellect but the full range of human life and action, in accordance with the broader excellences of moral virtue and practical wisdom. This view connects eudaimonia with the conception of human nature as composite, that is, as involving the interaction of reason, emotion, perception, and action in an ensouled body.

The *Eudemian Ethics* exhibits a similar indecision, less elaborately expressed. Most of the work expounds a comprehensive account, but the following passage appears at its close:

Therefore whatever mode of choosing and of acquiring things good by nature—whether goods of body or wealth or friends or the other goods—will best promote the contemplation of God, that is the best mode, and that standard is the finest; and any mode of choice and acquisition that either through deficiency or excess hinders us from serving and from contemplating God—that is a bad one. This is how it is for the soul, and this is the soul's best standard—to be as far as possible unconscious of the irrational part of the soul, as such. [1249b17-24]

Although this passage is admittedly somewhat isolated, it seems to support the conclusion that Aristotle was tempted by an intellectualist (or perhaps spiritualist) account of the ends of life in the *Eudemian Ethics*. In fact, considering the emphasis on the divine element in our nature at the end of the *Nicomachean Ethics* (1178b7-33), it does not seem out of line to bring God into the matter at the end of the *Eudemian*. "Intellectualist" may be rather too dry a term for the almost Augustinian sentiments that can be detected in both works.

Since the philosophical issue between these two positions arises in virtue of the ambivalence of the *Nicomachean Ethics* alone, I shall discuss it largely in that setting. I shall also comment on the relation of this issue to the psychology of the *De anima*. There is a connection between intellectualist tendencies in the *Ethics* and Aristotle's view of the relation between *nous* and the rest of the soul. But the latter view appears to me to contain as much indecision as the former. It is because he is not sure who we are that Aristotle finds it difficult to say unequivocally in what our eudaimonia consists, and how the line is to be drawn between its constituents and its necessary conditions. Moreover, I shall argue that intellectualism has strong defenses even without a two-substance theory of human beings.

Aristotle's program is compactly set out in *NE* 1.7, beginning at 1097b-22. If we are not to stop with the truism that the supreme human good is eudaimonia, we must inquire into the *ergon* of man, since if something has an ergon, that thing's good is a function of its ergon. The ergon of a thing, in general, is what it does that makes it what it is. Not everything has an ergon, for there are things to be which is not to do anything. But when something has an ergon, that thing's good is specified by it. The proper ergon of man, by which human excellence is measured, is that which makes him a man rather than anything else. Humans do a great many things, but since some are done equally well, or better, by plants, fish, and animals, they are not among the things to do which is to be human.

This lands us immediately in difficulty, for the inference seems unsound. If the feature of life unique to humans could exist in the absence of those features which humans share with the beasts, the result would be not a human being but something else. And why should we take the highest good of a rarefied individual like that as the ultimate end for complicated and messy individuals like ourselves? One would expect at the very least that the *interaction* between the function that differentiates us from animals and the functions that we share with them would play a role in the definition of eudaimonia. This would mean including the *practical* exercise of the rational faculty as well as the contemplative.

Suppose we pursue this line of criticism further, however, by asking whether we should not demand the inclusion of still more functions in the definition of human ergon and hence of human good. What about health, for example, or fertility? It will be objected that these fail to meet an essential condition for inclusion: the condition of autonomy.[2] This condition states that the fundamental elements of human good cannot be due simply to luck. And health, for example, can be the result of sheer good fortune rather than of a man's own efforts.

But the basis of this objection must be examined. It stems, presumably, from the condition that good is tied to ergon or functioning; and what simply *befalls* a thing, whether that thing be a man or a plant, is not an instance of its functioning or malfunctioning. Therefore, if I contract cholera, the intrusion of the hostile bacilli is a calamity, but not a malfunction of mine, hence not to be weighed in counting me *eudaimon* or not. Its *effect* on me, however, is certainly a malfunction. And why should this purely physical malfunction not be *in itself* a deviation from my human well-being (rather than just because of its deleterious effects on the life of reason)? If it is excluded on the ground that sweating, throwing up, and shuddering with fever are not things that *I do*, then the question has been begged. For the issue is precisely whether the account of what a person is and does should include or exclude the bodily functions that he shares with animals and even plants. If digesting, for instance, is something a clam does, why is it not something a human does as well—and something to do which is part of being human, even though it does not require *effort*?

In neither the *De anima* nor the *Nicomachean Ethics* is the nutritive element excluded from the human soul; yet it is not one of the aspects of human functioning which Aristotle is willing to regard as a measure of eudaimonia. This position has considerable intuitive appeal. If we could see why nutrition is assigned such a low status, we might have a clue to the train of thought that tempts Aristotle to pare away everything except the intellect, till the only thing that intrinsically bears on eudaimonia is the quality of contemplative activity.[3]

Let me introduce a homely example. A combination corkscrew and bottle-opener has the function of removing corks and caps from bottles. This is a simple ergon, which allows us to evaluate the implement in terms of its capacity for successful performance. However, it does not seem simple enough to escape the question Aristotle has raised. It removes bottle-caps, to be sure. But since it has that function in common with any mere bottle-opener, *that* cannot be the special ergon (*to idion*) of our implement—the ergon by which its excellence is judged. So, by elimination, *to idion* must be removing corks. Unfortunately that is a capacity it shares with mere corkscrews, so that can't be part of its special ergon either. Obviously this argument is no good. The thing must have a simple conjunctive ergon, and its excellence is a function of both conjuncts.

Why won't such a reduction work for the case of the human soul and eudaimonia? We have dispensed with digestion and procreation on the ground that clams do it too. Sensation and desire are common to dogs. So we are left with reason. But the gods have reason without having these other capacities, so *that* isn't the peculiar ergon of man, either. Therefore we must abandon this method of arguing by elimination and acknowledge that man has a conjunctive ergon that overlaps the erga of gods and dogs as a combination corkscrew and bottle-opener combines the functions of corkscrews and bottle-openers. They just happen to find themselves in the same ergon box.

If this argument were correct, it would support not just a comprehensive position extending to nonintellectual areas of consciousness and activity but the inclusion of all the lower life functions in the measure of human excellence. But in fact the conjunctive picture of the component capacities of the human soul is absurd, and if we can say why it is absurd, we may be able to understand why Aristotle accords to reason the title of *ergon idion* of man, despite the fact that it, like digestion, might be shared by other beings as well.

The operative idea is evidently that of a hierarchy of capacities. The life capacities of a complex organism are not all on a level: some serve to support others. This is not so easy to account for clearly. Take for example the prima facie subservience of nutrition to perception and locomotion. That might be a ground for denying that nutrition is part of the special ergon of a higher animal. But perception and locomotion—for example, in a giraffe—largely serve the ends of nutrition and reproduction, so the case is unclear. What is the point of being a giraffe? A giraffe leads a certain type of active life supported by complex metabolic, digestive, and circulatory processes and ordered in such a way as to permit those processes to proceed efficiently. One thing is clear: its walking and seeing and digesting are not simply three separate activities going on side by side in the same individual, like a doll that wets, cries, and closes its eyes. A giraffe is one organism and its functions are coherently organized. Its proper excellence is not just the conjunction of the special excellences of its component functions but the optimal functioning of the total system in the giraffe's *life*. And the highest-level account of this will be concerned not with blood pressure and peristalsis but with activity— some of which, admittedly, helps to control blood pressure and provide material for peristalsis.

The main difference between a human being and a giraffe is that a human being has reason and that his entire complex of organic functions supports rational as well as irrational activity. There is of course feedback as well: in humans not only perception and locomotion but also reason is employed in the service of nutrition and reproduction. Reason is also involved in the control of perception, locomotion, and desire. Nevertheless the highest-level account of a human life puts all the other functions into a supportive position in relation to rational activity. And although reason helps us to get enough to eat and move around, it is not subservient to those lower functions. Occasionally it may have to serve as the janitor or pimp of the passions, but that is not basically what it is *for*. On one plausible view reason, despite its continual service to the lower functions, is what human life is all about. The lower functions serve it, provide it with a setting, and are to some extent under its control, but the dominant characterization of a human being must refer to his reason. This is why intellectualism tempts Aristotle, and why a conjunctive position, which lets various other aspects of life into the measure of good, is less plausible. Neither a conjunctive nor a disjunctive view about eudaimonia is adequate to these facts. The supreme good for man must be measured in terms of that around which all other human functions are organized.

But at this point it is essential to recall that much of the practical employment of reason is in the service of lower functions. Is this a proper exercise of that faculty, or does it have a point beyond the uses of cleverness, prudence, and courage, beyond the rational calculation of the most sensible way to spend one's time and money or to organize society? This question prompts Aristotle to pass from the vague characterization that human life, as opposed to other life, is rational, to a consideration of the *objects* best suited for the exercise of this capacity. This is a peculiar question, which did not arise about giraffes. The nonrational activity of giraffes and its feedback on the metabolic functions seems at first sight a perfectly satisfactory model, and we might be tempted to apply it to humans. Why can't we reach a parallel account of proper human functioning by just adding reason to the top of the class of capacities that cooperate in an organized fashion to further the life of the individual? Why should there be any doubt that the use of reason to earn a living or procure food should belong to the central function of man?

The answer is as follows. Human possibilities reveal that reason has a use beyond the ordering of practical life. The circle of mutual support between reason, activity, and nutrition is not completely closed. In fact all of it, including the practical employment of reason, serves to support the individual for an activity that completely transcends these wordly concerns. The model of feedback does not work for the ergon of humans, because the best and purest employment of reason has nothing to do with daily life. Aristotle believes, in short, that human life is not important enough for humans to spend their lives on. A person should seek to transcend not only his individual practical concerns but also those of society or humanity as a whole.

In *NE* 6.7, while arguing that *sophia* is the highest type of knowledge, and knowledge of the highest objects, he says (1141a21-23): "For it is absurd to think that Political Science or Prudence is the loftiest kind of knowledge, inasmuch as man is not the highest thing in the universe." Theoretical and practical matters must compete for the attention of the rational faculty; and the capacity that enables humans to concentrate on subjects more elevated than themselves at the same time spoils them for lowlier concerns. The imperfection of applications of reason to practical matters is that these applications make human life the primary object of rational attention, whereas with reason man has become the only creature capable of concentrating on what is higher than himself and thereby sharing in it to some extent. His time is, so to speak, too valuable to waste on anything so insignificant as human life.

This does not mean that there is no distinction between excellence and depravity in the practical domain. It is certainly better to exercise reason well in providing for one's needs and in dealing with others—that is, to have moral virtue—than to exercise it badly. But this is essentially a caretaker function of reason, in which it is occupied with matters—that is, the sordid details of the life of a complex person—far below those which it might be considering if it had more time and were less called upon merely to *manage*.

It is this point of view, I believe, which dominates chapters 7 and 8 of Book 10, where the intellectualist account of eudaimonia receives its strongest endorsement. Even there the possibility of doubt is acknowledged. Aristotle appears uncertain whether the result is to be described as a strictly human good. Having argued the claims of the contemplative life on a variety of grounds, he breaks in at 1177b27 with the remark that such a life would be higher than human. It is achieved not in virtue simply of being a man but in virtue of something divine of which men partake. Nevertheless this divine element, which gives us the capacity to think about things higher than ourselves, is the highest aspect of our souls, and we are not justified in forgoing its activities to concentrate on lowlier matters—namely, our own lives—unless the demands in the latter area threaten to make contemplation impossible. As he says at 1177b-33, we should not listen to those who urge that a human should think human thoughts and a mortal mortal ones. Rather we should cultivate that portion of our nature which promises to transcend the rest. If anyone insists that the rest belongs to a complete account of human life, then the view might be put, somewhat paradoxically, by saying that comprehensive human good isn't everything and should not be the main human goal. We must identify with the highest part of ourselves rather than with the whole. The other functions, including the practical employment of reason itself, provide support for the highest form of activity but do not enter into our proper excellence as primary component factors. This is because men are not simply the most complex species of animal but possess as their essential nature a capacity to transcend themselves and become like gods. It is in virtue of this capacity that they are capable of eudaimonia, whereas animals are incapable of it, children have not achieved it, and certain adults, such as slaves, are prevented from reaching it.

Perhaps this is an unsatisfactory view of human nature and hence an unsatisfactory view of what it is for a human being to flourish. I believe it is a compelling position, however, and one that does not have to depend on a denial of the hylomorphic doctrine of the soul. It might be challenged in either of two ways. One might simply deny that the ergon of man is single and allege that it is a collection of sub-erga without orderings of priority and support—like those of a many-bladed knife. This leaves us uncertain how to draw the line against good digestion as a component of eudaimonia (rather than just as a contribution to it). A second method would be to preserve the assumption that the ergon of man is one, but to offer a different account of its organization, according to which the highest-level specification of human capacities is not just intellectual but involves both theoretical and practical concerns. While this seems to me the most promising line of attack, I shall not pursue it here.

NOTES

1. These remarks derive from comments on a paper by John M. Cooper, "Intellectualism and Practical Reasoning in Aristotle's Moral Philosophy," presented at a meeting of the Society for Ancient Greek Philosophy, in New York, 28 December 1969. My research was supported in part by the National Science Foundation.

2. Cooper is responsible for pointing out the importance of this condition. His paper cites three textual statements of it: *EE* 1215a12-19, *NE* 1099b18-25, and most explicitly *Politics* 1323b24-29.

3. This conclusion would require explanation even if a two-substance reading of the *Ethics* were correct. That is, even if the psychology of the *Nicomachean Ethics* included a soul composed of both a form or primary actuality of the body

and a pure intellect that was distinct from this, we would still have to ask why the proper function of the hylomorphic section was not counted in the assessment of eudaimonia. And I suspect that any account that made sense of the restriction in light of the two-substance theory could be applied with equal success to justify corresponding restrictions on what counts toward eudaimonia on a purely hylomorphic theory of persons, where nous, instead of being another soul, was just the highest type of first-order actuality in the complex—distinguishable only in thought from the other parts of the soul, and not really *distinct* from them. That Aristotle shares this view is shown by a parenthetical remark in *NE* 1.13, where he is considering which part of the soul possesses the excellence that is to be identified with eudaimonia. "Whether these two parts are really distinct in the sense that the parts of the body or of any other divisible whole are distinct, or whether though distinguishable in thought as two they are inseparable in reality, like the convex and concave sides of a curve, is a question of no importance for the matter in hand" (1102a30-34).

2

Aristotle on Eudaimonia

J. L. Ackrill

Like most great philosophical works Aristotle's *Nicomachean Ethics* raises more questions than it answers. Two central issues as to which it is not even quite clear what Aristotle's view really is are, first, what is the criterion of right action and of moral virtue? and, second, what is the best life for a man to lead? The first question is raised very explicitly by Aristotle himself at the beginning of Book 6, where he recalls that moral virtue (or excellence of character) was defined as a mean determined by the rule or standard that the wise man would employ, and now says that this statement though true was not clear: we need also to discover what *is* the right rule and what *is* the standard that fixes it. Unfortunately he does not subsequently take up this question in any direct way. The difficulty about the second question is not that he fails to discuss it—it is after all the center of his target—or that he fails to answer it, but that he seems to give two answers. Most of the *Ethics* implies that good action is—or is a major element in—man's best life, but eventually in Book 10 purely contemplative activity is said to be perfect *eudaimonia*; and Aristotle does not tell us how to combine or relate these two ideas.

One way of answering the two questions brings them into close connection. For if Aristotle really holds, in the end, that it is contemplation (*theoria*) that is *eudaimonia*, a possible or even inevitable answer to the first question is that right actions are right precisely in virtue of their

15

making possible or in some way promoting *theoria*, and that the states of
character commendable as virtues or excellences are so commendable
because they are states that favor the one ultimately worthwhile state
and activity, the state of theoretical wisdom (*sophia*) and the activity of
theoria. Professors Gauthier and Jolif, in their admirable commentary,[1]
take some such view; and since they recognize that Aristotle sometimes
stresses the "immanent character" of moral action they find here a major
incoherence in his thought. They themselves seek to explain why he falls
into this incoherence (recognizing the moral value of virtuous actions
and yet treating them as "means to arrive at happiness") by suggesting
that in his account of action he brings into play ideas that properly apply
not to actions but to productive activities—he fails to free himself from
an inappropriate way of speaking and from the associated way of
thinking.

Professor Hintikka too has argued recently[2] that Aristotle remained
enslaved to a certain traditional Greek way of thought ("conceptual teleology") and that this is why his analysis of human action uses the ends-
and-means schema though this "does not sit very happily with some of
the kinds of human action which he considered most important."
According to Hintikka, since Aristotle could not "accommodate within
his conceptual system" an activity that did not have an end (*telos*), he
had to provide a *telos* even for activities he wanted precisely to distinguish from productive activities, and so he fell into the absurdity of
speaking of an activity of the former kind as *its own end.*

Mr. Hardie,[3] also believing that Aristotle fails in Book 1 of the *Nicomachean Ethics* to think clearly about means and ends, claims that this
fact helps to explain why he confuses the idea of an "inclusive" end and
the idea of a "dominant" end. Hardie attributes to Aristotle as an "occasional insight" the thought that the best life will involve a variety of aims
and interests, but finds that the other doctrine—that *eudaimonia* must be
identified with one supremely desired activity—is Aristotle's standard
view, and not merely something to which he moves in Book 10. Dr.
Kenny[4] agrees in interpreting Book 1 as treating the pursuit of *eudaimonia* as the pursuit of a single dominant aim: "Aristotle considers happiness only in the dominant sense."

II

In this lecture I should like to question some of the views about the *Nicomachean Ethics* that I have been outlining. In particular I shall contend
that in Book 1 (and generally until Book 10) Aristotle is expounding an

"inclusive" doctrine of *eudaimonia,* and that there is no need to suppose that he was led into confusion on this matter by some inadequacy in his understanding of means and ends.

III

It may be useful, before turning to the text, to make two preliminary points. First, the terms "inclusive" and "dominant," which have been prominent in recent discussion, need to be used with some care. The term "inclusive" suggests the contrast between a single aim or "good" and a plurality, while the term "dominant" suggests the contrast between a group whose members are roughly equal and a group one of whose members is much superior to the rest. When used as a contrasting pair of terms how are they to be understood? By "an inclusive end" might be meant any end combining or including two or more values or activities or goods; or there might be meant an end in which different components have roughly equal value (or at least are such that no one component is incommensurably more valuable than another). By "a dominant end" might be meant a *monolithic* end, an end consisting of just one valued activity or good, or there might be meant that element in an end combining two or more independently valued goods which has a dominant or preponderating or paramount importance. The former (strong) sense of "dominant end" is being used when Hardie claims that in Book 1 (apart from his occasional insight) Aristotle "makes the supreme end not inclusive but dominant, the object of one prime desire, philosophy"; the latter (weak) sense when he says that "some inclusive ends will include a dominant end." It is clearly in the strong sense of "dominant" (and the contrasting weak sense of "inclusive") that Hardie and Kenny claim that Book 1 expounds *eudaimonia* as a dominant and not an inclusive end.

The second point concerns the nature of Aristotle's inquiries about *eudaimonia* in Book 1. It is not always easy to decide what kind of question he is answering—for example, a linguistic, a conceptual, or an evaluative question. At one end of the scale there is the observation that all agree in using the *word eudaimonia* to stand for that which is "the highest of all practicable goods," and that all take the expressions "living well" and "doing well" to be equivalent to it. At the other end there is the substantial question "what is *eudaimonia*?," a question that invites alternative candidates and to which Aristotle offers, with his own arguments, his own answer (or two answers). In between there are remarks about *eudaimonia,* and about what we all think about it, which could be construed as helping to elucidate the very concept of *eudaimonia* or as moves towards answering the question "what is *eudaimonia*? what form of life satisfies the concept?" It will not be necessary to attempt exact demarcations. But it is important to bear in mind that two things might be meant by the assertion that Aristotle makes *eudaimonia* a dominant end: first, that, according to him, consideration of the logical force of the term *eudaimonia*, and of its place in a network of concepts ("good," "end," etc.), shows that *eudaimonia* is necessarily a dominant end; or (secondly) that, according to him, although it is not part of the very *concept* of *eudaimonia* that it should be a single activity, yet it is in fact so— the life that fills the bill proves on inquiry to be "monolithic" although this is not directly deducible from the terms of the bill itself. In claiming that Aristotle expounds in Book 1 an "inclusive" and not a monolithic doctrine of *eudaimonia* I was referring both to his account of the concept itself—or what one might call in a broad sense the meaning of the word— and to his view about the life that satisfies the concept and deserves the name.

                                    IV

At the very start of the *Nicomachean Ethics* (1.1) we find Aristotle expounding and using the notion of an end, and connecting it with terms like "good" and "for the sake of." He distinguishes between activities that have ends apart from themselves (e.g., products like bridles or outcomes like victory), and others that are their own ends. After remarking that where an activity has a separate end that end is better than the activity, he says that one activity or skill, *A*, may be subordinate to another, *B*, and he gives some examples, cases in fact where what *A* produces is used or exploited by *B*. He then makes a statement that is often neglected and never (I think) given its full weight: "it makes no difference whether the activities themselves are the ends of the actions or something else apart from these, as in the case of the above-mentioned crafts" (1094a16-18). He is clearly saying here that his point about the subordination of one activity to another has application not only where (as in his examples) the subordinate activity produces a product or outcome which the superior activity uses, but also where the subordinate activity has no such end apart from itself but is its own end. Commentators have not been sufficiently puzzled as to what Aristotle has in mind. It is after all not obvious what is meant by saying that one action or activity is for the sake of another, in cases where the first does not terminate in a product or outcome which the second can then use or exploit. It is no doubt true, as Stewart remarks, that a builder may walk to his work. But it is not clear that walking to get to the building-site is properly to be regarded as an activity that is its own end. Walking to get somewhere is more like fighting for victory: its success or failure depends on the outcome, and that is its point.

It would be natural to expect that corresponding to the initial distinction between activities there would be a fundamental distinction between the ways in which activities of the two different types could be subordinate to another activity. The idea of the use or exploitation of a product or outcome being inappropriate where the subordinate activity is not directed to a product or outcome, what immediately suggests itself instead is a relation like that of part to whole, the relation an activity or end may have to an activity or end that includes or embraces it. Many different types of case could be distinguished. But, to seek no more precision than immediate needs require, one may think of the relation of putting to playing golf or of playing golf to having a good holiday. One does not putt *in order to* play golf as one buys a club in order to play golf; and this distinction matches that between activities that do not and those that do produce a product. It will be "because" you wanted to play golf that you are putting, and "for the sake" of a good holiday that you are playing golf; but this is because putting and golfing are *constituents of* or *ingredients in* golfing and having a good holiday respectively, not because they are necessary preliminaries. Putting *is* playing golf (though not all that playing golf is), and golfing (in a somewhat different way) *is* having a good holiday (though not all that having a good holiday is).

Now the idea that some things are done for their own sake and may yet be done for the sake of something else is precisely the idea Aristotle will need and use in talking of good actions and *eudaimonia*. For *eudaimonia* —what all men want—is not, he insists, the result or outcome of a lifetime's effort; it is not something to look forward to (like a contented retirement), it is a life, enjoyable and worth while all through. Various bits of it must themselves be enjoyable and worth while, not just means for bringing about subsequent bits. That the primary ingredients of *eudaimonia* are for the sake of *eudaimonia* is not incompatible with their being ends in themselves; for *eudaimonia* is constituted by activities that are ends in themselves. More of this in a moment. The main point I want to make about *Nicomachean Ethics* 1.1 is that it is unreasonable to suggest that Aristotle is slipping into an inherited usage when in fact he is very obviously introducing and expounding distinctions vital for what follows. Hintikka, in the paper from which I have quoted, seems to assume that the world *telos* ("end") must mean an end produced by (instrumental) means, and that "for the sake of" necessarily brings in the idea of an end separate from the action. But the word *telos* is by no means so narrowly confined, and it is absurd to rely on the implications (or supposed implications) of a translation rather than on the substance of what the philosopher is evidently saying. Why should Hintikka, in any case, identify having a "well-defined end or aim" with doing something as a means to producing an outcome? If I play chess because I want to enjoy myself, is not that a well-defined aim? And can we ourselves not speak of "doing something for its own sake"? Of course an action cannot be "a means to performing itself"—but Aristotle's words are not, like these, nonsensical; and his meaning seems clear enough.

Unlike Hintikka, Gauthier and Jolif have no trouble over action being its own end. They recognize the importance of "l'affirmation par Aristote, dès les premières lignes de l'Éthique, du caractère immanent de l'action morale," though they add regretfully that its force is "limitée par les lignes 1094a16-18 [quoted above] et par la contradiction qu'elles incluent." In their note on this last sentence they say: "on ne voit pas... comment les actions morales, dont c'est la nature d'être à elles-mêmes leur propre fin, pourront ultérieurement être ordonnées à autre chose pour former une série hiérarchisée." They call this one of Aristotle's "incohérences foncières." "Au lieu d'être sa fin à elle-même, l'action morale devient un moyen de *faire* autre chose qu'elle-même, le bonheur." I have tried to suggest that this offending sentence may in fact invite us to think of a kind of subordination which makes it perfectly possible to say that moral action is for the sake of *eudaimonia* without implying that it is a means to producing ("faire") something other than itself.

V

Aristotle's thought on this matter is more fully developed in the first part of chapter 7 (1097a15-b21), where he starts from points about "good" and "end" and "for the sake of" which come from chapter 1 and concludes with the statement that *eudaimonia* is something final and self-sufficient, and the end of action. In asking what we aim at in action, what its "good" is, Aristotle says that if there is just one end (*telos*) of all action, this will be its good; if more, they will be its good. Now, he goes on, there evidently *are* more ends than one, but some are chosen for something else, and so they are not all *teleia* ("final"). But the best, the highest good, will be something *teleion*. So if only one end is *teleion*, that will be what we are looking for; if more than one are *teleia*, it will be the one that is most *teleion* (τελειότατον).

No reader or listener could be at all clear at this point as to what is meant by "most *teleion*." The word *teleion* has been introduced to separate off ends desired in themselves from ends desired as means to other ends. What is meant by the suggestion that there may be degrees of finality among ends all of which are desired for themselves? Aristotle goes on at once to explain how, among ends all of which are final, one end can be more final than another: *A* is more final than *B* if though *B* is sought for its own sake (and hence is indeed a final and not merely intermediate goal) it is also sought for the sake of *A*. And that end is more final than any other, final without qualification (τέλειον ἁπλῶς), which is always sought for its own sake and never for the sake of anything else. Such, he continues, is *eudaimonia*: there may be plenty of things (such as pleasure and virtue) that we value for themselves, but yet we say too that we value them for the sake of *eudaimonia*, whereas nobody ever aims at *eudaimonia* for the sake of one of them (or, in general, for anything other than itself).

Surely Aristotle is here making a clear conceptual point, not a rash and probably false empirical claim. To put it at its crudest: one can answer such a question as "Why do you seek pleasure?" by saying that you see it and seek it as an element in the most desirable sort of life; but one cannot answer or be expected to answer the question "Why do you seek the most desirable sort of life?" The answer to the question about pleasure does not imply that pleasure is not intrinsically worth while but only a means to an end. It implies rather that pleasure *is* intrinsically worth while, being an element in *eudaimonia*. *Eudaimonia* is the most desirable sort of life, the life that contains all intrinsically worthwhile activities.

This idea, that takes up the thought suggested in the last sentence of chapter 1, is expressed again in the following lines, where the term "self-sufficient" is introduced. That is self-sufficient (αὔταρκες) in the relevant sense which, taken alone (μονούμενον), makes life desirable and lacking in nothing (μηδενὸς ἐνδεᾶ). *Eudaimonia* does just that. For, Aristotle says, we regard it as the most worth while of all things, *not* being counted as one good thing among others (πάντων αἱρετωτάτην μὴ συναριθμουμένην)—for *then* (if it *were* simply the most worth while of a *number* of candidates) the addition of any of the other things would make it better, more worth while—and it would *not* have been lacking in nothing. He is saying, then, that *eudaimonia*, being absolutely final and genuinely self-sufficient, is more desirable than anything else in that it *includes* everything desirable in itself. It is best, and better than everything else, not in the way that bacon is better than eggs and than tomatoes (and therefore the best *of the three* to choose), but in the way that bacon, eggs, and tomatoes is a better breakfast than either bacon or eggs or tomatoes— and is indeed the best breakfast without qualification.

It is impossible to exaggerate the importance of this emphatic part of

chapter 7 in connection with Aristotle's elucidation of the concept of
eudaimonia. He is not here running over rival popular views about what
is desirable, nor is he yet working out his own account of the best life. He
is explaining the logical force of the word *eudaimonia* and its relation to
terms like "end," and "good." This is all a matter of report and analysis,
containing nothing capable of provoking moral or practical dispute.
Aristotle's two points are: (i) you cannot say of *eudaimonia* that you seek
it for the sake of anything else, you can say of anything else that you seek
it for the sake of *eudaimonia*; (ii) you cannot say you would prefer *eudaimonia* plus something extra to *eudaimonia*. These points are of course
connected. For if you could say that you would prefer *eudaimonia* plus
something extra to *eudaimonia*, you could say that you sought *eudaimonia* for the sake of something else, namely the greater end consisting
of *eudaimonia* plus something extra. The first point is that *eudaimonia*
is inclusive of all intrinsic goods; and if that is so by definition, it is unintelligible to suggest that *eudaimonia* might be improved by addition.
This ends and clinches one part of Aristotle's discussion, and he marks
quite clearly the transition to the different and more contentious question to be dealt with in what follows: "*eudaimonia*, then, is something
final and self-sufficient, and is the end of action. However, while the
statement that *eudaimonia* is the chief good probably seems indisputable
(ὁμολογούμενόν τι), what is still wanted is a clearer account of *what it is*."

It is not necessary to claim that Aristotle has made quite clear how
there may be "components" in the best life or how they may be interrelated. The very idea of constructing a compound end out of two or
more independent ends may rouse suspicion. Is the compound to be
thought of as a mere aggregate or as an organized system? If the former,
the move to *eudaimonia* seems trivial—nor is it obvious that goods can
be just added together. If the latter, if there is supposed to be a unifying
plan, what is it? For present purposes it is enough to claim that Aristotle
understands the concept of *eudaimonia* in such a way that the *eudaimonia* necessarily includes all activities that are valuable, that he applies
the notion of *A*'s being for the sake of *B* to the relation between any such
activity and *eudaimonia*, and that it is in this sense that he holds that
good actions are for the sake of *eudaimonia*.

Commentators have not, I think, given due weight to these interlock-
ing passages about the finality and self-sufficiency of *eudaimonia*.
Gauthier and Jolif follow Burnet in giving a correct account of the latter
passage, and they say: "le bonheur ne saurait s'*additioner* à quoi que ce
soit pour faire une *somme* qui vaudrait mieux que lui; il est en effet lui-
même la somme qui inclut tous les biens." Unfortunately they fail to connect this with the earlier passage in which Aristotle speaks of ends that

are indeed final yet subordinate to one supreme end, *eudaimonia*. Nor do they refer to this text when considering (and rejecting) the suggestion that Aristotle's general idea of *eudaimonia* is of a whole composed of parts.

Mr. Hardie also recognizes that the self-sufficiency passage suggests an inclusive end; yet he offers the previous sections as part of the evidence that Aristotle's main view is different. Aristotle's explicit view, he says, "as opposed to his occasional insight, makes the supreme end not inclusive but dominant, the object of one prime desire, philosophy. This is so even when, as in E.N. I.7, he has in mind that, *prima facie*, there is not only one final end"; and Hardie then quotes: "if there are more than one, the most final of these will be what we are seeking." I do not think that "*prima facie*" does justice to "if more than one, then the most final." It seems to imply that Aristotle is saying that though there may seem at first sight to be several final ends there can really be only one final end, and the others must really be only means to it. But there is, of course, no "seems." The hypothesis is that there *are* several final ends. When Aristotle says that if so we are seeking the most final he is surely not laying down that only one of them (*theoria*) is *really* a final end. What he has in mind with this use of "most final" must be discovered by considering the explanation he immediately gives (an explanation which Hardie, very remarkably, does not quote). For certainly the idea of degrees of finality calls for elucidation. The explanation he gives introduces the idea of an objective that is indeed a final end, sought for its own sake, but is nevertheless also sought for the sake of something else. So the *most* final end is that never sought for the sake of anything else because it includes all final ends. That there *is* such an end whenever there are several final ends is not then a piece of unargued dogma; it follows naturally from the very idea of an "inclusive" end. Such, Aristotle immediately continues, is *eudaimonia* (not, we note, *theoria* or *nous*)—and he then passes to the self-sufficiency point which, as Hardie himself recognizes, implies the inclusive approach.

Dr. Kenny, on the other hand, in his paper "Happiness," actually reverses the sense of the passage about self-sufficiency. He attributes to Aristotle the remark that "other goods added to happiness will add up to something more choiceworthy," and he says that this "makes it clear that Aristotle did not consider happiness an inclusive state made up of independent goods." This interpretation will not, I am convinced, survive a careful consideration of the immediate context (especially Aristotle's description of the "self-sufficient" as "lacking nothing" and his statement that *eudaimonia* is best "not being counted as one good thing among others"). Nor are other passages in which the quite special character of the concept *eudaimonia* is dwelt upon compatible with this interpretation of *eudaimonia* as happiness. It is indeed only if one is willing, with Kenny, to treat "happiness" as a fair translation of the word *eudaimonia* that one can feel the slightest temptation to take the self-sufficiency passage as he does. This willingness is the fatal flaw in his paper considered as a contribution to the understanding of Aristotle. The point is important enough to deserve a brief digression.

It may be true, as Kenny says, that happiness is not everything, that not everyone seeks it, and that it can be renounced in favor of other goals. What Aristotle says, however, is that *eudaimonia* is the one final good that all men seek; and he would not find intelligible the suggestion that a man might renounce it in favor of some other goal. Nor is Aristotle here expressing a personal view about what is worth while or about human nature. It is in elucidation of the very *concept* that he asserts and emphasizes the unique and supreme value of *eudaimonia* (especially in 1.4, 7, 12). The word *eudaimonia* has a force not at all like "happiness," "comfort," or "pleasure," but more like "the best possible life" (where "best" has not a narrowly moral sense). This is why there can be plenty of disagreement as to what form of life *is eudaimonia*, but no disagreement that *eudaimonia* is what we all want.

Kenny points out that someone might renounce happiness because the only possible way to achieve his own happiness would involve doing wrong. He writes: "In such a case, we might say, the agent must have the long-term goal of acting virtuously: but this would be a goal in a different way from happiness, a goal identified with a certain kind of action, and not a goal to be secured by action." How would the situation envisaged be described by Aristotle? If I find it necessary to undergo privation or suffering in order to do my duty I shall have to recognize that my life will fall short of *eudaimonia*. But what I *renounce* is comfort in favor of right action, not *eudaimonia* in favor of right action. Nor could Aristotle possibly contrast *eudaimonia* with acting virtuously on the ground that *eudaimonia* is "a goal to be secured by action" while acting virtuously is "a goal identified with a certain kind of action." Comfort and prosperity may be goals to be secured by action, but *eudaimonia* is precisely *not* such a goal. It is doing well (εὐπραξία), not the result of doing well; a life, not the reward of a life. Nearly everything Kenny says about happiness goes to show that the word "happiness" is not a proper translation of the word *eudaimonia*.

VI

On what other grounds, then, may it be contended that Aristotle's idea of *eudaimonia* in Book 1 is the idea of a "dominant" end, a "single object of desire"? Hardie takes the notorious first sentence of chapter 2 as expressing this idea—not indeed as asserting it, but as introducing it hypothetically. The sentence and following section run as follows in Ross's translation:

If, then, there is some end of the things we do, which we desire for its own sake (everything else being desired for the sake of this), and if we do not choose everything for the sake of something else (for at that rate the process would go on to infinity, so that our desire would be empty and vain), clearly this must be the good and the chief good. Will not the knowledge of it, then, have a great influence on life? Shall we not, like archers who have a mark to aim at, be more likely to hit upon what is right?

It is commonly supposed that Aristotle is guilty of a fallacy in the first sentence, the fallacy of arguing that since every purposive activity aims at some end desired for itself there must be some end desired for itself at which every purposive activity aims. Hardie acquits Aristotle. He writes:

Aristotle does not here prove, nor need we understand him as claiming to prove, that there is only *one* end which is desired for itself. He points out correctly that, if there are objects which are desired but not desired for themselves, there must be *some* object which is desired for itself. The passage further suggests that, if there were *one* such object and one only, this fact would be important and helpful for the conduct of life.

It is, however, not so easy to acquit Aristotle. For what would be the point of the second part of the protasis—the clause "if we do not choose everything for the sake of something else" together with the proof that we do not—unless it were intended to establish as true the first part of the protasis—"there is some end of the things we do, which we desire for its own sake (everything else being desired for the sake of this)"? If the second part were simply a correct remark—irrelevant to, or a mere consequence of, the first part—it would be absurdly placed and serve no purpose.

The outline structure of the sentence is "if *p* and not *q*, then *r*." Nobody will suggest that the not-*q* is here a condition additional to *p*. The one natural way to read the sentence as a coherent whole is to suppose that *q* is mentioned as the only alternative to *p*. In that case a proof of not-*q* would be a proof of *p*. So when Aristotle gives his admirable proof of not-*q* he is purporting to prove *p*; and the sentence as a whole therefore amounts to the assertion that *r*.

This interpretation is confirmed by the fact that in what follows Aristotle does assume that *r* is true. Hardie attributes to him the suggestion that if there *were* only one object desired for itself, this fact *would* be important. But what Aristotle says is that knowledge of it "*has* (ἔχει) a great influence"; and he says we must try "to determine what it *is* (τί ποτ᾽ ἐστί), and of which of the sciences or capacities it *is* the object"; and he proceeds to try to do so.

There is, then, a fallacious argument embedded in the first sentence of chapter 2. But further consideration of the context and Aristotle's general approach may help to explain and excuse. What, after all, is the conclusion to which Aristotle's argument is directed? That there is some end desired for itself, everything else being desired for it. This need not be taken to mean that there is a "single object of desire," in the sense of a monolithic as opposed to "inclusive" end. Indeed the immediately following references to the political art as *architectonic* and as having an end that *embraces* the ends of other arts are themselves (as Hardie allows) indicative of an inclusive conception. If, however, the idea is admitted of an end that includes every independently desired end, the possibility presents itself of constructing one (inclusive) end from any plurality of separate ends and of speaking of the one compound or inclusive end as the highest good for the sake of which we seek each of the ingredient ends.

Enough has been said about other passages to suggest that this notion is indeed central to Aristotle's account of *eudaimonia* in Book 1. The sentence at the beginning of chapter 2 precedes a passage that points to the inclusive conception. It immediately follows (and is connected by an inferential particle with) the remark I discussed earlier to the effect that activities that have no separate product can nevertheless be subordinate to and for the sake of higher activities—a remark which itself invites interpretation in terms of "inclusive" or "embracing" ends. This being the context and the drift of Aristotle's thought it is perhaps not so surprising that he should commit the fallacy we have found it impossible to acquit him of. For the fallacy would disappear if an extra premise were introduced—namely, that where there are two or more separate ends each desired for itself we can say that there is just one (compound) end such that each of those separate ends is desired not only for itself but also for *it*.

VII

Up to the middle of 1.7, then, Aristotle has explained that the concept of *eudaimonia* is that of the complete and perfectly satisfying life. He has also mentioned various popular ideas as to what sort of life would fulfill that requirement, and he has accepted without discussion some fairly obvious views about certain goods that presumably deserve a place in the best life. Next, in the second part of chapter 7, he develops the *ergon* argument, thus beginning to work out his own account. Something must now be said about the way in which this argument terminates.

Consideration of man's *ergon* (specific function or characteristic work) leads Aristotle to the thesis that *eudaimonia,* man's highest good, is an active life of "the element that has a rational principle." This would of course cover practical as well as theoretical rational activity. However, Aristotle's final conclusion adds what is usually taken to be a restriction to theoretical or contemplative thought, *theoria,* and to express therefore a narrow as opposed to an inclusive view of *eudaimonia.* For he says: "the good for man turns out to be the activity of soul in accordance with virtue, and if there are more than one virtue, in accordance with the best and most complete" (or "most final," *teleiotaton*); and it is supposed that this last must refer to *sophia,* the virtue of *theoria.* However, there is absolutely nothing in what precedes that would justify any such restriction. Aristotle has clearly stated that the principle of the *ergon* argument is that one must ask what powers and activities are peculiar to and distinctive of man. He has answered by referring to man's power of thought; and that this is what distinguishes man from lower animals is standard doctrine. But no argument has been adduced to suggest that one type of thought is any more distinctive of man than another. In fact practical reason, so far from being in any way less distinctive of man than theoretical, is really more so; for man shares with Aristotle's god the activity of *theoria.*

Aristotle does have his arguments, of course, for regarding *theoria* as a higher form of activity than practical thought and action guided by reason. He will even come to say that though it is not *qua* man (but *qua* possessing something divine) that a man can engage in *theoria,* yet a man (like any other system) is most properly to be identified with what is best and noblest in him. But it is clear that these arguments and ideas are not stated in the *ergon* argument and involve quite different considerations. The only proper conclusion of the *ergon* argument would be: "if there are more than one virtue, then in accordance with all of them." This is precisely how the conclusion is drawn in the *Eudemian Ethics* (1219a35-39): "Since we saw that *eudaimonia* is something complete [*teleion*], and life is either complete or incomplete, and so also virtue—one being whole virtue, another a part—and the activity of what is incomplete is itself incomplete, *eudaimonia* must be the activity of a complete life in accordance with complete virtue (κατ᾽ ἀρετὴν τελείαν)." The reference to whole and part makes clear that by "complete virtue" here is meant all virtues.

If, then, the *Nicomachean Ethics* addition—"if there are more than one virtue, in accordance with the best and most complete"—is a reference by

Aristotle to a "monolithic" doctrine, the doctrine that *eudaimonia* is really to be found in just one activity, *theoria*, it is entirely unsupported by the previous argument, part of whose conclusion it purports to be. Moreover, it is not called for—and has not been prepared for—by the conceptual clarification of the notion of *eudaimonia* earlier in the book and chapter; for it has not there been said that the end for man must be "monolithic" (or even contain a dominant component). Thus such a restriction will be an ill-fitting and at first unintelligible intrusion of a view only to be explained and expounded much later. Now this is certainly a possibility, but not, in the circumstances, a very strong one. For we are not dealing with a work that in general shows obvious signs that marginal notes and later additions or revisions have got incorporated but not properly integrated into the text. Nor is the case like that of the *De anima*, in which there are several anticipatory references to "separable reason" before that difficult doctrine is explicitly stated. For there the remarks do not appear as part of conclusions of arguments; they are the lecturer's reminders of a possibility later to be explored, they keep the door open for a new character's later arrival. Here, however, in the *Nicomachean Ethics*, something is being affirmed categorically, and at a critical stage of the work, and as a crucial part of the conclusion of a carefully constructed argument.

Is there not any alternative to construing "the best and most complete virtue" as an allusion to *sophia*? After all it must be allowed that the meaning of the expression "most complete virtue" or "most final virtue" (τελειοτάτη ἀρετή) is not perfectly obvious. An alternative may suggest itself if we recall that earlier passage in the same chapter, concerning ends and final ends. For there too there was a sudden baffling use of the term "most final"—and there it was explained. "Most final" meant "final without qualification" and referred to the comprehensive end that includes all partial ends. One who has just been told how to understand "if there are more than one end, we seek the most final" will surely interpret in a similar or parallel way the words "if there are more than one virtue, then the best and most final." So he will interpret it as referring to total virtue, the combination of all virtues. And he will find that this interpretation gives a sense to the conclusion of the *ergon* argument that is exactly what the argument itself requires.

This suggestion is confirmed by two later passages in Book 1, where Aristotle uses the term *teleia arete* and clearly is not referring to *sophia* (or any one particular virtue) but rather to comprehensive or complete virtue. The first of these passages (1.9.10) is explicitly taking up the conclusion of the *ergon* argument—"there is required, *as we said*, both complete virtue (*aretes teleias*) and a complete life." The second (1.13.1) equally obviously relies upon it: "since *eudaimonia* is an activity of soul in accordance with complete virtue (*areten teleian*), we must investigate virtue." And the whole further development of the work, with its detailed discussion of moral virtues and its stress upon the intrinsic value of good action, follows naturally if (but only if) the conclusion of the *ergon* argument is understood to refer to *complete* and not to some one *particular* virtue.

VIII

It is evidently not possible here to survey all the evidence and arguments for and against the thesis that Aristotle's account of *eudaimonia* in Book 1 is decidedly "inclusive"; but one question should be touched on briefly. If such is indeed Aristotle's account it may well be asked why he does not state it more plainly and unambiguously, using the terminology of parts and whole as in the *Eudemian Ethics*. One possibility worth considering is that he realizes in the *Nicomachean Ethics* that the notion of *parts* is really much too crude. To say that *eudaimonia* is a whole made up of parts does indeed make it quite clear that you are expounding an "inclusive" and not a "dominant" or "monolithic" end. But it leaves quite unclear what kind of partition can be meant and how such "parts" are put together. Plato already brings out in the *Protagoras* the difficulty of understanding the suggestion that there are different virtues which are "parts" of complete virtue. Aristotle is particularly conscious of the variety of ways in which different factors contribute to a good life, and also of the fact that the distinguishable is not necessarily separable. So it may be that the reason why he does not speak of parts of a whole in *Nicomachean Ethics* 1 is not that he now sees *eudaimonia* as other than inclusive, but that he now has a greater awareness of how difficult it is to say exactly how the notion of "inclusion" is to be understood. It may have seemed less misleading to speak (rather vaguely) of "contributing to a final end" than to use an expression like "parts of a whole" which sounds entirely straightforward but is not really so.

IX

I have argued with respect to *Nicomachean Ethics* 1 that when Aristotle says that A is for the sake of B, he need not mean that A is a means to subsequent B but may mean that A contributes as a constituent to B; that this is what he does mean when he says that good actions are for the sake of *eudaimonia*; and that he does not argue or imply that *eudaimonia* consists in a single type of activity, *theoria*. This is a defense of Aristotle against the charge that in Book 1 a confusion about means and ends leads him to hold that action has value only as a means to *theoria*. But the original questions are now, of course, reopened: what, according to Aristotle, does make virtuous actions virtuous? and how are action and *theoria* related in his final account of the best life for man? I shall conclude with some exceedingly brief remarks on these questions.

It might be suggested that Aristotle's answer to the first question is that actions are virtuous insofar as they promote *theoria*, even if that answer is not argued for or implied in the first book. But although Book 10, using new arguments, certainly ranks *theoria* above the life of action as a higher *eudaimonia* it does not assert roundly—let alone seek to show in any detail—that what makes any good and admirable action good and admirable is its tendency to promote *theoria*. Nor can this thesis be properly read into Aristotle's statement in Book 6 (1145a6-9) that practical wisdom does not use or issue orders to *sophia* but sees that it comes into being and issues orders for its sake. He is here concerned to deal with a problem someone might raise (1143b33-35): is it not paradoxical if practical wisdom, though inferior to *sophia*, "is to be put in authority over it, as seems to be implied by the fact that the art which produces anything rules and issues commands about that thing"? Aristotle's reply does not amount to the unnecessarily strong claim that *every* decision of practical wisdom, *every* correct judgment what to do, is determined by the single objective of promoting *theoria*. It is sufficient, to meet the difficulty proposed, for him to insist that since *theoria* is an activity valuable in itself the man of practical wisdom will seek to promote it and its virtue *sophia*, and that *that* is the relation between practical wisdom and *sophia*. To say this, that practical wisdom does not control *sophia* but makes it possible, is not to say that making it possible is the only thing that practical wisdom has to do.

It has sometimes been thought that the last chapter of the *Eudemian Ethics* offers an explicit answer to our question. Aristotle says here that whatever choice or acquisition of natural goods most produces "the contemplation of god" is best; and any that prevents "the service and contemplation of god" is bad. However, Aristotle is not addressing himself at this point to the question what makes good and virtuous actions good and virtuous. Such actions he has described earlier in the chapter as praiseworthy and as done for their own sake by truly good men. It is when he passes from good actions to things like money, honor, and friends—things which are indeed naturally good but which are nevertheless capable of being misused and harmful, and which are not objects of praise—that he raises the question of a criterion or test (ὅρος). The test is only to determine when and within what limits natural goods should be chosen or acquired, and it is to provide this test that the promotion of contemplation is mentioned. So while here, as in *Nicomachean Ethics* 10, the value of contemplation is emphasized, it is clearly not put forward as the foundation of morality or as providing the ultimate criterion for the rightness of right actions.

Aristotle does not then commit himself to the thesis that actions are valuable only insofar as they promote *theoria*. But no alternative answer to our first question seems to present itself. He holds no doubt that good actions spring from and appeal to good states of character, and that good states of character are good because they are the healthy and balanced condition of a man. But it will be obvious sooner or later that this is a circle or a blind alley. Again, it is no doubt true and important that the good man does what he does "because it is noble" (ὅτι καλόν) and that the right thing to do is what the good man would do. But such remarks do not begin to reveal any principle or test whereby the man of practical wisdom can decide what *is* the noble or the right thing to do. Perhaps indeed he can "see," without having to work out, what to do; and that will make him an admirable adviser if we want to know what to do. But if we are inquiring about the "why?" rather than the "what?" references to the good man's settled character and reliable judgment are not helpful.

The other question—what is the best life for a man to lead—also remains without a satisfactory answer. A life of *theoria* would certainly be the best of all lives—and such indeed is the life Aristotle attributes to his god. But, as he himself allows, *theoria* by itself does not constitute a possible life for a man. A man is a sort of compound (*syntheton*), an animal who lives and moves in time but has the ability occasionally to engage in an activity that somehow escapes time and touches the eternal. So you do not give a man a complete rule or recipe for life by telling him to engage in *theoria*. Any human life must include action, and in the best life practical wisdom and moral virtue will therefore be displayed as well as *sophia*. But then the question is unavoidable: if *theoria* and virtuous action are both valuable forms of activity—independently though not equally valuable—how should they be combined in the best possible human life? What really is, in full, the recipe?

Aristotle's failure to tackle this question may be due in part to the fact that he often considers a philosopher's life and a statesman's life as alternatives, following here a traditional pattern of thought, the "comparison of lives." They are indeed alternatives, if (as is presumably the case) concentration on *theoria* is incompatible with concentration on great public issues. But the philosopher's life here in question as one alternative is not a life simply of *theoria*, any more than the statesman's is a life of continuous public action. To contrast the philosopher with the statesman is to leave out of account the innumerable activities common to both. But it is precisely the relation, in the best life, between *theoria* and such activities —the ordinary actions of daily life—that requires elucidation. Insofar then as he is concerned to pick out the philosopher's life and the statesman's life as the two worthiest ideals and to rank the former higher than the latter, Aristotle is not obliged to ask how in the philosopher's life the distinctive activity of *theoria* is to be combined with humbler practical activities—any more than to ask how in the statesman's life domestic claims are to weigh against public ones.

However, there must surely be some deeper explanation why Aristotle so signally fails to attempt an answer to the question how *theoria* and virtuous action would combine in the best human life. The question is theoretically crucial for his project in the *Ethics*, and must also have been of practical importance for him. The truth is, I suggest, that the question is incapable of even an outline answer that Aristotle could accept. For he does not wish to claim that actions have value only insofar as they (directly or indirectly) promote *theoria*; and it would have been desperately difficult for him to maintain such a claim while adhering reasonably closely to ordinary moral views. But if actions can be virtuous and valuable not only insofar as they are promoting *theoria*, the need for Aristotle to give a rule for combining *theoria* with virtuous action in the best life is matched by the impossibility of his doing so, given that *theoria* is the incommensurably more valuable activity.

It may seem that one could say: maximize *theoria*, and for the rest act well; and Aristotle's own famous injunction "to make ourselves immortal as far as we can" (ἐφ᾽ ὅσον ἐνδέχεται ἀθανατίζειν) might be understood in this way. Such a rule, giving absolute priority to *theoria*, would certainly avoid conflicting claims: it will only be if and when *theoria* cannot be engaged in and nothing can be done to promote *theoria* in any way that the other value will enter into consideration. However, the consequences of such a rule would be no less paradoxical than the consequences of the outright denial of any independent value to action. For the implication of the denial is that one should do anything however seemingly monstrous if doing it has the slightest tendency to promote *theoria*—and such an act would on this view actually be good and virtuous. The implication of the absolute priority rule is also that one should do anything however monstrous if doing it has the slightest tendency to promote *theoria*—though such an act would on this view actually still be monstrous.

The only way to avoid such paradoxical and inhuman consequences would be to allow a certain amount of compromise and trading between *theoria* and virtuous action, treating the one as more important but not incomparably more important than the other. But how can there be a trading relation between the divine and the merely human? Aristotle's theology and anthropology make it inevitable that his answer to the question about *eudaimonia* should be broken-backed. Just as he cannot in the *De Anima* fit his account of separable reason—which is not the form of a body—into his general theory that the soul is the form of the body, so he cannot make intelligible in the *Ethics* the nature of man as a compound of "something divine" and much that is not divine. How can there be a coalition between such parties? But if the nature of man is thus unintelligible the best life for man must remain incapable of clear specification even in principle. Nor can it now seem surprising that Aristotle fails also to answer the other question, the question about morality. For the *kind* of answer we should expect of him would be one based on a thesis about the *nature* of man, and no satisfactory account of that kind *can* be given while the nature of man remains obscure and mysterious.

Aristotle is, of course, in good company—in the company of all philosophers who hold that one element in man is supremely valuable, but are unwilling to embrace the paradoxical and extremist conclusions about life that that view implies. And a parallel difficulty is felt in many religions by the enthusiastic. How can the true believer justify taking any thought for the future or devoting any attention to the problems and pleasures of this mortal life? *Sub specie aeternitatis* are not such daily concerns of infinitely little importance? In fact compromises are made, and theologians explain that nobody need feel guilty at making them. But the suspicion remains that a man who really believed in the supreme importance of some absolute could not continue to live in much the same way as others.

NOTES

1. R. A. Gauthier and J. Y. Jolif, *L'Éthique à Nicomaque* (Paris and Louvain, 1958-59). Quotations are from 2:5-7, 199, 574, 886.

2. J. Hintikka, "Remarks on Praxis, Poesis, and Ergon in Plato and in Aristotle," *Studia philosophica in honorem Sven Krohn—Annales Universitatis Turkuensis*, ser. B, 126 (1973), 53-62. Quotations are from pp. 54, 55, 58.

3. W. F. R. Hardie, "The Final Good in Aristotle's Ethics," in *Philosophy*, 40 (1965), 277-295. Quotations are from pp. 277 and 279. (See also Hardie's *Aristotle's Ethical Theory* [Oxford, 1968], especially chap. 2.)

4. A. Kenny, "Happiness," in *Proceedings of the Aristotelian Society*, n.s. 66 (1965-66), 93-102. Quotations are from pp. 99 and 101.

3

The Metaphysical and Psychological Basis of Aristotle's Ethics

T. H. Irwin

The beginning of Aristotle's *Ethics* is surprising. Aristotle assumes that there is some ultimate good for man, called "happiness" (*eudaimonia*), and that it is the right focus for ethical theory.[1] But what does he mean, and why does he believe this with so little argument? When he insists on this ultimate good, does he endorse an alleged psychological law that everyone pursues his own happiness? Or does he mean to advise everyone to pursue his own happiness? However we take these remarks, we may reasonably be less easily convinced by them than Aristotle is. The "law" seems to be no more than a false generalization. The advice seems less than obviously sound. And anyhow, what has all this to do with a work on ethics? Should ethical theory not be concerned with the good of others besides the agent? Does not Aristotle's egoistic assumption guarantee failure in answering the central questions of ethics? Or if we try to understand "happiness" in some way that escapes these objections, does not Aristotle's claim reduce to some useless triviality, saying that people desire most whatever they desire most?

A second surprise follows. When Aristotle offers to say what happiness is, he refers to the "function" or "characteristic activity" (*ergon*) peculiar to human beings: just as a hammer or a leg has a function, a living organism has one; a human being's function is some life of action belonging to what is rational, so that the good for man will be some realization of the soul according to virtue in action with reason. This argument is not easy to accept. Is the inference from artifacts and organs to human beings secure, or does it rely on the disputable assumption that a human being is an artifact, or else a limb of some larger organism? How is the peculiar function of human beings to be isolated, and why should it be rational activity rather than, say, combing hair or killing for pleasure? Is peculiarity a good test of anything important? What justifies the assumption that the function of a human being must be some function of his soul, and so, apparently, not of the whole human being? Is the conclusion about virtuous activity justified, and how is "virtuous" to be understood?

These questions challenge the basis of Aristotle's theory. If he has no good answers, he may still have interesting things to say on particular questions, but he has no coherent or plausible theory. To find his answers we might look at the *Ethics* itself—at the first book, where he presents these claims, and at later books where he uses them. I intend to try a different—complementary, not competitive—approach. It is familiar enough that Aristotle's ethics is supposed to be somehow closely connected to his view of human nature—whether we think that is one of his greater insights or one of his graver mistakes. But what exactly is the connection? To find it we must look outside the *Ethics*, first to his account of the soul in the *De anima*. But this account is not self-sufficient either; it relies on the results of his discussion of substance, form, and matter in the *Metaphysics*. These metaphysical questions should be our starting point.

This approach to Aristotle is not always welcomed. Some readers find in him a series of rather acute discussions of various philosophical topics rather than a comprehensive theory; and Aristotle himself insists strongly on the autonomy of different disciplines, with their own methods, assumptions, and standards of proof. He resists efforts to subordinate these disciplines to some overall view of knowledge and reality, rejecting these efforts as misguided Platonizing. Concentration on the individual treatises and discussions rather than on the Aristotelian corpus as a whole has obvious benefits; we do not have to swallow the system whole, and we avoid those scholastic codifying tendencies that force tentative inquiries from different points of view on different topics into some contrived system that may only conceal what is valuable in Aristotle. These antisystematic tendencies are especially appealing in ethics, where many doubt the legitimacy of attempted derivations of ethical conclusions from metaphysical premises—and Aristotle himself seems to be one of those doubters.

However, I do not think the attempt to find a metaphysical basis for these ethical doctrines in Aristotle is either anachronistic or philosophically fruitless; and I hope it will expose some questions of interest about his views. From his metaphysical doctrines I will try to construct an argument for Aristotle's view of the soul and for his basic ethical claims. I need to construct, not merely describe and expound; Aristotle himself does not present the continuous argument I will present. But I hope we will see why it is an Aristotelian argument. He suggests the connections between his metaphysical, psychological, and ethical doctrines, but leaves us to work them out in detail. As we try to work them out, we can see the strengths of Aristotle's position and some difficulties that he ought to answer. My brief, synoptic account of the arguments will inevitably repeat familiar points and oversimplify some difficult issues, both exegetical and philosophical. But it should isolate the main questions.

SUBSTANCE AND FORM

Aristotle claims that the soul is a substance because it is a form, assuming that substance is form. Why does he assume this? Sometimes he identifies the form with a universal—the species-property instantiated in particular material individuals.[2] In the *Metaphysics*, however, he claims that a form is a "this," a particular (*Met.* 1029a26-35; 1038b4-6; 1042a26-29); each thing is its form, or itself insofar as it has form (1035a7-8).[3] "Insofar as it has form" explains Aristotle's concern. Substances are the basic realities in the world. To find substances it is not enough to pick out the right things and identify them by properties that may be irrelevant to their being substances. Socrates is a substance insofar as he has a form, because he is a man, not because he is pale or six feet tall. The substances in the world are particular men and horses, not particular pale things or six-feet-tall things. To identify something's form is at least to identify the natural kind it belongs to.

Aristotle claims more than this, however. When he says that some substances are their form rather than their matter, he is not just saying that they belong to natural kinds but that they belong to them because of their form rather than their matter. Read one way, this claim is uncontroversial. Even a lump of gold belongs to the natural kind *gold* because it exemplifies a certain form—the structure and composition of gold. A square block of gold has a form—being square and composed of gold— and in this sense is not "mere matter." It is plain, however, that Aristotle speaks of form and matter, at least sometimes, in stricter and more controversial terms; from this point of view a form need not correspond to every natural kind, and shape or composition will be a property of the

matter, not part of the form. A natural substance's form is its characteristic function rather than its structure or composition, which are features
of its matter.

Taken this way, the claim that something is a substance because of its
form, not its matter, is controversial; it implies that Socrates is essentially a man, something performing human functions, not essentially
something with a certain kind of (nonfunctionally described) structure
and composition. How can Aristotle justify this claim? Why are the functional, not the material, properties essential to Socrates?

If something's essence is to provide a criterion of its identity at a time
and through time, then perhaps Aristotle thinks Socrates' human functions are essential to him because they provide this criterion. We know
that Socrates now is not the same kind of thing as that corpse beside him,
though they are made of the same kind of matter.[4] Socrates is a man, and
the corpse is not. We know that Socrates now and Socrates ten years ago
are the same individual even though Socrates now may have none of the
individual material particles that composed Socrates ten years ago. If
Socrates now has a wooden leg or an artificial kidney, he is not even
composed of the kind of matter that belonged to Socrates ten years ago.
But Socrates is still a man, and the same man that he was, because of his
continuous human functions.

But all this simply assumes a view about natural kinds and essences
and provides no new argument for it. If we identify Socrates with his
human functions, he does persist through changes of matter. But if we
identify him with this particular mass of material constituents, he does
not. Our judgments about his identity through time show that we are
concerned with his functions rather than his composition. They do not
justify that concern.

In any case these claims about identity fail to express Aristotle's view
of essence. Unlike some philosophers he does not identify essential properties with necessary properties.[5] For him some necessary properties are
"intrinsic concomitants" (kath' hauta sumbebēkota) that belong to something necessarily, because of its essence, but are not themselves part of
the essence (Met. 1025a30-34). Aristotle offers no clear rules for deciding
when a property is essential and when it is an intrinsic concomitant, but
he at least insists that reference to the essence explains why something
has the intrinsic concomitants it has (DA 402b16-18). A material property might be an intrinsic concomitant without being essential; certain
kinds of bodily organs may be intrinsic concomitants of animals because
the animals have the essential, nonmaterial properties they have (e.g.,
Met. 1036b28-30).

An essential property is explained by contrast with an intrinsic concomitant. If an intrinsic concomitant is a necessary property that belongs to something because of its essence, an essential property will explain the necessary properties of a natural kind. When Aristotle identifies a substance with its form, he claims that its essence is formal rather than material, that its functional properties explain its necessary properties. He needs to say more about the relevant kind of explanation; and the distinction between functional and nonfunctional properties is not always easy to draw. But at least we can see roughly what Aristotle claims about form and substance and what we should expect of any property taken to be essential.

FORM AND FUNCTION

Aristotle's natural teleology, outlined in *Physics* 2, defends the claim that a natural organism is its form by arguing that its functional properties are the essential, explanatory properties, explaining its behavior. The explanation involves the final and formal causes (here identified), two of Aristotle's "four causes." Many have remarked that Aristotle distinguishes the formal and the final cause from the efficient cause—the type of explanation closest to our conception of causal explanation—and have wrongly inferred that formal and final causation are quite separate from causal explanation as we understand it.[6] On the contrary, Aristotle defines something's nature as its internal origin of change and stability (*Phys.* 192b8-33)—his normal description of an efficient cause (cf. 192b-14 with 194b29). He then argues that something's form rather than its matter is its nature (193a28-b8); he must then associate form rather than matter with something's internal efficient cause.[7]

Later, Aristotle argues that some natural processes have final as well as material and efficient causes: they do not happen merely by necessity but also for the sake of something (198b10-199a8). An event or process is not goal-directed just because it actually achieves some result that might have been its goal; Aristotle recognizes that it may rain and spoil the crops on the threshing floor, but all the same that was not the goal of the raining (198b16-23). We are confident that the result of spoiling the crops "has nothing to do" with the rain's falling; and we are confident of this because the spoilage is causally irrelevant to the rain.[8] In genuine natural teleology, then, the result must be causally relevant to the process it explains.

Being causally relevant is different from being the cause; the future result need not be the cause of the past event, but it must be relvant to explaining why the event happened. This is easy with artifacts; screwdrivers are for driving screws because the designer intended to produce this result. Natural organisms could be understood the same way if they were artifacts produced by a cosmic designer aiming at their benefit. But this efficient cause is not necessary for Aristotle's teleological explanation. Natural selection will do as well, since here too the fact that this process produces a good for the organism does contribute to the causal explanation of the process. Natural teleology is not compatible with all conceivable efficient causes of an event; but it may be compatible with more than one.

Aristotle does not distinguish teleological description and teleological explanation, or not as clearly as he should. Teleological descriptions need not be causally relevant. Aristotle is free to remark that some processes in fact regularly benefit organisms. But to say that a process happens "for the sake of the result" or "to bring about the result" is normally to say more than that they are regularly correlated; it is normally to say that the result is causally relevant to the process. Since Aristotle wants to make the stronger claim, that some processes happen for the sake of their results, he should argue for causal relevance.[9]

We can now see how Aristotle must defend his view that substance is form. He must argue that the essential, explanatory properties of natural organisms are their form—their characteristic goal-directed activities aiming at their survival and maintenance. If this is true, then their form, not their matter, makes them the substances they are. The doctrine of natural teleology is a vital support for the claim that substance is form.

If this is Aristotle's best argument, some of his conclusions are unjustified. Perhaps the formal properties of natural organisms are essential and explanatory; for these things form is substance. But surely the same will not be true of all continuants; piles of bricks are essentially composed of bricks. For other substances besides Aristotle's favored candidates, natural organisms, substance is apparently matter.[10] Even for the favored candidates not only the formal properties are explanatory. Some features of organisms, as Aristotle himself recognizes, can be explained by reference to their material properties; why not say that they have a material as well as a formal essence? The doctrine of the four causes implies that for different explanations different essences must be recognized, since essential properties are explanatory; it therefore excludes the view that there is only one set of real natural kinds, that each thing belongs to one and only one real kind. Since kinds are identified by their essential properties, different explanations and different essential properties will place things in different natural kinds.

Aristotle does not take account of these consequences of his other views when he claims that substance is form. If he did, his unqualified claim would have to be qualified. The taxonomy that defines natural kinds by their formal and functional properties is only one correct taxonomy, reflecting one type of explanation. But if it is at least one correct taxonomy, that is what Aristotle needs for the defense of his view that the soul is form.

FUNCTION AND SOUL

Our examination of the formal and final causes in the *Physics* should help us to understand Aristotle's claim that the soul is the form of the living body and the body is matter (*DA* 412a16-21). Since form and essence are identified, Aristotle means that the soul is the essence of the living organism, that it is a substance insofar as it is ensouled. The soul is the form because the form of an organism is its life—its goal-directed pattern of activity (412b10-25). Aristotle does not insist, as he should, that this pattern of activity must be causally relevant for explaining the organism's behavior if it is to be the form (though cf. perhaps 415b8-28). But if we insist on this condition, why is the soul the form? Aristotle assumes that something's having a soul makes the difference between its being alive and its being dead. Those who have supposed that the soul is a substance, that it is not material, and that it is not the body are in a way right; for psychic states are types of goal-directed activity, not material states. But in this sense a carrot or a mollusk has an immaterial, substantial, nonbodily soul no less than a human being has.

Then is it simply an accident that both Aristotle and we speak of souls? When we speak of a soul or mind, we normally think of states of consciousness; Aristotle's theory seems to be a theory of something quite different from what concerns us in psychology or philosophy of mind. But this is a superficial answer. Aristotle's theory includes an important claim about thoughts, feelings, perceptions, and so on. A plant's digestive activities are psychic states because reference to them helps to explain the plant's behavior by seeing how it is goal-directed. Reference to perception and thought, on this view, does the same for animals and human beings.

Aristotle says that those organisms that have perception also have desire, pleasure, and pain (413b22-24).[11] An animal's action can be explained by reference to its perception and desire, and explained better than if these psychic states are neglected. If we assume with an animal as with a plant that only the organism's actual good is relevant to explanation of its behavior, much of its behavior will be hard to understand teleologically; a dog's eating a lump of red rubber or growling at a tree is no benefit to it. But if we suppose that the dog believes the rubber is a piece of meat or that there is a cat in the tree, and ascribe the right desires, its actions are intelligible. If we explain a dog's action by reference to its perceptions and desires, we can say—roughly, since some correction will be needed later (see below, "Soul and Reason")—that we attribute to it some conception of its good; we no longer explain its action only by our conception of its good but appeal to its conception too. As Aristotle suggests, perception, desire, pleasure, and pain must all be ascribed together; pleasure and pain explain what the animal desires, and without ascribing desires to the animal we would not know what perceptions to ascribe to it. Like other teleological explanations this explanation claims causal relevance: perception causes desire and desire causes action. The difference is that the action is explained by the animal's causally relevant conception of its good, not by its actual good.

This conception of the soul as form of the body does not imply that psychic states will be all and only the states we associate with consciousness; Aristotle recognizes conscious states as psychic states only insofar as perception, thought, desire, pleasure, and pain belong to an animal's conception of its good, which teleologically explains its behavior. This general conception will affect Aristotle's views of what creatures have psychic states and of when it is reasonable to ascribe psychic states to a creature. It will be easier to see what is relevant for our purpose in Aristotle's views if we compare them briefly with Descartes's more familiar views about what mental states are and when something has them. Descartes decides on quite different grounds from Aristotle's whether something has perceptions and thoughts or not.[12]

Descartes sometimes assumes that a certain kind of transparency is the mark of mental states—that I am in a mental state if and only if it seems to me that I am in it. For animals to lack mental states would be for them to lack this transparent awareness. But how do we decide that they lack it? Descartes might argue that an animal has no self-consciousness and so can never find that anything seems to itself a certain way. But what is required for self-consciousness? And if transparent awareness requires self-consciousness, might we decide that it is too much to require for mental states? Descartes begins with a criterion for mental states which each person apparently can apply in his own case; the question about animals will be whether they have anything like these familiar transparent mental states.

Descartes, however, does not leave it at that. He believes that animals are nothing more than machines and have no minds or mental states. But he does not argue that they lack transparent awareness. Instead he argues that since animals display no evidence of a capacity for such complex, creative activities as language-use, they need not have minds; they are just machines, since their movements can be explained mechanically.[13] This is an interesting but strange move by Descartes. For he does not explain why the states that must be ascribed to a language-user must be transparent introspectible states meeting his usual criterion of the mental.

Neither of Descartes's reasons for denying minds to animals is a reason for Aristotle to deny them souls. Souls need not include transparent, introspectible states, and they are not confined to creative language-users. Aristotle need not reject Descartes's claim that a mechanical explanation of all animal behavior—in Aristotle's terms, a material explanation—is possible. He can agree that every animal movement has a mechanical explanation and still insist that a teleological explanation referring to perceptions and desires is true and informative; if this is so, an animal has a soul. Descartes believes that since mind and body are different substances, the same thing cannot be both a body and a mind; if its movements can be explained in purely bodily, material, mechanical terms, it cannot have mental properties. For Aristotle it is not so simple; something that is essentially a soul can have the intrinsic concomitant of being a body, so that it necessarily has both psychic and bodily properties. The result is that for Descartes animals cannot have the transparent states introspectively familiar to us; for Aristotle animals and human beings have souls in the same way, with no appeal to introspection. The Aristotelian doctrine of soul is consistent with dualism; but it does not rest on the dualist assumptions supporting Descartes's position.

The important point to notice, for our purposes, in the rapid comparison of Aristotle and Descartes is the different role in the two theories of the subject's special access. For Descartes it has to be crucial; that is one way he identifies mental states; and it is one reason for him to deny that animals have mental states. Those who accept Descartes's conception of human mental states do not always follow him in denying mental states to animals. Instead they ascribe to animals reduced or analogical states, parasitic on the transparent states we have; but they ascribe those states that best explain the animal's behavior, since there will be no conflict with the subject's reports. For Aristotle animal psychic states are ordinary psychic states, not reduced or analogical or parasitic. It is not surprising that the explanatory constraints applying to them also apply to human psychic states. Aristotle has no reason to think that psychic states —perceptions, beliefs, desires—must be transparently accessible to the subject, and to him alone. Even if there are such states, this feature of them is not the feature that makes them psychic states. Psychic states, for human souls as for others, are those that are causally relevant to a teleological explanation of the movements of a living organism.

We have found that Aristotle recognizes a distinction between those en-souled creatures whose behavior is explained teleologically by reference to their good (plants) and those whose behavior is explained by reference to their perceptions and desires; with these creatures we appeal not just to our conception of their good but to their own conception. This is a reasonable first sketch, but it needs to be corrected. To see what is distinctive of human souls and why in particular the desire for happiness is essential to them, we must consider more carefully Aristotle's distinction between animal and rational souls.

Aristotle distinguishes them in several ways:

1. Animals lack reason and have only perception (*DA* 414b1-9).

2. They lack universal apprehension and have only perception and memory of particulars (*EN* 1147b3-5).

3. They lack deliberation and decision (*prohairesis*) (*DA* 434a5-10, *EN* 1111b8-9).

4. They lack rational desire or wish (*boulēsis*), which belongs to the rational part of the soul (*DA* 432b5); but wish is the desire for the good; without it animals can have only appetite (*epithumia*), nonrational desire for the pleasant (*DA* 414b5-6).[14]

The basic difference here is an animal's lack of reason; all the other differences are particular expressions of this one. If Aristotle's claim that they lack universal apprehension is to be at all plausible, it must mean that they are incapable of applying concepts reflectively, by rationally judging that this and that feature of a particular makes it one of a certain kind.[15] The same lack of reason makes them incapable of deliberation and decision and of any desire for the good. Desire for something as a good requires—so Aristotle assumes—the agent to consider and evaluate different options and to judge that this is better than that, not simply to be aware that he desires this more than that. To do this an agent must be able to reflect and deliberate about the different considerations affecting the desirability of this action. Since animals cannot do this, they have no desire for things as goods. They still, however, desire things as pleasant —they are aware of characteristics of things which make them desired.[16]

Animals, then, on Aristotle's view, have no *full* conception of their good; they are just aware of some things as pleasant and desire them for their pleasure. But some reference to their good is still essential. If we did not believe that an animal frequently desires what is *in fact* good for it (even though it is not aware of things as good), how would we know what desires to ascribe to it at all? If it is digging in the snow, does it want to bury itself, or does it want food and believe there is some in the snow, or does it want to keep warm and believe that the snow will keep it warm? If it finds a piece of meat, we have some reason to say that this was what it wanted.[17] If the animal is right at least fairly often, we have reasonable grounds for ascribing beliefs and desires, and some grounds for thinking they belong to genuine teleological explanations. We have no reason to ascribe to the animal itself any capacity for reflective coordination of its desires, but we cannot suppose they are totally uncoordinated and unsystematic or that they always frustrate each other; if we suppose this, we lose any reason to ascribe desires to the animal at all. If we follow Aristotle in insisting that psychic states teleologically explain behavior, we must recognize some system in the psychic states ascribed, even if we need not assume that the agent itself creates or recognizes this system.

REASON AND THE FINAL GOOD

Human, rational souls differ from animal souls in their desire for the good. A desire for something as a good is a rational desire, formed by rational reflection on the benefits of different options. I may have a rational and a nonrational desire for the same thing—I may simply be hungry for this food and also want it because I know I will not be eating for eight more hours—and either type of desire may persist without the other.

It is easy to agree with Aristotle that rational desire of this simple form is an essential feature of the human soul; and once we agree about that, the concept of a final good readily applies to a rational being's desires. Someone who can compare the benefits of different possible actions must have some conception of a final good that will be better promoted by one action than by another. Nothing very complex is needed here. If I can do x resulting in A or do y resulting in B and C, and I want A, B, and C equally, then I will choose to do y rather than x. In this case the final good I pursue is A + B + C; by reference to that I decide what is on the whole better to do.

This pattern of desire and choice, resting on a desire for a final good, is part of the human, rational, soul as Aristotle understands it; it is an essential feature, since it explains many of a human being's properties and actions. To this extent it is clear how Aristotle reaches the starting point of his ethical theory. The desire for a final good is part of the human essence and pattern of activity; Aristotle is not relying merely on common agreement or on some mere psychological generalization.

It is not quite so easy, however. For Aristotle's claims about the final good are not confined to those I have noticed. A rational agent might in particular conditions recognize that he wants A + B + C and that the rational choice is to choose A + B over C alone. But he may have no general view of what he wants in his life as a whole; he may not be able to supply the long list of elements or their complex weighting outside this or that particular situation. From the fact that in _every_ situation the agent has _some_ comparative view of the available goods Aristotle seems to infer fallaciously that there is some _one_ comparative view that the agent applies to _every_ situation.[18] The final good he assumes as an object of desire seems rather more elaborate than anything we have found in the choices of every rational agent. Surely it is clear that many human agents have no grand all-embracing desires of the kind assumed by Aristotle?

Perhaps, though, it is not so clear for someone who accepts an Aristotelian, as opposed to a Cartesian, conception of the soul and of psychic states. A Cartesian must agree that if an agent sincerely avows no desire for his final good, then he has none; the agent's own transparent access to his psychic states makes his avowal authoritative. Aristotle will not necessarily agree, if he finds that the desire for a final good explains actions that would otherwise be teleologically unexplained and unintelligible. Even if someone avows no such goal, it may guide his behavior. Someone who sees a conflict between the goals he pursues on one occasion and his longer-term goals will often try to remove the conflict by adjusting one goal to another so as to achieve the total result he prefers. We can explain and understand this pattern of choice by reference to his ultimate end, the goal he conceives as his final good. Often, indeed, we may misconceive someone's desires and actions if we do not consider his more ultimate ends. We might suppose correctly that a civil servant works hard to gain promotion; but we will not fully understand his action or his motives until we realize that he wanted promotion to some responsible position allowing him to pass secrets to the Soviet Embassy. The same action—or what looks like it—may be understood differently when we refer to his more ultimate aims; the same action coming from one person might be a rude insult, from another evidence of thoughtlessness, from a third ill-timed but well-meaning frankness. When we know the agent's ultimate motives and their connections, we understand his actions better. We saw that some system must be found in animals' actions if we are to ascribe desires to them at all. The same is true of rational actions too; but here we have reason to find the system in the agent's own reflective conception of his ends. Even if he does not realize that he conceives his ends this way, we will find evidence that he does in his actions and his views of them.

For these sorts of reasons, Aristotle can argue, the explanatory role of psychic states requires us to ascribe a desire for some overall good, some goal including the agent's other goals. Whether or not someone avows this desire does not matter. Indeed, on this view we will often trust his avowals just because they are reliable—because they generally ascribe a desire that explains his actions well. If Aristotle's general theory of the soul is understood, some common objections to his claims about the universal desire for a final good will justifiably leave him unmoved.

But this argument is not a complete defense of Aristotle. It proves at most that rational agents have some implicit, partial, not always completely coherent overall end reflecting a rough structure and order in their desires. This is not enough for Aristotle's purposes in the *Ethics.* The rational agent is supposed to aim at an overall end guided by some systematic reflective conception of his good, parallel to the political scientist's overall conception of the good of a political society (1094a26-b11). Aristotle cannot reasonably claim that everyone has this conception of his good. Perhaps we can justify the ascription of some rough conception of a final good to an agent when we seek to explain his actions. But Aristotle cannot use this argument to justify his demand for reflection about the final good; his demand requires us to reach a reflective conception which most people lack. Aristotle's claim about the final good seems to equivocate between psychological description and ethical advice; sometimes he appears to think that everyone has a conception of the final good, sometimes to advise people to acquire it, without realizing that he is making different claims.

But can Aristotle argue that the minimal, rough conception of a final good reasonably ascribed to everyone justifies his advice to acquire a clear and explicit conception of the final good? A rational agent choosing something as a good must weigh the benefits of different options on each occasion. But if he has no clear view of the preferable options from one occasion to another, he will become far less competent at deciding in particular cases too. For one relevant and important consideration is the effect of this choice on his future circumstances. If he has no view of what would be preferable in the future, or if his view is quite inconstant from one occasion to another, he is ill equipped to make a sensible choice; either he does not know how to evaluate the future effects of an action, or he may well change his mind about them later, and so he has no reason to take his present views seriously. Aristotle will correctly argue that a conception of a final good—the good to be achieved in a life as a whole —will help to avoid these faults in practical reasoning and choice. He can fairly claim that a conception of the final good is relevant for every rational agent; everyone either relies on it or has reason to rely on it because of what he already does.

Perhaps it is not so surprising after all that Aristotle sometimes seems to treat the final good as an end everyone does pursue and sometimes as an end everyone ought to pursue but may not pursue already.[19] The way in which everyone does pursue it—a rough, implicit way—gives a reason why everyone ought to pursue it—in a clear, explicit way. The human essence and form includes the pursuit of goods; it is an essential human property to reflect about comparative values; and someone who does this has reason to pursue a clearly and reflectively conceived final good, as Aristotle advises.

Aristotle's claim about happiness or the final good is a claim about human nature but not the sort of claim usually associated with psychological egoism. He is not accepting the psychological claim that people always or generally care more about benefiting themselves than about others; he is not beginning with a "realistic" assumption about the natural selfishness of human beings. He begins with an assumption about a rational being's attitude to his desires and goals, that a rational being compares the values of different actions and acts on the results of his evaluation; and he assumes that someone who acts and chooses this way has reason to follow Aristotle's advice and work out a clear and detailed conception of his final good. The final good or happiness involves the systematic satisfaction of someone's rational aims as a whole; it does not necessarily imply that everyone will or should care less about other people's interests than about his own. When we understand the grounds for Aristotle's claims about the status of the final good, we can also avoid some misinterpretations of these claims.

Aristotle's metaphysics and psychology, then, do support his ethical starting point. This starting point does not simply repeat his metaphysical conclusion about the human form and essence; he is not out just to understand and explain human action. But the metaphysical conclusion shows why someone whose action is understood and explained in this way has reason to accept Aristotle's ethical starting point.

HUMAN ESSENCE AND HUMAN FUNCTION

It is time to reconsider the function argument and the initial objections to it. The appeal to "function" or "characteristic activity" should not be challenged; the function of a living organism is just its form or essence, described in the *De anima* as its soul. Aristotle classifies the lives of different kinds of organisms just as he classifies their souls in the *De anima* (1097b33-1098a5; *DA* 414b32-415a13).[20] The doctrine of the soul as the form of the living organism explains Aristotle's conclusion that happiness will be a realization of the soul; he does not exclude the body from consideration but simply insists that happiness will involve the living being in its functional rather than its purely structural and material aspects.

The doctrine of the soul also shows why Aristotle's appeal to the peculiar activity of human beings is not as unreasonable as it might look. If x can do A, B, and C, and nothing else can do C, but other things can do A and B, we might describe x's peculiar function either as "doing A, B, and C" or as "doing C." Now it is fairly clear that Aristotle understands the peculiar activity of man in the first, inclusive way. The peculiar activity of man corresponds to the peculiar activity or way of life of plants and animals. When Aristotle says that a horse or an ox has a perceptive life (1098a1-3), he surely does not mean that it does or should spend all its life perceiving; he means that a life guided by perception is characteristic of it. Similarly, he does not mean that a human being does or should concentrate on rational thinking rather than action; he means that a human being characteristically guides his actions by practical reason.[21]

The function argument, then, summarizes the account of the human soul and essence which we have surveyed in the *De anima.* Its point is not that human beings should aim at the maximum possible difference from other living organisms but that living well for them will require the good use of characteristically human capacities and activities; the good use will be the use that promotes happiness. Aristotle makes clearer the point I have developed, that practical reason is part of the human essence and that the good life for human beings will involve the use of this essential property.

The function argument must now be clarified or corrected on one point. It is rather misleading to make it an argument about the peculiar characteristic activity of human beings, unless "human beings" is interpreted in a rather special way. According to Aristotle, it is essential to human beings that they guide their action by practical reason. Suppose we found a species of Martians who were also guided by practical reason but were anatomically and chemically quite different from us. Must we say that since practical reason is found not to be peculiar to us, it cannot be an ethically relevant characteristic?[22] On the contrary; Aristotle's argument here and his general view of the human soul require him to say that we have discovered a new variety of human beings, or perhaps that human beings and these Martians belong to a wider kind—call it "rationals"—and that the first principles of ethics rest on the characteristic activity of rationals. This possibility recalls a point noticed earlier which Aristotle does not consider enough—that from different points of view and for different purposes we may assign the same object, or even the same class of objects, to different kinds. If Aristotle recognized this, he would have to be more generous in recognizing substances than he seems to be in the *Metaphysics*. But the line of argument we have traced could still be constructed.

CONCLUSION

Our discussion has inevitably been rapid and superficial in places; we have had to survey several difficult Aristotelian doctrines to give some rough impression of how they might fit together. Moreover, we have avoided perhaps the most important and interesting question—whether Aristotle's starting points, as we have understood them, really are an adequate basis for his ethical theory. We might well suspect that the claims about happiness and the function of human beings, even if true, are too general and imprecise to support specific and precise answers to ethical questions. To see whether this suspicion is justified or not we need to examine more of Aristotle's theory and arguments. Here I have postponed that examination and simply tried to show why Aristotle starts where he does and why it is reasonable for him to start there.

If my argument has been correct, we have found that on these issues at least Aristotle is a systematic philosopher. His general reluctance to discuss nonethical topics in the *Ethics* (e.g., 1096b30-31; 1102a23-26) should not mislead us. His ethical theory is based on his psychology and therefore on his metaphysics; the starting point of ethics is a feature of human agents which is part of their soul and essence, as understood in Aristotle's general theory of substance. But I mean this to be of interest beyond its relevance to our understanding of Aristotle. I believe the line of argument traced in Aristotle succeeds in showing that the final good may be a sound starting point for ethical theory; and to that extent we have reason to take the ethical theory seriously. Aristotle's theory is not only a systematic presentation of the beliefs and prejudices of his contemporaries. It is also intended to be a theory of interest to all rational agents. I have tried to show why he is justified in saying this about the starting point of his theory; and it would be useful to see how far he is justified in saying it about the rest of the theory.

My conclusion raises a further question about Aristotle's ethical method, about the kind of argument he thinks appropriate for ethics, and about the kind he actually uses. He is sometimes supposed to regard ordinary language and ordinary beliefs as the final arbiter of the correctness of an ethical theory; the theory should begin from the difficulties raised by common beliefs and try to make the beliefs coherent, pronouncing all or most of them true. This conception of ethical argument is not just the misinterpretation of readers anxious to find their respect for common sense and ordinary language reflected in Aristotle; Aristotle himself describes his method in similar terms (1145b2-7). If my argument has been sound, it has shown that this conception of Aristotle's ethical method is at best a half-truth. His argument begins with his assumptions about happiness; and we have found that these are not arbitrary assumptions, and not merely common beliefs, but consequences of his general theory of the soul, form, and essence. Now Aristotle does not advertise these connections between his ethics on the one hand and his psychology and metaphysics on the other. But if they are real connections, they suggest a way of evaluating his ethical theory which goes beyond its fidelity to common beliefs. The argument of the *Ethics* depends on more than common sense. It depends on the whole view of natural substances outlined in Aristotle's metaphysics and psychology.

NOTES

Since this paper surveys several disputed questions, the notes are not meant to be exhaustive; they merely acknowledge some debts and mark some qualifications.

1. The *Nicomachean Ethics* begins with the good for man, the *Eudemian Ethics* with eudaimonia. For present purposes I do not distinguish the two; but I do not think Aristotle regards "The good for man is eudaimonia" as a tautology.

2. The *Categories* clearly identifies the *eidos* with the universal, the second substance. *Physics* 1-2 is less clear on this; but it *never* insists, as the *Metaphysics* does, that the eidos is a "this," or that there are particular as well as universal forms.

3. Some of the questions raised by Aristotle's remarks are well discussed in E. M. Hartman, *Substance, Body, and Soul* (Princeton, 1977), esp. chap. 2.

4. This point needs to be stated carefully, since Aristotle sometimes says that the matter of a man must be potentially a man; and a corpse is not. Though Socrates and the corpse may be made of the same kind of matter, they are not both made of the matter of a man.

5. Contrast, e.g., the account of essential properties in A. Plantinga, *The Nature of Necessity* (Oxford, 1974), esp. pp. 55 f. Locke's real essences, however, have the explanatory features of Aristotle's essences (though with a different kind of explanation). To be exact, essential properties, as Aristotle conceives them, need not all be necessary—but that requires further discussion.

6. See, e.g., J. M. E. Moravcsik, "Aristotle on Adequate Explanation," *Synthese* 28 (1974), 3-17. On teleological explanation and causal relevance see, e.g., L. Wright, "Functions," *Philosophical Review* 82 (1973), 139-168, and *Teleological Explanations* (Berkeley, Los Angeles, London, 1976), chap. 2.

7. This efficient-causal role of *phusis* and *eidos* is clear in *Phys.* 2.1-2, but it is

not mentioned in the account of the four causes in 2.3. Aristotle recognizes at 198a21-23 that the three kinds of explanation, final, formal, and efficient, sometimes "come to one"; but he relies on a different argument there.

8. I assume that Aristotle thinks this is a genuine case of coincidence with no teleological explanation. He need not be taken to argue in 198b32-199a8 that everything in nature happens for the sake of something. *Tauta* in 198b34 and 199a4 may refer to *hōsper kan ei heneka tou egigneto*, 198b29-30; it is only to the things that appear teleological that the disjunction "either by chance or for the sake of something" applies. On this view 198b36-199a3 should be taken as a parenthesis.

9. Instead of mentioning (efficient) causal relevance to distinguish real from apparent teleology Aristotle assumes that whenever apparent teleological effects happen always or usually, they will be really teleological (198b34-36). Here as in the discussion of luck (196b36-197a1) this reference to what happens always or usually is an imperfect substitute for an appeal to causal relevance.

10. Sometimes—e.g., *Met.* 1042a25-27, 32; *DA* 412a6-7—Aristotle allows matter to be one legitimate type of substance; but he relies on different reasons from those I have mentioned. *Met.* 8.2 argues that some analogy to form must be mentioned to indicate the essence of some nonsubstances.

11. Pleasure and pain, on Aristotle's view, also require *phantasia*; and so, if everything with perception has pleasure and pain, everything with perception must have phantasia (413b22-23, with the usual punctuation). Aristotle, however, is not quite consistent in allowing phantasia to everything that has perception; cf., e.g., 415a10-11. If he doubts that some perceiving things have phantasia, he ought to doubt that they have pleasure and desire; but as far as I know, he never expresses any doubt about this.

12. On Descartes's views I am indebted to N. Malcolm, "Thoughtless Brutes," in his *Thought and Knowledge* (Ithaca, 1977), chap. 2; Z. Vendler, *Res Cogitans* (Ithaca, 1972), pp. 152 ff.; A. J. P. Kenny, "Cartesian Privacy," in his *The Anatomy of the Soul* (Oxford, 1973), pp. 113-128.

13. See Descartes, *Philosophical Letters*, trans. A. J. P. Kenny (Oxford, 1970), pp. 53-54, 206-208, 243-245, 251. Descartes's position is more complicated than my summary suggests, and perhaps not finally consistent.

14. I have discussed these differences more fully in "Reason and Responsibility in Aristotle" (chap. 8 of this anthology).

15. This may be Aristotle's point at *DA* 428a18-24 and 419b10-21.

16. See G. E. M. Anscombe, *Intention* (Oxford, 1957), pp. 70-74, on "desirability characteristics." Aristotle is sometimes inconsistent, or at least unclear, about a sharp distinction between desire for the pleasant and desire for the good. *NE* 1094a1-3 is often (perhaps wrongly, given *praxis te kai prohairesis*) taken to mean that all desire pursues the good. *DA* 433a27-29 says that the object of desire is either the good or the apparent good. It is no use to say that pleasure is included as an apparent good; for it will be an apparent good only to someone who has the concept of a good, and animals do not. *NE* 1113a32-b2 is explicitly concerned only with those who have a concept of good; but *De motu animalium* 700b27-30 seems to imply that the pleasant is always an apparent good. *Rhetoric*

1369b18-20 distinguishes the apparent good and the apparent pleasant, consistently with Aristotle's normal view.

17. See D. C. Dennett, *Content and Consciousness* (London, 1969), p. 77.

18. Aristotle's position is discussed by Anscombe, p. 34; W. F. R. Hardie, *Aristotle's Ethical Theory* (Oxford, 1968), pp. 16 f.; J. L. Ackrill, in sec. VI of his "Aristotle on *Eudaimonia*," *Proceedings of the British Academy* 60 (1974), 339-359 (chap. 2 of this anthology). I am not sure that Aristotle commits the fallacy attributed to him by Anscombe and Ackrill.

19. It is not very clear at the beginning of the *NE* whether Aristotle thinks everyone already does pursue happiness or the good for man or a final good. *Boulometha* and *hairoumetha* in 1094b19-20 suggest that he is describing what "we" do—and perhaps "we" includes everyone; *prattetai* in 1097a19 is quite vague. (On Ackrill's and Anscombe's interpretation of 1094a18-22—see the previous note—Aristotle clearly endorses the descriptive view.) *EE* 1214b7-14 perhaps suggests that not everyone pursues a final good—though here Aristotle mentions the adoption of some specific goal such as honor or culture and does not quite say that someone might fail altogether to pursue a final good.

20. The *NE* speaks of types of life where the *DA* speaks of types of soul. But *DA* 414a4-14 shows that no difference of doctrine need be assumed here; cf. F. Dirlmeier, *Aristoteles: Nikomachische Ethik* (Berlin, 1969), ad loc. The close parallel with the *DA* casts doubt on the claim of R. A. Gauthier and J. Y. Jolif, *Aristote: L'Éthique à Nicomaque*, 2d ed. (Louvain and Paris, 1970) on 1098a3-4 that Aristotle here assumes a theory of the soul incompatible with the *DA*.

21. This interpretation is suggested by *praktikē* in 1098a3—though not proved, since *Politics* 1325b16-21 recognizes contemplation as a kind of *praxis*; see J. A. Stewart, *Notes on the Nicomachean Ethics* (Oxford, 1892), ad loc. However, Aristotle probably intends *praktikē*, introduced with no further warning or explanation here, to refer to a life of action in the ordinary sense (cf. 1139a18-22). (This interpretation is confirmed if the parenthesis in 1098a4-5 is genuine.) In that case the function argument is intended to justify not the contemplative life in particular but the life of practical reason; further argument is needed for the contemplative life, and Aristotle offers it in *NE* 10. See H. H. Joachim, *Aristotle: Nicomachean Ethics* (Oxford, 1951), ad loc., contrary to Stewart and to Gauthier and Jolif.

22. See R. Nozick, "On the Randian Argument," *Personalist* 52 (1971), 282-304. Several questions, including this one, are raised by T. Nagel, "Aristotle on *Eudaimonia*," *Phronesis* 17 (1972), 252-259 (chap. 1 of this anthology).

4
Self-Movers[1]
David J. Furley

Aristotle sometimes calls animals self-movers. We must try to determine what exactly he means by this. In particular, we must look at this thesis in the light of certain passages in the *Physics* which appear to deny that there can be self-movers. Is this apparent anomaly to be explained genetically? Are we to believe that Aristotle criticized and rejected his earlier thesis that animals are self-movers? Or is his position as a whole consistent? How then are we to explain away the apparent anomaly?

To anyone who reads *Physics* 2 a little incautiously it might appear that since nature is declared to be an internal source of change and rest (ἀρχὴ κινήσεως καὶ στάσεως, 1. 192b13-33), anything that has a nature must be a self-mover.[2] For what else is a self-mover but a thing that has *in itself* a source of change and rest? Thus all the things specified at the beginning of *Ph.* 2.1 would be self-movers: living things and their parts, plants, and the simple bodies, earth, water, air, and fire.

But this turns out, of course, to be too generous. We are told explicitly in *Ph.* 8.4. 255a5-10 that the bodies that move by nature up or down cannot be said to move themselves. Three reasons are given: (a) to move itself is a "life property" (ζωτικόν) and confined to things that have souls; (b) if they moved themselves, they would be able to stop themselves, and if it is "in its own power" for fire to move upward, it must likewise be in its power to move downward; (c) nothing that is homogeneous and continuous can move itself.

Clearly, then, things with souls have an ἀρχὴ κινήσεως καὶ στάσεως in

55

themselves in a stronger sense than lifeless natural bodies. The refinement, according to *Ph.* 8, is a difference in the voice of the verb: the natural bodies, as opposed to things with souls, have a source not of causing movement or of acting (κινεῖν, ποιεῖν) but of being acted on (πάσχειν). In fact, this gives too little to the natural bodies in Aristotle's theory. He should at least stress that they have an internal source of being acted on *in a fully determinate way.* But we do not need to pursue that subject here, and we can also leave aside the difficult question of what is the *active* mover of the natural bodies when they move according to their nature—a question to which Aristotle offers no wholly satisfactory answer.

In chapter 5 of *Ph.* 8 Aristotle starts from the proposition that we can distinguish chains of movers, such that A is moved by B, which is moved by C, and so on. He produces a number of arguments to show that such a series cannot be infinite: it must be stopped—or rather started—by something that is not moved by another but by itself: "If everything that is moved is moved by something, but the first mover, although moved, is not moved by another, it must be that it is moved by itself" (256a19-21).

Initially, Aristotle considers only the possibility that such a series is started by a self-mover, not the alternative that it is started by an unmoved mover. It is something of a surprise that he next (256b3 ff.) produces an argument from which he says "these same conclusions will follow," but from which he draws a conclusion in the form of a disjunction: "So either the first thing that is moved will be moved by something at rest, or it will move itself" (257a26-27).

The reason why Aristotle can regard this disjunctive conclusion as the same as the other is clear from its context in chapters 4 and 5, in which the concept of a self-mover is analyzed. As a whole, a thing may be said to move itself; but within the whole it must always be possible to distinguish a mover and a moved. This is argued a priori, on the ground that one and the same thing cannot simultaneously be active and passive, or in a state of actuality and potentiality, in the same respect. The conclusion is expressed in these words: "Well, it is clear that the whole moves itself not by virtue of having some part such as to move itself; it moves itself as a whole, moving and being moved by virtue of part of it moving and part of it being moved. It does not move as a whole, and it is not moved as a whole: A moves, and only B is moved" (258a22-27). This conclusion is quite general: for *any* self-mover we can distinguish a part (or aspect—the article with the genitive is as noncommittal as possible) that moves without itself being moved, and a part that is moved.

The same analysis is applied explicitly to living creatures in chapter 4 (254b14-33). There is no doubt, says Aristotle, that there *is* a distinction in this case between the mover and the moved, but it is not obvious how to draw the distinction. "For it seems that as in boats and things that are not naturally constituted, so in living beings also there is something that causes movement distinct from what is moved, and thus the whole animal moves itself." At first sight this explanatory sentence appears to support the statement that there *is* a distinction rather than the nearer statement that there is some difficulty about how to draw it. But Simplicius's interpretation probably gets the right nuance (*Ph.* 1208, 30 ff.). It is obvious, he says, that a living being is moved by its soul, but it is not clear how this is to be distinguished from that which it moves—whether it is altogether distinct in nature and place or in some other way. The movement of a living being looks like that of a boat or a chariot, in which the cause of motion is the helmsman and the driver (not, incidentally, the oarsmen or the horses); and these both have a distinct spatial individuality and their own nature. But, he implies, there is doubt about whether the soul is such an individual. Simplicius probably has an eye on *De anima* 2.1. 413a8, where Aristotle writes: "On the other hand, it is still unclear whether the soul is the ἐντελέχεια of the body as a boatman is of a boat."[3]

There is a qualification to be added to the conclusion that a self-mover includes an unmoved mover. What Aristotle has shown is that the first mover in a series must cause motion in some way other than *by* being moved itself. The first mover may be moved incidentally. This is true, of course, of living beings, which are moved by their souls and in turn carry their souls about with them (259b16-20).

Aristotle now faces the suggestion that if animals can initiate motion by themselves from a state of rest, without being moved by anything outside themselves, perhaps the whole cosmos might have initiated motion in itself in this way. He attempts to rebut this argument by showing that, after all, animals do *not* start moving from a state of rest without any external cause.

There are two passages where this point is made: (A) *Ph.* 8.2. 253a11-21 and (B) *Ph.* 8.6. 259b1-16. Aristotle seems to think of A as an outline sketch, the detail of which is to be filled in by B (see 253a20-21). But in fact each passage contains some details omitted from the other. There is some significance both in the differences and in Aristotle's attitude to them; so we shall have to look at them in detail. I number the points in A; B can be divided into three sections, in the middle one of which I number the correspondences with A.

A
But this [sc. that animals move from a state of rest, having been moved by nothing external to them] is false. [i] We always see one of the connatural parts of the animal in a state of motion, and [ii] it is not the animal itself that is the cause of the motion of this, but perhaps (ἴσως) its environment. [iii] In using this expres-

sion, that a thing moves itself, we speak not of every [kind of] motion but only of locomotion. [iv] So nothing prevents—perhaps rather it is necessary—that many motions come about in the body because of the environment, and some of these move the mind (διάνοια) or desire (ὄρεξις), and the latter then moves the whole animal—[v] as happens in sleep, for when there is no perceptive motion present, but there is *some* motion, animals wake up again.

B

[*a*] We see that there plainly are things that move themselves, such as the class of things with souls, and animals; and these suggested that it may be possible for motion[4] to arise in something from total nonexistence, since we see this happening in them (being immobile at some time, they are then put into motion, as it seems).

[*b*] Well, we must note this, [iii] that they move themselves with *one* motion, and this not strictly; for the cause is not in themselves, but [i] there are other natural motions in animals, [ii] which they do not have because of themselves—for example, growth, decay, respiration, which are motions undergone by every animal while it is at rest and not moved with its own motion. The cause of this is the environment, and many of the things that enter [the animal], such as food; for [v] while it is being digested they sleep, and while it is being distributed they wake up and move themselves, the first cause being outside themselves.

[*c*] Hence they are not always being moved continuously by themselves. For the mover is another, which is itself moved and in change with respect to every self-mover.[5]

We shall return to discuss these two passages shortly. Before doing so it may be as well to look around elsewhere in *Ph.* 8 to see the extent of the disharmony in Aristotle's attitude to self-movers.

Aristotle does not *reject* the concept of self-movers in *Ph.* 8. Chapters 4 and 5 are sometimes regarded as amounting to the rejection of the concept. Chapter 4 contains the sentence "It is clear, then, that none of these moves itself" (255b29), which has been taken as a general rejection of *all* self-movers.[6] But it is not. The reference of the pronoun is to inanimate natural bodies only—"the light and the heavy" (255b14-15). Nothing is said or implied about animals. Nor does the *analysis* of self-movers into a moved part and a moving part imply that there is no such thing as a self-mover. It is evidently quite legitimate, in Aristotle's view in these chapters, to call the whole a self-mover, provided that the moving part is itself unmoved except accidentally.

But passages A and B seem to deny that proviso and hence, taken together with chapters 4-5, to reject the possibility of self-movers. Yet Aristotle clearly does not want such a conclusion. Even at the end of B he continues to speak of self-movers ("the cause of its moving itself by itself," 259b17). Even in his final argument for the existence of an eternal unmoved mover he continues to allow the possibility of noneternal unmoved movers, and although he does not say so, commentators generally take him to mean animal souls (258b12, 20, 32). The *De motu animalium* summarizes the position reached in the *Physics* thus: "Now, that the ἀρχή of other motions is that which moves itself, and that the ἀρχή of this is the unmoved, and that the first mover must necessarily be unmoved, has been determined previously" (698a7-9). Self-movers here are still allowed the role of ἀρχή for other movements: he still has in mind the distinction between inanimate natural bodies, which have an ἀρχή of *being* moved, and animate beings, some of which have an ἀρχή of *causing* movement (*Ph.* 8.4. 255a5-10). He has neither rejected this distinction nor provided different criteria for drawing it. In *Eudemian Ethics* 2.6 and *Nico-machean Ethics* 3.5 he insists that a man is the ἀρχή of his actions. There is a class of actions that are voluntary, and one of the criteria for picking them out is that the ἀρχή is *in* the agent himself (*NE* 3.1. 1111a22).

The tension in Aristotle's thinking about this subject is set up by a clash of motives. He clearly wants to preserve the commonsense intuition that the movements of animals, and especially the actions of human beings, are not brought about by external agents in the same way that the movements of inanimate beings are. Yet he sees a danger that *all* the movements in the cosmos might be thought explicable on this principle of the self-movement of autonomous parts, and so insists that even this self-movement presupposes some external changes that are independent of animal movements.

What is particularly striking about the argument of passages A and B is the way in which it assimilates intentional action to mere mechanical movements. What moves the animal is διάνοια or ὄρεξις, but what moves this is the physical metabolism that goes on all the time in the animals, and what moves this is in the first place food and so forth, which enters from the environment. This is a pattern of explanation which one might think suitable, perhaps, for the movements of the periodical cicada of the eastern United States (*magicicada septemdecim*), which lies dormant in the earth until it emerges, noisily and with all its millions of congeners, every seventeen years (next in May 1987). It seems thoroughly inade-quate for explaining the action of a man signing a contract or even of a bird building a nest.

Passage B does not even mention ὄρεξις. Passage A does (iv), but instead of treating it teleologically, as Aristotle does in *De anima* and *MA*, it reduces it to a simple mechanical response. Even food is not some-thing the animal moves to get (an ὀρεκτόν), but only something that "enters from the environment" and eventually causes the animal to move when it wakes up from its postprandial sleep. The reason why Aristotle puts it this way is surely the nature of his argument. He has an a priori argument in *Ph.* 8.1 to show that both time and motion have no starting point. Observation of animals suggests that they do function as starting points for motion. All Aristotle needs to show is that their motions do not provide an example of a beginning of motion in a system in which *no* motion took place before, and that they could not be explained at all on the assumption that no motion took place before. It does not matter to his argument *how* the previous motion is related to the alleged beginning of motion, so long as it is a necessary condition for it. So he uses the simplest possible mechanical model: *A* is pushed by *B*, *B* by *C*, and so on.

The same oversimplified model seems to be in his mind in *De anima* 3.10. "There is good reason for the view that these two are the causes of motion, ὄρεξις and practical intelligence; for the object of ὄρεξις causes motion, and because of this the intelligence causes motion, because its ἀρχή is the object of ὄρεξις (433a17-20). The pronouns are slightly ambiguous; but presumably the sense is that the object in the external world which is desired stimulates the practical intelligence to search for means to get it and thus to put into practice the steps needed to get it.

"What causes motion would be one in form, the ὀρεκτικόν as such, but the first of all would be the ὀρεκτόν, since this moves without being moved, by being the object of thought or imagination (νοεῖν or φαντάζειν), although the causes of motion would be many in number [sc. because desires can oppose each other]" (433b10-13). Again, the unmoved mover of animals in this is the *object* of desire.

If we distinguish three items in a case of motion—(*a*) that which causes motion but not by virtue of being moved itself, (*b*) that which causes motion by virtue of being moved by (*a*), and (*c*) that which is moved by (*b*) without necessarily moving anything—then the role of (*a*) is played by the external object of ὄρεξις, that of (*b*) by the faculty of ὄρεξις in the soul, and that of (*c*) by the animal (433b13-18).[7] Here again the unmoved mover is not the soul or any "part" of the animal but something external to it—the object of ὄρεξις, here identified with the πρακτὸν ἀγαθόν. At the end of this section Aristotle sums up: "In general, then, as has been said, it is as appetitive (ὀρεκτικόν) that the animal is such as to move itself (ἑαυτοῦ κινητικόν)" (433b27-28). As in the *Physics*, we have both an account of an external mover and a claim that the animal is a self-mover.

The picture is not essentially different on this point in the *MA*: "The first cause of motion is the object of ὄρεξις and of διάνοια" (700b23-24). "ὄρεξις and the ὀρεκτικόν cause motion by being moved" (701a1). "According to the account that states the cause of motion, ὄρεξις is the middle item, which causes motion by being moved" (703a4-5).

This oversimplified model produces at first sight a very blatant clash with *De anima* 1.3-4, where it is explicitly denied that the soul is moved. The ὀρεκτικόν is certainly part of the soul or an aspect of it; in 3.10 it is described, deliberately, emphatically, and repeatedly, as a *moved mover*; yet in these early chapters of the *De anima* Aristotle has claimed that the soul is not moved. In a justly famous passage (408b1-18) he argues that the habit of saying that the soul is pained, pleased, encouraged, terrified, or angered, and that it perceives and thinks, might suggest that it is moved; but this, he says, does not follow. It would be better —that is, less misleading—to say that the *man* is moved to pity, or to learn, or to think, *with* or *in* his soul (the simple dative): "and this not in the sense that the motion is in the soul but in the sense that [sc. the motion proceeds] sometimes as far as the soul and at other times from it." The cryptic last clause is explained briefly in the next sentence: "Perception, from *these* [sc. objects in the perceptible world]; recollection, from *it* [sc. the soul] to the movements or cessations from movement in the sense organs." We can ignore the second part of this; but what does the first suggest? Perceptible objects, it seems, cause the motion (cf. 417b19-21, 426b29-31), and the motion proceeds "as far as" (μέχρι) the soul, which is not, however, moved by it.

In *De anima* 2.5 Aristotle says something about the difficulty of finding the right language to describe the relation between the soul and the objects of perception. αἴσθησις consists in being moved and in πάσχειν (416b33). We first proceed on the assumption that being moved and πάσχειν are the same as ἐνεργεῖν (417a14-16). But we have to distinguish different senses of πάσχειν and ἐνεργεῖν. A man who is ignorant of letters πάσχει something when he learns his letters from a teacher. His ignorance is destroyed, and his potentiality for knowledge is actualized. But this degree of actualization is itself a potentiality for further actualization when the man actually has in mind the letter A. In this latter move the state of potentiality is not destroyed but preserved: hence we ought not to say that the man is changed (ἀλλοιοῦσθαι), or at least we ought to recognize a different kind of ἀλλοίωσις (417b2-16). So with αἴσθησις. To have an αἴσθησις is to pass from the first to the second state of actuality, and what causes the actualization is the object of perception.

So the soul is not *moved* by the objects in the external world in any of the senses enumerated in 1.3 (φορά, ἀλλοίωσις, φθίσις, αὔξησις), except that it experiences this highly specialized form of ἀλλοίωσις.[8] Is this qualification sufficient to allow Aristotle to maintain his distinction between the movements of animals and the natural motions of inanimate bodies? It is certainly not sufficient in itself, because he uses the same pattern in his explanation of natural motion (*Ph*. 8.4. 255a30-b13). In this case too we can distinguish two stages: the change from (say) water, which is potentially air, into air, through an external agency; and then the full actuality of the element in attaining its natural place. Here too

Aristotle uses the simile of the man first learning, and then exercising, his skill. So if animals are self-movers but inanimate natural bodies are not, the difference in the explanation of their motions is not to be found in this point.[9]

The problem comes into particularly sharp focus in the *Ethics*. In the *Physics* and the biological works, including *De anima*, Aristotle was concerned with fitting the movements of animals into certain general patterns of explanation. In the *Ethics* he has to find the distinguishing characteristics of a subset of animal movements—namely, human actions for which we hold the agent morally responsible. It now becomes crucial for him to decide whether a man is really a self-mover, and in what sense, and when. The notion that the object of desire is what moves a man to action becomes a challenge to the whole concept of moral responsibility.[10]

Suppose someone says that pleasant and good objects are compulsive, since they exercise force upon us and are external to us. Then [1] everything would be compulsive on such a theory, since these are the objects for which everyone does everything. Moreover, [2] people who act because they are forced, involuntarily, do so with pain, whereas those who act because of anything pleasant and good do so with pleasure. But [3] it is absurd to blame external objects rather than oneself as being too easily caught by such attractions, and to take the credit for one's good behavior but blame pleasant objects for one's bad behavior. [*NE* 3.1. 1110b9-15]

The third point in this passage is the only one that gives an idea of *how* Aristotle proposes to rebut this challenge: the responsibility lies in the man's character and cannot be shifted to an external object of desire. "A man is the source and originator of his actions as he is of his children" (1113b17). We cannot go back to ἀρχαί beyond those that are in us. Aristotle considers a possible objection: perhaps our feeble moral character is itself given to us by nature and is out of our control:

But perhaps he is the kind of man *not* to take care. No; people are themselves responsible for having become men of this kind, by living in a slack way. They are responsible for being unjust or overindulgent, by cheating or by spending their lives drinking, and so on. In every field of action, actions of a certain kind make a corresponding kind of man. This is clear from the case of people who practice for any sort of contest or similar activity—they practice by continually repeating the action. [*NE* 3.5 1114a3 ff.]

He raises a similar kind of objection a little later, this time in a form more directly relevant to our present theme:

Suppose someone were to say that everybody desires what *appears* good (φαινόμενον ἀγαθόν) but is not master of the appearance (φαντασία) — the goal appears to each man in accordance with the kind of man he is. But (against this) if each of us *is* somehow responsible for his disposition, he will be somehow responsible for this appearance; otherwise no one is himself responsible for acting badly, but does these things through ignorance of the goal, believing that he will achieve what is best for himself by these means. And the desire for the goal is not a matter of choice, but it is necessary to be born with a natural faculty of sight, as it were, by which one will judge well and choose what is really and truly good; in that case, to be born well will be to have a good natural faculty of this kind. . . . Well, if this is true, how will virtue be any more voluntary than vice? To both alike, the good man and the bad man, the goal is presented and established by nature or however else it may be; and they both act in whatever way they do act by referring all the rest to this. So, whether the goal is presented to each man in whatever form it may be presented not by nature but with some dependence on the man himself, or the goal is natural but virtue is voluntary because the good man performs the actions leading to the goal voluntarily, in either case vice must be no less voluntary than virtue. [*NE* 3.5. 1114a31 ff.]

This passage suggests—admittedly in a very sketchy way—an important modification of the theory of desire set out in the *Physics*. In the latter, "the object of desire" (ὀρεκτόν) was presented as if it were simply an object in the external world. But people desire things in the external world, and exert themselves to get them, *under certain descriptions*, and their actions cannot be explained without some notion of what each of their goals means *for them*. The ὀρεκτόν cannot be identified as such independently of the ὀρεκτικόν, and in this sense the ἀρχή of action produced by desire is "inside" the agent.[11]

Does Aristotle recognize that the ὀρεκτόν, as the unmoved mover of human action, is always an intentional object? He does not say so explicitly. At first sight he appears to hedge his answer somewhat in the passage just quoted: "whether the goal is presented . . . not by nature but with some dependence on the man himself, or the goal is natural but virtue is voluntary because the good man performs the actions leading to the goal voluntarily . . ." One might think that Aristotle meant to suggest here that the goal, being natural, moves a man to action in some way that does not involve how it appears to him, by the properties inherent in the nature of the external object that constitutes the goal. But clearly that is not what he meant. He was still thinking rather of the nature of the *agent*. The suggestion is just that one's *perception* of the goal may be in some sense natural—the same suggestion that has just been rejected in the preceding twelve lines. Probably he revives it again here to forestall a possible objection that *some* human goals do after all have a claim to be called natural— εὐδαιμονία itself, for example. Even in that case, he suggests, virtue and vice would be equally voluntary, because the subordinate goals depend on moral character, which is in our power. The answer is given more clearly in *De anima* 3.10. Aristotle begins the chapter by observing that there are apparently two causes of motion, either ὄρεξις or νοῦς, "if one lays it down that φαντασία is a kind of νόησις" (the latter proviso is to take care of the case of animals that have no νοῦς). But these are not put forward as alternative causes of motion, as it seems at first sight: ὄρεξις is always involved, whether or not νοῦς or φαντασία is involved. Aristotle continues: "Now νοῦς is always right, but ὄρεξις and φαντασία are both right and wrong. Hence, although what causes motion is the ὀρεκτόν, this may be the good or the seeming good" (φαινόμενον ἀγαθόν, 433a26-29). Does this suggest that νοῦς is an alternative to φαντασία in this case and that either one or the other apprehends the object of desire? The same may be suggested by 433b12, where he says that the object of desire moves either by νοηθῆναι or by φαντασθῆναι. This would appear to be a consequence of Aristotle's regard for linguistic usage as a guide to the truth. When we are clear and in no doubt about something, we do not say "it appears so" (φαίνεται, 428a14), and hence we do not want to say there is a φαντασία in this case.[12] But it is awkward to use two different terms for what is evidently the same faculty according to whether it gets something right or possibly wrong. At the end of the chapter, in his summary, Aristotle lets νοῦς drop out of the picture: "In general, as has been said, an animal moves itself in that it is capable of ὄρεξις; and it is not capable of ὄρεξις without φαντασία. Every φαντασία is either rational (λογιστική) or perceptual (αἰσθητική). Animals other than man have a share of the latter too" (433b27-30). The discussion in *MA* repeats this point: "The organic parts are put into a suitable condition by the πάθη, the πάθη by ὄρεξις, and ὄρεξις by φαντασία; the latter comes about either through νόησις or through αἴσθησις" (702a17-19).[13]

This line of thought will give Aristotle most of what he wants in order to defend his distinctions in *Ph.* 8 and to make a consistent whole of the theses announced there. Animals are clearly distinguished from inanimate natural bodies in that although both require external things to explain their movements, only animals require external things perceived (or otherwise apprehended) as having significance *for them*. Note that this is not just a difference in the complexity of the response to a stimulus, but a difference in kind. Only a being with a soul can move in this way. An animal is correctly described as a self-mover, because when it moves, its soul moves its body, and the external cause of its motion (the ὀρεκτόν) is a cause of motion only because it is "seen" as such by a faculty of the soul.[14] There must *be* an external object, however, and hence the movement of an animal does not provide an example of a totally autonomous beginning of motion (as noted earlier, Aristotle thought that if such an example could be produced, his cosmology would be in danger).[15]

The suggestion made in this paper is not that Aristotle was ready with an articulate theory of intentionality to defend his view of animals as self-movers. It is that he was sufficiently aware of the intentionality of objects of desire to want to retain the notion that animals move themselves, in spite of finding that they are moved by the objects of desire. I think therefore that the apparent inconsistencies in his texts on this subject are not to be explained genetically but rather as coming from two different approaches that he has not fully articulated. I think they could reasonably well have been made into a consistent theory that would have required him to do only a little rewriting.

Although he could plausibly retain the proposition that animals are self-movers, I am not sure that it would be worth struggling to retain the concept of the animal soul as *unmoved* mover. The point is that external objects are not in themselves sufficient causes for the voluntary movements of animals. But they do have some effect on the soul, and it would be obstinate of Aristotle to deny that the effect can be called a movement.

There is one conspicuous loose end in the theory that the ἀρχή of human actions is "in" the agent. Aristotle maintains that people are moved to act by what appears desirable to them, that what appears desirable depends on their character, and that their character in turn depends on their actions and is *therefore* "in their power." His theory needs some explanation of these character-forming actions and of how it is that they are not caused by external pressures but proceed from an ἀρχή in the agent himself.

NOTES

1. During the preparation of this paper I had the opportunity of studying the manuscripts of two books not yet published at that time: Dr. Martha Craven Nussbaum's *Aristotle's "De motu animalium"* (Princeton, 1978) and Dr. Edwin Hartman's *Substance, Body, and Soul: Aristotelian Investigations* (Princeton, 1977). The problem investigated in this paper is one that has interested me for a long time; but the manner of treating it here is much influenced by these two works. I am also indebted to their authors for comments on the first draft of this paper.

I am especially indebted to Prof. D. J. Allan, Dr. Malcolm Schofield, and Dr. Richard Sorabji for their comments, which have greatly assisted me in revising the paper for publication.

2. For a review of this subject, especially in its relations with Plato and the pre-

Socratics, see F. Solmsen, *Aristotle's System of the Physical World* (Ithaca, N. Y., 1960), 92-102.

3. This very controversial sentence is also discussed by C. Lefèvre, "Sur le statut de l'âme dans le *De anima* et les *Parva naturalia*," in *Aristotle on Mind and the Senses: Proceedings of the Seventh Symposium Aristotelicum*, ed. G. E. R. Lloyd and G. E. L. Owen (Cambridge, 1978), pp. 21-67, at 23-24. Although it is not strictly relevant to my argument, it may be worth mentioning one or two points on which I differ from him.

(a) Grammatically, this sentence beginning ἔτι δὲ ἄδηλον... is coordinate with a4 ὅτι μὲν οὔ...οὐκ ἄδηλον.... It is neither a new beginning, as M. Lefèvre thinks, nor coordinate with a6 οὐ μὴν ἀλλά...(On this point see H. J. Easterling, "A Note on *De anima* 413a8-9," *Phronesis* 11 [1966], 159-162.)

(b) The boatman-boat analogy is not inconsistent with the ἐντελέχεια theory of soul. The problem raised in this sentence is whether the activity that constitutes soul is *localized* (in the heart, although Aristotle does not mention the heart here); that is what is still unclear. That Aristotle would not have thought localization in itself to be inconsistent with the ἐντελέχεια theory (as Sir David Ross thought, among others) may perhaps be shown by considering the analogies with which he introduces the ἐντελέχεια theory—the analogies of the axe and the eye (412b10 ff.). The "soul" of these is the ἐντελέχεια of the whole, but in both cases it is localized—the chopping power of the axe in its edge, and the seeing power of the eye in its pupil or wherever it may be.

4. Motion in general, not *a* motion, as in Apostle's translation.

5. For analysis of these two passages, see especially F. Solmsen, "Plato's First Mover in the Eighth Book of Aristotle's *Physics*," in *Philomathes, Studies...in Memory of Philip Merlan* (The Hague, 1971), pp. 171-182. I am not wholly convinced, however, either that these passages attack particularly the Platonic notion of a self-moving soul or that passage B interrupts the "triumphant progress of the thought" in the rest of chap. 6.

6. For example by G. A. Seeck, "*Nachträge*" im achten Buch der Physik des Aristoteles, Abhandlungen der Geister- und Sozialwissenschaftlichen Klasse, Akademie der Wissenschaften und der Literatur, Mainz, 1965, no. 3, p. 151; and by W. K. C. Guthrie, ed. and trans., *Aristotle: On the Heavens*, Loeb Classical Library (London and Cambridge, Mass., 1953), p. xxix. Guthrie interprets the cross-reference at *De caelo* 311a12 in the same sense.

7. For more comments on this passage see J. B. Skemp, "῎Ορεξις in *De anima* III 10," in *Aristotle on Mind and the Senses*, pp. 181-189. I do not differ from his interpretation.

8. Aristotle nevertheless freely uses the term ἀλλοίωσις of sense perception in *MA* (701a5, b17-18) and elsewhere.

9. This is explored further by Henri Carteron, *La notion de force dans le système d'Aristote* (Paris, 1923), pp. 142 ff.

10. I have examined Aristotle's theory about this at greater length in my *Two Studies in the Greek Atomists* (Princeton, 1967), pt. 2: "Aristotle and Epicurus on Voluntary Action."

11. "Systems to whom action can be attributed have a special status, in that

they are considered *loci* of responsibility, centres from which behaviour is directed. The notion 'centre' seems very strongly rooted in our ordinary view of such systems, and it gives rise to a deep-seated and pervasive metaphor, that of the 'inside.' Beings who can act are thought of as having an inner core from which their overt action flows.... What is essential to this notion of an 'inside,' however, is the notion of consciousness in the sense of intentionality" (Charles Taylor, *The Explanation of Behaviour* [London, 1964], pp. 57-58). Taylor quotes (pp. 68-69) Merleau-Ponty, *Structure du comportement* and *Phénoménologie de la perception* for an extension of this notion to include the goals of nonhuman animals.

Stuart Hampshire explains Aristotle's position thus: "The reason for an action has been given when the agent's conception of the end has been explained together with his calculation of the means to it. We then see the fusion of the thinking, which is an inhibited discussion of the desired end and the means to it, and the mere wanting. The reason for the action is a fusion of these two elements, because the representation to myself in words of an object desired modifies the direction, and sometimes the intensity, of the original, blind appetite" (*Thought and Action* [London, 1959], p. 167).

12. See M. Schofield, "Aristotle on the Imagination," in *Aristotle on Mind and the Senses*, pp. 99-140.

13. There is an excellent discussion of φαντασία and its role in action in Nussbaum, *Aristotle's "De motu animalium."*

14. There is no reason to think it is an internal *image* of the object that moves the animal, rather than the object itself, perceived in a particular way. Dr. Nussbaum has discussed this fully in her *Aristotle's "De motu animalium"* and has persuaded me that some of what I wrote in *Two Studies in the Greek Atomists,* pt. 2, about "mental pictures" was at least too hasty.

15. What about delusions, hallucinations, etc.? Aristotle could reply that although animals may on occasion move in pursuit of a purely imaginary goal, these cases are parasitic on genuine cases. They would not pursue the imaginary goal unless there were similar goals in reality.

5

Aristotle on Learning to Be Good

M. F. Burnyeat

The question "Can virtue be taught?" is perhaps the oldest question in moral philosophy. Recall the opening of Plato's *Meno* (70a): "Can you tell me, Socrates—can virtue be taught, or is it rather to be acquired by practice? Or is it neither to be practiced nor to be learned but something that comes to men by nature or in some other way?" This is a simple version of what was evidently a well-worn topic of discussion. Socrates' characteristic but still simple reply is that until one knows what virtue is, one cannot know how it is (to be) acquired (*Meno* 71ab). I want to reverse the order, asking how, according to Aristotle, virtue is acquired, so as to bring to light certain features in his conception of what virtue is which are not ordinarily much attended to. Aristotle came to these questions after they had been transformed by the pioneering work in moral psychology which the mature Plato undertook in the *Republic* and later dialogues; by his time the simplicities of the debate in the *Meno* lay far behind. Nevertheless, about one thing Socrates was right: any tolerably explicit view of the process of moral development depends decisively on a conception of virtue. This dependence makes it possible to read a philosopher's account of moral development as evidence for what he thinks virtue is. In some ways, indeed, it is especially revealing evidence, since in problems of moral education the philosopher has to confront the complex reality of ordinary imperfect human beings.

My aim, then, is to reconstruct Aristotle's picture of the good man's development over time, concentrating on the earlier stages. Materials for the construction are abundant in the *Nicomachean Ethics*, but scattered; the construction will be gradual, its sense emerging progressively as the pieces come together from their separate contexts. I shall have to forgo extended exegesis of the various discussions from which Aristotle's remarks are extracted, but I trust that it is not necessary to apologize for the undefended interpretative decisions this will involve; such decisions are an inescapable responsibility of the synoptic enterprise.

Aristotle's good man, however, is not the only character I have in view. I am also interested in the conflicted akratic, the weak-willed (incontinent) man who knows the good but does not always achieve it in action. I want to place his problem too in the perspective of his development through time. And while I am not going to attempt anything like a full treatment of Aristotle's account of *akrasia* (incontinence, weakness of will), my hope is that the temporal perspective I shall sketch will remove one major source, at any rate, of the dissatisfaction which is often, and understandably, felt with Aristotle's account of the phenomenon.

In both cases, the good man and the akratic, we shall be concerned with the primitive materials from which character and a mature morality must grow. A wide range of desires and feelings are shaping patterns of motivation and response in a person well before he comes to a reasoned outlook on his life as a whole, and certainly before he integrates this reflective consciousness with his actual behavior. It is this focus of interest that constitutes the chief philosophical benefit, as I conceive it, of what is a predominantly historical inquiry. Intellectualism, a one-sided preoccupation with reason and reasoning, is a perennial failing in moral philosophy. The very subject of moral philosophy is sometimes defined or delimited as the study of moral reasoning, thereby excluding the greater part of what is important in the initial—and, I think, continuing —moral development of a person. Aristotle knew intellectualism in the form of Socrates' doctrine that virtue is knowledge. He reacted by emphasizing the importance of beginnings and the gradual development of good habits of feeling. The twentieth century, which has its own intellectualisms to combat, also has several full-scale developmental psychologies to draw upon. But they have not been much drawn upon in the moral philosophy of our time, which has been little interested in questions of education and development.[1] In this respect Aristotle's example has gone sadly unstudied and ignored.

No doubt Aristotle's developmental picture is still much too simple, by comparison with what could be available to us. Let that be conceded at once—to anyone who can do better. What is exemplary in Aristotle is his grasp of the truth that morality comes in a sequence of stages with both cognitive and emotional dimensions. This basic insight is already sufficient, as we shall see, to bring new light on akrasia.

So let us begin at the beginning, which Aristotle says is "the *that.*" This somewhat cryptic phrase occurs in an admitted digression (cf. 1095b14) toward the end of 1.4. Aristotle has just begun the search for a satisfactory specification of happiness and the good for man when he pauses to reflect, with acknowledgments to Plato, on the methodological importance of being clear whether one is on the way to first principles or starting points or on the way from them (1095a14-b1). The answer to Plato's question is that at this stage Aristotle is traveling dialectically toward a first principle or starting point, namely, the specification of happiness, but in another sense his inquiry must have its own starting points to proceed from. As he explains (1095b2-13),

For while one must begin from what is familiar, this may be taken in two ways: some things are familiar to us, others familiar without qualification. Presumably, then, what *we* should begin from is things familiar to *us*. This is the reason why one should have been well brought up in good habits if one is going to listen adequately to lectures about things noble and just, and in general about political (social) affairs. For the beginning (starting point) is "the *that,*" and if this is sufficiently apparent to a person, he will not in addition have a need for "the *because.*" Such a person has, or can easily get hold of, beginnings (starting points), whereas he who has neither [sc. neither "the *that*" nor "the *because*"],[2] let him hearken to the words of Hesiod:

> The best man of all is he who knows everything himself,
> Good also the man who accepts another's sound advice;
> But the man who neither knows himself nor takes to heart
> What another says, he is no good at all.

The contrast here, between having only "the *that*" and having both "the *that*" and "the *because*" as well, is a contrast between knowing or believing that something is so and understanding why it is so, and I would suppose that Aristotle quotes the Hesiodic verses in all seriousness. The man who knows for himself is someone with "the *because*"—in Aristotle's terms he is a man of practical wisdom equipped with the understanding to work out for himself what to do in the varied circumstances of life— while the one who takes to heart sound advice learns "the *that*" and becomes the sort of person who can profit from Aristotle's lectures. These lectures are no doubt designed to give him a reasoned understanding of "the *because*" which explains and justifies "the *that*" which he already has or can easily get hold of. What, then, is "the *that*"?

The ancient commentators are agreed that Aristotle has in mind knowledge about actions in accordance with the virtues; these actions are the things familiar to us from which we must start, and what we know

about them is that they are noble or just.[3] This fits an earlier statement
(1.3. 1095a2-4, quoted below) that the lectures assume on the part of
their audience a certain experience in the actions of life, because they are
concerned with these actions and *start from them*. It also conforms to
what 1.4 says is the subject matter of the lectures for which knowledge of
"the *that*" is a prerequisite: things noble and just.

Now the noble and the just do not, in Aristotle's view, admit of neat
formulation in rules or traditional precepts (cf. 1.3 1094b14-16; 2.2.
1104a3-10; 5.10. 1137b13-32; 9.2. 1165a12-14). It takes an educated perception, a capacity going beyond the application of general rules, to tell
what is required for the practice of the virtues in specific circumstances
(2.9. 1109b23; 4.5. 1126b2-4). That being so, if the student is to have "the
that" for which the doctrines in Aristotle's lectures provide the explanatory "*because,*" if he is to be starting out on a path which will lead to his
acquiring that educated perception, the emphasis had better be on his
knowing of specific actions that they are noble or just in specific circumstances. I put it as a matter of emphasis only, of degree, because often, no
doubt, moral advice will come to him in fairly general terms; a spot of
dialectic may be needed to bring home to the young man the limitations
and imprecision of what he has learned. But even where the advice is general, this need not mean he is taught that there are certain rules of justice,
say, which are to be followed as a matter of principle, without regard for
the spirit of justice and the ways in which circumstances alter cases.
What Aristotle is pointing to is our ability to internalize from a scattered
range of particular cases a general evaluative attitude which is not reducible to rules or precepts. It is with this process in view that he emphasizes
in 1.4 that the necessary beginnings or starting points, which I have
argued to be correct ideas about what actions are noble and just, are not
available to anyone who has not had the benefit of an upbringing in good
habits.

We can put this together with some further remarks about "the *that*" at
the end of 1.7 (1098a33-b4):

We must not demand explanation [sc. any more than precision] in all matters
alike, but it is sufficient in some cases to have "the *that*" shown properly, just as
in the case of starting points. "The *that*" is a first thing and a starting point. Of
starting points some are seen by induction, some by perception, some by a certain habituation, and others in other ways again.

This time the wider context points to the outline definition of happiness
or the good for man as the particular "*that*" which Aristotle has initially
in mind. The search for a satisfactory specification of happiness and the

good for man has just been completed, and Aristotle is reflecting on the extent to which he should claim precision and proof for his answer: it has the status of "the *that*" merely, and, being general, no more precision than the subject matter allows. Thus it would obviously be wrong to think of the notion of "the *that*" as intrinsically tied to particular low-level facts. Nevertheless, in this passage the thesis that we have to start from "the *that*" without an explanation, without "the *because*," is re-asserted for starting points quite generally, and is complemented by a brief survey of various ways in which we acquire starting points. We already know that in ethics good habits are a prerequisite for grasping "the *that*." It is now added that habituation is actually a way of grasping it, on a par with, though different from, induction, perception, and other modes of acquisition which Aristotle does not specify (the ancient commentators fill out the list for him by mentioning intellectual intuition and experience).[4] Each kind of starting point comes with a mode of acquisition appropriate to it; to give a couple of examples from the ancient commentators, we learn by induction that all men breathe, by perception that fire is hot. In ethics the appropriate mode for at least some starting points is habituation, and in the light of 1.4 it is not difficult to see which starting points these must be.[5] The thesis is that we first learn (come to see) what is noble and just *not* by experience of or induction from a series of instances, nor by intuition (intellectual or perceptual), but by learning to do noble and just things, by being habituated to noble and just conduct.

In part, this is the well-known doctrine of 2.1 and 4 that we become just or temperate by doing, and becoming habituated to doing, just and temperate things. But the passages we have examined from 1.4 and 7 add to those chapters a cognitive slant. It turns out that Aristotle is not simply giving us a bland reminder that virtue takes practice. Rather, practice has cognitive powers, in that it is the way we learn what is noble or just. And on reflection we can see that this addition is quite in accord with 2.1 and 4, even demanded by them. For according to 2.4 the ultimate goal toward which the beginner's practice is aimed is that he should become the sort of person who does virtuous things in full knowledge of what he is doing, choosing to do them for their own sake, and acting out of a settled state of character (1105a28-33). The beginner would hardly be on the way to this desirable state of affairs if he were not in the process forming (reasonably correct) ideas as to the nobility or justice of the actions he was engaged in; if you like, he must be on his way to acquiring a mature sense of values.

Let me skip here to 7.3, where at 1147a21-22 Aristotle has an interesting remark about learners in general:

Those who have learned a subject for the first time connect together[6] the propositions in an orderly way, but do not yet know them; for the propositions need to
become second nature to them, and that takes time.

We shall come later to the significance of this learner as one of Aristotle's
models for the state of mind of the akratic man. At present I want simply
to connect the thought in 7.3 of ideas or beliefs becoming second nature
to someone with the thought in 2.4 of the learner in morals as someone
who is tending toward a firmly established state of character which
includes, and therefore must in part have developed out of, convictions
about what is noble and just. The fully developed man of virtue and
practical wisdom understands "the *because*" of these convictions—in
terms of 1.4's contrast between things familiar without qualification and
things familiar to us, he has knowledge or familiarity in the unqualified
sense—but this state is preceded by the learner's knowledge (in the qualified sense) of "the *that*," acquired by habituation so that it is second
nature to him. Although only at the beginning of the road to full virtue,
the learner has advanced to a stage where, having internalized "the *that*,"
he has or can easily get hold of the type of starting point which is seen by
habituation.

Thus the picture forms as follows. You need a good upbringing not
simply in order that you may have someone around to tell you what is
noble and just—you do need that (recall the Hesiodic verses), and in 10.9
and again in the *Politics* 8.1 Aristotle discusses whether the job is best
done by one's father or by community arrangements—but you need also
to be guided in your conduct so that by doing the things you are told are
noble and just you will discover that what you have been told is *true*.
What you may begin by taking on trust you can come to know for yourself. This is not yet to know *why* it is true, but it is to have *learned that* it
is true in the sense of having made the judgment your own, second nature
to you—Hesiod's taking to heart. Nor is it yet to have acquired any of
the virtues, for which practical wisdom is required (6.13; 10.8 1178a16-
19), that understanding of "the *because*" which alone can accomplish the
final correcting and perfecting of your perception of "the *that*." But it is
to have made a beginning. You can say, perhaps, "I have learned that it is
just to share my belongings with others," and mean it in a way that someone who has merely been told this cannot, even if he believes it—except
in the weak sense in which "I have learned such and such" means simply
that such and such was the content of the instruction given by parent or
teacher.

This is a hard lesson, and not only in the moralist's sense. How can I
learn that something is noble or just by becoming habituated to doing it?

Is it not one thing to learn *to* do what is just and quite another to learn *that* it is just? Clearly, we need to look further at what Aristotle has to say about learning to do what is noble and just. Let us begin again at the beginning presupposed by Aristotle's lectures. For more is said about good upbringing and its benefits in 10.9, the very last chapter of the *Nicomachean Ethics*, which is specifically devoted to moral education.

In this chapter Aristotle gives an explanation (1179b4-31) of why it is that only someone with a good upbringing can benefit from the kind of argument and discussion contained in his lectures.

Now if arguments were in themselves enough to make men good, they would justly, as Theognis says, have won very great rewards, and such rewards should have been provided; but as things are, while they seem to have power to encourage and stimulate the generous-minded among our youth, and to make a character which is well-bred,[7] and a true lover of what is noble, ready to be possessed by virtue, they are not able to encourage the *many* to nobility and goodness. For these do not by nature obey the sense of shame, but only fear, and do not abstain from bad acts because of their baseness but through fear of punishment; living by passion they pursue the pleasures appropriate to their character and the means to them, and avoid the opposite pains, and have not even a conception of what is noble and truly pleasant, since they have never tasted it. What argument would remould such people? It is hard, if not impossible, to remove by argument the traits that have long since been incorporated in the character; and perhaps we must be content if, when all the influences by which we are thought to become good are present, we get some tincture of virtue.

Now some think that we are made good by nature, others by habituation, others by teaching. Nature's part evidently does not depend on us, but as a result of some divine causes is present in those who are truly fortunate; while argument and teaching, we may suspect, are not powerful with all men, but the soul of the student must first have been cultivated, by means of habits, for noble joy and noble hatred, like earth which is to nourish the seed. For he who lives as passion directs will not hear argument that dissuades him, nor understand it if he does; and how can we persuade one in such a state to change his ways? And in general passion seems to yield not to argument but to force. The character, then, must somehow be there already with a kinship to virtue, loving what is noble and hating what is base.[8]

This important and neglected passage is not rhetoric but precise argument,[9] as I hope eventually to show. My immediate concern is the student Aristotle wants for his lectures. He is someone who already loves what is noble and takes pleasure in it. He has a conception of what is noble and truly pleasant which other, less well brought up people lack because they have not tasted the pleasures of what is noble. This is what gives his character a kinship to virtue and a receptiveness to arguments directed to encouraging virtue.

The noble nature here described—Aristotle's prospective student—we met earlier as the person with a starting point. He is one who has learned what is noble ("the *that*") and, as we now see, thus come to love it. He loves it because it is what is truly or by nature pleasant. Compare 1.8 1099a13-15:

Lovers of what is noble find pleasant the things that are by nature pleasant; and virtuous actions are such, so that these are pleasant for such men as well in their own nature.

This is from a context which makes clear that the word *love* is not idly used; Aristotle has in mind a disposition of the feelings comparable in intensity, though not of course in every other respect, to the passion of a man who is crazy about horses. And the point he is making is that what you love in this sense is what you enjoy or take pleasure in. But equally he insists (10.9 1179b24-26) that the capacity for "noble joy and noble hatred" grows from habituation. I should now like to suggest that the prominence given to pleasure in these passages is the key to our problem about how practice can lead to knowledge.

There is such a thing as learning to enjoy something (painting, music, skiing, philosophy), and it is not sharply distinct from learning that the thing in question is enjoyable. Once again we need to eliminate the weak sense of *learn*, the sense in which to have learned that skiing is enjoyable is simply to have acquired the information, regardless of personal experience. In the strong sense I learn that skiing is enjoyable only by trying it myself and coming to enjoy it. The growth of enjoyment goes hand in hand with the internalization of knowledge.

There is also such a thing as learning to enjoy something properly, where this contrasts with merely taking pleasure in it. This is a hard subject, but I can indicate roughly what I mean by a few examples of not enjoying something properly: enjoying philosophy for the sense of power it can give, enjoying a trip abroad because of the splendid photographs you are taking on the way, enjoying a party because you are meeting important people, letting a symphony trigger a release of sentimental emotion. Aristotle's virtue of temperance is about the proper enjoyment of certain bodily pleasures having to do with taste and touch. These are things that any man or beast can take pleasure in, but not necessarily in the right way. Take the example of the gourmand who prayed that his throat might become longer than a crane's, so that he could prolong his enjoyment of the feel of the food going down (3.10 1118a26-b1): this illustrates the perversion of a man who takes more pleasure in brute contact with the food than in the flavors which are the proper object of taste. Aristotelian temperance is also concerned with sexual relations:

All men enjoy in some way or other good food and wines and sexual intercourse, but not all men do so as they ought. [7.14 1154a17-18]

And this again is a thought we can understand, however difficult it might be to elaborate.

Now Aristotle holds that to learn to do what is virtuous, to make it a habit or second nature to one, is among other things to learn to enjoy doing it, to come to take pleasure—the appropriate pleasure—in doing it. It is in the light of whether a man enjoys or fails to enjoy virtuous actions that we tell whether he has formed the right disposition toward them. Thus 2.3 1104b3-13 (but the whole chapter is relevant):

We must take as a sign of states of character the pleasure or pain that ensues on acts; for the man who abstains from bodily pleasures and delights in this very fact is temperate, while the man who is annoyed at it is self-indulgent, and he who stands his ground against things that are terrible and delights in this or at least is not pained is brave, while the man who is pained is a coward.[10] For moral excellence is concerned with pleasures and pains; it is on account of the pleasure that we do bad things, and on account of the pain that we abstain from noble ones. Hence we ought to have been brought up in a particular way from our very youth, as Plato says, so as both to delight in and to be pained by the things that we ought;[11] this is the right eduction. [Cf. 1.8 1099a17-21; 2.9 1109b1-5; 3.4 1113a31-33; 4.1 1120a26-27; 10.1 1172a20-23]

Such passages need to be received in the light of Aristotle's own analysis of pleasure in Books 7 and 10 (cf. esp. 10.3 1173b28-31): the delight of the temperate man who is pleased to be abstaining from overindulgence, or that of the brave man who is pleased to be standing up to a frightful situation, is not the same or the same in kind as the pleasure of indulgence or the relief of safety. The character of one's pleasure depends on what is enjoyed, and what the virtuous man enjoys is quite different from what the nonvirtuous enjoy; which is not to say that the enjoyment is not as intense, only that it is as different as the things enjoyed. Specifically, what the virtuous man enjoys, as the passage quoted makes very clear, is the practice of the virtues undertaken for its own sake. And in cases such as the facing of danger, cited here, and others, the actions which the practice of the virtues requires *could* only be enjoyed if they are seen as noble and virtuous and the agent delights in his achievement of something fine and noble (cf. 3.9 1117a33-b16). That is why his enjoyment or lack of it is the test of whether he really has the virtues.

Next, recall once more the statement in 2.4 that virtue involves choosing virtuous actions for their own sake, for what they are. If we are asked what virtuous actions are, an important part of the answer must be that they are just, courageous, temperate, and so forth, and in all cases noble.

(It is common to all virtuous actions that they are chosen because they are noble: 3.7. 1115b12-13; 4.1. 1120a23-24; 4.2. 1122b6-7;[12] EE 1230a27-29.) Accordingly, if learning to do and to take (proper) enjoyment in doing just actions is learning to do and to enjoy them for their own sake, for what they are, namely, just, and this is not to be distinguished from learning that they are enjoyable for themselves and their intrinsic value, namely, their justice and nobility, then perhaps we can give intelligible sense to the thesis that practice leads to knowledge, as follows. I may be told, and may believe, that such and such actions are just and noble, but I have not really learned for myself (taken to heart, made second nature to me) that they have this intrinsic value until I have learned to value (love) them for it, with the consequence that I take pleasure in doing them. To understand and appreciate the value that makes them enjoyable in themselves I must learn for myself to enjoy them, and that does take time and practice—in short, habituation.

Back now to 10.9. We have come to see that the young person there spoken of as a true lover of what is noble is not simply someone with a generalized desire to do whatever should turn out to be noble, but someone who has acquired a taste for, a capacity to enjoy for their own sake, things that are in fact noble and enjoyable for their own sake. He has learned, really learned, that they are noble and enjoyable, but as yet he does not understand why they are so. He does not have the good man's unqualified knowledge or practical wisdom, although he does have "the that" which is the necessary starting point for acquiring practical wisdom and full virtue. He is thus educable. According to 10.9, argument and discussion will encourage him toward virtue because he obeys a sense of shame (aidōs) as opposed to fear. What does this mean?

Aristotle discusses shame in 4.9:

> Shame should not be described as a virtue; for it is more like a feeling than a state of character. It is defined, at any rate, as a kind of fear of disgrace....
> The feeling is not becoming to every age, but only to youth. For we think young people should be prone to the feeling of shame because they live by feeling and therefore commit many errors, but are restrained by shame; and we praise young people who are prone to this feeling, but an older person no one would praise for being prone to the sense of disgrace, since we think he should not do anything that need cause this sense. [1128b10-12, 15-21]

Shame is the semivirtue of the learner. The learner is envisaged as a young person who lives by the feelings of the moment and for that reason makes mistakes. He wants to do noble things but sometimes does things that are disgraceful, ignoble, and then he feels ashamed of himself and his conduct.[13] Now Aristotle holds that all young people (and many older ones) live by the feeling of the moment and keep chasing after what at a given time appears pleasant. A sample statement is the following from 8.3. 1156a31-33:

> The friendship of young people seems to aim at pleasure; for they live under the guidance of emotion, and pursue above all what is pleasant to themselves and what is immediately before them. [cf. 1.3. 1095a4-8]

The point about those of the young who have been well brought up is that they have acquired a taste for pleasures—namely, the pleasures of noble and just actions—which others have no inkling of. The less fortunate majority also live by the feelings of the moment (10.9. 1179b13, 27-28), but since they find no enjoyment in noble and just actions, the only way to get them to behave properly is through fear of punishment (10.9. 1179b11-13). They will abstain from wrongdoing not because it is disgraceful, not because of what the actions are, unjust, but simply and solely as a means of avoiding the pains of punishment. Whereas the well-brought-up person has an entirely different sort of reason for avoiding them. Insofar as he realizes they are unjust or ignoble, they do not appear to him as pleasant or enjoyable; insofar as he does not realize this and so desires and perhaps does such things, he feels badly about it, ashamed of his failure. The actions pain him internally, not consequentially. He is therefore receptive to the kind of moral education which will set his judgment straight and develop the intellectual capacities (practical wisdom) which will enable him to avoid such errors.

The fundamental insight here is Plato's. For in discussing the development in the young of a set of motives concerned with what is noble and just, we are on the territory which Plato marked out for the middle part of his tripartite soul. The middle, so-called spirited part strives to do what is just and noble (*Rep.* 440cd), and develops in the young before reason (441a; cf. Ar. *Pol.* 1334b22-25). It is also the seat of shame: implicitly so in the story of Leontius and his indignation with himself for desiring to look on the corpses, explicitly in the *Phaedrus* (253d, 254e). The connection with anger, which we shall also find in Aristotle, is that typically anger is this same concern with what is just and noble directed outward toward other people (cf. *NE* 5.8. 1135b28-29). Aristotle owes to Plato, as he himself acknowledges in 2.3, the idea that these motivating evaluative responses are unreasoned—they develop before reason and are not at that stage grounded in a general view of the place of the virtues in the good life—and because they are unreasoned, other kinds of training must be devised to direct them on to the right kinds of object: chiefly, guided practice and habituation, as we have seen, but Aristotle also shares with Plato the characteristically Greek belief that musical appreciation will teach and accustom one to judge rightly and enjoy decent characters and noble actions through their representation in music (*Pol.* 1340a14 ff.). In both cases the underlying idea is that the child's sense of pleasure, which to begin with and for a long while is his only motive, should be hooked up with just and noble things so that his unreasoned evaluative responses may develop in connection with the right objects.

To say that these responses are unreasoned is to make a remark about their source. The contrast is with desires—the reasoned desires to which we shall come shortly—which derive from a reflective scheme of values organized under the heading of the good. But where desires and feelings are concerned, the nature of the response and its source are connected. It is not that the evaluative responses have no thought component (no intentionality): on the contrary, something is desired as noble or just, something inspires shame because it is thought of as disgraceful. The responses are grounded in an evaluation of their object, parallel to the way appetite is oriented to a conception of its object as something pleasant; in this sense both have their "reasons." The point is that such reasons need not invariably or immediately give way or lose efficacy to contrary considerations. There are, as it were, pockets of thought in us which can remain relatively unaffected by our overall view of things. This is a phenomenon which the century of psychoanalysis is well placed to understand, but the Greek philosophers already saw that it must be central to any plausible account of akrasia. It is that insight which backs their interweaving of the topics of akrasia and moral development.[14]

From all this it follows not only that for a long time moral development must be a less than fully rational process but also, what is less often acknowledged, that a mature morality must in large part continue to be what it originally was, a matter of responses deriving from sources other than reflective reason. These being the fabric of moral character, in the fully developed man of virtue and practical wisdom they have become integrated with, indeed they are now infused and corrected by, his reasoned scheme of values. To return to temperance:

As the child should live according to the direction of his tutor, so the appetitive element should live according to reason. Hence the appetitive element in a temperate man should harmonize with reason; for the noble is the mark at which both aim, and the temperate man desires the things he ought, as he ought, and when he ought; and this is what reason directs. [3.12. 1119b13-18; cf. 1.13. 1102b28; 9.4. 1166a13-14]

This is Aristotle's version of the psychic harmony which Plato sought to establish in the guardians of his ideal republic.

But Aristotle, as 10.9 makes clear, draws an important conclusion from the requirement of unreasoned beginnings which is not, perhaps, so evident in Plato (though we shall come back to Plato in a while). In Aristotle's view it is no good arguing or discussing with someone who lacks the appropriate starting points ("the *that*") and has no conception of just or noble actions as worthwhile in themselves, regardless of contingent rewards and punishments. To such a person you can recommend the virtues only insofar as they are required in a given social order for avoiding the pain of punishment—that is, for essentially external, contingent reasons. You cannot guarantee to be able to show they will contribute to some personal goal the agent already has, be it power, money, pleasure, or whatever; and even if in given contingent circumstances this connection with some antecedent personal goal could be made, you would not have given the person reason to pursue the virtues for their own sake, as a *part* of happiness, but only as a means to it.

This casts some light on what Aristotle takes himself to be doing in the *Nicomachean Ethics* and on why he asks for a good upbringing as a condition for intelligent study of the subject. If he is setting out "the *because*" of virtuous actions, he is explaining what makes them noble, just, courageous, and so on, and how they fit into a scheme of the good life, not why they should be pursued at all. He is addressing someone who already wants and enjoys virtuous action and needs to see this aspect of his life in a deeper perspective. He is not attempting the task so many moralists have undertaken of recommending virtue even to those who despise it: his lectures are not sermons, nor even protreptic argument, urging the wicked to mend their ways. From 10.9 it is clear that he did not think that sort of thing to be of much use; some, perhaps most, people's basic desires are already so corrupted that no amount of argument will bring them to see that virtue is desirable in and for itself (cf. 3.5. 1114a19-21). Rather, he is giving a course in practical thinking to enable someone who already wants to be virtuous to understand better what he should do and why.[15] Such understanding, as Aristotle conceives it, is more than merely cognitive. Since it is the articulation of a mature scheme of values under the heading of the good, it will itself provide new and more reflective motivation for virtuous conduct. That is why Aristotle can claim (1.3. 1095a5-6; 2.2. 1103b26-29; 2.4. 1105b2-5; 10.9. 1179a35-b4) that the goal of the study of ethics is action, not merely knowledge: to become fully virtuous rather than simply to know what virtue requires.[16] Someone with a sense of shame will respond, because he wants to do better at the right sorts of things. Someone with nothing but a fear of punishment will not respond; the only thing to do with him is tell him what he will get into trouble for.

After these rather general remarks about the character of Aristotle's enterprise we can begin to move toward the topic of akrasia. We need first to round out the picture of the motivational resources of the well-brought-up young person. For the unreasoned evaluative responses with which his upbringing has endowed him are not the only impulses that move him to act. Being a human being he has the physiologically based appetites as well. The object of these is, of course, pleasure (3.2. 1111b17; 3.11. 1118b8 ff.; 3.12. 1119b5-8; 7.3. 1147a32-34; 7.6. 1149a34-36; *EE* 1247b20), but they can be modified and trained to become desires for the proper enjoyment of bodily pleasures; this, we saw, is what is involved in acquiring the virtue of temperance. There are also instinctive reactions like fear to be trained into the virtue of courage. In a human being these feelings cannot be eliminated; therefore, they have to be trained. It would also be wrong to omit, though there is not room to discuss, the important fact that Aristotle in Books 8 and 9 takes seriously his dictum that the human being is by nature a social animal: friendship is itself something noble (8.1. 1155a29), and among the tasks of upbringing and education will be to give the right preliminary shape to the feelings and actions bound up with a wide range of relationships with other people.[17]

That said by way of introduction, we can consider a passage that takes us from moral education to akrasia (1.3. 1095a2-11):

Hence a young man is not a proper hearer of lectures on political science; for he is inexperienced in the actions that occur in life, but its discussions start from these and are about these; and, further, since he tends to follow his passions, his study will be vain and unprofitable, because the end aimed at is not knowledge but action. And it makes no difference whether he is young in years or youthful in character; the defect does not depend upon time, but on his living, and pursuing each successive object, as passion directs. For to such persons, as to the incontinent, knowledge brings no profit; but to those who form their desires and act in accordance with reason knowledge about such matters will be of great benefit.

Reason will appeal and be of use to the well-brought-up student because he is ready to form his desires in the light of reasoning; that we have already discovered. Other people, the immature of whatever age, form desires in a different way, and this is what happens in akrasia; or rather, as we shall see, it is one half of what happens in akrasia. We have here two kinds of people, distinguished by two ways of forming desires. What are these two ways of forming desires and how are they different?

As Aristotle describes what he calls deliberation (cf. esp. 3.2-4), it is a process whereby practical thought articulates a general good that we wish for and focuses it on a particular action it is in our power to do, thereby producing in us a desire to do this thing. A desire is formed by the realization that the action will fulfill one of the ends endorsed by our reasoned view of the good life, and this more specific desire—more specific, that is, than the general wish from which it derived—is what Aristotle calls choice:

> The object of choice being one of the things in our own power which is desired after deliberation, choice will be deliberated desire of things in our own power; for when we have decided as a result of deliberation, we desire in accordance with our deliberation.[18] [3.3. 1113a9-12]

Or, to paraphrase his remarks in a later book (6.2. 1139a21-33), choice is desire pursuing what reason asserts to be good.

So much for the forming of desires in the light of reasoning, which means: reasoning from the good. If a piece of practical reasoning does not relate to one's conception of the good, Aristotle does not count it deliberation, nor its outcome choice. But that does not mean he denies that reasoning and thinking are involved when desires are formed by the alternative process mentioned in 1.3. On the contrary, he describes such thinking in some detail, as we shall see if we now turn to his discussion of akrasia in Book 7.

The akratic (weak-willed) man is one who acts against his knowledge (judgment) and choice of the good;[19] he has a reasoned desire to do one thing, but under the influence of a contrary desire he actually does another. Clearly, however, this contrary desire itself needs to be generated if we are to understand how it fixes upon some particular object and fits into an adequate explanation of the akratic's behavior. Equally clearly, at least one main purpose Aristotle has in 7.3 is to exhibit akratic behavior under a standard pattern of explanation which he schematizes in the practical syllogism. His model case turns on the point that bodily appetite can supply a major premise of its own having to do with the pleasant rather than the good ("Everything sweet is pleasant" or "Sweets are nice"). That is to say, appetite sets an end that is not integrated into the man's life plan or considered scheme of ends, his overall view of the good. Unlike the self-indulgent man, whose (perverted) reason approves of every kind of sensual gratification as good in itself, the akratic is tempted to pursue an end which his reasoned view of life does not approve. But he acts, Aristotle emphasizes (7.3. 1147a35-b1), under the influence of a sort of reason and an opinion. His action is to be explained on the standard pattern by a combination of desire and thought, articulated in the syllogism "Sweets are nice; this is a sweet; so I'll have this." For the akratic this is only half the story—we have explained the action he actually performs but not the conflict behind it—but it is presumably the whole story of the immature people in 1.3. They form desires and undertake actions not in accordance with reason because their ends are simply things that strike them as pleasant at a given moment; they have no steady conception of the good to reason from.[20]

But there are other sources of incontinence than the bodily appetites: most notably, the unreasoned evaluative responses we met before as an important characteristic of the well-brought-up beginner. A parallel procedure to the one we have just followed will give us a picture of the sort of error that makes Aristotle's prospective student ashamed of himself. What in him is a mistake is one half of the conflict involved in nonappetitive akrasia.

The details appear in 7.6. 1149a25-b2:

Spirit seems to listen to reason to some extent, but to mishear it, as do hasty servants who run out before they have heard the whole of what one says and then mistake the order, or as dogs bark if there is but a knock at the door, before looking to see if it is a friend; so spirit on account of the warmth and hastiness of its nature, no sooner hears—even though it has not heard an order—than it springs to take revenge. For reason or imagination informs us that we have been insulted or slighted, and spirit, reasoning as it were that anything like this must be fought against, boils up straightway; while appetite, if reason or perception merely says that an object is pleasant, springs to the enjoyment of it. Therefore spirit follows reason in a sense, but appetite does not.

The description, which owes much to Plato (*Rep.* 440cd again),[21] implies the usual pattern of practical thought and reasoning: "Slights and injustices must be fought against; I have been wronged/slighted; so I should take revenge." Aristotle does not specify in detail the better syllogism which must also be present if this is to be a case of full incontinence, but we can supply the order which spirit does not stop to hear—for example, "It is better to wait and investigate an apparent wrong before taking revenge; this is an apparent wrong; so wait and investigate." As in Plato, the overeager dog in us[22] is concerned with what is noble and just, with honor and self-esteem, without taking thought for the consequences or the wider view.

If, then, these evaluative responses are in us as a result of our upbringing, and the bodily appetites are in us as a part of our natural inheritance as human beings, the seeds of akrasia are going to be with us as we enter Aristotle's lecture room. He will encourage us to think about our life as a whole, to arrive at a reasoned view of the good for man; but to begin with, until our understanding of "the *because*" has had a chance to become second nature with us, this will be superimposed upon well-established, habitual patterns of motivation and response which it will take time and practice to integrate with the wider and more adult perspective that Aristotle will help us achieve.

This seems to me important. I think many readers feel that Aristotle's discussion of akrasia leaves unexplained the point most in need of explanation. What they want to know is why the better syllogism is overcome. Not finding an answer they look for one in what Aristotle says in 7.3 about the akratic's knowledge and the way this is not used, not had, or dragged about. And then they are dissatisfied because no adequate answer is to be found in the discussion of *that* issue, for the good reason, I believe, that none is intended. The treatment of knowledge pinpoints what is to be explained. It is not itself the explanation. Even in the relatively easy case where a man simply fails to bring to bear on the situation (fails to use) some knowledge that he has, the fact of his failure requires explanation: he was distracted, overanxious, in haste, or whatever. For the more difficult cases Aristotle announces his explanation at 1147a-24-25:

Again, we may also view the cause as follows with reference to the facts of human nature.

Thus Ross's translation, but I think that the scope of "also" is the whole sentence,[23] which means this: we may also give an explanation of the phenomenon we have been endeavoring, with some difficulty, to describe. The explanation that follows is in terms of the two syllogisms, which together account for the conflict, and one of which explains the action the akratic man performs. But the outcome of the conflict might have been different. In the continent man it is; his action is to be explained by the better syllogism. So what determines whether it is appetite or reason that is victorious?

I submit that the question is misguided, at least so far as it looks for an answer in the immediate circumstances of the conflicted decision. If there is an answer, it is to be found in the man's earlier history. We must account for his present conflict in terms of stages in the development of his character which he has not yet completely left behind. For on Aristotle's picture of moral development, as I have drawn it, an important fact about the better syllogism is that it represents a later and less established stage of development. Hence what needs explanation is not so much why some people succumb to temptation as why others do not. What calls for explanation is how some people acquire continence or, even better, full virtue, rather than why most of us are liable to be led astray by our bodily appetites or unreasoned evaluative responses. It is no accident that Aristotle gives as much space to the akratic as a type of person as to isolated akratic actions, and it is characteristic of him that he measures the liability to incontinence by comparison with the normal man. Thus 7.10. 1152a25-33:

Now incontinence and continence are concerned with that which is in excess of the state characteristic of most men; for the continent man abides by his resolutions more and the incontinent man less than most men can.

Of the forms of incontinence, that of excitable people is more curable than that of those who deliberate but do not abide by their decision,[24] and those who are incontinent through habituation are more curable than those in whom incontinence is innate; for it is easier to change a habit than to change one's nature; even habit is hard to change just because it is like nature, as Evenus says:

> I say that habit's but long practice, friend,
> And this becomes men's nature in the end.

I trust that this second set of verses will by now reverberate in their full significance.

Given this temporal perspective, then, the real problem is this: How do we grow up to become the fully adult rational animal that is the end toward which the nature of our species tends? How does reason take hold on us so as to form and shape for the best the patterns of motivation and response which represent the child in us (3.12. 1119a33 ff.), that product of birth and upbringing which will live on unless it is brought to maturity by the education of our reason? In a way, the whole of the *Nicomachean Ethics* is Aristotle's reply to this question, so that this paper is nothing but a prolegomenon to a reading of the work. But I would like, in conclusion, to make a few brief comments concerning one important aspect of the process.

Consider 2.3. 1104b30-35:

There being three objects of pursuit[25] and three of avoidance, the noble, the advantageous, the pleasant, and their contraries, the base, the injurious, the painful, about all of these the good man tends to go right, and especially about pleasure; for this is common to the animals, and also it accompanies all objects of pursuit; for even the noble and the advantageous appear pleasant. Again, it has grown up with us all from infancy; which is why it is difficult to rub off this feeling, dyed as it is into our life.[26]

There are three irreducibly distinct categories of value for the fully virtuous man to get right—the three we have been discussing. Pursuit of pleasure is an inborn part of our animal nature; concern for the noble depends on a good upbringing; while the good, here specified as the advantageous,[27] is the object of mature reflection. We have seen that each of the three categories connects with a distinct set of desires and feelings, which acquire motivating effect at different stages of development. It has also become clear that Aristotle's insistence on keeping these distinctions is a key tactic in his vindication of akrasia against Socratic intellectualism.

Historically, the greatest challenge to the intelligibility of akrasia was the argument mounted by Socrates in Plato's *Protagoras* (351b ff.), which showed that weakness of will is unintelligible on the assumption, precisely, that there is only one "object of pursuit"—one category of value, within which all goods are commensurable, as it were, in terms of a single common coinage. Pleasure was the coinage chosen for the argument, but the important consideration was that if, ultimately, only one factor counts—call it F—and we have measured two actions X and Y in terms of F, and X comes out more F than Y does, there is nothing left to give value to Y to outweigh or compensate for its lesser quantity of F. The supposed akratic cannot possibly find reason to do Y, the less valuable action, rather than the better action X, because Y offers him less of the only thing he is after: pleasure or whatever else the F may happen to be. If what Y offers is less of the only thing the man seeks, pleasure, its offering that pleasure cannot intelligibly function as a reason for doing Y instead of the admittedly more attractive X.[28] The moral is close to hand: Y must offer something different in kind from X if the temptation and the man's succumbing to it are to be intelligible. Plato came to see this, and in the *Republic* it was in part to make akrasia and other forms of psychological conflict intelligible that he distinguished different objects of pursuit for the three parts of the soul. The passage quoted is Aristotle's version of that Platonic insight.[29]

However, the fact that there are three irreducibly distinct categories of value need not mean that one and the same thing cannot fall under two or more of them at once. To vindicate akrasia it is necessary only that this need not happen. The continent and the incontinent man do find the good and the pleasant or, in the anger case, the good and the noble in incompatible actions. Therein lies their conflict. The self-indulgent man, on the other hand, has no use for the noble and identifies present pleasure with his long-term good (cf. 3.11. 1119a1-4; 7.3. 1146b22-23; 7.7. 1150a-19-21; 7.8. 1150b29-30; 7.9. 1152a5-6). It would seem to follow that what we need to do to become fully virtuous instead of merely continent or worse is to bring those three categories of value into line with each other. We have already seen how a good upbringing makes the noble a part, perhaps the chief part, of the pleasant for us. Aristotle's lectures are designed to take the next step and make the noble a part, perhaps the chief part, of one's conception of the good (cf. *EE* 1249a11). That is why in 2.4 he makes it a condition of virtue that virtuous actions be chosen for their own sake. Choice, which is reached by deliberation from a conception of the good, includes a desire for them as good in themselves as well as noble and pleasant. But then he adds a further condition, and rightly, since choice by itself is compatible with incontinence and indeed continence. The further condition is that all this must proceed from a firm and unchangeable character. That is, it is second nature to the virtuous man to love and find his greatest enjoyment in the things he knows to be good (cf. 8.3. 1156b22-23). In him the three categories of value are in harmony. They have *become* commensurable in terms of pleasure and pain, but not in the objectionable way which led to Socratic intellectualism, since the virtuous person's conception of what is truly pleasant is now shaped by his independent, reasoned conception of what is good, just as it was earlier shaped by his father's or his teacher's advice about what is noble. Indeed, one definition of the noble given in the *Rhetoric* (1366a34) is to the effect that the noble is that which, being good, is pleasant because it is good (cf. *EE* 1249a18-19). And with all three categories in harmony, then, and then only, nothing will tempt or lure him so much as the temperate or brave action itself. Nothing else will seem as pleasurable. That is how Aristotle can assert (7.10. 1152a6-8) that the fully formed man of virtue and practical wisdom cannot be akratic. Quite simply, he no longer has reason to be.[30]

NOTES

For details of the works cited in these notes see the Bibliography at the end of this essay. References by name alone, without page number, are to a commentator's note on or a translator's rendering of the passage under discussion.

1. One exception is John Rawls, *A Theory of Justice*, chaps. 8-9, but the exception that most completely exemplifies what I am looking for is Richard Wollheim, "The Good Self and the Bad Self: The Moral Psychology of British Idealism and the English School of Psychoanalysis Compared"; it is noteworthy that he too has to go to the history of philosophy—specifically, to F. H. Bradley—to find a serious philosophical involvement with developmental questions.

2. *Contra* Aspasius, Stewart, Burnet, Ross, and Gauthier-Jolif, who take Aristotle to be speaking of a person of whom it is true neither that he has nor that he can get starting points.

3. So Aspasius, Eustratius, Heliodorus ad loc. and on 1098a33-b4. Stewart agrees. Burnet's proposal that "the *that*" is the much more general fact that the definition of happiness is such and such is right for 1.7 (see below), but at the moment the definition of happiness is the first principle or starting point we are working towards. For sane remarks on this and other misunderstandings of 1.4, see W. F. R. Hardie, *Aristotle's Ethical Theory*, pp. 34-36, although Hardie's own suggestion ("the *that*" is "a particular moral rule or perhaps the definition of a particular moral virtue") also errs on the side of generality.

4. Some scholars (Peters, Grant, Stewart, Gauthier-Jolif) keep the modes of acquisition down to the three explicitly mentioned by reading καὶ ἄλλαι δ' ἄλλως (1098b4) as a summary rather than an open-ended extension of the list:

"some in one way, some in another" rather than "others in other ways again." The rendering I have preferred has the support of Ross as well as the ancient tradition.

5. Not, or at least not in the first instance, the definition of happiness, as Burnet thinks: although this is "the *that*" which initiates the passage, it was secured by argument, not habituation, and Aristotle has turned parenthetically to a survey of wider scope (cf. T. H. Irwin, "First Principles in Aristotle's Ethics," p. 269 n. 18). Of course, the starting points in question and the habituation they presuppose will lead further (cf. esp. 7.8. 1151a15-19), but we are still at the beginning of Aristotle's lectures and of the progress they are designed to encourage.

6. Ross translates "string together"; he may not have intended the disparaging note the phrase now sounds. The fact is, the verb συνείρειν is not invariably, or even usually, disparaging in Aristotle's vocabulary. It is disparaging at *Met.* 1090b30, *De div.* 464b4, but not at *Soph. El.* 175a30, *Met.* 986a7, 995a10, 1093b-27, *De gen. et corr.* 316a8, 336b33, *De gen. anim.* 716a4, 741b9, *Probl.* 905a19.

7. Ross translates "gently born," which has aristocratic overtones irrelevant to the argument, even if Aristotle's sympathies happened to run in that direction. In fact, in the *Rhetoric* (1390b22-25) Aristotle says that most of the products of noble birth are good for nothing, and he makes a sharp distinction between noble birth (εὐγένεια) and noble character (γενναιότης). His view in the *Politics* is that it is likely that good birth will go with moral merit, but no more than that (*Pol.* 1283a36 in its wider context from 1282b14).

8. From here on I quote Ross's translation, corrected in a few places.

9. Strictly, the argument occurs twice, each paragraph being a distinct version, as Rassow saw ("Zu Aristoteles," pp. 594-596). But all that shows is that Aristotle thought the material important enough to have had two goes at expressing it satisfactorily.

10. Strictly, as Grant observes, doing the right thing with reluctance and dislike is rather a sign of continence (self-control) than of vice proper (cf. 3.2. 1111b-14-15, *EE* 1223b13-14, 1224b16-18); the attributions of self-indulgence and cowardice should not be pressed.

11. The reference is to Plato *Laws* 653a; cf. also *Rep.* 395d, featuring the idea that habit becomes second nature.

12. In the first and third of these passages Ross rather misleadingly translates "for honour's sake."

13. The connection between shame and the desire to do what is noble is very clear in the Greek. Shame is felt for having done αἰσχρά (things disgraceful, ignoble, base), and αἰσχρά is the standard opposite of καλά (things noble, fine, honorable). Hence to do something from fear of disgrace is not incompatible with doing it for the nobility of the act itself. This is made clear at 3.8. 1116a27-29, on "citizenly" courage: the only thing that is "second best" about this form of courage is that the citizen soldier takes his conception of what is noble from the laws and other people's expectations (1116a17-21) rather than having his own internalized sense of the noble and the disgraceful (cf. 3.7. 1116a11-12).

14. For a twentieth-century philosophical discussion that makes interesting use of Greek ideas to bring out the significance of the different sources of desire, see

Gary Watson, "Free Agency." Watson goes so far as to claim (pp. 210-211) that there are desires carrying absolutely no positive favoring of their object, not even an idea that it is pleasurable. But the cases he cites (a mother's sudden urge to drown her bawling child in the bath, a man who regards his sexual inclinations as the work of the devil) cry out for treatment in terms of the thought of pleasure having to be kept unconscious.

15. An example to the point is the celebrated argument in 1.7 which uses considerations about the distinctive activity (*ergon*) of man to show that happiness is activity in accordance with virtue: it is not an argument that would appeal to anyone who really doubted or denied that he should practice the virtues—so much is made clear in the closing pages of Book 1 of Plato's *Republic*, where Thrasymachus remains totally unmoved by an earlier version of the same argument—but it would say something to the reflective understanding of someone with the basic moral concerns which Aristotle presupposes in his audience. (Irwin, pp. 260-262 seems to be more optimistic.)

16. Not that Aristotle ever suggests that attendance at lectures such as his is the only way to get practical wisdom nor that attendance is sufficient by itself for developing the needed intellectual virtues. But he is serious about aiming to help his students in that direction, in a quite practical way. This is the solution to the traditional problem (most sharply formulated by Joachim, pp. 13-16) about why Aristotle failed to recognize that the *Ethics* is not itself practical but a theoretical examination *of* the practical. The real failure here is in the impoverished conception of practical reason which finds it a puzzle to accept the practical orientation of Aristotle's enterprise (see further Irwin, pp. 257-259).

17. Here again Aristotle borrows from the middle part of Plato's tripartite soul: the *Republic* (375a ff.) likened the guardians to noble dogs, with special reference to their warm and spirited nature, and in the *Politics* (1327b38-1328a1) Aristotle expressly alludes to the *Republic* when he suggests that the capacity of the soul in virtue of which we love our familiars is spirit ($\theta \nu \mu \acute{o} \varsigma$).

18. It might be objected that Aristotle did not need to make choice a new and more specific desire. Given a wish for X and the realization that Y will secure X, explanation is not furthered by adding in another desire; it should be enough to say that the man wanted X and saw Y as a way of securing it (for intimations of this line of argument see Thomas Nagel, *The Possibility of Altruism*, chaps. 5-6). But a new and specific desire is not explanatorily redundant in Aristotle's scheme if it helps to explain the pleasure taken in a virtuous act, a pleasure that ought to be more specific to the particular action than the pleasure of simply doing *something* to fulfill one's wish to be virtuous.

19. Against knowledge or judgment: 7.1. 1145b12; 7.3. 1146b24 ff. Against choice: 7.3. 1146b22-24; 7.4. 1148a9-10; 7.8. 1151a5-7; 7.10. 1152a17.

20. That this is the point, not a denial that they engage in practical thinking at all, is clear from 10.9. 1179b13-14: "living by passion they pursue the pleasures appropriate to their character and *the means to them*." Cf. 6.9. 1142b18-20; *EE* 1226b30.

21. This is one of the reasons why it seems preferable to translate $\theta \nu \mu \acute{o} \varsigma$ "spirit" throughout, rather than "anger" (Ross).

22. The dog image of 1149a28-29 brings with it an allusive resonance to large tracts of Plato's *Republic:* cf. n. 17 above.

23. Compare W. J. Verdenius, " Καί Belonging to a Whole Clause." A good parallel in Aristotle is *An. Post.* 71b20-22, where καί emphasizes not the immediately following τὴν ἀποδεικτικὴν ἐπιστήμην, which merely resumes τὸ ἐπίστασθαι and the point that this must be of necessary truths, but rather the subsequent characterization of the premises from which these necessary truths are derived; that is the new point signaled by καί (here I am indebted to Jacques Brunschwig).

24. For these two forms of akrasia see 7.7. 1150b19-22.

25. Ross's translation "choice" badly misses the point, since not every pursuit (αἵρεσις) is a choice (προαίρεσις) in the technical sense explained earlier. Note that this means that Aristotle does not endorse in every particular the commonplace (*endoxon*) which forms the famous first sentence of *NE*: he does not, strictly, think that every action aims at some good—for one thing, akratic action does not.

26. The dyeing metaphor is yet another allusion to Plato's treatment of these topics: cf. *Rep.* 429d-430b.

27. Perhaps because Aristotle is making argumentative use of a commonplace (endoxon): cf. *Top.* 105a27, 118b27. For the sense in which the advantageous = the good is the object of practical wisdom see 6.5. 1140a25-28, 6.7. 1141b4-8: the man of practical wisdom deliberates correctly about what is good and advantageous to himself with reference to the supreme goal of living the good life; but of course the same equation can be made when the deliberation concerns a more particular end (6.9. 1142b27-33).

28. Here I can only sketch my account of the *Protagoras* argument, but various people have independently been propounding similar accounts for quite a time, and the key idea is beginning to emerge in print: see, for example, David Wiggins, "Weakness of Will, Commensurability, and the Objects of Deliberation and Desire."

29. In a different context (*Pol.* 1283a3-10) Aristotle expressly denies that all goods are commensurable (συμβλητόν); similarly *EE* 1243b22, *NE* 9.1. 1164b2-6. Earlier in life Aristotle may have been tempted to think otherwise. *An. Pr.* 68a25-b7 is a sketch toward a calculus of preference relations as envisaged in *Top.* 3.1-3, where 116b31-36 aspires to cardinal measurement, not just a relative ordering. Yet it is difficult to judge how far Aristotle thought he could take the project, for *Top.* 118b27-37 seems to be clear that there is no question of quantitative commensurability across the three categories of the noble, the pleasant, and the advantageous. Hence when Aristotle at *De an.* 434a8-9 says that deliberation requires the measurement of alternatives by a single standard, it is important that in the context he is concerned to mark the difference between rational agents and unreasoning animals, for which purpose the simplest achievement of deliberative calculation will suffice. ἀνάγκη ἑνὶ μετρεῖν need not be generalized to all deliberation.

30. This paper was one result of the leisure I enjoyed from my tenure of a Radcliffe Fellowship. I am grateful to the Radcliffe Trust for the gift of the Fellowship

and to University College, London, for allowing me to take it up. The paper has been improved by discussions at a number of universities (London, Cambridge, Reading, Sussex, Princeton, Berkeley, and the University of Massachusetts at Amherst) and by the comments of David Charles, James Dybikowski, Martha Craven Nussbaum, Amélie O. Rorty, Richard Sorabji, and Susan Khin Zaw. I only regret that to deal adequately with all their criticisms would require the paper to be even longer than it is. But perhaps my greatest debt is to the members of my graduate seminar at Princeton in 1970 (two of them now writing in the present volume), from whom I received my first understanding and appreciation of Aristotle's ethics.

BIBLIOGRAPHY

Aspasius. *In Ethica Nicomachea quae supersunt commentaria.* Edited by G. Heylbut. Berlin, 1889.

Burnet, John. *The Ethics of Aristotle.* London, 1900.

Eustratius. *Eustratii et Michaelis et Anonyma in Ethica Nicomachea commentaria.* Edited by G. Heylbut. Berlin, 1892.

Gauthier, René Antoine, and Jean Yves Jolif. *L'Éthique à Nicomaque,* 2d edition. Louvain and Paris, 1970.

Grant, Sir Alexander. *The Ethics of Aristotle,* 4th edition. London, 1885.

Hardie, W. F. R. *Aristotle's Ethical Theory.* Oxford, 1968.

Heliodorus. *In Ethica Nicomachea paraphrasis.* Edited by G. Heylbut. Berlin, 1889.

Irwin, T. H. "First Principles in Aristotle's Ethics," *Midwest Studies in Philosophy* 3 (1978), 252-272.

Joachim, H. H. *Aristotle: the Nicomachean Ethics.* Oxford, 1951.

Nagel, Thomas. *The Possibility of Altruism.* Oxford, 1970.

Peters, F. H. Translation of *Nicomachean Ethics.* 10th ed. London, 1906.

Rassow, H. "Zu Aristoteles," *Rheinisches Museum,* N.F. 43 (1888), 583-596.

Rawls, John. *A Theory of Justice.* Oxford, 1972.

Ross, Sir David. Translation of *Nicomachean Ethics* in *The Works of Aristotle Translated into English,* vol. 9. Oxford, 1925.

Stewart, J. A. *Notes on the Nicomachean Ethics.* Oxford, 1892.

Verdenius, W. J. " Καί Belonging to a Whole Clause," *Mnemosyne,* 4th ser. 29 (1976), 181.

Watson, Gary. "Free Agency," *Journal of Philosophy* 72 (1975), 205-220.

Wiggins, David. "Weakness of Will, Commensurability, and the Objects of Deliberation and Desire," *Proceedings of the Aristotelian Society,* n.s. 79 (1978-79), 251-277 (chap. 14 of this anthology).

Wollheim, Richard. "The Good Self and the Bad Self: The Moral Psychology of British Idealism and the English School of Psychoanalysis Compared," *Proceedings of the British Academy* 61 (1975), 373-398.

6

Aristotle on Action

J. L. Ackrill

Aristotle's statements about action and choice seem to involve serious inconsistencies—and on topics central to ethics and to his *Ethics*. Here are some samples.[1]

(a) Aristotle holds that when we choose to do something we always choose with a view to some end, for the sake of something; but he also insists that a man who does a virtuous act is not doing it virtuously—is not displaying virtue—unless he has chosen it "for itself."

(b) Actions are done for the sake of other things, and things we can do are not themselves the ends with a view to which we do them; yet action (*praxis*) differs from production (*poiesis*), according to Aristotle, precisely because it is its own end.

(c) In recommending the theoretical life Aristotle says that whereas contemplation "aims at no end beyond itself" fine actions do "aim at some end and are not desirable for their own sake"; but in recommending the life of action he says that doing noble and good deeds is a thing desirable for its own sake, and that "those activities are desirable in themselves from which nothing is sought beyond the activity."

Passages like these suggest two problems. First, how can action be good in itself if it is valued as a means to *eudaimonia*? Secondly, how can an action be something done to bring about an outcome and yet be distinguished from a production because done for its own sake? The first

93

problem invites discussion of Aristotle's view of morality and its foundation: is it valuable in itself or only because it promotes something else?
The second—with which the present note is concerned—calls for an
examination of Aristotle's concept of an action, and of his distinction
between *praxis* and *poiesis*.[2]

Commentators discussing this distinction often fail to face the real difficulty, that actions often or always *are* productions and productions
often or always *are* actions. (The idea that some periods of the day are
occupied by action-episodes and others by production-episodes would
obviously be absurd even if "production" referred only to the exercise of
special techniques or skills, since a period of such exercise could certainly
be a period during which an action, of promise-keeping for example, was
being performed. In fact, however, Aristotle's notion of production is
not limited either to technical performances or to the making of material
objects.) The brave man's action *is* fighting uphill to relieve the garrison,
and the just man is paying off his debt *by* mending his neighbor's fence.
How then is one to understand the thesis that paying off a debt is an
action but mending a fence is a production? I propose to examine one or
two passages in which Aristotle speaks of choosing to do something "for
itself" or of doing something *hekousiōs* (intentionally), in order to see if
they throw any light on the problem. For Aristotle closely connects the
concept of *praxis* with choice; and a man's actions, properly speaking,
for which he can be praised or blamed, are confined to what he does if
not from choice at least *hekousiōs*.

In *Nicomachean Ethics* 2.4 Aristotle confronts a puzzle: how can he
say—as he has said—that men become just by doing just things, when
surely men who do just things are already, *eo ipso*, just? He first remarks
that even in the case of skills correct performance does not suffice to
prove the performer's possession of the relevant skill. He goes on to make
further points specially relevant to virtues as opposed to skills. It is not
enough that the thing done should itself have a certain character, say justice, in order to justify the inference that it is done justly and that the
agent is a just man; it is necessary that he should do it knowingly, choosing to do it for itself, and from a settled disposition. Actual things done
(*pragmata*) are called just if they are such as a just man would do. But it
is not he who does them that is just, but he who does them in the way in
which just men do.

Aristotle thus draws a strong contrast between *what* is done—which
might have been done from various motives or inadvertently—and *why*
it is done. If inferences to the character of the agent are to be made from
the character of the thing done, it must have been done "for itself." This
last, however, seems to be an unhappy formulation. For the "actual thing

done" must be some performance—such as mending a neighbour's fence —which is in fact (in the circumstances) just, though it might be done by someone ignorant of or indifferent to its justice. But when it is asked whether the doer chose to do it for *itself* the question is of course whether he chose to do it because it was just, not whether he chose to do it because it was mending a neighbor's fence. How can doing something because it is ϕ be doing it for itself or for its own sake unless the thing done is specified precisely as ϕ? Only if the action is designated not as mending a fence but as *the ϕ act* does the expression "for itself" get the necessary grip. Yet the ϕ act *is* some such performance as mending a fence, and it does not seem natural to say in such a case that the agent has done two things at the same time. It is easy to understand how Aristotle, not having addressed himself to this theoretical difficulty, should have said of an action both that it is done for itself and that it is done for the sake of something else: the ϕ act *is* done for itself, the mending of a fence is *not* done for its own sake but for its ϕness.

It may be thought that to take mending a fence as one's example of an "actual thing done" is to make it unnecessarily difficult to interpret the requirement that the just agent should choose to do what he does "for itself." Mending a fence is all too obviously something in itself unattractive, nor is it by any means always the just thing to do. However, Aristotle's position would hardly be easier if an example like repaying a debt were used. It is not always just to repay a debt either. In any case, even if what is done could be given a description such that *any* such act would be just, yet such an act would inevitably have other characteristics too. What "for itself" points to will be clear only if the act is brought before us precisely *as* having the relevant characteristic, e.g. *as* the just act: it is not enough that it should actually or even necessarily have it.

One way of bringing out the point at issue is to distinguish two ways of understanding the expression "do something that is ϕ." It may mean "do something (that is ϕ)," where there is no implication that the doer necessarily knows or supposes that what he does is ϕ. Or it may mean "do something-that-is-ϕ," where it is implied that the doer knows or supposes it to be ϕ (whether or not he does it *because* it is ϕ, "for itself"). Aristotle comes close to this kind of formulation in *Nicomachean Ethics* 5.8. Here, before contrasting the character of what is done with the character of the agent (along the same lines as 2.4), he raises a preliminary question: before asking whether someone did a just act "for itself" (or for ulterior motives) we must ask whether he *did a just act* at all, properly speaking.

Aristotle first distinguishes between "doing a thing that is in fact wrong" and "doing-wrong" (*adikein*, a single word). To do-wrong is to do something wrong knowingly and intentionally. If one does what is as a matter of fact wrong but does not know that what one is doing is wrong, one cannot be said to do-wrong (save *per accidens*) (5.8.1). Later in the chapter (5.8.4) Aristotle applies the same principle to expressions like "doing what is right" and "doing things that are wrong." A man who has been *compelled* to return a deposit cannot be said to have done-right or even to have *done what is right*, save *per accidens*. So it seems that what a man can be said to have done strictly, without qualification, not *per accidens*, is what he has done unforced and knowingly.

The contrast between doing something, properly speaking, and only doing something *per accidens*, differs from the earlier contrast between doing something for itself and doing it for an ulterior motive. But here again what is involved is a context that does not permit free substitution of alternative descriptions of the agent's performance. In the strict use a man "does—" only if he "does—knowingly." An action of his, then, is not something some of whose features or circumstances he may be ignorant of. Rather it must be *defined* by features he is aware of, since it is only *as* so defined that he can be said to have done it *knowingly* and hence to have *done* it at all (strictly speaking).

Aristotle implies then that nothing a man does unknowingly can count as an action of his. Does he recognize that, since there are on any occasion a great number of facts an agent knows about what he is doing, there will be a great number of different ways of characterizing what he is doing knowingly? Does he see that what is done may be subject to praise under one description and blame under another, or may constitute one offense under one description and a different one under another, or may invite moral appraisal under one description and technical appraisal under another?

In *Nicomachean Ethics* 5.8, between the sections already summarized, Aristotle explains what counts as *hekousion*: "whatever of the things in his power a man does in knowledge and not ignorance of either the person, the instrument, or the result—e.g. whom he strikes, what he strikes with, and with what result—and [knowing] each of them not *per accidens*."[3] This last requirement is explained by an example: you may know that you are striking a man but not know that the man is your father; so, Aristotle implies, you do not know *whom* you are striking (your father) save *per accidens*. Similarly, he adds, as regards the result and the whole action.

Here, then, Aristotle touches on some of the various factors or circumstances of any practical situation—whose number and diversity he often, of course, stresses; and he uses the notion of knowing *per accidens*, a notion that is essentially connected with the idea that free substitution of extensionally equivalent expressions is not always permissible. Yet he conspicuously fails to remark that though on his account you do not strike your father *hekousiōs*, you do strike a man *hekousiōs*; or that, in virtue of different known factors in a given situation, a man may be accused of—and offer diverse excuses for—different offenses. Aristotle's mind is clearly on giving conditions for ascribing responsibility for an act as already specified in the accusation: "he struck his father a fatal blow with a sword."

We must, however, examine Aristotle's fuller account of actions and excuses in *Nicomachean Ethics* 3.1. He starts with the privative term, *akousion*: a man can deny responsibility for something done—claim that it was *akousion*—if he can plead force or ignorance. By "force" is meant real physical force, where it would in fact be misleading to say that the man had *done* anything—"the *arche* [originating principle] is outside and nothing is contributed by the person who acts or rather is acted on." By "ignorance" is meant ignorance of facts, circumstances, and consequences, not ignorance of "the universal," of what is good or lawful. Corresponding to these negative tests for *akousion*—not due to an *arche* in the person, not known—is the positive formula: the *hekousion* is "that whose originating principle is in the agent himself, he being aware of the particular circumstances of the action."

Various questions arise as to the interpretation of the ignorance test, and Aristotle discusses some of them. But the point of concern to us he does not bring out, and indeed his way of speaking serves to conceal it. I give someone a drink not knowing it to be poison—I think it will refresh but in fact it will kill. Ignorance makes my act *akousion*. *What* act? Clearly what I did through ignorance was to poison my friend, not to give him a drink. The ignorance that makes my act *akousion* is ignorance of a feature that goes to define that act and not ignorance of a feature that simply characterizes it. Now some of Aristotle's formulations could perhaps be construed in such a way as to accommodate this point. When, after referring to the various circumstances of action, he says that "the man ignorant of any of these acts *akousiōs*" (3.1.15), we might take him to mean that corresponding to ignorance of any factor there will be some act the man can be said to have done *akousiōs*. And when he says that that is *hekousion* which a man does in knowledge of person, instrument, and result (5.8.3), we might take him to be using only by way of example a case where the performance in question is specified as the bringing about of a certain result by using a certain instrument on a certain person. This would then be consistent with his allowing that that is also *hekousion* which a man does in knowledge of person and instrument (but in ignorance of result): he struck his father *hekousiōs* (though he struck his father a fatal blow *akousiōs*).

These would, however, be very forced ways of interpreting Aristotle's words. His own approach is indicated by the fact that, after going through a number of things of which one might be ignorant, he says that one who was ignorant of any of these is thought to have acted *akousiōs* —and especially if he was ignorant on the most important points (3.1.18). It is clear that Aristotle is not associating knowledge or ignorance of this, that, or the other with various act-descriptions involving this, that, or the other, with respect to each of which the question "did he do it *hekousiōs?*" could be asked. Rather he is asking simply whether a man "acted *hekousiōs*" on some occasion, and saying that he did so only if he knew all the important circumstances.

It is easy to understand why Aristotle should have spoken as he does. In a simple exposition he considers simple and striking cases. We all know what Oedipus did, and we are quite willing to say simply that he "acted *akousiōs.*" The enormity of the charge of striking his father a fatal blow pushes aside any minor infelicities of which he may simultaneously have been guilty, and even submerges the quite serious charge (which he might well find it harder to evade) of having struck a man. In such a dramatic case one can ask simply whether a man "acted *hekousiōs,*" or whether he "did it *hekousiōs,*" without entering into or even noticing theoretical questions about the identification of actions.

It is difficult, however, to see how closer consideration could have left Aristotle satisfied with his way of speaking. For whether he identified the thing done ("it") with the person's bodily movement M or with the total package M (a, b, c . . .)—where the letters in brackets stand for various circumstances etc.—he would find it impossible to raise the questions that we (and the courts) want to raise. But if he treated M(a), M(b), etc. as different things done (perhaps different offenses), about each of which separately the question whether it was done *hekousiōs* could be asked, he could not say that the knowledge required for an affirmative answer was knowledge of all or of the most important factors in the situation. The knowledge required for an affirmative answer to the question about M(a) would be simply the knowledge that M would be M(a).

It might be said that, though what a man does on a particular occasion must be (as it were) taken apart in this way—the question about intention or "voluntariness" being directed not at the whole package but at the elements in it, M(a), M(b), etc.—yet what a man does *hekousiōs* on a particular occasion can be treated as a single action (*the* action he performed)—say, M(a, g, m . . .), where the letters in brackets stand for the circumstances etc. known to the agent. Certainly, however much he disliked some of the circumstances, however much he regretted that doing M(a) would be doing M(g), he did know that it was precisely this package

—M(a, g, m . . .)—that he was taking, and he took it because on the whole he wanted to do so rather than not.

There are, nevertheless, still reasons for picking M(a, g, m . . .) apart. First, he may well have to go to different courts to meet different charges in respect of M(a), M(g), etc. In one court M(a) will be the action complained of, and that it was also M(g) will be, perhaps, a mitigating circumstance. Secondly, even if our knowledge that he took the package because on the whole he wanted to make it superfluous to ask separately whether M(a) was *hekousion*, whether M(g) was *hekousion*, etc., we may well want to ask with respect to each whether he was glad or sorry (or indifferent) that he was doing *that*. Was *that* what made him take the whole package, or was it perhaps an element he regretted but had to accept in order to get some other? He wanted M(a, g, m . . .) on the whole. Was it perhaps only (or precisely) M(a) that he *really* wanted?

This takes us back to the first part of Aristotle's account of the *hekousion*—"that whose *arche* [originating principle] is in the agent himself, he being aware of the particular circumstances." The *arche* relevant for action is no doubt desire, *orexis*. (For, as Aristotle recognizes, not every internal *arche* leads to performances classifiable—even given knowledge—as *hekousia*. Many processes of a biological kind are not influenced by our wishes and desires; they are not *hekousia* and they are not *akousia* either. 5.8.3. 1135a33-b2.) But of what exactly is desire the originating principle? Is it, to use the above crude symbolism, M or M(a) or M(a, g, m . . .) or M(a, b, c . . .)? Does Aristotle's general account of human and animal movement throw any light on this?

The central features of this account are familiar. If an object of thought or imagination becomes an object of desire, a man's faculty of desire is stimulated and moves him towards realizing or achieving it. Three "causes"—or explanatory factors—are mentioned here: the final cause, the object of desire; the efficient cause, the man's actual desire; and the formal cause, the essence or definition of the movement produced. In a certain way these three "causes" coincide, as Aristotle says, for example in *Physics* 2.3, where he takes his illustrations from productive crafts.

It would appear then that *what* action precisely has been performed— what action is genuinely explained by the *arche* in the agent—depends on what the object of thought and desire was. Unfortunately, difficulties at once arise. Aristotle often gives as the object of desire (or of its species, appetite and wish) a *characteristic* (like the pleasant, the noble), and not something that could strictly be *done*. When he does speak of what we may want to *do* he is naturally often concerned with cases in which deliberation is involved, where one thing is done as a means to another or where the pros and cons of a course of action have to be weighed up. So an immediate distinction presents itself between what one primarily wants to do and what one wants to do derivatively, insofar as one thinks it necessary to achieve one's real aim. Should we then say that what we *really* want to do, or want to do without qualification, is only what we want nonderivatively to do? Aristotle comes close to this in *Nicomachean Ethics* 7.9.1: "if a person chooses or pursues this for the sake of that, *per se* it is that that he pursues and chooses, but *per accidens* it is this. But when we speak without qualification we mean what is *per se*." This suggests a series or hierarchy of descriptions of what a man does because he desires to, each successive description coming nearer to revealing exactly what he aims at. In our simple case, M(a, g, m . . .) comes first, and is followed by M(a): his wanting the package was derivative from his wanting M(a). But if it is always for some desirable characteristic that a possible line of action appeals, there will be M(φ) after M(a) in the series. Desire is then the *arche* of M(a, g, m . . .), M(a) and M(φ)—but primarily of the last and only derivatively of the others.

It is clear, I think, that what Aristotle says about desire as the originating principle of action does not provide an answer to the sorts of questions about actions and action-descriptions that were left unanswered by his discussions of responsibility. Moreover, his account of the *physiology* of animal movement, which shows how desire operates as a physical (non-intentional) process leading to muscular and limb movements (how desire is in a way the *arche* of M), gives no clue as to how the physiological story is connected to the psychological one, or how questions about the individuation of movements are related to questions about the individuation of actions.

I conclude that while Aristotle has much to tell us about the responsibility for actions, the motives of actions, and the physiology of actions, he does not direct his gaze steadily upon the questions "What *is* an action?" and "What is *an* action?" It is not that such questions would be beyond him. He revels in questions of this kind, and he has the conceptual and linguistic equipment needed to tackle them. Whatever the reasons why he did not tackle these questions head-on, it seems likely that this failure is itself the reason for many of the "incoherences" and "contradictions" to be found in passages such as those I quoted at the beginning.

NOTES

1. *Nicomachean Ethics* 1.1; 2.4; 3.3; 6.2, 4, 5, 12; 10.6, 7.
2. In October 1974 I delivered at the Chapel Hill Colloquium in Philosophy a paper entitled "Aristotle on Action." The first part discussed the place of action

in *eudaimonia*, and it expressed views similar to those in "Aristotle on *Eudaimonia*," *Proceedings of the British Academy* 60 (1974), 339-359 (chap. 2 of this anthology). It is the second part of that paper that is here published, more or less as it was given. A number of workers in the Aristotelian vineyard have suggested that it would be useful to have it in print, in spite of its evident limitations.

3. The flow of the sentence is in favor of understanding "knowing" rather than "doing" before "each of them." (For "knowing *per accidens*" see for example *Posterior Analytics* 76a1, 93a25, 93b25.)

7

Being Properly Affected: Virtues and Feelings in Aristotle's Ethics

L. A. Kosman

I

A moral virtue, or as we might say, a good state of character, is for Aristotle an established disposition for free and deliberate conduct of the right sort, a *hexis prohairetikē,* as he puts it.[1] In providing an account of the moral life in which the concept of a virtue or state of character is central, Aristotle reveals what is clear throughout the *Ethics*: that he, like Plato, thinks of the question of moral philosophy as not simply how I am to conduct myself in my life, but how I am to become the kind of person readily disposed so to conduct myself, the kind of person for whom proper conduct emanates characteristically from a fixed disposition. Of course the good life is a life of activity—a life, that is, in which such dispositions are realized and not simply possessed by persons of worth. Otherwise a perfectly desirable life might be spent asleep. But the good life is one whose activities are not simply in accord with the virtues but are the appropriate realizations of these virtues, and the virtues themselves are ready dispositions toward these activities. The good person is not simply one who behaves in a certain way, but one who behaves that way out of a certain character.

II

When we recognize the Aristotelian virtues to be dispositions toward deliberate and proper human conduct, it becomes tempting to take Aristotle to be thinking in terms of human action, of the virtues as fixed tendencies toward modes of *praxis*. But is that right? It is clear that no thoughtful reading of the *Ethics* can help but note the centrality of praxis in Aristotle's moral theory and its important connections to the other key notions in that theory—for example, responsibility, choice, and practical reasoning. But virtues are not in Aristotle's view dispositions solely toward modes of acting. Throughout his discussion of the moral virtues, and particularly in his earliest account of them in Book 2, Aristotle makes clear that the activities for which virtues are dispositions are of two sorts, actions and feelings, *praxeis kai pathē*. He rarely mentions virtue in Book 2 with respect to action alone, but rather in terms of this dual phrase. The first account of the notion of a disposition with which moral virtue will be identified, indeed, is exclusively in terms of feelings: *kath' has pros ta pathē echomen eu ē kakōs*.[2] So the virtues are dispositions toward feeling as well as acting.

Acting and feeling are not simply two modes of human conduct among others. This can be seen if we use the older and more etymologically parallel English renderings of Aristotle's *praxis* and *pathos* and describe the moral virtues as dispositions toward *action* and *passion*—toward characteristic modes of conduct, in other words, in which the virtuous person acts and is acted upon—is the moral subject, as it were, of active and passive verbs.

A view of feelings and emotions as passions or affections—that is, as instances of a subject being acted upon, of an agent, so to speak, as patient—is embedded in the very word which we translate by "feeling" or by "emotion," the Greek word *pathos*. This word, like the verb *paschein*, of which it is a derivative form, has an earliest sense of what is experienced or undergone by way of misfortune or harm—what is, as we say, *suffered*—but comes subsequently, as with "suffer," to have a general sense simply of what is experienced, a mode of a subject's being acted upon.[3]

Insofar as Aristotle sees fear, anger, desire, pleasure, and pain as pathē, as passions, he views what we would call feelings or emotions as modes of a subject being acted upon. This fact is further revealed in the list Aristotle offers us of emotions with which moral virtues are concerned and in which there can be excess, deficiency, and right measure. The majority of items on this list are described by passive verbs; in thinking of fear, anger, pleasure, or pain, Aristotle is thinking of being frightened, being angered, being pleased, being pained. When I am afraid, something is frightening me; when I am angry, something is angering me. When in general I am experiencing an emotion or feeling of the sort which Aristotle would call a pathos, something is affecting me; I am being acted upon in some way, where the concept of being acted upon is reciprocal to that of my acting in some way.[4] Actions and feelings are thus for Aristotle modes of human being—action and passion—seen in terms of reciprocal concepts basic to our understanding of entities in general, the concepts of acting and being acted upon.

The opposition between acting and being acted upon, that is, the praxis/pathos opposition, is, to be sure, peculiar to human activity, because praxis is according to Aristotle peculiar to human activity. But it is only a special instance of a more general structural duality, that of *poiein* and *paschein*, doing and being done.[5] This dualism is encountered early in and throughout Aristotle's writings, from its special appearance as an apparently reciprocal pair of relatively minor modes of being in the *Categories* to the important cosmological role recognized in the treatise *On Generation and Corruption.*[6]

This more general opposition of *poiein/paschein*, insofar as it governs and structures the most basic forms of being, understood as activity, is thus a central and fundamental structural principle of Aristotle's ontology. Action and passion then similarly represent terms of a fundamental structural principle of human activity. "Activity" here must take on a sense broad enough to include both acting and being acted upon—must, that is, include modes of active human being in which the human individual is both subject and object of the action, both agent and patient.

The notion of including as an aspect of human activity what an individual suffers, what is done to an individual in addition to what the individual does, may go against our intuitions. It is only an individual's actions, we might feel, which truly belong to the being of a human individual in its most basic sense. This intuition is something to which we shall have to return. But it should not blind us to the fact that the affections and passive sufferings of entities seem to be among the authentic characteristics which such entities have, and this is true for both human and nonhuman beings.

If the kinds of human activity now understood in this broader sense include not only what are, more strictly speaking, instances of human action but also instances of human passion in the sense of being acted upon, and these latter are understood as paradigmatic instances of feelings or emotions, then Aristotle's moral theory must be seen as a theory not only of how to *act* well but also of how to *feel* well; for the moral virtues are states of character that enable a person to exhibit the right kinds of emotions as well as the right kinds of actions. The art of proper living, we should say, includes the art of feeling well as the correlative discipline to the art of acting well.

III

Moral philosophy, then, should count as an important question that of sentimental education and should recognize the proper cultivation of our feelings as within the domain of our moral concerns. But how could this be? It appears to be a distinction between our actions and our passions that actions are within our control, whereas passions are not; we are the initiating principle of what we do, but not of what is done to us. Aristotle seems to make exactly this point in claiming that we are angered or frightened, for example, not by choice—*aprohairetōs*, as he puts it.[7]

But if we give allegiance to the meta-ethical dictum that "ought" implies "can," then it seems problematic how a moral philosophy could concern itself with questions of our feelings in contrast with questions of how we ought to act in response to or in light of those feelings. What is, as Aristotle would say, *eph'hēmin*—within our power—is surely what we do, but not what is done to us.

One way in which this objection might be met is by pointing out what I have emphasized earlier: the important role of the concept of *virtue*. Since we are primarily called upon by a moral theory not to act and be acted upon in certain ways but rather to be the kinds of persons disposed so to act and be acted upon, the question of what feelings are or are not immediately within our powers may be moot.

But could a moral theory be concerned with sentimental education even in this sense, namely, with the cultivation of proper sentimental dispositions? For in what sense might such dispositions themselves be said to be within the domain of choice or *prohairesis*? Why, in other words, wouldn't the question be pushed one step further back? And how then could we be said in the first place to have a *disposition* to be acted upon rather than to act in certain ways? Let me first say something preliminary about this latter question.

Aristotle's claim that virtues are dispositions toward feeling as well as action can be seen, in light of our recognition that feelings are passions, to rest upon a theory of potentiality which recognizes the existence of passive as well as active powers. For since a disposition is a power—that is, a potentiality that renders an entity capable of a mode of actual being —and since feelings are passions, the virtues in question must be passive powers—the potentialities, that is, for being actively affected in a certain way.

That Aristotle has a *general* theory of passive powers is evident. The discussion of potentiality in Book 9 of the *Metaphysics* makes this clear (in the context of a discussion that once again reveals the reciprocal relation and basic dialectical unity of *poiein* and *paschein*). Passive potentialities, we there learn, are elements within an entity's nature, not simply external to it, and are connected to other more obviously integral aspects of the entity's being. To say that oil is *burnable* is to ascribe to the oil a power that belongs to it and is a potentiality for being affected in a certain way, for having something done to it, and is at the same time to link this capacity to certain positive states and characteristics of the oil.[8]

More obvious forms of potentialities with respect to being affected are those by virtue of which an entity is capable of withstanding or not suffering a certain affection. Aristotle often refers to such a type of power both in the discussion in the *Categories* and in that in the *Metaphysics*.[9] In both cases, however, we are considering powers exhibited by an entity for discrimination among affections, for being affected in this way and not that.

Another class of such powers, and one that for Aristotle is paradigmatic and important, includes the faculties of the soul. The perceptual capacities, and the faculties of reason and thought as well, are potentialities of the sensitive and intelligent subject to be *affected* in certain ways, to be acted upon by the sensible and intelligible forms of objects in the world.[10] When we think of them in this way, there is nothing particularly mysterious about these powers: they are simply the abilities to be open to certain affections and closed to certain others—the reciprocal capacities, we might say, of being discriminatingly receptive and resistant.

The doctrine of passive potentiality enables Aristotle to envision a state of character by virtue of which an individual has the power to be affected in certain ways, the capacity to undergo certain passions and avoid others. A moral virtue with respect to feelings or emotions is just such a capacity; it is the power to have and to avoid certain emotions, the ability to discriminate in what one feels.

IV

But this suggests only how there might be said to be powers to be acted upon in certain ways; what concerned us was whether such powers might be said to be dispositions involving choice. We still therefore need to be concerned with the question of choice, and that question may now be put this way: how is it possible for Aristotle to see a virtue as a disposition toward a feeling or emotion, given the following facts about choice? In his first characterization of virtue Aristotle denies that virtues might be feelings themselves by pointing out that a feeling is not the sort of thing that is chosen; our anger and fear are, as he might have said, "aprohairetic," whereas the virtues are kinds of choice or at least not aprohairetic, not devoid of choice. But then we should ask: how could choice be involved in a fixed tendency toward that which does not involve choice, indeed for which we are in no wise praised or blamed? Won't there have to be a radical asymmetry between the relation among dispositions, actualizations, and choice in the case of feelings and that relation in the case of actions? For in the latter case a virtue appears to be a disposition toward prohairetic acts; the actions themselves are instances of choice, and it seems to be only by virtue of this fact that the hexis or disposition which is a virtue with respect to these acts is said to be prohairetic. But in the case of feelings, virtues would, on the view we are considering, themselves be chosen but at the same time be dispositions toward actualizations that are not chosen.

One solution to this problem which I hinted at before would be to abandon the notion that virtues are dispositions with respect to feelings in the sense of being fixed tendencies to feel in a certain way. It is not that courage as a virtue with respect to fear disposes us to feeling fear in certain ways or in certain circumstances or to a certain degree but rather that it disposes us to certain actions with respect to and in light of our fear. Some support may appear to be given to this reading by Aristotle's description of a disposition as a state by virtue of which we are ill or well disposed with respect to the emotions: *kath' has pros ta pathē echomen eu ē kakōs*.[11]

This is the view of Joachim in his commentary on the *Ethics*; he writes:

In the development of the orectic soul there is a hexis when the soul *echei pōs* (viz. *eu ē kakōs*) *pros ta pathē*: i.e. when a permanent attitude towards his emotions (towards any possible disturbances of his orectic self) has been reached—an attitude which expresses itself in actions which are either the right or the wrong response to such disturbances.[12]

But this reading is surely wrong: Aristotle, in the passage in question, immediately goes on to explain:

if for instance, with respect to being angered we do so excessively or insufficiently [*sphodrōs* or *aneimenōs*: if we're too violent or too easygoing] we're badly disposed, but if moderately [*mesōs*] then we're well disposed.[13]

Aristotle's more detailed discussions of the virtues make clear that it is with respect to how one feels and not simply how one acts in light of one's feelings that one is said to be virtuous. The courageous person is one who is frightened by the right things, in the right way, in the right circumstances, and so on, and who is not frightened when it is appropriate not to be. The temperate person is one who is pleased by the right things, in the right ways, and so on. The so-called "gentle" person (whose virtue Aristotle finds to have no proper name) is angered by the right things, in the right way, and so on.[14] There is here no indication that these moral virtues defined in terms of feelings are dispositions toward some range of actions appropriate in light of these feelings, and, on the contrary, every indication that they are dispositions toward appropriate feelings themselves.

What emerges in addition, however, is the recognition that these feelings are accompanied by concomitant actions. I have talked so far as though feelings could be understood as particular affects of an individual independent of anything else that might be true of the individual. In a sense this is exactly Aristotle's theory and is why he says that pathē are those things with regard to which we are said to be moved.[15] But considered more broadly, there is no way to identify a feeling or emotion without taking into account (1) what we might call the cognitive element in emotions and (2) actions on the part of the agent which are characteristically and naturally associated with such feelings.[16] Fearing is related to fleeing, desiring to reaching for, anger to striking out at, in no accidental way. In each of these cases, a certain action or range of actions is connected to a pathos in some important logical sense. That connection is defeasible, but it is not a merely accidental connection.

These considerations suggest that there may be two elements to the actuality corresponding to any given virtue. A virtue is a complex disposition in the sense that its actualization is complex, and specifically in that its actualization consists of a characteristic set of feelings *and* a correspondent characteristic set of actions.

But if this is true, our discussion of virtues has been seriously misleading. The fact that virtues are dispositions with respect both to actions and to feelings ought not to suggest to us that there are a number of virtues that are dispositions with respect to actions and a number of other virtues that are dispositions with respect to feelings, any given virtue being a disposition with respect to one or the other, but rather that a given virtue is a disposition with respect to a characteristic set of actions *and* feelings. These feelings are not, as in the view we have just been considering, merely the occasion for actions that are the proper realizations of the virtue; they are part of the concept of that virtue considered as a disposition. But neither are they the sole realizations of the virtue; they are part of the set of corresponding actions and feelings for which the virtue is a disposition.

V

With this understanding in mind, let us, as Aristotle would say, make a fresh start. Recognizing that virtues are dispositions toward feeling as well as toward action, we found ourselves perplexed by Aristotle's apparent claim that virtues involve choice, while feelings do not. It appeared to us that there was an unexplained asymmetry in Aristotle's understanding, such that virtues might involve choice without their appropriate feeling-realizations involving choice, even though virtues seemed to involve choice in the first place because they are dispositions toward actualizations that are deliberate and chosen. Is it possible to make sense of the notion that a virtue involves choice even though the feelings that are its realization do not? Could a person be said to be courageous in a deliberate and chosen manner without it being the case that the feelings which such a person characteristically exhibits by virtue of being courageous are themselves chosen?

Consider a parallel situation in the case of actions. A person may exhibit a vice such that the actions performed as a result of that vice are involuntary considered in themselves, and we may still want to say that the vice itself is voluntary. Thus someone, as Aristotle notes, may in one sense not be responsible for individual actions performed while he was intoxicated or ignorant of what he was doing or in general acting in accordance with some trait of character that made it impossible or extremely difficult for him to do the right thing, and yet in another sense clearly be responsible, at least for being in the first place unaware or drunk or in general of such and such a vicious character.[17]

These examples provide only a partial parallel to our case. In the first place, they concern the somewhat weaker notion of voluntariness, not that of choice. In the second place, they concern only instances of vice and the concomitant breakdown of moral action. Nowhere do we find an instance of Aristotle's characterizing as voluntary a virtue whose resultant actions could be said to be involuntary. Finally, the examples that come most readily to mind—cases of drunkenness, ignorance, or negligence—concern what seem to be in a sense "meta-vices": states that condition our general capacity for virtuous conduct. As a consequence the relationship between the action and the vice that occasions it is not a straightforward relationship of disposition to realization. Only under a partial description could an act of negligence be said to be the actualization of the vice of negligence in the same sense in which an act of courage is the realization of an agent's courageous disposition.

But we could extend the basic point to cases of specific vices. It seems a part of Aristotle's views on moral responsibility that vicious actions are in some important sense not chosen, and indeed under certain descriptions not voluntary, though the vices that occasion them are, and are therefore the responsibility, like their actions, of the moral agent.

This is an enormously complex and difficult topic in Aristotle's thought, and an important one for Aristotle and for moral philosophy in general; the respect in which vicious acts are not willed but nevertheless our responsibility may be central to an understanding of the moral life (compare Kant). I introduce the question here only because it suggests that certain predicates which we might think of as features of actions and only derivatively of characteristics or dispositions relative to those actions may be applied independently to one or the other in a variety of ways. Most importantly we see here a sense in which predicates appropriate to dispositions (in this case the predicate of being voluntary) may apply to these dispositions not only with reference to their actualizations but also with reference to the mode of their acquisition.

It is a part of Aristotle's moral theory which I have alluded to but not stressed that virtues are acquired. They are, as he says, not *phusei*, but neither are they *para phusin*: neither natural nor contrary to our nature.[18] This is what makes them dispositions—*hexeis*—rather than simply potentialities—*dunameis*. They must therefore be acquired, and their acquisition cannot be effected simply by an act of choice; we do not decide to be virtuous and straightaway become so. Virtues are cultivated and not chosen in any simple sense, for it is not as a direct result of calculation, deliberation, resolution, or any other relatively simple mode of human activity that we become courageous, temperate, or wise. We become these through a process of *ethismos*, or habituation, through the habitual acting out and embodying of those actualizations which the dispositions are dispositions toward.[19] This mode of acquisition is part of the logic of a virtue, because it is part of the logic of a hexis, a disposition, and a virtue is a hexis. It is therefore part of the logic of a moral theory which, as I have suggested, places the notion of virtue at its center.

Perhaps this sense in which we would want to say that a virtue is not chosen—think how easy the moral life would then be!—may have been what led us to say that a virtue's involving prohairesis must depend on the actualizations of that virtue being prohairetic. But there now emerges an alternative way of thinking about the issue: instead of supposing that the quality of being prohairetic flows backward, as it were, from actualization to disposition, suppose we say that a virtue is prohairetic which is acquired through acts that are themselves prohairetic. What happens when we try this model?

Note first that there is a sense in which a virtue might be said to be chosen, and on a specific occasion. A person might decide on such an occasion to act virtuously and see that act as the first in a series designed to effect a transformation in her life to being virtuous. So she chooses on this occasion to be virtuous and so acts, acting virtuously now this time, now another time, now another time, until the fixed disposition of virtue becomes a hexis that characterizes her moral self. Why shouldn't we say in such a case that the virtue has been chosen, from the beginning, and precisely because the acts that fix that virtue are chosen?

This notion accords well with the view of Aristotle's we have just been looking at. On this view one becomes virtuous by impersonating a virtuous person, and in that impersonation, through the process of habituation, becomes the virtuous person whom one impersonates. The direction of self-constitution is seen as leading from actions to states of character as well as the other way around; indeed, we should perhaps say that the other way around is subsequent, is only a logical feature of the relationship between our character and the individual moments of our conduct once they have been established.

But how does this help us with the question of virtues and feelings? For our initial problem with feelings was that they are said by Aristotle not to be chosen; an account according to which virtues are prohairetic because the acts that fix them are prohairetic seems therefore to be of little help in understanding the relation among choice, virtues, and feelings. This question supposes that virtues whose actualizations are feelings may be acquired only through the direct and deliberate choice of feelings. But given our recognition that the actualization of a virtue is a complex and related set of actions and feelings, a different view is now open to us. A person may act in certain ways that are characteristically and naturally associated with a certain range of feelings, and through those actions acquire the virtue that is the disposition for having the feelings directly. Acts are chosen, virtues and feelings follow in their wake, though in logically different ways.

On this view the structure of becoming virtuous with respect to feelings reveals itself to be of the following sort: one recognizes through moral education what would constitute appropriate and correct ways to feel in certain circumstances. One acts in ways that are naturally associated with and will "bring about" those very feelings, and eventually the feelings become, as Aristotle might have said, second nature; that is, one develops states of character that dispose one to have the right feelings at the right time. One does not have direct control over one's feelings, and in this sense the feelings are not chosen; but one does have control over the actions that establish the dispositions, the virtues, which are the source of our feeling in appropriate ways at appropriate times and in appropriate circumstances. Although we may in some narrow sense not be responsible for our feelings, we are responsible for our character as the dispositional source of those feelings.

This picture has much to recommend it. In the first place, it seems correct. My anger or jealousy may not be an emotion which I choose, and yet it may be true that I have become a person disposed to such anger or jealousy by a series of actions that would make it perfectly reasonable to describe my character as something I have chosen. In the second place, it points to what seem important differences between feelings and actions which become clear only when we talk about the modes of acquisition of virtues. Much of the picture I have sketched depends upon the fact that one can simulate an action but can only pretend to have a feeling. Thus the mode of inculcation with regard to feelings must be by some other method than that of habituation. There is, in other words, no way to come to feel a certain way by practicing feeling that way, and this is precisely because in some sense our feelings are not in our control. But it is nonetheless possible to engage in a certain range of conduct deliberately designed to make one the kind of person who will characteristically feel in appropriate ways, at appropriate times, and so on. And in this sense, feelings are deliberate and chosen, since the hexeis from which these feelings emanate are deliberate and chosen, since (in turn) the actions that lead to these hexeis are deliberate and chosen, and deliberately chosen to make one the kind of person who characteristically will have the appropriate feelings.

VI

This picture seems to me on the whole correct and, broadly speaking, faithful to Aristotle's vision of the moral life, but it fails in important respects as a solution to the problems that initially perplexed us. Note in the first place how far we have come from our initial characterization of a virtue as a disposition for deliberate and chosen conduct. That characterization interpreted Aristotle's description of a virtue as a *hexis prohairetikē* to mean that the virtue was the agent's ready capacity to act (in the broadest sense) prohairetically, not that the virtue had been acquired through some mode of prohairetic action. In the second place, the rather elaborate account into which we have been led seems curiously otiose; once we recognize that actions and feelings are linked together as the realizations of a virtue, why not simply say that a virtue is prohairetic because it is a disposition for those elements of its realizations which are actions? For there is no special problem, apart from the general problem of giving an account of what prohairesis is, about actions being prohairetic. Finally, the most important flaw in the account I have suggested is the following. The account depends upon actions that lead to the establishment of a virtue but are not the expressions of an already established virtue being prohairetic. But this is not a view which Aristotle seems to hold. Such actions are voluntary, but it is by no means clear that they are for him in the fullest sense prohairetic. Just as acts are in a sense virtuous when they are acts of the kind which a virtuous person would perform, but are fully virtuous only when performed by a virtuous person (one who performs such acts in the way that a virtuous person would perform them—that is, out of the fixed character that is virtue),[20] just so an act may be like a prohairetic act, but not be one because it is not properly embedded in the larger context of the character and disposition of a moral agent—because it is not a realization of that agent's virtue. There is, Aristotle says, "no prohairesis without intelligence and thought, nor without moral character."[21] Prohairesis involves, as we might say, not simply deciding, but willing, where the notion of will is sufficiently rich to demand reference to the larger context of central and properly integrated goals and habits of an agent's moral life.

The recognition that choice for Aristotle is a concept governing not individual actions in a life divorced from this framework of goals and habits, but rather actions only as moments within a larger context of the character and intentions of the moral subject, reveals our picture to be inadequate as a solution to the problems I have raised. But it should, I think, contribute to the dissolution of these problems. For it should suggest the necessity of rethinking our initial denial that feelings may be chosen. That denial arose, I think, from our attending to a description by Aristotle of passions without reference to the context of virtue and character in which they occur. But why should we not be prepared to say that a person of steadfast and cultivated virtue who exhibits appropriate feelings in circumstances which he understands correctly and in which those are precisely the feelings which he would want to exhibit, taking into account the entire fabric of his desires, goals, plans, and hopes for himself—why should we not be prepared to say that such a person has chosen those feelings?

Nowhere, I believe, does Aristotle say this. What we would like, but do not find, is an extension of the theory of deliberation and practical reasoning to account for the ways in which virtuous persons might be said to have the proper feelings which they have by prohairesis. Such an account would need to provide a sense in which we might be freed to feel what would be appropriate to feel by something like deliberation and choice, by some mode of coming to understand properly the circumstances in which our feelings arise, the place of these feelings and circumstances in our experience, and the ways in which we hold these circumstances and feelings in the larger contexts of our lives. In a sense, the theories behind certain religious traditions, psychoanalysis, and disciplines that promise self-transformation and self-mastery might be thought to represent attempts at such an account.

But any such account, I think, would have to recognize the primacy of praxis in the shaping and execution of our moral lives. It is this primacy that finally dominates the concerns of the *Ethics*. To say then that there is a strict parallelism for Aristotle between actions and passions would not be quite correct. On the one hand, he is led by the *paschein/prattein* structure and by the understanding of emotion as pathos to view virtue as a disposition equally for action and feeling, and as a consequence to recognize correctly the important place which our feelings occupy in the structure of our moral conduct. But on the other hand, the distinction between passion as something that happens to one and action as something that one does, coupled with the recognition that ethics must be concerned with prohairesis, leads him to turn his attention from feelings in the latter parts of the *Ethics*. It is not that he simply leaves the question of feelings out, but that their importance fades in the context of a particular theory of deliberation and choice and their place in moral conduct.

Nor is it the case, however, as I have argued, that feelings are for Aristotle simply not chosen. The reason for this, I have suggested, is that choice for him is not a concept having to do with individual moments in an agent's life, nor with individual single actions, but with the practices of that life within the larger context of the character and intentions of a moral subject, ultimately within the context of what it has become fashionable to call one's life plan.

The question of moral choice in the deepest sense finally concerns questions of creating the conditions in which our actions and our feelings may be as we would wish them. These conditions include our states of character—the virtues—which we acquire through the complex practices of our moral life. So long as we consider moral questions in terms of individual moments in the agent's life, we will not be able to understand this fact. This is why it should be clear that questions of virtue and feeling as moral categories are importantly connected.

NOTES

1. *Nicomachean Ethics* 2.6. 1106b36; *Eudemian Ethics* 1.10. 1227b8.

2. *Nicomachean Ethics* 2.5. 1105b26; 2.2. 1104b14; 2.6. 1106b17, 1106b25, 1107a9.

3. See the article on *paschō* in G. Kittel, *Theological Dictionary of the New Testament* (Grand Rapids, Mich., 1964-1974), 5:904 ff.

4. *Nicomachean Ethics* 2.6. 1106b17 ff. Compare English *afraid* as originally the passive participle *affrayed*.

5. All this is on the assumption that *prattein* is a special case of *poiein* and not, as Aristotle comes to understand it, vice versa. Compare his uses of *kinesis* and *energeia* for a similar reversal of the common understanding.

6. *Categories* 9. 11b1 ff.; *On Generation and Corruption* 1.7. 323b1 ff.

7. *Nicomachean Ethics* 2.5. 1106a2.

8. *Metaphysics* 9.1. 1046a11 ff., 1046a19 ff.

9. *Categories* 8. 9a23; *Metaphysics* 9.1. 1046a13.

10. *On the Soul* 2 and 3. passim.

11. *Nicomachean Ethics* 2.5. 1105b26.

12. H. H. Joachim, *Aristotle, The Nicomachean Ethics* (Oxford, 1951), p. 85.

13. *Nicomachean Ethics* 2.5. 1105b26 ff.

14. See the table of the virtues in *Nicomachean Ethics* 2.7. 1107b1 ff., and the specific discussions of virtues in Books 3 and 4.

15. *Nicomachean Ethics* 2.5. 1106a4.

16. Thus *On the Soul* 1.1. 403a25, and the discussion of the emotions in the *Rhetoric.* See W. W. Fortenbaugh, "Aristotle: Emotion and Moral Virtue," *Arethusa* 2 (1969), 163-185.

17. *Nicomachean Ethics* 3.5. 1113b30 ff.

18. Ibid., 2.1. 1103a14 ff.

19. Ibid., 1103a28 ff.

20. Ibid., 2.4. 1105a26 ff.

21. Ibid., 6.2. 1139a33. See G. E. M. Anscombe, "Thought and Action in Aristotle," in *New Essays on Plato and Aristotle*, ed. Renford Bambrough (London, 1965).

8

Reason and Responsibility in Aristotle

T. H. Irwin

INTRODUCTION

Aristotle's account of responsibility has often been praised by philosophers who like to keep these things simple and unmetaphysical. At first sight he seems to avoid any ambitious attempt to identify "the common property of responsible actions"; he does not seem to be bothered by questions about whether and when we are "really free." He seems to define responsibility negatively: I am responsible for an action if and only if I do it neither by force nor because of ignorance. We do not decide that someone is responsible because we see that he exemplifies some common property of responsible agents, but simply because we see that neither of these supposedly well-defined excuses applies to this action.[1] Depending on our views on this question, we can either praise Aristotle for avoiding mystifying and misguided efforts to tackle the free-will problem or blame him for evading the central problem he should have faced.

I believe both the praise and the blame are misdirected. Despite the apparent simplicity and negative procedure of Aristotle's account, I believe he needs and assumes a positive account that raises more complex questions about the general conditions for responsibility. When we consider difficulties in the account as it stands and try to solve these difficulties by appeal to other Aristotelian doctrines, the resulting theory will be less simple, but more interesting, and more capable of answering some hard questions about responsible action. I will set out this "Aristotelian" theory—I will call it Aristotle's "complex theory"—partly for an exegetical purpose, to show what Aristotle is committed to, whether he realizes it or not. But I have a philosophical purpose too, to show that the account is worth consideration in its own right. I certainly do not claim that it is the adequate answer to every fair question about responsibility and free will. I am not confident enough about the right answers to be able to evaluate particular answers so decisively. But I hope it is right to find that Aristotle's views are worth our attention, though not for the reasons often alleged.

First we must decide what question to ask. Aristotle is not explicitly asking when someone acts responsibly but when someone acts voluntarily (hekousiōs).[2] But he examines voluntary action for ethical and jurisprudential reasons. He is concerned with virtue of character; virtue involves actions (praxeis) and affections (pathē) since it is the source of praiseworthy actions and affections; to know if a man is virtuous we must know if his actions are praiseworthy; but only voluntary actions can be assessed for praise and blame (Nicomachean Ethics 1109b30-34). To find a voluntary action is to find an action it is reasonable to consider for praise and blame.[3] Aristotle thinks this same inquiry will help legislators, since they are concerned with rewards and punishments (1109b34-35), which—he assumes—are reasonably applied only to voluntary actions. He assumes that the same conditions make actions candidates for moral and for legal scrutiny and reactions—praise, blame, reward, punishment, and so on. We normally suppose that someone is a proper candidate for this kind of scrutiny and reaction if and only if he is responsible for his actions; and so I will ask how far Aristotle's theory of voluntary action is a good theory of responsibility. Our judgments about responsibility may not always be confident or clearly correct. But they raise some of the right questions about Aristotle.

Like most of those who discuss Aristotle on responsibility, I refer to the Nicomachean Ethics, and especially to 3.1-5. But I will also refer sometimes to the account—often fuller, interestingly different, and not always inferior—in the Eudemian Ethics. One difficulty must be faced at once. Though we cannot fully elucidate the chapters on voluntary action without looking elsewhere in the NE, we must be cautious. Three of the most important books for our purpose, NE 5, 6, 7 (the "Common Books"), were probably written originally for the EE, and it is hard to say how little or how much they may have been revised for the NE. Though we must use these books to understand NE 3, we cannot too hastily assume that they always express the doctrine of the rest of the NE.

THE ATHENIAN BACKGROUND

When Aristotle speaks of legislators, he assumes that the voluntariness of an action affects its legal status. He is right about Athenian law; it exempts involuntary action from the normal legal procedures and punishment (Demosthenes 18.274-275; 21.43). But the question is more complicated. Athenian law recognizes two classes of criminal action (e.g., homicide or assault): action from forethought (*ek pronoias*), liable to the severest punishment, and involuntary action (Aristotle *Ath. Pol.* 57.3; Dem. 23.24, 77; 21.42-44). Apparently the law takes actions from forethought to be coextensive with voluntary actions; no nonphilosophical writer ever suggests that the law recognizes voluntary action that is not from forethought.[4]

"Forethought," however, is not clearly defined, and can raise difficulties. If A has been plotting against B, lays a trap for B, and kills B, we will normally be confident that A has acted from forethought; his murder was premeditated. But suppose A has no grudge against B, and then sees B kill A's children, and in his fury kills B in retaliation; does A act from forethought? He knows what he is doing—he acts with foreknowledge—but his action is not planned or premeditated. Perhaps we are inclined to be lenient to A here. Suppose now that A dislikes B but has no plans to kill him; one day A finds himself with B on the edge of a station platform with an express train approaching; a sudden impulse makes A push B under the train to kill B. A might deny premeditation, even say, "I don't know what came over me." He has not plotted and schemed against B or premeditated B's murder. But almost certainly he would not have had this murderous impulse if he had not disliked B already; he knew what he was doing; and he suffered no special provocation at the time. Does A act from forethought?

The attitude of Athenian law and—a different question—of Athenian juries to these sorts of cases is not clear; our incomplete evidence makes it hard to know whether there was a single consistent attitude. Sometimes a defendant denies forethought by arguing that he had not been plotting against the victim—here forethought is identified with premeditation (Antiphon 5.57, 59; Lysias 3.34, 41-43; 4.7). Nonetheless, defendants seem to have been convicted even though they killed because of anger or impulse (Dem. 54.25, 28; 21.71-75).[5] The assumption that an action is either from forethought or involuntary causes trouble. Some actions seem neither premeditated nor clearly involuntary—in our last two cases no one pushes A, and he knows what he is doing.[6] Two attitudes to these cases might attract us. Perhaps, since they are not premeditated, they are not from forethought, and therefore not voluntary, and should not be punished in the normal way. Since they are done with foreknowledge, perhaps they are voluntary, and therefore done with forethought.[7] A skillful advocate can appeal to the jury's sympathy, invite them to pardon actions done in anger or on impulse, and suggest to them that such actions display no forethought (Dem. 21.66, 71-75).[8] But people were still convicted of voluntary homicide for such actions, since they plainly intended harm to the victim. Since the law did not try to define "forethought," and no legal experts advised Athenian juries about what counted as forethought, it is not surprising that they faced ambiguities and difficulties. We are not surprised to find that these ambiguities and difficulties are an opportunity for ingenious advocates, and a puzzle for perplexed juries.

Now if Aristotle were trying to explain the concept of voluntary and involuntary action in common use, we might expect him to be especially concerned with forethought and its relation to voluntary action. This is not what we find. Though he mentions forethought sometimes, it is not the central concept in his account of voluntary action. This is surprising; it shows at once that Aristotle does not merely seek to describe or analyze the ordinary concept of voluntary action. At the same time Aristotle means his account to be relevant to ordinary judgments about responsibility. It will be easiest to see how and why after we have examined the account. We will consider first the simple theory Aristotle offers and then the more complex theory he needs and implies.

THE SIMPLE THEORY

In the *EE* Aristotle begins with the assumption that what is voluntary seems to be according to desire or decision or thought (*ētoi kat' orexin ē kata prohairesin ē kata dianoian*) and what is involuntary seems to be contrary to one of these (1223a23-26).[9] Aristotle argues that no one of the three types of desire is necessary for voluntary action, seems to conclude fallaciously that desire is not necessary, argues that decision is not necessary (1223b37-39), and concludes that thought is necessary and sufficient.[10] He isolates thought as the necessary and sufficient condition for voluntary action by showing how force (*bia*) or compulsion (*ananke*) and ignorance make action involuntary (1224a8-1225b6). The resulting account of voluntary action is this:

(1) A does x voluntarily if and only if A does x (a) because of himself; (b) not in ignorance; (c) when it is up to him not to do x (1225b7-9).

In this definition, clause (b) shows how the action is "according to thought." The contrast with external force explains (a); force was assumed to move an animal against its own impulse (1224a13-23), as when a wind blows me away. "Because of himself" just means "because of his own impulse." But when is (c) satisfied? Aristotle seemed to agree that someone sometimes acts on his own impulse, but because of some irresistible compulsion acts involuntarily, if he is under threat of death or some extreme penalty; "for what is up to himself—to which the whole matter is referred—is what his nature is capable of bearing" (1225a25-27). These cases count as involuntary action because of (c). But (c), so interpreted, is unfortunately obscure; how do we decide what someone's nature is capable of bearing?

The *Magna Moralia* begins the discussion with a different initial claim: that the voluntary is what we do without being compelled (*mē anankazomenoi*, 1187b34-36).[11] The rest of the discussion corresponds to the procedure of the *EE*; it concludes that since the involuntary is what happens by force and compulsion and not with thought (*meta dianoias*), the voluntary is what happens from thought (*ek dianoias*). This result can be presented in positive and negative terms:

(2) A does x voluntarily if and only if A does x from thought.
(3) A does x voluntarily if and only if A does x neither (a) by force nor (b) by compulsion nor (c) not with thought.

The author illustrates (c) by reference to the legal distinction between actions done with and without forethought, where some factual error excludes forethought (1188b28-38).

This definition raises the questions raised by the *EE*. It does not try to offer a general condition, such as (1c) for excluding cases of compulsion, mentioned in (2b).[12] And insofar as (2c) is explained by common views about forethought, difficulties with these common views are difficulties in understanding (2c).

The *NE* tries a different approach. The common beliefs considered are not about conditions of voluntariness but about conditions of involuntariness (1109b35-1110a1): Aristotle finds it more fruitful to begin there than to begin with positive conditions. The discussion of types of desire and their relations to voluntary action is drastically abbreviated (1109b9-17, 1111a24-b3). Instead Aristotle defends and clarifies the two conditions of involuntariness. He distinguishes force from compulsion and insists that only force makes action involuntary; compelled action, even when something overstrains human nature, is voluntary (1110a23-26, b3-7; contrast *EE* 1225a25-33). The discussion of ignorance is far more elaborate. The result is a definition of voluntary action which can again be stated negatively or positively:

(4) A does x voluntarily if and only if (a) the origin is in him, and (b) he knows the particular facts of the case (1111a22-4).

(5) A does X voluntarily if and only if he does x neither (a) by force nor (b) because of ignorance.[13]

The argument shows that the negative definition is meant to explain the positive, especially for (4a). To decide that the origin is in A we need only decide that A does not do x by force; A's movement is forced only when the origin of A's doing is outside A altogether, and A contributes nothing (1110a1-4, b15-17).

Definition (5) corresponds fairly well to (1a) and (1b) in the *EE* and to (3a) and (3c) in the *MM*. The *NE* rejects (3b), since it does not agree that compulsion makes an action involuntary. Nothing in (4) or (5) corresponds to (1c), requiring that it should be up to A not to do x. But (1c) is not neglected. Aristotle often insists in the *NE*, especially in 3.5, that some things are up to me; and he argues that whenever the origin of the action is in me, the action is up to me, and I do it voluntarily (1110a17-18). If this is so, (4a) captures (1c). One source of obscurity in the *EE* has apparently been removed. Deciding whether something is up to me is not obviously easier than deciding whether I do it voluntarily; both "voluntarily" and "up to me" should be explained by reference to some third concept, not only by reference to each other. The *NE* offers the further explanation: "the origin in me" in (4a) is held to explain "up to me" in (1c). But (4a) is not left unexplained either, since the negative test of (5a) is taken to show whether or not the origin is in me. Aristotle might reasonably hope to have clarified and simplified the account of voluntariness in the *EE*.

His hope would be premature. For if (4a) is explained fully by (5a), some things I do can have their origin in me, be known to me [as required by (4b) and (5b)], and still not be voluntary. My sweating, the beating of my heart, my digestive processes, my growing older—these all have their origin in me, and may well be known to me, but are strange cases of voluntary action. Elsewhere—in a Common Book, *NE* 5—Aristotle mentions this; some natural and unforced processes are not voluntary because they are not "up to us" (1135a31-b2).[14] These exceptions show that internal origin is not sufficient for something's being up to me, and therefore not sufficient for its being voluntary. The attempted simplification in the *NE* seems to fail.

However, Aristotle's account is not yet to be rejected out of hand. A fairly small change will avoid this objection. I may know that my heart is beating, but it will beat away whether I know it or not, and my knowing it does not explain why it happens. But in normal voluntary action my knowledge or belief does explain the action. And so (4b) should be amended to "because he knows the particular fact." This amendment clarifies (5b). Aristotle insists that ignorance makes an action involuntary only if it is done "because of ignorance," when the agent's ignorance explains why he did it. Similarly a voluntary action should be done "because of knowledge (or belief)." This amendment makes (4) and (5) no longer equivalent, since an action could be done neither because of ignorance nor because of knowledge. But we are merely extending Aristotle's own point in his own account of involuntary action.[15]

But this is not yet enough. Someone's knowledge can also explain involuntary action. I may know that I sweat when I go into hot rooms, and this knowledge may explain why I start to sweat before I go into a hot room when I know I am about to go in; but my sweating is still involuntary. Not all explanations through the agent's beliefs make the action voluntary. Some desire must be added to the belief. But desires can also cause involuntary action. My anxious desire to speak fluently may cause me to be tongue-tied, quite involuntarily. If it causes me to speak fluently in the normal way, the desire and the belief together cause my action, as reasons; the fact that they give me reasons for doing the action explains my doing it.[16]

We are still not far from Aristotle. He will agree that voluntary action requires both thought and desire (1139a35-b4); they present an end— something apparently good or pleasant—to be achieved, and present this action as a way of achieving the end. When the action is done because of the desire for the end and the belief about the means, it will be voluntary. It is curious that the *NE* does not mention the role of desire in voluntary action. Perhaps Aristotle takes it for granted. Or perhaps he thinks it is superfluous to mention it, since all and only the actions that count as voluntary by his criteria in (4) and (5) are actions on desire. If this is his view, he is wrong; he must mention the role of belief and desire to show why digestion and growing older are not voluntary.[17]

A moderate revision of Aristotle's definition now allows us to capture his apparent intentions, and perhaps to express what he takes for granted. The revised definition will be this:

(6) A does x voluntarily if and only if A's beliefs and desires, as reasons, cause his doing x.

Now consider two cases. Suppose first of all that A wants to cause B bodily harm, and stabs B. Now suppose alternatively that A stabs B to get B's money, knowing that he will cause B bodily harm. In both cases A voluntarily causes bodily harm to B. This is the point of Aristotle's condition (4b); what A intends may be taking B's money rather than causing bodily harm to B, but if he knows that he will cause bodily harm to B, he causes it voluntarily. To show that (6) covers this case, we might revise it as follows:

(7) A does x voluntarily if and only if (a) A believes x is F; (b) x is F; (c) A's beliefs and desires, as reasons, cause A to do x.

This definition allows A to do x both voluntarily and involuntarily; for perhaps x is also G, and A does not believe it is G. A's stabbing B may cause B's death; but it does not follow that A voluntarily causes B's death, though the event of causing B's death is a voluntary action of A's. We can say that the same action is both voluntary and involuntary, because the stabbing (done voluntarily) is also a causing death (done involuntarily), or that the same event is both a voluntary action of stabbing and an involuntary action of causing death. Any appearance of paradox here is deceptive, and does not threaten Aristotle's account.[18]

AN OBJECTION TO THE SIMPLE THEORY

These amendments to Aristotle's simple theory help us to see what is more seriously wrong with it. He makes the difficulty plain in two replies to objections:

1. First, he denies that action on emotion (thumos) or appetite (epithumia) is involuntary; if that were involuntary, he says, then neither the other animals nor children would act voluntarily—clearly meant to be an absurd consequence of the objection (1111a24-26). This is the only reference in the NE to a question discussed more fully in the EE; and this argument is not used in the EE.

2. Later, when he distinguishes voluntary action from action on decision (prohairesis), Aristotle again claims, as though it were obvious, that animals and children act voluntarily, but not on decision (1111b6-9). The EE agrees in distinguishing voluntary action from action on decision (1223b40-1224a4), but does not give this reason.

Has Aristotle overreached himself in replying to these objections? His ascription of voluntary action to animals and children is reasonable, but dangerous. It is reasonable, since nothing seems to exclude animals and children from satisfying the definition of voluntary action in the NE—in (7). The EE does not explicitly allow them voluntary action, and perhaps Aristotle would argue from (1c) that it is not up to them to refrain from acting as they act; but he does not argue this way and gives no other argument against the position of the *NE*.[19] This position is dangerous for Aristotle; for he insists that an action is a candidate for praise and blame if and only if it is voluntary, and partly for this reason rejects the claim that action on emotion or appetite is involuntary (1111a27-b3). He confirms elsewhere what he implies in 3.1, that an action is an injustice (*adikēma*) open to moral and legal sanctions if it is voluntary (1135a19-33).[20] Aristotle seems to believe these things:

(8) A is responsible (a proper candidate for praise and blame) for doing x if and only if A does x voluntarily.
(9) Animals and children act voluntarily.
(10) Animals and children are not responsible for their actions.

His account of voluntary action and responsibility seems to result in a contradiction.

The contradiction is not to be resolved by denying (10). I do not know where Aristotle affirms (10). But he clearly assumes that animals and children are not to be subject to legal and moral sanctions. He never suggests any radical extension of the recognized class of responsible agents.

When we notice this, we might try rejecting (8). Animals and children are not the only nonresponsible but apparently voluntary agents. Aristotle remarks that bestial and insane people are beyond the limits of virtue and vice (1148b19-31, 1149b22-1150a5). He does not say that the extremely insane and extremely brutish are not responsible for their actions; but it would be strange if they were, when they are so far beyond normal ethical assessment. Nothing prevents them, however, from meeting Aristotle's definition of voluntary agents in (7).[21] Perhaps his real views are better captured if (8) is replaced with this:

(11) A is responsible for doing x if and only if (a) A is a normal adult, and (b) A does x voluntarily.

But (11) will not do by itself. If the restriction to normal adults in (11a) cannot be further explained, it seems to be merely arbitrary; no reason is given for restricting responsibility to a subset of voluntary agents. To justify (11) and to say more precisely what a "normal adult" is, we should find some further feature distinguishing responsible agents from animals, the insane, and other voluntary nonresponsible agents.

A different solution would retain the test of responsibility in (8) and reject (9). Perhaps Aristotle's conditions for voluntary action are too generous and ought to be restricted so that only normal adults are voluntary agents. This solution isolates the class of responsible agents isolated by (11), but by a different route. As we saw, the *EE* does not explicitly concede voluntary action to animals and children; perhaps Aristotle ought to take this hint and explain better why it is not really "up to them" not to act [as required by (1c)]. St. Thomas chooses this way out of Aristotle's difficulty. He insists that voluntariness is necessary and sufficient for responsibility, agreeing with Aristotle on (8), and tries to define voluntariness to fit. He finds that animals act voluntarily only in a reduced way, because voluntary action in the primary way is determined by will (*voluntas*).²² St. Thomas exposes one crucial feature of Aristotle's doctrine of responsibility but still reaches a different answer from Aristotle's. We can best appreciate this later on.

I want to accept Aristotle's definition of voluntary action, agree that animals and children act voluntarily, and see how he might justify the restriction of responsibility to normal adults, as implied in (11). I will draw some of the distinctions that St. Thomas draws to justify his solution; but the differences between his solution and a more Aristotelian doctrine will not be merely verbal.

SOME RELEVANT DISTINCTIONS

I will review some of Aristotle's various ways of distinguishing normal adults from animals or children or both, to see how far they support his view on the conditions for responsibility and the sort of agent who is responsible.

1. Aristotle believes that neither animals nor children are capable of happiness, because they are not capable of "realization of the soul according to virtue" (1099b32-1100a5). Animals can never achieve virtue, and children can achieve it only when they cease to be children and mature. Happiness also requires a complete life. It is easy to see why children lack this. It is not clear whether Aristotle thinks animals lack it too.

2. In *NE* 6, a Common Book, Aristotle denies "activity" (*praxis*) to animals, with no mention of children (1139a18-20). We might suppose that this remark flatly contradicts the view in *NE* 3 that they act voluntarily. But parallels from—significantly—the *EE* suggests that "activity" is construed rather narrowly here. Animals suffer no conflict between reason (*logos*) and desire (*orexis*) but live by desire alone; but man has both, at the time of life when we also ascribe activity to him—since we do not say that an animal or child "acts," but say this only about someone acting because of reasoning (1224a25-30; cf. 1222b18-21). Here Aristotle clearly uses "act" and "activity" more narrowly than we would use

these terms, and more narrowly than he uses them when he says that an animal or child "acts" or "does something" when it eats or drinks. He can still say that animals do these things voluntarily. We should be careful in using this evidence from the *EE* and a Common Book unless we find that it makes the best sense of *NE* 3 too.

3. In another Common Book, *NE* 7, Aristotle says that animals have no "universal apprehension" but only "imagination and memory of particulars," so that they cannot be incontinent (1147b3-5); presumably they cannot then be continent, virtuous, or vicious either. This difficult comment is best understood by reference to Aristotle's rather strict claims about "apprehension" (*hupolēpsis*). He suggests once that animals have imagination (*phantasia*), not belief (*doxa*), since belief requires confidence (*pistis*), and confidence requires reason, which animals lack (*De anima* 428a18-23).[23] Aristotle allows animals "perceptive" but not "deliberative" imagination, and no belief from reasoning (*DA* 432a5-11).[24] He thinks animals do not hold beliefs for reasons and so do not think there is *reason* to apply a universal predicate to a situation. They may be aware of this as good; but he denies that they can decide that since there is this to be said for an action and that to be said against it, overall the action is worthwhile. Here is why animals cannot be incontinent. Incontinence is more than a conflict of desires; it is a conflict between a desire based on an overall assessment of an object as good or bad and a desire not based on such an assessment. Since animals cannot have the first sort of desire, they cannot be incontinent.

4. In his discussion of luck (*tuchē*) Aristotle says animals and children cannot perform lucky actions, because lucky action implies action (praxis), action requires decision (prohairesis), and animals and children lack decision (*Physics* 197b1-8). As in the *EE* and *NE* 6, Aristotle denies action or activity to animals and children, insisting that any real activity must be caused by a decision (*NE* 1139a31). Animals lack decision because it requires the kind of reasoning they lack. In *NE* 1 he perhaps associates activity with decision in the same way (1094a1-2).[25]

5. In the introductory remarks on decision Aristotle says animals and children act voluntarily but lack decision (1111b8-10); and he justifies himself by saying that nonrational animals have appetite and emotion (*epithumia kai thumos*) but no decision (1111b12-13). The *EE* agrees that animals have appetite and emotion without decision (1225b26-28), but it does not concede that they act voluntarily.[26] Aristotle does not say in the *NE*, but does imply, that animals and children lack "wish" or "rational desire" (*boulēsis*).

These different distinctions between rational agents and others are connected. The crucial distinction is drawn in the last passage; the reasoning lacking in nonrational agents is the reasoning that forms a decision. This will be clearer when we have discussed decision further. We can fairly guess that decision is meant to distinguish agents responsible for their voluntary actions from animals and children who act voluntarily without responsibility. But to show exactly how decision affects responsibility we must ask more questions about Aristotle's view of decision.

DECISION AND RATIONAL CHOICE

Decision is "deliberative desire" or "thinking desire" (1139a23, b4) or "desiring intellect" (b5), when "judging by deliberation we decide according to rational wish" (1113a11-12).[27] An animal's lack of "deliberative imagination" (*DA* 434a5-10) explains why it is incapable of decision. But what sort of deliberation and deliberative desire is needed for an Aristotelian decision? Aristotle's emphasis on decision may mislead us.

We might suppose that a decision rests on a desire that is to some extent formed by deliberation. If I want a cigarette, and deliberate about how to get it, my resulting desire to walk down to the slot machine is partly formed by deliberation. But Aristotle does not count this as a rational decision; he recognizes that someone, even an incontinent, can deliberate about the satisfaction of an appetite, but denies that this deliberation results in a decision (1142b18-20, 1111b13-14). To the extent that the incontinent acts against his own rational wish (boulēsis; 1136b5-9) he acts against his decision.[28]

Why is the incontinent's frustrated desire his *rational* desire? His desire to go to the slot machine is not a rational desire, because it results from deliberation about the means to the satisfaction of his nonrational desire to smoke. If he deliberated about the components of his nonrational end, his resulting desire would still be nonrational; if he wants to amuse himself when he realizes it would be better to exercise, he may choose to play poker as a way of amusing himself; and his desire to play poker will be a nonrational desire. A rational desire must be formed by some special kind of deliberation that does not depend on some single nonrational desire for some single end. The incontinent's desire to amuse himself is—in these circumstances—nonrational, because it is not influenced by his other ends; he is not influenced by the thought of his future ill health and its bad effects on his other aims and plans. A rational desire results from someone's deliberation about what would be best to do in the light of all his aims.[29]

In Aristotle's view this conception of a rational desire demands a special object—happiness (*eudaimonia*). Happiness is the ultimate end, and the proper object of a rational person's desire, because it is the achievement of everything that deserves to be achieved for its own sake, and is therefore the most complete of goods (1097a25-b21). A desire is rational insofar as it is formed by deliberation about the role of this action in the agent's plans for his happiness. We might infer that happiness cannot itself be the object of a rational desire, since a desire for happiness must be assumed before any rational desire can be formed. Aristotle, however, thinks it is the object of rational desire (1111b26-30). He is justified. For he has argued that we have reason to pursue happiness just because it is the ultimate end that includes everything that we have reason to choose for itself; when we understand this, we have a rational desire for happiness.

This is only a sketch of Aristotle's views on happiness and on rational desire. But it may be enough for us to go on with. A decision is formed by rational desire and deliberation, and is itself a rational desire, directed on a particular action believed by the agent to be in his power (1111b26-30, 1113a2-12). When Aristotle says that animals and children lack decision, he means that they cannot form deliberative desires reached by deliberation on their final good; they lack rational wish, the desire belonging to the rational, deliberative part of the soul (*DA* 432b5-6, *EE* 1223a27-28).[30] An incontinent agent has a rational wish and deliberates about it to reach a decision (1149a9-10, 1150b29-31, 1151a5-7, 28-33, 1152a10-17), but does not act on it (1111b12-14).

THE ROLE OF DECISION IN RESPONSIBILITY

Our inquiry into Aristotle's conception of animals, children, and rational agents allows us to return to our question about the definition of responsible agents in (11). Instead of saying that "normal adults" are responsible, we can now be more precise:

(12) A is responsible for doing x if and only if (a) A has effective decision, and (b) A does x voluntarily.

Now is this a reasonable view? If we have correctly understood Aristotle's conception of decision, why should decision divide responsible from nonresponsible agents?

Why is an animal not responsible? We are inclined to say it "can do nothing about" its desires; it just has them and acts on them. If a human being could do nothing by further thought to alter his desires, we would be inclined to say that he is no more responsible for his action on those desires than an animal would be; no further reflection or deliberation would change the desire he now has and acts on. Such a person's desires and actions are totally compulsive, and it would be unreasonable to hold him responsible for acting on them.

Now deliberation can influence action to different degrees. Sometimes A might have a compulsive desire to eat this sweet thing he sees in front of him; there is no room for deliberation. Sometimes he may compulsively desire a sweet thing, but realize that both this cake and that fruit are sweet things, and consider whether to get the cake, which is three feet away, or the fruit, which is six feet away. We could not hold him responsible for eating a sweet thing rather than refraining; but we might hold him responsible for eating the cake rather than the fruit, since he could do something about which he ate. If he failed to deliberate about what to eat, and we know that he could have deliberated, we might criticize him and persuade him to deliberate before eating.

Sometimes an agent may have more control over his present desires. Suppose that B is different from A and can do something about his desire to eat. He has a stronger desire to keep his body free of artificial chemicals. Deliberation may show him that eating this cake will fill him with artificial chemicals. In this case we might reasonably hold B responsible for eating the cake rather than not eating it; and we might criticize him for failing to deliberate about the effects of eating the cake when he could have deliberated about them. But we cannot reasonably hold him responsible for choosing to stay free of chemicals. This desire is not an Aristotelian rational desire and cannot produce a rational decision; the strength of the desire is not affected by rational deliberation about his other ends. Even if in this case he realized that freedom from chemicals is less important than eating something, he would desire just as strongly to be free from chemicals and would act on the desire.

To find a genuine Aristotelian decision and rational desire, consider C, who, unlike B, does not have the relative strength of his desires fixed beyond his control. Deliberation about his overall good, considering all his rational aims, affects the strength of particular desires, so that they produce the best actions. We can criticize C both for his actions and for having desires of that strength. If, like B, he foolishly chooses to stay free of chemicals rather than eat something he needs, we can criticize him for that choice; either he deliberated badly or he should have deliberated and did not.

These cases suggest why Aristotle might be right to associate responsibility with deliberation, since deliberation makes the agent more than a passive subject or spectator of his desires; it makes him able to do something about them. But why should the deliberation that belongs to Aristotelian decisions and rational desires be important? It is not necessary for all responsibility. But it is necessary for the type of responsibility we normally ascribe to human agents. We normally suppose that a responsible person can do something about the desire he acts on—that it is not compulsively strong but is responsive to his reasoning and deliberation. We assume that rational agents are capable of doing more than simply acting on the desire they find to be strongest; they can also affect the strength of their desires by further deliberation. Here Aristotle is right to suggest that decision and rational desire, as he understands them, are important for responsibility.[31]

VARIETIES OF RESPONSIBLE ACTION

But our discussion of the role of decision has exposed some ambiguities. What is the relation between being an agent who decides and being responsible for particular actions? In presenting Aristotle's views in (12) I suggested that if A is responsible, he must "have decision." Two ways of understanding this will not do:

(13) A is responsible for doing x if and only if (a) on some occasions A effectively decides, and (b) A does x voluntarily.

(14) A is responsible for doing x if and only if (a) A effectively decided about doing x, and (b) A does x voluntarily.

Here (13) is too weak. Some of A's desires and actions may be susceptible to rational decision, but the desire to do x may not be. If A's desire to do x is one of his compulsive desires, it would be a mistake to hold him responsible for doing x. Aristotle does not mention this sort of difficulty; but he probably recognizes that the compulsive desires of insane people cause nonresponsible action, since they lack decision and reasoning (1149b34-1150a1); and he does not show why some of a rational agent's desires cannot be compulsive.

But (14) is too strong and too restrictive.[32] Aristotle certainly thinks effective decision to do an action is sufficient for responsibility for that action. But he does not think it is necessary. Someone is open to praise or blame for an action as long as he does it voluntarily (1135a19-23). Appetite, anger, sudden passion or impulse are all possible causes of voluntary and responsible actions. Aristotle does not suggest that in all these cases the agent's "will" or rational desire is involved, assenting to the other desires; this is St. Thomas's way of amending Aristotle's account. But though voluntary action without decision can be responsible action, desire cannot be ignored altogether. As our previous discussion of cases has shown, we believe that rational agents who act impulsively or without deliberation could have deliberated effectively; and this is why we hold them responsible for acting on that desire. The best way to clarify (12) without the errors of (13) and (14) is this:

(15) A is responsible for doing x if and only if (a) A is capable of deciding effectively about x, and (b) A does x voluntarily.

We can see from (15) why voluntariness is normally a good test of responsibility in normal adults, as (11) earlier claimed. But now we can explain this, and say why the voluntary actions of normal adults, not of other voluntary agents, are responsible. What makes someone a "normal" adult for this purpose is his capacity for effective decision.

Here it is useful to return to our earlier comparison between Aristotle and Athenian law, and see how far he has refined or improved the ordinary legal classification. Different remarks in the Aristotelian ethical works suggest different ways of fitting the Aristotelian view onto Athenian law. These may reflect different Aristotelian views; but they may also reflect the ambiguities in the legal distinction.

The *MM* identifies voluntary action with action on thought and with the action from forethought recognized by Athenian law; ignorance of fact is taken to prove absence of forethought, and absence of forethought is taken to make an action involuntary (1188b28-32).[33] Later, however, the author distinguishes voluntary action from action on decision and praises those few legislators who seem to distinguish the two. We do not know which legislators he has in mind. If he is referring to the distinction between forethought and the lack of it, he contradicts his previous endorsement of the view that actions on forethought and voluntary actions are coextensive.

The *EE*, however, clearly associates decision with forethought (1226b-31-1227a2); here Aristotle claims that legislators divide actions in three, involuntary, voluntary, and done from forethought, and thinks they have some grasp of the truth, though they have not made the distinction clearly (1126b37-1227a1). Aristotle does not say he is referring to Athenian law here. But he is contradicting the claim in the *MM* that lack of forethought implies involuntary action; and our knowledge of Athenian law generally supports the report in the *MM*. There is no evidence to suggest that action on a decision was distinguished from action from forethought.[34]

The Common Book *NE* 5 returns to the three-way distinction between involuntary actions, voluntary actions, and actions on forethought (cf.

EE 1227a1-2). When he distinguishes action on decision from other voluntary action, Aristotle says it is right to judge that what comes from emotion (thumos—here especially anger) is not from forethought; for it is not the man who acts from emotion who starts it, but the man who makes him angry (1135b25-27).³⁵ Here, as in the *EE*, Aristotle appeals to the legal distinction between forethought and the lack of it to support his distinction between action on decision and other voluntary action. But if he is appealing to Athenian law, it is a dangerous appeal; for the Athenian law regarded actions without forethought as involuntary—the very thing Aristotle wants to deny.

It is perhaps not so surprising that in *NE* 3 Aristotle avoids mention of the legal distinctions and does not suggest that his distinctions correspond to the law's. The *MM* and *EE* show that appeals to different aspects of legal distinctions could cause trouble; and the *NE* tries to avoid this trouble by presenting a clearer set of distinctions. Aristotle recognizes two conditions unsatisfactorily combined in the legal conception of "forethought": foreknowledge and premeditation. He agrees that foreknowledge is necessary for voluntary action when he argues that action caused by ignorance of fact is involuntary. Premeditation is part of deliberation and decision, but, in Aristotle's view, is not necessary for voluntary action or for responsibility. The legal notion of forethought does not correspond exactly to any part of Aristotle's analysis; and this is just as well, since the legal notion combines two conditions that are better separated. On Aristotle's view, unpremeditated action can still be fully voluntary; and the agent is fully responsible for it if he is capable of effective deliberation about it. Aristotle does not try to describe or analyze ordinary legal criteria of responsibility; he tries—successfully—to replace them with something better.

ADVANTAGES OF ARISTOTLE'S ACCOUNT

We have now replaced a simple Aristotelian theory of responsibility, summarized in (8), with the more complex theory expressed in (15). I do not think we have replaced Aristotle's theory with someone else's. We have simply explored the implications of Aristotle's restriction of the class of responsible agents to those who are capable of decision. It is not unreasonable to call this Aristotle's conception of responsibility, even though he never presents it as explicitly as he should; we can now understand his judgments about who is responsible, and when, better than we could from the simple theory.

Is the complex theory a good theory? It is fair to expect a good theory of responsibility to explain and justify our treatment of someone we hold responsible for his actions. This expectation may turn out to be mistaken: perhaps there is no justification for the ways we hold people responsible. But at least we should begin with this kind of treatment. This is not the same as defining responsibility as liability to these forms of treatment; they may or may not be justified in particular cases, and we should look for ways to decide when they are justified. Aristotle says praise and blame are the proper reactions to responsible agents; this will do as a rough summary, if we include gratitude, resentment, thanks, indignation, admiration, condemnation, with simple praise and blame. Aristotle will agree with this, since he thinks that responsible actions are open to appraisal as virtuous or vicious, in a way that shows something about the character of the agent. To be responsible for an action is not to be the object of these attitudes—sometimes it may be pointless or inappropriate to praise or blame—but being responsible is being a reasonable candidate for these attitudes, the sort of agent doing the sort of action for which praise and blame are normally justified.[36]

Now why should we follow Aristotle in associating praise and blame with the capacity for deliberation and decision? At first sight the connection is not obvious. We may change the behavior of some animals, and certainly of children, by praise and blame; and in general, vigorous praise or blame may affect someone's behavior whether or not he reflects or deliberates about it.[37] But this is not our normal attitude to responsible agents. When we react with praise, blame, resentment, gratitude, and so on, we do not normally mean to cause some irresistibly compulsive desire in the agent to do what we approve of; we do not normally expect that he will be incapable of resisting his reformed desires even if he thinks it better not to act on them. Normally praise and blame and the other attitudes are intended to affect someone's deliberation, so that on reflection he will come to choose what he has been praised for and avoid what he has been blamed for. Indeed, we would normally reject a method of changing someone's behavior which caused him to have irresistible desires to do what we would like him to do; that would be an illegitimate interference with a responsible agent. When Aristotle identifies responsible agents with agents capable of effective decision, he explains and justifies these reactions to responsible agents.

It is worth comparing Aristotle's doctrine with another effort to explain and justify normal reactions to responsible agents—Hume's attempt. Hume agrees with Aristotle's condition (1a) in insisting that someone is open to praise or blame only if he is himself the cause of his actions. But Hume understands this requirement in two nonequivalent ways: responsible actions must proceed (a) from a person's character, and (b) from something durable in him.[38] These are not equivalent demands; animals and children satisfy the second condition but not the first. The first condition is too restrictive. Hume may be right to say—and Aristotle agrees—that someone will be blamed less for what he does "hastily and unpremeditatedly" than for what proceeds from his character. But he is wrong to identify every durable element in a person with his character; someone's tendency to eat when he is hungry is a very durable element of him but is not a part of his character. Aristotle is much more nearly right in finding someone's character in the result of his deliberation and decision about the ends he is to pursue. But it is not surprising that Hume cannot use this test to distinguish someone's character from other durable elements of him. He does not think ends can be chosen by rational deliberation and decision; for Hume, deliberation and practical reason are never practical except when they discover means to ends pursued by nonrational desires. For Aristotle it is important to distinguish character traits, the product of deliberation, from other constant features; Hume cannot draw this distinction.

Hume's reference to durability is a poor substitute for Aristotle's reference to deliberation and decision. We may sometimes be justified in blaming someone rather severely when he acts "out of character"; if we rely on a normally honest person in a position of trust and he once embezzles the money, he may be liable to severe and justified blame. The question should not be how frequent this lapse is likely to be, but whether he was capable of deliberating about what he did. The Aristotelian test gives us the right answer, the Humean test the wrong answer.

We can now return to an issue treated very briefly in the *NE* and see whether the complex theory allows a better treatment. Aristotle rejects the view, discussed more fully in the *EE*, that action on emotion or appetite—types of nonrational desire—is involuntary. First he remarks that this view will make the action of animals and children involuntary, which is absurd (1111a24-26). We have noticed that this reply is not as decisive as Aristotle seems to think. Even if it is correct, it does not prove what he wants, that we are responsible for acting on nonrational desires: they might be as compulsive in us as they are in animals. His important reply is the next one, that we ought to have certain kinds of emotional and appetitive desires; someone can reasonably advise us to acquire them, and we can be praised or blamed for having or lacking them (1111a27-b3). These are the sorts of things we can affect by our deliberation, and to that extent we are responsible for them.[39] This is the answer Aristotle needs, though he does not set it out here.

Aristotle discusses questions about compulsion when he discusses "mixed actions"—the ship-captain abandoning his cargo in a storm, the victim handing over money at gunpoint to a thief. In the *EE* Aristotle conceded that these could sometimes be cases where the kind of duress might be stronger than human nature could bear, and that then it would be compelled and forced, and an involuntary action (1225a12-34). The *NE* sharply distinguishes external force (bia) from compulsion (anankē), insisting that mixed actions are compelled, but not forced, and therefore not involuntary. In all these cases the origin is in the agent, and therefore the act is voluntary (1110b1-5). This is not enough for Aristotle's purposes. He wants to prove that we are responsible for these actions, that they do not remove us from praise and blame. If they are caused by compulsive desires and so are voluntary only in the way that the actions of animals and children are, they are not responsible actions.

Nor does Aristotle's answer show what is "mixed" about these mixed actions. Presumably they are supposed to be a mixture of the voluntary and the involuntary; but this account of the mixture does not distinguish them from most other voluntary actions. Aristotle seems to say that action-tokens of mixed action-types are tokens of types which I would not choose to do, but are tokens which I do choose to do in particular circumstances (1110a8-19). "Handing over my money" is an action-type I normally do not choose; but in these conditions, when I am being threatened at gunpoint for ten dollars in my wallet, I will choose to do a token of that type. But this account of the mixture fails to explain what Aristotle wants to explain, why we should think there is some special duress or compulsion in mixed action-*tokens* which makes us doubt their voluntary and responsible character. For he has not distinguished mixed action-tokens from many other kinds of voluntary action including no duress. I do not choose the action-type "drinking bitter liquid"; but I do choose a token of that type when the liquid is a medicine and I want to recover. Any action chosen as a means to some other end seems to meet Aristotle's conditions for being a mixed action; but this is surely not what he intends.

The complex theory allows a better defense of Aristotle's position here than he provides for himself. He is quite right in the *NE* to distinguish mixed action from action on compulsive desires.[40] The captain abandoning his cargo is not moved by a compulsive desire that would move him even against his rational decision; clearly the rational decision is to abandon the cargo. Aristotle argues correctly that in fact the desires causing mixed actions are not irresistible; we reasonably expect someone to suffer death himself rather than kill his mother (1110a26-29). Mixed actions are candidates for praise and blame, and sometimes are praised and blamed, though often excused and pitied. They are compelling, not because they compel someone against his rational desires, but because he is compelled to choose rationally actions that are against his rational plan. The contradiction here is only apparent. The captain's rational plans include delivering his cargo, not abandoning it; but if he is to be a rational planner at all, he must survive, and to do that he must violate part of his rational plan and do what is needed to stay alive. In these cases the differences between one person's rational plan and another's are usually irrelevant—for each of them, staying alive is necessary for any rational plans at all.

These compelled actions may look like mixtures of voluntary and involuntary, insofar as they seem to conflict with a person's rational decision—and Aristotle sometimes recognizes that action on reason is most of all voluntary (1168b35-1169a1). But his definition of voluntary action, as formulated in (4) or (7), makes mixed actions straightforwardly voluntary. It is better to rely on the complex theory to show what is odd about mixed actions; this theory shows how they are responsible actions, caused by rational deliberation, and yet not fully expressive of the ends someone has chosen by rational deliberation. Aristotle correctly admits that some conditions overstrain human nature (1110a23-26); this is not because they appeal to compulsive and irresistible desires, but because no rational person could rationally decide differently in those conditions. He rightly resists the claim that such actions are not voluntary or not responsible. He still insists that some actions in these "compelling" conditions can reasonably be praised or blamed; a person's rational decisions and plans make some difference.

Aristotle is quite right to separate mixed action from action on compulsive desires and to insist that it is voluntary and responsible. The *NE* seems to be clearer about this than the *EE*. But the simple theory of responsibility does not properly clarify or defend his views. The complex theory does much better, better than Aristotle does for himself.

DIFFICULTIES IN ARISTOTLE'S THEORY

Aristotle's complex theory of responsibility is clearly better than his simple theory. We have found that it is a reasonable theory itself, clarifying and justifying our judgments about responsibility. But, like many worthwhile philosophical theories, it raises further difficulties. Our statement of Aristotle's position in (15) makes A's responsibility for doing x depend on A's capacity for effective deliberation about x; we hold A responsible if we hold that he might reasonably have been expected to deliberate effectively about x, even if he did not deliberate this time. The appeal to capacities in the analysis of responsibility is a notorious source of philosophical difficulties.[41] We might try this analysis:

(16) A is capable of deliberating effectively about x if and only if A would deliberate effectively about x if he chose to.

But this analysis faces the familiar objection that A might be incapable of choosing to deliberate effectively about x, even if the conditional in (16) is true.

Aristotle offers no help in answering these questions, since he does not introduce or discuss capacity for deliberation in his account of responsibility. But perhaps he does not need the analysis of (16), which involves the troublesome reference to choosing to deliberate. We can avoid the difficulties of inability to choose if we understand capacity to deliberate in a different way:

(17) A is capable of deliberating effectively about x if and only if there is some deliberative argument which, if it were presented to A, would be effective about his doing x.

The deliberative argument might be presented to A by A himself, or by someone else; there is no need for A to choose to present it to himself, and so no question arises about his capacity to choose. Perhaps no one knows the particular deliberative argument that will be effective on A; but if we believe there is one, we have reason to hold A responsible for x.

If we accept (17), we can restate Aristotle's view of responsibility:

(18) A is responsible for doing x if and only if (a) there is some deliberative argument which, if it were presented to A, would be effective about A's doing x; (b) A does x voluntarily.

This is simply a fuller version of (15), explaining capacity for deliberation by the analysis in (17).

But when is it reasonable to hold A responsible? Normally we hold someone responsible for an action that he did in the past, and our holding him responsible implies certain treatment of him in the future. Suppose A did x yesterday, and today we are considering his action. We might believe from what we know about A's past that a deliberative argument applied yesterday before he did x would have prevented him from doing x and that therefore he was responsible for doing x when he did it. What A decided, however, was to have a radical brain operation that makes him incapable of effective deliberation. It is pointless and inappropriate for us to apply to A the normal kinds of praise and blame that we apply to responsible agents; and so in one way A is not responsible now for doing x. It is still true that the attitudes appropriate for responsible agents were appropriate then; but they are no longer appropriate. If they are still appropriate, A must still be capable of effective deliberation about that type of action now, not only when he did it yesterday. To make this explicit, and to summarize Aristotle's conception, we can modify and expand (18) as follows:

(19) A is responsible for doing x at a time t if and only if (a) there is some deliberative argument which, if it were presented to A before t, would be effective at t about doing x; (b) A believes at t that x is F; (c) x is F; (d) A's beliefs and desires, as reasons, cause A to do x.

This analysis supplies the necessary temporal references to the analysis of capacities for deliberation in (18) and the analysis of voluntary action in (7). The analysis in (19) implies that if A is responsible for doing x, then there is some time at which the treatment appropriate for responsible agents is appropriate for A. It does not imply that the treatment is still appropriate at some later time. For a later time we need a different analysis:

(20) At t2, later than t, A is justifiably treated as a responsible agent because of his doing x at t if and only if (a) (19a)-(19d) are all true; (b) there is some deliberative argument which, if it were presented at t2, would be effective at t2 about doing G-type actions; (c) at t A wanted to do x because he believed x was G.

These elaborations make the definition unfortunately unwieldy; and probably it takes only moderate ingenuity to show that they are not enough. But it is useful to mention them, not only for the entertainment of those who like reading strings of ever more complicated definitions, but to show how Aristotle's complex theory can perhaps cope with reasonable objections, and to prepare ourselves for some further hard questions.

RESPONSIBILITY, ACTION AND CHARACTER

On this theory of responsibility, someone can be responsible for an action without being responsible for his character or for the traits of personality that cause him to deliberate and act as he does. Someone may have been so strongly conditioned to be a Nazi that we must regard his Nazi outlook as compulsive, beyond his power to change even if he thought it better to change it; for these values of his, neither (19) nor (20) is satisfied. But we can still hold him responsible for breaking the speed limit, or stealing from fellow Nazis. We can also hold him responsible for inefficient Nazi activity, since Nazi values themselves make him susceptible to deliberative argument against this. We cannot, however, hold him responsible for his Nazi values: they are not open to deliberation.

Aristotle holds that at least some people can justly be held responsible for being the sort of people they are.[42] Indeed, he suggests no exceptions; but he must admit some, since the mad and bestial people he considers elsewhere are no more responsible for being what they are than for doing what they do. If these are left aside, why does Aristotle think other people are responsible for their characters?

At first sight, he seems to rely wholly on his simple theory of responsibility [expressed in (8)], with predictably bad results. Most of his argument seeks to show that we acquire our states of character voluntarily. This is not hard to prove, if the conception of voluntary action in (7) is assumed. But it does nothing to show that we are responsible for our characters. The difficulties presented in (8)-(10) reappear. For probably most of us began to have our characters formed when we were children, when we acted voluntarily but were not responsible for our actions. Here voluntariness is clearly a bad criterion of responsibility.[43]

Suppose Aristotle assumes, or we assume on his behalf, the complex theory of responsibility; is his argument more reasonable? This theory rules out any appeal to the voluntary actions of children, since they lack the capacity for deliberation and decision. Aristotle must claim that most adults have not been so strongly conditioned that no deliberative argument will move them; he must argue that adults are still capable of effective deliberation about the sort of people they should be. And indeed Aristotle seems to be thinking of adults rather than children when he argues that we are responsible for our characters. He rejects someone's plea that he did not know his vicious activities would produce vice: "To be ignorant that from each kind of exercise the corresponding states come to be belongs to someone altogether insensible. Further it is unreasonable that the man doing injustice should not wish (boulesthai) to be unjust or the man doing intemperate things should not wish to be intemperate" (1114a9-12). Only an adult could be expected to know that his actions will form his states of character; and only an adult can reasonably be assumed to wish to be intemperate when he does intemperate actions. If "wish" is taken strictly here, Aristotle is considering someone who has deliberated and formed a rational desire to be vicious and then acts on that desire. This man clearly satisfies Aristotle's criteria for responsibility. Aristotle is wrong to suggest that mere voluntariness is sufficient for responsibility. But he might have conceded that some people doing vicious actions do not have a rational desire to be vicious, and still maintain his main point; as long as they have the capacity to deliberate about their character, they can be praised or blamed for the results of their deliberation or failure to deliberate.

Aristotle recognizes—indeed insists—that a state of character, once formed, does not depart overnight. It is not only a set of beliefs but also the result of training of nonrational desires—emotions, feelings, appetites, desire for pleasure, and rejection of pain—in a particular direction, so that they are attached to particular objects. These attachments, once formed, are hard to shift. This is why Aristotle suggests that once someone has become vicious, it is no longer up to him by wishing to change to being virtuous (1114a12-14). Here the point would be clearer if Aristotle distinguished the questions answered in (19) and (20). Someone who has become vicious by voluntary actions that he could have effectively deliberated about is responsible, in the sense of (19); at some time the treatment suitable for a responsible agent would have been suitable for him. But according to (20), he cannot now reasonably be treated as a responsible agent because of those past actions; there is no point in praising or blaming him any more, since that will not change anything. Aristotle does not mark the distinction between (19) and (20), and might not agree with the conclusion I have drawn. But if he had marked the distinction, his account would have been clearer and more persuasive.

But perhaps it is not so simple. In one way the irreversibly corrupted person may still be blamed for his condition. Vice requires the agreement of someone's rational and nonrational desires. Someone may be incapable of changing his nonrational desires but still capable of changing his rational desires by deliberation; Aristotle may be considering such a person when he says that someone's wishing to be just rather than unjust will not make him just (1114a13-14). Someone may form the rational desire to be just, but he will not adjust his pleasures and other attachments so easily. Such a person will perhaps be incontinent or, if he is lucky, continent; or perhaps he will lose his rational desire to be virtuous when he sees it will not entirely succeed. But if he fails to form this rational desire and to try to execute it, he can reasonably be blamed for being the way he is. It is not clear whether Aristotle means this; but he should say it.[44]

Aristotle's discussion of responsibility for character begins by considering how character is formed by decision and action on it (1113b3-7).[45] But the later discussion concentrates on voluntary formation of character. Our previous argument helps to explain why Aristotle speaks in these two ways. He sees that responsibility is somehow related to decision; and he sees that the relation is not straightforward: we can be responsible for more than we decide. He does not clearly formulate the answer he needs, suggested in (19) and (20), and so he does not ask exactly the right question about responsibility for character. But when the right question is asked, the complex theory allows a reasonable defense of Aristotle's claim about responsibility for character.

CONCLUSION

I have discussed some questions about Aristotle's views on responsibility to show how far the complex theory can and cannot be represented as Aristotle's own theory and to see how good a theory it is. It is not his explicit theory of responsibility. Nor is it an implicit theory he follows perfectly without articulating it; for sometimes his discussion is obscure or wrong in ways that can be corrected by the complex theory. However, it is not just a gift to Aristotle either. The complex theory allows us to understand why he thinks only some voluntary agents are responsible and why voluntary action normally is responsible action. And it allows us to state more clearly and defensibly Aristotle's arguments about responsibility for action on nonrational desires, for mixed actions, and for character. Aristotle needs the complex theory; he has all the concepts and distinctions needed to formulate it; it is the reasonable conclusion to draw from his discussion of responsibility, though he does not explicitly mark that conclusion himself.

Modern readers have often asked whether Aristotle is a determinist or a libertarian about responsibility, whether he thinks that human freedom requires the causes of some human actions to be uncaused.[46] If my account has been correct, nothing in the *Ethics* or in the complex theory constructed from it suggests that for Aristotle, responsibility for one's actions and character excludes causation of the choices forming them. Responsibility for character does not require some uncaused event or undetermined choice in the past; it requires capacity for effective deliberation at relevant times in the past and the future. All that Aristotle says and implies about this is perfectly compatible with his being a determinist. Whether he ought to think determinism and responsibility are compatible is a larger question than I can answer now.

However, these reflections on Aristotle's theory may help us to assess briefly one argument against the compatibility of determinism and responsibility. Some incompatibilist critics argue that our attitudes to people as responsible agents would be unjustified unless we were justified in believing that their actions are not fully determined; these critics rightly urge that someone can satisfy Aristotle's simple theory and still not be fairly held responsible. Kant defends a libertarian, nondeterminist view of human action by arguing that responsibility and free will require more than mere causation by desires:

> Freedom in the practical sense is the will's independence of coercion through sensuous impulses. For a will is sensuous, in so far as it is pathologically affected, i.e. by sensuous motives; it is animal (*arbitrium brutum*) if it can be pathologically necessitated. The human will is certainly an *arbitrium sensitivum*, not, however, *brutum* but *liberum*. For sensibility does not necessitate its action. There is in man a power of self-determination, independently of any coercion through sensuous impulses. [*Critique of Pure Reason*, A 534]

Now Aristotle's complex theory agrees with Kant on the conditions of human responsibility. For Aristotle too, responsible human action is not coerced or necessitated through sensuous impulses; there is a power of self-determination. Aristotle, however, finds the power of self-determination in the capacity for effective decision, not in uncaused acts of will. He offers an alternative answer to Kant's question which avoids Kant's libertarian metaphysics. If Aristotle's theory of responsibility is a good one and adequately justifies our treatment of responsible agents, it removes one—only one—temptation to deny the compatibility of determinism and responsibility. And so, while the *Ethics* takes no position on the truth of determinism, it may encourage us to be more skeptical about some antideterminist arguments.

Someone who argues, as I have argued, that Aristotle's complex theory of responsibility is implied and required by what he says ought to ask why Aristotle himself does not see this, or at least does not say it. I can only speculate. Aristotle presents the simple theory of voluntary action in (5) perhaps to replace the more complex and obscure statement of (1). The treatment of responsibility in the *NE* reflects a reasonable desire for simplicity—in this case causing oversimplification. Aristotle may wrongly have thought he could explain responsibility by clear and simple conditions for voluntary action without taking proper account of the inadequacy of voluntariness for responsibility.

One important influence on Aristotle's thought about responsibility has not appeared in my discussion: Plato's argument in *Laws* 9. Aristotle constantly and correctly rejects the claim he may ascribe to Plato that only action on rational desire is really voluntary and responsible. Perhaps anxiety to disagree with Plato leads Aristotle—here and elsewhere —to lose sight of the Platonic parts of his own position. For his complex theory of responsibility depends heavily on the Platonic division of the soul which is always accepted in the Aristotelian ethical works. Perhaps

Aristotle omits, consciously or unconsciously, those parts of his theory which make the Platonic position seem attractive.

The demands of the complex theory perhaps suggest one reason why Aristotle does not formulate and advertise it. Responsibility depends on rational desire and decision—on the formation of someone's conception of his good by deliberation, and the execution of this conception in decision and action. This rational deliberation is practical reasoning about ends. Now many of the central doctrines of the *Ethics* reflect Aristotle's view that such reasoning is possible and necessary for a good life. At the same time Aristotle has some reasons for being skeptical about the power of practical reason to form someone's ends. The *Ethics* never completely resolves this conflict in his views, and perhaps his treatment of responsibility is one symptom of the conflict.[47]

The complex theory of responsibility offers us a further benefit. It not only gives us better answers to questions about responsibility than the simple theory gives. It also allows us to appreciate the coherence of Aristotle's ethics from a new point of view. We know that he begins his *Ethics* by considering the ultimate good for man, or happiness.[48] The complex theory of responsibility shows why that is not an arbitrary starting point and why the discussion of responsibility might usefully have come at the beginning of the *Ethics*. Human responsibility depends on human capacity not merely to choose actions but to choose to act on one or another desire in the light of some more general plans and aims constituting some overall conception of the agent's good. But to have these overall plans, even in some vague and inexplicit form, and act on them is already to aim at one's overall good. I have not challenged Aristotle's right to describe an agent's overall plans as his conception of *his own* ultimate good; this description certainly deserves examination. But if he is right to explain conditions for being a responsible agent this way, his ethical theory should be of interest to every responsible agent. That is indeed what Aristotle claims in addressing his advice to "everyone who is capable of living by his own decision" (*EE* 1214b7). In the *Ethics* he tries to find the virtues which every responsible agent has reason to accept; and the complex theory of responsibility shows us why he should choose to begin where he begins. It is only the complex theory that illuminates other parts of the *Ethics* in this way. We should again be surprised and puzzled that Aristotle himself should not have stressed this important connection; but we should also perhaps be more confident that the complex theory is not our charitable, perhaps misguided, attempt to help Aristotle out, but his own implied position, explaining and illuminating other aspects of his work.[49]

NOTES

1. See J. L. Austin, "A Plea for Excuses," in *Philosophical Papers*, ed. J. O. Urmson and G. J. Warnock, 2d ed. (Oxford, 1970), p. 180: "Like 'real,' 'free' is used only to rule out the suggestion of some or all of its recognized antitheses. . . . Aristotle has often been chidden for talking about excuses or pleas and overlooking 'the real problem'; in my own case, it was when I began to see the injustice of this charge that I first became interested in excuses."

In this paper I sometimes speak unidiomatically of "responsible action," meaning "action for which the agent is responsible," and of "acting responsibly" in the same way.

2. It has often been suggested that the term *hekousion* is only imperfectly translated "voluntary"; and this is true in the sense that both voluntary and compulsory military service are normally cases of *hekousion* action for Aristotle. Perhaps "intentional" is as near as we can come. But I will continue to use "voluntary" as a conventional and convenient rough equivalent, irrespective of English idiom. See also F. A. Siegler, "Voluntary and Involuntary," *Monist* 52 (1968), 268-287, at 268 f.

3. By "consider for praise and blame" I mean that questions about praise and blame can reasonably be raised, that the agent is a candidate for praise and blame, not that praise or blame always will or always should result.

4. I cannot claim to have investigated these questions thoroughly. For some divergent views see J. H. Lipsius, *Die attische Recht*, 3 vols. (Leipzig, 1905-1916), p. 607; L. Gernet, *Recherches sur le développement de la pensée juridique et morale en Grèce* (Paris, 1917), pt. 3, chap. 2; D. M. Macdowell, *Athenian Homicide Law* (Manchester, 1963), pp. 44-47, chap. 6; J. W. Jones, *The Law and Legal Theory of the Greeks* (Oxford, 1956), pp. 261-273; R. S. Stroud, *Drakon's Law on Homicide* (Berkeley and Los Angeles, 1968), p. 41; W. T. Loomis, "The Nature of Premeditation in Athenian Homicide Law," *Journal of Hellenic Studies* 92 (1972), 86-95. The relation of Athenian law to Aristotle on responsibility is explored by H. D. P. Lee, "The Legal Background of Two Passages in the *Nicomachean Ethics*," *Classical Quarterly* 31 (1937), 129-140.

5. These cases are discussed by Loomis, who cites them against Stroud's suggestion that Drakon's law made special provision for homicides that were voluntary but were not from forethought. Macdowell agrees that "not from forethought" is used interchangeably with "involuntarily." (Macdowell actually says that the two expressions are synonymous, which is further than I would go; contexts like Antiphon 1.5 suggest that they add something to each other; but they do seem to be coextensive.)

6. It is not surprising that Plato is especially concerned in *Laws* 866d-867b with the voluntary or involuntary character of killing in anger.

7. R. A. Gauthier and J. Y. Jolif, *Aristote: L'Éthique à Nicomaque*, 2d ed. (Louvain and Paris, 1970) on 1111a24-25 assume that Athenian law would count killing in anger or on impulse as involuntary, because not from forethought. I know of no clear evidence for this claim, which overlooks the ambiguities and obscurities in "forethought."

8. Loomis, "Premeditation," does not mention Demosthenes' suggestion that unpremeditated actions deserve to be excused. Apparently an advocate could make a jury feel uneasy about treating such actions as being from forethought. He does not try to persuade the jury that such actions are involuntary. But a resourceful advocate on the other side could argue that since these actions are clearly voluntary, and done in full knowledge, they must be from forethought. The defendant in the case mentioned in Dem. 21.66 was convicted by only one vote; perhaps this suggests ambivalence in the jury.

9. I assume that the *EE* was written earlier than the *NE*. I believe the two accounts of voluntary action support this assumption, though I can also see ways of arguing for the opposite conclusion from the differences in the accounts. The account in the *Magna Moralia* is too interesting to ignore; but I do not claim confidence about the authenticity of the *MM* or its relation to the other two works. The structure of its discussion is parallel to that in the *EE*, not to the *NE*; and to that extent we might suppose it is Aristotle's first attempt. But *MM* 1195a15 ff. includes material not found in *NE* 5.8 (assuming this to be Eudemian) and somewhat closer to *NE* 3.1-5.

10. Cf. J. L. Ackrill, *Aristotle's Ethics* (London, 1973), p. 268. This may be unfair to Aristotle. Some of the tentative dialectical arguments claim to show that appetite and emotion are not always sufficient for voluntary action (1223b5-18, 22-28). These arguments suggest that there is something involuntary in incontinent action. Aristotle does not reject these arguments yet, though they conflict with his own views elsewhere. Instead he makes a new start at 1224a8 by considering force, which has been invoked in the previous arguments to show that incontinent action is involuntary because it is forced. The final account of voluntary action is reached by consideration of force. It is still puzzling and unjustified that desire is not mentioned in the definition. Ackrill, however, remarks that it is implicitly recalled. At *EE* 1224a21-23 Aristotle says that animals do or undergo something by force when something external moves them "against the impulse (*hormē*) in them," and in 1224b12-15 he says that compulsion is contrary to their impulse, when agents resist by wish and appetite. Apparently, then, voluntary action should be according to wish or appetite. The *NE* does not mention desire in its account of force and compulsion.

The *MM* considers the claims of the three types of desire, with different arguments from those in the *EE*. It does not at once draw the illegitimate conclusion of the *EE*; at 1188a37-38 it says that when we find these oppositions in arguments we should speak more clearly about the voluntary. But after discussing force and compulsion it does draw the illegitimate conclusion, at 1188b25-26, with no further grounds than the dialectical arguments about the three types of desire.

11. Cf. *Rhetoric* 1368b9-10, which, however, adds the requirement of knowledge.

12. The *MM* may omit (2b) because it is an earlier and less sophisticated account or because it is a later account that agrees with the *NE* in excluding "up to him" from the definition. Similarly, we might explain the reference to legal practice as Aristotle's first attempt, made in the hope of keeping close to common beliefs, or as a disciple's attempt to relate the Aristotelian theory to legal practice.

13. *EE* 1225b10 has "in ignorance," *agnoōn*, where the *NE* has "because of ignorance," *di' agnoian*. While the *NE* uses these two terms to mark a sharp distinction between two different roles of ignorance, the *EE* uses both indifferently in this context. But the combination "in ignorance and because of being ignorant" in 1225b10-11 may be intended to indicate the condition described more fully in the *NE*; 1226b31-33 uses "because of ignorance." *NE* 5. 1135b12 uses "with ignorance," where *NE* 3 would use "because of ignorance." *MM* 1188b25-39 does not mention *agnoia* explicitly but uses *meta dianoias* to cover the requirement of knowledge. 1195a15 ff., however, has more to say about agnoia, and marks some of the distinctions drawn in *NE* 1113b30-1114a3.

14. Aristotle says that these processes are neither voluntary nor involuntary (1135b1-2). J. A. Stewart, *Notes on the Nicomachean Ethics* (Oxford, 1892), ad loc. proposes to delete "nor involuntary," following Rassow and Spengel, and appealing to 1113b26-29. But this passage says that such processes are not voluntary, not that they are involuntary. Aristotle may mean that I do something involuntary only if I could (on some other occasion) do it voluntarily; the question about voluntariness could reasonably be raised about this type of action. This causes a difficulty for the second example in 1135b1-2, dying—for I surely can do this voluntarily. Perhaps Aristotle means by "dying" only "dying a natural death," which I cannot do voluntarily. J. Burnet, *The Ethics of Aristotle* (London, 1900), ad loc. may have the same point in mind; and *De motu animalium* 703b3-10 may also suggest it.

15. I understand "explain" here as "causally explain," and I think Aristotle understands it the same way. But the amendment can be accepted by those who deny that explanations of action by beliefs and reasons are causal.

16. This amendment is simply meant to recognize the difficulty about "odd" causal chains, where the causal role of beliefs and desires does not depend on their being reasons for the actions they cause. See D. Davidson, "Freedom to Act," in *Essays on Freedom of Action*, ed. T. Honderich (London, 1973), pp. 153 f. *MA* 703b6-10 mentions movements of the heart and penis which are involuntary though caused by something appearing. However, the explanation of why they are involuntary—"when the intellect (*nous*) has not commanded" (b7)—does not properly distinguish them from voluntary actions on emotion or appetite.

17. Perhaps Aristotle thinks a reference to desire here would involve a vicious circle. Desire does not explain all movements of animals but only those that are neither forced movements nor natural processes such as digestion; and how is the relevant subset of movements to be isolated except as voluntary actions? In that case Aristotle might think "voluntary action" should be explained without reference to desire. If this is his view, I doubt whether he is right. It is better to show why reference to desire and goals helps to explain some actions and then to use our account of action on desire to understand voluntary action.

18. We can say either (a) that Oedipus voluntarily struck the stranger but did not voluntarily kill his father or (b) that he voluntarily killed his father. But (b) must be taken to mean "he voluntarily did an action identical to the killing of his father" (or otherwise appropriately related to the killing of his father, depending on our views on the individuation of actions and events). The limits of his respon-

sibility will normally be determined by "striking the stranger," not by "killing his father." It is not clear whether Aristotle firmly grasps the importance of descriptions of actions for assessing responsibility; but I do not think he makes any serious mistake. At *EE* 1223b25-28 Aristotle says that we cannot do something both voluntarily and involuntarily at the same time and "according to the same of the action" (*kata to auto tou pragmatos*). In *kata to auto* he may well have in mind (e.g.) "hitting the stranger" and "killing his father." Ackrill, *Aristotle's Ethics*, p. 25, and in "Aristotle on Action," *Mind* 87 (1978), 595-601 (chap. 6 of this anthology), thinks Aristotle is more seriously astray.

19. *EE* 1224a13-20 argues that force (*bia*) and compulsion (*anankē*), are sources of involuntariness insofar as they go against something's own impulse (*hormē*). Since animals act by their own impulse, Aristotle gives no reason here for denying that they act voluntarily. A possible reason might be found in 1225a-25-28, where Aristotle might say that animals are never able to "bear" external pressure: they always just react compulsively to external stimuli, and so it is never up to them to refrain from doing what they do. However, he does not draw this conclusion. Indeed, he seems to insist that compulsion must not belong to one's own reasoning (*logismos*) or desire (*orexis*); this allows noncompelled action to animals. On 1224a25-30 see below, "Some Relevant Distinctions."

20. Admittedly, this precise statement may be from a Eudemian book. But the same thing is said briefly at 1109b31 and implied throughout *NE* 3.1-5.

21. Again we must be cautious, since *NE* 7 may be an originally Eudemian book. But it is hard to believe that in *NE* 3.1-5 Aristotle does not intend to exempt similar people from responsibility. In 1113b26-30 and 1114a21-30 he does not mention insane people as exempt from blame; but he does allow that natural disorders are exempt, and in 7 he regards some forms of insanity as natural disorders. It seems safe to say that *NE* 3 is not intended to justify blame for insane people. See further R. Löning, *Die Zurechnungslehre des Aristoteles* (Jena, 1903), chap. 14.

22. See *Summa Theologiae* 1-2. 6.2 in corp.: Perfectam igitur cognitionem finis sequitur voluntarium secundum rationem perfectam, prout scilicet apprehenso fine aliquis potest deliberans de fine et de his quae sunt ad finem moveri in finem vel non moveri. Imperfectam autem cognitionem finis sequitur voluntarium secundum rationem imperfectam, prout scilicet apprehendens finem non deliberat sed subito movetur in ipsum. . . . voluntas nominat rationalem appetitum, et ideo non potest esse in his quae ratione carent. Voluntarium autem denominative dicitur a voluntate et potest trahi ad ea in quibus est aliqua participatio voluntatis secundum aliquam convenientiam ad voluntatem; et hoc modo voluntarium attribuitur animalibus brutis, inquantum scilicet per cognitionem aliquam moventur in finem.

This doctrine of two grades of *voluntas* is not applied explicitly to Aristotle in St. Thomas's *In X Libros Ethicorum Aristotelis*, ed. A. M. Pirotta (Turin, 1934). But it is needed to support his account of how action on passion and appetite is voluntary. Thomas agrees that voluntary action is so called because of its relation to voluntas, an *appetitus rationalis* (iii, lect. 4, §426). But he also thinks it is so called "non quia moventur ex voluntate sed quia proprio motu sponte agunt, ita quoad a nullo exteriori moventur. Hoc enim dicemus voluntarium quoad quis sponte et proprio motu operatur" (§427). These two accounts of the voluntary are consistent only if the second describes a reduced grade of voluntary action. Gauthier and Jolif on 1111a22-24 criticize St. Thomas for importing rational choice and voluntas into the analysis of Aristotle's concept of *hekousion*. I agree that St. Thomas reaches his view of Aristotle by misinterpretation of some Aristotelian texts; but I do not agree that it is a sheer mistake—merely a result of uncritically reading later philosophy back into Aristotle—to believe that voluntas is relevant. Insofar as voluntariness is linked to responsibility, St. Thomas's desire to find a connection with rational choice is justified by Aristotle's own claims. (The history of the concept of voluntas is explored by Gauthier in 1:255-266.)

23. I retain *DA* 428a22-24, deleted by Ross in his Oxford Text. I take *hepetai* and *akolouthei* to have a logical rather than a temporal force, as in the logical works. This passage is relevant to Aristotle's conception of *hupolēpsis*, since 427b24-26 makes *doxa*, *epistēmē* and *phronēsis* and their opposites the species of hupolēpsis. Now epistēmē and phronēsis clearly require *logos*, and if doxa requires it too, all hupolēpsis requires logos.

EE 1235b27-29 seems to reflect the strict construal of doxa as requiring logos. Similarly *NE* 1140b25-26 (from a Common Book) makes *to doxastikon* a part of the soul which has logos.

Perhaps St. Thomas alludes to the same kind of distinction when he separates perfect and imperfect cognition of ends; in perfect cognition "non solum apprehenditur res quae est finis, sed etiam cognoscitur ratio finis et proportio eius quod ordinatur ad finem ipsum," *Summa Theol.* 1-2. 6.2 "Cognoscitur ratio finis" implies that the agent appreciates something as a good, as contributing to some overall good, not merely as an object of desire.

24. In *DA* 434a11 I retain *hautē de ekeinēn*, deleted by Ross. Following G. Rodier, *Aristote: Traité de l'âme* (Paris, 1900), ad loc., I translate: "This is the reason why the other animals seem not to have belief: because they do not have the imagination that comes from reasoning [i.e., the deliberative imagination], while it [the deliberative imagination] includes the other one [the perceptive imagination which animals have]." Aristotle does not assert (as D. W. Hamlyn wrongly claims, *Aristotle: De anima II-III* [Oxford, 1968], ad loc.) that animals have belief. He does not say whether the reason for its seeming that animals lack belief is a good one or not. But he may be suggesting that there can be belief, as well as imagination, without reasoning. This suggestion is stronger if *doxan* rather than *phantasian* should be understood with *tēn ek sullogismou;* but then *hautē de ekeinēn* is more difficult: it would have to mean "belief from reasoning includes belief without reasoning," making the sentence even more elliptical than it is on the other translation.

25. Perhaps *praxis te kai prohairesis* in 1094a1-2 refers only to a praxis in the strict sense, proceeding from a prohairesis. If so, Aristotle does not commit himself here to saying that everything we do—including, e.g., what we do on appetite—is done for the sake of some good, since action on appetite is not strictly praxis.

It is not clear how often Aristotle observes his other restriction on praxis, that it is an end in itself (1140b6-7). This restriction may be reflected in 1094a1, which may begin with varieties of *poiēsis* and of praxis; cf. a3-5. It is easy to see that all cases of praxis in this sense will be cases of praxis in the sense "action on a prohairesis." The converse is not so clear. If I decide to build a house to keep me warm, my building is a praxis in one sense (based on a prohairesis) but not in another (chosen for itself). The most Aristotle can say is that all actions on a prohairesis ultimately aim at a praxis in his strictest sense, since they all aim at happiness that is praxis. Aristotle's shifting use of the term *praxis* raises questions he does not answer.

26. *MM* 1189a1-4 makes the same point in different terms, saying that animals have praxis but lack prohairesis, since prohairesis requires logos, which animals lack. Like the *EE*, the *MM* does not concede here that animals act voluntarily.

27. In 1113a12 I read *boulēsin* instead of *bouleusin*; see Gauthier and Jolif, ad loc. I use "decision" as an equivalent for Aristotle's term *prohairesis*, which may be more restrictive than the normal English use of "decision."

28. Aristotle is not quite consistent in saying that the incontinent has no bad prohairesis. In *Rhet.* 1368b12 he mentions *kakia* and *akrasia* as the causes of someone's having a prohairesis to do harm and do bad action. He then speaks of *mochthēria*, implying that akrasia is a mochthēria. Since this is inconsistent with his views in the Ethics, it is possible that he does not mean by *akrasia* here what he means in the *Ethics*. 1136b5-9 and 1152a4-6 say that the incontinent does not believe he ought (*dein*) to do the action he does. This perhaps speaks against accepting *dein* instead of *idein* in 1142b19. 1136b5-9 displays another apparent inconsistency. Aristotle defines "suffering injustice" as suffering harm contrary to one's own boulēsis; he agrees that someone can be harmed and suffer unjust things voluntarily but denies that anyone ever suffers injustice voluntarily—no one wishes (*bouletai*) this, not even the incontinent, but he acts against his boulēsis. It is hard to make sense of this argument unless Aristotle is taken to assume that the incontinent acts voluntarily only if he acts on his boulēsis. But that assumption is clean contrary to his usual conception of voluntary action. (Conceivably he is influenced by the conception of voluntary action in 1168b35-1169a1.)

29. *DA* 434a7-10 does not make it clear what kind of deliberation animals cannot do. Reasoning is needed for the question "whether to do this or this," which might include a choice between two means to a single end (e.g., will I buy cigarettes here or there?), or a choice between two ends (e.g., will I go for a walk or read a book?). The next words—"and it is necessary to measure by one [sc. standard]; for he pursues the greater"—suggest that we are choosing between two ends; but this may involve either simply registering that one desire is stronger than another (e.g., when I remember that I could go to a film, I realize I would rather do that than read a book) or discovering by reflection that one action is better than another (e.g., I realize it would be better for my health, and so in this case best overall, to go for a walk). It is this last kind of deliberation that is necessary for incontinence, rather than a mere clash of desires (cf. *NE* 1111b15-16); and since in 434a11 ff. Aristotle considers incontinence, this may be the kind of

deliberation he denies to animals. But then why should they not be capable of the deliberation mentioned at *NE* 1142b17-20?

30. On some difficulties in Aristotle's conception of wish see T. H. Irwin, "First Principles in Aristotle's Ethics," *Midwest Studies in Philosophy* 3 (1978), 252-272, at 256 f. *NE* 1111b19 ff. might lead us to think a wish is just an unfocused desire, which we cannot try to fulfill now. But some such desires might be purely appetitive, even potentially incontinent; in the middle of the desert I might wish I could eat a seven-course meal at Maxim's. But this should not count as a boulēsis, for Aristotle, since a boulēsis is said (though not in the *NE*) to belong to the rational part of the soul. "Wish," then, is an imperfect rendering of boulēsis; I have used "rational wish" and "rational desire" as well; and sometimes "will," following *voluntas* (see n. 22 above), is suitable.

On wish and deliberation see especially G. E. M. Anscombe, "Thought and Action in Aristotle," in *New Essays on Plato and Aristotle*, ed. R. Bambrough (London, 1965). On deliberation about happiness see especially David Wiggins, "Deliberation and Practical Reason," *Proceedings of the Aristotelian Society*, n.s., 76 (1975-76), 29-51 (chap. 13 of this anthology), in the sec. entitled "Rejection of the First Thesis"; J. M. Cooper, *Reason and Human Good in Aristotle* (Cambridge, Mass., 1975), pp. 19-32; T. H. Irwin, "Aristotle on Reason, Desire, and Virtue," *Journal of Philosophy* 72 (1975), 567-578, at 570 f.

31. Here and in what follows I am especially indebted to H. G. Frankfurt, "Freedom of the Will and the Concept of a Person," *Journal of Philosophy* 68 (1971), 5-20, and to G. L. Watson, "Free Agency," ibid. 72 (1975), 205-220. The type of reflection required for responsibility for self is explored by C. Taylor, "Responsibility for Self," in *The Identities of Persons*, ed. A. O. Rorty (Berkeley, Los Angeles, London, 1976).

In speaking of "effective deliberation" I mean deliberation that, as a reason (cf. n. 16 above), determines action (where "determines" is to be understood with the reservation in n. 39 below).

32. H. H. Joachim, *Nicomachean Ethics* (Oxford, 1951), p. 51, seems to accept (14). He sees the importance of decision in Aristotle's account but exaggerates it. He suggests that when a man acts on appetite or emotion (or "passion"), "since he has acted without reflection—on the impulse of the moment, from passion or appetite—the punishment or reward will take the form of hurting him or giving him pleasure; the way in which animals or children are treated." Aristotle never says anything like this, and should not; it should make some difference whether the agent's deliberation is capable of affecting his desires. Later, Joachim seems to go further: "Roughly, Aristotle's answer is: 'An act is imputed to a man so far as it is traced to his deliberate decision.' A man is the efficient cause of his action so far as he acted *ek prohaireseōs* . . ." (p. 96). Burnet's view is somewhat similar (*Ethics*, pp. 109, 122 f.). He suggests that we are morally, as distinct from legally, responsible only when "we adopt the act as our own as a means to the realization of some end" (p. 122)—i.e., apparently, when we act on a prohairesis. This also seems too restrictive. Lee, "Legal Background," p. 139, also wrongly suggests that someone is "fully responsible" only for what he does on a prohairesis; this

misinterpretation of Aristotle makes it easier to associate his view with the Athenian legal conception of *pronoia*.

33. The terms *prodianoeisthai* (1188b30) and *ouk ek pronoias* (b35) make it clear that an action is taken to be voluntary if and only if it meets the Athenian test for being done from forethought.

34. Aristotle's term *prohairesis* is found elsewhere in fourth-century Greek; see Gauthier-Jolif, 2:189 f., and for more examples E. Kullmann, *Beiträge zum aristotelischen Begriff der "Prohairesis"* (Basel, 1943), pp. 43-50. Dem. 21.43 first mentions killing *ek pronoias*, then killing *ek prohaireseōs*, with no obvious difference in sense; cf. Dem. 6.16, Lycurgus *Leocr.* 148. I know of no nonphilosophical context where action ek prohaireseōs is recognized as a proper subset of voluntary action.

35. Comments such as Dem. 21.66, 71-75; Lys. 3.34, 41-43; 4.7 (see above, "The Athenian Background") suggest that Aristotle's claim represents at least something that advocates might try on a jury with some hope of success. But it is most likely that Athenian law drew no such distinction and that Athenian juries at least did not always draw it (see Dem. 54.25, 28; 21.71-75, mentioned above in "The Athenian Background"). Burnet says that Athenian law "distinguished *phonos ek pronoias* from ordinary homicide even of the voluntary kind" (p. 109). He cites no evidence; he perhaps represents how Aristotle would like Athenian law to be rather than how it was. Jones suggests (*Law and Legal Theory*, p. 261) that *ek pronoias* was thought to be more precise than *hekousios*, again citing no evidence.

36. These remarks are meant to suggest briefly what is wrong with a conception of responsibility which makes someone responsible when he *is* the object of these kinds of treatment. Such a theory is presented in a simple form by M. Schlick, "When is a Man Responsible?" in *Free Will and Determinism*, ed. B. Berofsky (New York, 1955), pp. 60 f. (from M. Schlick, *Problems of Ethics*, trans. D. Rynin [New York, 1939]): "Hence the question regarding responsibility is the question: Who, in a given case, is to be punished?" Here "is to be" might mean "will be" or "ought to be." By "punishment" Schlick seems to understand any educative and deterrent measures that form a man's motives and that someone ought to suffer these measures if they will affect his behavior in the expected way (or other people's behavior, by deterrence?). Many difficult questions about punishment and responsibility are ignored here.

37. On the punishment and correction of animals and children see F. H. Bradley, *Ethical Studies*, 2d ed. (Oxford, 1927), pp. 31 f. As Bradley sees, the question about responsibility is related to the question whether to punish only for what has been done rather than to apply corrective preventive measures: "I was once told of a west-country sportsman who, on starting for the field before the day's work was begun, used regularly to tie up his dogs to a gate and thrash them, and at intervals during the day's sport repeat the *nouthetēsis*. Whether it was wise to correct for no fault is a question for the dog-breaker; but surely no man in his senses would call it punishment. And yet it was good utilitarian punishment. And that is what is meant, when it is said that such punishment is the treating a man like a dog."

38. See *An Enquiry Concerning Human Understanding*, sec. 8, pt. 2, in *En-*

quiries Concerning the Human Understanding and Concerning the Principles of Morals by David Hume, ed. L. A. Selby-Bigge, 2d ed. (Oxford, 1902), p. 98: "Actions are, by their very nature, temporary and perishing; and [a] where they proceed not from some *cause* in the character and disposition of the person who performed them, they can neither redound to his honour, if good; nor infamy, if evil. . . . [b] as they proceeded from nothing in him that is durable and constant, and leave nothing of that nature behind them, it is impossible he can, upon their account, become the object of punishment or vengeance." Here (a) and (b) mark Hume's two nonequivalent conditions.

39. "To that extent" is needed since he arguably might still be responsible for the action. If he decides to do something and also has an effective compulsive desire to do it, his action is overdetermined. If the decision is a sufficient condition for the action—i.e., if it would have been effective even if he had no compulsive desire—he can be held responsible for the action as he would be if he had not acted on a compulsive desire. This sort of case is mentioned by Frankfurt, "Freedom of the Will," p. 19.

40. The *NE* associates mixed actions with compulsion (ananké: 1110a26, 32, b1), but not with force. *EE* 1225a3-33 speaks of both force and compulsion in the actions called "mixed" in the *NE* (the *EE* does not call them "mixed") and is less sure that they are voluntary. (1228a14-15 is puzzling, but may suggest, contrary to the *NE*, that mixed actions cannot be the result of decision; Aristotle may think they result from nonrational desire.) Here Aristotle says, "for what is up to him, to which the whole thing is referred, that is what his nature is able to bear" (1225a25-26), while the *NE* mentions "what overstrains human nature" (1110a25) as mixed actions, which are voluntary. The *EE*'s view is less precise—partly because it defines voluntary action as what is up to us rather than as what has its origin in us, as the *NE* defines it. *MM* 1188b13-34 distinguishes compulsion from necessity, unlike the *EE* (which it usually agrees with on voluntary action), and describes mixed actions as cases of compulsion. But unlike the *NE*, 1188b18-19 tries to explain the compulsion as the result of what is outside the agent, suggesting that compulsory action is not voluntary—but the *MM* does not say whether such action is voluntary or not.

Aristotle's use of "compulsion" and "overstraining human nature" in these cases might lead us to think of "duress" or "coercion." We should notice that he does not think mixed actions are coerced in the sense defined by Frankfurt. "Coercion," in *Essays on Freedom of Action* (see n. 16 above), p. 77. He makes it a requirement for coercion that the victim should not be morally responsible for submitting, and argues that a coercive threat must therefore appeal to desires or motives which are beyond the victim's ability to control or which he believes to be beyond it. When Frankfurt cites 1110a22-25 as the epigraph of his essay, we should not be misled; Aristotle thinks—perhaps surprisingly—that even those things that overstrain human nature do not exempt from responsibility. This much is fairly clear in the *NE*. It is less clear in the *EE*. Perhaps Aristotle rejects the treatment of ananké in the *EE* and its tendency to associate ananké with bia because that treatment makes mixed actions look too much like the quite different cases of psychological compulsion.

I omit one important but complicated further question: whether and how Aristotle can distinguish incontinent action from action on compulsive desires and show that—as he believes—it is responsible action.

41. Some difficulties are discussed by R. M. Chisholm, "Freedom and Action," in *Freedom and Determinism*, ed. K. Lehrer (New York, 1966), pp. 14-16, and by Davidson, "Freedom to Act," pp. 141-144.

42. The *EE* has no connected discussion corresponding to *NE* 3.5 on responsibility for character. But at 1225b11-17 and 1223a5-14 the *EE* makes claims that raise the questions considered in the *NE*. *MM* 1187a5-29 raises some of the questions in a different context.

43. Aristotle's failure to consider early training as a possible threat to responsibility is criticized by D. J. Furley, *Two Studies in the Greek Atomists* (Princeton, 1967), pp. 194, 235 f., citing R. Jackson, "Rationalism and Intellectualism in the Ethics of Aristotle," *Mind* 51 (1942), 343-360, at 349. Furley remarks, "It is odd that Aristotle never (to my knowledge) asks himself why the discipline of parents and teachers is not to be taken as an external cause of a man's dispositions" (p. 194). Furley does not cite 1095a2-11, b4-6, 1179b21-34, which suggest that Aristotle thinks it is possible for someone to be so badly brought up that he is incapable of becoming good even if he wants to be. This might be true even though each of the actions that cause the permanent damage is itself voluntary. Either Aristotle just neglects these other comments of his when he writes 3.5, or he takes them for granted. I see no reason not to accept the second possibility.

44. Aristotle's comparison between the vicious man and the invalid in 1114a-21-31 does not make it clear whether the invalid can still do something about his illness. We might think that in these conditions, if he satisfies (20), he can justly be blamed, as Aristotle assumes, but that otherwise he cannot justly be blamed. The comparison between the man who has become vicious and the man who has thrown a stone (1114a17-18) fails to distinguish (19) from (20).

45. Commentators differ about whether 1113b3-7 refers to (a) the actions forming a virtuous character (e.g., perhaps, Burnet) or (b) the actions proceeding from the state of character (Grant and more clearly Ackrill, *Aristotle's Ethics*, p. 251). *Hai tōn aretōn energeiai*, b5, might be taken to support (b). But this is not clear. The relevant "realizations belonging to the virtues" may include those actions that form, not only those that express, a virtue (Aristotle normally calls the latter *energeiai kata tēn aretēn*, e.g., 1100b10-13, 1177a10, though *hai tēs aretēs energeiai*, 1173a14-15, seems to refer to them too; 1177b6-8 is less definite). Aristotle calls the formative actions *energeiai* elsewhere, e.g., 1103b21-23. Someone who is acquiring the right state of character must act on the right wish and deliberation; since he is responsible for this action on these motives, and this action and these motives cause the formation of a virtue, he is responsible for the formation of the virtue itself. If we assume (a) here, it is easier to explain why in b13, *touto d'ēn to agathois kai kakois einai*, Aristotle assumes that the doing of virtuous actions amounts to being virtuous or at least that responsibility for them amounts to responsibility for being virtuous. This is false, as Aristotle often insists, unless restricted to actions on wish and deliberation. These are reasons for assuming that (a) is Aristotle's point, though (b) would admittedly be a more

natural way to take b5-6. Here I have benefited from J. L. Ackrill, "An Aristotelian Argument about Virtue," *Paideia: Special Aristotle Issue* (Buffalo, N.Y., 1978), pp. 133-137.

46. Aristotle's position on questions about free will and determinism is discussed by P. M. Huby, "The First Discovery of the Free Will Problem," *Philosophy* 42 (1967), 353-362, well answered by W. F. R. Hardie, "Aristotle and the Free Will Problem," *Philosophy* 43 (1968), 274-278. Their discussion is sometimes confusing since each of them thinks that Aristotle's rejection of the view that nature or desire for pleasure compels all of someone's actions implies his rejection of determinism. Apart from other contexts in Aristotle I do not see anything in the ethical works implying a claim that human responsibility requires uncaused events.

47. I have discussed these questions more fully in "Aristotle on Reason, Desire, and Virtue" and in "First Principles in Aristotle's Ethics."

48. The *EE* begins with happiness (1214a17). The *NE* begins with the good for man (1094a22, b7) and argues for its identification with happiness (1095a14-22, 1097a15-b21).

49. I have benefited from discussion of versions of this paper at Cornell, Syracuse, Harvard, and the University of Texas, Austin, and especially from the help of G. J. Fine, J. M. Fischer, and W. H. Wilcox.

Additional note:

I had finished this paper before reading the instructive discussion of some of these issues in R. R. K. Sorabji, *Necessity, Cause and Blame* (Ithaca and London, 1980) and A. J. P. Kenny, *Aristotle's Theory of the Will* (London and New Haven, 1979). Kenny and Sorabji differ widely from each other and from my own view. I have discussed some of Kenny's account in a review in the *Journal of Philosophy*, June 1980.

9

Aristotle's Doctrine of the Mean

J. O. Urmson

Aristotle's account of excellence of character, of which the doctrine of the mean is a part, seems to me to be both interesting and bold. In spite of some difficulties in detail, it is quite possibly true. In many current interpretations of the doctrine, however, Aristotle is made to say things that are either uninteresting, or manifestly false, or both false and uninteresting. It will, therefore, be as well to begin by offering an interpretation of what he has to say on this topic. But I shall spend the minimum of time attacking alternative interpretations and on points that are primarily of philological interest; I want to get on to the question whether what Aristotle, as interpreted by me, says is true.

Though Aristotle has said that the *end* of ethical philosophy is practical, the doctrine of the mean is not introduced by Aristotle as a piece of moral advice but as part of the definition of excellence of character (*ethike arete*). At 1105b19 he asks, "What is excellence?" which is his regular, formal way of setting the question of definition (in the Aristotelian, not the modern, sense of "definition"). To give a definition one must first state the genus and then the differentia of the kind of thing to be defined. Accordingly Aristotle immediately shows that excellence is a settled state (*hexis*) and says (1106a12) that this is the genus. He then starts at once to look for the differentia, for merely to know the genus does not get us very far. For intellectual excellence is also a settled state, and so is badness of character. What distinguishes excellence of character from all other settled states is, in his own words, that it is "concerned

157

with choice, lying in a mean, that is, the mean relative to us, this being determined by the rational procedures by which a wise man (*phronimos*) would determine it." Like badness of character, but unlike intellectual excellence, it is a settled state concerned with choice; unlike all other states, it is in a mean relative to us.

Now there are, according to Aristotle, six possible states of character. At the top of the list, in order of merit, there is heroic excellence (*NE* 7.1). Second comes (ordinary) excellence. Third comes *enkrateia* or self-control, the state of the man who, unlike the previous two, wants to act badly but makes himself act as they would. Fourth comes *akrasia*, or lack of self-control, the state of the man who wants to act badly, tries to act properly, but fails. Fifth comes badness of character, the state of the man who wants to act badly and does so without resistance, thinking it to be a good way to act. Finally there is brutishness, the state of the man who from congenital defect or disease has to be regarded as subhuman and not a proper object of normal moral appraisal. So the doctrine of the mean, as part of the differentia of excellence of character, ought to enable us to distinguish it from all the other five states of character that have just been listed. In fact Aristotle gives us no indication how heroic excellence could be distinguished from ordinary excellence as a different state; it seems to be merely ordinary excellence to the highest possible degree. But this perhaps does not matter, since Aristotle makes no serious use of the notion of heroic excellence. I think that we may safely ignore it as being merely part of a Kant-like architectonic, something brought in to be the opposite of brutishness. But we must certainly be able to distinguish excellence of character from all the other states if Aristotle's account of the mean is to be vindicated.

Now we cannot distinguish the good man, the man with an excellent character, from the self-controlled man either by his actions or by his beliefs and reasoning. They both act in the same way, and do so under the guidance of the same practical thinking. The only way in which the good man differs from the self-controlled man is that he wants to act in the way that he does, whereas the self-controlled man does so with difficulty. In this one way, indeed, the good man is like the bad, though in all other ways they are at opposite extremes; both the good man and the bad act as they want to act, without any internal conflict.

In the *Nicomachean Ethics* Aristotle discusses excellence and badness of character fully before he more than incidentally mentions those who have or lack self-control. Nonetheless, as he very well realizes, he has to make room for them, and does so. Interpreters who forget this tend to underemphasize or misinterpret two points about excellence of character which Aristotle makes very clearly, but the significance of which he does not fully explain. These two points are that (1) excellence of character is concerned with both emotions (*pathe*, passions) and actions, not with actions alone. In the *Eudemian Ethics*, indeed, Aristotle says simply that it is concerned with emotions, without mentioning actions (e.g., *EE* 1106b16); (2) excellence of character is concerned with likes and dislikes (*hedonai* and *lupai*, traditionally translated as "pleasures and pains").

When Aristotle says that excellence of character is concerned with emotions and actions, he does not mean that it has two distinct fields. He means that (temporarily neglecting the complicated cases of self-control and lack of it) an action can be regarded as manifesting and embodying some emotion. As emotions, he says (*NE* 1105b21) he has in mind desire, anger, fear, confidence, envy, joy, friendship, hatred, longing, emulation, pity, and, in general, conditions that involve likes and dislikes. Whenever one acts in a way that displays character, Aristotle believes, one will be manifesting one or another of these and similar emotions. If we cease to put the complicated case of self-control on one side, we can now see one way in which to distinguish the good man from the self-controlled man; whereas the action of the good man is a natural manifestation of his emotion and he therefore acts in accordance with his likes and dislikes, the action of the self-controlled man is not. He makes himself act contrary to his emotions and therefore contrary to his likes and dislikes.

We can readily imagine a situation in which the bad man, the self-controlled man, and the good man all act in the same way. If this is so, it can only be that the bad man is externally compelled to act that way—otherwise he would act differently. The self-controlled man will make himself act that way. Neither of them wants to act that way, neither likes acting that way, neither enjoys acting that way, neither takes pleasure in acting that way. But the good man is, without friction, manifesting and responding to his emotion. So he does it liking it, wanting to, enjoying it, taking pleasure in it. So Aristotle can say (*NE* 1104b3 ff.) that a criterion of the nature of the state is the liking, enjoyment, or pleasure with which an act is performed or the dislike, distress, or distaste with which it is done. If, say, one abstains from some bodily indulgence, liking and wanting to abstain, that shows that one has a character of a certain sort. So excellence of character is concerned with likes and dislikes in this way: if a man has excellence of character, he likes acting in a proper way, feeling emotions which he can manifest with pleasure, since there is no internal struggle.

One can get confused at this point because there is one special excellence, temperance, which is concerned with certain pleasures, bodily pleasures, in a quite different way. In the way in which bodily pleasure and distress are the field of temperance, other special excellences have as their field, not pleasure and distress or likes and dislikes, but emotions like anger and fear. So temperance is doubly concerned with pleasure or enjoyment. As is the case with all excellences, temperance is concerned with the pleasure or dislike with which you act; but, unlike other excellences, it is concerned with the pleasure or dislike which you find in indulgence in bodily pleasures. If you are temperate, you will like abstaining from orgies.

We have here, incidentally, one very good reason in addition to many others for not accepting the thoughtless traditional translation of *ethike arete* and *kakia* as "moral virtue" and "vice." No doubt the fact that the great translator Cicero translated *kakia* as *vitium* should be enough to warn us off those English translations. For in classical Latin *vitium* does not mean "vice." But, more relevantly, it is an insult to Aristotle's good sense to make him say that taking insufficient pleasure in the pleasure of food, drink, and sex is a moral vice, though he regards it as an *ethike kakia*. Moreover, the encratic man can be said to have moral virtue with as good or better reason than the Aristotelian man of excellent character. Thus the man who makes himself stand and fight the enemy, while longing to run away, is at least as entitled to be regarded as possessing the moral virtue of courage as the man who takes his stand without inner conflict. But, for Aristotle, having to make oneself behave properly, however admirable the deed, betrays a defect of character. Excellence of character is not the triumph of grace over the old Adam; it is that state of character which entitles a man to be called *eudaimon*. Clearly one is more eudaimon if one acts properly without friction, without effort, enjoying it, than if one has to struggle to do so through faulty education. That is how Adam would have acted when eudaimon before the fall.

So in the case of excellence of character both emotions and actions are in a mean, whatever that signifies; in the case of self-control, actions, but not emotions, are in a mean; in the case of bad character neither actions nor emotions are in a mean. But what is it for emotions and actions to be in a mean?

If one takes the doctrine of the mean to claim that one should always feel and exhibit a moderate, though (since it is a relative mean) not a mathematically fixed, quantity of a given emotion, the doctrine is plainly absurd. It is perfectly plain that in any given situation one should feel and exhibit a zero amount of almost every emotion. Let us suppose that in a normal context you invite me to dinner with you; how much anger, fear, pity, and confidence should I exhibit as my reaction? Plainly, in normal circumstances, none. Or should we take Aristotle as saying that when some amount of a certain emotion is appropriate, the right amount is always a moderate amount? But this is very stupid. If you are trivially rude to me, should I be moderately angry with you, and also when you torture my wife? To be moderately angry would be absurd on both occasions.

It is perfectly plain, in fact, that for Aristotle what is primarily in a mean is a settled state of character. In his definition he says that excellence of character is a settled state in a mean; thus an emotion or action is in a mean if it exhibits a settled state that is in a mean. The man whose character is such that he feels only mild annoyance at a trivial slight and is enraged by torture has a character that is in a mean between one that exhibits rage on trivial as well as important occasions and one that can coolly contemplate the greatest outrages. On each occasion his reaction exhibits a mean state, and thus his actions are on each occasion in a mean.

To have one's emotions and actions in a mean, says Aristotle, is to feel and manifest each emotion at such times, on such matters, toward such people, for such reasons, and in such ways as are proper. To diverge from the mean in the direction of deficiency is as much not to experience and exhibit emotions at all when one should, or not about matters about which one should, or not toward people toward whom one should as it is to exhibit the emotions to the wrong degree. The same holds of the defect of excess, *mutatis mutandis.* That the doctrine concerns the *mean* and is not merely the doctrine that excellence of character is a settled state of exhibiting the *proper* amount of emotion is sufficiently obvious. One's character may err in two opposed ways; one may exhibit an emotion too often or too rarely; about too many or too few things; toward too many or too few people; for too many or for too few reasons; when it is uncalled for and not even when it is called for. A point that Aristotle, who admits to be talking in outline only, fails to notice is that it is possible, if unlikely, that one's character should exhibit deficiency in some respects, the mean in others, and excess in others, even with regard to a single specific excellence.

One could summarize the point that has just been made by saying that Aristotle holds excellence of character to be a mean or intermediate disposition regarding emotions and actions, not that it is a disposition toward mean or intermediate emotions and actions. This latter view is, as we have seen, absurd, if taken strictly. Interpreted more charitably it is the doctrine of moderation, the view that *medio tutissimus ibis.* No doubt Aristotle was, in general, like most Greek sages, inclined to accept a doctrine of moderation, though in Book 10 of the *Nicomachean Ethics* he seems to believe in a rather immoderate indulgence in contemplation of the immutable. But no doubt he was inclined to hold that usually, when some people said "None of that at any price" and others "As much of that as possible," the sanest view would be that a fair amount was all right, but one should always go easy on it. So Aristotle was probably a believer in the doctrine of moderation, sensibly interpreted. But what I wish to emphasize is that the doctrine of moderation is no part of the doctrine of the mean, nor is it a consequence of the doctrine of the mean, though it is perfectly compatible with it. The doctrine of moderation holds that a character in a mean state will never, or very rarely, require such extreme action as some people are sometimes inclined to believe. Everyone would agree that one should be very angry, for example, at extreme gratuitous cruelty; but extreme emotion and action is far less often justified than one may be inclined to believe. So the doctrine of moderation is a doctrine about where the mean lies; as such it is a partial sketch of how the man of wisdom would determine where the mean lies, which is quite a different thing from the doctrine that excellence is in a mean to be determined by the wise man (perhaps making use of the principle of moderation).

That the doctrine of the mean does not require the doctrine of moderation can be easily shown. Let us suppose that I were to hold that one should rarely drink alcohol, but that when one did one should make a real night of it, while you held that a regular daily glass of wine was in order but one should never take much. Presumably your view is more in line with the doctrine of moderation than mine. But we can both readily assent to the doctrine of the mean as part of the differentia of excellence of character. Both can allow that the right way lies between two errors of excess and deficiency. I for my part can recognize that regular nightly swilling is excess and total abstention a deficiency. We certainly disagree about what the wise man would regard as proper, which is important but quite a different matter.

If the foregoing is correct, it must be wrong to hold that Aristotle thought that we should decide how to act on particular occasions by working in from the extremes. For this view clearly supposes that Aristotle viewed excellence of character as a disposition toward the mean, not a mean disposition. If one were to ask Aristotle how to decide how to act on particular occasions, his initial answer would be that one must do so by bringing to bear the intellectual excellence of (practical) wisdom. If we then ask in what wisdom consists, we shall get a long answer about its involving, among other things, planning ability, experience, ability to appreciate a situation, and executive ability (*deinotes*). There is no simple decision procedure for the wise man to use. How could there be when there are so many variables? If one is generous, one has a settled disposition to do gladly whatever is found to be the generous thing; but what the generous thing to do is depends on a full appreciation of all the factors in the situation by an experienced man who has acquired sound general principles. As Aristotle was well aware, the doctrine of the mean does not begin to answer the question of how rationally to decide how to act, a topic to which most of Book 6 of the *Nicomachean Ethics* is devoted.

Aristotle's account of excellence of character is then, in summary form, as follows:

(1) For each specific excellence of character that we recognize there will be some specific emotion whose field it is.
(2) In the case of each such emotion it is possible to be disposed to exhibit it to the right amount, which is excellence.
(3) In the case of every such emotion it is possible to be disposed to exhibit it either too much or too little, and each of these dispositions is a defect of character.
(4) "Too much" includes "on too many occasions" and similar possibilities as well as "too violently"; "too little" includes "on too few occasions" and similar possibilities as well as "too weakly."

I believe that Aristotle is prepared to go even further and also accept the following proposition:

(5) There is no emotion that one should never exhibit.

The ground for attributing this view to him is that he considers certain emotions and actions that are alleged to be always wrong and claims that this is because they are in fact cases of excessive emotion, of which it would be proper to exhibit a proper amount (*NE* 1107a9-26). Another is that if there were emotions in regard to which excellence was not in a mean, Aristotle's definition of excellence of character would be defective.

The differences between excellence of character, self-control, lack of self-control, and badness of character can be schematically displayed with reference to the doctrine of the mean as follows:

	Emotion displaying mean state	Action displaying mean state	Choice displaying mean state
Excellence of character	Yes	Yes	Yes
Self-control	NO	Yes	Yes

	Emotion displaying mean state	Action displaying mean state	Choice displaying mean state
Lack of self-control	NO	NO	Yes
Badness of character	NO	NO	NO

In saying, in the above table, that the acratic man makes the same correct choice as the excellent man I am obviously saying something oversimple, which would require much qualification, but not retraction, in a full discussion of Book 7 of the *Nicomachean Ethics*.

So much for exposition of the doctrine of the mean. The exposition has been selective; nothing has been said about the difference between relative and mathematical means or the theory that the doctrine is related to certain theories to be found in the *Physics*, among other omissions. But I hope that the positive view that I wish to attribute to Aristotle has emerged with reasonable clarity.

I now turn from exposition of Aristotle to critical discussion. I have claimed that the doctrine of the mean is interesting and bold; if any reader should disagree with me on this point, I should be very perplexed but should not wish to argue. I have also claimed that it is very possibly true. But it is certainly not obviously true, and certain difficulties in it need examination.

Aristotle's attempt to show that the doctrine is true takes the form of running through a quite large set of specific excellences of character and showing that the doctrine of the mean fits them all. But in doing so he gets into some serious difficulties, some of which he notices and some of which he does not. It is by no means clear that he succeeds in clearing up even the difficulties that he does notice. It would be well to start by an examination of the most notorious of these, concerning "particular" justice, or justice in the narrower of the two senses that Aristotle distinguishes.

Particular justice is stated by Aristotle to have two forms, distributive and rectificatory, and justice consists in fair distribution and redistribution according to certain principles. But Aristotle notoriously has great difficulty in finding the specific emotion that is displayed in just and unjust action, and equal difficulty in distinguishing the two errors of excess and deficiency that the theory of the mean requires. From time to time he suggests that greed (*pleonexia*, desire for an unfairly large share of distributable goods) is the characteristic excessive emotion displayed by the unjust man. But it is not at all clear that there is some other degree of the same emotion, let us call it desire for a fair share, that is characteristically displayed by the just distributor or rectifier. Qua distributor and rectifier neither gets anything, and the desire would seem irrelevant. Even the unjust distributor and rectifier need not be motivated by greed, though he clearly may be; he may treat one party unfairly out of a desire for revenge. Aristotle toys now with the suggestion that this is a special case of greed and that the judge is greedy for revenge. But this is a mere piece of verbal jugglery that would reduce all other excellences of character to being special cases of particular justice; we could say, for example, that the coward is greedy for safety. Further, if greed were the characteristic excessive emotion of excess and desire for a fair share the characteristic emotion of excellence in the field of justice, there should be, according to the doctrine of the mean, a desire for less than one's fair share which would inform the characteristic defect of injustice at the extreme of deficiency. But apart from the fact that Aristotle thinks it rather grand to forgo one's claims, he rightly is unwilling to count voluntary acceptance of a loss as a case of injustice. Moreover, to get less than one's fair share, even unwillingly, which seems to be the opposite extreme to getting more than one's fair share, may be an evil, but it is not a defect of character. Aristotle cannot find a second defect of deficiency to lie on the side of justice opposite to injustice. We need not follow out all Aristotle's desperate attempts to save the day. In the end he admits that justice is not a mean in the same way as the other excellences of character (*NE* 1133b34) but only insofar as it aims at a mean between two evils consisting in people getting more and less than their fair entitlement.

So Aristotle admits failure, in spite of allowing himself an uncharacteristic quantity of very dubious argument in an attempt to mitigate it. But if he fails, he ought to admit that the doctrine of the mean is incorrect. However, I think that Aristotle goes wrong, not in his general account of the nature of excellence of character but in his account of justice. It is reasonably clear that distributive and rectificatory justice fail to conform to Aristotle's general account of excellence of character, not because the latter is defective but because they are not excellences of character alongside the rest. To be a just distributor or rectifier one needs to have many excellences of character and plenty of wisdom, but there is no specific state of character that is displayed in acting as a judge. This sort of justice is what Hume called an artificial, not a natural, virtue. To conform to it is to conform to certain social rules of distribution, and there is no special motive for their observance or breach; Hume's "natural" virtues are, his "artificial" virtues are not, settled states in regard to specific emotions.

If, on the other hand, we wish, with Aristotle, to say that greed is a specific defect, we must not try to associate it specially with particular justice. It will be a matter of claiming more than one's fair share, not just of accepting it. If, at a picnic, you offer me a portion of your share of the sandwiches, I am not exhibiting a defect of character if I accept your kind offer. But then why should not claims falling short of what one is entitled to be the defect at the opposite extreme to greed, just as Aristotle holds the man who "thinks himself worthy of less than he is really worthy of" in other respects to be "small-souled" or unduly humble (1123b10)? No doubt it is grand to forgo or give up what one has a right to; it is part of "magnificence." One is no more being faulty in giving away some of one's sandwiches than one is in accepting such an offer. But to give up what one has a right to is very different from being a low-spirited door-mat who cannot stick up for his rights; why should that not be a defect of character? So we could have excessive, proper, and deficient concern with one's rights to things, parallel to vanity, proper pride, and excessive humility but concerned with property rather than with honor and esteem. But it is not clear that we need to recognize a specific character trait of excessive and deficient self-assertiveness for each domain in which they can be exhibited.

My conclusion is that Aristotle fails to show that the doctrine of the mean holds in regard to justice because of his defective treatment of the latter rather than because the former is mistaken. In particular, it is a mistake to try to link greed specially with fair distribution.

We may now pass on to another difficulty. We have already noted that Aristotle appears to claim not only that some defects of character are excesses or deficiencies with respect to some emotion but that all are. Thus Aristotle appears to hold that every emotion is in itself capable of being legitimate; there is no emotion that one should never experience— it is only a matter of avoiding over- and underindulgence in each. He duly notes that certain actions such as murder, adultery, and theft, and certain emotions such as spite, shamelessness, and envy are *ex vi terminorum* bad (*NE* 1107a9 ff.), which might seem to contradict this. But he goes on to claim that all these are simply names for excesses and deficiencies. Envy is necessarily bad since it is the name for an excess of an emotion which one may have to a proper extent.

This is a very bold doctrine, though Aristotle must in consistency hold it. To some extent it presents no very serious difficulty. Theft would normally be an excessive desire for goods, adultery is excessive sexual activity, and murder may exhibit excessive anger. But how about *epichairekakia*, usually translated "spite" but literally meaning "rejoicing in others' misfortunes," and envy? What Aristotle says about these two is very odd (*NE* 1108b1 ff.): *nemesis* is a mean between envy and spite, and their field is distress and pleasure about the fortunes of one's neighbors. The man of nemesis experiences distress when people fare well undeservedly, the envious man goes beyond him and is distressed when anyone fares well, while the spiteful man so far falls short of distress as to rejoice.

Now this will not do at all. First, it is arbitrary and absurd to call rejoicing a deficiency of distress. Second, Aristotle incredibly says that the spiteful man rejoices when others fare well, when in fact he rejoices when others fare ill; and it is hard to see how this could be the deficiency of an emotion of which envy is an excess. Aristotle, as Ross notes in his translation, has made a careless slip, but it is not clear how he would rectify it.

If one had to try to find some related triad, it might seem best to start from the requirement that the field be that of pleasure and distress about the fortune of neighbors. The man in a mean state would presumably both rejoice and be sorry to the right extent and on the right occasions about their fortunes. He will rejoice at deserved good and bad fortune and regret undeserved good and bad fortune, to the right extent and on the right occasions. Now we could imagine a man who was too concerned about his neighbors' fortunes, who rejoiced and sorrowed about them too much and inappropriately; he could be said to be in excess. Similarly we could imagine a man whose concern about neighbors' fortunes was deficient. But neither bears the slightest resemblance to the envious or spiteful man; one is simply overinvolved emotionally and the other underinvolved. If we consider envy to be regret at neighbors' good fortune and spitefulness to be rejoicing in their bad fortune, neither seems to be particularly in excess or deficient with regard to any common feeling or emotion.

So it is hard to see how envy and spite could be seen as excess and deficiency of some emotion of which a proper amount could be felt. Nor could it have seemed obvious to Aristotle that he was right, since in the *Eudemian Ethics* he gives a table in which envy is said to be an excess where *nemesis* is the mean, and the deficiency is said to have no name. It is surely possible and even likely that the same man should be both envious and spiteful, as Aristotle himself notes in *Rhetoric* 2.9.5. Nor can I think of two emotions of which envy and spite are wrong amounts, though unconnected, nor can I see why either should be called an excess or deficiency rather than vice versa.

It might seem then that we have found two faults of character that are not excesses or deficiencies, two emotions that are always a mark of a bad character, if felt in any degree. If this is so, then the doctrine of the mean cannot be an all-embracing account of good and bad character. But the matter is not clear, because of a passage in the *Nicomachean Ethics* which may safeguard Aristotle on this point but is by no means easy to interpret.

In chapter 7 of Book 2 of the *Nicomachean Ethics* Aristotle has rapidly run through the trilogies of excellences and defects, roughly sorted into similar groups. Having given a group concerned with cooperation in words and deeds, he goes on: "There are means both in pathemata and concerning emotions. For shame is not an excellence, though the modest person is praised" (*NE* 1108a30 ff). In the sphere of shame the extremes are said to be bashfulness and shamelessness. If shame is not an excellence of character, then the extremes are presumably not defects of character, though no doubt blameworthy in some way. The bogus trilogy of envy, *nemesis*, and rejoicing in the misfortunes of others immediately follows. It is thus a reasonable hypothesis that the bogus trilogy is also not one of excellence and related defects of character. If so, then though Aristotle's treatment of envy and rejoicing in misfortune may not be satisfactory, the flaw will not be in his account of goodness and badness of character.

But why are shame and, presumably, nemesis not excellences of character? Aristotle gives us no further account of nemesis and related defects, but he does tell us more about shame in the last chapter of Book 4 of the *Nicomachean Ethics.* Shame, we are there told, is a largely physiological reaction to ill repute, manifested in such ways as a tendency to blush. Aristotle also says that it is an emotion, not a settled state or hexis; but then no emotion is a settled state. I take him to mean that whereas in the case of some emotions there can be a settled state in which one regularly manifests them to a proper or improper degree, in the case of shame, a mere reaction, there is no associated settled state of choice. At *EE* 1234a Aristotle explicitly says that such feelings are not excellences of character because they are without choice. Let us see if we can develop this meager clue.

Aristotle's list of emotions in Book 2, chapter 5, begins with desire. Could it be that all the emotions manifested in character are to be regarded as forms of desire or motivation? Certainly Aristotle was prepared to define anger as something like desire for retaliatory suffering (*De anima* 403a30). Can we regard fear as essentially involving a desire for safety, and pity as involving desire that the misfortunes of those pitied should end? These emotions can then be regarded as at least having an appetitive component and thus suitable to be embodied in choice and action. Again, in akrasia or lack of self-control the errant emotion could hardly conflict with rational choice if it did not include some form of desire.

But in the case of, say, shame and rejoicing over the misfortunes of others we seem to be faced with a mere passive reaction involving no desire. Shame is largely a physiological reaction; and rejoicing in misfortune is merely to take a nasty pleasure in contemplation of the misery of others and does not involve procuring their misery. Neither is a motive to action. Shame may, indeed, hold me back from action; but perhaps we have to distinguish a desire not to do something from an inability to bring oneself to do it.

It would be excessive to claim that these speculations are either clearly true or clearly what Aristotle had in mind. But, if tentatively accepted, they would constitute a defense of Aristotle's position. He could still claim that all states of character were connected with some specific emotion and that every emotion that embodies desire might be exhibited to an excessive or proper or deficient extent. Such feelings or nonappetitive emotions as shame and envy and rejoicing in misfortune would fall outside his theory of excellence of character. But his few short remarks about envy, nemesis, and rejoicing in misfortune certainly cannot be defended as they stand.

I wish finally to consider a further difficulty in the doctrine of the mean which has been raised, as exemplified in the account of bravery (*andreia*). Ross considered that rashness was not an opposite extreme to cowardice and suggested that Aristotle's triad should be replaced by two dyads:

Defect or "vice"	*Excellence or "virtue"*
Rashness	Caution
Cowardice	Courage

I agree with Ross in finding Aristotle's triad unsatisfactory, but would prefer, in accordance with Aristotle's general theory, to replace his one triad with two triads. For if rashness is, as Ross says, an insufficiency of caution, is there not also a possible fault, not very uncommon, which is excess of caution, overcautiousness? If we can think of *tharros* as an indeterminate degree of daring, then one can be overdaring, overbold, or rash, insufficiently daring or overcautious, or also daring to the right degree. If one is daring to the right degree, then one will be called cautious in comparison with the overbold man or bold in comparison with the overcautious man, as Aristotle explains in Book 2, chapter 8. The same form of behavior can be called either, depending on which extreme it is being contrasted with.

Now cowardice is not the same thing as excessive caution. One might be brave but overcautious temperamentally. Unwillingness to take a proper risk need not result from excessive fear, or from fear at all.

Andreia as opposed to *deilia* (cowardice) is not courage but bravery or valor. One may be called courageous if one masters one's fears, but there is a fearless bravery that is quite different, and it is this that Aristotle would count as an excellence of character. In a well-known story, Socrates was left unmolested by the enemy during the retreat from Delium because he was clearly, from his demeanor, not afraid of them. Now Aristotle says, rightly, that there are things that any sane man would fear; to be totally fearless is to be a lunatic. But probably there are some men who would not fear some things that a well-integrated man of sense would fear. If a man is not afraid under heavy fire there is something wrong with him, as there is if he is afraid to cross a road in a rear area, lest some stray shell should hit him. There is here, too, the possibility of excess and deficiency, even if excessive fearlessness is rare. So we have here two triads:

Defect	*Excellence*	*Defect*
overcaution	caution	rashness
cowardice	bravery	insensitive fearlessness

We should distinguish these two triads and not run them together as Aristotle does. But he incorrectly applies his theory, rather than, as Ross suggests, applying an incorrect theory.

Aristotle, then, makes mistakes. He wrongly treats particular justice as an excellence of character and thereby gets into difficulties he cannot solve. He is inclined to look for a different emotion for each different excellence, whereas empty vanity and graspingness are better seen as showing the same emotion toward different objects—greed for honor and greed for money. He gives a very unsatisfactory account of envy and spite. He confounds two triads in one when he discusses andreia. But provided that we realize that he is discussing that excellence of character that is manifested in the practical life of the eudaimon, not Christian virtues, I cannot see that the mistakes we have noted are major, or render his account seriously inadequate in principle. At the very least it is a substantial doctrine worthy of Aristotle's genius.

10

Courage as a Mean

David Pears

Aristotelian courage involves two distinct feelings, fear and confidence. It cannot, therefore, lie in a mean in quite the same way as his other virtues. In fact it is hard to see how a single virtue could be placed on two different graduated scales. If courage finds a place on the scale of fear and actions exhibiting fear, how can it also find a place on the scale of confidence and actions exhibiting confidence? Or is there only one scale here, continuous in fact and discontinuous only in name? Aristotelian virtue requires that feelings be medial as well as actions. Whatever mediality is, the requirement excludes self-control from the virtues. But courage seems to be a matter of feeling and controlling fear. How then can it be a virtue? Or is the man of true Aristotelian courage literally fearless?

True Aristotelian courageous actions are performed on the field of battle by citizen-soldiers both for victory and for the nobility of the actions themselves. How are these two goals related to one another? Must there always be an external goal, such as victory, or could a man cultivate courage purely for its nobility, like Hemingway, or, to take a passive case, like a prisoner waiting helplessly in a cell for his own execution? When there is an external goal, why must it be victory? There certainly seem to be other good things for the sake of which an agent might exhibit courage. Does the external goal even have to be good in order that courage may be exhibited? If so, this ought not to be a trivial matter of labels but a consequence of the structure of courage.

These are all questions of interpretation, but that is not their only interest. They are all equally interesting when they are rephrased as questions about the structure of our concept of courage. They are also difficult to answer in both forms. It would be unrealistic to expect a simple account of a virtue as complex as courage. It would also be unrealistic to expect all its instances to conform to a single pattern. Complex concepts combine many elements and often allow untypical instances in which one element is lacking. Aristotle must have felt these difficulties when he tried to fit courage into the theory of the mean.

The first question was "How does Aristotelian courage involve two distinct feelings, if indeed fear and confidence are two distinct feelings?" The best way to appreciate the difficulty of placing a single virtue on two different graduated scales is to look first at a virtue that does not face that predicament. That will give us a background against which the contrasting case of courage will show up in striking detail. It will also lay the foundation for a theory about the relation between courage and self-control.

Moderation is a clear case of a virtue medially placed on a single scale of feelings and matching actions. The feelings are varying desires for food, drink, and sex, and so the scale has a kind of homogeneity that a single scale of fear and confidence might not have. Desires for food, drink, and sex may be excessive, deficient, or medial, but their objects are always the same three kinds of thing. It is questionable whether this is true of the desires associated with fear and confidence, whatever they may be.

The actions that match the feelings at each point on the scale of moderation are related to them in a straightforward way. They are the actions that are the objects of the desires that are the feelings. There is also the possibility of mismatch. Aristotle marks three points on the scale of feelings and three corresponding points on the scale of actions: excess, mediality, and deficiency. It follows that there are nine cases of mismatch, the most interesting of which is, perhaps, self-control. This is how Aristotle distinguishes self-control from moderation: "If self-control involves having strong and bad appetites, a moderate man will not be self-controlled and a self-controlled man will not be moderate: for a moderate man will not have excessive or bad appetites" (Nicomachean Ethics 7.2.6); and "Both a self-controlled man and a moderate man are such as to do nothing contrary to reason for the sake of bodily pleasure, but the former has bad appetites, while the latter does not have them, and the latter is the sort of person who would not feel pleasure contrary to reason, while the former is the sort of person who would feel it but is not led by it" (NE 7.9.6). Aristotle refuses to regard self-control as a virtue. "Self-control is not a virtue but a kind of mixed state" (NE 4.9.8).

This sets the stage for my second question about Aristotelian courage.

If it is a matter of feeling and controlling fear, how can it be a virtue? Or is the man of true Aristotelian courage literally fearless? If so, the virtue must be rare, and it may be unintelligible. This is a stark dilemma, and interpretation would be easier if there were a third possibility. However, the structure of courage is complex, and the third possibility, if there is one, might be more readily discernible in the simpler structure of moderation.

Aristotle says that the moderate man does not have excessive or bad appetites. That suggests an almost saintly match between his feelings and his medial actions. But he also says that the appetites of the self-controlled man are both strong and bad, and this suggests that there is a third possibility, bad but weak appetites that the agent does not indulge. However, he does not mention this possibility, and all that we can say is that he may not have intended to imply that such a character would not be moderate.

He says that in the self-controlled man appetites obey reason but that they are even more obedient to reason in the moderate man (*NE* 1.13.17). Now the appetites of the moderate man are more obedient to reason because they have become medial. So Aristotle must be thinking of the alteration of feelings by long training and habituation (see *NE* 3.12.7-9), but he may also be allowing for the possibility that an appetite could be immediately transformed by reason. Certainly this possibility exists in the case of fear. But that is because fear is based on an assessment of the disvalue of its object, and it is not clear that appetite is similarly based on an assessment of the value of its object.

There is another interesting hint in what he says about the pleasures of the moderate man. "He would not feel pleasure contrary to reason" (*NE* 7.9.6). This might merely mean that, if his actions were excessive, he would not feel pleasure, because he would lack the necessary appetites. But it might also mean that, even if he had been going to derive pleasure from excesses, it would be immediately transformed into nausea and revulsion by the pronouncements of reason.

These hints do not amount to much. Aristotle's usual picture of the relation between appetites and reason is a simple one. If appetites are nonmedial, reason can tell them not to interfere, and this command is obeyed in cases of self-control. This leaves no room for the third possibility that excessive appetites might occur but be transformed by reason, perhaps because they were weak. The third possibility would be interesting, because it would lead to a more realistic account of the inner life of the moderate man. However, there is not much evidence for ascribing such a view to Aristotle, and if the third possibility exists in the case of courage, it is probably for reasons peculiar to that virtue.

The question whether Aristotelian courage is a form of self-control cannot be answered before the question how it involves fear and confidence. If it were a form of self-control, the courageous man would curb his own fear. So let us take fear first and inquire how it fits into the structure of courage.

The simplest answer would be that fear and confidence lie on a single homogeneous scale, because fear shades into confidence as it diminishes and vice versa. This would give Aristotelian courage the same structure as moderation. But moderation has a single homogeneous scale of feelings only because the feelings are always desires for the same kinds of things: food, drink, and sex. Now fear is not itself a desire, but it is arguable that it always involves a desire. So, in order to test the simple interpretation of Aristotle's account of courage, we need to identiy the desire involved in fear and to ask whether it allows fear to be placed on a single homogeneous scale with confidence.

On the battlefield, where true Aristotelian courage is shown, the desire involved in fear must be the desire to save one's own skin. In the *Eudemian Ethics* the courageous man fears "things that are painful and destructive" (*EE* 1229a32-40), and the implication is that in general he wants to avoid such things. In the *Nicomachean Ethics* this is explained in some detail: "It is for facing what is painful . . . that men are called 'courageous.' Hence courage also includes pain. . . . Yet the end that courage sets before itself would seem to give pleasure but to be concealed by the concomitant circumstances. . . . Death and wounds will be painful to the courageous man, and they will go against his inclination; but he will face them because it is noble to do so or base not to do so" (*NE* 3.9.2-4).

I shall mark this point by calling death and wounds "the countergoals" of courage on the battlefield. So three kinds of goal are put before the citizen-soldier: the external goal, which is victory; the nobility of courageous action, which may be called "the internal goal"; and on the negative side, the countergoal, wounds and death, which in general he wants to avoid.

Since Aristotle recognized that courage needs a countergoal, the object of the aversion involved in fear, it is curious that in the *Nicomachean Ethics* he gives a nondesiderative definition of fear, "expectation of harm" (*NE* 3.6.2). This definition is obviously incomplete. For it omits all reference to avoidance, and gives an adequate account only of cases in which fear is simply the opposite of hope, and has no connection with taking avoiding action because all such action is known to be impossible. It is in this way that a person caught in an earthquake feels fear. But a soldier can run away, and, in order to cover this kind of case, the desire to take avoiding action must be built into the definition of this kind of fear, and then, for the sake of uniformity, of all kinds of fear, because when the situation is hopeless, the desire is still there but it has become a mere wish. In the *De anima* Aristotle gives a hint of how the definition would go. He gives a list of feelings, which include fear and anger, and he defines anger from a formal point of view as "the desire to return pain for pain" (*DA* 403). So it is plausible to credit him with a parallel definition of fear, which would go something like this: "Fear is the desire to avoid harm that is judged probable." This is confirmed by a passage in the *Rhetoric*, where he says that fear is impossible unless there is some hope of safety, because fear makes one deliberate, and nobody deliberates in a situation already accepted as hopeless (*Rh.* 1383a). It is interesting that this passage goes too far in its correction of the excessively intellectual definition of fear given in the *Nicomachean Ethics* (3.6.2). That definition is adequate only in cases where nothing can be done, but the remedy need not be to deny that these are cases of fear.

In the light of this, let us ask again whether fear can be placed on a single homogeneous scale together with confidence. This might appear possible if confidence involved a desire for harm, but there are only too many reasons for rejecting such an absurd idea. In the *Rhetoric* Aristotle defines confidence as "an expectation that what brings safety will be close at hand, while what produces fear will not exist or will be far away" (*Rh.* 1383a17-19). Even if this definition overintellectualizes confidence, it would be absurd to supplement it by requiring confidence to involve a desire for harm. The furthest that we could possibly go in that direction would be to say that it involves a desire for risk, relying on Aristotle's characterization of the rash man whose confidence is excessive (*NE* 3.7). I would not take this step, for reasons that I shall give later. The point to be made now is that even if we do take it, we still shall not have fear and confidence on a single homogeneous scale, unless the desire involved in fear can be shown to be the desire to avoid risk. But it cannot be. Aristotle explicitly says that the objects of fear are "painful and destructive" (*EE* 1229a32-40), and though it is true that anyone who wants to avoid such things will also want to avoid the risk of them, that does not show that the direct object of the aversion involved in fear is risk.

However, let us grant, for the sake of argument, that confidence involves the desire for a lot of risk, and fear the desire for little or none. What then? We seem to be able to postulate a virtue lying on a single homogeneous scale of feelings, like Aristotelian moderation. However, that virtue would not have an external goal and therefore would not be Aristotelian courage. True, its manifestations would look like those of courage, but its inner structure would be quite different. It would be cultivated purely for its own sake, rather like Hemingway's "courage," but not exactly like it, because this idea would be that people would have a general appetite for risk, just as they do for food, drink, and sex.

Let us call this virtue "darage." We need a new name for it because, unlike daring, it is supposed to be based on a general appetite for risk. Darage has no external goals. On the contrary, it is dysfunctional and might well extinguish the species. The man of darage exposes himself to risks medially but pointlessly, and his appetite matches his performance. We may suppose that darage has the same countergoals as courage, because those who practice it want, in general, to avoid things that are painful and destructive. But they also want to expose themselves to the risk of such things both because they have a general appetite for risk and because they see the nobility of it.

Evidently, darage is a trait that differs from courage. We do have some desire for risk, but the theory of darage vastly exaggerates its scope. When we expose ourselves to risk, there is nearly always an external goal motivating us; and when the risk is pointless, nobility is ascribed to our deeds only if they are of a kind that are usually done for the sake of some external goal. We need not discuss the question whether darage is a form of courage but an untypical one, or a trait quite distinct from courage. It is obvious that darage is not Aristotelian courage and what the difference is.

We are trying to discover how fear and confidence figure in the structure of Aristotelian courage. We have witnessed the collapse of the hypothesis that the two feelings involve desires for the same kind of thing and so lie on a single homogeneous scale. Is it possible that there are two different scales, one for fear and the other for confidence? It seems obvious that this possibility must be realized in one way or another, but everything depends on the way in which we take it to be realized.

One suggestion would be that each of the two feelings involves a basic desire and that the two scales exhibit the varying degrees of the two different basic desires. Sir David Ross suggested a theory of this kind in his book *Aristotle* (5th ed. [London, 1949], pp. 205-207). I shall not criticize the details of his theory, though I shall have to give them in order to make the theory intelligible. My criticisms will be general criticisms of all theories of this kind. I shall argue first that if confidence involved a basic desire for risk, and fear a basic aversion from risk, they could be placed on a single homogeneous scale and the related virtue would be darage; and second, that in fact fear does not involve a basic aversion from risk, and confidence does not involve any basic desire.

We need a statement of Ross's theory. His theory is offered in the context of his general criticism that Aristotle failed to realize that all virtue is really self-control. However, Ross concedes that in the particular case of courage Aristotle did take the first step toward realizing this truth. For he did connect courage with two different feelings, fear and confidence, and he did distinguish between the two scales on which these feelings vary, because he says that deficiency of fear is not the same thing as excess of confidence (*NE* 3.6.7-8). This is Ross's interpretation of part of Aristotle's account of courage. His next step is to apply his general criticism and to argue that Aristotle failed to realize that each of these two scales of feeling has its own virtue and that in each case the virtue is a form of self-control. On the scale of fear the virtue is courage, which is control of fear, and the vice is cowardice. On the scale of confidence the virtue is discretion, which is control of the desire for risk, and the vice is rashness. So Ross ends his criticism of Aristotle's ideas and his development of his own with two dyadic systems instead of a single triadic one. Naturally, most of what he says is criticism rather than interpretation. For example, Aristotle insists that there is only one virtue in this area. But Ross's idea is that he began with an important insight but failed to exploit it.

I am concerned only with one feature of Ross's theory, the structure of the two scales of feeling. The crucial point is that they exhibit varying degrees of desire for the same kind of object: risk or danger. The rash man wants too much, and the coward wants too little or none at all. So these two characters are related to one another in the same way as the self-indulgent man and the insusceptible man on the scale of desires for food, drink, and sex. True, there is a difference, because the insusceptible man simply lacks physical appetites (*NE* 2.2.7), while the coward has a positive aversion from danger. However, that does not affect my criticism of Ross's theory, which is that if both fear and confidence involve desires for the same kind of thing, and if Ross's two scales are based on desires, then they collapse into a single scale. It follows that his two virtues also collapse into a single virtue, which would be darage but for his thesis that all virtues are forms of self-control. It is irrelevant that one man might achieve this virtue by moving inward from the direction of cowardice and another by moving inward from the direction of rashness, because the destination is the same even if the journey is different. So, though Ross produces the illusion of two dyadic systems and two virtues, in fact he is offering a single triadic system and a single virtue.

This criticism is reinforced when we add that the proper object of the aversion involved in fear is not risk but "what is painful and destructive" (*EE* 1229a32-40), or, more briefly, harm. It would also be further reinforced by the addition of my second criticism, that confidence does not involve any basic desire differentiated by its proper object. However, before I can make that criticism good, I must go back to fear and interpret Aristotle's doctrine that people ought to fear things medially. The interpretation of that doctrine will put us in a position to solve the problem of courage and self-control. Having done that, I shall return to the interpretation of Aristotelian confidence. So in relation to that topic I am about to start on a digression, but, for reasons that will soon appear, a necessary digression. Before I start on it, I must emphasize that my criticism of Ross's theory does not show that fear and confidence do not have two different scales, but only that they do not involve basic desires whose varying degrees can be exhibited on two different scales. It remains possible that the two scales can be constructed in some other way, and it will appear later that this possibility is realized.

There is an important distinction between two uses of the words *fearless* and *fearlessly*. A man may behave fearlessly because he lacks the appropriate fear or because, although he has it, he behaves like a man who lacks it. The adverb sometimes makes a point about both the causation and the manner of the agent's conduct and sometimes makes a point only about its manner. This distinction runs through the whole of Aristotle's exposition of his doctrine that people should fear medially. It is not always visible on the surface of his text, because it occasionally disappears, like a geological fault; but it is always at work shaping his thought even when it is invisible. Since it is so important, it is best to begin with his clearest explanation of it.

In the *Eudemian Ethics* (1228b4 ff.) he says that the man of courage is on the whole fearless. He explains this by saying that he either does not feel fear or feels it slightly and not readily and seldom and only when the thing is very fearful; but, he adds, he faces very fearful things. Now things that are very fearful produce extreme fears, even, we may presume, in the man of courage. How then can he be fearless? Aristotle solves this problem in two steps. First, he points out that average human nature determines what things are in general fearful. Second, he maintains that "the man of courage is fearless in relation to such fearful things and faces them. In one way they are fearful to him, but in another way they are not. As a man he finds them fearful, but as a man of courage he finds them either slightly fearful or in no way fearful. Yet they really are fearful, because they are fearful to most people" (*EE* 1228b4-30).

This is not pellucid, but its main point must be that the man of courage goes into the dangerous predicament with the appropriate human fear of the countergoal. Perhaps others would have to alter their fears in order to make them conform to this standard, but his fear already conforms to it. It cannot be that he goes into the general predicament without any such general fear, because if that were so, there would be nothing for him to face. We may call this fear of the countergoal "contributory fear," because it will contribute to the action; but it will not necessarily be the only feeling that contributes to it. Contributory fear need not produce conduct that is fearful in the second sense distinguished just now. So "the man of courage is fearless in relation [to things that are in general fearful] and faces them" (*EE* 1228b26-27). This must be the second use of the word *fearless*, because Aristotle goes on to say that "he finds them fearful as a man." Also, on the next page, he tells us that "he is fearless because courage follows reason, and reason bids him choose what is noble" (*EE* 1229a1-2). Let us call this "the behavioral use" of the word *fearless*, because it comments only on the manner of the agent's conduct.

I believe that the attribution of this distinction to Aristotle is not only essentially correct but also very important, because it yields a solution to the problem of courage and self-control. However, the dividing line is not so clear in Aristotle's mind as I have just made it appear. So before I approach the problem of courage and self-control, I must put in some qualifications. There are two points at which I have oversimplified his thought. First, although it is true that he uses the word *fearless* in the behavioral way toward the end of the first quoted passage, it is not the whole truth. Second, more needs to be said about the general standard of contributory fearfulness and about the possibility that some people might have to adjust their fears in order to conform to it.

At the end of the first quoted passage, Aristotle says that the man of courage may find the countergoal in no way fearful. This cannot merely mean that he will not act fearfully, because it clearly refers to his feelings. Nor can it mean that he has no general fear of the countergoal because without it he could not be courageous. So it must mean that he will not be troubled by emotional perturbation. There are two places in the *Nicomachean Ethics* where Aristotle makes this requirement explicit: 3.8.15 and 3.9.1.

The second point at which qualification is needed is much more important. In any field of feeling and action Aristotle fixes the mean in relation to human nature (*NE* 2.6.5-9), and when he fixes the standard of correct fear in this way, he is simply applying his general doctrine to this particular case. Now there are various ways in which he thinks that people may feel incorrect fears. They may fear things that should not be feared at all (*NE* 3.7.3), and this would be a human failing if it were fear of poverty or illness (*NE* 3.6.4) and a subhuman failing if it were fear of the squeak of a mouse (*NE* 7.5.5). Or they may fear things that should be feared, but fear them in the wrong way or at the wrong time or for the wrong reason (*NE* 3.7.4-5). The commonest form of fearing the right things in the wrong way is fearing them too much or too little (*NE* 2.6.10), and this failing is frequently mentioned in both versions of Aristotle's account of courage (e.g., *EE* 1228a23-1230a34 and *NE* 3.6-9).

It would be an exaggeration to suggest that all these remarks about medial fear apply to the general, contributory fears with which agents enter dangerous predicaments, but that is certainly how Aristotle means most of them. The man of courage has medial fears while others often have deviant fears, and these fears are general fears that will contribute to the agents' actions in particular predicaments.

But can a man alter his fears? That was the question asked earlier about physical appetites. The answer in that case was that, though Aristotle clearly believes that a man can alter them over a long period of time, there is not much evidence for taking him to believe that he could alter them immediately. There is a stronger case for taking him to believe that a man can sometimes alter one of his own fears immediately. For he often says that a man can fear a thing too much or too little, and this must mean that his fear is disproportionate to the disvalue of that type of thing, and so it opens up the possibility that a man might argue himself out of an excessive fear by telling himself that the object really was not so bad. Fear is amenable to reason because it is based on an assessment of the disvalue of its object.

There is also another way in which fear is amenable to reason. In a particular predicament a man may change his estimate of the probability of the countergoal. That would lead to an increase or decrease of his fear of this particular instance of the type, but not of the type itself. Now Aristotle does not introduce probability as a second parameter determining the medial point for a particular fear. He merely observes that courage is shown on the battlefield when the circumstances that bring death are close at hand (*NE* 3.6.10; cf. *Rh.* 1383a17-19 and *EE* 1229b10-12). But I shall argue later that it would be a very natural extension of his theory to bring in probability at this point.

If a man's fear is sensitive to his realization that its object is not so bad as he thought or is worse than he thought, fear is amenable to reason in the deeper of the two ways distinguished earlier. Reason can make good the deficiency or remove the excess in the fear. However, reason may fail in this task, and then the only thing left for it to do is to oppose the excess or deficiency in the fear. In the first case, contributory fear is controlled, and in the second, contributory fearlessness is controlled. So here is one way in which fear might create a need for self-control.

It might be supposed that even when a man enters a predicament with medial fear of the countergoal, his fear still has to be controlled. That is what is left of the original problem about courage and self-control. We are now in a position to solve it. A medial fear does not have to be controlled, because it makes a correct contribution to the action. If the external goal has a high value, the desire to avoid the countergoal will be outweighed in the balance. Even if the countergoal is death, the desire to avoid it will be outweighed if the external goal is victory. But if the external goal has a comparatively low value, the agent's decision may go the other way. A medial desire to avoid the countergoal does not have to be controlled, because it makes a correct contribution to the action. Even when it is outweighed, it may still rightly modify the way in which the agent tries to attain the external goal. Control is needed only when the desire is nonmedial, and then mainly when its nonmediality would lead to the wrong action if it were not controlled.

This solution depends on the fact that courage is a virtue exhibited in predicaments in which two different values conflict with one another, the value of the external goal and the disvalue of the countergoal. In this conflict there is no need to control the outweighed value, because it has been outweighed. No such solution would be possible if courage lay on a single homogeneous scale of feeling involving a desire for a single type of object, like risk, and a single value, like the medial pursuit of risk.

How does confidence fit into this structure? It certainly does not involve a desire for the external goal. Aristotle took the external goal to be victory in cases of true courage, and safety in other cases (*NE* 3.6.11). His definition of confidence in the *Rhetoric* (1383a17-19), "an expectation that what brings safety will be close at hand," suggests that "safety" or "survival" might possibly cover all his external goals. However, confidence evidently does not involve the desire for safety in the way in which fear involves the desire to avoid harm.

Does confidence involve a desire for risk? I argued earlier that even if it did, that would not place it on a single homogeneous scale with fear, because the proper object of the desire involved in fear is not little or no risk. I also argued that Ross assumes that different amounts of risk are the proper objects of the desires involved in the two feelings, and so, when he tries to place each on a separate scale, the two scales merge into a single homogeneous scale. The question whether confidence does involve a desire for risk was postponed.

The answer must be that it does not. It is true that the man of courage takes a risk and takes it gladly (*NE* 2.3.1), from which it follows that he wants to take it. However, this is not a contributory desire, like the desire involved in fear, but a total desire in which the various contributory desires have been weighed against one another. The two most important contributory desires are the desire for the external goal and the desire to avoid the countergoal. There is also a third contributory desire, the desire for the internal goal, courageous action for the sake of its nobility; but that desire often makes a different kind of contribution, because nobility is a property that often does not help the agent to identify the courageous project in a particular predicament. Now a contributory desire may be a basic ingredient in a feeling, as the desire to avoid the countergoal is a basic ingredient in fear. But a total desire cannot be. Therefore the fact that the man of courage wants to take a risk and takes it gladly does nothing to support the theory that this is a basic desire, still less that it is a basic ingredient in confidence.

It is true that Aristotle says that spirited behavior is the most natural form of courageous behavior (NE 3.8.12). However, spirit is not the same as confidence, and there is no implication that spirit involves a basic desire for risk. Aristotle's point is that spirit is a natural ally of rational courage because nature has locked it automatically onto the same goals (see EE 1229b20-32 and NE 3.8.10-11). There is no suggestion that those goals include risk pursued for its own sake.

There is, however, a simple way of constructing a homogeneous scale for fear and confidence without too much implausibility and without the corollary that the medial virtue would be darage. Instead of saying that confidence involves a basic desire for risk, we could say that it involves a basic lack of aversion from harm. It would then lie on the same scale as fear. In order to avoid the conclusion that the medial virtue would be darage, we could then bring in the external goal and the conflict of values that is essential to the solution of the problem of courage and self-control. However, this solution does not fit the text. For though many passages could be read to mean that fear and confidence are related in this way, some are incompatible with the interpretation. The clearest incompatible passage occurs in the Nicomachean Ethics, where Aristotle distinguishes between excessive confidence and excessive fearlessness (NE 3.7.7-8).

If it is implausible to credit Aristotle with the view that confidence involves a basic desire for risk or a basic lack of aversion from harm, it seems equally implausible to credit him with the view that it involves any other basic desire. There is, therefore, no case for regarding the definition of confidence given in the Rhetoric (1383a17-19) as overintellectualized, like his definition of fear in the Nicomachean Ethics (3.6.2). How then does confidence fit into the structure of Aristotelian courage?

The only remaining possibility seems to be that confidence has something to do with the odds. That would fit the general idea behind the purely intellectual definition given in the Rhetoric. It is true that there would be a misfit in an important detail, because there is no hint of conflict in that definition. However, that is explicable. Confidence is not confined to conflicts in which courage can be exhibited, and so the definition of confidence must fit other cases besides this special one.

But what does happen to confidence in the special case in which courage can be exhibited? Obviously, a man in a tight corner will not "[expect] that what will bring safety is close at hand" (Rh. 1383a17-19).

Something has to be added to the definition to allow for the odds in a typical dangerous situation in which two values conflict. But what?

At this point Aristotle's text fails us. For though it contains some suggestive observations about confidence, there is no explicit theory. The observations give us the phenomena and some hints about how he would deal with them, but he does not really explain how he would deal with them or how he would fit confidence into the structure of courage. So what follows is speculative. But it is controlled by the constraints of his observations, and I cannot see that any other reconstruction is possible.

First, we must distinguish the desperate courage of the Spartans at Thermopylae from the sperate courage of men in a more hopeful strategic position. Now the Spartans' courage was desperate because they were certain to be killed but not because their self-sacrifice seemed pointless to them. They expected to delay the Persian advance and did delay it. However, they knew that they had no chance of safety whatsoever, and so the definition of confidence given in the *Rhetoric* would not apply to what they felt, even if it were modified to allow for odds. They did not feel any confidence, if confidence involves some belief in the possibility of safety. Therefore, if they were confident, it was only in the behavioral sense of "being confident," parallel to the behavioral sense of "being fearless" that was explained earlier. The verb θαρρεῖν is often used by Aristotle in this way. It takes a direct object and means "to face confidently."

However, he does not discuss desperate courage, and so it is a conjecture that he would say that the Spartans at Thermopylae were confident only in this behavioral sense. But it is hard to see what else he could say, except, of course, that their behavior was produced by an intention steadfastly maintained. There is no room for any feeling remotely related to the expectation that what would bring safety was close at hand.

Desperate courage is the limiting case, but Aristotle does make some interesting observations about the more frequent and central cases of sperate courage. So the reconstruction of his theory about the role of confidence in these cases is less conjectural. The first step is to qualify the simple definition given in the *Rhetoric* in order to allow for the odds. The man whose confidence is medial will assess the chances of safety correctly, neither exaggerating them nor minimizing them. He will then have in one pan of the balance a countergoal with a certain disvalue and a certain probability. In the other pan he will have the external goal, and it too will have a certain probability and a certain value. If he decides to go for the external goal, he will do so with a correct and steadfast assessment of the chances of safety and a conviction that the external goal is worth it.

If this is right, there is a graduated scale on which both fear and confidence are placed. It is the scale on which the agent's estimates of the probabilities of the countergoal are marked. These estimates are made in particular predicaments, and they are independent of the agent's general fears of types of countergoal, which are marked on a different scale. So the earlier account of fear was not complete. It dealt only with fears of types of countergoal. We now have to add something that was mentioned earlier but put aside—namely, the modification of the agent's general fear by his assessment of the probability of the countergoal in the particular predicament. These estimates lie on a second scale. On this scale fear and confidence are related to the same factor of probability but in opposite ways. This corresponds to a common view of the two feelings and possibly to some of the things that Aristotle says about them. On the other hand, his distinction between excess of confidence and excess of fearlessness can still be justified: when he draws that distinction, he is thinking of the other scale, on which the agent's fears of types of countergoal are marked.

Aristotle's observations are not enough to support this interpretation, but they do point towards it. He says that people who are confident of victory because they have been victorious so often are not courageous (*NE* 3.8.13). Now these people fit the simple definition of confidence given in the *Rhetoric*. But we know that courage involves confidence. Therefore the confidence that it involves must be based not on certainty but on an assessment of the odds. This is confirmed by his argument against Socrates' equation of courage with expertise; expert soldiers may look courageous, but often they are not really courageous because they know that there is no risk (*NE* 3.8.6). Finally, he points out that the excessively confident are impetuous and willing when the danger lies in the future but that they give up when the moment of danger actually arrives. His explanation is that they overestimate the chances of safety and, when the crisis comes, revise their estimate downward (*NE* 3.7.12 and 3.8.16).

There remain the questions asked at the beginning about the goals of Aristotelian courage. The countergoal of courage is "pain that tends to destroy life" (*EE* 1229a40). The supreme instance is death met in battle for the sake of its nobility. However, Aristotle does not completely exclude all other countergoals and external goals (*NE* 3.6.6-10). He allows that courage may involve fears of other countergoals, provided that they are not the kind of thing that should not be feared at all, but he claims that in such cases the word *courageous* is being used in an extended sense (*NE* 3.6.3). He also allows that courage may be exhibited off the battlefield. His examples are "at sea and in cases of illness" (*NE* 3.6.7-8). He does not develop the second of these two examples, but what he says about the first shows that the external goal is survival in a storm. There is no trace of the idea that there might be examples of external goals less closely related to safety and survival. So his views about the external goals of courage are restrictive in two different ways. He requires the external goal to be closely related to safety and survival, and he takes the paradigm to be the safety and survival of a city at war.

These views are of great interest, but they do not affect his conception of the structure of courage, provided that there is always some external goal. But is there always an external goal in cases of illness? And what would he have said about a purely passive case, like a prisoner waiting helplessly in a cell for his own execution, or about the Spartans if they had believed their self-sacrifice to be pointless?

The answers to these questions are not clear, but it is clear that at this point Aristotle's theory was restricted to two possible lines of development. He could have allowed passive cases of courage, and he could have treated such courage as "a mean in respect of feelings [but not also actions]" (*NE* 3.7.14). The doctrine was available for this use, but in fact he did not use it in this way, perhaps because courage seemed to him to be too closely tied to action. The second possible line of thought is compatible with the first one, because it deals with a different question. It is to say that the nobility of what the Spartans did at Thermopylae in order to delay the Persian advance would have remained a property of their deeds even if they had believed them to be pointless. His insistence on the nobility of courageous action and his tendency to attach nobility to types of action make it likely that this would have been, or perhaps was, his line of thought.

However, that immediately raises the question how the internal goal of courageous action, its nobility, is related to its external goal. Part of an answer to this question has already been given: often the nobility of a courageous project will not enable an agent to identify it in his deliberations, and so he will have to weigh the external goal against the counter-goal. That answer now has to be qualified. There are occasions when the type of the project—for example, to obey orders and stand and fight—is enough to identify it as the courageous project, and the agent might put this to himself by saying, "Obviously, that would be the noble thing to do." But even on an occasion like this, the commander has to ask himself whether it really is what courage requires, and reflections on possible nobility will seldom put him in a position to answer this question. For in such cases nobility is a resultant property and not a constitutive property. Therefore, the commander will usually have to go more deeply into the structure of the particular project. Nevertheless, he will sometimes be able to attach nobility to the type of action in the particular case without further thought about the structure of the particular case. If the Spartan commanders at Thermopylae had believed self-sacrifice to be pointless, and if they had not already had orders from home, that would have been the only rational way in which they could have decided that it would be courageous to stand and fight.

In the normal case the agent does weigh the external goal against the countergoal, decides on a project, and carries it out for the sake of the external goal and in spite of the countergoal. How then can he also carry it out for the sake of its nobility?

The first thing that needs to be said is that the external goal could not conflict with the internal goal in the way in which it conflicts with the countergoal. The conflict of motive, if there is one, is of a different kind. It is not a question of different actions, but of the same action from different motives. But is there any conflict even of this kind? A simple answer would be "No, because the two things are yoked together and cannot be separated" (cf. *NE* 10.4.11). This is what Aristotle says about life and pleasure. Is he in a position to say the same thing about the structure of a courageous action and its nobility? The answer depends on his theory about the better kind of egoism (*NE* 9.8), which would need more discussion than there is space for here.

The only question remaining from the list at the beginning of this paper is: "Does courage require a good external goal?" If not, it might be exhibited both by an intentional and by an unintentional wrongdoer. This too is a complex question, and I shall only make one point about it. If the attribution of courage depends partly on the correctness of the agent's valuation of the countergoal, as Aristotle believed, why should it not depend equally on the correctness of the agent's valuation of the external goal? A countergoal is essential to courage, but an external goal is equally or almost equally essential. So why distinguish between the effects of incorrect valuations of the two goals? Indeed, why not take the agent's actual feeling about the countergoal, correct or incorrect, as the relevant factor? This is what we often do in our assessments of courage.

Of course. But that is only because some of us have a general conception of virtue that is more like Ross's than Aristotle's. But if Aristotle does give virtue the structure that I have described, surely he faces a difficulty when he moves from moderation, which involves only one value, to courage, which involves two? The difficulty is not verbal but real, and it takes the form of a dilemma: either courage requires only that the agent actually have certain feelings about both the countergoal and the external goal, or it requires that he have correct feelings about both the countergoal and the external goal.

Aristotle may have accepted this dilemma. It is not clear whether he did accept it, because he confines his discussion of courage to cases where the external goal is unquestionably good. This is a pity. The *Nicomachean Ethics* contains an interesting discussion of the parallel question about another executive characteristic, self-control (*NE* 7.9.1-4). The solution offered is that we must distinguish between unqualified and qualified attributions of self-control. This solution would have allowed him to get between the horns of the dilemma about courage. But perhaps he would have rejected the dilemma. If so, that would be a symptom of his tendency to separate the virtues from one another in a way that suits their presentation in individual character-sketches but not their operations in real life.

11

Justice as a Virtue

Bernard Williams

I shall consider some points in Aristotle's treatment of justice in Book 5 of the *Nicomachean Ethics*, in order to raise certain questions about justice as a virtue of character. I am concerned with what Aristotle calls "particular" justice, that is to say, with justice considered as one virtue of character among others. This disposition is said to have two basic fields of application, the distributive and the rectificatory; this distinction will not concern us, and almost all the discussion can be referred to the first of this pair. Particular justice and injustice are concerned with a certain class of goods—"those which are the subjects of good and bad luck, and which considered in themselves are always good, but not always good for a particular person" (1129b3-5). These are listed at 1130b3 as honor, money, and safety: these are "divisible" goods, which are such that if one person gets more, another characteristically gets less.

From the beginning, Aristotle associates particular injustice with *pleonexia*—variously, greed, the desire to have more, the desire to have more than others: *pleonektēs ho adikos* 1129b1. This characteristic Aristotle treats as the defining motive of particular injustice:

If one man commits adultery for the sake of gain, and makes money by it, while another does so from appetite, but loses money and is penalized for it, the latter would be thought self-indulgent rather than *pleonektēs*, while the former is unjust and not self-indulgent: this is obviously because of the fact that he gains. Again, all other unjust acts are ascribed in each case to some kind of vice, e.g.

189

adultery to self-indulgence; deserting a fellow soldier, to cowardice; assaulting someone, to anger. But if he makes a gain, it is ascribed to no other vice but injustice. [1130a24 f.]

This passage occurs in chapter 2 where Aristotle is concerned to find the distinguishing mark of particular injustice. It seems clear that the reference to "unjust" acts is to acts that are unjust in the general sense—that is to say, roughly, wrong—and a similar interpretation is given to *adikei* at 1130a17.[1] Aristotle's point is that the way to pick out acts that are unjust in the particular sense from the whole range of acts that are contrary to justice in the general sense is by reference to the motive of pleonexia (which, on any showing, is excessively restricted, at this point of the discussion, to the desire for monetary gain). This is what the passage means; but its exact conclusion is unclear, and discussions of it do not pay enough attention to the Aristotelian distinction between unjust acts and an unjust character. It is one question whether particular injustice as a vice is characterized by the motive of pleonexia; it is another question whether all acts that are unjust in the particular sense are motivated in that way. The two questions come together only if some quite complex assumptions are made, which I shall try to bring out.

Later in the book, Aristotle directly addresses the distinction between acts and character, and also applies his usual distinctions about responsibility. In chapter 8, he first considers acts done from ignorance, and makes various distinctions among these: of a person acting in this way involuntarily, he says that they act neither justly or unjustly except *kata sumbebēkos*—they do things that merely happen to be just or unjust (1135a17-18). Beyond this, if someone acts, not out of ignorance, but also not from deliberation (*ek prohaireseōs*) and, rather, from some passion, the act will indeed be an unjust act, but the agent will not be an unjust person: *adikei men oun, adikos d' ouk estin* (1134a21, the first paragraph of chapter 6, a passage evidently displaced from its context). One who acts unjustly *ek prohaireseōs* is a person who possesses in the full sense the vice of injustice, and is fully an unjust person.

This, so far, is standard Aristotelian doctrine about bad acts and their relation to character and intention. Leaving aside acts that are involuntary through ignorance (more simply, unintentional), we can concentrate on the distinction, among intentional acts, between those that are the product of passion and later regretted, and those that are the expression of a settled disposition or vice of character.

This distinction bears a close relation, of course, to that between the *akratēs* and the *mochthēros*, but it is not exactly the same. *Akrasia* is itself a disposition, a trait of character, and as with any other bad characteristic, one can draw the distinction between someone who has this characteristic and is regularly disposed to give in to certain kinds of impulse, and someone who on some few occasions does so. We need not be concerned here to fit the *disposition* of akrasia into the account.

For the present purpose we need only a distinction between *acts*. With respect to some undesirable characteristic V, it is the distinction, among acts that are, in the relevant aspect, intentional, between:

(A) those that are V acts but are not the acts of a V person

and

(B) those that are both V and the acts of a V person.

The usual situation with the vices of character, in Aristotle's treatment, is that it will be a necessary condition of an act's being V that it is the product of some particular motive—lust, fear, or whatever.

To be put alongside this is another distinction among acts, in terms of their motives: the distinction between those that are motivated by a desire for gain, and those that are motivated otherwise. Now the distinction between (A) and (B) standardly consists in this, that (A) acts are the episodic and later regretted expressions of a motive that regularly motivates the person who does (B) acts, that is to say, the person who is V. But it is obvious that an (A) unjust act need not be motivated by desire for gain at all. To take Aristotle's paradigmatic distribution case, a person could on a particular occasion, be overcome by hopes of sexual conquest, or malice against one recipient, and so knowingly make an unjust distribution, and his act would surely be an unjust act.

Another of Aristotle's claims, admittedly an obscure one, indeed leads to this conclusion. In his rather unhappy and perfunctory account of the application of the mean to justice, he says:

. . . just action is intermediate between acting unjustly and being unjustly treated; for the one is to have too much and the other to have too little. Justice is a kind of mean, but not in the same way as the other virtues, but because it relates to an intermediate amount, while injustice relates to the extremes. [1133b3 f.]

It is not worth pursuing all the difficulties raised by these remarks, but one thing that the passage seems awkwardly to acknowledge is that if X has been unjustly treated, then someone else (chap. 11), Y, has acted unjustly toward him. But it cannot be a necessary condition of X's being unjustly treated by Y that Y be motivated by the desire for gain, rather than by lust, malice, anger, or whatever.

However, Aristotle is certainly tempted by his standard model, according to which, since pleonexia is the motive of the unjust person, (A) acts of injustice must be episodic expressions of pleonexia. This idea issues in a desperate device at 1137a1 f.:

> If (the distributor) judged unjustly with knowledge, he himself gets an unfair share of gratitude or revenge. As much, then, as if he had shared in the plunder, one who judges unjustly for these reasons gets too much. . . .

There must be something wrong in extending pleonexia to cover someone's getting more of this kind of thing. What would it be in such a case to get the right amount of gratitude or revenge?

Aristotle correctly holds:

(a) one who knowingly produces an unjust distribution acts unjustly.

He also explicitly claims:

(b) the characteristic motive of the vice of injustice is the desire for gain.

In addition, he seems disposed to accept the standard model from which it will follow that:

(c) the difference between (A) acts and (B) acts of injustice is not of motive, but only a difference in the dispositional grounding of that motive,

and the consequence of accepting all these claims is obviously false. There are acts that are unjust, and in the "particular" sense, but which are the products of fear, jealousy, desire for revenge, and so on. Moreover, they may be not just episodic expressions of motives of that kind, but rather of some related dispositional trait. The cowardly man who runs away in battle acts not only in a cowardly way, but also unfairly, and does so because of his cowardice. Unjust acts that are not expressions of the vice of injustice can thus stem from other vices. But the motives characteristic of those other vices are not the motive of pleonexia supposedly characteristic of the vice of injustice. So we cannot, granted these truths, accept both (b) and (c).

It might be said that the cowardly man's act of injustice is in fact motivated by pleonexia, the desire for gain, as well as by fear: he is aiming at an unfair share of the divisible good of safety. That description, unlike the nonsense about an unfair share of gratitude or revenge, could contain some truth. But it will not do in order to straighten out Aristotle's account of the matter, since 1130a17 f. makes it clear that pleonexia is seen as *contrasted* with such motives as fear, and not as coexisting with, or being a product of, such motives. The broader question of what pleonexia exactly is I shall come back to at the end.

(c) is one of the assumptions that I referred to earlier as needed to bring together the two questions, whether the unjust character is characterized by the motive of pleonexia, and whether all unjust acts are the product of that motive. (c) states that each unjust act must have the same motive as the unjust acts that are the product of an unjust character; and that is surely wrong. We can recognize that it is wrong, however, only because we can identify certain intentional acts as unjust in the particular sense, and can do this without referring to their motive. Indeed, we are helped by Aristotle in doing this, by his drawing our attention to such basic cases as the intentional misdistribution of divisible goods. Aristotle himself gives us a clear indication of the areas in which some unjust acts are to be found; in doing so, he also puts us in a strong position to deny, as he does not seem clearly to have done, the assumption (c).

However, the fact that some unjust acts can be located without referring to their motive does not entail that they all can be. It might be that some other unjust acts could be identified simply from their motive; in particular, by their flowing from a settled dispositional motive characteristic of the unjust character. In this case, they would not all have to be of the same types as those unjust acts that are identified independently of motive, such as misdistributions of divisible goods. They might, for instance, be acts of a sexual kind which, if motivated in a more usual way, would not be identified as having anything to do with particular injustice at all. Aristotle clearly thinks that there are acts of this kind. He associates the vice of *adikia* so closely with a certain motive (or rather, I shall suggest later, a certain class of motives), pleonexia, that he calls a person who is dispositionally motivated by that an *adikos*, and holds, in chapter 2, that any act which that person does from that motive is an act of particular injustice. Aristotle could of course go further, and hold that any act, of any kind, which is even episodically motivated by pleonexia is an unjust act in the particular sense. He would then have completed the equation of adikia and pleonexia, not only with respect to character, but with respect to acts. It is not clear to me, however, that he does hold that: chapter 2, at any rate, seems to commit him only to the view that any act of a dispositionally pleonektic man which is an expression of his pleonexia is an unjust act.

Aristotle, then, certainly equates the character-state of adikia with that of pleonexia. He certainly thinks that any act, whatever its other characteristics, which flows from that state is an unjust act. He may think, though it is not absolutely clear that he does, that any act that is even episodically motivated by pleonexia is an unjust act. He is strongly disposed to think, lastly, that any act that is an unjust act is motivated, even if only episodically, by pleonexia; but since he himself suggests some plausible ways of identifying some unjust acts independently of their motive, this is an unsound conclusion for him to hold, and insofar as he tends to hold it, it is probably because of the unsound theoretical assumption (c).

Treated in this way, adikia comes out as something rather different from anything that we would now be disposed to call "injustice." One must certainly recognise that the *dikaiosunē-adikia* scheme does not exactly match even a part of our *justice-injustice* scheme. The point, however, can also be put more critically. Since Aristotle leads us so clearly, as has already been said, to some areas in which dikaiosunē undoubtedly overlaps with justice, his dealings with the question of motive can be seen as an imperfection in his attempt to relate those areas to the virtues of character. Even in his own terms, the assumption (c), if indeed he made it, would be a mistake. His willingness, further, to equate the character state of adikia with that of pleonexia and to call an unjust act any act that arises from that state, can be seen as the other side of the same coin. In both ways his theory inclines him to think that the state of character that stands opposed to dikaiosunē must have a characteristic motive; and dikaiosunē is enough like justice to make it convenient, and perhaps even fair, to call this a mistake.

I now turn to some questions about justice and injustice as states of character, independently, to some degree, of Aristotle's treatment. I shall concentrate on the area where our concepts most clearly overlap with Aristotle's, that of distributive justice. As a way of dealing with justice as a virtue, this concentration is obviously very selective, but the general shape of the conclusions will, I believe, apply more widely. In discussing distributive justice, I will not always assume, as Aristotle does, that we are concerned with some unallocated good that is, so to speak, "up for grabs" and waiting to be distributed by some method or other to some class of recipients. We can, besides that, recognize also the case in which the good is already in somebody's hands, and the question is rather whether he justly holds it. We can extend the term *distribution* to cover such possibilities,[2] though since I am mainly concerned with justice as a virtue of character and am discussing the case of distributive justice in the interest of that concern, the case where there is no distributor will be of secondary interest.

In the distributive case, we can distinguish three items to which the terms *just* and *unjust* can be applied: a distributor (if there is one), a method, and an outcome. The question basically raised by Aristotle's treatment concerns the relation between the first of these and the other two; but it is worth saying something about the priority between method and outcome in determining what is just. Is a just outcome to be understood as one reached by a just method, or is a just method, more fundamentally, one that leads to just outcomes? At a first glance there seem to be examples that tell either way. Aristotle's own preferred examples tend to be ones in which the relevant merit or desert of the recipients is understood (at least by the distributor) beforehand, so that the basic idea is of a just outcome, namely, that in which each recipient benefits in proportion to his desert, and a just method will be, derivatively, a method that brings about that outcome. It seems different, however, if one takes a case in which some indivisible good has to be allocated among persons who have equal claims to it, and they agree to draw lots (a method that can be adapted also to cases in which they have unequal claims to it). Here the justice is not worn in its own right by the outcome of, say, Robinson, getting it, nor is it the fact that it has that outcome that makes the method just; it is rather the other way round.

This distinction is more fragile than it first looks, and it is sensitive to the ways in which the outcome and the method are described. Thus if the method is itself described as that of allocating, say, the food to the hungry, the "desert" can come to characterize the method itself, and not merely the outcome. Not all the difficulties here are very interesting; they flow from an evident indeterminacy in the notions of method and outcome. But, even allowing for the difficulties, there is a class of cases in which the justice very specially rests in the method rather than in the particular outcome. In these, when we ask "what makes it fair that A has it (*or* has that amount of it)?" the answer refers to a process by which A came to have the good in question, and, moreover, no characteristic of A which does not relate to that process is appropriately cited as grounding his claim to the good. This is true of Nozick's "entitlement theory,"[3] under which someone justly holds an item if he received it by an appropriate process (e.g., buying it) from someone who justly held it. Under such a theory, the process by which someone receives something is constitutive of the justice of his holding, and there is no independent assessment of the justice of the outcome at all.

This bears a resemblance, illuminating and also politically relevant, to another kind of case that also satisfies the condition for primacy of method, the case of allocation by lot. If Robinson draws the long straw, then what makes it fair that he gets the good is simply the fact that it was he who drew the straw. We may of course want to go further than that, and add that the straw-drawing was itself a method that, for instance, was agreed upon in advance. The fact that we can do this does not mean that the justice of the method ceases to be primary over the justice of the particular outcome: in explaining the fairness of Robinson's getting the good, we still essentially refer to the method. However, the point that we can, in the case of lots and similar processes, relevantly go on to say such things as that the method was agreed upon in advance, serves to bring out an important contrast with entitlement theory. In the case of lots, it is possible to ask questions about what makes the method a just or fair method.

The answers to those questions may even refer, in a general way, to outcomes. They will not refer to the particular outcome, and relative to that, the method remains primary, but some general relation of the method to outcomes may be relevant. For instance, a familiar argument in favor of a particular method of allocating some indivisible good would be that the probability it assigned to any given person of receiving the good was the same ratio as the share which that person, under the same general criteria, would appropriately receive of a divisible good (he gets one fifth of the cake, and a one-in-five chance of getting the chess set). A similar point emerges from the fact that lot-drawing can be modified, in certain circumstances, to allow for repeated trials; for instance, earlier winners may be excluded from later draws because it is thought fairer to increase over time the chances of a given person's winning. In such ways it is possible to criticize the fairness of methods such as drawing lots, by reference to general patterns of outcome, and by applying a notion of justice to such general patterns. But this resource seems mysteriously not available with Nozick's entitlement theory, and no other considerations, it seems, can be brought to bear on the question whether established methods of transfer are fair methods. But if we are to be convinced that the favored transactions are not only just but unquestionably just, some special argument needs to be produced: it certainly does not simply follow from the truth that, relative to the particular case, the concept of "justice" applies primarily to the method and derivatively to the outcome. That is a feature which Nozick's preferred methods of transfer share with other methods of distribution, where criticism of the methods is nevertheless possible.

For our present purposes, however, the priorities of method and outcome are a secondary issue. The main question concerns the relations of either of these to the notion of a just person, and from now on I shall speak of a "just distribution" to cover both those cases in which the method would naturally be considered primary, and those in which it is more natural to pick on the outcome. The notion of a fair distribution is prior to that of a fair or just person. Such a person is one who is disposed to promote just distributions, look for them, stand by them, and so on, because that is what they are. He may also be good at inventing just distributions, by thinking of a good method or proposing an acceptable distribution in a particular case: this will be a characteristic of Aristotle's *epieikēs* (1137b34), the person who is good at particular discriminations of fairness. But even there, it is important that, although it took him, or someone like him, to think of it, the distribution can then be recognized as fair independently of that person's character. It cannot rest on his previous record that some particular distribution, which perhaps seems entirely whimsical, is just (except in the sense, uninteresting to the present question, that his past record may encourage us to believe that there are other considerations involved in the present case, known to him though invisible to us).

The disposition of justice will lead the just person to resist unjust distributions—and to resist them *however they are motivated*. This applies, very centrally, to himself. There are many enemies of fair conduct, both episodic and dispositional, and the person of just character is good at resisting them. This means that he will need, as Aristotle himself insists, other virtues as well: courage, for instance, or *sōphrosunē*. But the disposition of justice can itself provide a motive. The disposition to pursue justice and to resist injustice has its own special motivating thoughts: it is both necessary and sufficient to being a just person that one dispositionally promotes some courses as being just and resists others as being unjust.

What then is the disposition of injustice? What is it to be a dispositionally unjust or unfair person? The answer surely can only be that it is to lack the disposition of justice—at the limit, not to be affected or moved by considerations of fairness to all. It involves a tendency to act from some motives on which the just person will not act, and indeed to have some motives which the just person will not have at all. Important among the motives to injustice (though they seem rarely to be mentioned) are such things as laziness or frivolity. Someone can make an unfair decision because it is too much trouble, or too boring, to think about what would be fair. Differently, he may find the outcome funny or diverting. At the end of that line is someone who finds the outcome amusing or otherwise attractive just because it is unfair.

It is important that this last condition is not the central or most basic condition of being an unjust person. The thoughts that motivate the unjust do not characteristically use, in this upside-down way, the concepts of justice and injustice. Those concepts, however, as has just been said, do characteristically figure in the thought of the just person. It is not untypical of the virtues that the virtuous person should be partly characterized by the way in which he thinks about situations, and by the concepts he uses. What is unusual about justice is that the just person is characterized by applying to outcomes and methods, in an analogous sense, the concept under which he falls; this is itself connected with the priority of the justice of distributions over justice of character.

On this account, there is no one motive characteristic of the unjust person, just as there is no one enemy of just distributions. In particular, the unjust person is not necessarily greedy or anxious to get more for himself, and insofar as Aristotle connects injustice essentially with pleonexia, he is mistaken. The mistake can, moreover, be fairly easily diagnosed at the systematic level: the vice of adikia has been overassimilated to the other vices of character, so that Aristotle seeks a characteristic motive to go with it, whereas it must be basic to this vice, unlike others, that it does not import a special motive, but rather the lack of one.

The point is not merely that "injustice" is not the name of a motive. Beyond that, there is no particular motive which the unjust person, because of his injustice, necessarily displays. In particular, he does not necessarily display pleonexia, which, whatever else needs to be said about it, certainly involves the idea of wanting something for oneself. Not all the motives that operate against justice, and gain expression in the unjust person, fit this pattern—not even all the important ones do so.

Beyond this, however, what is pleonexia? Is it even a motive itself? To call someone pleonektēs surely does ascribe certain motives to him, but motives that are very indeterminately specified. The pleonektēs wants more, but there must be something in particular of which in a given case he wants more. But "more" than what? More than is fair or just, certainly, but he does not characteristically want it in those terms—he has no special passion for affronting justice, and, like the unjust person generally, he is not specially interested in using the concepts of justice and injustice at all. It is rather that he wants more than he has got, or that he wants more than others. Now anyone who wants anything that admits of more or less wants more than he has got, or at least more than he thinks that he has got; but when this becomes a recursive condition, it is called greediness, and that is certainly one sense of *pleonexia*. Such a person does not necessarily, or even typically, worry about comparisons with others. But in another, and probably the most important, sense of *pleonexia*, comparisons with others are the point, and the notion of having more than others is included in the motivating thought. The application to such goods as money or honor or the Nobel Prize is obvious.

The case of Aristotle's third divisible good, safety, is more difficult. To want *more safety than others* is surely an odd want, if that is its most basic intentional description; what one wants is *as much safety as possible*—enough, one hopes, to keep one safe. Of course, since safety is in the circumstances a divisible good, the steps taken to satisfy this want will involve, and may be aimed at, taking away other people's safety (pushing them out of the fallout shelter). Thus the actions involved are much the same as with cases of pleonexia, but there is still a significant difference. With the Achillean pleonektēs of honor, an essential part of his satisfaction is that others do not have what he has; but the Thersitean pleonektēs of safety does not mind how many are eventually saved, so long as he is, and for this reason, his pleonexia is a different thing. The important point is that pleonexia is not, in his case, ultimately a motive at all: he is a coward, with a keen understanding that safety is a divisible good, and no sense of justice. Thus even in some cases of the egoistic desire for a divisible good, pleonexia is not the most basic or illuminating way of characterizing what is wrong with the man who does not care about justice. The love of competitive honor, however, is essentially pleonektic, and straightforwardly directed at making sure that others do not get it instead of oneself.

The word *pleonexia* can cover both greed and competitiveness. It certainly refers to a class of motives, rather than to any single motive. Those who are pleonektic of some things are not usually pleonektic of everything: as Aristotle well knew, those who are pleonektic of honor are not necessarily pleonektic of money, and conversely; and if there is anyone who is pleonektic of safety, it is certainly not Achilles. These various motives have no doubt at all times fueled some of the most settled indifferences to justice; but it is a mistake, one that dogs Aristotle's account, to look for something other than that settled indifference itself to constitute the vice of injustice, and, having looked for it, to find it in such motives.

NOTES

1. So commentators, e.g. Joachim and Gauthier-Jolif, ad loc.; W. F. R. Hardie, *Aristotle's Ethical Theory* (Oxford, 1968), p. 187.

2. Robert Nozick, who strongly emphasizes this point in his *Anarchy, State and Utopia* (New York, 1974), calls the chapter in which this is discussed "Distributive Justice."

3. Nozick, *Anarchy*, chap. 7.

12

Aristotle on the Role of Intellect in Virtue

Richard Sorabji

How large a role does Aristotle give to the intellect in his account of virtue? Commentators have minimized its role in three interrelated ways. They have derationalized the *prohairesis* (choice) involved in virtue, they have reduced the part played by *phronēsis* (practical wisdom), and they have treated habituation as a mindless process sufficient for making men good. I wish to challenge each part of this threefold case.

PROHAIRESIS (CHOICE)

In order to be just, or otherwise virtuous, it is not enough to do what a just man would do. One must *prohaireisthai* (choose) to do the just act. This is the clear opinion of *NE* 2.4. 1105a31; 6.12. 1144a19.[1] It implies that every virtuous act involves exercising *prohairesis* (choice).

What is prohairesis? The chapters of *NE* devoted to it (3.2-3) make it out to be a very intellectual thing. It is a matter of desiring to do what deliberation has shown to be conducive to our goal (1111b26-30; 1112a-30-1113a12; repeated 6.2. 1139b4). But many modern commentators see a problem here. They consider that the definition of *prohairesis* in 3.3 talks in terms of choosing the *means* to one's goal, and then they object that elsewhere in the *Ethics* the conception of choosing *means* does not fit Aristotle's use of the word *prohairesis*. I have noticed sixteen[2] commentators who claim that elsewhere in the *Ethics* Aristotle uses the word *prohairesis* in a different way.

There are at least two differences. First, D. J. Allan argues that outside
Book 3 Aristotle thinks in terms of choosing to perform an action as an
instance of some desirable kind of action, rather than as a *means* to some
goal. Allan does recognize that the "instance" use and the "means" use of
the word *prohairesis* are analogous. But many writers fasten on a further
point, which makes Aristotle's uses of the word *prohairesis* seem even
more divergent. Whereas Aristotle claims in 3.2 and 3.3 that one chooses
means, not ends, elsewhere choice is of ends, and indeed the word means
no more than one's general purpose. This latter interpretation,[3] far more
than the first, weakens the link between prohairesis and rationality. It is
no longer clear that one chooses something for a reason—that it conduces to something else. The most extreme version of this view is W. D.
Ross's. He claims that outside the two passages in which prohairesis is
formally discussed (3.2-3 and 6.2) it hardly ever refers to the means. Both
in the remainder of the *Ethics* and in Aristotle's other works it generally
means "purpose" and refers not to means but to an end. He cites 22 passages in support of this claim.

The passage (2.4. 1105a31) where Aristotle first says that in order to be
virtuous we must choose to do our virtuous acts is often cited as a case
where Aristotle is unfaithful to his definition of choice. For he says that
we must choose to do the virtuous act *for its own sake.* Surely, it is
argued, choosing the act for its own sake excludes choosing it as a *means*
to a goal.

Let us look at these claims more closely, starting with Allan's and
going on to Ross's, and using the assumption that there is an onus of
proof on the interpreter who says that Aristotle is contradicting his official account. Where commentators have talked simply of *means* to an
end, Aristotle uses a variety of terms. Some critics have already pointed
out that when he says we choose what is *pros* some goal, this need mean
no more than that we choose what is *related to* a goal. The word *pros*
does not imply means. But it should be further pointed out that according to 3.3 we choose[4] sometimes the means (*dia*) and sometimes the manner (*pōs*) of doing something (1112b15; 30). It looks as if at b30 a difference is intended between means and manner parallel to that between
choosing a tool and choosing how to use it.

Turning now to 2.4, what are we to make of Aristotle's statement that
the virtuous man chooses to do the virtuous act for its own sake? Must
we construe this, with Allan, as meaning that he chooses to do the courageous act as an *instance* of courageous activity? Whether *instance* is more
appropriate a word than *means* depends on how the goal is specified.
Perhaps as well as choosing the courageous act because it is an instance
of courageous conduct, the brave man can also be said to choose it as a

means to his goal of continuing to be a courageous man. Thus if the goal is specified not as courageous conduct but as courageous character, talk of *means* is quite appropriate. And in 3.7, as Allan remarks, there are signs that Aristotle does sometimes think of the matter this way. The end of every activity, he says, is conformity with the corresponding disposition (1115b20-21). The corresponding disposition for the courageous man is courage. Presumably, then, he can be said to choose his courageous act as the means to retaining his courageous character.

It may, incidentally, be felt that a courageous man should act from different motives, neither because his act is an instance of courageous conduct nor because it is a means to remaining courageous, but rather, for example, to save his friends. In cases of private adversity, however, we surely would not disapprove of his acting courageously (remaining cheerful) for the sake of being courageous.

The man who chooses to do the virtuous act for its own sake may choose it not because it is required by some particular virtue, such as courage, but because it is required by virtue in general. Thus Aristotle often speaks as if this man thinks in rather general terms of what is required by *to kalon* (the noble). But it makes little difference either way, for the man who thinks more specifically in terms of what is required by courage will at the same time have to think generally in terms of what is required by virtue. This will become clearer later when we discuss the unity of the virtues. We shall then see that considerations of what courage requires involve considerations of what the other virtues require.

Let us return to the dichotomy between instance and means. I have suggested that the courageous man may have both attitudes, in Aristotle's view, choosing to act courageously both as an instance of courageous conduct and for the sake of being a courageous man. I have been allowing that the two attitudes are slightly different from each other. But in other examples this would not necessarily be the case. It may come to the same thing whether we say of the man who is looking for a just solution that he is seeking the means to a just solution or that he is seeking what would count as such. Nor should it be supposed that *instance* and *means* are the only possibilities. Manner, which Aristotle mentions in 3.3, may be more appropriate than either. For example, the liberal man may be best described as choosing a *way* of bestowing his wealth. Again, the *Eudemian Ethics* allows that one can choose moneymaking (*EE* 2.10. 1226a8), presumably as *part of* the good life.

So far we have challenged the claim that in 3.2-3 we are said to choose only means, while in 2.4 the virtuous man is said to choose only instances. But the more important thing for our purposes is that choice remains in all these contexts connected with rationality. Whether the vir-

tuous man is choosing a *means* to being courageous, or an *instance* of
courageous conduct, or a *way* of bestowing his wealth, the choice
involved is still a rational thing. This brings us to W. D. Ross's claim that
Aristotle usually violates the assertion in 1111b26-30, 1112b11-16, 33-34
that we do not choose ends but only (as Ross construes it) means. A companion assertion in Aristotle is that we choose only things in our power
(1111b20-33; 1112a30-b8, 1112b24-28, 1112b31-32, 1113a9-11). It is not
always noticed how little restriction this places on our choice. Aristotle
means that on any particular occasion of deliberation we take some goal
for granted and choose what conduces to it. But there is nothing to prevent our treating that goal on another occasion as the means to some further goal. Moreover, even such general goals as moneymaking can be
viewed as required for the good life and can be in our power. This is why
moneymaking is cited in the *Eudemian Ethics* as something we can
choose. The mild restriction that we choose only what is in our power is
close to one that applies to the English verb *intend*. We can intend to do
something only if we think it is in our power. And in saying that we
choose only in relation to ends, what Aristotle means to do is to preserve
a certain link between choice and rationality. If we choose an end, we
choose it in relation to a yet further end. Ross may be right that outside
the *Ethics* the word *prohairesis* loses this link with rationality and comes
to mean no more than purpose. But of Ross's citations from within the
Nicomachean Ethics only a very few seem to me to demand such a loose
interpretation. While it would be tedious to go through them all, a good
number will come to seem implausible on the basis of what has already
been said. We need only remember that we can choose ends, so long as
they are related to further ends, and that the relationship may be that of
instance, manner, or part, as well as that of means.

    Choice, then, is a rational thing. But it may be wondered whether Aris-
totle remains faithful to his claim that it involves *deliberation*. There is a
passage that seems to dissociate virtue, choice, and deliberation. *NE* 3.8.
1117a17-22 speaks of courage (or what is thought to be courage, a18)
being shown in sudden dangers, where there is no time for calculation
and reasoning (*logismos* and *logos*). A first reading might suggest that
here we have an instance of courage in which there is no time for choice.
And this impression might be confirmed by 3.2. 1111b9, which says that
we do not describe sudden actions as being in accordance with choice.
But this interpretation is almost certainly wrong, for according to
1117a22 the sudden acts of daring we are here concerned with *are* chosen.
(The verb is presumably to be understood from the preceding line.) The
point made elsewhere that we do not describe sudden acts as being in
accordance with choice need not worry us. For Aristotle does not say

that the common usage (*legomen*) to which he refers applies to *all* sudden acts without exception, nor that he endorses it, if it does. It is not even clear that the present acts of daring are sudden in the relevant sense, for though they are responses to sudden danger, they flow from the agent's character, and from this point of view are not unexpected.

An objector may still protest that if there is choice here, it is choice in a debased sense, choice divorced from deliberation. I am not sure that we must accuse Aristotle of abandoning the link with deliberation. The reasoning for which he says there is no time is reasoning about precautions that will make one more confident of safety. This is clear from the immediate context and could be confirmed, if necessary, by passages in the *Rhetoric* (1389a33-35; 1390a15-17), which suggest that the reasoning that is contrasted with character is reasoning about *advantage*. This leaves open the possibility that choice in these cases may be linked with a different kind of reasoning. And there certainly is something analogous to the deliberation described in 3.3. For there is the perception that one thing (the particular act) is conducive to another (the ideal of courage and the noble, 1117a17). The biggest obstacle to saying that this is a form of deliberation is the fact that Aristotle defines deliberation as involving search (*zētēsis* 1112b20-23; 1142a31-b15). In order to stand by his claim that choice involves deliberation, Aristotle would have to take the implausible view that in the present cases of sudden danger the courageous man always has to *ask himself* what courage requires of him. Perhaps the implausibility did not strike Aristotle. He would have noticed it more readily if he had paid more attention to those cases in which it is a foregone conclusion what the virtuous man will do (e.g., pay for his shopping). Here it is clearer that the virtuous man need not ask himself what to do. But it is best to acknowledge that rather than taking so implausible a view, Aristotle may to this extent have contradicted his original account of choice. I intend to leave these alternatives open, but we shall need to recall them later.

PHRONĒSIS (PRACTICAL WISDOM)

There is a second way in which Aristotle brings in the intellect. He insists that the virtues require *phronēsis* (practical wisdom *NE* 6.13. 1144b17-1145a6; 10.8. 1178a16-19; *EE* 3.7. 1234a29). Practical wisdom involves the ability to deliberate (6.5. 1140a25-b6; 6.7. 1141b8-14; 6.9. 1142b31; *Rhet.* 1366b20). The man of practical wisdom deliberates with a view not merely to particular goals but to the good life in general (*pros to eu zēn holōs* 6.5 1140a25-31), with a view to the best (*to ariston* 6.7. 1141b13;

6.12. 1144a32-33), and with a view to happiness (*eudaimonia Rhet.* 1366-b20). At the same time he is concerned not only with universals, such as the good life in general, but also with particular actions (6.7. 1141b15; 6.8. 1142a14; 20-22; 6.11. 1143a29; 32-34).

Whatever other roles practical wisdom may or may not play, I suggest that one role is this. It enables a man, in the light of his conception of the good life in general, to perceive what generosity requires of him, or more generally what virtue and to kalon require of him, in the particular case, and it instructs him to act accordingly. A picture of the good life will save him from giving away too much, or too little, or to the wrong causes, in particular instances.

This account fits, I believe, with everything Aristotle has to say about practical wisdom. First, it assumes that the man of practical wisdom is virtuous, not vicious, as is made clear at 6.12. 1144a22-b1. Next, it presupposes that practical wisdom is concerned with what ought to be done and that it gives orders. This is explicit at 6.10. 1143a8-9. Then it maintains that practical wisdom involves knowing what is required in the particular case. We have already noted Aristotle's insistence that it is concerned with particulars. But Aristotle starts making his position clear early in the *Nicomachean Ethics.* Already in 2.6 the definition of virtue reveals that it is the man of practical wisdom who knows where the mean lies between prodigality and meanness in particular cases. Virtue is defined (1107a1-2) as lying in a mean position which the man of practical wisdom defines. It is sometimes said instead that the mean position is defined by *orthos logos* (the right rule 2.2 1103b31-34; 3.5. 1114b29; 6.1. 1138b20), but this makes no difference, for it is finally revealed that the orthos logos is in accordance with, or actually is, practical wisdom (6.13. 1144b21-28). We see, then, that practical wisdom is concerned with knowing just what to do in particular cases in order to hit the mean and in order not to give the wrong amount or to the wrong causes. That it calls for something like perception to recognize at what point one's action would become blameworthy was stated as early as 2.9. 1109b20 and 4.5. 1126b2. In Book 6 practical wisdom is compared with sense-perception five times (1142a27-30; 1143b14; 1144a29; 1144b1-17; cf. 1143b5 discussed below). In 6.13 Aristotle, repeating the analogy for the last time, compares how a man stumbles without sight (1144b1-17). The point seems to be that a natural impulse to give does not yet amount to generosity without practical wisdom to tell us what to give and to whom. On the contrary, without this we will be like a sturdy body stumbling for want of sight.

Though practical wisdom involves the perception of what to do in particular cases, it also involves more. Such perception can come from mere experience (6.11. 1143b11-14). But practical wisdom is contrasted in 6.7. 1141b16-21 with experience, because it involves perceiving what to do in particular cases in the light of knowledge of something more universal. Book 6, chapter 1, gives a vivid description. When you want to hit the mean, there is a mark (*skopos*) at which you must look (*apoblepein*) as you relax or tighten the string (1138b22-23).⁵ The mark at which the man of practical wisdom looks is, presumably, his conception of the best (*to ariston*), at which he is said to aim (1141b12-14) and from which his reasoning is said to start (1144a31-33). And this is further confirmed by 1094a23-24, which is talking of knowledge of the highest good (*t'agathon* and *to ariston*) when it says that such knowledge will have a great influence on life, since, like archers who have a mark, we shall better hit what is right. The point from which the reasoning of practical wisdom starts is compared with the first premises of a theoretical science (*EE* 2.11. 1227b-24-25; 28-30; *NE* 7.8. 1151a16-17). And there is a further indication that it consists in a very general conception of the good. For this helps to explain the statement that as soon as we have practical wisdom, we must have all the virtues together, not merely some of them (6.13. 1144b32-1145a2).

Some of these ideas may seem strange. Why should all the virtues go together? And why should we need a conception of the good life in general in order to be virtuous? Why should it not suffice to have a conception of each of the separate virtues? The answer is that the virtues are not separate, for courage is not a matter of facing any danger for any reason but of facing the right danger for the right reason (e.g., 3.7. 1115b15-20). And what is right here depends partly on the claims of other virtues, such as justice, and also on what kind of life we should be aiming at, one of leisure and philosophy, for example. So we cannot know what courage requires of us now without knowing what the good life in general requires. The man who has only experience without a picture of the good life in general can achieve only limited success in seeing what courage requires.

We are now in a position to see how extensively the intellect is involved in virtue. If Aristotle does not mean that our conception of the good life has in every case to be *consciously* reflected on, his view seems very reasonable. We cannot decide what we ought to do in a particular situation by reference to some single isolated consideration, such as fearlessness. Many considerations will influence us. And for the virtuous man, according to Aristotle, these many considerations will add up to a unified picture of the best life, a picture which he no doubt did reflect on at the period when he was acquiring it, and which he will reflect on again in difficult cases. But what about easy cases, where the outcome is a foregone conclusion? Even here it would be reasonable for Aristotle to hold that a man is influenced by a whole set of ideas about how to live (that it is more important, for example, to pay for his groceries than to keep the money dishonestly for buying books). We should expect, though, that the picture would influence him in these cases without his consciously reflecting on it. But we have already seen that it is unclear whether Aristotle recognizes that virtuous actions need not involve conscious reflection. For according to his official account, every virtuous act involves choice, choice involves deliberation, and deliberation involves search (*zētēsis*).

The role we have ascribed to practical wisdom is not the only one it has. Indeed, discussion has often centered on other roles, or putative roles, and drawn attention away from the importance and scope of this one. There has been a major controversy involving Trendelenberg, Teichmüller, Loening, and Allan on one side, Walter and some distinguished followers on the other.[6] According to Trendelenberg, practical wisdom has a further function as a rational intuition of what our ultimate goals should be. I shall later argue that we acquire our conception of these goals through a process that involves induction followed by teaching. However greatly desire is involved, the intellect is as well, contrary to Walter's view. Whether Aristotle labels the intellectual element as an exercise of practical wisdom is of secondary importance.

One task for practical wisdom, not yet mentioned, is this. When we see in the light of our conception of the good life that courage requires us to attack the enemy, action may follow at once. But it may be that the enemy has not yet arrived, and in that case we will not yet attack, but only resolve to attack. Action will not follow until we see the enemy has arrived. It may also be that we need to work out the best means or manner for attacking the enemy, perhaps by an ambush. And after this is worked out, the action again will not follow until the enemy is seen to be at hand. All this further reasoning is said to be a task for practical wisdom, or at least for the component of practical wisdom called cleverness (1144a21-29).

Aristotle thinks the whole chain of reasoning can be represented in syllogistic form. No single reconstruction fits everything he says about practical syllogism, since he uses the idea to make different points in different passages, but the following fits one strand of his thought.[7] Our conception of the good life (to ariston) is a sort of major premise (1144a-32). Our perception that attack is required, so we shall argue later, is a minor premise (1143b3). The conclusion is either an action (attack) or a resolution to attack, which forms a major premise for further reasoning. If the next minor premise is about the means or manner of attack ("ambush is the best means"), this premise will be based largely on military knowledge. But it will presumably still have to be controlled by an intuitive perception of what courage requires, since not any and every means would be compatible with courage and the good life. This is why there is a reference (brief and overrestrictive) at 3.3. 1112b7 to choosing the noblest means and at 1142b23-24 to choosing a means that is not only effective but also right (*di' hou dei*). And (so we shall argue) it is why Aristotle says we need intuitive perception (*nous* 1143b5) of the last minor premise (b3) in the series, without restricting the point to cases where the last minor premise is "attack is required." The point can also apply even where it is "ambush is required." These premises will be last in the series of premises about what to do, but not necessarily last altogether. For a final minor premise may be needed of an entirely different kind, one that is supplied by sense-perception (1147a26; b9-10), "here is the enemy." The ultimate conclusion is an action (*De motu* 701a20-24), though the interim conclusions in these cases[8] will be resolutions.

There is a difficulty. Aristotle says (so we shall argue) that reasoning (logos 1143b1) does not grasp what courage requires of us, and there is a suggestion that the judgment of practical wisdom at this point is not one that can be deduced (1143b12). Aristotle does not deny that the judgment about what courage requires enters into a chain of reasoning, but only that it is discovered by that reasoning. Does this go against my claim that the intuitive judgment is made in the light of a conception of the good life? I think there is no conflict. Aristotle's point is that the judgment about what courage requires cannot be derived syllogistically with the aid of a minor premise from our conception of the good life. This is not to deny that it is influenced by that conception.

This is a convenient point to make clear where choice (prohairesis) comes in. The resolution to attack the enemy can be a choice, and so can the resolution to attack them by ambush. I agree with G. E. M. Anscombe[9] that choice can occur well in advance of there being an opportunity for action. This is clear from Aristotle's treatment of weak will, among other things—that is, from his view that it is hard to abide by the decision we have chosen (1110a29-31) and that in giving in to temptation we may be acting against our own choice[10] (1148a9; 1151a7; a29-b4; 1152a17).

Let us now return to the role of intellect in virtue. In spite of all the evidence we have been looking at, some writers have tried to play down the role of intellect. The best known case is that of Walter, who insisted that our goals are decided by virtue and that virtue, so far from being a rational thing, is a state of the faculty of desire, which simply approves certain goals. Thus Aristotle is assimilated to Hume and the emotivists.

Closer to our interests is the view of William Fortenbaugh, from whom I have learned a great deal about the other side of the case. He has argued that the virtuous man can act virtuously without his practical wisdom being in play at all.[11] Fortenbaugh concentrates on a role of practical wisdom which certainly need not be exercised on every occasion. Like Walter,[12] he connects it chiefly with calculating the means to immediate goals such as revenge.[13] Indeed, he connects it with calculating the safest and most advantageous way to achieve these goals. As *NE* 3.8 points out, such calculation, so far from being required in every courageous act, can actually make one doubt a man's courage. If this is its main role, one wonders why Aristotle thinks practical wisdom so necessary. Unlike Fortenbaugh, I have emphasized the moral functions of practical wisdom, which explain why Aristotle thought it so important. Fortenbaugh does not altogether neglect these functions, for a footnote (15) acknowledges that practical wisdom can consider whether revenge itself is called for by reference to more general goals. But this is thought of as something that does not happen in the majority of cases, and it is said that for the most part the calculations of practical wisdom are technical deliberations concerning means, and so lacking in independent moral significance. A ground for this is Aristotle's claim that virtue makes the goal right, which is taken to mean that normally it is moral virtue, a sort of consistent disposition (*hexis*) or character (*ethos*), which makes the virtuous man pursue the right immediate goals, and that practical wisdom normally plays no part in this. I have argued, on the contrary, and will argue again, that though moral virtue is a disposition, it is one directed by practical wisdom. And I shall give a quite different interpretation to the claim that virtue makes the goal right. What may seem more arguable is Fortenbaugh's denial that the virtuous man's practical wisdom is in play every time he acts virtuously. Yet certainly he makes a choice every time (2.4; 6.12), and choice, according to the official account, involves deliberation and search. If the virtuous man really deliberates what to do every time, it is likely that he will answer by reference to his conception of the good life, and such deliberation is said to be the task of practical wisdom. Even if Aristotle abandons the link with deliberation and search, I have suggested he may still quite reasonably hold that the virtuous man is influenced every time, albeit sometimes unconsciously, by his conception of the good life.

We ought to go behind Fortenbaugh's claims to some of the statements in the *Ethics* which may seem to support not only his interpretation but also the more extreme view that virtue can exist in someone who lacks practical wisdom altogether. A case in point is Aristotle's assertion that the kind of virtue we have been discussing, virtue of character, must be distinguished from the virtues of intellect and that practical wisdom is among the latter (1.13. 1103a1-8; 6.1. 1138b35-1139a3; 6.3. 1139b14-17). Coupled with this is the view that virtue of character belongs to the desiring part of the soul, which can only listen to reason, whereas practical wisdom belongs to the part of the soul that can reason for itself. If virtue of character is not intellectual, someone may ignore that it involves listening to reason and leap to the conclusion that it can exist without practical wisdom. And it may begin to seem that the *Ethics* is arranged in conformity with this idea, virtue of character being treated first in books 2-5, while practical wisdom is not discussed till 6. It may also be tempting, with Fortenbaugh, to construe virtue of character as a consistent disposition, or hexis, which need not be directed by practical wisdom. I shall say more at the end about how false this separation would be. For the moment let us notice that the texts cited do not support the conclusion but instead count against it. It is reasonable for Aristotle to endorse the Platonic distinction between virtue of character and virtues of intellect and to include practical wisdom among the latter. For virtue of character is regarded as a disposition to desire the mean that is found and dictated by deliberative skill, while practical wisdom is a disposition to use one's deliberative skill in order to find the mean and dictate it. This way of distinguishing between the two does not imply that one can exist without the other but on the contrary precludes it. The most we should acknowledge is that while listening to the dictates of reason is *part* of virtue, working out where the mean lies is considered not so much as a part, but rather as a *prerequisite*, of virtue.

There is just one place where Aristotle does present the distinction in a misleading way. In the first three chapters of Book 2 he is influenced by Plato, to whom he refers at 1104b12. The passage that has influenced him in the opening lines (1103a14-17) is *Laws* 653a-c (cf. 643b-645c; 659c-e; 951b; *Republic* 402a; 518e; 619c; *Phaedo* 82a-b). Here, like Plato (653a7-9), Aristotle points out that intellectual virtue takes time to acquire, and, like Plato (b5-6), he says that virtue of character is acquired through habituation. One worrying thing is that he seems to speak almost as if habituation were sufficient to instill virtue, an impression he will later correct. But it may lend color to the idea that he is here regarding virtue of character as something that does not need practical wisdom. What has happened? As we shall later see, there is some reason to think that Aristotle is simply overemphasizing habit, thinking it the most important factor, but not the sole one, for producing virtue proper. However, we must also notice an alternative interpretation. Having followed Plato so far, Aristotle may intend Plato's further point that there is such a thing as habit-virtue, which takes less time to acquire than intellectual virtue and is developed before reason (b3-4). For producing this kind of virtue, habituation is sufficient. But it must be pointed out that it is not unlike Aristotle to use Plato's words while giving a different twist to his thought. Aristotle's remark that intellectual virtue takes time to acquire (1103a16-17) may be entirely parenthetical and does not necessarily imply endorsement of Plato's further point that there is such a thing as habit-virtue, which can be acquired in less time. If, however, Aristotle is endorsing the rest of what Plato says, we still need not worry. For Plato makes it very clear that habit-virtue is not complete virtue (*sumpāsa* b6). So Aristotle too will be talking only of incomplete virtue and not suggesting that virtue proper can develop before practical wisdom. His talk of virtue as something that can be "increased" (*auxetai* 1105a14-15) lends some support to the idea that he is thinking of incomplete virtue.

There is another line of thought in Aristotle which may be taken to suggest that virtue can be acquired before practical wisdom. For he says that virtue makes our goal right, practical wisdom being only the steps to the goal (*NE* 1140b11-20; 1144a7-9; a20-b1; 1145a5-6; 1151a15-19; *EE* 2.11). He seems to be thinking of our most general goal, the kind of life we aim at. The statement may be interpreted as meaning that virtue *teaches* us what general goal to adopt and therefore exists in us as a teacher before we have acquired that goal. If so, virtue cannot require, as I have claimed, that we already possess the right general goal in the light of which we decide what to do. A closely associated claim is that not only does virtue involve practical wisdom, but also practical wisdom involves virtue (1144a28-b17; 30-32). It has been supposed[14] that some sort of vicious circle is involved, unless the virtue presupposed by practical wisdom is virtue in an impoverished sense, virtue not yet enriched by practical wisdom.

In fact, however, the last statement says that practical wisdom requires, but not that it is preceded by, virtue, while the first statement is not on the whole concerned with teaching. Rather, in several of the passages the point seems to be the different one that vices destroy our conception of the good life while virtue preserves that conception (1140b11-20; 1144a34-b1; 1151a16-16; cf. *EE* 1227b12-19). This talk of *preserving* a conception, incidentally, may seem to fit badly with my claim that virtue by definition *presupposes* a conception of the good life. But I think the two descriptions (preserving and presupposing) are compatible, for virtue involves not only a conception of the good life but also a desire for it, and it is the desire that "preserves" the conception. The important point for us is that preserving a conception is not the same as teaching it. So it cannot be inferred that virtue must already exist in us to act as a teacher *before* we have a conception of the good life.

Only one of the passages about making the goal right discusses *teaching* (7.8. 1151a15-19), and it is very tentative. It is not reasoning (logos) that teaches us the basic hypotheses in mathematics, or the goal in conduct. Instead, in connection with conduct Aristotle talks of habit, and indeed of *virtue* produced by habit, as what teaches us (or causes us?) to have right opinion about our goal. The emphasis on habit as producing virtue is familiar from 2.1. What seems to be added is the suggestion that the resulting virtue exists in us as a teacher *before* we have acquired right opinion about our goal. It may be that we should understand a word like *aitios* and take it that virtue is what *causes* us (thanks to its preservative power), rather than what *teaches* us, to have this right opinion. This would fit better with the talk in a16 of virtue *preserving* the goal. Even so, the doctrine is unexpected if right opinion is to be contrasted with knowledge, as it is in the somewhat comparable passage in Plato's *Republic* (429c-430b). For habit-virtue will then exist in us as the preserver of right opinion before we have acquired *knowledge* of our goal. But all this is very tentative, for Aristotle also considers that the teacher or preserver of right opinion (I take it he means right opinion about *moral* goals, not *mathematical* hypotheses) may after all only be natural virtue, a benign inborn disposition that falls short of virtue proper. It is no surprise to be told that *this* can exist in us before we have right opinion or knowledge of our goals. I conclude that even if the passage is tempted to postulate virtue preceding knowledge of the good life, it is also hesitant about doing so.

The claim that virtue makes the goal right also fails to support Fortenbaugh's more modest conclusion that normally it is virtue that makes us pursue such *immediate* goals as revenge on the right occasions, and that practical wisdom normally plays no part. On our interpretation, Aristotle is not denying a role to practical wisdom in the selection of *immediate* goals. Rather he is talking about what protects our general conception of the good life from distorting influences, and he assigns this task to the desire involved in moral virtue. There is no denial that when the virtuous man decides on an immediate goal such as revenge, his practical wisdom is in play and is guided by his conception of the good life.

What does need to be acknowledged is that the *Politics* greatly expands Aristotle's account. For it considers many new kinds of virtue, that of slaves, women, children (1.13), and subjects in the city state (3.4). And these inferior kinds of virtue are possessed by people who lack practical wisdom. For slaves are incapable of deliberating (1.5. 1254b22); women can deliberate, but their deliberations fail to control their passions; in children the power to deliberate is immature (1.13. 1260a12-14); and subjects have only true opinion: it is the rulers alone who have practical wisdom (3.4. 1277b25). *Rhetoric* 2.12 agrees that virtue may exist without practical wisdom, for it speaks as if people who are still young may have virtue even though they have been trained merely by convention (*nomos* 1389a35).

These claims do not actually contradict the *Nicomachean Ethics* but only extend its teaching. For it is explicitly said that the virtue in question is of a distinct and inferior kind. Only the ruler's virtue is perfect (*telea* 1.13. 1260a17). There are two kinds (*eidē* 3.4. 1277b19) of moral virtue, one which a man manifests in ruling, the other in being ruled. The inferior kinds of virtue were not discussed in the *Nicomachean Ethics*, apart from the possible exception of incomplete virtue in 2.1. They are quite distinct from the natural virtue that was described there.

What has happened here is parallel, I think, to what happens in Plato's *Republic*. Plato's Socrates says that virtue is knowledge. Yet in five places in the *Republic* we find him defining the virtues of courage, temperance, and justice in terms of mere opinion, or else assigning these virtues to lower classes in the state which have been described as lacking knowledge (*Republic* 429a-c; 430b; 431d-432a; 442d; 500d). When we ask why, we notice that the courage in question is merely political or popular courage (430c; 500d), a courage appropriate to citizen subjects (cf. *Laws* 710a; 968a; *Phaedo* 82a-b). And we are given other warnings that this is not virtue proper. 472b says "if we find out what justice is," as if the preceding account did not tell us, and 504b reminds us that a longer journey is needed if we are to get a better view of the virtues. When Plato and Aristotle come to the context of politics, they both have to think about instilling virtue into new classes of people, and they both are led to recognize new and inferior kinds of virtue.

MORAL EDUCATION

This brings us to the third context in which the role of intellect has been concealed: moral education. Someone who reads in isolation *NE* 2.1 could be forgiven for concluding that Aristotle thinks habituation sufficient to make men virtuous. It is tempting to combine this with the further assumption that habituation is itself an unthinking process.

But first this view must cope with the fact that induction, as well as habituation, forms part of moral education. The main account of moral induction is brief and cryptic. It comes in five lines at 6.11. 1143b1-5. We are told that certain judgments are starting points for the goal (b4). I take it Aristotle means starting points from which we learn what goals to adopt. He goes on, "for universals come from particulars." This implies that the goals are universal but that the judgments from which we start are particular, so that the process is one of induction. We were already told in 1.7. 1098b3 that some principles are reached by a process of induction.

No examples are given of the starting judgments. But from the clues supplied I suggest that a typical one would be the judgment, uttered by a father, "this is what courage requires of us now," or, more generally, "this is what virtue and to kalon require of us now." This suggestion fits everything we are told. First, it is the sort of judgment that could well start the moral education of a young man. For it would supply the initial materials for building up a conception of what is required not merely now but in general. It is also a particular judgment. It also fits the three descriptions given in line b3. There the starting judgment is said to be *eschaton* (literally, "last"), contingent, and a minor premise. This all fits, because the judgment "this is what courage requires of us now" (or in other cases "ambush is what is required of us now") is the last judgment the father makes about what he ought to do. It is also *eschaton* in the different sense of being particular. *Eschaton* came to mean "particular," because the particular is the last thing you arrive at, if you work your way down from the universal. The father's judgment is clearly contingent, which is mentioned in order to distinguish it from the necessary truths of scientific reasoning. Can it serve as a minor premise? Yes; we have already seen how it does so.[15]

We have not yet exhausted the evidence that the starting judgments are of the form, "this is what courage requires of us now." For such judgments it is true to say, as Aristotle does, that it takes something like perception to make them (b5) and that this perception can come from experience (b13-14). Even where military knowledge is also in play (as it is when we judge that *ambush* is required), we have argued that an intuitive perception is needed that ambush is compatible with courage and the good life. The need for intuitive perception is clearer in the nonmilitary judgment that *attack* is required. The perception in question is called nous (intuitive reason) both here and in chapter 13, 1144b8-13. In both chapters nous is very closely linked with practical wisdom, which, as we have seen, also involves something like perception, and which, as I have independently argued, also grasps propositions of the form "this is what courage requires now." I suggest the relation is this, that the word *nous* is applied to the perception of such facts but that this perception sometimes comes not from practical wisdom but from mere experience. It is only when the perception is influenced by our knowledge of the good life that it is called a judgment of practical wisdom.

At first, the child will not be able to perceive for himself what is required in the particular situation. That is why he is told at b11-14 to listen to the judgments of his elders who have experience or practical wisdom. But in time, experience will enable him to make these particular judgments for himself. And it will also generate in him the inductive process described at b4-5, so that he will begin to get a more general idea of what courage and virtue require. Experience does enable us to make judgments of some limited generality, even before we have practical wisdom. The example at 6.7. 1141b14-21 is that we may know from experience that chicken is good for health, even if we do not know that all light meat is good for health.

It makes little difference whether the starting judgments take the more specific form, "this is what courage requires of us now," or the more general form, "this is what virtue and to kalon require of us now." It might be thought that the second more general form would serve better to steer us toward a general unified conception of the good life, whereas the first would make us think instead only of separate virtues. But this is not so, because of the point already made that the virtues form a unity and that considerations about what courage requires involve considerations about what other virtues require.

Now that we have seen how the learner passes from particular perceptive judgments to more general ones, we are better placed to appreciate the process of habituation described in 2.1. The first thing to notice is that it is not a mindless process. If someone is to become good-tempered, he must not be habituated to avoid anger come what may. The habit he must acquire is that of avoiding anger on the right occasions and of feeling it on the right occasions. This is clear from Aristotle's account of what good temper is. As a result, habituation involves assessing the situation and seeing what is called for. So habituation is intimately linked with the kind of intuitive perception (nous) that we have been discussing. The learner must get into the habit of avoiding anger, or feeling it, in accordance with his intuitive perception of what the occasion demands. The process is not a mindless one.[16] Nonetheless, habituation is concerned with desire as well as with reason. The learner is being habituated to like reacting in accordance with his intuitive perception of what is required. And as induction gives him an increasingly general conception of what is required, habituation makes him like that general ideal.

Habituation is not mindless, but is it sufficient for producing virtue? We have mentioned that the beginning of NE 2, read in isolation, seems to speak almost as if it is. For it repeatedly claims that the virtues arise out of habituation and that we become good by being habituated (1103a14-17; a25; a34-b4; b14-25; 1104a33-b2; 1105a14-16). It contrasts habit with teaching (1103a14-17) and says that early habits make all the difference (1103b23-25). A particularly striking claim is that we are perfected by habit (1103a25). However, we know it is not Aristotle's view elsewhere that habituation alone is sufficient. Such a view neglects induction and, as we shall see, much else besides. I have already suggested alternative explanations of Aristotle's remarks in 2.1, either that he is talking of incomplete virtue or that he is simply overemphasizing the role of habit, because he thinks it the most important, though not the sole, factor in producing virtue proper. There is a reason why he might well have been doing the latter. For he wants to establish his position vis-à-vis the old controversy broached at the beginning of the chapter: does virtue come from nature, habit, or teaching? This question had long engaged poets and tragedians as well as sophists and philosophers. Aristotle is anxious to show that habit is much more important than Socrates had realized and that of the three it is the most important.

Nonetheless, through the rest of the *Nicomachean Ethics* Aristotle issues a series of warnings. Even within 2.1 he allows some role to nature, saying that we are naturally fitted to acquire the virtues, though made perfect by habit. The first major warning comes in 2.4, which is where he tells us that to become virtuous we must learn to choose our actions for the sake of virtue (1105a31-33). It is not enough to acquire the habit of doing what conforms to the virtues. We must do it in order to conform.

Aristotle returns to the trichotomy, nature, habit, teaching, at the end of the *Nicomachean Ethics* (10.9. 1179b4-31) and in the *Politics* (1332a40-b11; 1334b6; 1338b4), and he grants a role to each of the three. Some *natures* are more easily molded than others, some more receptive to teaching than others. As for *teaching*, this will not work on everyone, but it will on some, he says. Indeed, the *Nicomachean Ethics* is itself intended to provide teaching and would otherwise fail of its purpose. What Aristotle does insist on repeatedly is that habituation and experience are a necessary prerequisite for teaching (1.3. 1095a2-4; 1.4. 1095b2-8; 10.9. 1179b24-26; *Pol* 1334b6; 1338b4). Habituation is compared with preparing the soil for seed (1179b26). The man who has been habituated will have some ethical facts available at a not very high level of generality, from which teaching can start (1095b3-8).

What sort of things can be learned through teaching? The *Nicomachean Ethics* itself shows us. Among other things the pupil will get from Aristotle's lectures a fuller and clearer conception of the good life, and this conception will be grounded in a discussion of human nature. This reminds us of a further condition that must be met by the virtuous man. He must be able to decide, in the light of his conception of the good life, what is to be done in the particular case. And Aristotle's teaching will help with this, insofar as it completes and justifies a conception of the good life and bears on the application of that conception to daily affairs. Habituation alone could not give us the ability to apply the universal in this way to the particular.

I have maintained that Aristotle ascribes a major role to the intellect and that he does not contradict this ascription. But it needs to be acknowledged that he does something else. He tends to present the various parts of his view in isolation and to concentrate on each part in turn to such an extent as to give us the wrong impression of what the whole view will be. The emphasis on habit at the beginning of Book 2 is only one of many cases. Nonetheless, he does not always fail to prepare us for his total view, and I would in particular resist the suggestion that he has left us unprepared for the account of practical wisdom in Book 6. On the contrary, he begins to pave the way in Book 1, when he says in chapter 13 that virtue of character belongs to the part of the soul that listens to reason. Books 2-4 continue the preparation, by repeatedly saying that the mean in virtue is in accordance with logos or orthos logos. 2.2. 1103b-32 promises a later discussion of what this orthos logos is, and 6.1 repeats the promise. Both chapters thus point forward to the final answer (6.13), that it is, or is in accordance with, practical wisdom. The very definition of virtue in 2.6 had already pointed out that practical wisdom defines the mean. Thus the role given to practical wisdom in Book 6 represents no change of direction and should come as no surprise. In its turn the account of practical wisdom in 6 is completed by the conception of the good life, which is built up throughout the *Ethics* and concluded in Book 10.

I must apologize for having concentrated on asking what Aristotle's view is and for having said comparatively little about the philosophical merits and demerits of that view. I do think it is rewarding to consider whether our own conceptions of a good or courageous man bring in the intellect in the ways canvassed in the foregoing interpretation, and if not, why not. I also believe the view just ascribed to Aristotle is better worth discussing than the view that virtue is the product of a mindless habituation.[17]

NOTES

1. Bekker's chapter numbering. Cf. 1106a3; b36; 1113b3-7; 1139a22.

2. See esp. W. D. Ross, *Aristotle*, 5th ed. (London, 1949), pp. 195-196; D. J. Allan, *The Philosophy of Aristotle* (London, 1952), p. 177; idem, "Aristotle's Account of the Origin of Moral Principles," *Proceedings of the XIth International Congress of Philosophy, Brussels, August 20-26, 1953* (Amsterdam, 1953), 12:

120-127 (henceforth "Origin"), at 124; idem, "The Practical Syllogism," in *Autour d'Aristote: Recueil d'études... offert à Mgr Mansion*, Bibliothèque philosophique de Louvain, vol. 16 (Louvain, 1955), pp. 325-340.

3. Allan accepts it as well as the first one.

4. Strictly, we consider (*skopein* 1112b16) and seek (*zētein* b28) these, and deliberate about (*bouleuesthai peri* b11-12) them. But this implies that we choose them, for we choose what is decided upon as a result of deliberation (*ek tēs boulēs krithen* 1113a4, and see the other phrases at 1112a15; 1113a2; 10; 11-12).

5. Are the archers here and at 1094a23 trying to shoot a certain *distance*, aided by a marker that marks that distance, rather than shooting at a marker?

6. See Allan, "Origin," and R. A. Gauthier and J. Y. Jolif, *L'Éthique à Nicomaque*, 2d ed. (Louvain, 1970), 2:563-578.

7. The examples of syllogism in *NE*, unlike those in *De motu*, are all about health, and all start by considering some general policy of diet rather than a single action (like the attack in our example). Again unlike *De motu*, the *Ethics* includes no resolutions in its examples, though in some cases (not all) it may be intending to offer minor premises which we can intersperse with resolutions.

8. See n. 7 above.

9. In *New Essays on Plato and Aristotle*, ed. R. Bambrough (London, 1965). Pace W. F. R. Hardie, *Aristotle's Ethical Theory* (Oxford, 1968), pp. 180-181; Allan, "Origin," p. 124.

10. That the weak-willed man has in some cases made a choice which he violates is quite compatible with the point that he acts without choosing (1111b14; 1148a6; a17), i.e., without choosing to act as he does.

11. William W. Fortenbaugh, "Aristotle: Emotion and Moral Virtue," *Arethusa* 2 (1969), 163-185, at 169-173.

12. Julius Walter, *Die Lehre von der praktischen Vernunft in der griechischen Philosophie* (Jena, 1874), pp. 208-212.

13. There was a more extreme view in *Trans. and Proc. Amer. Philol. Assoc.* 95 (1964), 77-87; practical wisdom cannot decide what is good in the particular situation, i.e., presumably, cannot decide that revenge is good, but only how to take revenge.

14. E.g., W. Frankena, *Three Historical Philosophies of Education* (Chicago, 1965), p. 59.

15. It would not greatly alter my account if the eschaton in 1143b3 were distinct from the minor premise, and were the conclusion, as it is in 1141b28.

16. So also R. S. Peters, "Reason and Habit: The Paradox of Moral Education," in *Moral Education in a Changing Society*, ed. W. R. Niblett (London, 1963).

17. I have learned a very great deal toward this paper from William Fortenbaugh, who put the other side of the case in a seminar that we gave jointly. I have also benefited richly from other friends and colleagues who offered comments and criticisms. I have made revisions in response to those of J. L. Ackrill, Leslie Brown, M. F. Burnyeat, James Dybikowski, Richard Kraut, Keith Mills, G. E. L. Owen, Trevor Saunders, Malcolm Schofield, and Michael Woods. In spite of all this help I still feel uncertain about a number of these difficult passages.

13

Deliberation and Practical Reason[1]

David Wiggins

Consider the following three contentions:

(1) In Book 3 of the *Nicomachean Ethics* Aristotle treats a restricted and technical notion of deliberation which makes it unnecessary for him to consider anything but technical or so-called productive examples of practical reason. It is not surprising in the context of Book 3 that deliberation is never of ends but always of means.

(2) When he came to write Books 6 and 7 of the *Nicomachean Ethics* and *De anima* 3.7, Aristotle analyzed a much less restricted notion of deliberation and of choice. This made it necessary for him to give up the view that deliberation and choice were necessarily of *ta pros to telos*, where it is supposed that this phrase means or implies that deliberation is only of means. Thereafter he recognized two irreducibly distinct modes of practical reasoning, *means-end* deliberations and *rule-case* deliberations.[2]

(3) The supposed modification of view between the writing of Book 3 and that of Books 6-7, and the newly introduced (supposed) "rule-case" syllogism, bring with them a radical change in Aristotle's view of the subject—even something resembling a satisfactory solution to the problems of choice and deliberation. Thus 6-7 do better in this way than vaguely suggest what complexities a lifelike account of practical deliberation would have to come to terms with.

Taken singly these doctrines are familiar enough in Aristotelian exegesis. Their conjunction, the overall picture I have given, represents some-

221

thing of a conflation or contamination of what I have read or heard people say.[3]

It is my submission that, both as a whole and in detail, the view constituted by (1) (2) (3) is substantially and damagingly mistaken and that it obstructs improvement in our understanding of the real philosophical problem of practical reason. The examination of (1) (2) (3) will lead (in the final part of this paper) into some general consideration of that problem and Aristotle's contribution to it.

I shall begin by trying to show that for all its simplicities and over-schematizations, Aristotle's Book 3 account is in fact straightforwardly continuous with the Book 6 account of deliberation, choice, and practical reasoning. Both accounts attempt to analyze and describe wide and completely general notions of choice and deliberation. Both accounts are dominated, I think, by Aristotle's obsession with a certain simple situation of the kind described in Book 3. 1112b—the geometer who searches for means to construct a given figure with ruler and compass. Aristotle is acutely and increasingly aware of the limitations of this analogy, but (in spite of its redeployment at 1143b1-5) he never describes exactly what to put in its place. Twentieth-century philosophy is not yet in a position to condescend to him with regard to these questions. For all its omissions and blemishes, Aristotle's account is informed by a consciousness of the lived actuality of practical reasoning and its background. This is an actuality which present-day studies of rationality, morality, and public rationality ignore, and ignore at their cost.

REJECTION OF THE FIRST THESIS. BOOK 3 OF THE *Nicomachean Ethics*

The supposition that Book 3 set out to analyze a restricted notion of deliberation[4] or a restricted notion of choice gives rise to some internal difficulties within the book.

One apparent difficulty is this. *Bouleusis* (deliberation) is inextricably linked in Book 3 to *prohairesis* (choice). "Is prohairesis then simply what has been decided on by previous deliberation?" Aristotle asks at 1112a15, later to define it at 1113a10 as *deliberative desire of what is in our power.* About choice Aristotle remarks at 1111b6-7, "choice is thought to be most closely bound up with (*oikeiotaton*) virtue and to discriminate characters better than actions do." Now this is at least a peculiar remark if deliberation is construed as narrowly as some have been encouraged by the geometrical example at 1112b20 to construe it, and if we construe Aristotle's assertion that choice and deliberation are of what is toward the end (*tōn pros to telos*) to mean that choice and deliberation are concerned only with means. The only straightforward way to see it as a cardinal or conceptually prominent fact about choice that it accurately or generally distinguishes good from bad character, and has a certain constitutive relation to vice or virtue, is to suppose choice to be a fairly inclusive notion that relates to different specifications of man's *end*. The choices of the bad or self-indulgent man, the *mochtheros* or *akolastos*, would seem to be supposed by Aristotle to reveal this man for what he is because they make straightforwardly apparent his *misconceptions of the end*. The thought ought not to be that the choices such men make reveal any incapacity for technical or strictly means-end reasoning to get what they want—the ends they set themselves. For these they may well achieve —and, in Aristotle's view, miss happiness thereby. Their mistakes are not means-ends or technical mistakes. (Cf. 1142b17 f. and 6.12 on *deinotēs*.)

It may be objected that the thought is neither of these things but that by seeing a man's choices one can come to see what his ends are; and to know what his ends are is to arrive at a view of his character. But this interpretation, which scarcely does justice to *oikeiotaton*, must seem a little unlikely as soon as we imagine such an indirect argument to a man's ends. Typically, *actions* would have to mediate the argument. But actions are already mentioned by Aristotle in an unfavorable contrast. "Choice . . . discriminates characters better than actions do."

The interpretation of this passage is not perfectly essential to my argument, however. Let us go on, simply remarking that the onus of proof must be on the interpretation that hypothesizes that *prohairesis* or *bouleusis* means something different in Book 3 and Books 6 and 7. The first effort should be to give it the same sense in all these books. I hope to show that this is possible as well as desirable and that if anything at all gets widened in Book 6, it is the *analysis* of choice and deliberation, not the sense of the word. Each must be one *analysand* throughout. As so often, there has been confusion in the discussion of this issue because a *wider analysis of notion N* has sometimes been confused with an *analysis of a wider notion N*. "Wider conception" is well calculated to mask the difference between these fatally similar-looking things. But let us distinguish them.

There are certainly reasons why some scholars have seen the Book 3 notions of deliberation and choice as technical notions that were superseded by wider notions and then by wider philosophical analyses of either or both notions. These reasons derive from Aristotle's frequent assertions that, unlike *boulēsis* (wish), choice and deliberation are not *of the end* but of *what is toward the end (pros to telos)*. See 1111b26, 1112b-11-12, 1112b34-35, 1113a14-15, 1113b3-4. If *what is toward the end* in

Book 3 is taken (as it is for instance by Ross in his translation) to be a *means to an end*, then that must certainly suggest that as regards prohairesis and bouleusis we have a wider *analysand* as well as a wider analysis in Books 6-7. But I argue that they need not be taken so.

It is a commonplace of Aristotelian exegesis that Aristotle never really paused to analyze the distinction between two quite distinct relations. (A) the relation x bears to *telos* y when x will bring about y, and (B) the relation x bears to y when the existence of x will itself help to constitute y. For self-sufficient reasons we are committed in any case to making this distinction very often on behalf of Aristotle when he writes down the words *heneka* or *charin* (for the sake of). See, for example, Book 1. 1097-b1-5. The expression *toward the end* is vague and perfectly suited to express both conceptions.

The first notion, that of a means or instrument or procedure that is causally efficacious in the production of a specific and settled end, has as its clear cases such things as a cloak as a way of covering the body when one is cold, or some drug as a means to alleviate pain. The second notion that can take shelter under the wide umbrella of *what is toward the end* is that of something whose existence counts in itself as the partial or total realization of the end. This is a constituent of the end: cf. *Met.* 1032b27 (N.B. *meros* there), *Politics* 1325b16 and 1338b2-4. Its simple presence need not be logically necessary or logically sufficient for the end. To a very limited extent the achievement of one end may do duty for that of another. Perhaps there might even be some sort of *eudaimonia* (happiness) without good health, or without much pleasure, or without recognized honor, or without the stable possession of a satisfying occupation. But the presence of a constituent of the end is always logically relevant to happiness. It is a member of a nucleus (or one conjunct, to mention a very simple possibility, in a disjunction of conjunctions) whose coming to be counts as the attainment of that end. Happiness is not identifiable in independence of such constituents (e.g., as a feeling that these elements cause or as some surplus that can be measured in a man's economic behavior).

If it commits us to no new interpretative principle to import this distinction into our reading of Book 3 and to suppose that both these relations are loosely included within the extension of the phrase *what is toward the end*, then on this understanding of the phrase Aristotle is trying in *NE* 3 (however abstractly and schematically) to treat deliberation about means and deliberation about constituents in the same way. Optimistically he is hoping that he can use the intelligibilities of the clear means-end situation and its extensions (how to effect the construction of this particular figure) to illuminate the obscurities of the *constituents-to-*

end case. In the latter a man deliberates about what kind of life he wants to lead, or deliberates in a determinate context about which of several possible courses of action would conform most closely to some ideal he holds before himself, or deliberates about what would constitue eudaimonia here and now, or (less solemnly) deliberates about what would count as the achievement of the not yet completely specific goal which he has already set himself in the given situation. For purposes of any of these deliberations the means-end paradigm that inspires almost all the Book 3 examples is an inadequate paradigm, as we shall see. But it is not easy to get away from. It can continue to obsess the theorist of action, even while he tries to distance himself from it and searches for something else.

There are two apparent obstacles in Book 3 to interpreting the passages on choice and deliberation in this way and to making the crudities of the book continuous with the sophistications of Books 6-7.

(a) Three times Aristotle says, "We do not deliberate about *ends* but about *things that are toward ends*," and the plural may have seemed to anyone who contemplated giving my sort of interpretation to rule out the possibility that any part of the extension of *things that are toward ends*, that is, things that are deliberated, should comprise deliberable constituents of *happiness* (singular), that is, ends in themselves. If we do not deliberate about ends (plural), then it seems we do not deliberate about the constituents of happiness, which are ends, or about things that are good in themselves and help to make up happiness *(tele)*. So, it will be said, "that which is toward the end" cannot ever comprehend any constituents of happiness—these being according to Aristotle undeliberable. But on my interpretation it may include such constituents. Therefore, it may be said, Ross's translation of *pros* in terms of *means* is to be preferred.

(β) To deliberate about that which is toward happiness in the case where the end directly in question in some practical thinking is happiness might, if *that which is toward happiness* included constituents, involve deliberating happiness. But this Aristotle explicitly excludes.

Reply to (a). The first passage of the three in question, 1112b1, reads:

We deliberate (*bouleuometha*) not about ends but about what is towards ends. For a doctor does not deliberate whether he shall heal, nor an orator whether he shall persuade, nor a statesman whether he shall produce law and order, nor does anyone else *deliberate about his end*. They assume the end and consider by what means it is to be attained, and if it seems to be produced by several means they consider by which it is best and most easily produced, while if it is achieved by one only they consider how it will be achieved by this, and by what means that will be achieved till they come to the first cause, which in the order of discovery is last. For the person who deliberates seems to investigate and analyze in the way described as though he were analyzing a geometrical construction (not all seeking is deliberation, but all deliberation is seeking), and what is last in the order of analysis seems to be first in the order of being brought about.

I submit that the four words I have italicized show that the *bouleuometha* (we deliberate) and the use of the plural *telon* (ends) are to be taken distributively. Each of these three gentlemen, the orator, doctor, or statesman, has *one* telos (for present purposes). He is already a doctor, orator, or statesman and already at work. That is already fixed (which is not to say that it is absolutely fixed), and to that extent the form of the eudaimonia he can achieve is already conditioned by something no longer needing (at least at this moment) to be deliberated. If I am right about this passage, then there seems to be no obstacle to construing the other two occurrences of the plural, 1112b34-35 and 1113a13-14 (both nearby), as echoes of the thought at 1112b11, and taking *toward the end* (singular) as the canonical form of the phrase (cf. 1113b3-4, 1145a4-5 for instance). Provided only that difficulty (β) can be met, this end may (where required) be a man's total end, namely, happiness.

This reply prompts another and supplementary retort to the difficulty. Suppose I were wrong so far and that *that which is toward the end* (singular) had no special claim to be the canonical form of the phrase. Consider then the case where Aristotle is considering deliberations whose direct ends are not identical with happiness. (Presumably the indirect end will always be happiness: cf. 1094a.) Such ends need not be intrinsically undeliberable ends but simply ends held constant *for the situation;* cf. 1112b11 "assuming the end" *themenoi to telos.*

Reply to (β). It is absurd to suppose that a man could not deliberate about whether to be a doctor or not; and very nearly as absurd to suppose that Aristotle, even momentarily while writing Book 3, supposed that nobody could deliberate this question. It is so absurd that it is worth asking whether the phrase *deliberating about the end* or *deliberating about happiness* is ambiguous. It is plainly impossible to deliberate about the end if this is to deliberate by asking "Shall I pursue the end?" If this end is eudaimonia, then qua animate and men we have to have some generalized desire for it (a generalized desire whose particular manifestations are desires for things falling under particular specifications of that telos). Simply to call eudaimonia the *end* leaves nothing to be deliberated about whether it should be realized or not. That is a sort of truism (cf. 1097b23 *homologoumenon ti*), as is the point that, if the desirability of eudaimonia were really up for debate, then nothing suitable by way of practical or ethical concern or by way of desire would be left over (outside the ambit of eudaimonia itself) to settle the matter. But this platitude scarcely demonstrates the impossibility of deliberating the question "what, practically speaking, *is* this end?" or "what shall *count* for me as an adequate description of the end of life?" And so far as I can see, nothing Aristotle says in Book 3 precludes that kind of deliberation. The only examples we are given of things that we might conclude are intrinsically undeliberable are health and happiness (1111b26). The first is arguably (at least in the philosophy of the Greeks) an undetachable part of the end for human beings. The second is identical with the end as a whole (and no more practically definite an objective than "the end"). So we are not given examples of logically detachable constituents of the end or of debatable specifications of the end to illustrate Aristotle's thesis in *NE* 3. But on the traditional interpretation of the undeliberability thesis these were what was needed. So what I think he is saying that one cannot deliberate is *whether* to pursue happiness or health. It is not in any case excluded that (as described in *NE* 6) a man may seek by deliberation to make more specific and more practically determinate that generalized telos of eudaimonia which is instinct in his human constitution.

If this is right so far, then I think another step is taken beyond what was achieved in Allan's discussion to dissociate Aristotle's whole theory of deliberation from that pseudorationalistic irrationalism, insidiously propagated nowadays by technocratic persons, which holds that reason has nothing to do with the ends of human life, its only sphere being the efficient realization of specific goals in whose determination or modification argument plays no substantive part.[5]

REJECTION OF THE SECOND THESIS. THE TRANSITION TO BOOK 6.

On the reading of Book 3 so far defended, the transition from *NE* 3 to *NE* 6 is fairly smooth.

Regarding *practical wisdom* we shall get at the truth by considering who are the persons we credit with it. Now it is thought to be the mark of a man of practical wisdom to be able to deliberate well about what is good and expedient for himself, not in some particular respect, e.g. about what sorts of thing conduce to health or to strength, but about what sorts of things conduce to the good life in general (*poia pros to eu zēn holōs*). [1140a24-28, Ross's translation—note the *pros*.]

And again:

Practical wisdom on the other hand is concerned with things human and things about which it is possible to deliberate; for we say this is above all the work of a man of practical wisdom, to deliberate well.... The man who is without qualification good at deliberating is the man who is capable of aiming in accordance with calculation at the best for man of things attainable by action. Nor is practical wisdom concerned with universals only—it must also recognize particulars. That is why some who do not know, and especially those who have experience, are more practical than others who know. [1141b8-18, Ross]

Aristotle is saying here, among other things, that practical wisdom in its deliberative manifestations is concerned both with the attainment of particular formed objectives and also with questions of general policy— what specific objectives *to* form. He contrasts the two components, and in doing so he commits his investigation to the study of both (cf. 1142b-30). On my view of *NE* 3 we ought not to be surprised by this. But there is a philosophical difficulty about this kind of deliberation which becomes plainer and plainer as *NE* 6 proceeds.

Aristotle had hoped in *NE* 3 to illuminate examples of nontechnical deliberation by comparing them with a paradigm drawn from technical deliberation. The trouble with both paradigm and comparison is this. It is absolutely plain what counts as my having adequate covering or as my having succeeded in drawing a plane figure of the prescribed kind using only ruler and compass. The practical question here is only what means or measures will work or work best or most easily to those ends. But the standard problem in a nontechnical deliberation is quite different. In the nontechnical case I shall characteristically have an extremely vague description of something I want—a good life, a satisfying profession, an interesting holiday, an amusing evening—and the problem is not to see what will be causally efficacious in bringing this about but to see what really *qualifies* as an adequate and practically realizable specification of what would satisfy this want. Deliberation is still *zetēsis*, a search, but it is not primarily a search for means. It is a search for the *best specification*. Till the specification is available there is no room for means. When this specification is reached, means-end deliberation can start, but difficulties that turn up in this means-end deliberation may send me back a finite number of times to the problem of a better or more practicable specification of the end. And the whole interest and difficulty of the matter is in the search for adequate specifications, not in the technical means-end sequel or sequels. It is here that the analogy with the geometer's search, or the search of the inadequately clothed man, goes lame.

It is common ground between my interpretation and the interpretation of those who would accept the three tenets given at the outset, contentions (1) (2) (3), that Aristotle sensed *some* such difficulty in his dealings with practical reason. But according to the other interpretation [see (2) and (3)], Aristotle was led at this point to make a distinction between the situation where the agent has to see his situation as falling under a rule and the situation where the agent has simply to find means to encompass a definite objective.

Professor Allan gives the most argued form of this interpretation. Speaking of the practical syllogism he says, "in some contexts actions are subsumed by intuition under general rules, and performed or avoided accordingly. . . . In other contexts it is said to be a distinctive feature of practical syllogisms that they start from the announcement of an end [he then instances *NE* 1144a31, 1151a15-19, and *EE* 1227b28-32]. . . . A particular action is then performed because it is a means or the first link in a chain of means leading to the end." (2) In support of this he claims to find Aristotle making such a distinction in the syllogisms mentioned at *De motu animalium* 701a9 ff. In Forster's Loeb translation that passage reads as follows:

The conclusion drawn from the two premises becomes the action. For example, when you conceive that every man ought to walk and you yourself are a man, you immediately walk; or if you conceive that on a particular occasion no man ought to walk, and you yourself are a man, you immediately remain at rest. In both instances action follows unless there is some hindrance or compulsion. Again, I ought to create a good, and a house is a good, I immediately create a house. Again, I need a covering, and a cloak is a covering, I need a cloak. What I need I ought to make; I need a cloak, I ought to make a cloak. And the conclusion "I ought to make a cloak" is an action. The action results from the beginning of the train of thought. If there is to be a cloak, such and such a thing is necessary, if this thing then something else; and one immediately acts accordingly. That the action is the conclusion is quite clear; but the premises which lead to the doing of something are of two kinds, through the good and through the possible.

Now I think Allan understands this passage in a strange way. For he writes "Aristotle *begins* with an example of the former [sc. rule-case] type [the walk syllogism] . . . , but includes among other examples one of the latter type [the cloak syllogism] . . . and he adds that the premises may be of two forms, since they specify either that something is good, or how it is possible (*hai de protaseis hai poiētikai dia duo eidōn ginontai, dia te tou agathou kai dia tou dunatou* [the premises that lead to the doing of something are of two kinds, concerning the good and the possible])."[6] This is a strange reading. The walk syllogism like the next syllogism would have to be treated as a dummy syllogism, a mere variable in any case. For even if Allan's distinction between two kinds of syllogism could stand, the syllogism would be an idiotic example of either. No conclusion could safely rest on its "rule-like" appearance. It would also be difficult to settle which sort the house-syllogism belonged to if any such distinction were intended.

In truth, the sentence about two kinds of premises seems to be no more than an allusion to the general form often manifestly displayed and always present (I believe) in Aristotelian action-syllogisms. The first or major premise mentions something of which there could be a desire, *orexis,* transmissible to some practical conclusion (i.e., a desire convertible via some available minor premise into action). The second premise details a circumstance pertaining to the feasibility, in the particular situation to which the syllogism is applied, of what must be done if the claim of the major premise is to be heeded. In the light of these *De motu* examples nothing could be more natural than to describe the first premise of a practical syllogism as *pertaining to the good* (the fact that it pertains to some good—either a general good or something which the agent has just resolved 's good in this situation—is what beckons to desire) and to describe the second or minor premise as *pertaining to the possible* (where "possible" connotes the feasibility, *given* the circumstances registered by the minor premise, of the object of concern mentioned in the first premise). I can find no textual support for Allan's attempt to make the distinction into a distinction between different kinds of major premises. Indeed, no syllogism could be truly practical or be appropriately backed by orexis if its major premise were simply of the possible.

So much for the alleged presence of the distinction between rule-case and means-end syllogisms in the *De motu* passage. But even if I were wrong (and even if a distinctive rule-case type of syllogism were found at *NE* 7), still contention (3) would founder on other rocks. Allan's distinction of syllogisms is not the right distinction to solve Aristotle's problem, or *the* problem, of practical deliberation. The deliberative situations that challenge philosophical reflection to replace the means-ends description do not involve a kind of problem which anybody would think he could solve by subsuming a case under rules, whereas the comparatively trivial technical problems that are treated by Allan as means-end cases might often be resolved by recourse to rules. Nor can this difficulty be avoided by suggesting that if a policy question becomes too general or all-embracing, then there is no longer any rational deliberation about it. For Aristotle there is. He is convinced that the discovery and specification of the end is an intellectual problem, among other things, and belongs to practical wisdom. See 1142b31-33, for instance:

If excellence in deliberation, *euboulia,* is one of the traits of men of practical wisdom, we may regard this excellence as correct perception of that which conduces to the end, whereof practical wisdom is a true judgment.

It is one of the considerable achievements of Allan's interpretation to have resolved the dispute about this sentence and to leave it meaning what the ancient tradition took it to mean and what it so obviously does mean. The good is the sort of thing which we wish for *because we think it good*, not something we think good because it is what we wish for. Thought and reason (*not without desire*, I must add) are the starting point.[7]

If all this were not enough to wreck contentions (2) and (3), then Aristotle's own remarks elsewhere about the character of general rules and principles would be enough to discredit the rule-case approach. There *are* no general principles or rules anyway. "Matters concerned with conduct and questions of what is good for us have no fixity, any more than matters of health. The general account [of practical knowledge] being of this nature, the account of particular cases is yet more lacking in exactness; for they do not fall under any art or precept, but the agents themselves in each case consider what is appropriate to the occasion, as happens also in the art of medicine and navigation" (1104a7, cf. 1107a28). From the nature of the case the subject matter of the practical is indefinite and unforeseeable, and any supposed principle would have an indefinite number of exceptions. To understand what such exceptions would be and what makes them exceptions would be to understand something not reducible to rules or principles. The only metric we can impose on the subject matter of practice is the metric of the Lesbian rule:

In fact this is the reason why not everything is determined by law and special and specific decrees are often needed. For when the thing is indefinite, the measure of it must be indefinite too, like the leaden rule used in making the Lesbian molding. The rule adapts itself to the shape of the stone and is not rigid, and so too a special decree is adapted to the facts. [1137b27-32, cf. *Politics* 1282b3]

I conclude that what Aristotle had in mind in Book 6 was nothing remotely resembling what has been ascribed to him by his Kantian and other deontomaniac interpreters. Certainly contention (3) must seem absurdly overstated if the only new material which we can muster on Aristotle's behalf for the hard cases of deliberative specification is the "rule-case" syllogism.

THE BOOKS 6-7 TREATMENT OF DELIBERATIVE SPECIFICATION—A GENERAL FRAMEWORK FOR ITS INTERPRETATION AND EVALUATION

NE 6 can be seen in a more interesting light than this. On the interpretation to be presented I admit that the new materials largely consist of sophistications, amendments, and extensions of the means-ends paradigm. Nor is the alleged problem of the "validity" of the practical syllogism solved. But Aristotle has a number of ideas to offer that seem to me to be of more fundamental importance than anything to be found now in utility theory, decision theory, or other rationality studies, however sketchily and obscurely he expressed them. That Aristotle's ideas are inchoate, however, is only one part of what is troublesome in establishing this claim. There is also the difficulty of finding a perspective or vantage point, over a philosophical terrain still badly understood, from which to view Aristotle's theory, and the difficulty (in practice rarely overcome) of sustaining philosophic momentum over a prolonged examination of a large number of obscure but relevant passages of the *Ethics* and *De anima*.

To these difficulties my practical response is to adjourn all discussion of *akrasia* and, proceeding as if Aristotle had avoided what I regard as the errors of *NE* 7, to give the bare outline (a)-(g) of a neo-Aristotelian theory of practical reason. After that I shall amplify one cardinal point in this theory by giving an expanded paraphrase of two of the most obscure and most important passages about practical reason in *NE* 6. The only excuse I can offer to scholars, whom this style of interpretation will scandalize, is the Society's limitation of length. Your only defense against so prejudicial a method of exposition is to compare the paraphrase with the Ross translation.

(a) There are theories of practical reason according to which the ordinary situation of an agent who deliberates resembles nothing so much as that of a snooker player who has to choose from a large number of possible shots that shot which rates highest when two products are added. The first product is the utility of the shot's success (a utility that depends in snooker upon the color of the ball to be potted and the expected utility for purposes of the next shot of the resulting position) multiplied by the probability P of this player's potting the ball. The second product is the utility (negative) of his failure multiplied by $(1 - P)$. It is neither here nor there that it is not easy to determine the values of some of these elements for purposes of comparing prospects. There is no problem about the end itself nor about the means, which is maximizing points. What is more, there do exist deliberative situations, apart from snooker, which are a bit like this. But with ordinary deliberation it is quite different. There is nothing which a man is under antecedent sentence to maximize; and probabilities, though difficult and relevant, need not be the one great crux of the matter. A man usually asks himself "What shall I do?" not with a view to maximizing anything but only in response to a particular context. This will make particular and contingent demands on his moral or practical perception, but the relevant features of the situation may not all jump to the eye. To see what they are, to prompt the imagination to play upon the question and let it activate in reflection and thought-experiment whatever concerns and passions it should activate, may require a high order of situational appreciation, or, as Aristotle would say, perception (*aisthēsis*). In this, as we shall see, and in the unfortunate fact that few situations come already inscribed with the names of all the concerns which they touch or impinge upon, resides the crucial importance of the minor premise of the practical syllogism.

(b) When the relevant concerns are provisionally identified, they may still be too unspecific for means-end reasoning to begin. See the account of "deliberative specification" in the section entitled "Rejection of the Second Thesis" (above). Most of what is interesting and difficult in practical reason happens here, and under (a).

(c) No theory, if it is to recapitulate or reconstruct practical reasoning even as well as mathematical logic recapitulates or reconstructs the actual experience of conducting or exploring deductive argument, can treat the concerns which an agent brings to any situation as forming a closed, complete, consistent system. For it is of the essence of these concerns to make competing and inconsistent claims. (This is a mark not of irrationality but of *rationality* in the face of the plurality of ends and the plurality of human goods.)[8] The weight of the claims represented by these concerns is not necessarily fixed in advance. Nor need the concerns be hierarchically ordered. Indeed, a man's reflection on a new situation that confronts him may disrupt such order and fixity as had previously existed, and bring a change in his evolving conception of the point (*to hou heneka*), or the several or many points, of living or acting.

(d) A man may think it is clear to him in a certain situation what is the relevant concern, yet find himself discontent with every practical syllogism promoting that concern (with major premise representing the concern). He may resile from the concern when he sees what it leads to, or what it costs, and start all over again. It is not necessarily true that he who wills the end must will the means. (The same would have to apply to public rationality, if we had that. In a bureaucracy, where action is not constantly referred back to what originally motivated it, the acute theoretical and practical problem is to make room for some such stepping back, and for the constant remaking and reevaluation of concerns. Also for the distinction that individual citizens make effortlessly for themselves between projects on the one hand and concerns of another sort, which define and delimit the space within which deliberation operates unconstrained. In the difficulty of this referring back, and in the chronic inability of public agencies to render transitive between situations reviewed and/or brought about by planning the relation *is found better overall than*, lies one of the conceptual foundations for a reasoned hatred of bureaucracy, and for the demand for "public participation" in planning. If one dislikes the last, or has no stomach for the expenditure of time and effort that it entails, then one should go back to the beginning, defy certain demands often represented as imperatives, and reexamine the ends for which a bureaucracy of such a size was taken to be needed, or at least the means chosen to realize the said ends.)

(e) The unfinished or indeterminate character of our ideals and value structure is constitutive both of human freedom and, for finite creatures who face an indefinite or infinite range of contingencies with only finite powers of prediction and imagination (NE 1137b), of practical rationality itself.

(f) The man of highest practical wisdom is the man who brings to bear upon a situation the greatest number of genuinely pertinent concerns and genuinely relevant considerations commensurate with the importance of the deliberative context. The best practical syllogism is that whose minor premise arises out of such a man's perceptions, concerns, and appreciations. It records what strikes such a man as the in the situation most salient feature of the context in which he has to act. This activates a corresponding major premise that spells out the general import of the concern that makes this feature the salient feature in the situation. An analogy explored by Donald Davidson,[9] between a *judgment of probability*, taken in its relation to judgments of probability relative to evidence, and a *decision*, taken in its relation to judgments of the desirability of an action relative to such and such contextual facts, will suggest this idea: the larger the set of considerations that issue in the singling out of the said feature, the more compelling the syllogism. But there are no formal criteria by which to compare the claims of competing syllogisms. Inasmuch as the syllogism arises in a determinate context, the major premise is evaluated not for its unconditional acceptability, nor for embracing more considerations than its rivals, but for its adequacy to the situation. It will be adequate for the situation if and only if circumstances that could restrict or qualify it and defeat its applicability at a given juncture do not in the practical context of this syllogism obtain. Its evaluation is of its essence dialectical, and all of a piece with the perceptions and reasonings that gave rise to the syllogism in the first place. The analogy with probability is imperfect also because, as John McDowell has made me see,[10] certain virtues may demand that we *count for nothing* certain pertinent facts—for example, the likelihood of sustaining wounds in combating an adversary of implacably evil intent. (In most cases of the proper exercise of a virtue, we definitely do not want to say that the demands of the virtue are irrational. It is to be noted, though, that this is *not* to say that we shall expect there to be an *independent* account of prudence or rationality which itself shows these demands to be rational without reference to the virtue.)

(g) Since the goals and concerns that an agent brings to a situation may be diverse and incommensurable, and may not in themselves dictate any decision, they need not constitute the materials for some psychological theory (or any empirical theory above the conceptual level of a theory of matter) to make a prediction of the action.[11] Nor need anything else constitute these materials. There is simply no reason to expect that it will be possible to construct an (however idealized) empirical theory of the rational agent to parallel the predictive power, explanatory nonvacuity, and satisfactoriness for its purpose of (say) the economic hypothesis that under a wide variety of specifiable circumstances individual firms will push every line of action open to them to the point where marginal cost and marginal revenue are equal. If prediction were essential, then a phenomenologist or someone with a strong interest in the value consciousness of his subject would do best. But what is needed here is not prediction, but the subject's own decision processes, constantly redeployed on new situations or on new understanding of old ones.

My first translation-cum-paraphrase is of 1142a23 ff.:

That practical wisdom is not deductive theoretical knowledge is plain. For practical wisdom is, as I have said, of the ultimate and particular—as is the subject matter of action. In this practical wisdom is the counterpart or dual of theoretical intuition. *Theoretical* intellect or intuition is of the ultimate, but in this sense—it is of ultimate universal concepts and axioms that are too primitive or fundamental to admit of further analysis or of justification from without. [At the opposite extreme] practical wisdom [as a counterpart of theoretical reason] also treats of matters that defy justification from without. Practical wisdom is of what is ultimate and particular in the distinct sense of needing to be quite simply perceived. By perception here I do not mean sense perception but the kind of perception or insight one needs to see that a triangle, say, is one of the basic or ultimate components [of a figure which one has to construct with ruler and compass]. [For there is no *routine procedure* for analyzing a problem figure into the components by which one may construct it with rule and compasses.] The analysis calls for insight, and there is a limit to what one can say about it. But even this sort of insight is more akin to sense perception than practical wisdom is really akin to sense perception.

Comment: On this reading the geometer example turns up again. The method which the geometer discovers to construct the prescribed figure has a property unusual in a technical deliberation and ideal for making the transition to another kind of case, that of being in some sense constitutive of the end in view. It counts as the answer to a question he was asked (and would be proved to count so). *Caution.* Paraphrase and interpretation is not here confined to square-bracketed portions.

The other paraphrase-cum-translation I offer is of *NE* 1143a25 ff.:

...when we speak of judgment and understanding and practical wisdom and intuitive reason, we credit the same people with possessing judgment and having reached years of reason and with having practical wisdom and understanding. For all these faculties deal with ultimates, that is, with what is particular; and being a man of understanding and of good or sympathetic judgment consists in being able to judge about the things with which practical wisdom is concerned; for the equities are common to all good men in relation to other men. Now all action relates to the particular or ultimate; for not only must the man of practical wisdom know particular facts, but understanding and judgment are also concerned with things to be done, and these are ultimates. And intuitive reason is concerned with ultimates in both directions [i.e., with ultimates in two senses and respects, in respect of extreme generality and in respect of extreme specificity]. For intuitive reason [the general faculty] is of both the most primitive and the most ultimate terms. Its proper province is where derivation or independent justification is impossible. In the case of that species of intuitive reason which is the theoretical intuition pertaining to demonstrative proof, its object is the most fundamental concepts and axioms. In its practical variety, on the other hand, intuitive reason concerns the most particular and contingent and specific. This is the typical subject matter of the minor premise of a practical syllogism [the one which is "of the possible"]. For here, in the capacity to find the right feature and form a practical syllogism, resides the understanding of the reason for performing an action, or its end. For the major premise and the generalizable concern that comes with it arise from this perception of something particular. So one must have an appreciation or perception of the particular, and my name for this is intuitive reason. [It is the source both of particular syllogisms and of all the concerns however particular or general that give a man reason to act.]...we think our powers correspond to our time of life, and that a particular age brings with it intuitive reason and judgment; this implies that nature is the cause.... Therefore we ought to attend to the undemonstrated sayings and opinions of experienced and older people or of people of practical wisdom not less than to demonstrations; for because experience has given them an eye they see aright.

Comment. It is the mark of the man of practical wisdom on this account to be able to select from the infinite number of features of a situation those features that bear upon the notion or ideal of existence which it is his standing aim to make real. This conception of human life results in various evaluations of all kinds of things, in various sorts of cares and concerns, and in various projects. It does not reside in a set of maxims or precepts, useful though Aristotle would allow these to be at a certain stage in the education of the emotions. In no case will there be a rule to which a man can simply appeal to tell him what to do (except in the special case where an absolute prohibition operates). The man may have no other recourse but to invent the answer to the problem. As often as not, the inventing, like the frequent accommodation he has to effect between the claims of competing values, may count as a modification or innovation or further determination in the evolution of his view of what a good life is. *Caution.* As before, paraphrase has not been confined to square-bracketed sentences.

Conclusion. Against this account, as I have explained it, it may be complained that in the end very little is said, because everything that is hard has been permitted to take refuge in the notionof aisthēsis or *situational appreciation* as I have paraphrased this. And in aisthēsis, as Aristotle says, explanations give out. I reply that, if there is no real prospect of an ordinary scientific or simply empirical theory of all of action and deliberation as such, then the thing we should look for may be precisely what Aristotle provides—namely, a conceptual framework which we can apply to particular cases, which articulates the reciprocal relations of an agent's concerns and his perception of how things objectively are in the world; and a schema of description *which relates the complex ideal the agent tries in the process of living his life to make real to the form that the world impresses, both by way of opportunity and by way of limitation, upon that ideal.* Here too, within the same schema, are knitted together, as von Wright says, "the concepts of wanting an end, understanding a necessity, and setting oneself to act. It is a contribution to the molding or shaping of these concepts."[12] I entertain the unfriendly suspicion that those who feel they *must* seek more than all this provides want a scientific theory of rationality not so much from a passion for science, even where there can be no science, but because they hope and desire, by some conceptual alchemy, to turn such a theory into a regulative or normative discipline, or into a system of rules by which to spare themselves some of the agony of thinking and all the torment of feeling and understanding that is actually involved in reasoned deliberation.

NOTES

1. The first two parts of this essay ("Rejection of the First Thesis" and "Rejection of the Second Thesis") have been circulating in typescript since 1962, and as a result I have had the inestimable benefit (from which they will feel I had the time and ought to have had the ability to profit better) of comments from J. L. Ackrill, M. J. Woods, M. F. Burnyeat, R. Sorabji (without the support of whose article "Aristotle on the Role of Intellect in Virtue," *Proceedings of the Aristotelian Society*, n.s. 74 [1973-74], 107-129 [chap. 12 of this anthology] I should have had to postpone publication yet further), J. C. Dhybikowski, T. H. Irwin, Martha Craven Nussbaum, and G. E. L. Owen. To the last-named I owe also the

invitation to continue the first two parts into the third part and on to a section on *akrasia* as James Loeb visiting fellow in Classical Philosophy at Harvard in Spring 1972 (see chap. 14 of this anthology).

2. I think that those who employ these or similar terms usually intend the distinction of two kinds of reasoning, and the two distinct kinds of nontheoretical syllogism allegedly recognized by Aristotle, to correspond in some way to Aristotle's distinction of production (*poiēsis*) and practice (*praxis*).

3. (1) (2) (3) is to be sharply distinguished from the (worse mistaken) subjectivist interpretation still in some quarters defended. This enlarges the role of moral virtue at the expense of intellect and, so far as possible, assimilates *NE* 6 to *NE* 3 —where *NE* 3 is read in an exclusively means-end fashion. (1) (2) (3) is closer to the reason-oriented naturalist interpretation I shall commend and, like my interpretation, it owes much to Professor D. J. Allan. See his "Aristotle's Account of the Origin of Moral Principles," *Proceedings of the XIth International Congress of Philosophy, Brussels, August 20-26, 1953* (Amsterdam, 1953), 12:120-127 [hereinafter referred to as Allan (1)] and "The Practical Syllogism," in *Autour d'Aristote: Recueil... offert à Mgr Mansion* (Louvain, 1955), pp. 325-340 [hereinafter referred to as Allan (2)]. These publications represent so considerable an advance in clearing away the mass of captious misinterpretation to which Aristotle's praxeology had been previously subjected that I have preferred to consider the composite view given above rather than dwell on Allan's special version of it. But I shall allude frequently to his treatment of single passages.

What principally distinguishes Allan's view from the composite view (1) (2) (3) is that Allan is inclined to say that the changes he postulates between the view of Book 3 and the view of Books 6-7 leave Aristotle's analysis of *deliberation* itself more or less unaffected. Against this, I say either the alleged rule-case reasoning, which is admitted by Allan to be *prohairetic*, can be properly termed deliberative or it cannot. If it can, then, if choice needed radical alteration, then so *on Allan's interpretation of it* did the Book 3 account of deliberation. It could not remain unaffected. For precisely the same considerations then operate on both. If we say it cannot be termed deliberative, however, we contradict 1140a27-28. Cf. also 1139a23, 1141b8-15.

4. Cf. Allan (1), p. 124: "...the good propounded may be (a) distant or (b) general. Thus there is fresh work for practical reason to perform. In the former case, we have first to calculate the means which will, in due course, achieve the end. In the latter, we have to *subsume the particular case under a general rule*. Both these processes are analysed by Aristotle in a masterly fashion, *in different parts of his work, the former in the third book* of the Ethics, the latter in Books VI and VII and in his psychological writings" (my italics). And cf. (2) "His *first* position in the *Ethics* is that all virtuous action involves choice, that all choice follows up a deliberation and *that all deliberation is concerned with the selection of means*" (my italics).

5. Cf., at random, Jeremy Bray, *Decision in Government* (London, 1970), p. 72: "...the individual consumer's own decision processes which are the more complex for not being wholly rational in any economic sense." (Is there really, or

should there be, a special sense of "rational" in economics?) Bray goes on to suggest that anyone who thinks there is room for reason in this sphere, or sets much store by the concept of *need*, must wish to deny freedom: "However the concept of minimum need may be used in social security arrangements, it is a poor guide to consumer behaviour whether at the minimum income or other levels, and whether in an advanced or primitive society. The particular purchases made by a family reflect not only their immediate tastes such as a liking for warmth, bright colours, and tinned fruit, but also their spiritual life and fantasy world—the stone fireplace as a safe stronghold in a morally insecure world, the Jaguar car to release frustration or bolster a waning virility, the tingling toothpaste as a ritual purification. Far from being a matter for ridicule, consumer choice is something to nurture, cultivate and protect." In the name of liberty, yes, but not because these ends are really outside the reach of reason or rational appraisal. Lest Bray's seem to be a purely Fabian doctrine, I quote a Chicago School economist, Milton Friedman: "Differences about economic policy among disinterested citizens derive predominantly from different predictions . . . rather than from fundamental differences in basic values, differences *about which men can only fight*" (my italics) (*Essays in Positive Economics* [Chicago, 1953], p. 5). For a protest see Alan Altshuler, *The City Planning Process* (Ithaca, N.Y., 1965), *ad init.*

6. Allan (2), pp. 336-337.

7. See *Politics* 1332b6 and *Metaphysics* 1072a20: "We desire it because it seems good to us, it doesn't seem good to us because we desire it." It is the beginning of wisdom on this matter, both as an issue of interpretation and as a philosophical issue, to see that we do not really have to choose between Aristotle's proposition and its apparent opposite (as at e.g., Spinoza, *Ethics*, pt. III, proposition 9, note). We can desire it because it seems good *and* it seems good because we desire it.

8. Jonathan Glover speaks of "the aesthetic preference most of us have for economy of principles, the preference for ethical systems in the style of the Bauhaus rather than Baroque" (*The Aristotelian Society, Supplementary Volume* 49 [1975], 183). Against this I say that only a confusion between the practical and the theoretical could even purport to provide reasoned grounds for such a preference. (For the beginnings of the distinction, see Bernard Williams, "Consistency and Realism," *The Aristotelian Society, Supplementary Volume* 40 [1966], 1-22.) Why is an axiom system any better foundation for practice than, e.g., a long and incomplete or open-ended list of (always at the limit conflicting) *desiderata*? The claims of all true *beliefs* (about how the world is) are reconcilable. Everything true must be consistent with everything else that is true. But not all the claims of all rational concerns or even all moral concerns (that the world *be* thus or so) need be reconcilable. There is no reason to expect they would be; and Aristotle gives at 1137b the reason why we cannot expect to lay down a decision procedure for adjudication in advance between claims, or for prior mediation. By the dragooning of the plurality of goods into the order of an axiom system I think practice will be almost as rapidly and readily degraded (and almost as unexpectedly perhaps) as modern building, by exploitation of the well-intentioned efforts of the Bauhaus, has been degraded into the single-minded pursuit of profit. The last

phase of Walter Gropius's career, and the shady and incongruous company into which his ambitions for modern architecture drew him so irresistibly, will repay study by those drawn to Glover's analogy.

9. Cf. "How is Weakness of Will Possible?" in *Moral Concepts*, ed. Feinberg (Oxford, 1969).

10. Cf. "Are Moral Requirements Hypothetical Imperatives?" *The Aristotelian Society, Supplementary Volume* 52 (1978), 13-29. The possibility of being wounded is in one way relevant—for the demands of courage presuppose that the evil to be avoided is commensurate with the risk—but in another way not relevant. Once the demand is there, the brave man par excellence cannot as such allow the possibility to weigh.

11. See Donald Davidson, "Mental Events," in *Experience and Theory*, ed. Foster and Swanson (London, 1971). Also my "Towards a Reasonable Libertarianism," in *Essays on Freedom and Action*, ed. T. Honderich (London, 1973), pp. 36-41.

12. G. H. von Wright, *Varieties of Goodness* (London, 1963), p. 171. Both for the quotation and in the previous sentence I am indebted to Martha Craven Nussbaum. In her *Aristotle's "De motu animalium"* (Princeton, 1978) she writes: "the appeal of this form of explanation for Aristotle may lie in its ability to link an agent's desires and his perceptions of how things are in the world around him, his subjective motivation and the objective limitations of his situation . . . animals are seen as acting in accordance with desire, but within the limits imposed by nature."

14

Weakness of Will Commensurability, and the Objects of Deliberation and Desire[1]

David Wiggins

> It is hard to struggle with one's heart's desire. It will pay with soul for what it craves.
>
> —Heraclitus (fragment 85 Diels)

I

Almost anyone not under the influence of theory will say that, when a person is weak-willed, he intentionally chooses that which he knows or believes to be the worse course of action when he could choose the better course; and that, in acting in this way, the weak-willed man acts not for *no* reason at all—that would be strange and atypical—but irrationally.

The description just given appears to be a consistent description of the inconsistent (not necessarily perverse) conduct that is characteristic of weak will. In this paper something will be done to show that it is a satisfiable and frequently satisfied description. But there are philosophers of mind and moral philosophers who have felt a strong theoretical compulsion to rewrite the description, rather than allow the phenomenon of weakness of will to appear as an incontrovertible refutation of the theories of mind or morality that they are committed to defend. I cannot claim that it is inconceivable that this pretheoretical description of weakness of will should be strictly and literally true of nothing; but I do venture to say that he who values his pet theory above the phenomenon, and wants to hold that weakness of will as I have described it is simply an illusion, will need to command some formidable conceptual-cum-explanatory leverage in the philosophy of value and mind—and an Archimedean fulcrum of otherwise inexplicable facts of human conduct. Pending the emergence of such a theoretician—a man of some different stuff from any ordinary philosopher, psychologist, decision theorist, or economist —I assert that we should feel some provisional gratitude for the rich philosophical suggestiveness by which *akrasia* compensates us for the harm it so repeatedly does us.

In the first place, the phenomena of weakness of will helps us to adjudicate certain ideas that have important dependencies in moral theory:

(1) that there is something a man invariably acts to maximize;
(2) that a man invariably acts in order to maximize something;
(3) that there is something such that all actions we have reasons to do are actions that will maximize that.

If I am right in the principal contention of this paper, then (1) (2) and (3) can all be traced to the same oversimplified conception of value (and consequentially mind) as can (5) and (6) below. (See section VIII.) But the dubiety of (1) (2) (3) does not exhaust even the moral philosophical interest of weak will. The phenomenon also endangers certain variants of the idea

(4) that, whatever the assertibility condition of a normative judgment may lack in objective factuality, this deficit can be made up by some affect in the maker of the judgment whose seriousness or sincerity may be ascertained by testing whether he acts out the commitment that his judgment purports to express.

In the philosophy of mind there are at least two positions that are impugned by weakness of will as pretheoretically conceived (both formulations influenced by Christopher Peacocke[2]):

(5) is the position that results from conjoining two principles, the principle (a) that the desire one acts on intentionally is the strongest deliberated desire, and the principle (b) that it is irrational to act against the strongest deliberated desire.

(6) is the position that results from combining principle (a) above with the principle (c) that the best criterion for someone's making the deliberated judgment that course x is better than course y is his wanting more strongly to choose x than he wants to choose y.[3]

Only the conjunctions (a) *and* (b), (a) *and* (c) are directly impugned by weakness of will. But anybody who takes it seriously will suspect each of (a) and (c). (Especially perhaps if he is disposed to accept (b); but, even if he thinks (b) arises from a flawed conception of rationality, he may be led to suspect both of the other principles.) Such a philosopher is likely, I think, to recover the following almost prephilosophical picture of the progress from thought to action:

(i) Faced with choice between courses of action x and y one may appraise or evaluate each. (In a favorable case it may be possible and desirable to compare them in respect of one simple or complex feature: but let us bracket the question whether that is always possible.)

(ii) By whatever deliberative route, one may come to decide that x is the better course. In a favorable case one may decide that x is better *all things considered.*[4] But an agent may disbelieve altogether in the possibility of arriving at such a judgment—in which case, if he is able to decide at all, then he dispenses with the "all things considered" and goes straight to the next stage.

(iii) One decides *to* follow course x; and thereafter one has the intention to do that. There is no need for a chronological differentiation between this and phase (ii) above. But some conceptual differentiation seems imperative. One can decide for x rather than y without thinking either of them the better. And, where there is a judgment of comparison, it is surely one thing to think that x is better than y [phase (ii)], and another to *find it so* and, finding it so, to choose it.

(iv) Having decided in favor of x, one may stick by the decision when the relevant moment comes—or not stick by it and change one's intention. This is usually weakness. But when one sticks by the decision even where the original deliberation and judgment stand in need of review (e.g., in the light of new perception), that is *obstinacy.* If one holds the judgment open to relevant new perception and, subject only to that, one abides by the practical decision, then that is *continence*, or *strength of character.* (It may even be *temperance.*) In the special case where fear obtrudes, it is *courage.*

Continence and courage are states of character. If states of character are dispositions (as I suppose they are), then it will help to allay some gratuitous perplexities about the failures that have just been rehearsed under (iv) to remember what certain ordinary dispositions are like.[5]

Just occasionally a horse that is surefooted may miss his step. He may even trip at the point where a less surefooted animal was lucky enough to have passed recently without slipping. Again, aviation spirit is very inflammable. But, just once, someone may get away with it when he throws a lighted match into a tankful of the stuff—even as someone far less rash pays with his life for the risk that he took in throwing a match into a tankful of paraffin.[6] When these things happen, we think that there is always an explanation to be found. We do not always find it (and there is no one place where we always need to look). Nor can we write down a list of conditional sentences (still less a list of reduction sentences in the manner of Carnap) such that a horse is surefooted—or a stuff is inflammable—if and only if these conditionals are true. In special cases we can leave all that behind and give a scientific account of the secret nature of the disposition in question. In ordinary cases the most we can do is to specify the disposition as *that disposition* in virtue of which *normally*, if for instance . . . be the case, then —— will be the case, leaving theory, anecdotal knowledge, and whatever else to lend content to the "normally" and the "for instance."

Similarly (somewhat similarly, rather: see below, section V), when a man of some character fails to persevere in his decision, we look for an explanation. But the task of the philosophy of mind is not to chronicle in advance the conditions under which this failure will happen, or to provide one explanation schema to cover all cases. It is to describe such phenomena as weakness of will in such a way that there is room for the case-by-case explanations that we normally accept. Some of the explanations that we sometimes accept describe what happens from the inside. They give the man's *reason* for departing so weakly from his decision. In that case it is of capital importance that our philosophy of value should accommodate such reasons *as* reasons, even as the philosophy of mind measures up to the question of what quality and degree of weakness is evidenced by the lapse, and the even harder question of what it shows about character. ("Moral insight, as communicable vision or as quality of being, *is* something separable from definitive performance, and we do not always, though doubtless we do usually, require performance as, or allow performance to be, the test of the vision or of the person who holds it."[7])

We can make perplexities for ourselves in moral philosophy and philosophy of mind by promoting arbitrary construction in invented vocabulary to the place that should be occupied by ordinary description of mental phenomena, or by ignoring the special character of dispositional concepts. But above all we perplex ourselves by failing to heed the subject matter of deliberation and decision. To ignore the nature of the scheme of values between which deliberation and decision have to arbitrate is the most potent source of perplexity about weakness of will.

II

If we are to describe phases (i)-(iv) at all, then we need autonomous and mutually irreducible notions of believing, desiring, deciding *that*, deciding *to*, intending. And, in correspondence with these, we need to speak not only of a man's capacity for evaluation and appreciation, his nerve and resolve, but also of his executive virtues or dispositions, like courage and continence.[8] Or so I should argue. Once we are embarked on this descriptive project, and once we seek to draw out the mind's picture of the mind, it is like building one's own house and then economizing on ink and postage stamps in order to offset the mounting expense, to try to describe all this exclusively in terms of belief and desire. But how do wanting and desiring fit into the picture? I described phases (i), (ii), (iii), and (iv) as if wanting scarcely figured at all—a salutary exaggeration or defect, perhaps, but scarcely one that can be allowed to go uncorrected. To fill the lacuna will bring us just one step closer to Aristotle,[9] though the account of weakness of will that would result if the picture were made complete is not Aristotle's own account.

In the first place, desire or something that brings in desire is involved at phases (i) and (ii). It is hard to conceive of there being an evaluation of *x* and *y* in the absence of a structure of preexisting concerns that both will *direct* the imagining of what *x* amounts to and of what *y* amounts to and will *focus* the evaluator's attendant perceptions of the circumstances. I cannot see that such standing concerns, which jointly determine what Aristotle called a conception (*hupolepsis*) of the good, have necessarily to be *identified* with desires. (Does there really need to be an exact correspondence between such concerns and actual desires?) But I concede that such concerns cannot exist unless there are some standing desires that they organize. Again, although I should insist that the imagination and perception that phases (i) and (ii) call for are needed to *prepare* desire to embrace course *x* at phase (iii), I will concede that deliberative imagination and the other cognitive capacities involved do have to be energized by something that belongs on the side of affect—if only the readiness and capacity to *form* desires that will make real that which is judged to be good.

It must then be conceded to the side of desire that both imagination and perception at phase (i) and deliberative integration at phase (ii) will require an organizing conception that is in some sense (the sense just given) sustained or held in place by desire. But, so long as we avoid all technical uses of "want" and "desire," we shall not be in the least tempted to *identify* evaluative or integrative thinking with desire. Nor, I should now add, do we need to hasten to the conclusion that an organizing conception, which is not itself a desire, is sure to be ineffective at either the integrative or the subsequent stages (iii) (iv) if there is a desire contrary to the desire for course x, and this contrary desire (the desire to escape danger now, for instance) constantly presents itself as stronger than the desire for x.

As regards this last claim, everything depends on what one ought to mean by strength in a desire.[10] There is one sense in which a strong desire is a desire that is a winner; the desire either knocks out its rivals or defeats them on points. Just as the strongest fighter is the fighter who is such as to win, so the strongest desire is the desire that is such as to get itself acted upon (so to speak). Philosophers have noted this usage and gone so far as to make it analytic that the strongest desire is the desire that wins. What is unfortunate about this is not so much the stipulation itself of analyticity—needless though it is (consider—by an unseen foul or by bad luck, the stronger fighter can lose against the weaker)—as the bad effect the stipulation appears to have had upon the comprehension of the other sense of "strong" as predicated of desires.

In the other and commoner sense of "strong," a desire is strong if, in respect of vividness or appeal to the imagination, exigency, or importunity, it is *like* a desire that is a strong desire in the first sense. A strong desire is a desire that has the subjective character typically enjoyed by desires that do in fact get their way. But a desire can have this felt character without getting its way. And a desire can get its way without having this subjective character.

I strove to keep phases (ii) and (iii) apart. But, even when (iii) itself is achieved and when there is a consequential desire to *implement* the decision in favor of x (so much we should expect), I think one can now see that there is still no reason why the desire to do that which is involved by x should be stronger than all other desires—unless that simply means that, where the decision *is* actually adhered to, this desire is shown to have been the strongest. So stage (iii) can be reached without there being any guarantee (even if there is some presumption) that some desire is present that will *see to it* that the decision will be implemented. *At most* the achievement of stage (iii) guarantees that there is a positive desire to implement the decision. And hence the need for the executive virtues of which I spoke under (iv), virtues that can refresh and recollect deliberations under (i) (ii) (iii) but are conceptually distinct from anything we find there. The more a man needs to overcome subjectively stronger desires to keep to his decision, the more need he will have of continence. The less susceptible he is to attractions that run counter to the desires that support his decision at (iii) and supervene upon that, and the less susceptible he is to pleasures that compete with the distinctive pleasures that are accessible to the man of temperance and fortitude, the less need he will have of continence as such. At the ideal limit, he will have no need of it according to Aristotle, because all counterattractions are simply "silenced" (to borrow John McDowell's phrase[11]).

III

It may seem that what is most required to conclude this description of the passage from thought to action is an account of the distinctiveness and desirability of the objects of the particular kinds of desire that a man needs continence to insure him against the attractions of. The comparison between cowardly and incontinent actions and the very Aristotelian character of the notions here employed of desire, disposition, and executive virtue may even suggest that the account of weakness that I recommend as satisfactory is the existing Aristotelian account. But nobody who looks at either account in detail will confuse the account I have begun here with Aristotle's own description of incontinence. Let me say why I prefer my Aristotelian account to Aristotle's own.

Aristotle writes in Book 7 of the *Nicomachean Ethics:*

> One may be puzzled how a man with a correct view of a situation can be weak of will. For some deny that this is possible if he really knows what is the right thing to do. For if the knowledge is present, it is strange, as Socrates thought, for something else to overcome knowledge and manhandle it like a slave. Socrates was totally opposed to that view. He denied that there was any such thing as weakness of will. For knowing that it *is* the best, nobody, he said, acts contrary to the best. If he does act contrary to the best, it must be through ignorance. This account of Socrates' conflicts plainly with what seems to be the case and what people say [the *phainomena*].... [1145b21]

After such an introduction, someone who read the book for the first time might conceivably anticipate the sort of description of akrasia that was begun in the previous sections of this paper, a description exploiting the conceptual riches of *hexeis* (dispositions) that Aristotle was the first philosopher to appreciate and then building on Aristotle's own account of the education of the emotions and perceptions and the maturation of such virtues as courage and temperance. If however we follow G. E. L. Owen's analysis of "phenomena" in the works of Aristotle,[12] then we shall not be altogether unprepared for the possibility that, at the end, Aristotle will conclude that, in at least one important respect, Socrates was more right than wrong about weakness. (Phainomena are not necessarily facts.) And an examination of the ensuing text of Book 7 will suggest that this possibility is indeed realized. It is a strangely Socratic account compared with the account Aristotle might have given; and we need to understand how this came about.

Aristotle's fullest and final treatment of akrasia is at 1147a24-1147b19, and it presupposes the doctrine of the practical syllogism. I shall first declare the general interpretation I accept of the practical syllogism, then cut a long interpretative story short by an expanded translation-cum-paraphrase of the particular passage.

Practical syllogisms offer explanations of actions. These explanations are causal, but they reconstruct the reasons an agent himself has for his action. They usually comprise a major and a minor premise. The first or major premise mentions something of which there could be a desire (*orexis*) transmissible to some practical conclusion (i.e., a desire convertible via some available minor premise into action). The second or minor premise details a circumstance pertaining to the feasibility in the particular situation of what must be done if the claim of the major premise is to be heeded. In the light of the examples Aristotle gives in *De motu animalium,* nothing seems more natural than to describe the first premise of a practical syllogism as *pertaining to the good* (the fact that it pertains to some good—either a general good or something which the agent has just resolved is good for this situation—is what can beckon to desire); and to describe the second or minor premise as *pertaining to the possible* (where "possible" connotes the feasibility *given* the circumstances registered by the minor premise of the object of concern of the major premise).

Aristotle calls such patterns of reasoning "syllogisms" because of an analogy that interests him between *deductively concluding or asserting* and *coming to a practical conclusion or acting.* He says that the conclusion of a practical syllogizing is an action. What matters for present purposes is that agents can see in the truth of the minor premise a way of ministering to some concern to which the major affords expression, and that their seeing this explains what they do.

The translation-cum-paraphrase that I offer of 1147a24 following is this:

Again, we may also view the cause of akrasia by reference to the facts of human nature. The one premise [the major] is universal, the other premise is concerned with the particular facts, which are the kind of thing to fall within the province of perception. When a single proposition results from the two premises, then [in the case of scientific or deductive reasoning] the soul must of necessity affirm the conclusion; while in the practical sphere it must of necessity act. For instance, if one had better eat of anything that is sweet, and the object presented in some

specific situation is sweet, then the man who can act and is not physically prevented *must* at the very moment [at which he brings the premises together] act
accordingly. So when there is some major premise or other [which combines with
some minor premise to] constrain the man from eating of something [when for
instance a major premise indicating that ϕ things are bad for the health combines
with a minor premise that a certain x is ϕ]; and when there is another practical
syllogism in the offing with the major premise that everything sweet is nice to eat
and a minor premise that x is sweet (this being the premise that is active) and
appetite backs this syllogism; then the former syllogism forbids the man to taste
but appetite's syllogism pushes him on. (For each part of the soul has the power
of originating motion.) So it turns out that a man behaves incontinently under
the influence (in some sense) of reason and belief. For he has argued himself to his
practical conclusion from true beliefs, and these beliefs are not in themselves
inconsistent with reason. It is the appetite itself that opposes reason, not the
premises of the appetite's syllogism. It also follows that this is the reason why the
lower animals are not incontinent, viz., because they have no universal judgments of the kind that figure in practical syllogisms, but only imagination and
memory of particulars.

The explanation of how this sort of ignorance is dissolved and the incontinent
man regains his knowledge is the same as in the case of the man drunk or asleep
and is not peculiar to his condition; we must go to students of natural science for
it. Since the second premise (the minor) is a judgment deriving from perception
and is the hinge on which all action must turn, it is of this premise that the incontinent man is prevented by his condition from properly possessing himself. Either
that, or, if he does possess it, he does so only in the sense in which possessing does
not mean comprehension but only talking, as a drunken man recites the verses of
Empedocles. And so, because the second premise is not universal (still less an
object of scientific knowledge) in the way the major premise may be universal,
the point that Socrates most insisted upon turns out to be correct.[13] For passion
does not worst [reading *perigignetai* with Stewart] anything with the status of
demonstrable knowledge. It is not demonstrable knowledge that is manhandled
like a slave [which would be absurd]. What passion overwhelms is a man's perception or appreciation of a particular situation.

This account of weakness is inconsistent with common sense, and
almost as inconsistent as Socrates' own account was with the account
that we should naturally give of the cases where we think we know we
are doing what we should not do. Either the incontinent man reaches the
conclusion of the better syllogism, or he doesn't. If he does, then there
can be no conditional necessity of the kind Aristotle alleges that he act on
the conclusion. For he doesn't act and he does reach it. Still less can the
conclusion of the syllogism be action itself. On the other hand, if the
agent does not get to the conclusion, then there is no room for the struggle that Aristotle himself observes to be characteristic of incontinence (cf.
1102b17, 1136a31). There is no ambiguity in "know" which can reduce
the severity of this dilemma. Nor does it help if the story is that the con-

clusion is reached, secures momentary abstinence, and is then eclipsed by appetite's syllogism. On any premises that makes conceptual trouble for weakness, the two syllogisms cannot struggle, because they cannot co-exist—even for one moment.

IV

There has already been occasion to refer to John McDowell's appealing interpretation of Aristotle's thoughts about continence, incontinence, and virtue. For Aristotle there really is some important way in which the incontinent man's cognitive conception of a situation may be expected to differ from a temperate man's conception. (There is full allowance for that in our account of the stages (i)-(iv) of sections I and II above.) But this is only half of what is needed. It is important to see that McDowell can be right about the interpretation of Aristotle on temperance, and right about what temptation or fear is *at that ideal limit* of temperance, and yet a difficulty can still arise that McDowell does not acknowledge. For the difficulty we are now concerned with relates not to the difference between temperance and continence but to the difference between conti-nence and incontinence as these occur in ordinary adult people who fall short of the ideal, and to the distinction that Aristotle is obliged to postu-late between the continent man's and the incontinent man's knowledge and perception of a situation. These two men are neither of them temper-ate. In a sense, then, they are very much the same sort of men, and *sus-ceptible* at least to the same sorts of excess. (Indeed, on different occa-sions one and the same man may do the continent thing or the inconti-nent thing.) How then can it be maintained, even in the face of all the phenomenological findings, that the continent and incontinent man see things differently? (Unless the claim is *ex post facto* and the supposed dif-ference is not even represented to be a subjective difference.)

V

When what I almost venture to call a more Aristotelian account than Aristotle's was possible (see sections I, II), why did Aristotle give such a Socratic account of the phenomena of weakness?

It is true that in order to give another account he would have had to effect some modification of the doctrine that the conclusion of a practical syllogism is invariably an action (because on the rival account the conti-nent and incontinent men have normal, ready access to both competing syllogisms). But why should he have insisted on that doctrine just as it stood? There is also the conditional necessity Aristotle alleges that a man who both gets and puts together minor and major premise will act in accordance with them. But here we must ask what caused Aristotle to insist on this necessity in the first place. I suppose it may be suggested that he thinks that only in this way will either an explanation of action or an analogy between theoretical and practical syllogism be achieved. But neither of these points is enough.

The point about analogy is a point worthy of respect, but scarcely decisive. There can be analogy between very different sorts of thing. If we can find no room for the operation of the will when the two premises of a demonstrative syllogism are seen by him who puts them together to entail their conclusion, then that makes sense enough. For there is nothing the will can add here. Everything that bears on the criterion for belief is already present.[14] That is how it is with believing something. But we need not expect the analogy between pursuit and/or abstinence and belief and/or nonbelief to be perfect or complete. Least of all should we expect this in respect of that which distinguished the practical and theoretical in the first place, namely, what touches the will. And, coming now to the first point about explanation, nor need it weaken the rationalizing role of the practical syllogism (its power to display a course of action under what the agent sees as its rational title to be realized) that the claim made on the agent by the syllogism may be controverted or defeated. Why then, if Aristotle qualified his sentence about the necessity that a man act upon the syllogism unless prevented or unable, would the awareness of the syllogism come to lack force in the explanation of behavior? Surely he could put in another *unless*. Why should a syllogism-form lack explanatory force in the cases where the man acts by reason of the corresponding thought just because there are allowed to be cases where he might *not* act upon that sort of consideration? (Suppose someone asks why the waiter crossed the room. Suppose it be said that he crossed because I beckoned to him. Does this explanation get undermined by the fact that, when he's tired or others are beckoning or whatever, he ignores my beckoning to him?)

If the difficulty Aristotle would have in dropping or further qualifying the "necessarily" is meant to relate to the fact that all explanations seek after completeness, well then it may be allowed that, to complete the explanation of a man's actual behavior, we must add that nothing did controvert or defeat the consideration which, in thinking or syllogizing thus, the agent saw the force of and then acted because of. In the case of explanation the addition is completely otiose, however, because we already know that the action did take place and was not obstructed. If we insist on the symmetry of explanation and prediction, I suppose that some such condition will need to be added in a predictive case. And it is a difficulty when prediction is insisted upon that, so long as we stay on the purely psychological level, there is no guarantee that we shall be able to attach an operational or predictively useful content to this extra condition.[15] But what that illustrates is not the futility of the psychological sort of explanation given by the practical syllogism, but the real nature of the symmetry between explanation and prediction. At a given level of description the prospect of symmetry will correspond to the prospect of deterministic description at that level. There is nothing in Aristotle's philosophy or Aristotle's science to aggravate the disappointment that some will feel about this. And the undiminished beauty of explanation of what *has* happened is that it need not wait upon the distant or illusory prospect of fully deterministic description.

We shall come closer, I think, to the real difficulty that Aristotle must have supposed that he perceived in akrasia if we forget these irrelevancies and go back to an earlier sentence of the *NE*, 1111b13-15: "The incontinent man acts from his desire but not from his choice; whereas the continent acts from choice and not from his desire." Indeed, in Aristotle's special sense of "choice" (*prohairesis*), the incontinent man acts contrary to choice (1148a9). (Which is not yet to say that he acts nonintentionally in the ordinary sense of the English word *intentionally*.) This is a much more promising clue to what troubled Aristotle and what would have prompted him to reject very firmly the idea of developing the neo-Aristotelian account of incontinence that I began in sections I and II.

In the early books of the *Nicomachean Ethics* Aristotle develops special conceptions of happiness (*eudaimonia*), acting (*prattein*), and choice (*prohairesis*) such that all the purposive doings that a man chooses to do, in the special sense of "choose" and "do," he chooses for the sake of what he conceives as eudaimonia or activity in accordance with human excellence.[16] For a man to embrace a specific conception of eudaimonia just is for him to become susceptible to certain distinctive and *distinctively compelling* reasons for acting in certain sorts of ways. Now the difficulty that incontinence poses is not that it constitutes a counterexample to this generalization. (How could it? The generalization rests on a stipulation that simply excludes the weak-willed doings of the *akrates* from counting as chosen, or as actions in the special sense of "choose" and "act" employed in Aristotle's construction.) The difficulty is rather that the incontinent man as he was described at the outset is *party* to the Aristotelian conception of activity in accordance with human excellence, and understands the claims it makes. If he is party to that, then he understands these claims by virtue of being susceptible to them as claims of this sort. How then, understanding so much, can he prefer weaker and different claims, or allow himself to pursue a different goal whose pursuit is actually incompatible with what he recognizes as the supremely important goal? If he *can* do this with his eyes open—and if he can act sometimes and speak always in a manner so like the continent man's (so similar even in certain respects to the temperate man's) that there is no alternative but to credit him with a true view of eudaimonia, then his very existence may appear to constitute a quite special threat to Aristotle's construction.

Aristotle exacts from a rational disposition that is directed toward that which is the best of all humanly conceivable goods much more than he would exact from the common or garden physical dispositions that I turned to advantage in section I.[17] I think he exacts so much because, when a man has properly understood what Aristotle has described as eudaimonia, it must impugn the title of eudaimonia to satisfy the criteria of adequacy announced by Aristotle himself in Book 1 if someone who understands eudaimonia takes himself to have a reason to prefer something that he can see is less important. How could he prefer a smaller good when there was an overwhelmingly larger good staring him in the face and he understood what made it overwhelmingly larger? How, understanding the larger thing, could a man fail to pursue it?

Once an end is proposed that is both complete (in the sense of being chosen for itself and never for the sake of anything else, cf. 1079a33) and genuinely self-sufficient—in the sense of being such that a life qualifies by virtue of the sole achievement of that as worth living and lacking in nothing (1097b14-15)—a man has only to understand what is being proposed to him. If this *telos* or *skopos* has been correctly described (and sufficiently persuasively described to convince the akrates), then there ought to be no further problem of single-mindedness. For the man who knows what eudaimonia is will know that, if he attains it, then his life will merit the following description:

His opinions are harmonious, and he desires the same things with all his soul; and therefore he wishes for himself what is good and what seems so, and does it (for it is characteristic of the good man to work out the good), and does so for his own sake (for he does it for the sake of the intellectual element in him, which is thought to be the man himself); and he wishes himself to live and be preserved, and especially the element by virtue of which he thinks. For existence is good to the virtuous man, and each man wishes himself what is good, while no one chooses to possess the whole world if he has first to become someone else (for that matter, even now God possesses the good); he wishes for this only on condition of being whatever he is; and the element that thinks would seem to be the individual man, or to be so more than any other element in him. And such a man wishes to live with himself; for he does so with pleasure, since the memories of his past acts are delightful and his hopes for the future are good, and therefore pleasant. His mind is well stored too with subjects of contemplation. And he grieves and rejoices, more than any other, with himself; for the same thing is always painful, and the same thing always pleasant, and not one thing at one time and another at another; *he has just about nothing to regret.*[18]

Where this is the prospect and it is attainable by action, and where even approximations to this practical ideal represent approximations to the very same intrinsic goods, nothing else should hold out any prospect at all to practical reason. Just as, "if water chokes, then there is nothing else to wash it down with" (1146a34), so Aristotle's notions of practical reason and of eudaimonia are subverted—or so he seems to fear—if anything qualifies with men as they actually are as a counterattraction to the attractions of eudaimonia. It ought to be that, once that is described and understood, the force of practical reason is utterly spent and the philosopher is *functus officio.*

VI

It would be a serious misunderstanding of these claims to see the "oughts" and "shoulds" that were needed for their expression as in any way normative. What they represent are not requirements upon agents but theoretical conditions for the delineation of the unitary objective that Aristotle set himself to describe. Having described it for what it is, and commended eudaimonia to practical reason, it is not for philosophy to engage in exhortation. Insofar as moral philosophy is to be protreptic at all, the didactic effort is to be directed solely at the conditions for the cognitive understanding of the claims that eudaimonia enjoys to our undivided allegiance. And such claims as can be made for eudaimonia have to be true in virtue of what can be quite simply revealed to unblinkered perception and ordinary human understanding of the actual constitution of human values. If their actual constitution does not admit of the delineation of an ideal of eudaimonia with a purely rational claim upon us, then that is a defeat for philosophy as Aristotle conceives it.

There is another misunderstanding that I should deprecate. The argument rehearsed in section V is likely to have reminded the reader not only of the celebrated Socratic-Platonic arguments of *Gorgias* and *Meno* but also of the infamous argument of "the many" which is tied to Protagoras's tail in the *Protagoras* 354d-355d.

It is not easy to explain the real meaning of what you call being overcome by pleasure [i.e., akrasia], and any explanation is bound up with this point. You may still change your minds if you can say that the good is anything other than

pleasure, or evil other than pain. Is it sufficient for you to live life through pleasure and without pain? If so, and if you can mention no good or evil *which can-*
not in the last resort be reduced to these . . . you have to say that a man often recognizes evil actions as evil yet commits them . . . because he is led on and distracted by pleasure. . . . the absurdity of this will be evident *if we stop using all*
these names together, pleasant, painful, good, and evil, and since they have
turned out to be only two, call them by only two names. . . . What ridiculous
nonsense for a man to do evil knowing it to be evil because he is overcome by
good. . . . By being overcome you must mean taking evil in exchange for greater
good. . . .

Let ϕ be the universal or all-purpose predicate of favorable assessment. A
man will only be incontinent if he knows or believes the thing he doesn't
do is the thing with most ϕ to it. But if that is the alternative that has
most ϕ to it, and if nothing else besides ϕ-ness counts positively for anything, there is nothing to commend any other course of action over the
one that is most ϕ. He could have had no reason, *however bad*, for
choosing the other. The choice of a smaller amount of pleasure now
against a larger amount of pleasure later is explicitly described as a form
of ignorance in the supposedly single dimension ϕ; and the argument can
allow for now fashionable complications (which Plato anticipates at 356)
such as the rate at which the agent chooses to discount future ϕ. If everything with any relevance to choice is comprehended in the question how
ϕ a given course of action is, and how ϕ its competitors are, then no
rational sense can be made of weakness of will. This is the *Protagoras*
argument.

The misunderstanding I have in mind, and against which I now seek to
guard, is to suppose that Aristotle's argument against accepting weakness
of will unreconstructed would be of this reductive character, or would
depend on the idea that all values are in this sense commensurable. Certainly it would be unfortunate if this were so, because in that case the
interpretation would have Aristotle contradict himself. He states explicitly at *Politics* 1283a3 that the very idea of universal commensurability is
absurd.[19] And in the *Eudemian Ethics* he denies that knowledge and
money have a common measure (1243.22-23). Again, there are no signs
in the *Nicomachean Ethics* of Aristotle's supposing that there is a common measure to assess exhaustively the values of the noble, the useful,
and the pleasurable (even though the noble and the useful will in the formation of orexis appear to us also under the aspect of pleasure, cf. 1104b-
50-1105a1). What he has to maintain is only that, if eudaimonia is to
qualify by the formal criteria of autonomy and completeness, then it
must be that wherever a man has to act, he can subsume the question at
issue under the question of eudaimonia and discern which course of
action is better from that point of view:

Sensory imagination is found in other animals but deliberative imagination only in those which have reason. For whether one shall do this thing or do that thing it is the work of reason to decide. And such reason necessarily implies the power of measurement by a single standard. For what one pursues is the greater good. So a rational animal is one with the power to arbitrate between diverse appearances of what is good and integrate the findings into a unitary practical conception. [*De anima* 434a5-10][20]

There is no question even here of supposing that there is just one evaluative dimension ϕ, and one quantitative measure m, such that ϕ-ness is all that matters, and all courses of action can be compared with one another by the measure m in respect of ϕ-ness. What is assumed is only the weaker proposition, which is of the $\forall \exists$ not the $\exists \forall$ form, that for any n-tuple of courses of action actually available at time t to an agent x there is some way or other of establishing which of the n-tuple is the better course of action in respect of eudaimonia, and (consequentially upon that) the greater good.[21] There is no obvious inconsistency between holding this *De anima* doctrine and maintaining the thesis of value pluralism or incommensurability in the form of the denial of the $\exists \forall$ sentence.

VII

If the apparent menace of the akrates unredescribed to the soundness of Aristotle's construction has nothing to do with reductive commensurability in the *Protagoras* sense and everything to do with such formal requirements as self-sufficiency, and with the special prospect of having just about nothing to regret that eudaimonia holds out to rational intelligence, then it will be timely to review the question whether Aristotle could not have contrived to accommodate together both akrasia as pretheoretically described and eudaimonia as theoretically described (still appealing solely to reason). This will require some reexamination of the *autarkeia* or self-sufficiency condition that Aristotle seems to impose on happiness, and a preparedness to complicate his account of how contentment can exist in a world of value-conflict.

The *De anima* passage, taken as I have taken it, claims that there will always be a greater good. It does not imply that there will be no grounds for regret about that which is deemed to be the lesser good. And it does not itself imply that everything that matters about an alternative necessarily registers in the measurement of it in respect of eudaimonia. Nor does it imply that if course x is better in respect of eudaimonia than course y, then there is no desirable feature that y offers that x does not offer too, by way of an equal or greater degree of that very feature. One might call this last *the principle of compensation in kind*. To insist on it would be to attempt to restore a proposition of the ∃ ∀ form, taking "eudaimonia-promoting" or some such dimension as an all-inclusive and sole dimension of assessment. But, so soon as we clearly formulate this principle and see that it is false, I think we shall see room for the akrates to choose the smaller good when he could have the larger, and choose it for a reason that is a *real* reason, for all that it is a *bad* reason. This can happen wherever there is no prospect of compensation in kind, and y has some peculiar or distinctive charm that the incontinent man is susceptible to.

Perhaps Aristotle has some occasional slight tendency to believe something rather like the principle of compensation in kind. Perhaps this underlies his occasional claims that even the purely pleasurable appears to us under the aspect of good. ("The pleasure of the moment appears pleasurable quite simply and good quite simply because of lack of regard for the future." *De anima* 433b8-10.) But what is important is that it will take only a very slight change of focus to exempt his construction from this intolerable burden. In the definition of self-sufficiency, we need not take "lacking in nothing" to mean "lacking in nothing at all that would be found valuable by anybody pursuing whatever course," only "lacking in nothing that a man who had chosen the great good of eudaimonia would regard as worth bothering with." And that surely is all that the Book 9 passage really demands on behalf of eudaimonia. Both temperance and continence are still possible on these conditions. There is still room for some men to be temperate while others are merely continent. And it is not exhortation that makes the difference, but rationality generously conceived (i.e., not the instrumental rationality prescribed by an abstract a priori construction), ruling not a despotical rule but the constitutional rule of a statesman or prince over his free subjects, as Aristotle puts it at *Politics* 1254b3-5. Reason simply reveals the real possibility of eudaimonia.

Conceiving eudaimonia and the philosopher's task in these terms, we relinquish certain prospects we might have thought we ought to have had of proving conclusively the in all respects overwhelming superiority of the life or lives that can be shown by Aristotle's consensual-cum-descriptive method to be the best; and we are en route to further and comparable doubts, not only about whether Aristotle's problem of eudaimonia admits of a unique solution but also about whether there are external or independent notions of rationality or happiness to be had such that the other-regarding virtues can be non-question-beggingly represented as rationally required for our happiness. Aristotle's philosophy is not so innocent of all ambitions for unique solutions and reasons invincible that he himself is proof here against all disappointment. But the *Nicomachean Ethics* offers the reader all manner of consolation. It describes, elucidates, and amplifies the actual concerns of human life, and makes transparent to theory the way in which these concerns necessitate, where they do necessitate, the actions or decisions in which they issue. Those who find that this is enough in practice to retain their interest in the subject will find that they can drop Aristotle's doctrine of the akrates' ignorance of the minor premise and complete the neo-Aristotelian doctrine of incontinence that I began in sections I and II. But rather than prosecute that here, it is necessary for me to conclude by attending to two intermediate matters. The first relates to commensurability, and the second to the nature of the philosophical problem of weakness of will. (A name I hope to have done something to rehabilitate.)

VIII

The neo-Aristotelian position denies the strong, reductive commensurability we find in the *Protagoras*. Explicitly it also denies the nonreductive strong commensurability that is involved in the principle of compensation in kind. These are both $\exists \forall$ principles. It would recommend that Aristotle persevere cautiously in some however qualified form of the $\forall \exists$ thesis of the *De anima* 434a5-10. (Rather than draft the qualification, I indicated the nature of serious doubts about the unqualified claim.) But what would distinguish such a position from the utility-maximizing $\exists \forall$ models of man that are proposed by some social scientists? The question must be asked because it is a common charge among the tender-minded that economists and others disregard the plurality and mutual irreducibility of goods.[22] And Aristotle himself is sometimes cited as a witness for value pluralism.

The maximizing type of theory with which I have to contrast Aristotle's theory may be seen as a normative theory of rational individual choice (individual choice in the first instance, later social choice, but we shall scarcely reach out to that), where the rationality in question is relative to the objective of maximizing by reference to a utility measure actually specified for some individual consumer. Alternatively, the theory may be seen as a specification of the actual motivation of some individual consumer, this being ascertained and tested on the methodological assumption that this consumer tries consistently to maximize with respect to the said utility measure. For my purposes it makes no difference in which light the theory is seen. Either way what results is a would-be specification, not only of the subject's actual motivation, that is, his springs of action, but also of the constraints under which he is seen as a utility-maximizer; and either way the individual's utility measure is specified as a function from goods (X_i) and evils (A_j) to total utility, and given in the form $U = f(X_1 \ldots X_g, A_1 \ldots A_h)$. The function f is plotted as an indifference map in $g + h$ dimension, which orders as lesser or greater various, variably mixed, equally wanted packets of the g types of good and h types of evil.

Meaning can be given to incommensurability within this theory by reference to the case where choices actually made by the subject leave indeterminacy about how certain goods or evils trade off for him against certain other goods or evils. But, insofar as the theory aspires to any completeness in what it undertakes, it aims to state the terms on which anything will trade off against anything else with respect to utility contribution. The commensurability that results is nonreductive, and it contrasts sharply with the commensurability mooted in *Protagoras.*[23] One overreaching consideration is postulated, however—namely, maximization of the subject's total utility. There is something *u* (namely, utility) such that, for any decision the subject has to make between possible courses of action, there is an indifference curve on which each possible choice can be located for purposes of comparison in respect of *u* with the other possible choices.

This last is an $\exists \; \forall \; \exists$ proposition, and what I claim is that any similarity between what this promises and what is entailed by the neo-Aristotelian theory of "eudaimonia maximization" is superficial in the extreme.

First, even if the Aristotelian theory were seen as an empirically based proposal for an agent's rationality with respect to his eudaimonia, or were seen under another aspect as a theory of the subject's eudaimonia-valuations ascertained and tested on the assumption that he is consistently seeking eudaimonia, it would certainly not purport to describe or exhaust all his springs of action. Weak or perverse doings would have to lie outside the ambit of the theory. It would be expected that a separate enumeration of the springs of action would treat of the valuations of pleasures which the subject is susceptible to and is not compensated for in kind when he relinquishes them for the sake of eudaimonia. Such an enumeration could be autonomous and, say, phenomenological in character; and it would also be expected to describe in full the nature and grounds of all the other chagrins and regrets (*metameleiai*) the subject experienced in making the decisions he made under constraints of various kinds. Chagrin may sometimes speak more clearly than action itself of his values. (The difficulty of choice is not merely epistemological, which is all there is room for such problems to be when they are seen as problems of hitting on the utility-maximizing response.) An account like this of what an agent put a value upon and had *a* reason to choose (contrast a theory of what it would be rational all things considered for him to choose) could be expected to *feed into* an account of the subject's conception of eudaimonia and of the choices he would make for the sake of that.

Second, the *De anima* passage is wholly exempt from the principal difficulty or implausibility of the maximization theory:

> We can derive a rational choice for any given objective and constraint, but we must have both an objective and a constraint, and we must keep clear which is which. . . . the consumer is said to maximize utility, and utility is defined as that which the consumer attempts to maximize. This truism is completely general and cannot be false. Since he is motivated to make choices by a desire to achieve his objective, we can further say that the level of utility achieved depends upon the choices he makes. If he is choosing among goods, utility is a function of the volumes of the goods acquired.[24]

Here what is represented as a truism requires a prior premise to the effect that there is something the subject seeks to maximize. (What is at issue is no more innocuously truistic than the first premise of a well-known argument that begins "God is by definition that being which is omniscient, omnipotent, and benevolent [a being than which no greater being can be conceived].") The statement that there is something the subject seeks strictly to maximize is not itself a definition, and must be allowed to take its chance with other empirical sentences. It would be indirectly falsified if, in spite of heroic efforts to formulate the individual utility functions of the kind that theories of this general form assume or hypothesize that individual agents attempt to maximize, applied-utility theorists encountered no significant success, or no better success than theorists of other persuasions—psychologists or historians or entrepreneurs and their market researchers. Saying the very specific thing it does say, and the utility function having the special form it does have, the statement that individuals maximize their utility is anything but a truism. To defend it as a truism is to make into humbug everything that social scientists say in deference to Popper about falsification.[25]

What about the corresponding Aristotelian proposition about eudaimonia? It too is not immune from empirical upset. For there may be absolutely no specification of eudaimonia that will muster the appeal which Aristotle's construction depends upon. (See sections V, VI—requirements that survive the withdrawal of the principle of compensation in kind.) But, unlike utility, eudaimonia is not built up from a set of packages of goods (or *agatha kath' hauta*) which the theory claims the agent will seek to maximize if he is rational. So the theory does not require what the utility theory will require. The judgment that one course of action is better than another is not arrived at in this way at all, but by reference to the agent's preexisting conception (constantly informed and reshaped by circumstance) of the life that it is good for a man to attempt to realize.[26] The judgment that one course of action represents a greater good than some other course is *consequential* or *supervenient* upon that.

Third, precisely because the striving for eudaimonia, conceived as the explanation of some actions, reaches behind behavior and behind the desires that explain behavior to the thoughts and feelings that lie behind desire, the Aristotelian theory, however discursive and descriptive and low-level it may be, provides a much more intelligible theory of conduct than a utility theory, which has practically nothing to say about what organizes the indifference curves that make up an individual's total schedule of preferences—and still less to say about how extrapolation is even possible to the untested counterfactual choices of its subject from observations of the actual choices of its subject taken under quite different circumstances and different constraints. The utility theory needs to be a psychological theory at this point: but it does not even have the form of one, let alone the content.

A fourth and final difference is worth noting. Like the utility theory of individual choice, the Aristotelian theory has its social counterpart. In Aristotle's *Politics* that form of government is held to be best in which every man, whoever he is, can act well and live happily. But the theory does not subserve a program for social action to maximize anything. (See point two above.) *A fortiori* it does not extrapolate into (or project onto) the future, a future supposed to be Utopian,[27] desires conceived by men in circumstances held *ex hypothesi* to be unsatisfactory and intolerably constraining. Insofar as it suggests a social program, the program is only for the removal of the public impediments to eudaimonia.

IX

It is useful to distinguish between (i) giving an account of mind and value that *leaves room* for weakness of will, (ii) *describing* or *anatomizing* weakness of will in convincing detail, and (iii) *explaining* weakness of will. I have concentrated on (i) and on the discrediting of principles that make (i) difficult. There has been a little of (ii). And on the level of reasons a little about (iii). (Here, under explaining itself, there is a further distinction between explanation in terms of reasons and explanation in, say, physiological terms of why, of two men who saw a situation the same way, one acted weakly and the other matched his action to his evaluation.)

My strategy has been first to reduce the size of the explanandum by giving a nonreductive account of deciding that, deciding to, and so forth. This account demonstrates the exposure of the process of thinking and then acting to all sorts of mishap; according to it, none of these break-downs comes close to threatening a conceptual connection. As a result of our accepting the nonreductive account, I believe that we can then come to be satisfied by a smaller and less ambitious theory of weakness than other philosophical pictures of the phenomenon standardly make it re-quire. (There is in a sense less to explain.) By these means, I have also hoped to offer an explanation that works on the level of reasons but leaves knowledge intact. Incommensurability came into this, but I did not introduce it in order to ascribe any instability to understanding (if such instability be required for the weakness that is *moral* weakness, then that is something quite special to moral weakness) or to excite (what might nonetheless be welcome) any skepticism about that which is known. Incommensurability was introduced in conjunction with the idea of the falsity of the principle of strict compensation in kind, and in order to suggest the heterogeneity of the psychic sources of desire satisfaction and evaluation (both the evaluation consequential upon desire and the evaluation which desire is consequential upon). The notions of "dia-chronic rationality" and "the overall best course" inherit from this heter-ogeneity a certain liability to fragmentation.[28] They cannot live up to the standards that are set by most philosophical accounts of practical rationality.

The philosopher's business here is with the springs of action insofar as we can clarify these for ourselves as reasons for acting, and with the nature of desire. If I am right (and if I am right to take as central the weakness of will that does give itself reasons), then we cannot under-stand any of these things until we first understand values and the relation of values that conflict with one another.

NOTES

1. In October 1975 I read a paper called "Deliberation and Practical Reason" (chap. 13 of this anthology) to the Aristotelian Society. The present paper repre-sents a reworking with new beginning and ending of most of what had to be omit-ted from that paper. Except to reiterate my gratitude for the James Loeb Fellow-ship in Classical Philosophy at Harvard University in Spring 1972 under the aus-pices of Professor G. E. L. Owen, I shall not repeat all the acknowledgments reg-istered there, lest the deficiencies of this part should appear utterly inexplicable. There are new debts however to H. H. McDowell, M. F. Burnyeat, and C. A. B.

Peacocke. I have greatly benefited from discussion and correspondence with all of them and by the exchange of manuscripts on germane topics. McDowell's "The Role of *Eudaimonia* in Aristotle's Ethics" is in *Proceedings of the African Classical Associations* 15 (1979-80) and is chap. 19 of this anthology. Burnyeat's paper "Aristotle on Learning to Be Good" is chap. 5 of this anthology. Peacocke's paper "Intention and Akrasia" is forthcoming in *Essays for Donald Davidson*, ed. Merrill Provence Hintikka and Bruce Vermazen (Dordrecht, 1980). I am newly indebted also to Professor J. L. Ackrill, and would direct the reader to a book I regret I did not know at the time of writing either of my contributions to this anthology, namely, his *Aristotle's Ethics* (London, 1973). See esp. pp. 30, 32-33, and 272.

2. Op. cit.

3. Cf. Donald Davidson, "Weakness of Will," in *Moral Concepts*, ed. Feinberg (Oxford, 1969), p. 2.

4. The statement that *x* is the better course all things considered is to be read here not with a technical sense but with the ordinary sense which English invests it with.

5. I am much indebted here to J. C. D'Alessio, "Dispositions, Reduction Sentences, and Causal Conditionals," *Critica*, 1, 3 (1967), and to his thesis on dispositions (Oxford D. Phil., 1968).

6. People say that Lord Brabazon of Tara was in the habit of doing just this, in order to demonstrate the relative safety of paraffin as a fuel for aeroplane engines.

7. Iris Murdoch, "Vision and Choice in Morality," *The Aristotelian Society, Supplementary Volume* 28 (1954), 42.

8. For the notion of an executive virtue see D. F. Pears, "Aristotle's Analysis of Courage," *Midwest Studies in Philosophy* 3 (1978).

9. See especially *De anima* 433b29-30, *De motu animalium* 702a18-19, 700b17-35; and the account of *phantasia* offered by Martha Craven Nussbaum in Essay V in her *Aristotle's "De motu animalium"* (Princeton, 1978).

10. Cf. Susan Khin Zaw, "Irresistible Impulse and Criminal Responsibility" in *Human Values*, ed. G. N. A. Vesey (Hassocks, Sussex, 1978).

11. See "Are Moral Requirements Hypothetical Imperatives?" *The Aristotelian Society, Supplementary Volume* 52 (1978), 13-29.

12. "Tithenai ta Phainomena," in *Aristotle*, ed. J. M. E. Moravcsik (London, 1968).

13. It will be worth reckoning up the similarities and differences between Aristotle and Socrates here. Aristotle does not think *akrasia* is an unusable term. He merely redescribes the phenomenon. Socrates would appear to have thought the term itself was unusable and irremediably confused. Both think the phenomenon that goes under this name has to do with culpable ignorance: but the nature of the ignorance is different. For Socrates the ignorance is typically general in character; whereas for Aristotle the ignorance is of something particular, something here and now. (N.B. the careful stipulation *prin en to pathei genesthai* at 1145b30.) Both believe in the interpenetration of knowledge with virtue, and in *some* form of the thesis of the unity of virtue. But what Aristotle believes is weaker, and per-

mits him far greater theoretical freedom in the separate but interdependent characterizations of the individual virtues.

14. See B. A. O. Williams, "Deciding to Believe," in *Problems of the Self* (Cambridge, 1972); or D. Wiggins, "Freedom, Knowledge, Belief and Causality," in *Knowledge and Necessity*, ed. Vesey (London, 1970).

15. Compare here Donald Davidson, "Mental Events," in *Experience and Theory*, ed. Foster and Swanson (London, 1971).

16. As regards these terms and Aristotle's construction I have been both influenced and persuaded by John McDowell's "The Role of *Eudaimonia* in Aristotle's *Ethics*."

17. Cf. *NE* 1104a30-33, a requirement going well beyond the conceptual requirements suggested by the need to attend to the point that Socrates is represented in *Republic* Book 1 as making against Polemarchus—that on Polemarchus' definition of justice it might just as well be said that the concept of a just man and the concept of a thief overlap or coincide.

18. *NE* 1166a10-29 in the translation of W. D. Ross, except for the last sentence, on which see the translation and discussion of Martha Nussbaum, op. cit., pp. 223-224.

19. The passage is cited by Martha Nussbaum, op. cit., and by M. F. Burnyeat, op. cit., who provides at his n. 29 a comprehensive list of passages of Aristotle that bear on his views about evaluative commensurability.

20. The paraphrase of the last sentence quoted depends heavily on Martha Nussbaum's theory, op. cit., Essay 5, that the noun *phantasia* holds onto its connection with the verb *phainesthai* and stands for what results from being appeared to by something. In this case it is the good. The deliberator has two or more partial notions of the apparent good and has to harmonize or unify them here and now into a practicable plan for the actual realization of the good.

21. Similar remarks could be made about the theory of preferability adumbrated at *Prior Analytics* 68a25-b7, cited by Burnyeat. "Measure" is somewhat otiose, then, at 434a. See below, VIII, paragraph 7, on "greater good."

22. For references to modern writings on commensurability see my "Truth, Invention and the Meaning of Life," *Proceedings of the British Academy* 42 (1976), 368 n. 1; and add to the references to Williams, Berlin, Kolnai, etc. Leszek Kolakowski, "In Praise of Inconsistency," in *Marxism and Beyond* (London, 1969) and Stuart Hampshire, *Morality and Pessimism* (Cambridge, 1972).

23. Cf. Brian Barry, *Political Argument* (London, 1965), pp. 3-8, which also illustrates the method of indifference maps.

24. D. M. Winch, *Analytical Welfare Economics* (Harmondsworth, Middlesex, 1971), p. 17, a work I choose not because of any special vulnerability to the objection I shall attempt to make, but for its signal clarity and philosophical and historical sense.

25. No doubt some theorists will propose that the statement is a regulative maxim or a principle of interpretation of behavior, and above the melee of falsifiable sentences. Such a theorist should study the gruesome fate of the so-called Principle of Charity, which was defended by Quine and Davidson as a principle of radical interpretation. It *may* be a truism that, whatever an agent does, we can

represent his choices *ex post facto* by indifference maps. But such a description of choices need not be projectible in Goodman's sense. Nor is *this* truism equivalent to the claim, which must, if it be significant and true, import projectibility, that there is something an agent maximizes and this is his utility.

26. See "Deliberation and Practical Reason," concluding pages.

27. Or *Glanzbild der Zukunft* as Burkhardt put it, with an ambiguity Aurel Kolnai used to enjoy pointing out between "a resplendent image of the future" and "the mirage of the future."

28. Cp. Thomas Nagel, *Mortal Questions* (Cambridge, 1979), pp. 128-141.

15

Akrasia and Pleasure: Nicomachean Ethics Book 7

Amélie Oksenberg Rorty

Aristotle's discussion of *akrasia* in Book 7 of the *Nicomachean Ethics* is a natural continuation of his account of the contributions that the varieties of the intellectual virtues make to the virtuous practical life.[1] In Book 6 Aristotle has drawn a strong conceptual connection between at least some of the intellectual virtues—*phronesis* and *sophia*—and practical virtue (1144b15-25); must he, therefore, join Socrates in linking all forms of wrongdoing to ignorance? Like Socrates, Aristotle holds that the true (although opaque) object of desire is the good for man (*NE* 1.1-2); does it, therefore, follow that all ignorant action involves involuntary ignorance of the same thing: ignorance of what constitutes *eudaimonia*?

The Socratic position has three separable theses: (1) no person voluntarily does (what he takes to be) bad; (2) acting virtuously requires—indeed, is identical with—(acting from) knowledge; so acting badly is acting from or in ignorance; (3) there is fundamentally one object of moral knowledge, the Good. It follows that all forms of wrongdoing are essentially the same and that they all involve involuntary ignorance of the Good. Once Aristotle has tied virtue to phronesis, he must face the question whether he is committed to a version of the Socratic position: that wrongdoing involves a failure of practical wisdom (phronesis), that it essentially involves ignorance of what is good.[2]

Because he has already shown in Book 3 (1110b17ff. and 1113b30 ff.) that ignorance can be voluntary, or at any rate that some actions done in ignorance are voluntary, he need not dwell on the demonstration that at

least some forms of wrongdoing are voluntary, if anything is. But he
must still show that not all voluntary wrongdoing is alike. By building on
the distinctions he has drawn in Book 6 between varieties of intellectual
activity to which there correspond varieties of objects of knowledge,
Aristotle can show that there are varieties of ignorance. The next step is
to show that varieties of wrongdoing can be distinguished by distinguishing varieties of ignorance. But the Socratic problem might be thought to
remain: if each form of wrongdoing corresponds to a variety of ignorance, it might still be the case that each kind of ignorance is, in its own
way, involuntary. So Aristotle must also show that the varieties of ignorance that mark the varieties of wrongdoing are, by the canons set down
in Book 3, voluntary. This he does by diagnosing the sources, the charac-
terological sources, of akratic ignorance. Aristotle is forced to argue on
several fronts at once. While the first part of Book 7 focuses largely on
akrasia as a complex class of great interest, the task of the analysis is to
give a taxonomic mapping of the varieties of voluntary wrongdoing. But
having established in Book 3 that there is voluntary ignorant action and
in the beginning of Book 7 that the varieties of wrongdoing correspond to
varieties of ignorance, he has not yet established that the varieties of
ignorance involved in wrongdoing are the sorts of ignorance that are
blameworthy, rather than merely despicable.

For practical as well as for philosophic purposes it is important to be
able to diagnose the failures of the various sorts of wrongdoers, to understand the sources of their ignorance. Are they capable of some sorts of
responsible action? What are the chances of their improvement? We do
not know how to deal with the varieties of wrongdoers until we understand why they failed to act from knowledge that was in principle available to them. They could have acted otherwise, they might be thought
capable of knowing better: why did they not?

Aristotle's diagnosis of the sources of akratic ignorance picks up one
strand in the Socratic description of the phenomena: that the person is
led by pathe[3] like a slave, dragged around by (the thought of) pleasure.
For Socrates this shows that wrongdoing is involuntary: a person is misled by pleasure and could be misled by pleasure only because he does not
really know what is good. His response to pleasure is just another symptom of involuntary ignorance of what is really to his benefit. Aristotle
accepts one aspect of the Socratic description, that the wrongdoer, and in
particular the akrates, is misled by pleasure. But he stands the description
on its head: the akrates is not ignorant because he is misled by pleasure;
rather, his being misled by pleasure is an instance of, or sometimes the
consequence of, a culpable ignorance. It emerges that there are varieties
of akrasia, distinguishable by their origins. There are several ways that

the akrates can come to have forgotten the import of what he knows, different ways that a person can be misled by pathos. But to understand how a person can get pleasure (and honor) right *and* get them wrong, we need a full investigation of the character of pleasure. The taxonomy of voluntary wrongdoing remains incomplete until we have an explanation of the variety of ways that a person can be so mistaken about pleasure that he can be misled by it, and an account of how a person who is misled by pleasure can nevertheless be acting voluntarily. The discussion of pleasures at the end of Book 7 is a direct continuation of the analysis of akrasia. It is part of Aristotle's answer to Socrates: the intellectual failures of some wrongdoers rest in the sorts of character traits for which they are responsible, the ways they conceive of, and react to, pleasure.

I

What are the phenomena that, according to Aristotle, are denied by Socrates? The usual story is that the Socratic claims lead to a denial of akrasia. But the phenomena to be saved are those announced at the beginning of Book 7, the distinctions between varieties of wrongdoing (1145a15 ff.). The Socratic position not only denies that there is voluntary wrongdoing but also that there are significantly different ways (and not merely different degrees) of being ignorant and significantly different types of things of which to be ignorant. The part of the Socratic doctrine which makes all ignorant wrongdoing involuntary has already been discussed in Book 3; so the phenomena at issue in Book 7 cannot be simply that there is action that is both ignorant and voluntary. The issue at hand is then a different one: it is that of showing that there are varieties of wrongdoing, each of which involves a different sort of voluntary ignorance.

After laying out the range of dialectical views on the subject and dispatching Academic attempts to save both the phenomena and Socratic doctrine by distinguishing knowledge from opinion (*doxa*) (1145b31 ff. and 1146b24 ff.), Aristotle turns to his own attempts to save the phenomena and to do justice to the existing opinions. One of the first distinctions he introduces is that between active and potential knowledge (1146-b31 ff. and 1147a10 ff.). But Socrates is the last person to deny that it is possible to be ignorant in one way and not in another, or to have unactualized potential knowledge. The distinction between innate knowledge of the Good and the actualization of such knowledge is the cornerstone of Socratic ethics, just as the distinction between innate knowledge of the forms and recollected knowledge is the cornerstone of Socratic epistemology. Aristotle's distinction between actual and potential knowledge is a refinement of the Socratic distinction between innate knowledge and its active exercise. Aristotle introduces further subdivisions in the Socratic distinction: he first distinguishes knowledge that is actively used from knowledge that has been acquired and is available to be used without actually being exercised (1146b31 ff.). He then distinguishes two ways that a person can have knowledge without actually exercising it (1147a11 ff.). A person can have knowledge which he is not using but which he could straightway use when the occasion requires, because nothing about his condition prevents its actualization (as a mathematician knows the Pythagorean theorem when he is at the theater, absorbed in *Oedipus*). Or he may have knowledge that he is not using because his condition prevents his doing so even when the occasion is appropriate (as a drunken mathematician is [in a condition that will make him] unable to count money to pay for his drink). Such knowledge is doubly potential: both the circumstances and the person's condition would have to be changed for the knowledge to be brought into play. And yet the knowledge is not purely potential: the person has learned it, has exercised it, and could do so again when the impediment is removed. If the person is responsible for having got himself in the condition where he cannot use knowledge that he has, he is responsible for what he does in that condition because he is responsible for his ignorance (1110b9 ff.). It is this modification in the Socratic distinction between actual and potential knowledge—that a person can sometimes be held responsible for being in a condition where he cannot exercise his knowledge—which serves as the lever in Aristotle's analysis.

But Aristotle does not think that these distinctions are sufficient to explain or save the phenomena. After all, how could Socrates deny, while Aristotle saves, the phenomena, if Aristotle's explanation only involves a variation on what are cited as the grounds for the Socratic denial? A further battery of distinctions is required to supplement that between degrees and conditions of the actualization of potential knowledge.

As there are distinct intellectual virtues that are exercised in practical reasoning, so there are distinct modes of ignorance and irrationality. While a person could not be a rational, responsible agent without having some threshold level of the range of intellectual virtues, they are not as strongly interdependent as are the practical virtues. The Socratic position on wrongdoing rests on a doctrine of the unity of the intellectual as well as of the moral virtues; in both cases there are only variations in degrees of the actualization of innate knowledge and virtue, where these are always coordinated. Aristotle's distinction between at least some of the practical and some of the theoretical virtues rests on his distinctions between the varieties of intellectual virtues. A person can be clever without being wise, or superbly intuitive about discerning the general in the particular without being good at demonstrating or deriving particulars from general principles (1152a10-14). Beyond a basic threshold level that sets a minimum condition for rationality, a person's knowledge may be at different stages of actualization for various types of intellectual activity. Since the various intellectual virtues have their respective proper objects, a person can be ignorant of general principles while being knowledgeable about particulars, and vice versa (1140b30 ff.; 1141b33 ff.; 1142a32 ff.; 1142b35 ff.).

Having sketched Aristotle's strategies in Book 7, we can turn to the details of his taxonomic analysis. The extreme case of the brutish man (*theriotes*) can almost be discounted as a variety of voluntary wrongdoing. The brutish person can hardly be called a responsible agent, because he only marginally knows what he is doing. Set a plate before him and he eats, hungry or not, good food or not. It is not even the thought of pleasure that moves him: his actions are not in any way thoughtful. Extreme akrasia or self-indulgence (*akolasia*) may resemble the behavior of the theriotes, but the resemblance is merely superficial: the condition of the theriotes is quite distinct (1148b24-1149a24).

The bad man (*kakos*), the self-indulgent man (*akolastos*), and the akrates are capable of voluntary and even deliberate action (1113b5-1115a3). They have the sorts of traits that make intentional action possible: they are constitutionally sound, capable of normal and relatively fine sensory discrimination, and constitutionally capable of acting and reacting within a mean. They also have a range of intellectual virtues that make inference possible: they have general principles, are able to apply them to draw conclusions in particular situations, and can engage in relatively long inductive and demonstrative inferences; having reasoned, they are able to act in accordance with their reasoning rather than from any stray cause.

Unlike the akrates, the kakos is a man who is ignorant of the general principles of human action: he is mistaken in his ends. He has ends—he is the sort of person who can act in the light of his ends—but he has the wrong ends. Since he is capable of voluntary action, he is the sort of person who could revise his ends: he has the constitutional and intellectual traits that make such revision possible, even though it remains unlikely that he will change. The akrates, however, does have the right ends: he really has a general knowledge of what is good and does not merely know the formulae that express such knowledge. Indeed, he may have the same general opinions as the *phronimos*. Behaviorally, the akrates is often confused with the akolastos because they both tend to go wrong about matters of pleasure. But they are ignorant of different sorts of things; their conditions are distinct (1150b29-1151a1).

Unlike the akrates, the self-indulgent man (akolastos) is a type of kakos. He is a bad man, not a weak one. He is self-indulgent as a matter of principle (1118a1 ff.; 1150b29 ff.). As we shall see when we turn to Aristotle's discussion of pleasure, this means that he separates his pleasure in an activity from the nature of the activity; he pursues his pleasure in the activity rather than finds his pleasures in pursuing the proper end of the activity. Because he misconceives what is really good about what he does, he finds his pleasure in the wrong place. The akolastos is misled by pleasure, because he does not know what is good. The akrates, in contrast, temporarily forgets his knowledge of what is good because he has put himself in a situation and in a condition in which his perceptions of pleasure are so affected that he acts from his reactions (pathe) rather than from his knowledge (1151a20-28).

Since getting matters right about pleasure is so central to the virtues, there is a question about whether the self-indulgent man (akolastos) is really distinguishable from the bad man (kakos). As Aristotle says in distinguishing political and practical wisdom, however, they are the same characteristic, but their essential aspect is different (1141b23 ff.). As the measured, temperate man (sophron) stands to the man of practical wisdom (phronimos), so the self-indulgent man (akolastos) stands to the bad man (kakos). While getting the mean in relation to pleasure is central to virtue, a person cannot acquire all the virtues by learning how to get proportions right for each occasion. The man of practical wisdom requires a large range of particular habits: he must know what to do as well as how to do it. Because the pleasure of each activity is determined by the nature of the activity, the analysis of sophrosune is formal: it must be supplemented by a substantive account of the other virtues that the phronimos has. The phronimos is a sophron; but the description of sophrosune does not give a sufficient or complete account of phronesis. Similarly, while being mistakenly self-indulgent about pleasures is central to kakia, the analysis of akolasia would be insufficient to account for the way the kakos fails to understand the good of each activity. It is because the akolastos does not understand the ends of his activities that he concentrates on his own pleasures, and not vice versa. His self-indulgence does not cause but rather consists in his mistaking the real ends of what he does (1117b22-1119b18).

The akrates has the general knowledge which the kakos lacks. His failure is a function of some other form of ignorance or irrationality. Yet the akrates is not necessarily stupid; indeed, like the vicious person, he can be quite clever. But a clever person can be quite irrational. Sometimes the akrates acts impulsively: he can fail to think about whether the situation before him falls under his general principles about what is good (1150b-19). Or if he does think about what he is doing, he does not see the particular case properly: he misperceives or misdescribes what is before him. Or even if he gets it right, he can fail to connect it with his general principles, fail to see the import of his knowledge. He then fails to draw the right conclusion about what to do, either making the wrong decision or failing to act from the decision implicit in his beliefs. These are varieties of failures of mind, whose origins lie in the sorts of failures of character for which a person can be responsible. They are failures that are compatible with a person's having the right general principles, having them to a relatively high degree of actualization.

When practical reasoning is articulated in the form of a practical syllogism, the failure of the akrates is identified either as a failure in his knowledge of the minor premise (the proper formulation of the state of affairs in which he finds himself) or as a failure to connect the major premise to the minor premise in such a way as to draw the appropriate conclusion (1147a24-1147b4). Some commentators have interpreted this as a difference between knowledge of value (in the major) and knowledge of fact (in the minor). Aristotle's position is far more subtle. He does not draw a sharp distinction between fact and value—not at any rate in a hard-and-fast way. He says, for instance, that the failure of knowledge in the minor premise may be a failure of knowledge about what sort of man one is (*De anima* 434a16-21; less directly: *NE* 1147a5-7 and 1147a29-34). Such a failure of knowledge is a failure to remember one's constitution or character; but this means forgetting what is good for that type of constitution or character. To forget, in the face of sweets, that one is diabetic is to forget what is good for oneself. Or for a man to forget that he is the sort of person who, when drunk, ignores his normal principled precision about the marital status of his lady friends is to forget a truth with practical import. To forget what sort of man one is can be to forget how one's character embeds one's ends. This is compatible with remembering those ends, but remembering them abstractly.

On the Socratic account, ignorance of pleasure entails ignorance of pain, and vice versa. Both are fundamentally ignorance of the Good, of proper proportion. But Aristotle distinguishes objects as well as modalities of knowledge: a person can be ignorant or irrational about pain independently of being so about pleasure. This distinguishes the "soft" man (*malakos*) from the akrates, the *enkrates* from the person of endurance. The malakos gives way to pain, acting so as to avoid it despite his judgment that in some situations it is inappropriate to do that; the man of endurance (*karterikos*) resists pain, gauging his actions by their general appropriateness rather than simply by their painfulness. The akrates gives way to pleasure, the enkrates resists it. He is tempted by pleasure: he can be affected by it as much as the akrates. The difference is that he does not act from his reactions: he holds out against them and continues to act in accordance with his ends (1150a9-32).

What then is the relation between the phronimos and the enkrates? Are they the same person, differently described, distinctively characterized? Characteristically, the phronimos does not have to use knowledge to resist the lures of pleasures (1145b13-14). Because he does not perceive what fails to accord with his ends as pleasurable, he is in the fortunate position, as the enkrates is not, of being unconflicted. Indeed, it is precisely this unconflicted condition that assures both his reliability and his pleasure in what he does. Because his pleasures are coordinate with his knowledge, acting from knowledge will be pleasurable for him; since his actions are pleasurable, they are all the more motivationally secure. But the phronimos does not differ from the akrates in being without passions: on the contrary, acting rightly with respect to his passions, having them in a mean, is one of the conditions of his virtue. In order to be courageous he must have the proper habits of fear; in order to be properly self-respecting he must have the proper habits of indignation. Sometimes, acting from his pathe *is* acting in accordance with reason; but there might also be times when even the phronimos might have to act as if he were an enkrates, exercising forethought as a form of *enkrateia*, to avoid putting himself in the position of naturally strong temptation, a position in which predictably he would at best be conflicted or at worst behave as an akrates. (It is just such foresight that Odysseus used in having himself bound and gagged, knowing that when he heard the song of the sirens he would head for the rocks.)

II

Once we have a taxonomy of wrongdoing which has reconciled dialectical opinion on the *aporiai* concerning voluntary wrongdoing, we still do not have a clear idea of what goes wrong and why. How can the akrates who has the same basic beliefs, the same general intellectual, emotional, and motivational equipment as the phronimos go wrong? The problem is particularly stark because Aristotle retains the Platonic connection between a person's ends, his principles, and his habits of action. How can what is so closely conceptually connected be dissociated in the action of the akrates?

It is helpful to look at the varieties of akrasia to see what sorts of things can go wrong with the akrates' habits about matters of pleasure and how these habits affect his ability to use his general knowledge. While the akrates has the right theoretical attitudes toward pleasures, he does suffer a weakness for them.

The standard Platonic explanation of the akrates' ignorance is that he is dragged about like a slave by *epithumia*, overcome by pleasure or the hope of pleasure. Again Aristotle's discussion begins with what is essentially a Platonic formula; but he finds it necessary to elaborate it, to add further distinctions. (Whether these additions are articulations or modifications of the Platonic positions seems to me to be a moot point. One could read the *Republic* as developing the theme that failures of knowledge also involve failures of character-based habits, that knowledge and character are correlative. Much of the argument, however, stresses the priority of knowledge. Whether the full account of that knowledge preserves its nonintellectualistic elements is an issue unlikely to be settled soon or to everyone's satisfaction.)

What then is it for the akrates to be diverted from his use of his knowledge, being dragged around by pathos? Of course, pathos is not necessarily passionate. The akrates need not be in the throes of anything intense or even powerful. His action can but need not be violent, abrupt, inelegant. To be moved by passion is simply to be moved by something primarily outside oneself, to react rather than to act. Passion-based actions are still voluntary when the person is responsible for putting himself in the position where he could predictably be so affected; or a person could be responsible for developing the habit of reacting that way (1114-a25 ff.). The akrates is affected by the thought of pleasure: he reacts to it, and it is the manner of his reaction rather than his end-defined desires which determines what he does. He has the right conceptions of the proper ends of his various activities, and so in principle he knows in what their goods and pleasures really consist. In reacting to situations, being moved by the thought of some pleasure, he is not (as Aristotle is careful to show in his discussions of both hedonism and antihedonism) acting compulsively, mindlessly, or involuntarily. It is precisely because the discussion of pleasure in Book 7 is a continuation and development of the discussion of akrasia that Aristotle is at pains to show that a person who is motivated by the thought of pleasure (whether or not he is correct in his conception of pleasure) can be acting voluntarily.

One of the ways of distinguishing varieties of pleasure is to distinguish their sources (1147b22-1148b33). In some cases this also defines their proper objects. There are (1) pleasures that are associated with necessary activities of the body, with food and drink and sex, the pleasure of taste and touch, and (2) pleasures that are not associated with necessary physical species-sustaining activities but (a) with activities that are intrinsically desirable (contemplation and virtue) or (b) with processes or activities that come to be desirable (only to some sorts of people) through accidents of development (the pleasures of recuperation or convalescence) or through some accident of perversion (the pleasures of the cannibal), or (c) with activities of the "intermediate class," neither intrinsically good nor only accidentally or perversely desirable: the assurance of material goods, wealth, victory, and honor. It is this last class, and its relation to basic epithumetic pleasures associated with necessary activities of the body, which is the most difficult, though not the paradigmatic, domain of akrasia (1147b20-1149a21).

Necessary bodily activities involve depletion and satiation; their pleasures are on a continuum with pains, and are identified in relation to them (1154a26-1154b32). The agent's conception of such necessary activities and their proper objects do not affect the cycle of wants and satisfactions. A person may be mistaken about the nature of sleep, having all sorts of false theories about it; and yet sleep will rest and refresh him independently of his theories. To a lesser extent this is true for eating: a person's theories about nutrition do not affect his digestion, although they can, by affecting his habits of eating, come to affect his pleasures of taste. To the extent that an activity comes to be intentionally defined, its pleasures and satisfactions are also intentionally defined. The more a person's behavior becomes intentional, the more his pleasures in his actions vary with their intentional descriptions. For those capable of seeing their actions—even actions associated with the satisfaction of species-defined epithumia—in the light of their ends, the range of behavior sensitive to intentional satisfaction is very great (1173b25-1174a1).

The primary way that a person can go wrong about the pleasures of necessary activities is to pursue them to excess or—what is, in view of the motivational force of pleasure, rarer—to fail to pursue them sufficiently.

Pleasures of the "intermediate class" are intentional in character; while they can be pursued moderately, deficiently, or to excess, they can also be pursued in the right way, under the right description, clustered properly in relation to other pleasures, with the right priorities; or they can be pursued in the wrong manner even when they are not pursued to excess. Perhaps even some of the epithumetic pleasures of the body are sensitive to misdescription in this way: a person can be misled so that he is pleased by an inappropriate feature of the activity. Someone can forget that the real point of eating is to be well nourished, and though he knows generally that granola is more nourishing than sweets, he forgets and feeds himself on sweets. He need not gorge himself on sweets; he need not eat more than the well-nourished person; indeed, he may eat quantitatively less than the person who eats properly. But when sweets are set before him, he forgets the proper pleasure of eating and concentrates on the pleasures of certain sorts of tastes rather than on the well-being that is the proper pleasure of nourishment (1152b26-1153a23; 1173b20-1171a1).

It is significant that the intermediate pleasures need not involve epithumetic pleasures: indeed, the class includes not only the satisfaction of *boulesis* but also the satisfactions appropriate to what, in Platonic terms, would be thumetic activity. For instance, a general can get carried away concentrating on winning a battle (taking the enemy on the hill) instead of assuring the victory (by defending the river valley) without being misled by an excessive zeal for fighting (he may know that there will be *more* fighting in the river valley) or a desire for *more* honor (he may know, abstractly, that honor lies in the victory rather than in high-risk boldness).

Sometimes a person's description of an action can mislead him to treat what is properly an *energeia* as if it were a process. He will then be misled in a particularly dangerous way, because he will tend to detach his pleasure as the end of a process, instead of its being embedded in and constituted by his activity. He can then come to pursue pleasure as his end, treating his action as merely what he does toward that end. Such a person is prone to the sorts of errors that arise from merely reacting to particular situations, forgetting how the point of his enterprises reflects his more general ends.

It is the manner of his reactions to pleasures that misleads the akrates: he acts from his reactions to what is before him, perceiving—misperceiving—what he does in terms of its pleasurable effects on him rather than seeing his situation, and his actions in it, as defined by his proper intentional ends. It is not that the akrates has, while the phronimos lacks, pathe. Indeed, many of the pathe of the akrates may be quite like those of the phronimos: he can fear what the phronimos fears. It is rather in the way he reacts, in the place that fear has in determining his actions, that he differs from the phronimos. If it is a question of epithumetic pleasures, his reactions fail to hit the mean: they are deficient or excessive, and their excesses determine what he does. If it is a question of intentionally defined pleasures, then he acts from his reactions rather than from those intentions that define his proper ends. For instance, the akratic general can get carried away by the excitement of the battle instead of acting from his understanding of a general's proper honor. Because this latter sort of mistake has a thought component, it is not the most base form of akrasia; but it is a form of injustice, because the person does not give his actions their proper weight (1149b20-27).

The question arises whether there is fundamentally one kind of akrasia

—akrasia haplos—a species of wrongdoing all of whose instances have common characteristics, or whether there are distinctive varieties of akrasia—akrasia kata meros—which only roughly resemble each other, and which are qualitatively distinguishable (1147b20 ff.; 1149a22-24). Aristotle treats this question by reverting to the distinction between epithumetic akrasia and akrasia that involves honor or indignation, akrasia concerning actions that are intentionally defined. The former is akrasia haplos, akrasia that involves either excess or deficiency. Presumably the reason that cases of akrasia concerning intentionally defined activities are cases of akrasia kata meros is that one would not be able to identify such cases as akratic without specifying the intentional description of the action. What goes wrong in the person's reactions is different in each type of case. Cases of akrasia kata meros form distinguishable varieties because the intentional descriptions of the actions vary. Akrasia haplos, epithumetic akrasia, is nevertheless said to be paradigmatic. Akrasia concerning the necessary pleasures of the body pursued to excess is the model for other forms of akrasia concerning, for example, honor and victory. Perhaps this is because even in the case of intentionally defined activities that involve honor and victory rather than physical pleasure, the akrates treats the good of the activity as if it were a pleasure independent of the activity that defines it. So a person might get carried away by the pleasure of being angry or the pleasures of indignation about matters of honor even when these pathe are not primarily epithumetic conditions, are not primarily matters of pleasure.

But haven't we brought Aristotle back to either the Socratic or the Platonic position? Aristotle moves to a discussion of pleasure because he must explain why the akrates is unexpectedly ignorant or forgetful. He continues with a dialectical discussion of the proper place of pleasure in the moral life, balancing the claims of hedonists on one side and of Platonists on the other. Against hedonists he argues that because pleasure is ingredient in and not product of activities, it cannot be evaluated or measured independently of the worth of the activity. For pleasures that are intentionally defined, the cause of akratic ignorance seems then to turn out itself to be a kind of ignorance, an ignorance of the real pleasures of what one does. Why does the akrates misdescribe his particular situation or fail to connect his general principles with the particular action before him, so that he emerges with an inappropriate action? He has failed to remember the pleasures proper to his situation. But isn't this just a restatement of the Socratic solution?

If Aristotle avoids the Socratic reduction of akrasia to ignorance by stressing the *condition* of the akrates at the time of his action, a condition that (like that of the drunken mathematician) makes him unable to exercise his knowledge, then he lands on the other horn of the Platonic dilemma: what he does is not voluntary (1147b6-9). It would seem that this interpretation does, after all, return Aristotle either to Socrates or to Plato. Either akrasia is ultimately a type of ignorance (the akrates being ignorant of how particular present pleasures should be connected to his general ends), or it is a sort of constitutional failure (the akrates is in a condition in which he fails to see the import of what he knows; he cannot exercise his knowledge). In either case the akrates seems not to be acting voluntarily. The only move toward saving the phenomena which Aristotle has made, it might then be argued, is his introducing the distinction between the ignorance of the akrates and that of the kakos.

But the akrates' failures of knowledge are not *merely* failures of knowledge; and the condition that generates akrasia is one in which he has voluntarily placed himself. That he has the wrong sorts of reactions, or that he acts from his reactions, or that he tends to place himself in the sorts of situations and conditions where he will predictably misperceive his pleasures and act from those misperceptions is a failure of character. He has habits that give his pathe undue dominance in the determination of his actions. He tends to treat them as if they were matters of necessity, which he could not forgo. When he is faced by certain sorts of situations—often situations he could have avoided—he detaches pleasures from their proper intentional weighting. He treats them as states he could get as the outcome of processes, quite independently of the real character of what he does. Pleasures that are *energeiai kata phusin hexeos* (1153a14-15) become pathe; he reacts to such pleasures in ways that lead him to forget what he knows. But his reacting that way falls—or can fall—within the realm of the voluntary.

III

But if the akrates' intellectual errors are based in failures of character, why is he blameworthy? His character is a result of his constitution, his early education, the habits he developed almost before he knew that they *were* habits. It is, I think, important to realize that Aristotle's attitude toward the issues of responsibility is primarily a practical one: he is interested in determining what type of person can be given responsibility to investigate the conditions for thoughtful action; he is not interested in the psychic condition of the post-Christian, post-Romantic individual. As long as it is within a person's power to have acted otherwise, as long as the person has the sorts of traits that can in their very nature be exercised in acting-or-not-acting in accord with ends, being directed by his thoughts about his ends, then that person is capable of voluntary and deliberate action. A person is not blamed or praised for the accidents of constitution and upbringing which make him capable of voluntary action. Rather, such capability is what qualifies him to be either praised or blamed. The virtuous, the vicious, and the akrates alike fill the conditions for responsible action: even when they act from habit, they do not act from compulsion. Even when (moved by pleasures) they react rather than act, they actively have all the traits and capacities that could have led them to act otherwise (1113b3-1115a6). But it is possible for a person who is incapable of voluntary actions to have bad ends. Because he is not the sort of person who can be held responsible for his character, there is a sense in which he is not capable of virtue or vice. He may be despicable, disgusting, and even dangerous, without being blameworthy. Similarly, the gods are not, in the usual sense of the term, virtuous; they are extolled, but not praised or blamed (1145a25-33).

It is a matter of fortune that a person has the traits that enable him to determine what sort of character he shall have. Few are endowed with the constitution, have the capacities or the good fortune to receive the early education that assures the sort of character that is capable of determining itself. Such people are not, among other things, capable of realizing the formative power of their habits, especially their habits of pleasure. But if one is the sort of person whose character is capable of self-determination, then one is responsible for having the sort of character one develops, because one has, by hypothesis, the sorts of traits that can determine the ends one adopts and how one acts from them (1114a30-1114b26).

The question, "Can a person voluntarily act contrary to his judgment of what, in general, is best?" has been answered. Such actions are voluntary when they are really a person's own actions: when (1) they are intentional, with the intentions being largely one's own, springing ultimately from one's ends, and (2) the agent's character is such that he could have done otherwise. The action is not determined by circumstances: the agent could have foreseen the circumstances and gauged his own situation to fit his ends. The agent does not depend on circumstances alone to actualize his dispositions and habits; he does not simply react to external events.

But doesn't this have the consequence of either making all actions voluntary or making no actions voluntary? For whether a person is capable of rational choice—whether he has the sort of character that can determine itself—depends on whether he developed the appropriate sorts of habits at a time before he could have determined those habits himself. If, however, voluntary action is simply action that flows from a person's character, even the theriotes acts voluntarily; for what he does grows out of what he is. The difference is that a person who is capable of acting voluntarily is simply one who—perhaps by accident—is capable of practical reasoning and of acting from, or in accordance with, practical reasoning. To be sure, a person could not have determined that he is that sort of person. But that is not what he is responsible for: if he is that sort of person, then he is responsible for what sort of character he has and what sorts of actions he performs. Like the kakos and the phronimos, the akrates is that sort of person.

IV

There are familiar criticisms of Book 7: that the book is an ill-organized set of random remarks, that the account of pleasure is older and cruder than that in Book 10, that Aristotle fails to notice that he has not succeeded in differentiating his position from that of Socrates.

I believe these criticisms to be unfounded. I have already argued that the book forms a coherent and unified analysis, properly placed after Book 6, and that the discussion of pleasure is a continuation of the discussion of akrasia as a form of wrongdoing. Aristotle differs from Socrates in his diagnosis of the causes of the akrates' ignorance: he emphasizes the character-sources of the akratic condition, viewing it as resting on badly formed habits concerning pleasures. Such failures have an intellectual dimension without necessarily being caused by an intellectual error. And of course Aristotle also differs from Plato in distinguishing varieties of wrongdoing and establishing that at least some are voluntary.

The question whether the distinction between Socrates' and Aristotle's positions on the issues of Book 7 marks a difference in emphasis or a difference in basic outlook has all the air of an idle question. Socrates had to direct his account largely to those who had to be persuaded of the central role of knowledge in virtuous action, while Aristotle—in the position of being able to take those arguments for granted—could concentrate on arguments against the Academy and against hedonists. The issue of whether this generates a difference in emphasis or a difference in position is not a genuine aporia but a set piece for the debater's arts.

The question whether the account of pleasure in Book 10 differs from that in Book 7 is a more serious question. It is true that the analysis of pleasure in Book 10 introduces considerations not mentioned in Book 7. But the issues at stake in the two discussions are quite different. In Book 7, in the context of a discussion of varieties of wrongdoing, we are given an account of how (despite its being a good) pleasure can mislead a person into forgetting what he knows. The account of pleasure in Book 7 appears as part of a discussion of the sources of akrasia. But in Book 10 Aristotle must make good his claim that the virtuous life assures not only Aristotelian eudaimonia but also the goods associated with traditional eudaimonia. Indeed, he wants to go further, to show how his analysis of happiness and virtue explains the plausibility of the traditional account (1098b22-30).[4]

On the traditional account, eudaimonia involves living well and faring well, having a pleasant life with the goods of a pleasant life; such a life is also honorable, worthy, and choiceworthy. That the life of the *eudaimon* contains virtue, phronesis, and sophia has already been shown in Book 6. Presumably this is sufficient to show that such a life is honorable and worthy. It remains, therefore, to show that Aristotelian eudaimonia, consisting in the actively virtuous life, is both pleasurable and compatible with the kinds of pleasure to be found in contemplation. The account of pleasure in Book 10 must, therefore, focus on the pleasures that are inherent in, and not merely consequent on, virtuous activity. And this is precisely what that account does: it shows that self-contained activities have their appropriate self-contained pleasures. Nothing in that account is incompatible with the traditional warnings of Book 7: that some sorts of pleasure can mislead.

There are other complaints. Why, it is asked, does Aristotle lapse into moralistic warnings against pleasure at all? He has, after all, established that pleasure is a good and, even more importantly, that when natural activities are properly performed, they are pleasurable, their proper pleasures revealed in the activity, the activity perfected by its pleasure. Besides his standard dialectical courtesy, the reasons for this are that the object of inquiry in the *Ethics* is, as he says, to determine how to become good and not merely to know, theoretically, what virtue is (1103b27-31). He warns against too close an attention to pleasures, and against some pleasures, in the same way as he gives counsel on how to aim at the mean for pleasures: some activities are very difficult to get just right. When they are specially tempting, one must aim at the farther side of one's goal in order to come close to getting it right (1109a3; 1109b12). While the pleasures of natural activities are, or can be, intrinsically good, a person who attends primarily to the activity as pleasurable will tend to separate out the pleasurable in the activity from the activity itself. He will come to value the activity for its pleasure instead of seeing the pleasure as dependent on the character of the activity. Even the best of men runs the danger of akrasia under those circumstances.

Aristotle might equally have warned the virtuous not to focus too much on the way their virtues empower them, or assure them with self-esteem, not to focus too closely on the ways in which the virtues work to make life conventionally successful and the virtuous self-respecting. Such a focusing would run the danger that the person might come to be primarily motivated by these considerations rather than see the extent to which they are dependent on the character of virtuous activity. The virtuous are no more virtuous for the sake of self-respect than they are for the sake of pleasure.

Aristotle is sometimes also charged with not having a clear understanding of moral conflict or of the unevenness of moral development. But his discussion of akrasia is just such an acknowledgment. The akrates is precisely the sort of person who is conflicted because his moral development is uneven. His knowledge of general principles is at a different level of actualization from his habits of perception and his habits of action. Because even general knowledge of practical principles is expressed in a tendency to action, the akrates will be conflicted: he regrets what he has done (1150b28-30).

NOTES

1. Because Aristotle has no notion corresponding to the *will, weakness of will* is a poor translation of *akrasia*. Because many cases of akrasia fall outside the moral domain, *moral weakness* is equally misleading. *Incontinence* also has unacceptable connotations. *Unrestraint* captures some of the sense, but it does not convey, as *weakness* does, the privative sense of the term. *Psychological weakness* and *powerlessness* are more appropriate, but both are too broad. For these reasons I shall simply retain the Greek.

2. The Socratic position on akrasia is stated primarily in *Protagoras* 352a-358d: it diagnoses wrongdoing as a form of involuntary ignorance. The Platonic account is advanced in the *Republic* 439a-441c. While that analysis also makes wrongdoing involuntary, it emphasizes the power of appetite (*epithumia*) in overcoming *logos* and *thumos*. The Platonic account is broader than the Socratic: ignorance would be only one explanation of the condition of the *akrates*; his constitution or upbringing might also explain his reaction. For our purposes, the distinction between the Socratic and the Platonic diagnoses of akrasia can be ignored.

3. Because the standard translations of *pathos* are unsatisfactory, I shall retain the Greek. Since *passion* has come to be thought of as a turbulent and even troubled emotional condition, it is a poor translation for *pathos*. In contrast, *passivity* suggests complete inertness; but even though pathe are not, in the strict sense, motives (because they are not determined by a person's ends and desires), a person can act from pathe. The condition can be the beginning of an action. Insofar as *affection* suggests being *affected by*, it provides a better rendering; but, of course, in ordinary discourse, *affection* is much narrower than *pathos*. *Feeling*

misleadingly suggests a subjective condition, the subject of introspection. But unnoticed bruises and scratches can be pathe. _Emotion_ is, of course, too narrow. _Modification_ correctly suggests that some expected normal condition is changed by an external event or object. But it is too broad, and is, in any case, awkward. _Reaction_ is helpful; it is paired with _action_, as _pathos_ is paired with _praxis_; and it can refer both to a person's condition in being affected and to the beginning of action or motion that can follow from that state.

4. Cf. my "The Place of Pleasure in Aristotle's Ethics," _Mind_ 83 (1974), 481-497.

BIBLIOGRAPHY

Ando, T. _Aristotle's Theory of Practical Cognition._ Kyoto, 1958.
Gauthier, R. A., and J. Y. Jolif. _Aristote: L'Éthique à Nicomaque._ 2d ed. Louvain, 1970.
Grant, A. _The Ethics of Aristotle._ London, 1958.
Hardie, W. F. R. _Aristotle's Ethical Theory._ Oxford, 1968.
Joachim, H. H. _Aristotle: The Nicomachean Ethics._ Oxford, 1955.
Kenny, A. "The Practical Syllogism and Incontinence." _Phronesis_ 11 (1966), 163-184.
Milo, R. D. _Aristotle on Practical Knowledge and Weakness of Will._ The Hague, 1966.
Owen, G. E. L. "Aristotelian Pleasures." In _Articles on Aristotle: Ethics and Politics_, edited by J. Barnes, M. Schofield, and R. Sorabji. London, 1977; New York, 1978.
Robinson, R. "Aristotle on Akrasia." In _Articles on Aristotle: Ethics and Politics_ (see preceding entry).
Rorty, A. O. "The Place of Pleasure in Aristotle's Ethics." _Mind_ 83 (1974), 481-497.
———. "Plato and Aristotle on Belief, Habit, and _Akrasia._" _American Philosophical Quarterly_ 7 (1970), 50-61.
Santas, G. "Aristotle on Practical Inference, the Explanation of Action, and Akrasia." _Phronesis_ 14 (1969), 162-189.
Stewart, J. A. _Notes on the Nicomachean Ethics of Aristotle._ Oxford, 1892.
Walsh, J. J. _Aristotle's Conception of Moral Weakness._ New York, 1963.
Wilson, J. Cook. _On the Structure of Book Seven of the Nicomachean Ethics._ Oxford, 1912.

The articles by Julia Annas, M. F. Burnyeat, L. A. Kosman, Richard Sorabji, and David Wiggins printed in this volume are also particularly helpful. I also benefited from unpublished papers that David Charles and Paul Grice were kind enough to let me read. For good counsel on an earlier draft of this paper I am grateful to Robin Jackson and to Gregory Vlastos.

16

Aristotle on Pleasure and Goodness

Julia Annas

Aristotle's two discussions of pleasure in *Nicomachean Ethics* 7 and 10 have justly been admired and have been discussed at length for their suggestions about the nature of pleasure and in particular for the striking differences between the two passages. In this paper I would like to concentrate on a different matter: a thesis which Aristotle holds about the relation of pleasure and goodness and which is common to both passages and independent of the differences between them. While he is not completely consistent about accepting the implications of this thesis throughout the *Ethics*, it is clearly his considered view and deserves attention.

The accounts in Books 7 and 10 notoriously differ over what pleasure *is*, but they agree in the thesis that pleasure is not a bad thing. In the good life it is something to be pursued, not shunned. Qualifications are necessary, however, before we speak of "pleasure" *simpliciter* at all, for pleasures differ in kind with their corresponding activities. Thus the good man takes pleasure in virtuous activities and finds the wicked man's pursuits not merely wrong but repellent. So it is right for the good man to seek pleasure; pleasure will point him in the right direction, for the pleasure proper to an activity encourages the performance of that activity, and the pain or boredom proper to it correspondingly discourages it; thus the good man's pleasure will encourage him in his tendency to perform good actions and will confirm the formation of virtuous habits. Pleasure will also, though this is less stressed, confirm the deplorable tendencies of the bad man, since it will strengthen his habits of wickedness

285

and weakness. But in either case it is wrong to think of pleasure as something that only the bad man goes in for while the good man has something better to aim at. What matters is not to avoid or minimize pleasure; this attitude is indeed castigated as a mistake. What is supremely important is to be right about pleasure, because it is only the appropriate pleasure that will lead in the right direction. Since only pleasure in good actions will lead to the performance of good actions, the good man must be right about what kind of pleasure to encourage; but when he is right, that kind is certainly to be encouraged.

This view is common to both discussions, regardless of their differing theories about the nature of pleasure. Book 7, with its doctrine that pleasure is unimpeded activity, says that "if certain pleasures are bad, that does not prevent the chief good from being some pleasure. . . . Perhaps it is even necessary, if each disposition has unimpeded activities, that, whether the activity (if unimpeded) of all our dispositions, or that of some one of them is happiness, this should be the thing most worthy of our choice; and this activity is pleasure"[1] (1153b7-12). The happy life is bound to involve pleasure as an essential part, and those who deny this are thinking of the wrong kind of pleasures. The good man will not go in for the kind of pleasures enjoyed by a child or an animal; these would indeed hinder his characteristic activities (1153a27-35), but "the pleasures arising from thinking and learning will make us think and learn all the more" (1153a22-23). There is a long diagnosis, in chapter 14, of the train of thought that leads people to claim that pleasure is in itself a hindrance to the good life. Most people who think this do so, according to Aristotle, because they are implicitly identifying pleasure with bodily pleasure—the kind of pleasure that arises from satisfying desires for food, sex, sleep, and so on, the desires that arise in the normal course of having a body. If pleasure were limited to pleasure from these sources, then it would be a hindrance to the good life, and to think of these as the only pleasures is a mark of lack of moral development. The good man's life will include these pleasures, but it will include far more, and it will be structured in such a way that the bodily pleasures have a place subordinate to intellectual and virtuous activities and the pleasures derived from these.

Book 7 also meets the objection of people who bring forward admittedly bad pleasures to support the claim that pleasure is a hindrance to the good life, and meets it with the picture of the good man as a norm. What is straightforwardly pleasant is what the good man takes pleasure in. The bad man's pleasures are only incidentally so: that is, we can only see what is pleasant about them when we take into account some feature of him or his circumstances. However, a claim that all pleasures are bad is too simplistic: "of those which are thought to be bad some will be bad if taken without qualification but not bad for a particular person, but worthy of his choice, and some will not be worthy of choice even for a particular person, but only at a particular time and for a short period, though not without qualification" (1152b29-31).

Book 10 holds that pleasure is in some way more than unimpeded activity: it perfects the activity. The discussion is more complex than that of Book 7 and notoriously differs from it in important respects. But the place of pleasure in the good life is not changed. There is the same contrast drawn between pleasures that are really pleasant and those that are only apparently so, and again the good man is said, at greater length, to be the norm: "If . . . virtue and the good man as such are the measure of each thing, those also will be pleasures which appear so to him, and those things pleasant which he enjoys. If the things he finds tiresome seem pleasant to someone, that is nothing surprising; for men may be ruined and spoilt in many ways; but the things are not pleasant, but only pleasant to these people and to people in this condition" (1176a17-22). And so again the people who say that pleasure is not a good are confuted by pointing out that the pleasures they are talking about are not the same as the pleasures of the good man. Disgraceful pleasures can be said not to be pleasant, since they depend for their pleasantness on some defect or perversion; or their sources are unacceptable in the good life; or "perhaps pleasures differ in kind; for those derived from noble sources are different from those derived from base sources, and one cannot get the pleasure of the just man without being just, nor that of the musical man without being musical, and so on" (1178b28-31). When discussing this issue in 10.3, Aristotle does not come down firmly on the side of any of these alternatives, but in 10.5 he develops the third alternative more strongly. Pleasures in general differ in kind according to the activities they complete. Activities like those of thinking and sensing differ in kind, and so therefore do the pleasures that complete them, each activity being encouraged and forwarded by its own proper pleasure and hindered by the pleasure taken in other activities. Further, pleasures differ in goodness according to the way their activities do (1175b24-29). Aristotle's position can be well summed up by what he says at 1174a1-4: "no one would choose to live with the intellect of a child throughout his life, however much he were to be pleased at the things that children are pleased at, nor to get enjoyment by doing some most disgraceful deed, though he were never to feel any pain in consequence."

Books 7 and 10, then, agree in rejecting the thesis that pleasure is in itself a bad thing, a hindrance to the good life or at best morally dubious. (Aristotle spends some time distinguishing the different versions of this

thesis, but the differences do not matter for present purposes.) Both discussions agree in rejecting this thesis because they agree that whether
pleasure is unimpeded activity or something further that "perfects" it, it
is so closely bound up with the activity that its moral worth is dependent
on that of the activity. Hence pleasure is not an aim equally available and
equally tempting to the good and the bad man alike, an aim which the
good man shows his worth by rejecting. The pleasures available to the
bad man are not a source of temptation to the good man, for he does not
choose to perform the activities that give rise to those pleasures. Since he
does not share the bad man's aims, the bad man's actions do not offer the
same attractions to him as they do to the bad man, just as the pleasures of
convalescence do not have the attraction for the healthy man which they
do for the invalid.

So, irrespective of which positive theory of the nature of pleasure he
accepts, Aristotle is committed by his analysis of it to certain theses that
are of great interest for what they exclude. For they exclude any form of
hedonism, and with it any form of utilitarianism that includes hedonism
as a part. Hedonism has traditionally been the claim, in some form, that
pleasure is the single end at which everyone aims. Now Aristotle does say
that pleasure is the natural end of all animate beings (1172b35-1173a5),
and he thinks it absurd to deny that pleasure is a good, because, he holds,
everyone does, in fact, aim at pleasure (1153b25-31). But he cannot be a
hedonist, because he cannot hold that pleasure is one single independently specifiable end which everyone pursues regardless of how they set
about it. For Aristotle, one cannot pursue pleasure regardless of the
moral worth of the actions that are one's means to getting it. Rather it is
the other way round: it is one's conception of the good life which determines what counts for one as being pleasant. The self-indulgent man
enjoys bodily pleasures, while the temperate man enjoys refraining from
them (1104b5-7). We are not to infer, however, that the temperate man is
getting more of what the self-indulgent man is getting, for they are not
getting comparable amounts of the same kind of thing at all. The pleasures differ as the activities do, and virtue and indulgence cannot be compared for efficacy as ways of achieving the good life. If we take what
Aristotle says seriously, a hedonist position cannot even get off the
ground. Of course, not every position is excluded straightaway which
has been put forward as being "hedonism." Notoriously the central
claims of hedonism weaken under pressure, so that pleasure as the universal end (or happiness defined in Mill's fashion as predominance of
pleasure over pain) fades into the vacuous notion of "whatever we aim at
in whatever we in fact do." But what *are* excluded are the interesting
forms of hedonism, which hold that pleasure in some form can be speci-

fied as an end of action in a way that is independent of any notions of the good or of virtue and determines the content of those notions. For Aristotle this is not a possibility because for him there is no such notion as pleasure as an independent aim in life regardless of how you get it. Of course he thinks that there is something in common to all pleasures; this is just what gives him such trouble when he tries to define it in Books 7 and 10. But in telling us what pleasure is, whether it is complete, whether it is an activity or a process, and so forth, he is not giving us a specification of what motivates all persons in the same morally indifferent way in everything that they do.

It should not need to be stressed how this theory of pleasure fits in with Aristotle's discussion of virtue and how it is acquired. In the discussions of pleasure we find merely a bare assertion that the good man is the norm. In Books 2-4 this idea is given some background, and we see why it is that virtue involves the notion of pleasure. Virtue, we find, requires the correct direction of desires, not just intellectual correctness, and so it is a mark of being good, and not merely continent, that one takes pleasure in performing virtuous actions. Only the truly good man will perform the actions required by virtue without objection or strain and feel the right kind of pleasure in doing them. When we turn to the discussions of pleasure, we find that the true and not merely incidental pleasures are those felt by the good man. This looks circular, and it is; but the circularity is not vicious, for it is, in a way, the point. One's notion of what is pleasant is not external to one's conception of the good life; and the truly good life involves a notion of pleasure that is essentially connected to the performance of virtuous activities. So the good life and the truly pleasant life *must* be explained in terms of one another. What is rejected is a notion of pleasure as an end that is common to good and bad and with equal appeal to both. Goodness does not consist in avoiding pleasure in the interests of some higher ideal but in being right about what is truly pleasant. What is required is not asceticism but intelligent choice that brings with it the redirection of pleasure to what is chosen. Learning to be virtuous involves learning to take pleasure in virtuous activities; the latter is not something added on to the former but is part of it and bound up with it.[2]

This may explain Aristotle's otherwise rather implausible-sounding claim that the exercise of the virtues is pleasant to the good man even in cases where this involves him in sacrificing his life or well-being. The prime case of this is of course courage. Aristotle fully admits that ". . . death and wounds will be painful to the brave man and against his will," even that the prospect of death will be *more* painful to the brave than to the cowardly man. "It is not the case, then, with all the virtues that the exercise of them is pleasant, except in so far as it reaches its end" (1117b7-16). Death and wounds are to be shunned by any standards, and so the exercise of courage which involves the risk of them is only pleasant insofar as it reaches its end, attainment of what is noble; one cannot expect the prospect to appeal to someone who does not want to attain the noble. The coward does not, like the brave man, have a conception of the good life which includes the idea that it is unthinkable to flee danger when a noble cause is at stake; and so, while he may stand firm to avoid shame or bad consequences, he cannot share the brave man's attitude of doing so willingly and ungrudgingly. The performance of virtuous deeds, especially those demanded by a virtue like courage, cannot be assessed for pleasure in a way that has appeal to virtuous, vicious, and indifferent alike. The pleasantness of some virtuous actions cannot be appreciated in a way that makes no reference to the viewpoint of the agent, or to his conception of the good life and what it demands of him, or to what is seen by him as valuable.

It is understandable that Aristotle takes his opponents, who deny plea-sure any value, to be confusing pleasure with bodily pleasure. In giving what he sees as their reasons for doing this he stresses the insistent and unavoidable nature of the desires that give rise to these pleasures. But he also sees that these are the pleasures that are common to all people to the greatest extent regardless of their view of the good: "the bodily pleasures have appropriated the name both because we oftenest steer our course for them and because all men share in them" (1153b33-35). Aristotle actu-ally thinks that there is a right and a wrong way even of enjoying food and sex (1154a17-18); but all the same, these pleasures are those of which it is most plausible to hold that they appeal to just and unjust alike. The error of taking them to be the only, or the paradigmatic, pleasures is the error of thinking that all pleasure is something that people aim at inde-pendently of their conception of what is worthwhile.

This view of the relation of pleasure to goodness represents a consider-able philosophical achievement. But Aristotle does not hold it with per-fect consistency. After the discussions of pleasure in Books 7 and 10 we are somewhat startled to find, when we turn back to the end of 2: "Now in everything the pleasant or pleasure is most to be guarded against; for we do not judge it impartially. We ought, then, to feel towards pleasure as the elders of the people felt towards Helen, and in all circumstances repeat their saying; for if we dismiss pleasure thus . . . we shall best be able to hit the mean" (1109b7-12). The reference is to *Iliad* 3.156 ff., where the Trojan elders marvel at Helen's amazing beauty but urge that, perfect though she is, she be sent back to the Greeks for fear that she may cause Troy's destruction.

This passage is surprising because it embodies the idea that pleasure is in itself inherently dangerous or dubious; the good man should avoid it, like a seductive but fatal Helen. This tone of popular moralizing sits oddly with the repeated insistence throughout this book that the good man is the man who takes pleasure in virtuous activities; for if this is the case, then the good man should not avoid pleasure but should positively pursue it, if it is of the right kind.

Although there are not many passages as negative about pleasure as this one, there is a certain amount of wavering between Aristotle's own viewpoint and the popular moralizing viewpoint. From his own point of view, one's conception of pleasure is internal to one's notion of the good, and so the good man should at the same time pursue pleasure and be careful that he takes pleasure in the right things. Taking pleasure in what one does is the reward and confirmation of virtue. From the popular viewpoint, pleasure is something that we all want, irrespective of our moral view; it is something that can make even the good man go wrong, and he will tend to avoid or minimize it or at least be wary of it, since his aim is virtue and the noble, and pleasure may interfere with this. Aristotle stresses (as has been pointed out already) that the popular viewpoint derives a great deal of its strength from covertly identifying pleasure with bodily pleasure; this is clearly the basis of the popular views Aristotle mentions in Book 1, which identify happiness with the "life of pleasure" and have the life of Sardanapallus in mind (1095a22-23; 1095b14 ff.). It is perhaps not too surprising that Aristotle wavers between these viewpoints, especially when we bear in mind his respect for ordinary moral intuitions.

Thus, while he often says that the good man goes right, and the bad man wrong, about all the ends of action, the noble, the prudential, and the pleasant (e.g., 1104b30-35; 1113a25-33), we also sometimes find him talking as though the good man aimed at the noble and the bad man at the quite distinct end of pleasure—for example, at 1121b7-10, where most people are said to incline toward pleasures because they do not live with a view to what is noble, and 1080a10-12, where the good man is said to be open to rational persuasion, because his aim is the noble, whereas "a bad man, whose desire is for pleasure, is corrected by pain like a beast of burden." In discussing the intellectual virtues in 6.5 Aristotle says that objects of pleasure and pain destroy judgments about what ought to be done; we would expect him to say the opposite—namely, that pleasure and pain confirm these judgments (1040b13-20). Clearly in these passages he means pleasure and pain as most people think of them, not the pleasure and pain appropriate to the corresponding activities.

Even in Books 2-4 there is some wavering. It is emphasized over and over again that pleasure in acting is a mark of the truly virtuous man as opposed to the merely continent and that the exercise of the particular virtues is marked by pleasure (1121a3-4; 1120a26-27 [liberality]; 1122b7 [magnificence]). Yet there are odd comments of an inappropriately negative kind. It is important to get pleasure right, we are told, because it makes us do bad things (1104b9-12); it is harder to fight pleasure than anger (1105a7-8); we tend naturally to pleasure and so to self-indulgence (1109a14-16); we should beware of pleasure as a temptress (1109b7-12, quoted above); most errors about the good are due to pleasure (1113a33-b2). Pleasure, we are told at 1104b34-35, is common to us and the animals; whereas we are told later that it is only the bodily pleasures, and not all of those, that we share with the animals (1118a23-26), and that the temperate man has pleasures of his own and avoids pleasure solely in the sense of not pursuing pleasures that appeal to children and animals (1153a27-35).

These passages do not represent a serious split in Aristotle's considered thought about pleasure; they merely show how difficult it is to sustain an ethical discussion from a viewpoint that corrects common views on an important and central matter and how easy it is to slide back into employing current terms and distinctions. The passage comparing pleasure to Helen is perhaps the only really surprising one, because Aristotle seems there to adopt quite consciously the moralizing view that, given his considered position, is a mistake.

Finally, I would like to make a few comments on what I have put forward as Aristotle's main thesis about pleasure and goodness: pleasures vary in goodness with the activities that give rise to them, and so pleasure cannot be thought of as an ethically neutral aim. The good man and the bad man will find different activities pleasant, and so when they both aim at pleasure they are not aiming at the same thing in any interesting sense. Pleasure is a universal end of action only in a vacuous way. It gives the good man a reason only for doing good actions, not for doing bad actions. This is a thesis that in the tradition of modern moral philosophy has not found much support; various forms of hedonism and utilitarianism have had more philosophical appeal. We tend to reject Aristotle's thesis because it runs up against two very deep-seated assumptions that we tend to make about pleasure. I would like to suggest that these assumptions are not as solidly based as we might think and that the force and attractiveness of the Aristotelian position ought to make us examine them and wonder whether we might have reason to reject them, at any rate in their commonest forms.

The first assumption we tend to make is that in any moral choice the pleasures available must be commensurable. Even if we accept that a

Benthamite calculus of pleasures is absurd, and that pleasure is not quantifiable and not the kind of thing quantities of which can be measured between people, it is something else to give up the idea that pleasures can be measured on some morally neutral scale available to the agent's practical choice. To let go of this seems to deprive us of any rational basis for choosing between morally differing courses of action that will lead to pleasure, at least given the notion of rationality with which we feel most at home, namely, one that requires that the objects of the agent's practical choice be commensurable on some scale. The hedonist utilitarian has no problem as to why it should be rational to do what will produce the greatest pleasure; his problems come rather over the question of why the nature of any action should put a constraint on achieving pleasure thereby. But if the pleasures to be derived from two morally differing courses of action themselves differ morally to just the extent that the courses of action do, then pleasure can in itself provide no independent rational basis for choosing between them. This may seem extreme, even if we reject the hedonist view that the pleasure to be obtained is the *only* relevant factor in the moral choice. But Aristotle's position does lead to the view that just in itself pleasure does not provide an independent rational basis for moral choice; it is not an ethically neutral yardstick. We must take seriously the idea that my notion of pleasure and what I find pleasant is internal to my conception of the good. If I have to do either X or Y, and I think X right and Y wrong, then the pleasures of doing X give me reason to do X, but the pleasures of doing Y do not give me reason to do Y. If they *do* tempt me, then I do not really think that Y is wrong. This is certainly the picture we get from remarks already mentioned (1173b25-27): wealth is desirable, but not as the reward of betrayal. The good man who appreciates what treachery really is cannot think of the money he would get from it as a real source of temptation. "Mere" money would be no incentive to him to do such a thing, and he might well be insulted at the idea that it could be. But someone who did think of the money as inviting would already have ceased to think of betrayal as completely wicked. If the thought of money could weigh with him at all as a temptation, he would already be the kind of person capable of living comfortably with a bad conscience; the pleasures of a clear conscience would no longer be such as to rule out any consideration of the pleasures to be got from money.

A defect of this picture[3] is that pleasures cannot be compared rationally between different conceptions of what is worthwhile. The pleasures of what I think wicked can offer me no real temptation until I cease to think of them as really being wicked. But, we may ask, what of the person who is good in some respects but not in others—surely the most common form of the human moral predicament? If the choices made by Aristotle's good man are all the result of a unified and coherent system of deliberation, then surely the good man is being presented as a person emotionally unified to an unrealistic extent. This does, I think, point up a major weakness in Aristotle's treatment of the moral agent. Although he lays much stress on the process of learning to be virtuous, he pays scant attention to the possibility of uneven moral development and the problems that this raises where true moral choice involves directed desire. What of the person who is brave but stingy: how is he to choose between the pleasures of saving money and the pleasures of doing courageous deeds? Aristotle does not face this kind of problem, and this is not the only way in which he betrays an implicit commitment to the unity of the virtues.

We are also faced, very sharply, by the problem of *akrasia*. For the incontinent man is, *ex hypothesi*, the man who acts because of some factor that arouses desire in him and thus promises pleasure to him, but who has a conception of the good and of the worthwhile life which excludes this or at least gives it a degree of prominence incompatible with his action. Surely the incontinent man is the prime counterexample to the thesis that what one finds pleasant is internal to one's notion of the good, for he is precisely the man who acts to gain pleasure in defiance of his concept of the good.

This is a major difficulty, about which I shall make only two remarks concerning Aristotle. First, Aristotle does see akrasia as posing a real problem. How *can* anything motivate an agent over and above the considerations that are already allowed for in his notion of the good life? If he has a coherent concept of the worthwhile way to live and has the emotional commitment that attends this, how can anything else appear pleasant in a way leading to action incompatible with this conception? Aristotle is aware that the incontinent man appears to give weight to a pleasure that strictly should not weigh with him at all. He recognizes akrasia as exactly the problem it would be for the view of pleasure being attributed to him.

Second, Aristotle makes things comparatively easy for himself by limiting akrasia proper to the area of behavior concerning the self-controlled and self-indulgent agents: the area of bodily pleasures. He emphasizes at length that behavior in this area alone is properly akrasia, and that cases where the agent follows pleasure against his considered better judgment are not cases of akrasia where this area of behavior is not in question; they are so called only by courtesy or an extension of the term (1147b21-1148b14, esp. 1148b6-14). But this is extremely artificial, and Aristotle does recognize cases that have the same structure as the cases that he is prepared to call akrasia, denying them the name somewhat arbitrarily: ". . . it was for the sake of pleasure that he [Neoptolemus] did not stand fast—but a noble pleasure; for telling the truth was noble to him, but he had been persuaded by Odysseus to tell the lie. For not everyone who does anything for the sake of pleasure is either self-indulgent or bad or incontinent, but he who does it for a disgraceful pleasure" (1151b-17-22). Surely, we want to say, this is an exemplary case of akrasia, and Aristotle should have treated it as such instead of excluding it on the ground that it does not involve a "disgraceful" pleasure (and are all bodily pleasures disgraceful?). Why does Aristotle arbitrarily confine akrasia to bodily pleasures? One answer is that, as he is aware, these are the pleasures whose appeal is most independent of the agent's conception of the good. Hence they are the easiest cases when we are considering the problem of how pleasures can be rationally compared by an agent when they come from morally conflicting activities. They do not wholly avoid the problem, of course, but it does seem that the really hard cases of akrasia are precisely cases like that of Neoptolemus rather than the would-be healthy man who eats a sweet.

There is, then, a serious problem here. Aristotle's account of pleasure and its place in the good life cannot properly account for either the incontinent man or the unevenly developed moral agent. I suspect, however, that the troubles here do not flow inevitably from the way Aristotle links pleasure and goodness. They flow rather from the assumption that if moral choice is to be rational, the objects of choice must all be comparable on some single scale in terms of some single principle. The modern versions of this assumption have been on the whole more destructive, because the notion of rationally choosing between comparable alternatives has been conceived more crudely. We have got used to the idea that if moral judgments are to be rational, they must be made with reference to some one supreme and independently specifiable first principle. This is the idea which Mill puts forward as an argument for utilitarianism. We tend still to follow Mill in thinking that the only alternative to this is to accept that moral judgments will be an incoherent chaos of unrelated intuitions. But perhaps this is not the only alternative. Perhaps the good man who prefers the pleasure of a good conscience to the pleasures offered by money is being rational even though the pleasures are not comparable on a single scale. This is an idea whose further development seems profitable. It would involve a deep reconsideration of the notion of rationality and of acting on, and accepting, a reason. This seems to me an area where paying attention to Aristotle may show us a way between two unprofitable courses that have seemed exclusive alternatives in twentieth-century moral philosophy. On the one hand we find rigid insistence on a single principle (or hierarchy of principles) and on the other an unimaginative and unargued intuitionism paying no attention to the coherence or emotional basis of moral judgments. It would be profitable to seek a development of Aristotle's views which will avoid his particular difficulties over akrasia and his overinsistence on the internal unity of the good agent.[4]

The second assumption we make about pleasure which stands in the way of accepting what Aristotle has to say about it and its relation to goodness is the assumption that pleasure is essentially subjective: by which I understand the thesis that something is pleasant if someone honestly reports that it seems so to him, and that it is senseless to claim that even if X reports honestly that he enjoys ϕing, still ϕing is not enjoyable. Even if we are objectivists about good and bad, right and wrong, we still tend to be subjectivists about pleasure. What other standard could there be for the pleasantness of an activity than someone's honestly claiming to be pleased by it? Who is to judge between the reports of the good man and the bad man and say that what the good man claims to enjoy is really pleasant while what pleases the bad man is not? How could there be an objective standard that could override someone's honest claim that some activity was pleasant?

Aristotle rejects subjectivism about pleasure, and it is no accident, or prejudice, that he does so, although the bearings of this on his ethics as a whole have perhaps not been sufficiently appreciated. For if one is an objectivist about the good, and the good and the truly pleasant are internally connected, then one is bound to be an objectivist about the truly pleasant. It would be incoherent to link pleasure and goodness as Aristotle does, and also to admit that anyone's say-so was as good as anyone else's about what is pleasant, whatever their moral views.

I am inclined to think that Aristotle is right to be an objectivist about the good, and right to draw the internal connections between pleasure and the good which he does draw; and since this commits him to being an objectivist about pleasure, our response ought to be to stop and see whether this is as unacceptable a position as we tend to assume.

We tend to be put off here by the claim that the good man is the norm, because we find the notion of "the good man" too general and vacuous. The analogy of the healthy man and the invalid is questionable and opens up as many problems as it solves. We can, however, make better sense of the claim at the level of the exercise of the particular virtues. The self-indulgent man pours himself another drink; the temperate man refuses. Aristotle claims that the temperate man is right and the self-indulgent man wrong; but he also claims, and this is harder to take, that the pleasure the temperate man feels in refraining is more genuinely to be called pleasure than that felt by the self-indulgent man in indulging. This is where we jib. Admittedly they both feel pleasure; admittedly the pleasures they feel are different in kind, and neither tempts the other; neither man is capable of experiencing the other's pleasure. But who is to say that one is really pleasant and the other not?

Aristotle's answer is that the good man is to say. If the temperate man is right to refuse, then his choices and his way of life set the standard, and the self-indulgent man's pleasures are substandard. We may jib less at this if we take seriously two of Aristotle's points: the implications of the thesis that pleasures differ in kind according to their activities, and the nature of the distinction Aristotle makes between true pleasures and other pleasures.

We are tempted to reject the downgrading of the pleasantness of indulging because we think that it involves denying an obvious truth—namely, that the self-indulgent man may honestly report immense pleasure, may indeed feel more pleased at the time than the temperate man. But this way of looking at it is still under the influence of the hedonist picture; it interprets Aristotle as claiming, implausibly, that the temperate man must be getting more of what the self-indulgent man is getting. But there is no one thing, be it a state of feeling pleased or whatever, which they are both competing to get amounts of. The pleasures of self-indulgence lie in the gratification of immediate desires; Aristotle's claim is that these are less appropriately called pleasant than the lasting condition of health and balance produced by temperance. He is not rejecting any claims about how people feel, merely rejecting feeling as the measuring rod for all pleasures. (Someone who did this would be making the familiar mistake of interpreting all pleasures as bodily pleasures.) The pleasures of temperance have no appeal to someone whose only or main interest is the gratification of immediate desires; but the appropriate response to this is, So what? It is the *good* man's pleasures that count, and they count *because* he is good, because he is *right* about what to do. The criterion for what is truly pleasant is thus a moral one; but this should occasion no surprise. We tend to think that the onus lies on Aristotle to show us that there can be an objective criterion of pleasure which could override what an agent honestly claims. But Aristotle would surely see it the other way round: we cannot say what is pleasant without some reference to what is good, since pleasure and good are internally connected; so why should we take seriously someone's claims about pleasure when we reject his claims about the good? They stand or fall together. If I think sadism is morally wrong, then I cannot think that it is really pleasant, whatever the sadist says. If he convinces me that it is pleasant, then he has already at least half-convinced me that it is not wrong, or at least not as wrong as I thought it was. (If we think of the works of de Sade, we can see that this idea has some plausibility.) So the claim that the good man's pleasures are truly pleasant while the bad man's are not is not unrealistic moralizing; it is just the natural result of taking seriously both the idea that pleasures differ in kind and the idea that there is a right and wrong about what kinds of action are really good and bad. Aristotle is not denying any claims made by any agents; he is merely denying that this is the proper criterion for judging what is pleasant. We may disagree; but it is not so obvious that we are right as is often thought.

The second consideration is that what Aristotle opposes to true pleasure is not false or unreal pleasure but *qualified* pleasure. Again, he is not making the palpably false claim that when the bad man honestly says that he is pleased we can tell him that he is *not* pleased; rather the claim is that what he is doing is not really pleasant, and this is a very different kind of claim. The bad man really is pleased; but his activities are only pleasant *for him*, not generally and without qualification. The sadist really does enjoy what he is doing; but what he is doing is not something that is pleasant, period. It is pleasant only for him, and given his circumstances. Virtuous activities, by contrast, are according to Aristotle pleasant in an unqualified way. They are pleasant for anyone in a normal state, not uncorrupted by bad upbringing or some defect.

No doubt we feel that ideas like this, presenting goodness and its pleasures as the natural human state, are overoptimistic and that they rely on notions of normality and the natural which may not bear much examination. But whether they do or not, they do not involve Aristotle in denying the report of the bad man who says he is pleased; they merely downgrade the status of that report. I have not tried to defend Aristotle's ideas *in toto*; but I do think that it is worthwhile to show that his objectivism about pleasure is not silly or unrealistic. Rather, it is the natural product of a view about the relation of pleasure and goodness which is worth serious consideration.[5]

NOTES

1. All quotations are from Ross's Oxford translation.

2. At this point I am heavily indebted to M. F. Burnyeat, "Aristotle on Learning to be Good" (chap. 5 of this anthology).

3. I am grateful to Martha Craven Nussbaum for conversation that made me aware of the importance of this point and of the issue of akrasia.

4. David Charles's (unpublished) work on akrasia is the most important original work in this field that I am aware of.

5. Apart from the people already mentioned, I have benefited from reading J. Gosling, "More Aristotelian Pleasures," *Proceedings of the Aristotelian Society,* n.s. 74 (1973-74), 15-34; Friedo Ricken, *Der Lustbegriff in der Nikomachischen Ethik des Aristoteles,* Hypomnemata, no. 46 (Göttingen, 1976); and J. McDowell, "Are Moral Requirements Hypothetical Imperatives?" *The Aristotelian Society, Supplementary Volume* 52 (1978), 13-29.

17

Aristotle on Friendship[1]

John M. Cooper

If the number of published discussions is a fair measure, the two books of the *Nicomachean Ethics* devoted to friendship (φιλία) have not much engaged the attention of philosophers and philosophical scholars. Yet such neglect is not easily justifiable. Both in his account of what friendship is and in the various considerations he brings to bear to show what is good about friendship Aristotle displays psychological subtlety and analytical ingenuity of an unusually high order. And on a number of topics that are undeniably central to his moral philosophy (moral virtue, character development, and pleasure, for example) Aristotle's views can only be fully understood and properly evaluated if due attention is paid to his theory of φιλία—both what it is and what role it plays in the good person's life.

THE FORMS OF FRIENDSHIP

I

All the standard treatments of Aristotle on φιλία point out that the Greek concept expressed by this word is much wider than our "friendship" (or the equivalents in other modern languages). Its field covers not just the (more or less) intimate relationships between persons not bound together by near family ties, to which the words used in the modern languages to translate it are ordinarily restricted, but all sorts of family relationships (especially those of parents to children, children to parents, siblings to one another, and the marriage relationship itself);[2] the word also has a natural and ordinary use to characterize what goes in English under the somewhat quaint-sounding name of "civic friendship." Certain business relationships also come in here, as does common membership of religious and social clubs and political parties. It is not enough, however, just to list the fairly diverse sorts of relationship that form the field of Aristotle's investigation; one wants to know, if possible, what it was about them that inclined the Greeks to group them together under this common name. W. D. Ross suggests that the word "can stand for any mutual attraction between two human beings,"[3] but, to judge from Aristotle's discussion itself, this is not true: aside from the fact that "mutual attraction" might seem to have erotic, or at any rate passionate, overtones that make it unsuitable as a characterization of, for example, business and citizenly ties, this account clearly lets in too much. People can be "mutually attracted" to one another without in any way developing active ties —without doing anything together, or for one another—and such mere attraction would not be counted as φιλία. Aristotle is himself always careful to emphasize the practical and active element in the relationships he investigates under this name, as for example in the *Rhetoric* (whose discussion of friendship and hatred, 2.4, is essential reading on this topic), where he defines liking (τὸ φιλεῖν)[4] as "wanting for someone what one thinks good,[5] for his sake and not for one's own, and being inclined, so far as one can, to do such things for him," and then characterizes a friend (φίλος) as someone who likes and is liked by another person (1380b36-1381a2). This account suggests, in fact, that the central idea contained in φιλία is that of doing well by someone for his own sake, out of concern for *him* (and not, or not merely, out of concern for oneself). If this is right, then the different forms of φιλία listed above could be viewed just as different contexts and circumstances in which this kind of mutual well-doing can arise; within the family, in the state at large, and among business partners and political cronies, well-doing out of concern for other persons can arise, and where it does so, there exists a "friendship." I suggest that if we want some indication of what is common to all the personal relationships which the Greeks counted as φιλίαι, we cannot do better than follow Aristotle's lead here. At any rate, I shall argue that this definition from the *Rhetoric* does state the core of Aristotle's own analysis of φιλία. According to him, φιλία, taken most generally, is any relationship characterized by mutual liking as this is defined in the *Rhetoric*, that is, by mutual well-wishing and well-doing out of concern for one another.[6]

If this characterization is correct, it should be clear why Aristotle's theory of friendship must be considered a cardinal element in his ethical theory as a whole. For it is only here that he directly expresses himself on the nature, and importance to a flourishing human life, of taking an interest in other persons, merely as such and for their own sake. In fact, Aristotle holds not only that active friendships of a close and intimate kind are a necessary constituent of the flourishing human life but also that "civic friendship" itself is an essential human good. That is to say, he holds not only that every person needs to have close personal friendships in which common and shared activities are the core of the relationship but also that fellow citizens who are not otherwise personally connected ought nonetheless to be predisposed to like one another and to wish and do each other well. In holding this he is in effect declaring that the good man will conduct himself towards other persons in a spirit, not merely of rectitude (mere justice) but actually of friendship.[7] Hence it is clear that Aristotle's discussion of friendship contains a very significant amplification of the theory of moral virtue expounded in the middle books of the *Nicomachean Ethics* and that his theory of virtue cannot be completely understood unless read in the light of it.

But does Aristotle really make well-wishing and well-doing out of concern for the other person's good a condition of friendship of all these diverse types? He seems to be widely interpreted as holding this to be a condition of only one form of friendship, while the others involve exclusively self-centered motivations. To settle this question will require a complete examination of Aristotle's theory of the forms of friendship and his views on what is essential to each.

II

At the center of Aristotle's analysis of $\phi\iota\lambda\iota\alpha$ in the *Nicomachean Ethics* stands his theory that there are three basic kinds or species ($\epsilon\check{\iota}\delta\eta$, 1156a7, 1157b1) of friendship, depending on what it is that attracts and binds the one person to the other. In some cases what cements the association is the pleasure, in others some advantage, that the one gets from the other; in a third set of cases it is the recognition of the other person's moral goodness. Aristotle counts the resulting relationships friendships of different types in virtue of the differences in what forms the bond between the associated parties. Furthermore, Aristotle thinks that the central case, by comparison with which the others are to be understood, is friendship based on the recognition of moral goodness. This much is clear. On many important details, however, Aristotle is notably obscure. I shall begin by mentioning two of these.

First, when exactly does Aristotle recognize a friendship as one involving mutual recognition of moral goodness? He usually refers to this kind of friendship by such phrases as "the friendship of people who are good and alike in virtue" (1156b7-8) or "the friendship of good persons" (1157a20, b25; similarly 1158a1, b7). He also calls this friendship "perfect" (τελεία, 1156b7, 34), since it exhibits fully and perfectly all the characteristics that one reasonably expects a friendship to have. By calling the parties to such a relationship "good men" (ἀγαθοί) and describing their friendship as "perfect" Aristotle seems to imply that only to fully virtuous persons—heroes of intellect and character—is it open to form a friendship of this basic kind. So, it would follow, ordinary people, with the normal mixture of some good and some bad qualities of character, are not eligible partners for friendships of the basic type; they would be doomed, along with thoroughly bad people (1157a16-19, 1157b1-3; EE 1236b10-12, 1238a32-33), to having friendships of the other two types, at best. Does Aristotle mean to imply that one who is not completely virtuous can only be befriended for the sake of some pleasure or advantage he brings, that no one can associate with him (unless under deception: cf. 1165b8-15) for the sake of his good qualities of character?

The second point that calls for comment concerns the two deficient types. In the course of laying the ground in *Nicomachean Ethics* 8.2 for his distinction between the three types of friendship, Aristotle remarks that not every case of liking (φιλεῖν) something occurs within the context of a friendship: one can like wine, for example, but this is not evidence of a friendship between oneself and wine, because (1) the wine does not like you back, and (2) you don't wish well to the wine. Thus, he goes on, a friendship exists only where you wish to the other party what is good for him, for his own sake, and this well-wishing is reciprocated: "people say that one ought to wish to a friend what is good, for his own sake; but those who wish what is good [to someone else] in this way people call 'well-disposed' (εὔνους) [and not 'friends'], if the other person does not return the wish: for friendship is good will (εὔνοια) when reciprocated" (1155b31-34). Here Aristotle seems to endorse the central idea contained in the *Rhetoric's* definition of friendship, that friendship is mutual well-wishing out of concern for one another; he makes it characteristic of friendships, of whatever type, that a friend wishes well to his friend for his friend's own sake.[8] That he means to make this sort of well-wishing a component of all friendship and not just of some special type is clear from the context; he has not yet distinguished the three species of friendship (he only does this in the following chapter) and is at this point merely marking off, in order to set it aside, the wine-drinker's sort of liking. The cases of liking that he retains for study, he says, are all ones in which one finds reciprocal well-wishing of the parties for one another's sake. The implication is that not only in "perfect" friendship but also in pleasure- and advantage-friendship a friend wishes his friend well for the friend's own sake. On the other hand, Aristotle repeatedly contrasts the two derivative types of friendship with the basic type by emphasizing the self-centeredness of pleasure- and advantage-friends; thus he says that in erotic relationships (one class of pleasure-friendships) people "love not one another but their incidental features" (1164a10-12), that is, what gives pleasure to themselves. Similarly for advantage-friendships: "Those who are friends on account of advantage cease to be such at the same time as the advantage ceases; for they were not friends of one another but of the benefit to themselves" (1157a14-16; similarly 1165b3-4). This seems to suggest that in pleasure- and advantage-friendships each party is concerned *solely* with his own good, and this would mean that they could not have the sort of concern for one another that Aristotle seems in 8.2 to attribute to friends. Other evidence, to which we shall turn in section IV below, seems to indicate the same thing. Which is Aristotle's considered view? Or is he simply inconsistent on this point?

It should be observed that if Aristotle holds both that pleasure- and advantage-friends are wholly self-centered and that only perfectly virtuous persons are capable of having friendships of any other type, he will be adopting an extremely harsh view of the psychological capabilities of almost everyone. For, clearly enough, there are few or no paragons of virtue in the world, and if only such paragons can have friendships of the basic kind, then most people, including virtually all of Aristotle's readers, will be declared incapable of anything but thoroughly self-centered associations. This would be a depressing result, and one that, given Aristotle's generally accommodating attitude toward the common sense of the ordinary man, should occasion surprise, at least in the absence of compelling general reasons on the other side. In what follows I shall argue that despite initial appearances Aristotle does not make friendship of the central kind the exclusive preserve of moral heroes and that he does not maintain that friendships of the derivative kinds are wholly self-centered: pleasure- and advantage-friendships are instead a complex and subtle mixture of self-seeking and unself-interested well-wishing and well-doing.

III

As already remarked, Aristotle distinguishes the three types of friendship from one another by reference to what it is that causes the parties to like one another: τριῶν ὄντων δι᾽ ἃ φιλοῦσιν (1155b27)—διὰ τὸ χρήσιμον, διὰ τὸ ἡδύ, and δι' ἀρετήν. Strictly, of course, it is not the actual properties of a person but those that someone else conceives him as possessing that are responsible for the existence of a friendship: in the case of pleasure, perhaps, there is hardly room for mistakes, but, plainly, one can be mistaken about whether someone is advantageous to know, or morally good. Though Aristotle in describing friendships usually neglects this distinction and speaks of friends of the various types as *actually* pleasant or advantageous to one another, or morally good, he does on occasion take explicit note of the decisive role of appearances here. Thus in *Nicomachean Ethics* 9.3 he discusses what becomes of the friendship you have made with someone, taking him to be a good person (ἐὰν δ᾽ ἀποδέχηται ὡς ἀγαθόν, 1165b13), when you find out otherwise. While such a friendship lasts, the deceived party will like his friend "for his virtue" (δι' ἀρετήν), even though he may in fact have none; so the friendship, from his side at least, will be a "friendship of the good." What gives a friendship its character as a friendship of a particular kind is the state of mind of the partners—their intentions toward and their conceptions of one another. Now, clearly enough, in the case of pleasure- and advantage-friends it is *some* (conceived) pleasure or advantage that their friends give them that makes them like them; the friend need not be thought to be pleasant or advantageous in every way or every context, but only in *some*, in order for the friendship to exist. One may well be friends with someone because he is a pleasant drinking-companion, even while recognizing his unsuitability as a companion in other pleasant pursuits. Up to a certain point, perhaps, a pleasure-friendship is more complete and perfect of its kind the greater the variety and scope of the pleasures the friends may share; but this is a difference in scope and perfection within a class of friendships that all belong to the same basic type. The type is determined by what it is about the other person that forms the bond, and this may perfectly well—indeed, typically will—involve a very limited and partial view of him as a pleasant companion.

It would be natural to suppose that within the class of virtue-friendships there could be a similar variation. Some virtue-friendships might involve the recognition of complete and perfect virtue, virtue of every type and in every respect, in the associates; other friendships of the same type might be based not on the recognition by each of perfect virtue in the other but just on the recognition of some morally good qualities that he possesses (or is thought to possess). Thus, one might be attached to someone because of his generous and open spirit, while recognizing that he is in some ways obtuse or not very industrious or somewhat self-indulgent. Such a friendship would belong to the type *virtue-friendship*, because it would be based on the conception of the other person as morally good (in some respect, in some degree), even though the person does not have, and is not thought to have, a perfectly virtuous character —just as a pleasure-friend need not be, or be thought to be, perfectly pleasant or pleasant in every way. Here again, the question of what type of friendship a given relationship belongs to would be settled by examining the conception of the person under which one is bound to him; if it is good qualities of the person's character, and not pleasure or advantage to oneself, that causes one to like him, it will be a virtue-friendship, even though these qualities may be, and be known to be, limited in their goodness and/or conjoined with other not so good, or even positively bad, personal characteristics.

Now it is clear, I think, that this must be how Aristotle understands virtue-friendship, considered as one of the three basic types of friendship, despite the prominence in his exposition of that most perfect instance, the association of two perfectly good men. This comes out most clearly from his discussion of friendship between unequals. Ideally, he recognizes (1158b30-33), friendship demands absolute equality—equality of status between the partners and equality of pleasure or advantage, given and received, or moral goodness, as the case may be. But in each of the three basic types (1162a34-b4) there occur also unequal friendships. Sometimes one party gives more pleasure than he gets, or benefits less from the association than his friend does; and similarly friendships exist, Aristotle claims, where one party is recognized to be morally better than the other. One class of unequal virtue-friendships is that between husband and wife (1158b13-19). Here Aristotle's idea seems to be that men as such are morally superior to women, so that a friendship between the absolutely best man and the absolutely best woman, each recognized as such, would be an unequal friendship. In such a friendship the disparity in goodness does not imply any deficiency on the side of the lesser person with respect to her own appropriate excellences; she will be perfect of her kind, but the kind in question is inherently lower. But Aristotle also recognizes unequal virtue-friendships between those whose natural status is equal (1162b6-13), and in that case the inequality must consist in one of the partners being not only less morally good than the other but deficient with respect to his own appropriate excellences. So in this case we will have a virtue-friendship where the superior person likes the inferior for such virtues as he has (or some of them), while recognizing that his character is not perfectly good. Even more significant for our purposes is Aristotle's discussion in 9.3. 1165b23 ff. of a virtue-friendship that starts out equal but is threatened with dissolution as one party improves in character and accomplishments and eventually outstrips the other. In this case it is clear that Aristotle is willing to countenance a virtue-friendship where *both* parties are quite deficient with respect to their appropriate excellences.

There can be no doubt, then, that on Aristotle's theory what makes a friendship a virtue-friendship is the binding force within it of *some*—perhaps, for all that, partial and incomplete—excellence of the character, and the perfect friendship of the perfectly virtuous is only an especially significant special case of this. For this reason, it seems preferable to refer to friendship of the central kind not, as Aristotle most often tends to do, as "friendship of the good" but, as he sometimes does, as "friendship of character" (ἡ τῶν ἠθῶν φιλία, 1164a12; διὰ τὸ ἦθος φιλεῖν, 1165b8-9; ἡ ἠθικὴ φιλία, EE 1241a10, 1242b36, 1243a8, 32, 35; cf. ἐκ τῆς συνηθείας τὰ ἤθη στέρξωσιν, NE 1157a11, and ἔοικε ... τῆς κατὰ τὸ χρήσιμον φιλίας ἡ μὲν ἠθικὴ ἡ δὲ νομικὴ εἶναι, 1162b21-23). The expression "character-friendship" brings out accurately that the basis for the relationship is the recognition of good qualities of character, without in any way implying that the parties are moral heroes. I will hereafter adopt this alternative terminology. One should not, however, overlook the significance of the fact that Aristotle himself prefers to characterize the central type of friendship by concentrating almost exclusively on the friendship of perfectly good men. For it is an aspect of the pervasive teleological bias of his thinking, which causes him always to search out the best and most fully realized instance when attempting to define a kind of thing. Aristotle does not himself mistake the perfect instance for the only member of the class, and there is no necessity for us to do so. But because in this case I believe his readers have often been misled, it seems best in expounding Aristotle's views to depart from his own preferred terminology.

IV

The central and basic kind of friendship, then, is friendship of character. Such friendships exist when two persons, having spent enough time together to know one another's character and to trust one another (1156-b25-29), come to love one another because of their good human qualities: Aristotle's word for "love" here is στέργειν, a word which is used most often to apply to a mother's love for her children and other such close family attachments.[9] Each, loving the other for his good qualities of character, wishes for him whatever is good, for his own sake, precisely in recognition of his goodness of character, and it is mutually known to them that well-wishing of this kind is reciprocated (1156a3-5). They enjoy one another's company and are benefited by it (1156b12-17) and in consequence spend their time together or even live with one another (συνημερεύειν καὶ συζῆν, 1156b4-5). Provided that no contingency physically separates them for any considerable period (1157b11-13), such a friendship, once formed, will tend to be continuous and permanent, since it is grounded in knowledge of and love for one another's good qualities of character, and such traits, once formed, tend to be permanent (1156b-11-12).

Pleasure- and advantage-friendships are, according to Aristotle, counted as friendships only by reason of their resemblance to this central case.[10] Thus character-friends are both pleasant and beneficial to one another, and pleasure-friends, though not necessarily beneficial, are of course pleasant to one another, while advantage-friends derive benefits, though perhaps not pleasure, from their association (1156b35-1157a3, 1156a27-28). But are there further, direct resemblances, based on properties that all three types of friendship have in common? If, as I suggested above, Aristotle means to adopt in *Nicomachean Ethics* 8.2 the *Rhetoric*'s definition of friendship as always involving well-wishing to one's friend for his own sake, then the types will have much in common: in every friendship, of whichever of the three types, the friend will wish his friend whatever is good, for his own sake, and it will be mutually known to them that this well-wishing is reciprocated.[11] As I have said, I believe that Aristotle does hold this view, but there are complications that must now be entered into.

The chief complication is caused by the qualifications which Aristotle immediately imposes on his statement in 8.2 that mutually known, reciprocated εὔνοια is essential to friendship. He says that friends must "wish well to (εὐνοεῖν) and want what is good for one another, and be known to one another as doing this, on one of the aforesaid grounds" (1156a3-5), that is, because they find their friend pleasant, or beneficial, or possessed of admirable qualities of character. But what does Aristotle mean by this "because"? What kind of ground does he have in mind here? Perhaps he means that in a pleasure-friendship the one person wants the other to prosper *in order that* his own (the well-wisher's) pleasure may be continued or increased. Similarly, an advantage-friend would want and be willing to try to secure what his friend needed, in order that his friend might continue to be in a position, or be better able, to see to *his* needs in due course. That is, well-wishing on the ground of pleasure or advantage would mean well-wishing in order to get pleasure or advantage for oneself. But this interpretation runs into an immediate objection. For although it is certainly possible to wish someone well both for one's own sake (because his success will bring advantages or enjoyments to oneself) and for his, it does seem incoherent to suggest that someone might wish well to someone else for that other person's sake *in order to* secure his own interests or enjoyments. To wish for someone else's good for his sake entails (perhaps means) wishing for his good *not* as a means to one's own (or anyone else's) good. But on this interpretation Aristotle would be guilty of this incoherent thought: he does not say merely that a pleasure-friend wishes for his friend's prosperity because the friend is pleasant to him, but that he has εὔνοια for his friend for this reason, and εὔνοια is defined in this very context (1155b32, where οὕτω is to be explicated by ἐκείνου ἕνεκα, b31) as wishing someone well *for his own sake* and does not mean wishing him well *tout court*.

It might be suggested that Aristotle, despite the apparent definition of εὔνοια at 1155b32, intends the word to be understood in the reduced sense of "wishing well (*period*)" when, a few lines later, he says that friends of all types wish each other well (εὐνοεῖν). Such a reduction in sense is in itself unlikely within the context of a single argument, however, and the evidence about Aristotle's usage of the word elsewhere seems to show that he always understands by it "well-wishing for the other person's sake." There is no doubt that this is how εὔνοια is understood in his official account of it in the *Nicomachean Ethics* 9.5, and in the corresponding passage of the *Eudemian Ethics* 7.7 (1241a1-14) Aristotle actually denies that εὔνοια exists in pleasure- and advantage-friendships at all, precisely on the ground that "if one wishes for someone what is good because he is useful to oneself, one would not wish this for his sake but for one's own, while εὔνοια is for the sake not of the well-wisher himself but for that of the person to whom one wishes well" (1241a5-8). We shall have to return to this passage of the *Eudemian Ethics* later; for the moment it is enough to point out how decisive and explicit Aristotle is here that εὔνοια requires not just well-wishing, but even well-wishing for the other person's sake. The apparent definition of εὔνοια in *Nicomachean Ethics* 8.2 is therefore not something put forward in passing, easily subject to immediate unannounced dilution; it is a statement of Aristotle's fully considered understanding of what εὔνοια is.

It should be recalled that the necessity for taking εὐνοεῖν in a reduced sense in 1156a4 was caused by interpreting the claim that a pleasure- or an advantage-friend wishes his friend well *because* his friend is pleasant or advantageous to him (διὰ τὸ ἡδύ, διὰ τὸ χρήσιμον) as meaning *in order to* secure his own pleasure or advantage. If διά is taken in this prospective way, as expressing merely what the well-wisher hopes to produce or achieve by his friend's prosperity, then it is impossible to interpret Aristotle coherently. But there is another, in itself more plausible, interpretation of the force of διά here. Notice first that if διά does mean "for the sake of," it ought to mean the same thing in the parallel remark about character-friendships: a character-friend wishes well to his friend δι' ἀρετήν, that is, on this interpretation, for the sake of excellence of character. One might, of course, make some sense of this: a person wants his friend to prosper so that he (the friend, presumably) can wax more virtuous or continue to do virtuous deeds. But it is not the only, nor even the most natural, way of understanding the claim that character-friends wish each other well because of excellence of character. In this case, the "because" (διὰ τὴν ἀρετήν) seems more likely to mean "in recognition of their friend's having a good character," so that it expresses a consequence or result of the friend's being morally good rather than some purpose that the well-wisher has in wanting him to prosper.[12] Thus, a character-friend wishes his friend to prosper because he recognizes his good character and thinks that it is fitting for those who are morally good to prosper. Understanding the "because" in this causal way makes it at least as much retrospective as prospective; the well-wishing and well-doing are responses to what the person is and has done rather than merely the expression of a hope as to what he will be and may do in the future. Now, if one interprets the "because" in this causal way in all three cases, as one must if one is to take it so in any of them, there is no special difficulty in understanding Aristotle's attribution of εὔνοια to all types of friends. For the pleasure-friend will now be said to wish well to his friend for his friend's own sake, in consequence of recognizing him as someone who is and has been an enjoyable companion, and the advantage-friend wishes his friend well for his friend's own sake, in consequence of recognizing him as someone who regularly benefits him and has done so in the past. Aristotle will here be making, in effect, the psychological claim that those who have enjoyed one another's company or have been mutually benefited through their common association will, as a result of the benefits or pleasures they receive, tend to wish for and be willing to act in the interest of the other person's good, independently of consideration of their *own* welfare or pleasure. A full-fledged friendship will exist, then, when such intentions are recognized by both parties as existing reciprocally.[13]

Before this interpretation can be accepted, however, we must see how it fits with what Aristotle says in 8.3-4, where he marks off character-friends, as "friends without qualification" (ἁπλῶς, 1157b4), from the other types, whom he counts as friends only "incidentally" (κατὰ συμβεβηκός, 1156a17, b11, 1157b4). Friends wish each other well, he says, "in that respect in which they are friends" (ταύτῃ ᾗ φιλοῦσιν, 1156a9-10): so, he explains, an advantage-friend or a pleasure-friend wishes his friend well "qua beneficial or pleasant" (ᾗ χρήσιμος ἢ ἡδύς, a16). Hence, he implies, advantage- and pleasure-friends are only incidentally one another's friends, while character-friends are friends in an unqualified way. In interpreting this passage I want to take up two points. First, what does Aristotle mean by saying that a friend of one of the lesser types wishes his friend well (merely) qua pleasant or qua advantageous to himself? Does this amount to saying that these types of friends regard each other exclusively as means to their own satisfaction or advancement? And second, how is it that to wish someone well "qua pleasant" or "qua advantageous" is a ground for saying that someone who does this is only "incidentally" a friend? I will take up the second point first.

Clearly enough, whether one person is beneficial or pleasant to another is an incidental characteristic of him: his being so results from the purely external and contingent fact that properties or abilities he possesses happen to answer to needs or wants, equally contingent, that characterize the other person. If, then, the conception of the other person under which one is his friend—as beneficial or as pleasant to oneself—is something that is only incidentally true of him, the same thing must also be said of that property which one acquires as a result of so regarding him: that one is a friend of the other person must be something that holds true only incidentally. By contrast, Aristotle claims, character-friends are friends of one another essentially (καθ᾽ αὐτούς, 1156a11, δι᾽ αὐτούς, 1156b10, 1157b3) or without qualification (ἁπλῶς). Admittedly, it is not a necessary truth about any individual that he has those good qualities of character for which he is loved (just as it is not a necessary truth about the pleasant or advantageous friend that he has those properties that yield pleasure or advantage). But on Aristotle's theory of moral virtue the virtues are essential properties of humankind: a person realizes more or less fully his human nature according as he possesses more or less fully those properties of character which count as moral excellences. And since individual persons are what they essentially are by being human beings, it can be said that a person (any person) realizes his own essential nature more fully the more completely and adequately he possesses the moral excellences. So if one is the friend of another person, and wishes him well, because of good moral qualities he possesses, one will be his friend because he is something that he is essentially and not incidentally (cf. 1156b8-9: οὗτοι [sc. character-friends] γὰρ τἀγαθὰ ὁμοίως βούλονται ἀλλήλοις ᾗ ἀγαθοί, ἀγαθοὶ δ᾽ εἰσὶ καθ᾽ αὐτούς). And in consequence the property that one acquires as a result of so regarding him, that of being his friend, can be said to relate one to him essentially and not incidentally. It is because his friend is just what he essentially is, a human being, that a character-friend wishes him well; pleasure-friends and advantage-friends wish their friends well not, or not merely, as what they essentially are.

In this train of thought the operative consideration is the conception of the other person under which one wishes him well, and since the argument here is developed directly out of the passage in 8.2, in which Aristotle declares that friends wish each other well on account of pleasure, advantage, or moral goodness, we can find support in it for the interpretation proposed above of that earlier passage. Properly understood, neither passage denies that friends of the derivative types wish their friends well for the friend's own sake; instead, they specify what it is about the other person that supports this response. In this respect all three types of friendship run parallel. There is, however, an important difference between the well-wishing that forms part of a character-friendship and the well-wishing in the other two cases. This follows from the fact, developed in 8.3-4, that only character-friends are friends essentially and without adventitious qualification. For given the close connection that Aristotle asserts between moral excellence and what a human being essentially is, a character-friend's well-wishing is more unrestricted, less hedged about by special assumptions and special expectations, than the well-wishing of the other types of friend. A character-friend wishes for his friend's well-being as, and because he is, a good man. But good qualities of character are, once fully acquired, permanent or nearly so (1156b12), since these properties belong to one's essential nature as a human being, and one's essential nature, once fully realized, is a permanent part of what one is. By contrast, pleasantness and advantageousness, just because they are incidental properties of a person (and depend upon the special circumstances, interests, etc., of other persons as well) are subject to change (1156a21-22, 1156b1). So character-friendships are much more permanent attachments than pleasure- and advantage-friendships are.

But these temporal limitations carry with them another limitation: in wishing well to one's friend because of his pleasantness or advantageousness to oneself, one is implicitly imposing limits of a special and narrow kind upon one's well-wishing. One's concern for the other person's good extends only so far as and so long as he remains a particular sort of person, pleasant or advantageous as the case may be: one likes and wishes well to someone conceived of as pleasant or advantageous to oneself, and the good one wishes him to have, for his own sake, is therefore restricted to what he can acquire without, thereby or in consequence, ceasing to be pleasant or advantageous. One wants him to prosper, for his own sake, and not merely as a means to one's own good; nevertheless, one does not want him to prosper in such a way or to such an extent that one no longer gets the pleasure or benefits one has received from associating with him. In short, in wishing someone well, for his own sake, because he is pleasant or advantageous, one's first commitment is to his retention of the property of pleasantness or advantageousness, and any good one wishes him to have, for his own sake, must be compatible with the retention of that special property under which, as his friend, one wishes him well in the first place.[14]

This, at any rate, I take to be the burden of Aristotle's claim that friends want good things for their friends "in that respect in which they are friends" (ταύτῃ ᾗ φιλοῦσιν, 1156a10), that is, qua persons pleasant or advantageous to themselves (a16) or qua persons of good character (ᾗ ἀγαθοί, b8-9). He does not say explicitly that the conception of the other person under which one is his pleasure- or advantage-friend implies these limitations to one's well-wishing, but he does draw the parallel inference about character-friends. Thus, Aristotle says, friends do not wish that their friends should become gods (although being a god is a very good thing) because to become a god is to cease to be a human being, and it is of a human being that one is the friend and, therefore, as a human being that one wishes for his prosperity: εἰ δὴ καλῶς εἴρηται ὅτι ὁ φίλος τῷ φίλῳ βούλεται τἀγαθὰ ἐκείνου ἕνεκα, μένειν ἂν δέοι οἷός ποτ᾽ ἐστὶν ἐκεῖνος· ἀνθρώπῳ δὴ ὄντι βουλήσεται τὰ μέγιστα ἀγαθά (1159a8-11).[15] If, then, the well-wishing of a character-friend is tacitly restricted to such goods as the friend can acquire while still remaining what he essentially is (a human being), pleasure- and advantage-friends, in accordance with their more restricted conceptions of other persons as their friends, will want their friends' prosperity only within the limits imposed by the existence and continuance of those special properties of pleasantness and advantageousness as possessors of which they are their friends.

Friends of all three types, then, on Aristotle's theory in the *Nicomachean Ethics*, wish for their friend's well-being out of concern for the friend himself. This is as true of a businessman who, through frequent profitable association, becomes friends with a regular customer as it is of a husband and wife or two intimate companions who love one another for their characters. Such a businessman looks first and foremost for mutual profit from his friendship, but that does not mean that he always calculates his services to his customer by the standard of profit. Finding the relationship on the whole profitable, he likes this customer and is willing to do him services otherwise than as a means to his own ultimate profit. So long as the general context of profitability remains, the well-wishing can proceed unchecked; the profitability to the well-wisher that is assumed in the well-wishing is not that of the *particular* service rendered (the particular action done in the other person's interest) but that of the overall fabric of the relationship.[16] Here, then, one has a complex and subtle mixture of self-seeking and unself-interested well-wishing and well-doing. The overriding concern of the advantage-friend is for his own profit. But this does not mean that every action and wish of his is ultimately aimed at the realization of something profitable to himself. He genuinely likes his friend and has a genuine and unself-interested concern for his good, and he will do him services that are not motivated, at least not entirely, by self-interest. Of course, some services he will refuse, because they will cost him too much, thus endangering the general profitability to himself of the association which is the basic presupposition of the friendship and therefore of any friendly service falling within it. Other services, however, no doubt small ones for the most part, he will freely perform. The same pattern of unself-interested well-wishing and self-seeking will be found in pleasure-friendships, with mutual pleasantness taking the place of mutual advantageousness.

The admixture of self-seeking in character-friendships is significantly less than in pleasure- and advantage-friendships. A character-friend loves his friend because of properties that belong to the friend essentially and not merely incidentally. This means that he loves him for what he himself is and not for merely external properties or for relations in which he stands to other persons. Hence the well-wishing characteristic of such a friendship does not take place within so restricted a context as that imposed by the self-centered desires for pleasure and profit which operate in the other types of friendship. The assumption in the case of character-friends which corresponds to the assumption of the pleasantness or advantageousness of the other person in the derivative friendships is just that the other person is a good human being. So the character-friend wishes his friend well in any way that is not inconsistent with his being the good human being he is assumed to be. He wants and expects both pleasure and advantage from his association with his friend, but aiming at these is not an essential condition of the friendship itself. He associates with a good person because of his goodness; pleasure and advantage may follow in due course, but his intention in maintaining the friendship is fixed on the goodness of the other person, not on his pleasantness or profitability. So, although there is unself-interested well-wishing in all three types of friendship, it is both broader and deeper in a character-friendship than in the other two. For it is only in this case that the conception of the other person under which one is his friend and wishes him well for his own sake is a conception that corresponds to what he himself essentially is.

V

If I am right, then, Aristotle's views on what is essential to friendship do not, as prevailing interpretations imply, commit him to holding that almost everyone has nothing but selfish motivations. On his theory ordinary decent people are capable even of character-friendship, with all that that implies in the way of unselfish interest in others, and in any event pleasure- and advantage-friendship themselves already involve a considerable degree of unselfish concern for the good of other persons. In concluding this discussion I want to make two further comments about Aristotle's theory, so understood.

First of all, Aristotle does not make the mistake, which a superficial reading would seem to convict him of, of counting as φιλίαι even of a diluted sort, just any established relationship in which two or more persons to their mutual knowledge receive pleasure or profit from associating together. That it would be a mistake to call in English all such relationships friendships (in no matter how relaxed a sense) I take to be obvious; a businessman is no friend of all his regular customers, and when a personal relationship is more or less purely exploitative, it would be taken for irony to describe the persons in question as friends. Friendship requires, at a minimum, *some* effective concern for the other person's good (including his profit and his pleasure) out of regard for him. Aristotle seems to feel, as we do, that the expectation, at least, of interest in the other person's good for his own sake was part of what the word itself conveyed. In conceding (as, e.g., at 1157a25-36) that because general usage counts as friends those bound together merely by advantage or pleasure, philosophical theory must allow that such people are friends (though of a derivative type), Aristotle is not reluctantly being forced to recognize as φιλίαι certain classes of wholly self-centered relationships. His reluctance is fully explained by the facts, which he argues for at length, that these relationships are less permanent, are based less on knowledge of and interest in the other person and his character, and involve to a much lesser degree the merging of one's interests and the sharing of one's life with another person, all of which are contained as ideals and, in that sense, as norms within the very idea of φιλία. Second, I should emphasize that Aristotle's theory is a theory of what a friendship is, that is, what is true of those who are friends; it does not, except incidentally, have anything to say about how friendships are formed in the first place. In some sense, no doubt, it is on Aristotle's view the desire for pleasure or profit, or the interest in moral excellence, that brings together those who then become friends. But clearly enough, in the actual course of events the first meeting may well be quite accidental and subsequent stages in the development of the relationship quite unmotivated by any explicit form of these interests. The casual, even unexpected, discovery of pleasure, profit, or moral qualities may elicit the responses that lead to the establishment of a friendship, without there being any premeditation or planning on either side. It may well be only in the clear light of hindsight that one could say that the desire for pleasure or profit, or the interest in moral excellence, was working to bring these people together; Aristotle's theory does not imply any stronger connection than this between these motives and the formation of the corresponding types of friendship.

FRIENDSHIP AND THE GOOD

VI

In the *Nicomachean Ethics* Aristotle faces the question what the value of friendship is in 9.9; but before considering his answer it is important to be clear exactly what question he means to be asking. On Aristotle's theory of the good there is a distinction to be drawn between what is good absolutely and without qualification (good "by nature" he sometimes calls it) and what is good for a particular person or class of persons. A thing is good absolutely if it is good for human beings as such, taken in abstraction from special and contingent peculiarities of particular persons: these peculiarities may provide additional interests, needs, and wants, and on the basis of them one can speak of additional, possibly divergent, things as good for this or that particular person. Hence in asking whether friendship is a good thing and what the good of it is, Aristotle neglects the question whether, and how, it may be good for special classes of person (bad or weak or mediocre people, for example, of one kind or another). He wants to know instead whether it is a good for human beings, as such. Now the morally good, flourishing person is a perfect human being, leading the perfect human life; so anything that is good for human beings as such (that is, good without qualification) will necessarily be good for him. So Aristotle's inquiry into the value of friendship takes the form of seeking an answer to the question whether or not a flourishing person, the perfect human being, will have any need of friends (ἀμφισβητεῖται δὲ καὶ περὶ τὸν εὐδαίμονα εἰ δεήσεται φίλων ἢ μή, NE 9.9. 1169b23-24).

This question itself is open to two sorts of misunderstanding. One of these Aristotle himself points out. To speak of someone's need for friends might be taken to imply some deficiency or defect in him and his mode of living—as if some essential element of his own good would be lacking to him unless he had friends to acquire or provide this for him. And of course to flourish is to be already leading a perfect, completely fulfilled life, so that, understood in this way, a flourishing person can have no *need* for friends. Since his life is already, *ex hypothesi*, perfectly complete, he cannot, as Aristotle puts it, need any adventitious (ἐπείσακτον) pleasure (or other good) as a means of improving his condition (1169b23-28). When Aristotle asks, then, whether a flourishing person needs

friends, he is inquiring whether the having of friends is a necessary constituent of a flourishing life—not whether friends are needed as a means
of improving a life that was already flourishing.

In the second place it is important to emphasize that the question to be
pressed concerns the value to a person of his *having* friends. That is, one
wants to be given reasons for believing that, so to say, anyone who sets
out to design for himself a life that shall be a flourishing one ought to
arrange things so that he forms friendships—so that he becomes attached
to certain people in ways that are characteristic of friendship, spends
time with them, does them services out of unself-interested goodwill, and
so on. It seems clear that this is the question that Aristotle means to be
asking in NE 9.9 (and in the corresponding passage of the *Eudemian
Ethics*, 7.12. 1244b1-1245b19). At any rate it is possible, as I shall argue
below, to discern in this chapter two quite profound, mutually independent attempts to answer this question, so understood.

Unfortunately, however, the largest part of Aristotle's response in
the NE (the long argument beginning at 1170a13, honorifically described
as the way people who consider the question "more scientifically"—
φυσικώτερον —will answer it) is hard to follow unless it is construed as
answering a different question. When one cuts through the complications
of a very convoluted argument (Ross sets it out in a series of eleven syllogisms),[17] Aristotle's final and grandest effort, on this interpretation,
comes to the following:

(1) For a good person, life itself is a good and pleasant thing; it is
always pleasant to be aware of oneself as possessing good things; therefore, the good person's awareness of himself as being alive is very pleasant and highly desirable to him (1170b1-5).

(2) A man's friend is to him a "second self," so that whatever is good
for him as belonging to himself will also be good for him when possessed
by his friend (1170b5-8).

(3) Since the good man's life and his awareness of it are pleasant and
desirable to him, he will find the life of his "second self" and his awareness of it also pleasant and desirable (1170b8-10).

(4) But he cannot satisfy this desire to be aware of his friend's existence
except by living in company with him, so he will need his friend "to live
with and share in discussion and thought with—for this is what living
together would seem to mean for human beings, and not feeding in the
same place, as with cattle" (1170b10-14).[18]

Now it is quite plain that in step (2) of this argument Aristotle simply
assumes, altogether without explicit warrant, that a good man will have
friends. It is only if one assumes that he *will* have friends that one can
apply to him, as Aristotle does in the remainder of the argument, the
consequences that flow, or are alleged to flow, from the fact that a friend

is to his friend as a second self. If the good man *has* friends, then of course, granted the "second self" thesis, he will take pleasure in being aware of his friend's life, as he also does in being aware of his own, and will want to be near him in order to have this pleasure. This I think is obvious and unobjectionable.[19] But until we are given some independent reason for thinking that the good man will need or want to form friendships in the first place, we are not entitled to assume that he will have the sort of attitude toward any other person which will enable him to get this pleasure and, in consequence, desire this close association. But there is not the slightest hint in this argument, so interpreted, of any reason for thinking *this*.[20]

It might be suggested that Aristotle has in mind (though certainly he does not say this here) that the pleasant self-awareness on which this argument turns is only satisfactorily obtainable through the awareness of a friend and his activities. On that basis one might be able to construct a more plausible-looking argument for Aristotle's conclusion. Thus Stewart:[21]

In seeing, hearing, walking, etc., a man is conscious of himself—of his own existence.... This perception of self, however, would hardly be possible to man if his only objects of experience were his own sensations.... [H]is experience of his own actions would be accompanied by only a dim consciousness of a self distinguished from them. But man is not confined to his own actions. He has a "sympathetic consciousness" of the actions of his friend—of actions which are still in a sense "his own" (for his friend is a ἕτερος αὐτός), and yet are not in such a way "his own" as to make it difficult to distinguish "himself" from them.... In other words—it is in the consciousness of the existence of another that a man becomes truly conscious of himself.

Why, however, should one believe this? No reason is given, and offhand it does not seem true that merely in order to be distinctly conscious of oneself one needs to be aware of other persons first. But even granted that one cannot attain self-consciousness except through consciousness of another person and his actions, it would still not follow that one needs friends for this purpose. Why wouldn't a casual acquaintance do just as well? Stewart describes a psychological process whereby a person, having noted the fairly gross distinction between himself and the actions of another person, is able to make the same distinction, or make it more sharply, in the case of his own actions. I do not see how the step from others' actions to one's own is made any the easier by the fact that the other person in question is a friend; the purely verbal point that, on the "other self" thesis, one can call the actions of a friend "one's own" does not seem to me to add anything to whatever psychological plausibility the process as described without it might seem to have.

In any event, as already noted, Aristotle does not here (or, so far as I can discover, elsewhere) claim the priority of other-awareness to self-awareness. He argues instead from the assumption of robust, pleasant self-consciousness in the good man to the pleasantness of his consciousness of his friend; this latter consciousness is represented, as it were, as an overflow from the good man's self-consciousness, not as something needed to create it in the first place. Interestingly, however, in the chapter of the *Magna Moralia* corresponding to *NE* 9.9 one does find the related point argued for, that self-*knowledge* depends upon knowledge of others:

Now supposing a man looks upon his friend and marks what he is and what is his character and quality (τί ἐστι καὶ ὁποῖός τις ὁ φίλος); the friend—if we figure a friend of the most intimate sort—will seem to be a kind of second self, as in the common saying "This is my second Heracles." Since, then, it is both a most difficult thing, as some of the sages have said, to attain a knowledge of oneself (τὸ γνῶναι αὑτόν), and also a most pleasant (for to know oneself is pleasant)—now we are not able to see what we are from ourselves (αὐτοὺς ἐξ αὑτῶν . . . θεάσασθαι) (and that we cannot do so is plain from the way in which we blame others without being aware that we do the same things ourselves; and this is the effect of favour or passion, and there are many of us who are blinded by these things so that we judge not aright); as then when we wish to see our own face, we do so by looking into the mirror, in the same way when we wish to know ourselves we can obtain that knowledge by looking at our friend. For the friend is, as we assert, a second self. If, then, it is pleasant to know oneself, and it is not possible to know this without having someone else for a friend, the self-sufficing man will require friendship in order to know himself. [1213a10-26]²²

It should strike one immediately that the focal point of this argument is self-knowledge and not, as in our *NE* passage, self-consciousness. Thus in the *NE* we find τὸ αἰσθάνεσθαι αὐτοῦ, 1170b9, with repeated use of αἰσθάνεσθαι and its derivatives throughout the argument, whereas in the *MM* αἰσθάνεσθαι and its derivatives are wholly lacking, and we find instead τὸ αὐτὸν γνῶναι, 1215a15, 23, εἰδέναι a16, 25, γνωρίζειν a23, 26. Nor are these mere stylistic variants: one can be conscious of one's self as an entity active in one's affairs even without knowing very fully or explicitly what kind of person one is, whereas self-knowledge as presented in the *MM* argument is precisely knowledge of one's character and qualities, motives, and abilities. No doubt this kind of self-knowledge presupposes self-consciousness, but it is plainly not the same thing. The *MM* is arguing not that friendship is a necessary prerequisite to mere self-consciousness but that it is necessary for self-knowledge.

One seems forced, then, to regard the "more scientific" argument of the *NE* as abortive. The argument from the *MM*, however, seems more promising. Self-knowledge is certainly a more complex matter than mere self-consciousness, and the idea that it depends upon knowledge of others might strike one as plausible and important. But this argument, too, has its difficulties. First, how, exactly, is knowledge of others supposed to make possible self-knowledge? And, even more, why does self-knowledge (at any rate for the good and flourishing person) depend upon knowledge of one's friends—why wouldn't enemies or casual acquaintances do as well? Finally, it is not enough merely to say, as this text does, that self-knowledge is pleasant; for the argument to be sound, self-knowledge must be actually indispensable to the good and flourishing person. But is it?

To take the last point first. It is certainly plausible to hold, and Aristotle presupposes throughout, that a person's life could not be called flourishing unless in addition to leading the sort of life that is as a matter of fact the best (doing acts of kindness and courage and so on) he knew what sort of life he was leading and chose it partly for that reason. Human flourishing, in short, does not consist merely in conformity to natural principles but requires self-knowledge and conscious self-affirmation. Self-knowledge is thus an essential part of what it is to flourish.[23] As such it is an extremely pleasant thing, and this is perhaps why in our text so much emphasis is laid on its pleasantness. But however that may be, there is no difficulty in granting on general Aristotelian grounds the indispensability of self-knowledge which the *MM* argument needs.

But how is self-knowledge to be attained? Notoriously, people tend to notice faults in others that they overlook in themselves; and they are equally inclined to attribute to themselves nonexistent virtues. Thus there is a double tendency to deny the presence in oneself of what one recognizes in others as faults and to claim for oneself virtues that one does not really have at all. These threats to one's objectivity must be reckoned with by everyone, the person who in fact possesses all the good qualities of character and intellect and no bad ones no less than other people. To be sure, the qualities in himself he thinks virtuous are so, and he has no faults; but how is he to be sure that he is not deceiving himself in thinking these things, as he must be if he is to *know* what he is like? It is plausible to suggest, as our text does, that mistakes of this kind are not so apt to occur where one is observing another person and his life; here the facts, both about what are faults and what are virtues, are more likely, at least, to speak for themselves. But that just points to the problem: how attain the same objectivity about oneself that is so comparatively less difficult about others?

This is where friendship is supposed to come in. At least in friendships of the best sort, where the parties love one another for their characters and not merely because they enjoy or profit from one another's company,

intimacy (it is alleged) bespeaks affinity: my friend is, in the *MM*'s striking phrase, a second me (τοιοῦτος οἷος ἕτερος εἶναι ἐγώ, 1213a12), myself
all over again. Now no doubt the sense of kinship among friends, even
among character-friends, can be exaggerated. Some people are certainly
drawn together partly by the presence of character-traits in the one
which the other lacks. Even in such cases, however, it seems reasonable
to think that there must be a strong underlying similarity of character
and views and that this similarity, intuitively felt by each in the other,
forms an important part of the bond between them. In any event, on
Aristotle's theory (cf. 1156b7-8) the perfect friendship is one where the
parties are fully good persons who are alike in character. If one supposes
that in this perfect character-friendship, as in other lesser ones, the
friends may feel a sense of their own kinship without necessarily knowing antecedently, on both sides, in what their similarity consists, then
such a friendship could well serve as the needed bridge by which to con-
vert objectivity about others into objectivity about oneself. For knowing
intuitively that he and his friend are alike in character, such a person
could, by studying his friend's character, come to know his own. Here
the presumption is that even an intimate friend remains distinct enough
to be studied objectively; yet because one intuitively knows oneself to be
fundamentally the same in character as he is, one obtains through him an
objective view of oneself. In the *MM*'s image, one recognizes the quality
of one's own character and one's own life by seeing it reflected, as in a
mirror, in one's friend.[24]

This is the nub of the argument. It is certainly ingenious, but is it
cogent? The principal weaknesses would seem to be two. First, one might
doubt whether, if, as seems true, people tend to be biased in favor of
themselves and blind to their own faults, they are any less so where those
with whom they are intimate are concerned. And second, one might feel
uneasy about the weight apparently being laid on the effectiveness and
reliability of one's intuitive sense of kinship with another person. Plainly
the argument only works if one can justifiably have more initial confidence in these feelings than in one's own unaided attempts to judge the
quality of one's life and character. But however difficult the latter may
be, is one any less open to deception through the former?

Although these are genuine doubts, not easily allayed, I think the argument nonetheless contains considerable force. For it must be admitted
that self-knowledge is, under any conditions, an extremely precarious
accomplishment. Neither this nor any other argument is likely to show
the way to an absolutely assured knowledge of what one is really like,
proof against all possible doubt. The question is just whether character-
friendship provides the best means available to a human being for arriv-

ing at as secure a knowledge of his own life and character as such a creature can manage. Considered in this light I think this argument has a certain weight. For it does seem fair to believe that objectivity about our friends is *more* securely attained than objectivity directly about ourselves. And the reliance we are being invited to place on our intuitive feelings of kinship with others is not, after all, either unchecked or unlimited. For it is on the sense of kinship as it grows up, deepens, and sustains itself within a close and prolonged association that the argument relies. And it does seem right to trust such tried and tested feelings. They are not "*mere* feelings" but are developed through long experience both of the other person and of oneself. This is, indeed, one reason why knowledge of one's friends might make self-knowledge possible where knowledge of a mere acquaintance, however detailed, would not: the sense of affinity, if it existed at all, could not be relied upon in this latter case, since it would not be based on prolonged and deep familiarity with him.

Admittedly, while granting some weight to the considerations advanced here, one may well feel that this argument hardly exhausts the sources of self-knowledge or even the most important ways in which friendship might help to advance it. Still, the recognition, which lies at the center of this argument, of the social bases of a secure self-concept and of the role intimacy plays in providing the means to this is a notable achievement.

In any event it deserves emphasis that this argument from the *Magna Moralia*, unlike the professedly more profound argument from *NE* 9.9 examined above, does give reasons, however strong or weak, why one ought in designing one's life to make explicit provision for friendships. It would be wrong, of course, to conclude that in the *Nicomachean Ethics* Aristotle argues only ineffectively for this conclusion. For there are other arguments in *NE* 9.9, and one of them (1169b28-1170a4), though certainly not without obscurities of its own, has pronounced affinities to the *MM* argument just examined.

For at the outset it was said that flourishing is an activity, and an activity clearly exists as something continuous and is not possessed like a piece of property. If flourishing consists in living and being active, and the activity of a good person is good and pleasant in itself, as was said at the outset, and what is peculiarly one's own is pleasant, and we can study ($\theta\epsilon\omega\rho\epsilon\hat{\iota}\nu$) our neighbors better than ourselves and their actions better than those that are peculiarly our own, and the actions of good persons who are their friends are pleasant to good people (for they are characterized by both the natural marks of pleasantness)—if so, then the fully flourishing person will need friends of this kind, given that he chooses ($\pi\rho\sigma\alpha\iota\rho\epsilon\hat{\iota}\tau\alpha\iota$) to study ($\theta\epsilon\omega\rho\epsilon\hat{\iota}\nu$) actions that are good and peculiarly his own, and the actions of the good person who is his friend are of this kind.

Here, as in the MM passage, we find two principal claims: that the good
and flourishing man wants to study (θεωρεῖν, 1169b33, 1170a2;
θεάσασθαι, 1213a16) good actions, and that one cannot, or cannot
so easily, study one's own actions as those of another.[25] But why does
the good person have reason to want to study good actions? Here the NE
is silent. This gap in the argument can, however, be filled in naturally
from the MM: it is because, for reasons we have already noted, the self-
knowledge that is a prerequisite of flourishing can hardly be attained by
other means. And at the same time it is clear, as it would not otherwise
be, why the other person whose actions these are must be an intimate and
not merely a casual acquaintance. If I am right, then, this passage of the
Nicomachean Ethics is intended to convey essentially the same argument
in favor of friendship as we find set out in full in the Magna Moralia. The
claim, here again, seems to be that it is only or best in character-friendship that one can come to know oneself—to know the objective quality
of one's own actions, character, and life.

VII

A second argument, independent of this one, follows in the NE immediately after the passage just quoted. At 1170a4-11 we read:

> Further, people think a flourishing person should live pleasantly. Now life is hard
> for a solitary person: for it is not easy to be continuously active apart by oneself,
> but this is easier together with others and toward them. So, [in living with others]
> his activity, which is pleasant in itself, will be more continuous, as it ought to be
> for a fully flourishing person (for the good man, qua good, takes pleasure in
> morally virtuous actions and dislikes vicious ones, just as a musician enjoys
> beautiful melodies and is pained by bad ones).[26]

Aristotle's central claim here is that living in isolation causes one to be
less continuously active at the things one cares most about than is consistent with leading a flourishing life. By contrast, he claims, one can be
more continuously active at these pursuits if one engages in them together
with others, by which he clearly means not just living in their company—
sitting by the side of others, as it were, but absorbed in one's own private
pursuits[27]—but making one's fundamental life activities themselves activities shared in common with others: μεθ' ἑτερων δὲ καὶ πρὸς ἄλλους, ῥᾷον
(1170a6). Why should there be this difference in continuity of activity
between a life made up of shared and a life made up of purely private
activities? Aristotle does not say. Several things might be in his mind.
Perhaps in a solitary life, where one has to see to all one's needs by one-

self and cannot rely on others, or the products of others' work, one is simply forced to be too busy too much of the time at menial and uninteresting things to be free to concentrate uninterruptedly on one's most cherished pursuits. But though this might well be true, it is hard then to see the point of Aristotle's proposed remedy: one does not have to *share* one's activities with anyone in order to have the benefits of others' assistance. Again, it might be suggested that if one tries to complete one's favorite projects all on one's own, it may simply require physical exertions of such magnitude that one has to take many pauses for rest, thus rendering one's activities intermittent and discontinuous. But again this cannot be all that Aristotle has in mind, since the natural remedy here would be to induce someone else to cooperate by making his skills, interests, and so on, available for one's private purposes, perhaps in return for occasional assistance from oneself: sharing one's projects with anyone else would surely not be necessary. In order to give Aristotle a reasonably plausible case for the preferability of a life of shared activities one must, then, at least supplement these points. A natural suggestion is this: Aristotle may be thinking that living in isolation causes one to lose the capacity to be actively interested in things. Even if the activity that delights one most is something that can be enjoyed by a solitary person (as is true of most intellectual pursuits), it tends not to be pursued with freshness and interest by someone living cut off from others. One tends to become apathetic and inactive without the stimulation and support which others, especially those whom one likes and esteems, provide by sharing one's goals and interests. If so, then one can see why Aristotle claims a special and essential place in any truly satisfactory human life for the sort of shared activities that only friendship makes possible: it will only, or especially, be through such activities that a human being finds his life continuously interesting and pleasurable.

Now whether or not this is what Aristotle has in mind, it is at any rate an interesting idea, and one that merits quite extensive consideration. I shall not attempt such a full-scale treatment here; still, the following points should be noted.[28]

First, by "shared activities" here I mean (and understand Aristotle to have in mind) activities that are performed by two or more persons together, and not just activities that are common to more than one person or mutually known to several persons to be common to them all. Thus two persons might be solitaire-devotees and so have a common interest, and each might know of the other's attachment to the game, so that one could speak of their mutual interest in solitaire; but neither of these conditions is sufficient to make their attachments to the game count as a shared interest (nor of course would their solitaire games count as shared activities), for the reason that solitaire is not a game that they play together. The playing of the game is not something in which they jointly share. Now some activities are shared activities, in this sense, by one sort of necessity or another. Thus perhaps games like baseball and tennis are so defined by their rules that they cannot be played at all unless some specified number of persons, greater than one, is actively involved. In other cases, such as playing a string quartet or doing many industrial and agricultural jobs, the work will normally have to be done together by more than one person, simply because of the physical limitations of the human body. Many activities, however, that can perfectly well be performed by single individuals in private (so far, at any rate, as the definition of what is being done, and physical capabilities, go) can also be shared. One can worship in private, or together with others; solve a mathematical problem, or write a book, alone or jointly; bathe by oneself or in company. Artistic and cultural activities are an especially interesting case. Here, many activities that, narrowly considered, might seem to be personal and private are nonetheless engaged in by those who do them in such a way as to make them shared. Thus, even though a single author may be solely responsible for a scholarly article, he presumably wrote it as a contribution to an ongoing subject of study to which he thinks of himself as attached jointly with others. His attitudes to his own work may be construed on the model of a game in which there are various positions, occupied from time to time by different persons, linked together by a common set of rules and shared purposes. The individual player's move, looked at in isolation, may well seem quite private to himself, but given the system of positions, rules, purposes, and so on, it is thought of by him as a contribution to the game in all the moves of which all the players share. Thus the individual author's acts of writing can be seen as part of a shared activity, namely, the shared activity of advancing the discovery of the truth in the subject in question. In general, where an activity is shared, one finds the following features: (1) there is a shared, and mutually known, commitment to some goal (whether something to be produced or something constitutive of the activity itself), (2) there is a mutual understanding of the particular role to be played by different persons in the pursuit of this common goal, and (3) within the framework of mutual knowledge and commitment, each agrees to do, and in general does do, his share in the common effort.

What then is there about shared activities which might make Aristotle think them in general more continuously interesting and enjoyable, in comparison with strictly private pursuits? Two things come to mind. First, the fact that others, especially if they are people one likes or admires, share with one in a commitment to the goal that gives the activity its sense is likely to strengthen one's own perception of the worth or value of the activity and thereby enable one to engage in it with interest and pleasure; that others, too, find a thing worth doing will be at least a welcome confirmation of one's own attitudes. Of course, it is possible to know that others agree in finding a thing worth doing even though each engages in it in a completely private way, so that if it is a good thing to know one's own views confirmed by the experiences of others, this good is available even if one does not share one's activities with anyone. What is in question here, however, is not a person's mere abstract knowledge that something is valuable and worthwhile but his actual direct experience of it *as* worthwhile. And it must not be overlooked that it is possible to know on sufficient grounds that something is good but be unable to actually experience it as such; and it is the latter that is crucial to the enjoyment of one's own life. In a shared activity one knows of the commitment of others to the goodness of the activity in no mere abstract, theoretical way. It is concrete and immediate. Hence it is only through participation in such activities that the confirmatory knowledge of others' evaluations is likely to be both constantly and directly present to one's consciousness. It seems not unreasonable to suggest, then, that the sort of confirmation of the worth of one's endeavors and pursuits which is so valuable, perhaps necessary, to a human being if he is to sustain his interests is hardly available outside of the context of a shared activity.

Second, where an activity is shared, each of the participants finds himself engaged in a number of different ways and at a number of different points: to be sure, he participates directly only in the parts of the enterprise to which it falls to himself to contribute, but indirectly he is, in principle, involved in every stage of the process, whoever the direct agent may be. What others do as their share of the joint activity he experiences as his doing as well, insofar as he is a member of the group, and it is the group that is the agent primarily at work in it. Admittedly, in not all shared activities does every participant retain a very full sense of his own involvement in all the varied operations that go to make it up; but it follows from my characterization above of shared activities that in some degree this sense of extended participation must be present in any person who conceives of himself as engaging with others in a joint activity. One's involvement in what one is doing is thus much broader in a shared activity than it is in the case of a completely private one: there are, so to speak, many more places and types of contact with a shared activity than there can be for a private one. In a shared activity one's enjoyment, and so one's interest in what one is doing, is not limited just to what one directly does oneself. This fact has two consequences that support Aristotle's claims for shared activities. First, insofar as the agent sees his own personal activity as a contribution to a larger whole, to which he is attached and in which he is interested also through the contributions of others, the sources of his continued interest in what he directly does are much expanded. His multiple involvements in the whole activity naturally enhance the interest which he can take in the activities that he personally undertakes as a participant in the larger group activity. He is thus much more likely to sustain his interest in his own personal doings and to get pleasure continuously from them. Imagine, for example, someone who enjoys mathematics as a purely private exercise. Numerical relationships fascinate him, and he wants to spend a lot of time exploring them. Such a person is likely to neglect this pursuit after a time and be only intermittently active at it; but if he comes to regard his activity as part of a larger group activity—so that he takes an interest not just in his own but also in others' research—he will be much more capable of sustaining his active interest in his own work because of its connection with the group activity of which he now sees it as part and in which he also has an interest. The tendency of anything long continued to become boring is thus avoided, to some extent, by finding in it additional things to be interested in. Second, insofar as he participates at second hand in the doings of others engaged with him in the shared activity, he can be said to be active—indirectly—whenever and wherever any of the group is at work. In this sense one could say that a participant of a group activity is active even when he is not himself directly making any contribution. So, if one takes into account the activities that a participant is indirectly sharing in, one can say that those who engage in shared activities will continue to be active even when they are not directly active at all—that is, not active at all in the only way in which one can be active in a purely private pursuit.

Now I do not claim that these considerations were actually in Aristotle's mind when he said that it is easier to be continuously active with others and toward others than in isolation. His failure to explain why he held this view makes it impossible to say with certainty what his reasons were. But it is hard to imagine what he could have meant if he did not have in mind at least some of these points. In any event I think the account I have just given does show that Aristotle's view, whatever exactly he may have rested it on, is sound. Shared activities are especially valuable for any human being since they, more than purely private activities, enable one to be continuously and happily engaged in things. This is so, in sum, for three reasons: (1) they provide one with an immediate and continuing sense that what one finds interesting and worthwhile is really so, since the experience of others is seen to agree with one's own in this respect; (2) they enhance one's attachment to and interest in one's own personal, direct activities by putting them within the context of a broader group activity that is itself a source of pleasure and interest; and (3) they expand the scope of one's activity by enabling one to participate, through membership in a group of jointly active persons, in the actions of others. It is reasonable, I think, to assume that human nature is inherently such that no human being can provide entirely from within himself the sources of his interest and pleasure in his life and the activities that make it up. Nothing can be made, as it were, automatically and continuously interesting for any human being, just because of what *it* is like. A human being has to invest things with his interest, by responding in appropriate ways to them; but these responses, though no doubt subjective, are not for that reason under one's own control. They depend in part upon the firm and continued sense of the value of what one is doing, and as Aristotle's argument plausibly suggests, this can hardly be secured except through the sense that others agree with one in this. If this is so, then I think one is entitled to infer, with Aristotle, that no life can be satisfactory for a human being which does not make explicit provision for a considerable range of activities shared with others. Only by merging one's activities and interests with those of others can the inherent fragility of any human being's interests be overcome.

Now this is obviously an extremely important conclusion to reach. But Aristotle must go even further and hold, not just that shared activities, but that activities shared with friends, are a necessary ingredient in the flourishing human life, if he is to derive from his emphasis on the greater continuousness of shared activity a defense of friendship. For even if, as I have implied, the benefits to be derived from shared activities are in many cases dependent on one's esteeming or respecting the judgment of one's fellow participants, this does not mean they must be one's friends. At any rate one does not need to have character-friendship, which is the fundamental kind and the kind which Aristotle wishes to defend, with those with whom one enjoys playing games or performing music or, notoriously, having sex. It is clear enough, however, that the satisfactions that derive from shared activity are especially needed in connection with those activities, whatever they may be, that are most central to a person's life and contribute most decisively to his flourishing, as he himself conceives it. For here the flagging of one's commitments and interests will be particularly debilitating; here more than anywhere else one needs the confirmatory sense that others too share one's convictions about which activities are worthwhile, and the other benefits of sharing pointed out above. Now on Aristotle's theory of *eudaimonia* the flourishing human life consists essentially of morally and intellectually excellent activities. So the flourishing person will have a special need to share *these* activities, if his own interests in life are to be securely and deeply anchored. But according to the account of shared activities that I have given, it is an essential condition of a shared activity that the parties to it should not just be committed to the goal or goals that give the activity its sense but should know about each other that they share this commitment. This requirement of mutual knowledge has substantial consequences where the activities to be shared include morally virtuous ones. For in order to know that someone is genuinely committed to moral values one must know him and his character pretty closely, since commitment here just is a matter of moral character or its absence. Superficial acquaintance is for this purpose quite insufficient, as it is not where there is question of someone's interest in music or baseball, because genuinely good moral character is what is required, and this is not easily distinguished from feigned or halfhearted attachment. So before one can share activities where the common pursuit of moral values is essential to what is to be done, one must come to know, and be known by, the other party or parties quite intimately. But this sort of mutual knowledge is hardly available outside of character-friendship. Hence, a human being cannot have a flourishing life except by having intimate friends to whom he is attached precisely on account of their good qualities of character and who are similarly attached to him: it is only with such persons that he can share the moral activities that are most central to his life.

It is possible, then, to defend both Aristotle's claim that shared activities are essential to any satisfactory human life and his implied conviction that true friendship is a necessary context within which at least some of these essential shared activities should take place.

VIII

I conclude that there are to be found in the Aristotelian corpus—and, if I am right about the purport of 1169b28 ff., in the *Nicomachean Ethics* itself—two interesting and telling arguments to show that true friendship is an essential constituent of a flourishing human life. If my interpretations are correct, Aristotle argues, first, that to know the goodness of one's life, which he reasonably assumes to be a necessary condition of flourishing, one needs to have intimate friends whose lives are similarly good, since one is better able to reach a sound and secure estimate of the quality of a life when it is not one's own. Second, he argues that the fundamental moral and intellectual activities that go to make up a flourishing life cannot be continuously engaged in with pleasure and interest, as they must be if the life is to be a flourishing one, unless they are engaged in as parts of shared activities rather than pursued merely in private; and given the nature of the activities that are in question, this sharing is possible only with intimate friends who are themselves morally good persons.

Three points about these arguments should be noted. First, in a certain way they both emphasize human vulnerability and weakness. If human nature were differently constituted, we might very well be immune to the uncertainties and doubts about ourselves which, according to Aristotle, make friendship such an important thing for a human being. As it is, we cannot, if left each to his own devices, reach a secure estimate of our own moral character; nor by ourselves can we find our lives continuously interesting and enjoyable, because the sense of the value of the activities that make them up is not within the individual's power to bestow. The sense of one's own worth is, for human beings, a group accomplishment. Hence we need each other because as individuals we are not sufficient—psychologically sufficient—to sustain our own lives. For a god things are different; the goodness of the divine activity of contemplation is continuously evident to a god, and he needs no other person or thing to enable him to see this or reassure him that it is so: as Aristotle says in the *Eudemian Ethics*, god is his own good activity, but human good consists in relationship to others (ἡμῖν μὲν τὸ εὖ καθ᾽ ἕτερον, ἐκείνῳ δὲ αὐτὸς αὐτοῦ τὸ εὖ ἐστιν, 1245b18-19). To argue thus the need of human beings for friendship from deficiencies in our psychological makeup both illuminates the nature of friendship and gives what I think is an entirely accurate account of its status in human affairs. Properly understood, there is nothing in this that should be construed as undermining or detracting from the intrinsic goodness, for human beings, of friendly relations with others. For Aristotle's point is that the deficiencies that make friendship such a necessary and valuable thing are inherent in human nature itself. There is no basis in his argument for one to accept one's friendships in a regretful, still less a provisional, spirit—pining away, as it were, for the day when one's deficiencies might be made up and one could live entirely out of one's own resources without having to depend upon others at all. Since the deficiencies in question are essential to being a human being— that is, essential to being what one is, to being oneself—it is irrational to form one's attitudes in the hope of adjustments in these respects. The only reasonable attitude is to accept one's nature as it is and to live accordingly. The arguments we have considered profess to show how and why someone who adopts this attitude will be led to form friendships and to value friendly relations as fundamental and intrinsically good ingredients of the life that is best for himself.

It is worth emphasizing that although in these arguments Aristotle defends the value of friendship only by showing that for human beings it is a necessary means to attaining certain broadly valuable psychological benefits, nothing in them commits him to denying that friendship is, or involves, anything intrinsically valuable. Indeed, in a few passages (1167b31-33 with 1168a5-9, and 1159a25-33), though they are not backed by much in the way of argument, Aristotle insists on the worthwhileness-in-itself of the active expression of love and on the direct pleasure that human beings take in the experience of being loved by others. These remarks are plainly not inconsistent with the arguments we have been examining, since there is no reason why something that is itself intrinsically good should not also be valued for other reasons. In fact, however, I think it is a mistake to see these two trains of thought even as separable, much more as competing, defenses of the place of friendship in a satisfactory human life. For, clearly, it does not follow from the mere fact that the active expression of love is found intrinsically good by human beings that a person who did not form friendships would be lacking something essential to his own good: there are lots of intrinsically good activities, and no human life can, in any event, contain them all.[29] To show that the active expression of love is necessary in any satisfactory human life requires further argument establishing the fundamental importance of *this* intrinsically good activity vis-à-vis others with which it might compete for a place in a person's life. Again, and for the same reason, it does not follow from the fact that people delight in being loved that one who had all the other goods in life would still want and need the love of others. This claim could only be made good by further argument showing why, for human beings constituted as they actually are, *this* experience in particular is indispensable.[30] The arguments we have examined (and, in the *NE*, only these) attempt this essential task—which is why I have focused principally on them. What they do is to characterize friendship from several points of view in such a way as to make it clear why human beings should find friendship and the activities and experiences that constitute it so interesting and valuable, in themselves, as they do. According to Aristotle we value, and are right to value, friendship so highly because it is only in and through intimate friendship that we can come to know ourselves and to regard our lives constantly as worth living. It must be granted, of course, that someone who was so constituted that he could achieve these results without forming friendships, as Aristotle plausibly thinks no actual human being could, would have been given no strong reason to form them; he would at most have been told that the active expression of love is something intrinsically good, and as we have seen, this is no more than a prima facie, defeasible reason to form friendships. Hence anyone who thinks that, nonetheless, such a friendless person would be leading a less than fully satisfactory life will not find in Aristotle anything to support his view. It may be that such a view cannot be defended; but even if it can, I think it must be granted that Aristotle's arguments capture an important part of what there is in love and friendship which is so valuable for human beings.

Finally, this emphasis on the psychological benefits of friendship is not at all incompatible with the claim that, necessarily, a friend cares for and about another person's good in the same way in which that other person himself does so. If Aristotle is right, the psychological benefits he appeals to are not available to human beings unless one takes up the altruistic attitudes toward others which on his theory are essential to friendship. This is obviously true for the argument that only within the context of a friendship can one establish and maintain active interests that are sufficiently secure and constant that a continuously active life can be constructed round them. This argument professes to show why one should want to become the sort of person who shares with others, on a basis of equality, his chief interests in life: the life of such a person, Aristotle argues, is more continuously active and interesting to him than anyone's life can be who lives in the sort of psychological isolation that the absence of friendship implies. But I think it is equally, though perhaps less obviously, true for his other argument, from the need for self-knowledge, as well. Admittedly, on this argument the benefit that accrues to a person from being someone else's friend is the firm sense that his own preferred activities are morally good. But Aristotle's point is that this sense is only achievable insofar as one first and more distinctly recognizes the moral goodness of the similar life and similar activities of another person. This means that one must regard the association with one's friend, through which one first comes to know him and in which one constantly renews one's knowledge thereafter, as an association with someone who is objectively good and whose life is worthwhile in precisely the same sense as one's own. The motif of the friend as a mirror, which is indeed at best implicit in the *Nicomachean* argument, is not to be interpreted as meaning that on Aristotle's view a flourishing person treats his friend as a mere instrument by which to enhance his own self-esteem. On the contrary, this image implies that his self-esteem only gets the support he seeks insofar as he first has precisely the same esteem for the other person and his life, taken by itself, as he will come to have for himself and his own life. Aristotle's argument, in short, is that *in* loving and valuing the other person for his own sake one becomes able to love and value oneself, and this he offers in explanation and illumination of the fact that a friend loves and values his friend for his own sake and places a high value on doing so. There is no reduction here of friendship to narrow self-love, nor, properly understood, does the need for self-knowledge emphasized in Aristotle's argument in any way undermine or render doubtful the recognition of the worth of the other person and his life which we think (and Aristotle emphasizes in his opening account of what friendship is) is essential to any relationship deserving of that name.

NOTES

1. This paper reassembles material I was forced to publish in two separate installments. The first part reproduces, with omissions and condensation, "Aristotle on the Forms of Friendship," *Review of Metaphysics* 30 (1977), 619-648. The second part is similarly related to "Friendship and the Good in Aristotle," *The Philosophical Review* 86 (1977), 290-315. The omitted material mostly deals with textual questions and other matters of interest primarily to scholars; such readers are advised to consult the original publications.

2. Such family relationships are in fact the original and, in some ways, the central cases of φιλία. It should be noted, as the Greeks were themselves quick to see (cf. Euripides *Phoenissae* 1446: φίλος γὰρ ἐχθρὸς ἐγένετ᾽, ἀλλ᾽ ὅμως φίλος), that unlike the other types of case, family-φιλία existed even despite the absence of goodwill, unself-interested well-doing and the other practical attitudes and actions that in Aristotle's account serve to define φιλία. This is because it was assumed, as a norm, that where family ties were of a certain sort, these modes of feeling and action ought to be forthcoming; their absence did not destroy the φιλία itself (as the quotation from Euripides just given illustrates).

3. *Aristotle* (New York: Meridian Books, 1959), p. 223.

4. Much harm is caused by translators who render this verb by "love," since then there is bound to be confusion when one comes to translate στέργειν and ἐρᾶν. I render φιλεῖν by "like," στέργειν by "love," and ἐρᾶν by "be in love." Ἔρως I translate "sexual attachment," reserving both "love" (noun) and "friendship" for φιλία itself.

5. Or: "what he thinks good." The Greek is ambiguous.

6. Aristotle consistently expresses this altruistic side of friendship by the use of a single Greek phrase (or its variants): the friend does well to his friend ἐκείνου ἕνεκα (1155b31). It is important to be clear from the outset what is and what is not implied by this phrase, taken by itself. (1) In Aristotle's usage, to say that one acts "for someone else's sake" means, at least, that the fact that the other person needs or wants, or would be benefited by, something is taken by the agent as by itself *a* reason for doing or procuring that something, and that he acts for that reason. (2) It seems also implied that this reason is by itself sufficient to determine the agent to action. (3) But it is not implied that this is the agent's *only* reason for acting as he does, nor, in particular, that he does not also have a self-interested reason for acting. (4) Nothing is implied about the relative strengths of the reason founded on the other person's good and such other reasons as may be at work at the same time; it is not, for instance, implied that the agent's concern, in the given

action, for the other person's good is stronger than his concern for his own. (5) Nothing specific is implied about the psychological source or nature of the agent's concern for the other person; it might be a deep emotional attachment, like the love of parent for child, or whatever passions are involved in the attachment of lovers to one another, or, as we say, the concern for the welfare of persons "just as such"; or any of various other motives might be at work in a given case. As we shall see, Aristotle does have special views about the strength and the psychological source of a person's concern for his friend's good, but these are further questions the answers to which are not determined in any way by saying merely that a friend acts to secure his friend's good for his friend's own sake. In what follows I frequently express Aristotle's point here by saying that friends act out of concern for one another, and refer to "unself-interested" or "disinterested" goodwill as characteristic of friends. All these expressions should be interpreted in the light of the qualifications just noted. In particular, "disinterested" is not intended to indicate the absence of passion or special attachment. The point is just that if one is someone's friend, one wants that person to prosper, achieve his goals, be happy, and so on, in the same sort of way in which he wishes these things for himself, whatever else one may want as well, and whatever explains one's having this desire.

7. For a brief exposition of Aristotle's conception of civic friendship as a form of what I call below advantage-friendship, and the importance which he attaches to it, see "Aristotle on the Forms of Friendship," pp. 645-648.

8. Strictly, of course, Aristotle only reports here what "people say," but he must be endorsing these views, since by the end of the chapter (1156a3-5) he is drawing inferences on his own behalf partly from them: friends, he says, "must wish well to (εὐνοεῖν) and want what is good for one another. . . ." That both "people" and Aristotle himself define εὔνοια as *disinterested* well-wishing (and not well-wishing *tout court*) has traditionally been taken as the burden of these lines. This reading is undoubtedly correct, especially in view of Aristotle's usage elsewhere (see *NE* 1167a13-17 and *EE* 1241a7-8 and my discussion in the fourth paragraph of sec. IV of this paper), and I adopt it in what follows.

9. The centrality of this emotional bond in Aristotle's analysis is sometimes overlooked, but it is there, nonetheless. In *NE* 4.6. 1126b16-28, in characterizing the nameless minor social virtue that shows itself in the right sort of behavior in ordinary social intercourse—the person who has it will openly assert his own views and preferences, as appropriate, while also heeding and yielding to those of others when this is right—Aristotle says that this kind of person behaves toward others in the sort of way that a friend does: "for the person in this intermediate condition is very like what, with love (τὸ στέργειν) added, we call a good friend. But his condition differs from friendship because he lacks passion (πάθος) and love (τὸ στέργειν) toward those with whom he associates." Aristotle does not in *NE* 8-9 (or *EE* 7) list στέρξις formally as a condition or component of friendship, but this seems to be only because he presupposes it as obvious. At any rate he refers frequently enough in *NE* 8-9 to friends as loving (στέργειν) one another, one another's characters, etc. Since Bywater's index omits all of these passages I add the following (I think complete) list of places where the word appears in these

books: 1156a15, 1157a11, 28, 1161b18, 25, 1162a12, b30, 1164a10, 1167a3, 1168a2, 7, 22.

10. The resemblance is partial at best: neither of the derivative friendships tends to be permanent (1156a19-20); neither requires an extended preparatory period of testing and getting to know one another (1156a34-35, 1158a14-18); advantage-friends do not even tend to spend their time together (1156a27-28). One can have many friends of these kinds but only very few of the other (1158a-10 ff.).

11. It should be noticed also that Aristotle does on occasion say that friends of the derivative types love (στέργειν) one another (1156a14-15, 1157a28, 1162a-12), thus implying at least a relatively close emotional attachment. He sometimes seems to deny this, however: see, e.g., 1164a10-11.

12. This interpretation is more in conformity with the predominant usage of διά, which, though it can sometimes express a purpose (cf. Liddell-Scott-Jones, A Greek-English Lexicon [Oxford: Clarendon Press, 1940], s.v. B III 3), normally expresses an antecedent causal condition. Had Aristotle wanted to refer here to the well-wisher's purpose he would presumably have written τοῦ χρησίμου (etc.) ἕνεκα.

13. It is, obviously, compatible with these intentions (see below) that a friend should also expect his friendship to bring pleasure and/or advantage to himself: indeed, Aristotle makes it very clear, as at 1156a22-24, that pleasure and advantage are both cause (δι' ὅ) and defining purpose (πρὸς ὅ) in the case of these lesser friendships. The point is that even though a person looks for pleasure or advantage from a relationship and would withdraw from it if he thought this end no longer attainable through it, he can still, on the assumption that the pleasure or advantage does remain firm, wish his friend well for his own sake. Here pleasure or advantage, assumed to be a stable property of the relationship, serves as cause, not as goal, of the well-wishing.

14. This consequence of Aristotle's theory of pleasure and advantage-friends is, from our point of view, perhaps not a very palatable one. One might, for example, rather think that people involved in a sexual liaison that is also a pleasure-friendship would, just to the extent that they regard one another as friends, be committed to sacrificing the liaison itself, if it came to that, if the welfare or prosperity (or some other important good) of one of them made this seem desirable. On Aristotle's account of pleasure-friendship, however, as I have interpreted it, there would be no such commitment. (If there were, that would show that the friendship was not purely a pleasure-friendship but was verging toward being a character-friendship: cf. 1157a8-12.) Pleasure- and advantage-friendships, on Aristotle's conception, are, despite his denial that they are wholly self-centered, much more self-centered than perhaps we would be inclined to think them. It should also, perhaps, be noted here that Aristotle, on my interpretation, does not have to deny that one might (out of simple gratitude, for example) wish and do well to someone who had ceased to be pleasant or advantageous to oneself. His point is that well-wishing *as an ingredient in friendship* is limited by the other person's continuing to (be thought to) be pleasant or advantageous. Nor is this an arbitrary restriction: if those who have once been close companions cease

to take pleasure in one another's company, then their friendship is dead, no matter how much they do for one another thereafter out of gratitude for past favors or pleasures. The same thing holds of business friendships. Friendship, of whatever sort, requires a continuing lively interest of one person in another, and *mere* gratitude for past pleasure or past services is not enough to provide this.

15. I follow here the traditional interpretation, found, e.g., in Ross's translation. J. Burnet (*The Ethics of Aristotle* [London: Methuen, 1900], p. 363), followed by R.-A. Gauthier (*Aristote: L'Éthique à Nicomaque* [Louvain and Paris: Publications Universitaires de Louvain, 1958-59], 2:693), takes the text to say instead that one does not wish his friend to become a god because to do so would be to wish to deprive *him* of a good, namely, one's friendship. This is textually more awkward, but just possible. Burnet and Gauthier apparently opt for it because they think it attributes a more seemly (because purely altruistic) intention to this well-wisher, who is presumed to be morally virtuous. But this is an illusion. After all, becoming a god might well entail a sufficient improvement in one's condition so that the loss of a human friendship would be more than compensated for, and in that case one's friend could hardly claim to be acting altruistically in refusing to want one to achieve this status. There is no incompatibility at all (*pace* Gauthier) in wishing for one's friend's good and wishing that he should be deified (or in some other way improve his condition at the cost of the friendship). Hence the passage only makes a coherent point if interpreted in the traditional way. Friendship, even the purest, essentially involves the desire for one's own good (as well as the desire for that of one's friend), and there is no reason to interpret away signs of Aristotle's recognition of this fact. Notice also that at the end of the passage Aristotle emphasizes (1159a11-12) that a person's first concern is (properly) with his own good, a remark that is perfectly in place on the traditional interpretation but hardly so on Burnet's and Gauthier's.

16. It is instructive in interpreting advantage-friendship to notice that Aristotle distinguishes two kinds (*NE* 8.13. 1162b21-1163a9): one that is νομική and ἐπὶ ῥητοῖς (1162b23, 25-26: i.e., governed by explicitly agreed-upon exchanges of services) while the other is ἠθική (1162b23, 31: i.e., it rests on the parties' characters, as decent people who do not need to buy one another's attentions). It is interesting to observe that in the latter sort of friendship Aristotle says the parties give to one another ὡς φίλῳ, i.e., in the spirit in which true friends do, without looking for or soliciting any particular, exact return. In fact, as this comment betrays, it is only what Aristotle calls ἠθικὴ φιλία κατὰ τὸ χρήσιμον that counts at all as a φιλία on his own announced criteria: so-called advantage-friends of the other type don't really have εὔνοια for one another, so that their association is a *purely* commercial affair and hence no friendship, not even an advantage-friendship. That Aristotle is not clearer on this point here shows, I think, a certain unwillingness on his part to embrace unreservedly the idea that no association can count as a friendship which does not involve disinterested well-wishing. A comparison of this passage with the corresponding argument in the *EE* (1242b31-1243b14) will serve to place Aristotle's inconsistency on this point into proper focus. The *EE* begins by marking off the same two types of advantage-friendship (1242b31-32), νομική and ἠθική. But as the argument pro-

ceeds, it becomes apparent (b38-1243a2) that this division is provisional only; the latter type is really a confused relationship, in which the parties cannot decide whether to treat one another as *real* friends (that is, character-friends, in which case they ought not to demand repayment for their services at all) or as advantage-friends (that is, friends of the type that has just been described as *one kind* of advantage-friend, the νομική, in which case commercial practice is the accepted model for their relationship). Thus, in this passage Aristotle actually implies that it is only where an association *is* purely commercial that it can count as an advantage-friendship, as his denial in the *EE* of εὔνοια to advantage-friends (1241a3-5) also implies. The *NE* discussion, in insisting that the ἠθικὴ φιλία κατὰ τὸ χρήσιμον is a legitimate type of advantage-friendship, is therefore a distinct improvement; as often, however, Aristotle, in reworking this passage to bring it into line with his later views, refuses to abandon completely the earlier ideas that are causing the trouble. What results is a halfway house in which both the νομική and the ἠθική count as legitimate advantage-friendships, even though his mature view would seem to imply that the νομική is not in reality a friendship at all.

17. See the footnote to 1170b19 in his translation (*The Works of Aristotle Translated into English* [Oxford: Clarendon Press, 1915], vol. 9).

18. Alternatively, the argument might be interpreted as follows (I state just the main points): Everything that is good by nature is choiceworthy in itself, and everything choiceworthy in itself is worthy of the good man's choice. Furthermore, the good and happy man must possess everything that is worthy of his choice, since without even one of these things his life will be lacking in something it ought to have (cf. 1170b14-19). But association with people who are one's friends is by nature a good thing: this is so because in being aware of a friend and his activities one is, given that friends are "other selves," aware of one's self, and being aware of oneself is admittedly good by nature. Hence it will be worthy of a good man's choice to have a friend, and therefore he must have a friend if his life is to be completely fulfilled and lacking in nothing.

This argument is unsound. First, it is not true that the good person's life will be defective if he lacks any of the things that are good by nature and in themselves. No one can have all the things that are good in themselves; there are too many such things, and of too many distinct types (cf. my *Reason and Human Good in Aristotle* [Cambridge: Harvard University Press, 1975], pp. 129-130). Card games are good in themselves, but it does not follow that a person who never learns to play cards leads a less than flourishing life for that reason. If having friends truly is necessary to the flourishing life it must, then, be because friends are more than merely good in themselves to have. Second, even if it was granted, as perhaps it ought to be, that self-awareness is a sufficiently important good-in-itself to be a compulsory component of the flourishing life, it would still not follow that friends are a compulsory component of this life. To show that, one would have to show that self-awareness is only or best obtainable through the observation of one's friends, and this does not seem true (see the eighth paragraph of sec. VI of this paper).

19. Despite the remarks of W. F. R. Hardie, *Aristotle's Ethical Theory* (Oxford: Clarendon Press, 1968), pp. 331 f. It is doubtless true, as Hardie points

out, that Aristotle pays no attention in this argument to the fact that, however closely one may be attached to another person, one can never experience his thoughts and actions in just the way one experiences one's own. But it is not clear how this is supposed to matter to Aristotle's argument. It remains true that friends do take interest in and derive pleasure from one another's thoughts and actions, and that the interest they take in them is akin to the interest they take in their own.

20. Nor is there a hint in this direction in the *EE* argument, 1244b23-1245b9.

21. *Notes on the Nicomachean Ethics* (Oxford: Clarendon Press, 1892), p. 392.

22. Translated by St. G. Stock (*The Works of Aristotle*..., vol. 9), except for the first sentence, which is taken from G. C. Armstrong's translation (Loeb Classical Library, *Aristotle*, vol. 18 [Cambridge: Harvard University Press, 1935]).

23. It should be borne in mind here and in what follows that having a good character, on Aristotle's theory, requires not merely correct practical *judgments* (having a certain reasoned conception of how one ought to live) but also, and even more, having this conception embedded in one's desires and thereby making it effective in one's actions. Thus to know one is virtuous requires knowing (1) what the desires are that in fact motivate one's actions and (2) that these desires depend upon the same scheme of ends as one's reasoned conception defines for one's life. And while it may not be hard to know what one's considered view of how to live is, and even that this view is the correct one, it is quite another, and much more difficult, thing to know what conception of how to live is embodied in the desires that actually motivate one's actions. In any event it is essential to keep in mind that the self-knowledge required for flourishing is knowledge of what actually motivates one's actions, not just of what intellectualized theory of living one is prepared to defend.

24. For the theme of self-knowledge through examination of a reflection of the self in the mirror of another self, see Plato *Alcibiades* I. 132c-133c. This passage may be the source of the *MM*'s analogy. In explicating the *MM*'s use of the analogy I have built especially on two features emphasized in the text. First, the good man is represented as looking at another person and his life in order to see a reflection of himself. And second, by observing this person's life he sees clearly what his own life is actually like: one cannot see what one is from oneself (1213a-16), but one can see this, i.e., one can overcome this bias, by looking to another who is one's friend. The author plainly is not saying that one evades the effects of bias by trying to find out by observing from someone's behavior toward oneself what his opinion of one is. It is by observing *his* personal qualities, not by guessing his judgment of one's own, that one receives the sort of confirmation that is at issue here. And it is impossible to see how this can be supposed to happen unless, as in my expansion, one takes the knowledge acquired in looking at the "mirror" and refers it back to oneself: knowing that this other person's qualities are the same as or very similar to one's own (this follows from his being a true friend, one's "other self") and having observed that his character is virtuous, one now knows that one's own personal qualities are virtuous as well.

25. I translate θεωρεῖν here as "study" (instead of "see" or "observe" or "contemplate") in order to make it clear that Aristotle is saying something much

stronger than merely that the good man wants to be aware of good actions and takes pleasure in that. In this context θεωρεῖν is no mere equivalent of αἰσθάνεσθαι; as often in Aristotle, even where it implies the use of the senses, the word carries overtones of concentrated study, of the sort involved in theoretical knowledge (its other principal meaning in Aristotle). So neither of the two central claims of this argument is found in the later argument at 1170a13-b19; nor, for the same reason, is the further claim made here, that the good man enjoys (i.e., enjoys studying) the good actions of his friend, equivalent to the later claim that he enjoys (i.e., enjoys perceiving) them. If MM 1213a10-26 corresponds to anything in NE 9.9, it must be to 1169b28-1170a4; certainly not to 1170a13 ff.

26. I take it that the clause in parentheses (ὁ γὰρ σπουδαῖος ... λυπεῖται) is meant to explain why one should expect the morally good person to be continuously active. A morally good person enjoys virtuous action and (cf. 1175a30-36, b13-16) what one enjoys doing one tends to keep on doing; hence a virtuous person should tend to be continuously active when engaged in virtuous pursuits. But as Aristotle has just pointed out, a solitary person cannot manage to be continuously active at anything. It follows that a solitary does not really enjoy anything very much. Hence the principle that virtuous action is pleasant for the virtuous person must be understood as carrying with it the tacit assumption that such persons live their lives in social union with others.

27. Cf. 1170b10-14: "[The flourishing person] needs, therefore, to be conscious of his friend's existence, and this would come about in their living together and sharing in discussion and thought: for this would seem to be what living together means for human beings, and not, as for cattle, feeding in the same place." Evidently the solitariness Aristotle finds so debilitating is at least as much a matter of psychological as of physical isolation.

28. Throughout the discussion that follows I am indebted to Annette C. Baier's "Intention, Practical Knowledge, and Representation," in Action Theory: Proceedings of the Winnipeg Conference on Human Action Held at Winnipeg, Manitoba, Canada, 9-11 May 1975, ed. Myles Brand and Douglas Walton, Synthese Library, vol. 97 (Dordrecht and Boston, 1976), and to conversations with her.

29. See n. 18 above.

30. Richard Kraut in "The Importance of Love in Aristotle's Ethics," available now from the Philosophy Research Archives, goes seriously astray in supposing that from these isolated remarks taken by themselves one can construct an adequate defense of the value of friendship (see sec. III of his paper, esp. p. 13, and further remarks at pp. 14, 16, 24). For the reasons noted in the text they are quite inconclusive.

18

The Good Man and the Good for Man in Aristotle's Ethics[1]

Kathleen V. Wilkes

It is notorious that Aristotle gives two distinct and seemingly irreconcilable versions of man's *eudaimonia*[2] in the *Nicomachean Ethics*.[3] These offer conflicting accounts not only of what the good man should do but also of what it is good for a man to do. This paper discusses the incompatibility of these two pictures of eudaimonia and explores the extent to which the notions of "the life of a good man" and "the life good for a man" can be successfully united in a single concept of eudaimonia.

I

One version of what eudaimonia is and how it might be attained, which shall for convenience be labeled the "life-plan" approach, recommends a life governed by practical reason and planned as an organic and optimally functioning whole: "Now it is thought to be the mark of a man of practical wisdom to be able to deliberate well about what is good and expedient for himself, not in some particular respect . . . but about what sorts of things conduce to the good life in general (*to eu zen holos*)"[4] (1140a25-28). This line of thought assumes that there are a number of choiceworthy and desirable elements which one wants or needs to include in one's life and which one aims at—always on condition that they are capable of being coherently integrated with one another.[5] A good or happy life becomes, in part at least, one that works, and works

341

over time—a life wherein the minimum is missing and the least inner conflict is found. To achieve this a man must analyze his amorphous notion of what a good life would be (cf. 1142b31 f.: one has a true grasp [*hupolepsis*] of the end [*telos*]); this involves a reflective assessment not only of his own short-term and long-term needs and interests but also of whatever other desiderata society in general, and the *phronimos* (the man of practical wisdom: see 1094b27 ff., 1143b11 ff.) in particular find important. After this assessment comes the more technical problem of achieving and integrating those aims. The correct distribution of relative weights to these varied pursuits can be settled by internal and pragmatic considerations; it will be, quite simply, the one that is found to work, and the distribution that works will be the one with the most completeness (*teleiotes*, 1097a28) and self-sufficiency (*autarkeia*, 1097b8). On this approach eudaimonia can be viewed either as an "emergent" property of such a life or, more plausibly, as identical with it.[6] It is described, as it were, in extension; it is a function partly of the range and nature of the desiderata included in any life plan and partly of the dynamic interrelation of these constituents—their organization and interplay. If this sketch is correct, then one task of the *NE* is to show that virtuous activity is an essential ingredient of every plan—that man cannot attain the good life, the good *for* man, unless he is a good man. Thus Aristotle grapples with the problem that Plato faced in the *Gorgias*, the *Republic*, and elsewhere: needing to show that the villain, whatever the appearances, is deluded in his pursuit of happiness and that his practical reason has organized his life inefficiently. Aristotle's solution to the problem is an interesting one but will more profitably be discussed later; for the "life plan" account of eudaimonia will soon turn up again, but seen from a different and illuminating angle. For the moment the above sketch will serve to introduce it.

II

The rival version of the good life is simple to state but difficult, in its extreme implausibility, to understand: it is a life devoted to nothing but the intellectual activity of *theoria*, contemplation. To grasp this idea properly it is necessary to examine in some detail the arguments by which Aristotle reaches this surprising conclusion; for as we shall see, the same evidence could quite plausibly be used to defend a quite different claim about the good life.[7]

The arguments begin in 1.7, where, moved perhaps by the apparent vagueness of his preceding remarks about eudaimonia, Aristotle asserts: "Presumably, however, to say that happiness is the chief good seems a platitude, and a clearer account of what it is is still desired. This might perhaps be given, if we could first ascertain the *ergon*[8] of man" (1097b22-25). The idea here is that eudaimonia requires to be understood via an examination of man's ergon; to discover what his ergon is requires a metaphysic of the person: one must examine what it is to be a man and must then specify human good in terms of what human beings are and can do. (Hence a reading of the account of human psychology in the *De anima* is essential to a proper understanding of this argument.) We must, then, look at the meaning of the expression "the ergon of man" and consider the relation that man's ergon has both to the life of the good man and to the life that is good for a man.

The ergon of any X is the function that it has; or, if it is the kind of thing that cannot readily be said to have a function, it is its characteristic activity. It is definitionally assigned; it is what X does that makes it just what it is, and if for any reason X becomes unable to perform its ergon, it is then no longer genuinely an X at all (cf. *De anima* 412b20 ff.). A sheepdog has the ergon of herding sheep; a good sheepdog is one that herds sheep well. Correspondingly, the good man is the one who performs admirably the activities specific to his kind (see 1098a11-15).

A study of man's ergon, then, can tell us what it is to be a good man, once we have discovered just what activities are indeed characteristic of mankind. But it is far from clear how this gets us any closer to the good *for* man—how, indeed, the superb functioning of any ergon-bearing creature is relevant to what that creature's greatest good is (this point is made clearly in an article by P. Glassen).[9] If happiness is indeed the greatest good for man, excellence of functioning seems neither to entail it nor to be entailed by it. The problem here is reflected by the two expressions that are most commonly used as synonyms for eudaimonia: doing well, *eu prattein,* and living well, *eu zen* (see 1095a18-20, 1098b20-22). The English translations echo the ambiguity that we suspect in the Greek; a man may do or live well, in the sense that he performs admirably the activities that his ergon ascribes to him, with or without doing well for himself or living a life that is good *for* him.

We cannot solve this problem without examining the nature of the activities that are characteristic of mankind and hence constitute man's ergon. Aristotle defines man's ergon as "activity of the *psuche*[10] in accordance with a rational principle" (198a7); but he complicates the issue by distinguishing two major forms of rationality: practical wisdom (*phronesis*) and philosophic wisdom (*sophia*) (see 1143b14-17).[11] So man's ergon may be the activity of the psuche in accordance with either or both of these. In the *Eudemian Ethics* as in the *NE* Aristotle eventually settles for an unequivocally intellectualistic (perhaps even spiritualistic) answer: the

ergon of man is to engage in contemplation, theoria—philosophic wisdom in its purest or most rarefied form. One may prefer the idea, shortly
to be discussed, that practical wisdom rather than theoria should determine the activities that comprise man's ergon. But should we even accept
that it is solely rational activity, of whatever sort, that is alone the ergon
of man?

The objection to a restriction of man's ergon to rational activity and
nothing else runs as follows (drawn largely from Nagel).[12] Even if one
agrees that the ergon defines the creature, one can disagree about how
man, and hence his ergon, should be specified. For there are many competing descriptions of man and his various abilities which would mark
him off from other animals while yet leaving room for the nutritive, loco-
motive, and sensory capacities which he evidently and crucially possesses
but which are ignored if he is described simply as a rational creature.
Animals indeed share in sensation, movement, and digestion, but in different measure and different ways. Further, the *De anima* allows man a
complex psuche, the description of which does include these nonrational
capacities. The psuche, being a form,[13] defines the creature whose psuche
it is. One way to discover the ergon of any X is to identify its form: that
is, sight is the form of the eye, so seeing is the eye's ergon; the power to
cut is the form of an axe, so that cutting is the axe's ergon (see *De anima*
412a6-413a6, passim). Hence if the psuche-form of man is complex, comprising rational and nonrational capacities, the ergon of man should be
correspondingly complex and should include the nonrational functions
of digestion, movement, and sensation, as well as rational activity. A
more varied, conjunctive ergon in the *NE* would therefore be more in
keeping with the outline of the psuche delineated in the *De anima*. If so,
then some activities of the body would count as part of man's ergon; and
this would allow in (for example) somatic pleasure as a constituent of
man's good, as indeed it is widely thought to be. The more Aristotle cur-
tails the scope of man's ergon, the further the notion of ergon drifts from
that of the psuche, and yet ergon and psuche should be two names for the
same thing. Moreover, the more restricted the description of man's ergon
becomes, the more likely it is that someone could, without obvious
inconsistency, assent to such a description while looking to find *happiness* from, say, the "life suitable to beasts" (1095b20). In sum, the more
curtailed the activities proper to "the good man" become, the more the
conceptually intertwined notions of ergon and psuche are forced apart,
and the wider looms the gap between what the good man does and what
it may be good *for* man to do.

Furthermore (the objection continues), Aristotle's own description of
man's ergon as nothing but contemplation does not even meet his own

condition that it should be *idion*—unique to, and thus defining, the creature whose ergon it specifically is: the gods do nothing else. Admittedly, uniqueness is secured if one conjoins practical reasoning with philosophic contemplation as equally an "activity of the psuche in accordance with a rational principle," since practical wisdom is irrelevant on Olympus.[14] But this would make man's ergon a conjunctive one (practical and philosophic thinking) anyway, and there seems no reason of principle why it should not be further extended so as to overlap with the capacities of animals at one end as it already does with those of gods at the other. Man is a hybrid and two-sided creature, who shares properties with both gods and animals. The ergon offered by Aristotle highlights the side of rationality at the expense of animality and thus oversimplifies the nature of man. With this oversimplification the gap between the life of a good man and the life that is good for a man appears to widen yet further.

To answer this objection and understand Aristotle's case we must return to the *De anima*. There we find that the capacities of the psuche are not all on a par but are hierarchically structured; some faculties are there primarily or solely to subserve others, to make their exercise possible. The above objection misleadingly suggests democracy, whereas in fact we have a monarchy; reason, in man, is at the top of the pyramid of capacities. Is this enough for the conclusion that the ergon of man is the activity of the reasoning part of the psuche alone? And if so, of which of the two principal forms of reason is it the activity? A parallel with a different creature may clarify these issues.

An ordinary dog eats; thus it is enabled to run, bark, see, smell, and hear. Nutrition subserves locomotion, vocalization, and sensation. But this alone does not show nutrition to be a lower-order capacity, for the dog runs to catch the rabbit that it sees, so that it may feed. Despite this feedback from locomotion and sensation onto nutrition, however, nutrition still *is* a lower-order capacity; for if the dog could run, bark, and see without eating, it would still be a *dog* (however unusual), whereas if it could only take in nourishment, it would be an oddly shaped vegetable, for all living creatures are defined by the capacities of their psuchai. This is why a dog's active life (running, barking, etc.) can be called "higher" than nutrition, defining the animal and coming at the top of the hierarchy of its bodily functions and canine activities. The fact that there is feedback—running and barking foster the efficiency of the digestive and metabolic processes—does not militate against this ordering. The ergon of a dog qua dog is presumably a matter of this kind of activity, which is made possible by the lower-order metabolic, circulatory, and digestive processes; its capacities are coherently and systematically arranged to promote optimal active functioning. Moreover, this activity that is characteristic of an ordinary dog is not only what a good (healthy) dog does but also seems to be what it is good *for* that dog to do, because of the feedback that ensures its health and fitness.

If we compare a sheepdog to the dog qua dog, the account is much the same except that a new activity is added (herding sheep) which is its ergon; and the ergon of a sheepdog is rather its "function" than merely its "characteristic activity." From this activity there is no feedback onto the other capacities; the activities of running, turning, crouching, and so on feed back onto nutrition and circulation but themselves subserve the herding capacity that per se generates no extra feedback. All the capacities a dog has qua dog are subordinated to this new one. The new capacity is justified by quite external grounds (the needs of the shepherd) and not by its contribution to the dog's own good. Hence what the good sheepdog does and what it is good *for* the sheepdog to do have no necessary correlation.

Is a man more like the dog or the sheepdog? In fact, of course, the analogy with neither is quite exact. The closest parallel to the dog would be a crudely egoistic hedonist, concerned solely with his own bodily ease and pleasure, and even then he would need to exercise more practical reason than the animal in order to coordinate and satisfy his bodily needs; while it is rather the slave (the "living tool": 1161b4) than the free man whom Aristotle would think to have a "function," a task imposed upon him, like the sheepdog. The main point of the analogy, however, lies in whether or not man's highest-order activity feeds back onto his lower-order capacities and whether in either case we can merge the good man's life with the life good *for* that man. Let us try first supposing that practical wisdom, phronesis, is man's highest-order capacity. It is certainly the most plausible candidate, for it does seem to be the capacity without which no entity could be fully a man; whereas on the one hand an inability to contemplate, and on the other blindness or paralysis, would not rule anything out of the category of mankind. Given that the ergon of a creature defines the creature, this is an important point. With practical reasoning as the supreme activity, then certainly there will be feedback onto all the other capacities. For man's practical reasoning is concerned above all with himself, his affairs, his health, and his interests (see 6.5). So he will try to order the maximally efficient functioning of his whole system. And this will not just involve—as it does with the dog or the crude hedonist—bodily ease and comfort. For man is essentially a social animal (see 1097b11),[15] and thus he has interests, desires, demands, and pursuits that require the cooperation of others and his own cooperation with them. So if his total system is to function as well as possible, and if his social as well as his material needs are to be met, he must live in and conform to a tolerably run state. The exercise of practical reason is rendered possible by his lower-order capacities and by the social circumstances in which he lives; his lower-order capacities function well partly because of practical reason's guidance and partly because of the social and economic conditions of the state. The state, in turn, is organized by the practical reason of some of its members and requires the intelligent assent of most of them; and so we have a complete circle, within which every exercise of practical reason is related to man's other capacities by feedback. The need to fit in with society will make it highly likely that the most successful man is one who has developed the moral (other-regarding) virtues, such as justice, generosity, and fairness; indeed, there is a place in this kind of life for nearly all private or social goods—active virtue, honor, pleasure, stamp collecting, and so forth. Theoria too may have a role to play; such an intellectual activity would certainly be thought good by many people. Thus we get a full and active life which we expect the "good man" to lead well (see 1144a36-b1, 1144b16-17) and one that is moreover a life that must be good *for* a man, since his practical reason is explicitly setting out to order all things for his own overall advantage. Finally, there is a further striking feature of this interpretation of man's *ergon:* it characterizes intensionally, so to speak, precisely the life that the life-plan account described extensionally; the two coincide at every point.

If, however, we take philosophic wisdom (sophia or theoria) as the highest of man's capacities, we certainly get Aristotle's own view, but we also find a multitude of problems. That it is Aristotle's own view is clear: "It would be thought strange if practical reason, being inferior to philosophic wisdom, is to be put in authority over it" (1143b33-35).[16] The problems are equally clear. The activity of contemplation has poor claim to be regarded as that activity the performance of which is definitive of mankind; not only is it the sole occupation of the gods, but many rational men are incapable of the heights of abstruse and abstract speculation. Moreover, theoria is an activity subserved by all but generating *no* feedback (the objects of contemplation are not the affairs of men but rather transcendental entities—the gods, unchanging first principles, Being). So the activity cannot be justified by the contribution it makes to the welfare of the man engaged in it (see 1143b19-20), nor can it be justified, as was the ergon of the sheepdog, by any contribution it makes to someone else's purposes. We need to know why Aristotle thinks that the life of contemplation is the life of the best sort of man (why it is the life of the good man) and why it is best for him (why it is a life good for a man).

Aristotle has several arguments for the supremacy of theoria over all else, some better than others. The fact that it has no bearing on, and hence no value for, the overall welfare of the man engaging in it he tries to use in 10.7 as a point in its favor:

And this activity alone would seem to be loved for its own sake; for nothing arises from it apart from the contemplating, while from practical activities we gain more or less apart from the action. [1177b1-4]

But of course the fact that theoria is irrelevant to any other pursuit can hardly be cited as proof of its superiority. Many trivial amusements are pursued for their own sakes too (see 10.6); and, practically speaking, philosophic wisdom can be counterproductive. Anaxagoras and Thales were "ignorant of what is to their advantage" (1141b5-6), and the latter, of course, is said to have fallen into a well.[17]

Another inconclusive argument for the supremacy of philosophic wisdom is derived from its subject matter. In 6.7 Aristotle claims:

Wisdom (sophia) must be intuitive reason (nous) combined with scientific knowledge (episteme)—scientific knowledge of the highest objects. . . . For it would be strange to think that the art of politics, or practical wisdom, is the best knowledge, since man is not the best thing in the world. [1141a18-22]

This seems to assume the unacceptable equation "knowledge of higher objects = higher knowledge." It will not do; we do not prefer biology to botany, if we do at all, on such grounds. Just because in Aristotle's cosmology the objects of practical wisdom (the affairs of men and the state) are less worthy than those of theoria, one cannot conclude that the knowledge theoria gives is therefore higher knowledge or that it should be indisputably superior to practical wisdom.

Aristotle needs, and employs, a quite new and independent argument to establish the dominance of theoretic over practical wisdom. He introduces a theological assumption: the gods also contemplate (1178b21-22), and since by definition a divine activity is better and higher than any mortal one, correspondingly the happiness that accompanies the contemplation is greater by definition than any gained through mortal pursuits. So if men participate in this godlike activity, they are eo ipso engaging in something greater and better than practical reason can provide; and the happiness they get is rather divine bliss (makariotes) than merely human eudaimonia. This is explicit in 10.7:

But we must not follow those who advise us, being men, to think of human things and, being mortal, of mortal things, but must, so far as we can, make ourselves immortal, and strain every nerve to live in accordance with the best thing in us; for even if it be small in bulk, much more does it in power and worth surpass everything. [1177b31-1178a2]

Hence the gap that loomed large in the theoretic life between what a good man did and what it was good for man to do is closed by these theological assumptions: the noblest and best man is the one who engages most in the divine activity of contemplation, and this activity is precisely what gives him the greatest and purest happiness.

III

I shall now sum up the results of the discussion of man's ergon. There are three candidate "good lives" for consideration—precisely the three listed in the *Eudemian Ethics*: "It is clear that all connect happiness with one or other of three lives, the 'political,' the 'philosophic,' and the 'voluptuary's'" (*EE* 1216a27-28). We find the "voluptuary's" life—crude egoistic hedonism—by assimilating man closely to the ordinary dog: his maximally efficient functioning is a matter of bodily health and physical pleasure, and all that distinguishes him from the dog is that he needs more practical reason than the dog to help him coordinate and satisfy his bodily needs. We need not linger over this life, as we would presumably agree with Aristotle that there is an important distinction between human eudaimonia and animal good: "The ox in Egypt, which they reverence as Apis, in most of such matters [concerning bodily needs] has more power than many monarchs" (*EE* 1216a1-3). It cannot be good *for* a man, as it is a life good for animals, and fails, for humans, the requirement that the goods in question should be "complete" and "self-sufficient": the hedonist of such a type is always at the mercy of circumstances, dependent on the society off which, as a parasite rather than a member, he lives. This dependence of his gratification renders his life not truly enjoyable, for "a thing's being one's own is one of the attributes that make it pleasant" (1169b31-32), and "the good we divine to be something proper to a man and not easily taken from him" (1095b26-27). Further, it cannot be the life of a good man if it is also the life of a good dog or ox; the ergon of man cannot be the same as that of another animal (see 1098a1-3).

But the second interpretation of man's ergon, which identifies that ergon with the "political" life, is a much more serious contender. The "political" life is a life governed by practical intelligence, and the active use of practical reason does seem to be the only genuine candidate for the role of man's characteristic activity, or ergon; theoria cannot play this part. It tallies with the life-plan account discussed earlier; it recognizes and exploits man's de facto position as a social animal; and it leaves room for countless combinations of diverse activities, subject only to the restrictions imposed by the demands and customs of social living. It will also satisfy well the conditions of completeness and self-sufficiency. For if a man has a number of interests and occupations, a sudden loss of one or two may often be made up by an emphasis upon new or different activities; for example, the runner who is past his prime may take to coaching athletes. Even in wretched circumstances the "political" man will be better off than the "voluptuary" similarly placed, as he has been trained always to maximize the minimum (see 1100b34 ff.). Living in society, he will need the social (other-regarding) virtues; and this brings pleasure, for Aristotle is confident that one cannot truly have any virtue without enjoying it (1099a18 ff.). Above all, this life closes the gap between what a good man does and what it is good for a man to do; for the good "political" man has reasoned that the surest way to his own good is to lead the best ("political") life possible.

The major conflict comes between this life and the "philosophic" one; and because of the theological assumptions cited, the cards are stacked in favor of the latter. Theoria cannot fail to provide happiness—and happiness of a divine kind—since it can be exercised at any time, and for longer (within certain limits set by human frailty) than any other activity (see 1177a22 ff.). But practical reason cannot so guarantee continual happiness, for one needs suitable circumstances in which to exercise it (e.g., the social engineer needs resources, power, and influence); and if the opportunities are not forthcoming, then, like a brilliant runner forced to be a spectator at the Games (1099a1 ff.), one must watch another running off with the prize of happiness. Further, theoria has no end other than its own exercise; as with seeing, attainment is predicated at the same time as the activity: means and ends coalesce. Since theoria is not part of any means/end pursuit chain, there are no frangible links and no unwanted consequences.[18] But this is not true of practical reason: it supplies good things, and yet "before now men have been undone by reason of their wealth, and others by reason of their courage" (1094b18-19). It is only with theoria that happiness is an ensured and certain concomitant, product, or form.[19] And finally, the theoretic man will be able, whenever necessary, to share the happiness of the "political" man, but not vice versa. For the "philosophic" man must be sure that he is free from distraction, has an adequate—but not excessive—supply of worldly goods (1178a23-25), and lives in a state that encourages and values the contemplative life. Now to secure all this, so that he has unlimited time for contemplation, the theoretic man must apply his own practical reason, or at least assent to and approve the arrangements of others; unless he does so, he can have no guarantee of the secure continuance of this background (see 1145a6-9; *Magna Moralia* 1198b9-20). He must then have practical wisdom, with the happiness that it brings, subserving the contemplative kind. Conversely, though, the "political" man can know none of the delights of theoria; it would be erroneous to suppose, as we did earlier, that the joys of contemplation can contribute to the happiness of a life governed by practical reason. For practical wisdom not only is unworthy to govern the exercise of the divine activity of contemplation (1145a9-11) but also is incapable of it; theoria is such that it cannot fail to wreck any scheme that attempts to contain it. The happiness it brings, being divine, is utterly incommensurable with that resulting from any other activity; so one could never prefer any other occupation to it. The activity of theoria has no built-in limit, as do other activities (see 1175a4-5; 1177a21-22)—for example, after a point one cannot be more virtuous in this situation or extract more bodily pleasure from that one. In other words, at t_1 we may need to exercise courage but at t_2 no longer, so we turn to stamp collecting, which palls after a time; there comes a point at which overmuch indulgence in one interest gives way to the desire or need to engage in another—which is what fitting items into a life plan is all about. But the only possible reason for ceasing to contemplate, according to Aristotle, is that if we did not occasionally relax from it, our theoretic capacity would diminish. We cannot (psychologically cannot) stop because we would rather be doing something else; we are forced to stop sometimes because of the animal element in human nature, which, if ignored, would so enfeeble us that theoria itself would become impossible: "thinking itself is sometimes injurious to health" (1153a20). Practical reason cannot be dispensed with, for man is not god (see 1178b33-35); but its success will be measured solely by the opportunities it creates for the exercise of theoria. Hence we get the extreme intellectualist sentiments of 10.7; and in the *Eudemian Ethics* comes the claim:

Therefore whatever mode of choosing and acquiring things good by nature—whether goods of body or wealth or friends or the other goods—will best promote the contemplation of God, that is the best mode and that standard is the finest; and any other mode of choice or acquisition that either from deficiency or excess hinders us from serving or from contemplating God—that is a bad one. This is how it is for the soul, and this is the soul's best standard—to be as far as possible unconscious of the irrational parts of the soul, as such. [*EE* 1249b16 ff.]

The "philosophic" life ultimately denies all value to the "political" one; the conflict could not be more pointed.

IV

Aristotle's position is thus not consistent; one cannot, and should not try to, juggle with the texts so that the conflict of the two lives is resolved.

The life governed by practical reason should be preferred *if* we regard the ergon of man straightforwardly as that activity the performance of which distinguishes man from all else; but Aristotle's psychology and theology debar us from so easy a conclusion. His psychology tells us that man is hybrid—caught in a constant tug-of-war between the claims of his divine and his hylomorphic nature; his theology tells us that the divine element is not commensurable with the hylomorphic (see 1154b20 ff.). The contemplative life is fully attainable only insofar as man can become godlike, and the constant and irremovable block to this is that he is biologically an animal. But the mixture of the divine and the animal is not a stable one; there could be no compromise effected between such disparate elements. No man may attain full divinity, but once he has tasted it in part he is, as it were, foredoomed to try for the impossible. Frustration is then evidently a permanent fact. The indecision in Aristotle's ethics arises directly from the bilateral nature of Aristotle's man and cannot be evaded.

But if that is so, it is comparatively easy for us today to settle the quarrel between the two kinds of life on offer: we can dispute the truth of two crucial premises. First, we may have no reason to accept the premise that establishes for Aristotle the supremacy of the theoretic life, namely, that theoria is the sole divine activity and engenders a correspondingly divine kind of happiness. Without this premise the "philosophic" life is not necessarily superior to all else: it need not be the only life liveable by the supremely good man, nor would it be the only life that is truly good for the best sort of man. Further, if the delights of contemplation are no longer of the superhuman, divine order, then theoria is compatible with numerous other activities; it no longer need provide a kind of bliss by comparison with which all other engagements pall. The predominantly philosophic life will now become the kind of life that would suit some kind of intellectual recluse, a man who would in fact get more pleasure and contentment from it than he would from more sociable activities; but it would not be the duty or desire of every man to strive after it.

The second of Aristotle's assumptions to dispute is his hard-and-fast distinction between philosophic thinking (sophia or theoria) and practical reasoning. Aristotle drew this firm line for the same reasons that persuaded Plato to distinguish just as sharply between knowing and believing: a difference of objects presupposes a difference of faculty (see 1139a-6-12). But this argument is exceedingly weak; and among philosophers and psychologists today there is little interest in the attempt to carve up rational activity into two or more clearly distinct sorts. The current tendency is rather to regard man's intellectual endeavors as comprising a whole host of techniques and behaviors that are intended to solve problems of various kinds. When the human intelligence is applied to problems of shoemaking, we call it craft; when applied to perplexities about the structure of the atom, it is science; if applied to organizational difficulties or to the best way of teaching little Johnny to tie his shoelaces, it is practical; if used on conceptual issues, it is philosophy; and there are many fields of inquiry apart from these. So philosophical inquiry, speculation, or reasoning is not importantly different in kind from practical thought: they are applications of the human intellect to different types of problem. *If*, then, the "philosophic" life is the life of the philosopher, the man who is particularly interested in specific sorts of tangles, then there can be no rivalry with the "political," or practically minded, man; they will allot the greater part of their time to the distinct issues that hold their interest most.

Perhaps, though, Aristotle does not mean this by "the philosophic life" —does not mean the endeavor to come to grips with and disentangle knots of a certain sort. In 10.7 the element of discovery is excluded from the activity of theoria: "it is to be expected that those who know will pass their time more pleasantly than those who inquire" (1177a26-27). He cannot mean that knowing is a way of passing time, for it obviously is not. Theoria must rather be something that follows on the solution of a problem, or on the discovery of a satisfactory theory, after research has shown how things must be or how they must hang together—a contemplation of something at last fully grasped and understood. And one can indeed grant that after a difficult piece of work—intellectual, practical, or technical—has been brought to a satisfactory conclusion, one can sit back and look with pleasure and approbation on the results achieved; and there may be a quasi-aesthetic delight in the very thought of the structure of the double helix, the design of a jet engine, or a philosophical theory. But such contemplation is not sustained indefinitely, and presumably we do not think it should be: this is not the end at which inquiry is directed. All research is intended to produce some answer, theory, or solution; but the point and pleasure of the work does not derive from the passive *post factum* contemplation of the results achieved but rather in the work itself and the discoveries. A sustained state (and it seems to be more of a state than an activity) of contemplation is occasionally claimed to accompany mystical or hallucinogenic experiences, and Aristotle believes that his god, who by definition knows everything, spends eternity in this manner; but in neither case is there sufficient evidence to justify the supposition that for men there could be a genuine, long-lasting, and wholly static state or activity of mental gazing. Inasmuch as the "philosophic" life is intended to consist of this improbable occupation, it seems neither feasible nor desirable. It would be more charitable to Aristotle—and fortunately in keeping with remarks of his elsewhere[20]—to stress the actively inquiring side of sophia and to play down the praise of contemplation. We could then resolve the conflict between the "philosophic" and the "political" lives by agreeing that although the ergon of man is indeed "activity of the psuche in accordance with a rational principle," the "rational principle" in question is, broadly, intelligence in general—intelligence that may be applied to art, craft, science, philosophy, politics, or any other domain.

The other question with which this paper began was the extent to which the notions of "the life of a good man" and "the life good for a man" can be successfully united in a single concept of eudaimonia. In this, surely, Aristotle is wholly successful, and his success is of great interest for contemporary moral philosophy. It is true that the way he links "the good man" with "the good for man" as far as the *theoretic* life is concerned—by claiming that a better-than-mortal happiness is, or is an immediate product of, a better-than-human activity—does not have much contemporary relevance once we have denied the reality or feasibility of a life devoted wholly to unproductive contemplation. But his argument that the better a man is at practical reasoning, the better a life he will lead, is of great importance; and its importance is enhanced if we extend the scope of phronesis, as we legitimately may, to include human problem-solving intelligence in general. For Aristotle's claim is then that the best man is the man who exercises his rational capacities to their fullest extent *to gain for himself the best life possible.* He arranges and patterns his entire way of life upon the basis of his deliberative reasoning about what short-term and long-term goals and interests will bring him most eudaimonia, taking into account his social, material, and intellectual endowments and limitations.

This thesis must be understood properly. For unless we understand it, we may agree with the kind of disapproval that Ross, for one, has expressed of "the self-absorption which is the bad side of Aristotle's ethics"[21] and may interpret the truth that Aristotle's ethics is ultimately selfish as a condemnation rather than a description. The essential thing to realize is that Aristotle—and Plato—wrote in a time when the distinction between the moral (other-regarding) and prudential (self-regarding) virtues had not yet been framed, and, perhaps even more importantly, that they would have denied any reality or importance to the distinction had it been explicitly presented to them. This is something that has, I believe, been almost completely ignored (or, what amounts to the same thing, tacitly or implicitly denied) by commentators. There are several reasons for its neglect. First, it is probably not entirely true that we do now equate morality *simpliciter* with other-regarding virtues and actions;

modern moral philosophy covertly equates the two but rarely does so explicitly. But if we fail to recognize that the current notion of morality *in fact* comprises centrally and essentially other-regarding behaviors and virtues alone, we will not recognize, either, the fact that Plato and Aristotle are not discussing our notion of morality at all. Second, we know well that the qualities approved of by Greeks of the fourth century B.C. are in many respects unlike those applauded by the twentieth century A.D.; and we use *this* fact to explain why Aristotle counts as *aretai* worth listing such things as magnificence, ambition, and ready wit. But this is only a partial explanation. More important is the fact that the three virtues listed are predominantly self-regarding and hence would never appear in any modern list of *moral* virtues. Third, a simple point of translation: *ethike arete* is almost invariably translated as "moral virtue," and so Books 2-5 get labeled the books about moral virtue, and Book 6, the book on intellectual virtue. But a far less misleading translation of *ethike* would be "of character," "of disposition," or "dispositional" and arete means "excellence" rather than "virtue." The distinction that Aristotle draws between the aretai of Books 2-5 and those of Book 6 is based in part on the presence or absence of an irrational, passionlike element (see 1102b13 ff.) and in part on whether they come primarily by teaching or by training (see 1103a14 ff.). Every criterion offered to distinguish the two kinds of aretai is one that (in our terms) includes self-regarding equally with other-regarding virtues in the Books 2-5 group. "Morality," in the contemporary sense of the term, is not something that Aristotle wished to discuss as such.

If that is so, then we can see that Aristotle's "good man" will indeed be a *morally* good man—that is, in morally demanding situations he will do the morally right thing. But the important notion of goodness here is rather that he is good at being the kind of man that he has deliberately chosen to be. If he thinks, and is right in thinking, that his greatest happiness will come from a solitary life as a philosophical recluse (to choose an extreme example), then the chances are that he will have comparatively little opportunity for exercising other-regarding aretai but much scope for the self-regarding aretai of self-discipline, perseverance, and the like. If, however, he thinks that his satisfaction will come from a life as a social worker, then evidently his exercise of other-regarding aretai will be much commoner. But neither life is, as such, better than the other; the ethical demand (*ethical* seems a better word to use than *moral*, as it is not so closely tied to other-regarding virtues and actions) is rather to cultivate to the utmost the excellences required by the life chosen by each man as being best for himself. P. F. Strawson quotes the professor who claimed, "For me to be moral is to behave like a professor";[22] with this Aristotle would have been in full agreement, once we had explained—and it would have been necessary to explain—the meaning of the term *moral*.

This discussion has two important consequences. First, when studying the ethical writings of Aristotle—and Plato—one should hesitate before accusing them of trading upon an ambiguity if we see them moving from one of *our* senses of "live well" and "do well" to the other. For although they may be doing so, it is more likely that they are not. Their shared conviction is that nothing can be an arete unless it benefits its possessor— that there is no *genuine* "doing well" that does not leave the doer better off, in some way, than before, and that real *eu prattein* and real *eu zen* are not ambiguous notions. The clearest, if slightly misleading, way of putting this into modern terminology is to say that an enlightened pru-dentiality presupposes or requires morality. Second, we should consider whether this is not a wise line to take. The attempt to derive "the good life" from the requirements of rationality is a worthy and an interesting aim; many contemporary moralists would like to answer the amoralist's challenge, "Why should I be moral?" by saying, "Because no other course of action is in your interests, placed in the circumstances in which you are." But if this is so, then the foundation of morality is identical with that of enlightened prudentiality. Certainly such an enterprise is more exciting and intellectually satisfying than the attempt to base morality in the emotions, in intuitions, in conscience, or in a social contract.

NOTES

1. I am grateful to M. F. Burnyeat and Thomas Nagel for valuable criticisms of an earlier draft of this paper.

2. To discover the content of the concept of eudaimonia is one aim of this paper. Thus I shall often transliterate rather than translate the term.

3. Hereafter *NE*. References from the *NE* will be given without the prefix *NE*. Citations from any other works will be prefaced by title.

4. *To eu zen* is one of the synonyms used by Aristotle for *eudaimonia*. It encapsulates the concealed ambiguity of *eudaimonia* well; is it the life of a good man or a life good for a man?

5. It will be evident that I am taking for granted the thesis that Aristotle's final good for man is an inclusive end, not a single paramount end. The literature of this dispute is extensive and well known; here I shall ignore it but for repeating one important point: the phrase *ta pros to telos* need not always mean "means to the end" but should often be taken to mean "constituents of the end"; and see also the crucial passage at 1097b16-20.

6. In the *Posterior Analytics* 90a15 and 93b8 it is argued that *ti esti* and *dia ti* amount to the same thing, so that what eudaimonia is and what produces it

would be answers to the same question. Thus to regard it as an "emergent" property seems harmless and may be useful.

7. The discussion of man's *ergon* which follows is heavily indebted to Thomas Nagel's "Aristotle on *Eudaimonia*," *Phronesis* 17 (1972), 252-259 (chap. 1 of this anthology), the influence of which will be so apparent that specific references would be otiose.

8. *Ergon* will be left in transliterated form. "Function" is a good translation in some cases; "characteristic activity" is nearer the mark in others, especially for human beings.

9. P. Glassen, "A Fallacy in Aristotle's Argument about the Good," *Philosophical Quarterly* 66 (1957), 319-322.

10. Again, *psuche* will generally be left transliterated. There is no adequate translation of this term in English; the commonly used "soul" is justifiable only if its shortcomings are well understood.

11. In fact the intellectual virtues that Aristotle cites are *episteme, techne, phronesis, nous, sophia,* and *politike.* But sophia is said to be the union of episteme and nous; and phronesis certainly is often considered to include techne and is said in 1141b23-25 to be of the same *hexis,* or disposition, as politike.

12. See n. 7 above.

13. All psuchai are forms; and the forms of all living things are psuchai. Psuchai are thus a subclass of forms.

14. See 10.8: "Will not the gods seem absurd if they make contracts and return deposits and so on? . . . If we were to run through them all, the circumstances of action would be found trivial and unworthy of gods" (1178b10-18).

15. Cf. *Politics* 1253a1 ff.: "Man is by nature a political animal. And he who by nature and not by mere accident is without a state is either above humanity or below it. . . . The proof that the state is a creation of nature and prior to the individual is that the individual, when isolated, is not self-sufficing, . . . but he who is unable to live in society or who has no need because he is sufficient for himself must be either a beast or a god." See also 7.1.

16. See also 1145a9-11.

17. But Thales is also reputed to have made a killing on a bumper olive harvest, by monopolizing all the olive presses; so legend counterbalances legend.

18. Unless one falls into a well. But such a consequence of contemplation is perhaps fortuitous.

19. It is thus unnecessary to add, as Aristotle does, the theologically highly dubious premise that the gods love and will reward whoever is most akin to them (1179a22 f.); this is presumably an extra claim brought in in the hope that *observable* good things will accrue to the theoretic man.

20. The highest science is the "first philosophy" of *Metaphysics* 1003a21-26, with no suggestion that inquiry is not essential. For it is a *science* of being, and as we have seen, episteme is an essential part of sophia.

21. W. D. Ross, *Aristotle,* 5th ed. (London, 1949), p. 208.

22. P. F. Strawson, "Social Morality and Individual Ideal," *Philosophy* 36 (1961) 8.

19

The Role of Eudaimonia in Aristotle's Ethics

John McDowell

1. In Book 1 of the *Nicomachean Ethics*, Aristotle evidently endorses the thesis that *eudaimonia* is the chief good, the end for all that we do. Following Anthony Kenny, we can distinguish at least two possible interpretations of that thesis: either as claiming that eudaimonia is that for whose sake all action is undertaken (an indicative thesis), or as claiming that eudaimonia is that for whose sake all action ought to be undertaken (a gerundive thesis).[1] Kenny is reluctant to attribute any doctrine of the former kind to Aristotle. But on the face of it an indicative thesis is what Aristotle appears to accept. At 1.12.8. 1102a2-3, he says: "... it is for the sake of this [sc. eudaimonia] that we all do all that we do"; and there seems to be no prospect of taking this to express a gerundive thesis.[2] And the general drift of Book 1 points in the same direction. At 1.2.1. 1094a-18-22, Aristotle says: "if, then, there is some end of the things we do, which we desire for its own sake (everything else being desired for the sake of this), ... clearly this must be the good and the chief good." Whether or not we suppose that the second "if" clause, which I have omitted, is meant as an argument for the truth of the first,[3] what I have quoted appears to say that if the indicative thesis about a single end of action is true, then the single end whose existence it asserts is the chief good; and it is hard to resist the impression that eudaimonia figures in the later chapters of Book 1 as verifying the antecedent of that conditional: first at 1.4.2. 1095a17-20, on the strength of general consensus, and then at 1.7.3-8. 1097a25-b21, on the strength of its satisfying the two conditions,

finality and self-sufficiency, which Aristotle argues that the chief good must satisfy.

2. Suppose someone says that everyone has a single end which he pursues in all his actions. We might ask: does he mean (i) that there is some end of action common to everyone? or (ii) that everyone has his own end, but one that may differ from his neighbor's?

1.4.2-3. 1095a17-28 indicates that Aristotle's answer would be "Both." Which answer is appropriate depends on the level of specificity with which ends are formulated. People have divergent views about what eudaimonia amounts to in substantive detail: if we formulate a person's end at a level of specificity at which such divergences appear, then *ex hypothesi* we cannot find *that* end shared by all (cf. (ii) above). But a thesis on the lines of (i) can be true nevertheless, in virtue of the availability of the term *eudaimonia* itself as a specification of the common end whose existence such a thesis asserts.

Aristotle himself has a specific view about what kind of life constitutes eudaimonia.[4] He certainly does not hold that everyone aims to lead that kind of life. But this yields no argument against attributing to him a thesis like (i). It would be a mistake—a missing of the nonextensionality of specifications of aim or purpose—to think one could argue on these lines: eudaimonia is in fact such and such a kind of life; there are people who do not have that kind of life as their aim; therefore there are people who do not have eudaimonia as their aim.

If it is the availability of the specification *eudaimonia* which permits the unification of substantively divergent ends in life, the question arises whether the unification is merely verbal. I shall revert to that question in due course (§§ 7 ff.).

3. Kenny's reluctance to attribute an indicative thesis to Aristotle deserves sympathy. Even if we bracket the question whether any interesting unification of divergent ends in life is effected by the specification *eudaimonia*, there is still room for suspicion of the claim that any one person has, in any interesting sense, a single end in all his actions. If "actions" means something like "voluntary or purposive doings," there is surely no plausible interpretation of the notion of eudaimonia which would make it true that all of anyone's actions are undertaken for the sake of what he conceives eudaimonia to be. Worse: that is conceded by Aristotle himself, when he recognizes the occurrence of incontinence. When someone acts incontinently in pursuit of a pleasure, he differs from an intemperate person—who would also pursue the pleasure—in that pursuit of the pleasure would conform to the intemperate person's con-

ception of the sort of life a human being should lead (hence, his conception of eudaimonia); whereas for the incontinent person that is precisely not so. The incontinent person has a different conception of what it is to do well (i.e., of eudaimonia), but allows himself to pursue a goal whose pursuit in the circumstances he knows to be incompatible with what, in those circumstances, doing well would be.[5] So his action, though voluntary, is not undertaken for the sake of (his conception of) eudaimonia.

4. But we can eliminate this counterexample, and so preserve the possibility of ascribing an indicative thesis to Aristotle, as Book 1 seems to require (§ 1 above), without accusing him of inconsistency. What is needed —and independently justifiable—is to equip Aristotle with a concept of *action* under which not just any voluntary or purposive doing falls.

The chief good is the end of the things we do (*telos tōn praktōn:* 1.2.1. 1094a18-19, cf. 1.7.1. 1097a22-23); and in the explicit statement of 1.12.8. 1102a2-3, quoted in § 1 above, the verb is *prattein.* Now we know in any case that *prattein* and its cognates have a quasi-technical restricted use at some points in Aristotle. At 6.2.2. 1139a19-20 and at *Eudemian Ethics* 2.6.2. 1222b18-21, *praxis* ("action") is restricted to man and denied to other animals. Voluntary behavior, however, is allowed to other animals by 3.2.2. 1111b7-10. That passage suggests that we should connect the field of application of the restricted use of *prattein* and its cognates with the field of application of the notion of *proairesis* (standardly translated "choice"), since proairesis is similarly denied to non-human animals (and also to children). As for proairesis, one might have thought, from 3.3.19. 1113a9-12, that just any deliberative desire to do something would count for Aristotle as a proairesis. But that does not square with the fact that, while denying that someone who acts incontinently acts on a proairesis (e.g., 3.2.4. 1111b13-15), he recognizes that an incontinent act can issue from deliberation (6.9.4. 1142b18-20). The best resolution is to suppose that a proairesis is a deliberative desire to do something with a view to doing well (*eupraxia:* see 6.2.4-5. 1139a31-b5).[6] "Doing well" (*eu prattein*) is by common consent a synonym for "having eudaimonia" (1.4.2. 1095a19-20). So, given the conjecture that praxeis— actions in the restricted sense—are doings that issue from proairesis, we have it guaranteed, by the implicit explanation of the restricted use, that all praxeis are undertaken for the sake of eudaimonia (i.e., eupraxia).

We might reach the same conclusion, without the detour through proairesis, from 6.5.4. 1140b6-7: "...while making has an end other than itself, action (*praxis*) cannot; for good action (*eupraxia*) itself is its end." This passage forces a further refinement into our picture. Aristotle here appeals to his distinction (cf. e.g., 1.1.2. 1094a3-5) between two sorts of application of the notion of an end, or of expressions like "for the sake of," according to whether or not that for whose sake something is done is distinct from that which is done for its sake. In the terminology which commentators have adopted from Greenwood, this is the distinction between *productive* means (where the end is distinct) and *constituent* means (where the end is not distinct).[7] Now in order to respect the distinction between praxis and making, we have to recognize that, even if undertaken for the sake of eudaimonia, a bit of behavior need not thereby be shown to be a praxis. To count as a praxis it must be undertaken as a *constituent* means to eudaimonia (that is, the agent's reason must be expressible on these lines: "Doing this is what, here and now, doing well is"), as opposed to a *productive* means (with the agent's reason expressible on these lines: "Doing well is doing such and such, and I cannot get into a position in which I can do such and such except by doing this").[8]

5. Kenny does consider (p. 28) the possibility of getting round the problem posed by incontinence (§ 3 above) in something like the way I have suggested: he contemplates the suggestion that since the incontinent person does not act on a proairesis ("choice"), one mist ascribe to Aristotle the thesis that whatever is *chosen* is chosen for the sake of eudaimonia. Kenny rejects this suggestion on the basis of 1.7.5. 1097b1-5: "for this [sc. eudaimonia] we choose always for itself and never for the sake of something else, but honor, pleasure, reason, and every virtue we choose indeed for themselves (for if nothing resulted from them we should still choose each of them), but we choose them also for the sake of eudaimonia, judging that by means of them we shall have eudaimonia." But this is inconclusive.

According to Kenny, it is clear that Aristotle "means not that on some particular occasion honor and pleasure are chosen both for their own sakes and for the sake of [eudaimonia], but that on some occasions they are chosen for their own sakes, and on other occasions for the sake of [eudaimonia]." This is open to dispute. Presumably Kenny's idea is this: the parenthesis shows that choosing those things for themselves is not choosing them as means to anything else; hence it can be true both that we choose them for themselves and that we choose them for the sake of (as means to) eudaimonia, only if the occasions of these choosings are different. However, the terminology of the parenthesis (note "resulted") suggests the possibility of a different construal, according to which what it shows is that choosing those things for themselves is not choosing them as *productive* means to anything else. With that construal of the parenthesis, the language of the passage is compatible with the idea that choosing those things for themselves, so far from excluding their being chosen, on the same occasions, for the sake of eudaimonia, actually *is* choosing them as constituent means to eudaimonia.[9]

However, although the language of the passage permits this interpretation, I am doubtful whether the substance does. Virtue and reason are surely not constituent means to eudaimonia (though they may be productive means); nor is it obvious that that is the right view of the relation of pleasure and honor to eudaimonia. Such a view has its plausibility in the context of a conception of eudaimonia as an aggregate of independently recognizable goods, and I shall be questioning (§§ 12-14 below) whether that conception is Aristotle's.

Suppose, then, that Kenny is right about the meaning of the passage: that, according to it, there are, or could be, choosings of, say, pleasure in the belief that the behavior motivated thereby will neither constitute nor produce eudaimonia—hence, choosings of pleasure other than for the sake of eudaimonia. Even so, my suggestion is not refuted. The verb translated "choose" in this passage is not *proaireisthai*, which, with its cognate noun, has the quasi-technical use discussed in §4, but *haireisthai*, which can mean (what *proaireisthai* in Aristotle's quasi-technical use does not mean, and what he must sometimes have needed a word for) simply "prefer," or "choose" in an ordinary sense. In that case the concession that in the sense appropriate to this passage, there can be choosings of pleasure other than for the sake of eudaimonia need involve no more than the familiar point about incontinence (§ 3 above); or a similar point about pursuit of pleasure, not contrary to one's conception of eudaimonia, as in incontinence, but engaged in by those (e.g., children or non-human animals) who do not pursue eudaimonia at all. Such points pose no threat to the thesis that all behavior that issues from proairesis is undertaken for the sake of eudaimonia.[10]

6. At *Eudemian Ethics* 1.2.1. 1214b6-12, Aristotle says: ". . . everybody able to live according to his own proairesis should set before him some object for noble living to aim at—on which he will keep his eyes fixed in all his praxeis (since clearly it is a mark of much folly not to have one's life regulated with regard to some End). . . ."[11] Kenny remarks (p. 29): "The fact that this is made as a recommendation shows that what is recommended is not something that is already the case in the behaviour of all men."

Curiously enough, the "should" that occurs in the Loeb translation I have quoted[12] corresponds to nothing in the text translated (although some manuscripts do have *dein*). One might argue that even if the text contains no "should," it needs in any case to be understood, because the parenthesis is evidently meant to back up a recommendation.[13] But it is not obvious that the parenthesis cannot be understood differently, as a sort of gloss on the restriction "able to live according to his own proairesis." In that case, with the Loeb text, the passage yields an indicative thesis about those to whom the restriction applies (sc. all but the very foolish).

In any case, once the character of the indicative thesis which I am ascribing to Aristotle is clear, it does not ultimately matter if this passage has to be read as making a recommendation. The recommendation is that those able to act on proairesis should do so, that is, should form a conception of eudaimonia and act for its sake; that this is made as a recommendation does not presuppose that a piece of behavior may both issue from proairesis and not be undertaken for the sake of eudaimonia.

7. Suppose Aristotle does wish to maintain that praxeis are (by definition) bits of behavior undertaken as constituent means to eudaimonia. What would be the point of such a thesis?

If we can find something more than merely verbal unification of divergent ends in life effected by the specification "eudaimonia," then "undertaken as constituent means to eudaimonia" marks out, in spite of the divergences, a distinctive sort of reason an agent can have for behaving as he does. In that case the point of the thesis can be to introduce us, by way of our grasp of that distinctive sort of reason, to a restricted class of bits of behavior which, because undertaken for that sort of reason, are of special interest in ethics. I suggest that we can indeed grasp such a distinctive sort of reason: it is the sort of reason for which someone acts when he does what he does because that seems to him to be what a human being, circumstanced as he is, should do. The ethical interest of such behavior is that the behavior, with its reasons, is indicative of the agent's character.[14]

8. It is important not to be misled about the kind of classification of reasons I have in mind. One possible classification of reasons is by general features of their content, into such categories as moral, aesthetic, or prudential. But that is not the kind of classification I have in mind.

To say that someone should do something is to say that he has reason to do it. Since reasons fall under categories of the sort I have just mentioned, it might seem to follow that uses of "should" fall under categories likewise. On this view, when "should" is used in characterizing the distinctive sort of reason that is involved in acting with a view to eudaimonia, what is involved would have to be one such specific kind of "should," say a moral or prudential "should." But that is not how I intend the suggestion.

Consider a dispute on the following lines. One party (X) says that a human being should exercise certain virtues, including, say, justice and charity. The other party (Y) says: "Nonsense! That's a wishy-washy ideal, suitable only for contemptible weaklings. A real man looks out for himself; he certainly doesn't practice charity, or justice as you conceive it." Now when X applies his view to specific circumstances, he will produce reasons which, according to him, people so circumstanced have for acting as he says they should; and the reasons will belong to one of the categories into which reasons fall. As his position has been described, the reasons will, at least in some cases, be moral ones. Y's reasons will be of a different category: namely, reasons of selfish interest. If we can nevertheless understand the exchange as a genuine dispute, with the recognizable topic "How should a human being behave?" then we cannot take the "should" in the question to have a sense that permits it to be backed only by one of the favored categories of reason. And surely we can so understand the exchange.

9. I have been using the word *moral* for a certain category of reasons to which a person may or may not think he should conform his life: a category of reasons on a level with, and distinguished by their content from, say, aesthetic reasons, so that if someone argues that human beings should not act in a certain way because it would be, say, inelegant, we might describe him as adducing not a moral but an aesthetic reason.[15] Some philosophers may want to object, in the interest of a use of "moral" according to which the reasons to which someone thinks a human being should conform his life are, *eo ipso,* the reasons he counts as moral. Thus, in the case I have just mentioned, the person is described, according to this view about the use of "moral," as thinking that the avoidance of inelegance is morally required; and similarly Y, in § 8, thinks looking out for oneself is morally called for. This is to insist that the "should" that fixes the topic of such disputes as that described in § 8 is a moral "should."

It is a terminological question whether we should use "moral" in this way. The terminological proposal does not conflict with the substance of my suggestion: namely, that we can make sense of a "should" (it does not matter whether we describe it as a moral "should") which, since it intelligibly locates disputes of the sort described in § 8, is not proprietary to any one specific mode of appraisal—in the sense in which, on this terminological proposal, moral appraisal is no longer a specific mode of appraisal.

Some will be tempted by a different way of insisting that the "should" in question does, contrary to my suggestion, belong to a specific category: namely, the thesis that ultimately it stands revealed as a certain sort of prudential "should." This is not merely a terminological proposal. I shall postpone discussion of it until I have related the suggestion to Aristotle's text.

10. At 1.7.9-16. 1097b22-1098a20, Aristotle exploits the thesis that the *ergon* of man consists in rational activity, and the conceptual connections between the notions of ergon, excellence, and activity, in order to reach the conclusion that eudaimonia, the good for man, is rational activity in accordance with excellence. This passage is commonly taken as a (purported) argument for Aristotle's own substantive view about what eudaimonia is. But it can be read in such a way that the conclusion is (so far) neutral, as between Aristotle's own substantive view and, say, a view of eudaimonia corresponding to the position of Y in the dispute described in § 8. With such a reading, the point of the passage can be, not to justify Aristotle's own substantive view, but rather to help the reader to comprehend the distinctive kind of reason which, according to the suggestion of § 7, the concept of eudaimonia serves to delimit.

What is the ergon of a kind of thing? Kenny (p. 27) objects to "function," and proposes the translation "characteristic activity." If that phrase is understood merely statistically, the required connection with the notion of excellence is not plausible. To underwrite that connection, we had better understand the ergon of an F as something like: what it is the business of an F to do.[16] This paraphrase leaves it open that, for different substitutions for "F," different sorts of consideration may be appropriate in justifying a candidate specification of the ergon of an F. For a range of cases it will be a matter of extracting, from an account of what it is to be an F, a specification of something that is indeed appropriately spoken of as the function of F's; but the concept of an ergon does not require the argument to take that shape in all cases.

Now disputes of the sort described in § 8 could evidently be conducted as disputes about what it is the business of a human being to do. Equally, they could be conducted as disputes about what human excellence is.[17] The thesis that man's ergon consists in rational activity obviously excludes what might otherwise have been a conceivable view of eudaimonia, namely, a life of unreflective gratification of appetite; in the spirit of the ergon argument, we might say that that embodies no recognizable conception of a distinctively human kind of excellence. But no other likely candidate is clearly excluded by the eliminative argument for that thesis (1.7.12-13. 1097b33-1098a7).[18] Aside from its exclusion of the brutish life, then, the ergon argument can be understood neutrally. Its upshot is not to identify eudaimonia with one of the disputed candidates, namely, Aristotle's own, but to bring out how the issue between the candidates can be seen as an issue between competing views about which specific properties of a person are human excellences; and the route to the conclusion brings out how the issue can be seen as an issue between competing views about what it is the business of a human being to do.

11. It will be protested that I have got this far only by ignoring that aspect of the sense of *eudaimonia* which makes the standard translation, "happiness," not completely inept. That aspect ensures that the term is correctly applied only to the life that is maximally attractive or desirable.

Thus if disputes about how a human being should live, like the one considered in § 8, are disputes about what eudaimonia is, then, according to the protest, that ensures that the "should" in the competing theses must claim its justification from considerations about the attractiveness or desirability, to a person wondering how to arrange his life, of the competing lives. Hence it is, after all, a "should" of a specific category, namely, a kind of prudential "should." (Of course the prudence in question need not be wholly self-centered.)

Again: even if the words "Eudaimonia is rational activity in accordance with excellence" can be accepted by all parties in substantive disputes about what eudaimonia is, still Aristotle thinks there is a correct position, namely, his own, on the topic of substantive dispute. According to the protest, now, even if the ergon argument does not actually constitute Aristotle's justification of his own position on the substantive issue, nevertheless, because it is eudaimonia that he identifies with rational activity in accordance with excellence, he is committed to the availability of a certain sort of justification for his own view about what rational activity in accordance with excellence is, namely, a kind of prudential justification: it must be possible to demonstrate, to a person who is wondering what sort of life to lead, that Aristotle's own recipe marks out that kind of life which is in fact most desirable for a human being.

If someone supposes that Aristotle undertakes this commitment, he will naturally suspect that there is more to the ergon argument than § 10 allowed. A natural speculation will be that the argument is meant to bring the investigation of human nature to bear on the specification of the good life, by way of the thesis that a specification of the ergon of F's is derivable from an account of the nature of F's. With this speculation, the ergon argument is conceived as a promissory note for something much more elaborate, in which the claim that Aristotle's own recipe marks out the most desirable life for a human being would be grounded in some prior doctrine about human nature.

12. This protest begins with something indisputable: the concept of eudaimonia is in some sense a prudential concept. When Aristotle says that activity in accordance with excellence is eudaimonia, what he says can be paraphrased as the claim that two prima facie different interpretations of phrases like "doing well" coincide in their extension: doing well (sc. in accordance with excellence: living as a good man would) is doing well (sc. as one would wish: living in one's best interest). But we need to ask which way round this equation is to be understood.

If, as in the protest, the prudential nature of the concept of eudaimonia is taken to show that that concept yields something like a decision procedure for disputes like the one described in § 8, then we have to suppose that we are meant to make our way into the equation at the right-hand side. The requisite idea of the most desirable life must involve canons of desirability acceptable to all parties in the disputes, and intelligible, in advance of adopting one of the disputed theses, to someone wondering what sort of life he should lead. Such prior and independent canons of desirability would presumably need to be constructed somehow out of the content of desires which any human being can be expected to have: thus, desires conceived as manifestations of a fairly stable and universal human nature, susceptible of investigation independently of adopting one of the disputed theses about eudaimonia.[19]

If someone demands that the exercise of moral excellences must be shown to make up a life that is maximally desirable, and his canons of desirability are of that independent sort, then he risks being accused of missing the point of moral thought; that the demand is a mistake is a well-known doctrine of H. A. Prichard.[20] Commentators who take Aristotle's equation this way round sometimes acquit him of this charge by alleging that his conception of the left-hand side of the equation is shaped precisely so as to make the equation come out true. Thus: Aristotle's admiration for what he regards as human excellences is not moral admiration, in the (it is alleged) peculiarly modern sense that makes Prichard's thesis plausible; what it is to be an excellence, in the sense in which that notion figures on the left-hand side of Aristotle's equation, is to be explained precisely in terms of the role played by states of character in enabling their possessors to secure for themselves maximally desirable lives.[21]

But this seems unsatisfactory. Certainly Aristotle's list of excellences of character includes states which it is difficult to believe anyone could find morally admirable; since he sees no noteworthy difference of kind among those excellences, it is plausible to conclude that he lacks our concept of moral appraisal as a distinctive mode of appraisal, to be contrasted, say, with aesthetic appraisal. But from the thesis that he lacks the conceptual equipment required to see it this way, it does not follow that, in the case of those of the excellences he recognizes which we can make sense of someone's morally admiring, his admiration for them cannot be classified by us as moral admiration; and if it can, then in respect of those excellences Prichard's objection tells against the equation, on the present interpretation, to exactly the extent to which it would have told if "excellence" on the left-hand side had been explicitly announced as a moral term. Moreover, if Prichard's thesis is plausible about the specifically moral dimension of thought, then it seems equally plausible about the not specifically moral (perhaps undifferentiatedly moral-cum-aesthetic) kind of appraisal apparently effected by the concept that unifies Aristotle's admiration for his excellences of character, namely, the concept of the fine or noble (*to kalon:* see, e.g., 3.7.2. 1115b11-13; 4.1.12. 1120a23-24; 4.2.7. 1122b6-7). The attempt to disarm Prichard's objection on the score of anachronism is, to say the least, not unproblematic.[22]

13. However, the equation can also be understood the other way round. If our way into it is meant to be at the left-hand side, then the point is this: if someone really embraces a specific conception of human excellence, however grounded, then that will of itself equip him to understand special employments of the typical notions of "prudential" reasoning—the notions of benefit, advantage, harm, loss, and so forth—according to which (for instance) no payoff from flouting a requirement of excellence, however desirable by the sorts of canons considered in § 12, can count as a genuine advantage; and, conversely, no sacrifice necessitated by the life of excellence, however desirable what one misses may be by those sorts of canons, can count as a genuine loss.[23]

Consider, for example, a specific conception of excellence which includes some form of temperance. The exercise of temperance will on occasion require sacrificing the opportunity of some otherwise attractive gratification of appetite. According to the way of employing the prudential notions which is appropriate to the position considered in § 12, that means that to live the life of excellence will be, on such an occasion, to incur a loss; and Aristotle's equation, on the interpretation considered in § 12, could be maintained in the face of such occasions only by claiming that acting temperately would involve a gain (in terms of the independent standards of gain and loss appropriate to the position of § 12) sufficient to outweigh that loss. In suitably described cases any such claim would be implausible to the point of being fantastic. On the different interpretation of the equation which I am considering now, the thesis is not that the missed chance of pleasure is an admitted loss, compensated for, however, by a counterbalancing gain; but, rather, that in the circumstances (viz., circumstances in which the missed pleasure would involve flouting a requirement of excellence) missing the pleasure is no loss at all.

How this derivative employment of the "prudential" notions comes about can be explained as follows. To embrace a specific conception of eudaimonia is to see the relevant reasons for acting, on occasions when they coexist with considerations that on their own would be reasons for acting otherwise, as, not overriding, but silencing those other considerations—as bringing it about that, in the circumstances, they are not reasons at all. Now for any way of employing the notion of a reason, we can make sense of a derivative way of employing the "prudential" notions, controlled by such formal interdefinitions as that a benefit is what one has reason to pursue and a harm is what one has reason to avoid. In the case considered in the last paragraph, even though the attractiveness of the missed pleasure would have been a reason to pursue it if one could have done so without flouting a requirement of excellence, nevertheless in the circumstances that reason is silenced. And if one misses something which one had no reason to pursue, that is no loss.[24]

There seems to be no obstacle to allowing this derivative employment of the "prudential" concepts to occur side by side with a more ordinary employment—except that there is a risk of confusing them. If we take seriously Aristotle's contention that a person's eudaimonia is his own doing, not conferred by fate or other people,[25] but also try to make room for his commonsense inclination to say (e.g., 1.8.15-17. 1099a31-68) that external goods make a life more satisfactory, we are in any case required to distinguish, on his behalf, two measures of desirability or satisfactoriness: one according to which a life of exercises of excellence, being—as eudaimonia is—self-sufficient (1.7.6-8. 1097b6-21), can contain no ground for regret in spite of great ill fortune;[26] and one according to which such a life would have been better if the fates had been kinder. The derivative employment of the "prudential" notions yields the former measure; and the strains in Aristotle's treatment of the relation between eudaimonia and external goods can be plausibly explained in terms of an intelligible tendency to slide between the derivative employment and a more ordinary conception of prudence.

With the equation understood this way round, it is because a certain life is a life of exercises of human excellence, or, equivalently, because it is a life of doing what it is the business of a human being to do, that that life is in the relevant sense the most satisfying life possible for its subject, circumstanced at each point as he is. How one might argue that this or that is what it is the business of a human being to do is left open. It does not have to be by showing that a life of such doings maximizes the satisfaction of some set of "normal" or "natural" desires, whose role in the argument would need to be justified by a prior theory of human nature.

We may still find an intelligible place, in the different position I am considering, for some such idea as this: the life of exercises of excellence is the life that most fully actualizes the potentialities that constitute human nature. But the point will be that the thesis—justified in the appropriate way, whatever that is—that this or that is what it is the business of a human being to do can be reformulated, with an intelligibly "value-loaded" use of "human nature," as the thesis that this or that is most in keeping with human nature; not that the justification of the thesis about the business of a human being is to be found in an independent, "value-free" investigation of human nature.

Such an explicit mention of human nature would be a sort of rhetorical flourish, added to a conclusion already complete without it. It is arguable, however, that human nature itself is more importantly involved in disputes like the one described in § 8. The suggestion would be that it is our common human nature that limits what we can find intelligible in the way of theses about how human beings should conduct their lives, and underlies such possibilities as there are of resolving such disputes, or at least of stably adopting one of the competing positions for oneself in a reflective way (aware that there are others). I do not intend to discuss these very difficult issues here. What I want to emphasize is that if, according to the position considered in this section, human nature is involved in this sort of way, then what it has is what David Wiggins calls "a causal and enabling role"; not the "unconvincing speaking part" which it would need to be credited with in the position considered in § 12.[27]

14. The price of supposing that Aristotle's equation is to be understood as in § 13 rather than as in § 12 would be to deprive him of what, in § 12, looked like a sketch of a decision procedure for disputes like the one described in § 8, and hence a program for a justification for his own substantive view of eudaimonia. But how high a price is that?

It is not obvious that Aristotle has any pedagogic purposes that require him to sketch a decision procedure for disputes like the one described in § 8; for he carefully stipulates (1.4.6. 1095b4-6) that he is not addressing people like the antimoralist Y.

It would be rash to suggest that there are no difficulties about making the position of § 13 cohere with everything Aristotle wrote.[28] But I believe the main reason why commentators tend to take for granted the interpretation considered in § 12, in spite of the philosophical difficulties it involves, is not textual but philosophical. A position on the lines of § 12 strikes them as so obviously what Aristotle needs that charity demands ascribing it to him; or they assume a philosophical framework within which the possibility of a position like that of § 13 is not so much as visible.[29]

Such a framework would be one within which it seems obvious that if disputes like the one described in § 8 are to be recognizable as genuine disputes, then it must be possible in principle to resolve them by means of the sort of external decision procedure, independent of any one of the disputed theses, which the position of § 12 envisages. Now that might be represented as an application of a quite general claim, to the effect that where there is a real question, there is a method for answering it. In that case discussion would need to focus on the question whether what truth there is in the general claim really does justify, in the case of disputes like the one described in § 8, the demand for an external decision procedure. But the philosophical framework I have in mind purports to justify that demand directly, by way of the Humean thesis that a genuine reason for acting owes its rational cogency ultimately to the fact that the action for which it is a reason will satisfy an unmotivated desire—a desire which the agent just has, without having any reason for it.[30] Given that thesis, an account of practical rationality—of the reasons to which we should conform our lives—cannot but be on the lines of the proposition of § 12: that is, in terms of the maximizing of some bundle of goods recognizable as such from outside any of the disputed positions about excellence. And the idea that there is an objective topic for disputes about how a human being should live must needs be anchored, as in the position of § 12, in a conception of human nature as a subject for prior investigation.

Prima facie conflicts arise in the application of an individual's conception of excellence, and this may seem similarly to necessitate a view of rationality as involving the maximizing of independently recognizable goods. For if there is no externally applicable method of resolution, does not the conception of excellence collapse, in virtue of the conflicts, into a mere random heap of intuitions?[31] The same philosophical framework is operative here. A possibility not being contemplated—rendered invisible by the subjectivism about reasons for acting which the Humean thesis seems to entail—is this. A coherent conception of excellence locates its possessor in what is, for him at least, a world of particular facts, which are often difficult to make out. Faced with a prima facie conflict, one has to determine how things really are, in the relevant corner of the world which one's conception of excellence makes more or less dimly present to one. What makes it the case that the conception of excellence is a unity, insofar as it is one, is not that prima facie conflicts are resolved by asking what will maximize some independently recognizable goods but that the results of those efforts at discernment tend to hang together, in the way that particular facts hang together to constitute a world.[32]

This is not the place to mount an attack on the Humean thesis about reasons. But whatever one's attitude to that thesis, one ought to be able to see that it would be a pity if commentators allowed their acceptance of it to blind them to the possibility that Aristotle may simply not be moving within the framework which it characterizes. Of course such blindness will seem more deplorable to those who would like to regard Aristotle as an ally in their opposition to the Humean cast of thought.

NOTES

1. Anthony Kenny, "Aristotle on Happiness," first published as "Happiness" in *Proceedings of the Aristotelian Society* 66 (1965-66), 93-102; revised version in *Articles on Aristotle,* ed. Jonathan Barnes, Malcolm Schofield, and Richard Sorabji, vol. 2, *Ethics and Politics* (London: Duckworth, 1977; New York: St. Martin's Press, 1978), pp. 25-32 (page references will be to this printing). Kenny further distinguishes two versions of the indicative thesis (logical truth and empirical observation); and he is concerned with a scope ambiguity in the thesis that everyone has a single end (see § 2 below).

2. *Pace,* apparently, Kenny's new footnote, p. 28. I quote (as throughout) from the translation of Sir David Ross, *The Nicomachean Ethics of Aristotle* (London: Oxford University Press, 1954): I shall sometimes substitute a transliteration for Ross's "happiness," in order not to prejudge the sense of *eudaimonia.* Citations and references are from the *Nicomachean Ethics* unless otherwise specified.

3. See, e.g., Kenny, p. 26; on the other side, sec. VI of J. L. Ackrill's Dawes Hicks Lecture, "Aristotle on *Eudaimonia*," *Proceedings of the British Academy* 60 (1974), 339-359 (chap. 2 of this anthology).

4. Or perhaps two specific views: an intellectualist view, and a different view that more easily accommodates the excellences of character discussed in Books 2-5. My concern is with the *role* of Aristotle's notion of eudaimonia and not with the *content* of his conception of it, so I shall not discuss this well-known problem of interpretation: for discussion and references see, e.g., John M. Cooper, *Reason and Human Good in Aristotle* (Cambridge, Mass. and London: Harvard University Press, 1975). I shall proceed throughout as if Aristotle were single-minded about what eudaimonia amounts to.

5. Cf. Kenny, pp. 27-28, presumably on the strength of, e.g., 7.3.2. 1146b22-24. Kenny seems to me to be clearly right about this, *pace* (by implication) Cooper, p. 16. (On 1.7.5. 1097b1-5, on which Cooper partly relies, see § 5 below.)

6. See G. E. M. Anscombe, "Thought and Action in Aristotle," in *New Essays on Plato and Aristotle,* ed. Renford Bambrough (London: Routledge and Kegan Paul, 1965), pp. 143-158 (also in Barnes, Schofield, and Sorabji, op. cit., pp. 60-71). "Deliberative desires" are desires the reasons for which can be reconstructed

in the form of a deliberation, not desires actually arrived at by deliberation: see Cooper, pp. 5-10.

7. L. H. G. Greenwood, *Aristotle: Nicomachean Ethics Book VI* (Cambridge: at the University Press, 1909), pp. 46-47.

8. See Anscombe, pp. 149-150 (pp. 64-65 in the reprinted version).

9. See Ackrill, sec. V. Cooper's idea, at p. 16, is a different one: that honor, etc. are chosen for themselves and *also* for the sake of eudaimonia.

10. The other objects of choice mentioned would require different treatment. A great deal more would need to be said in a full account of this difficult passage; all I have aimed to do is to show that Kenny's use of it is not conclusive.

11. Translation (with substituted transliterations) from H. Rackham, ed. and trans., *Aristotle: The Athenian Constitution; The Eudemian Ethics; On Virtues and Vices*, Loeb Classical Library (London: Heinemann, 1935).

12. And in the Oxford Translation quoted by Kenny.

13. Cf. Cooper, p. 94.

14. Perhaps in a sense of "character" stipulatively determined by this thesis itself; but that would not make the thesis any less worth considering. It is because they are undertaken for the distinctive sort of reason involved in proairesis (cf. § 6) that bits of behavior belong in the restricted class of praxeis; that explains why Aristotle says (3.2.1. 1111b5-6) that proairesis is more indicative of character than praxeis are.

15. I have deliberately left open the question what general features of their content mark out reasons as moral reasons in this sense.

16. Note the normative force that has to be attributed to "work," in Cooper's rendering "definitive work" (p. 145).

17. This is sometimes obscured because of the way in which "excellence," and still more "virtue," have been commandeered by those whose substantive view is a moral one, in the narrow sense. But obviously Y's position, in § 8, could be intelligibly expressed by saying "Genuine human excellence is the intelligence and strength needed to further one's own selfish ends."

18. *Pace* those who suppose that the ergon argument, as it stands, is meant to prove that eudaimonia is, as in Book 10, to be equated with a life of "contemplation": see, e.g., Cooper, pp. 99-100. Against that view, see Ackrill, sec. VII (and note the end of Cooper's n. 10, pp. 100-101).

19. Cf., e.g., Cooper, pp. 120-121.

20. "Does Moral Philosophy Rest on a Mistake?" in his *Moral Obligation* (reissued with *Duty and Interest*) (London, Oxford, New York: Oxford University Press, 1968), pp. 1-17.

21. See Kathleen V. Wilkes, "The Good Man and the Good for Man in Aristotle's Ethics," *Mind* 87 (1978), 553-571 (chap. 18 of this anthology); also Cooper, pp. 125 ff. (and for a remark about the modernity of the concept of morality, p. 77 n. 104). This view of the appropriate concept of excellence pervades Terence Irwin's account of Socratic and Platonic ethics, in *Plato's Moral Theory* (Oxford: Clarendon Press, 1977).

22. Wilkes combines this attempt with the claim that Aristotle's thesis, as she interprets it, is "exciting and intellectually satisfying" (p. 571). But if, for better or

worse, we are stuck with a notion of morality about which Prichard's doctrine is true (as I believe we are), the thesis cannot be intellectually satisfying to *us*. Wilkes's enthusiasm is unjustified unless Prichard is wrong about *our* notion of morality; and if he is (which she does nothing to show), then she did not need to make so much of the claim that Aristotle lacks that notion.

23. See D. Z. Phillips, "Does it Pay to be Good?" *Proceedings of the Aristotelian Society*, n.s. 65 (1964-65), 45-60; and D. Z. Phillips and H. O. Mounce, "On Morality's Having a Point," *Philosophy* 40 (1965), 308-319.

24. I exploit the idea of silencing in order to interpret Aristotle's distinction between virtue and continence, in my "Are Moral Requirements Hypothetical Imperatives?" *The Aristotelian Society, Supplementary Volume* 52 (1978), 13-29. The idea will seem unintelligible if one finds the following assumption plausible: if a certain general consideration (e.g., that something would be pleasant) is ever a reason for acting in a certain way, then it can be rational to act otherwise, on an occasion on which that consideration is known to obtain, only if the agent has weighed that reason against a reason for acting otherwise and found it outweighed. But we should not simply assume that the philosophical framework that makes that assumption plausible is Aristotle's: see § 14 below.

25. See Cooper, pp. 123-124, with reference to Aristotle.

26. Cf. 1.10.13-14. 1100b33-1101a8. Commentators who interpret the passage about self-sufficiency in terms of W. F. R. Hardie's notion of an inclusive, as opposed to dominant, end (see "The Final Good in Aristotle's *Ethics*," *Philosophy* 40 [1965], 277-295) tend not to notice, or sufficiently emphasize, the constraints which Aristotle's doctrine that eudaimonia is one's own doing places on the interpretation of the claim that it is "that which when isolated makes life desirable and lacking in nothing" (1.7.7. 1097b14-16). Kenny's construal (p. 31) has more to be said for it than Ackrill (sec. V) allows; though I do not think the upshot is felicitously expressed in terms of the notion of a dominant end either.

27. See "Truth, Invention, and the Meaning of Life," *Proceedings of the British Academy* 62 (1976), 331-378, at p. 375 n.: I have borrowed Wiggins's phrase; but when he accuses "Aristotelian Eudaemonism" of assigning human nature an "unconvincing speaking part," he does not have in mind the interpretation of Aristotle considered in § 12. (It is important to be clear that Wiggins is not interpreting Aristotle on those lines. If he were, then I should be about to suggest, in § 14 below, that he is reading Aristotle in the distorting framework of a Humean view about practical reason. But the rest of his lecture makes it obvious that Wiggins is hardly liable to such a temptation.) What Wiggins has in mind is a position in which, while the investigation of human nature is not conceived as prior to the specification of eudaimonia, claims about human nature are nevertheless thought capable of exerting some leverage in justifying candidate specifications. For my part, I should be inclined to view such a position (which I believe might meet with Aristotle's approval) as a response to the following fact (insufficiently recognized in the penultimate paragraph of § 13): the concept of human nature constitutes a natural focus for the rhetoric with which one might naturally try to recommend a particular conception of eudaimonia. (There is very nearly an example of this in my gloss, in § 10 above, on Aristotle's exclusion of the brutish

life.) If crediting this sort of speaking part to human nature is combined with a clear recognition that there is no question of an appeal to truths establishable independently of disputation about eudaimonia (that the leverage is not Archimedean), the position strikes me as innocuous. The speaking part *need* not be unconvincing—that depends on the quality of the rhetoric.

28. In particular, something needs to be said (but not here) about the "first principles" or "starting points" of 1.4.5-7. 1095a30-b13.

29. Cooper (p. 120) briefly considers something like the leading idea of that position but dismisses it as "trivial." (Similarly, on Plato, Irwin, pp. 9-10.) This complaint seems to issue from the philosophical framework I am about to describe.

30. David Hume, *A Treatise of Human Nature*, II. III. III (pp. 413-418 in the edition of L. A. Selby-Bigge [Oxford: Clarendon Press, 1896]): of course Hume does not express the thesis in terms of reasons for acting. The distinction between motivated and unmotivated desires is drawn in chap. 5 of Thomas Nagel, *The Possibility of Altruism* (Oxford: Clarendon Press, 1970).

31. See Cooper, pp. 95-96 (similarly Irwin, pp. 264-265).

32. The Humean thesis about reasons, suggesting as it does a quasi-hydraulic model of their cogency, underlies the assumption mentioned in n. 24 above.

20

The Place of Contemplation in Aristotle's Nicomachean Ethics

Amélie Oksenberg Rorty

Aristotle has often been charged with indecision and sometimes with holding conflicting views about the relative merits of a comprehensive practical life and one devoted primarily to contemplation.[1] He intimates that practical affairs might well be ordered so as to give the greatest opportunity for such theorizing (1177a12-18; 1145a6-11).[2] But he also regards growth, motion, perception, scientific understanding, and political activity as essential to a fully developed human life. *Eudaimonia* consists in the proper exercise of the essential potentialities of the soul, actualized for their own sakes because actualizing them just *is* living the life of a human being and not merely because they also promote and assure the sort of life that gives contemplation its widest play.

I want to investigate a way of reading Aristotle which shows how the contemplative and the comprehensive practical lives need not be competitors for the prizes of the best life. There is nothing about the practical life which prevents its also being contemplative, and even enhanced by being contemplated. Indeed, Aristotle remarks (1140b7-11) that men like Pericles are thought to possess practical wisdom because they have contemplative understanding of what is good. This is, he adds, our conception of an expert or leader in politics. Properly conceived, *theoria* completes and perfects the practical life, in the technical senses of those terms. And while of course practical wisdom cannot ensure theoria, it can assure the political conditions that allow contemplators to discover and exercise their potentialities. If there is a criticism of Aristotle in this area, it is political rather than conceptual. The interpretation I examine is not the one that Aristotle himself advances as a resolution to the tensions of the *Ethics:* it is not even clear that he was aware of the strains in his account. But this reading is woven entirely out of threads and materials provided by Aristotle. Though it is not the solution Aristotle himself explicitly formulates, it is an Aristotelian solution to the problems of reconciling the respective claims of the practical and the contemplative lives.

I shall argue that the range of contemplation is wider and its effects more far-reaching than has generally been allowed. In particular, we can contemplate the moral life in activity as well as the starry heaven above. It is only in a corrupt polity that the contemplative life need be other-worldly, and only in a corrupt polity that the policies promoting the development and exercise of contemplative activity would come into conflict with those establishing requirements for the best practical life. The discussion of friendship in Book 9 helps show what contemplation can contribute to the comprehensive practical life. By placing that discussion in the middle of his treatment of pleasure, Aristotle shows how virtuous friendship enables a person of practical wisdom to recognize that his life forms a unified, self-contained whole, itself an *energeia.* The discussion of friendship provides a transition from the Book 7 account of pleasure as the unimpeded exercise of basic natural activities to the Book 10 account of pleasure as perfecting activities—an account that makes sense of a person finding pleasure in contemplating the whole of a virtuous life. Finally, I shall suggest that the discussion of politics which follows the discussion of contemplation in Book 10 is meant to show that one of the aims of a statesman is the reconciliation of the contemplative and the practical lives.

I

What is this activity that is said to be the best, and why does it have such pride of place? Characterized by its attitude as well as by its objects, theoria is the self-contained activity par excellence. Not only is it done for its own sake, but it is complete in its very exercise: there is no unfolding of stages, no development of consequences from premises. It is fully and perfectly achieved in the very act (1177b1-5). When he contemplates the divine, or the fixed stars, the contemplator is no more interested in explaining them—no more interested in constructing the science of theology or astronomy—than he is in his achieving nobility or serenity.

Although the primary and paradigmatic objects of contemplation are the divine, the fixed stars, and perhaps mathematical objects, the condition for something's being contemplated is that it be necessary, unchanging, eternal, self-contained, and noble (1139a6-8). While objects that do not change at all are paradigmatic cases of what is contemplated, it is also possible to contemplate the unchanging form of what does change. Species meet that requirement: they have no external *telos:* they are eternal and unchanging (1035b3-1036a1; 1030a6-1031a14). Even when the definition of a species is a pattern of a temporal life, that pattern can be comprehended in one timeless whole.

The definition of a species gives not only the criteria for membership but also the essential attributes whose actualization is the *ergon* of the species (1034a5; 1016b33; 1032b1; 1139a16-20).[3] It is in the active exercise of these basic potentialities that virtue consists: in giving the final as well as the formal cause of the species, the definition sets the excellence of its members. The primary or natural energeiai of a species are those that involve the exercise of its essential potentialities; in performing these activities well the ergon of a species is fulfilled. To be a member of a species is just to have the potentiality for, and the bent to perform, these essential activities (1098a1-20). No particular motive or desire to perform them is required.

The minimal definition of a species gives the essential properties: they not only identify the members of the species but also are centrally explanatory of their activities. (The important debate about whether essential properties are analytically necessary and whether necessity is to be constured *de re* or *de dicto* do not affect our argument here.)[4] The expanded or explicated definition includes the various properties that are entailed by the essential properties, their intrinsic concomitants (73a34-73b15; 402b16-19). On the expanded account, to be human is to be a political and rational animal, that is, to be capable of practical wisdom and scientific knowledge (with all that that involves) as well as to be capable of growth and decay, perception, and desire (and all that they involve). Both minimal and expanded definitions can be apprehended in a single act of thought, in intuition as the beginning of scientific explanation, or in theoria, just for the sake of thinking.

In principle, then, the most general ends of human life, insofar as these are defined by the species, can be contemplated. For living creatures the formal and the final causes coincide: our general ends are the actualization and the exercise of the basic activities that define us. If eternal objects can be contemplated, and if species are eternal objects, Humanity and its proper ends can be contemplated. But of course such contemplation does not yet assure moral virtue: it is far too general for that. Before we can see what theoria and *phronesis* can contribute to one another, we must look more closely at the moral life in action.

II

In what does the well-lived practical life consist? What does the *phronimos* know, and what is the function of his knowledge in determining his actions?

The virtuous person performs the right action in the right way at the right time on the right objects. Getting the timing, the tempo, and the manner right requires a well-formed character, the right desires and beliefs embodied in habits (1106b36). It means, among other things, really knowing what one is doing, being aware of the circumstances and consequences of one's actions, with the right conception of the sort of action one is performing, one's own intentions conforming to the normic description of the action-type. Characteristically, such knowledge is manifest in a person consistently doing the right thing for the right reason, in view of general human ends.[5]

In having the right conceptions of ends, the virtuous do not merely have a different set of goals from the vicious. Sometimes the virtuous and the vicious have different conceptions of behavior that is, at a very general level of description, extensionally equivalent. At a finer level of description, however, the differences in the intentions of the virtuous and the vicious will be manifest in the *way* the action is performed. Sometimes the virtuous and the vicious have a different understanding of a general formula; a statesman can, for instance, have an appropriate general notion of his ends: to run the affairs of the *polis* for the well-being of its citizens. But he might mistake imperial expansion or Olympian victories for indices of political thriving. The phronimos has this just right: in him, virtue and knowledge are fused.

Two people can be doing the same things—discussing philosophy, passing legislation, writing poetry, or kneading dough—that is, they may be performing virtually the same physical motions and saying virtually the same things but be performing different actions. One person may be performing it as a self-contained activity that is intrinsically valuable, the other as a process structured and motivated by external goals.

(Consider three ways of writing tragedies: the tragedian can regard his activity as an end in itself. He can be writing-plays, without treating the play or the effect of the play on the audience as determining the structure of his craft. Or he may be writing: to produce a play. What he does as a writer will then be formed by the logically and psychologically prior end: the play. Or the end of his activity of writing-a-play can be: to produce a certain effect on his audience. It is then that end which structures both the play and the act of writing. The job of the philosopher writing on poetics is to analyze what the exemplary poet does by getting the description just right; the philosopher generates standards for criticism. The star poet need not be able to understand the philosopher, let alone be able to perform the analysis himself. And philosophy, too, can itself be done with different intentions by different practitioners: one person may be doing philosophy as a way of achieving fame, another as a way of engaging in intellectual combat, while still others "do philosophy" as a project in eccentricity or as a mode of poetry or politics. That the true philosopher does the activity for its own sake, for the sake of thinking-what-is-real, does not guarantee that he will find more truths than, for example, the intellectual prize-fighter. The philosopher does not hoard truths as a miser hoards gold. Truth-seeking as an energeia does not treat truths as separable end-products that can be made or discovered, possessed or hoarded, independently of the investigations that established them.)

It is the task of the moral philosopher to analyze the activity of the phronimos: to get the proper descriptions of his activities and processes, to determine their priorities in the light of general human ends (1094a1-1094b11). Not only can actions be performed under different descriptions, but they can also be nestled under different purposes, differently embedded in larger contexts. Although the phronimos sees the proper ends of processes, for example, he does not perform each process as if it were an energeia. He does not put his fingers on the stops of a flute as if that were a self-contained activity; his attention—which affects the manner of his performance—is on his playing the whole of a piece of music. Although the virtuous perform virtuous actions as ends in themselves (and not, for instance, as a means to self-respect or eudaimonia), they are not zealots of energeiai, trying to turn all their actions into self-contained activities.[6] When actions are processes, they are geared to the appropriate external telos; when they are energeiai, they are properly understood, under the right description, with the appropriate intrinsic telos. The ends of processes are of course eventually traced to ends that are goods in themselves. (But although the train of derivation may be quite long, virtue does not consist in shortcutting the stages, leaping to the final good for each process; it consists rather in getting the activities and processes properly nestled, with their ends properly understood.)[7]

In giving an account of the proper ends of process and activities the moral philosopher is guided by his understanding of the basic definitory properties of the species. Showing that an action (it is of course action-types and not action-tokens that are in question) qualifies as an energeia involves showing that it is a specification of the exercise of an essential attribute (1170a16-19). It is just for this reason that its end is contained in the activity itself: it is linked to a species-defining property. Because the purpose or end is contained in the very description of the activity, there need be no motive for performing it, though of course there may be additional benefits from doing so. It is for this reason, and not because they are instantaneous, that energeiai are timeless and that performing them at all counts as having performed them (1048b23-24; 1173a30 ff.).

But the ultimate ends of the species are, after all, very general indeed. While they give the general and basic energeiai that constitute human functioning, knowing them does not provide a set of rules or principles from which specific actions can be derived. If that were possible, *episteme* could replace phronesis, the philosopher would be a statesman, and deliberation would be unnecessary. The phronimos does not just perform actions that realize appropriate ends; his placing various ends in their appropriate priorities in quite different situations comes easily and even pleasurably from habit: he is acting from his second nature, his character. The phronimos' knowledge is characteristically expressed in particular choices and actions, not by mechanically applying rules or working out a syllogism. The ends are seen in the situation: such and such an action done in a certain manner is the actualization, the specification, of general human ends in a particular situation.[8] While the practical syllogism is the articulation of the phronimos' knowledge, he is not necessarily adept in theoretical argumentation, capable of demonstrating the priority of virtue to wealth. The phronimos' intentions are not merely antecedent causes of his actions; they are built into them and are manifest in the manner of their performance. After all, someone might be gifted at articulating appropriate practical syllogisms and yet suffer from *akrasia*, or even viciousness. Since thought and knowledge by themselves do not fix motives, the phronimos must also have the appropriate desires. His having the right desires conditions his perceiving: they fix his patterns of attention; and what he sees activates the appropriate directly motivating desires.

It is, Aristotle says, from a combination of thought and desire—*nous orektikos* or *orexis noetikos*—that we act (1139b3-5). The practical syllogism is the formulation and articulation of that *combination*. Its premises formulate the intentional components of the action. The phronimos need not run through the practical syllogism in order to act; it is logically, but not necessarily temporally, prior to the action.

But what is this metaphor of the nestling of ends in a train of practical reasoning? Perhaps we can get a clearer idea of the sort of knowledge that the phronimos has by looking more closely at the way in which a person's ends guides or determines deliberation. When Aristotle says that we do not deliberate about ends, he does not mean that we cannot deliberate about whether, for instance, a person should, in a particular situation, jeopardize his health and safety in order to achieve an important political good. Of course it is not deliberation but ethical inquiry that establishes whether health and political virtue are human ends, perhaps basic ends constitutive of eudaimonia. Nor can deliberation establish the principle that is used to evaluate the relative merits and priorities of health and political virtue. In evaluating competing goods one does not deliberate about which principle to use in determining their relative priorities. But having the principle, one can deliberate about how it applies.

If someone deliberately chooses to endanger his health and safety to achieve a political good, his action is not merely intentional and voluntary in the weak sense that he knows what he is doing and, coincidentally, desires to do it. It is intentional in the stronger sense that he does what he does in the light of his ends: they frame the dominant description of his action. The ends of the action, as he conceives it, and the satisfaction of his desires are the same. His operative desire is not merely, for instance, to have a statue of himself in the park or to get the better of a long-standing enemy—desires that he may also have. Rather, his operative desire is to achieve the political good in question. It is for this reason that Aristotle can speak indifferently of nous orektikos or orexis noetikos as *prohairesis* (1139b3-5) and can say that a choice is good when the thought and the desire are *homologoi*, the thought being true and the desire right (1139a30-31). Prohairesis is quite different from our notion of *choice*. Of course it requires that the standard conditions for voluntary actions be met: the action is not necessitated or compulsive. But prohairesis need not involve a selection among alternatives. Selective choices are not paradigmatic of prohairesis.

When Aristotle says that the true thought and the right desire of a good prohairesis are homologoi—when they have the same *logos* or reason—he means that the ends that determine the phronimos' operative desires are ends that do correspond to, or are specifications of, the ends that are established by the essential attributes of the species. The actions of such a life are rational in a strong sense: not only are they reasoned outcomes of a practical syllogism, but the premises of that syllogism are true. The intentional component of the action is true, and the desire that motivated the action was itself formed by the phronimos' general ends, ends that truly (i.e., not accidentally) coincide with those of the species.

It is his character rather than his purely theoretical capacities which assures the phronimos the right desires. Of course he must have good judgment, keen perception, and a range of intellectual virtues in order to gauge his situations well. But he must have developed habits of desire as well as habits of action. He doesn't just coincidentally desire things that happen to be truly good. His most general desires are just the human ends. He is, of course, committed to rationality, and committed to its exercise as a fundamental human energeia. But in ethics, rationality does not *by itself* provide the criteria for virtues. A rational inquiry requires an investigation into the variable and contingent conditions for human flourishing under different circumstances. The vexed question whether phronesis depends on virtue to provide the ends or supplies the ends itself (1144b1-1145a12) is settled by realizing that what the phronimos desires *is* what virtue requires. A person of practical wisdom has the same knowledge and desires as a virtuous person. To describe someone as practically wise and to describe him as virtuous is to pick out traits that are distinct but homologoi. Instead of a Platonic identification or reduction, Aristotle is proposing a conceptual interdependence among traits that can be independently identified.

Now let us take stock. This sketch may have touched on some very interesting Aristotelian doctrines; but what does it tell us about what contemplation can add to the practical life? After all, the phronimos knows what to do and how to do it. Why isn't practical wisdom in all its glory sufficient unto the day? This is just the difficulty: despite his knowledge of human ends the phronimos grasps those ends *in* the particular. His knowledge of the good is expressed in the appropriate action done in the right way, in the mean that suits each situation. It is in his actions that the phronimos specifies and articulates his knowledge of general human ends (1144b1-1145a11).[9] There is nothing the phronimos lacks to carry on properly, except the self-conscious, explicitly articulated placing of his knowledge in a reasoned whole. The phronimos is presumably aware of his virtue: because his actions involve the actualization of natural *hexeis*, they are characteristically pleasurable (1153a14-15). His life is characteristically, although not necessarily, *eudaimon*. It is triply well lived: its ends are characteristically realized, either in properly prized consequences or in intrinsically valuable activities; it is well lived because these activities involve the exercise of potentialities whose actualization constitutes the ergon and the well-being of a human life; and it is well lived because the actions that constitute such a life are *kala* performed well even when for contingent reasons they do not succeed.

Nevertheless a virtuous person might find himself in a situation where he cannot engage in the actions that are characteristic of him: the statesman who has become a political prisoner. Ill fortune can thwart the expectations of the actively virtuous: Priam witnessed the destruction of the life of Troy. It is not because he grieved at the deaths of Hector and many of the best and bravest of the Trojans, that Priam was not eudaimon. Until fortune changed its expected course, Priam's life had the shape and the substance of a life of eudaimonia. Had he been able to continue in the exercise of his virtues, active as king and citizen, his life might, despite its great sorrow, have been that of a eudaimon. Eudaimonia does not consist in reflecting on the nobility of one's character, basking in decent self-respect. Many of a virtuous person's actions are directed to the welfare of others, of the city, of friends, of one's children. While such actions may express virtue, the perfection of character is certainly not their aim. Not Achilles but Pericles is virtuous. And because of the fate of Athens and of his children, perhaps not Pericles. Yet if Pericles lacked eudaimonia, it was because of his implication in the tribulations of the Athenians and not because of his grief. Though it is fully enjoyable, a virtuous practical life is by no means without grief or regret: the death of one's parents, or of friends and sons in battle, or a failure to realize a good plan for a city (1166a27-30). It is part of virtue to know when and how to grieve: a practical life without any grief at all would be more than eudaimon, it would be *makarios*, supremely blessed. What distinguished Priam's griefs, making them incompatible with eudaimonia, was not their scope or intensity but their being of such a character as to prevent his exercising his virtues, let alone exercise them successfully and enjoyably. Because eudaimonia is an attribute of the whole of a person's life, with the natural intended consequences all called in, as it were, one cannot judge a person eudaimon until he is dead and the ends of his actions are achieved, even if these occur after his death (1100b30-1101b12). Although conceptually and characteristically the practical virtuous life is eudaimon, it is a life open to contingency. Although it is, taken as a whole, self-contained, still it is temporal and affected by accidents and contingencies.

Even when the pronimos can give a perspicacious account of the merits of a course of action, he need not necessarily have a reflective theoretical understanding of the connection between his virtues and the energeiai that constitute a well-lived life. The contemplative phronimos sees his ends as specifications of species-defining potentialities. Of course such contemplative reflection does not generate a more precise decision-procedure: contemplating humanity does not increase practical wisdom by a jot.[10]

It might be argued that this account gives too much scope to theoria and not enough to phronesis. After all, it is clear that the activities and decisions that constitute practical life are far too particular, too contingent, and insufficiently lofty to fall within the scope of sophia, let alone theoria. And that is right: it is not political debate as such, or a decision to strengthen the walls of the city rather than invade a neutral polis, that is contemplated. The energeiai that compose the virtuous life are not contemplated in their particularity but as instantiations of human ends defined by the essential properties of the species. It is our species-defined ends in action that are contemplated. In any case, no one engages in theoria in order to perfect the practical life. It has to be done for its own sake to be done at all.

It might be argued, however, that there is no need to make the phronimos quite as concentrated on the particular as I have suggested. After all, there are many situations in which being able to act well requires being able to reason well. There are many situations, especially those of rapid change or political instability, in which the phronimos must be able to calculate and even to articulate the nestling of ends in order to determine the best course of action. Of course the calculation of determinate means to determinate ends, as that is standardly conceived, gives a poor model of Aristotelian practical reasoning, since it fails to capture the way in which ends come to be specified by the activities that contribute to them and sometimes compose them. Nevertheless, just because the phronimos seems to resemble a stodgy well-brought-up gentleman, he need not be unintellectual, unreflective, or inarticulate, and there may be situations in which he had better be precise, articulate, and reflective.

Aristotle answers these objections for us by playing them off against each other. Theoria and phronesis are indeed quite distinct virtues: neither guarantees the other. And certainly the phronimos is often required to exercise a large range of intellectual virtues, but as the clever vicious man and the intelligent *akrates* attest, more is necessary. Still one might wonder why it is theoria, and not episteme, that best enhances the practical life. Doesn't scientific knowledge of the human species also show how the definition of the species structures the hierarchy of ends whose best actualization is the ergon and the excellence of the species?

The priority of theoria over episteme for enhancing the practical life rests on Aristotle's view that what is self-contained, unchanging, and necessary is more perfect than what is temporal or complexly structured in stages of dependency. Aristotelian episteme is a mode of explanation or demonstration: it is an attribute primarily of persons rather than of propositions or of a system of propositions. Because theoria is a self-contained, actualized realization, it is more perfected than episteme, conceived as a capacity to demonstrate and explain. If the systematic arguments of an entire scientific investigation were contained in a single act of mind—say the whole of Euclidean geometry treated as a complex self-contained truth—then we would have contemplated the whole of geometry but would not have engaged in scientific investigation or explanation.

Now of course just because contemplation can deepen moral understanding, the contemplator is not, as contemplator, interested in the moral consequences of his insight into human nature; nevertheless, the contemplator qua person can be. After all, there is nothing that says that the contemplator must forget what is realized in contemplation, as if the self-contained character of contemplation could only be achieved by a bad memory, "out of contemplation, out of mind" (1143b17-1144a1).

While this may tell us what contemplation can contribute to an understanding of the moral life, and even to its perfection, we have yet to see why the contemplative life is the most prizeworthy, the happiest—even the pleasantest—of lives. To see this we must sketch some of Aristotle's more difficult views about thinking and the thinker.

Since all the activities of the soul involve the exercise of some essential potentiality, an individual becomes realized as the sort of being that he is by performing the activities that are essential to his nature. Perceiving is not merely a psychophysical happening, a splendid event in one's life. It is by and in the activity of perceiving (among others) that we are actualized as the beings we are. Thinking, too, in its various forms, including theoria, is not merely a mental activity, although it certainly is at least that. It is, in every sense of the word, a realization of our potentialities (1166a17; 1169a2; 1178a2-8).

Most realizations of the soul are also physical realizations. This piece of flesh is so constructed that it is actualized as an eye by seeing (412b2-23). Aristotle means this literally: the nature of this stuff is realized by these activities. It is not that matter suffers a change by being bombarded by stimuli; it rather becomes what it *is* by doing its real work.[11]

When we are engaged in intellectual thought, no particular part of us is actualized as the sort of flesh it potentially is. Rather, the whole individual realizes his potentiality as Humanity by thinking (1166a17; 1169a2; 1178a2-8). This realization of an individual as thinker is not the becoming of ordinary change, the replacement of contrary predicates. It is the actualization of a potentiality in an activity, with the added and difficult characteristic that in thinking the mind becomes identical with the forms of its objects. For Aristotle the objects of thought are neither the efficient causes nor the products of a process. The divinities, the stars, the species, do not "strike" our minds.

An analogy may help us to see how Aristotle's view that the mind is active in thinking can be reconciled with his claim that *nous* becomes identical with the forms of its objects (430a15-25; 431a1-8).[12] Consider how a dance stands to dancing; the dance is only analytically separable from the activity itself. What we have to imagine is that there are necessary and universal species of dance that anyone who is dancing must be doing—the natural basic dances, as it were, that are the proper forms of dancing. These dances are complexly structured: in a sense their forms exist quite independently of anyone's dancing them; but an individual is a dancer only when he dances them; and they are instantiated in the dance. To complete the analogy we must imagine with Yeats that we cannot tell the dancer from the dance nor the dance from the dancing. Of course this analogy is misleading in several respects: as things now go, dances must be physically instantiated; not all thought must be. But it may be helpful in other respects: it may help us to see something that modern realism tends to blur, that truth is integral to the activity of thinking rather than a by-product of it, and that the formal causes of thought appear within the activity itself and not simply outside it, causing resemblances or simulacra within the mind. After all, Aristotle says the mind becomes the form of what is thought; if he meant to say that it becomes similar, that is what he would have said.

(While this analogy is of course farfetched to most of us, I suspect that it might not even have been thought of as an analogy by some of Aristotle's predecessors, who explain particular cases of knowledge by saying that an individual nous returns to, becomes identical with, or is absorbed in, the harmonic proportions of cosmic nous. Such views would have been in the background of Aristotle's account of the active intellect and of theoria.)

The objects of contemplation are the best and most perfect substances. By and in contemplation one becomes actively identical with the formal character of those substances. As contemplative persons, thinking the species, Humanity, and its essential energeiai, we realize those energeiai fully, being not only practically virtuous as the phronimos is—virtuous on each occasion as the occasion requires. As Mind, we become identical with our lives as unified wholes, the *eidos* Humanity. Contemplating the essential energeiai that define the species realizes our formal identity as the species. The contemplator of Humanity becomes a unified whole, a self-contained, self-justified, actualized Humanity, his essential and perfected life. Such a contemplator not only lives his life, he is that life as an eternal and unified self-contained whole. His contemplation and his living become one, immutable and unchanging, because contemplating is the best human activity and because the mind is actualized as and in what it thinks.

III

To see why this identity of thought and thinker contemplating Humanity is not only a good thing but the best and indeed the most pleasant component of the fully happy life, we need to consider the pleasures and fruits of friendship. The discussion of friendship interrupts an analysis of pleasure in Book 7; that analysis is resumed in Book 10, where it leads to an account of happiness and to the hymn to contemplation, which is in turn followed by a discussion of the tasks of the statesman. This interruption, this sequence, is no accident, no haphazard reshuffling of the note-taker's papyrus.

One objection can be got out of the way quickly. It has been thought that there is some problem in Aristotle's making friendship necessary to the well-lived life on the one hand, while at the same time emphasizing the priority of self-sufficient, self-contained *energeiai* on the other (1169b3-13). Self-sufficiency has of course nothing to do with isolation or even with self-development. A self-sufficient life is one whose activities are intrinsically worthy, have their ends in themselves, are worth choosing regardless of what may come of them. Aristotle is not concerned to justify friendship because it conduces to or promotes self-development but because it is part of a self-contained, fully realized life (1097b7-20).[13]

The sorts of friendships we need to examine are those between the virtuous, who share the activities of life together, wishing each other well, each for the sake of the other, because they see one another's characters as virtuous (1156b7-32). Other sorts of friendships, for pleasure or for utility, are incidental: they reveal neither the nature of *philia* nor why it is part of a well-lived life (1157b1-5).

What does Aristotle mean by saying that friends share the activities of life? And how can the mutual mirroring of friends observing (*theorein*) one another's virtues conduce, as Aristotle claims, to a sense of one's own life and to one's pleasure in one's own life (1169b33-1170a3)? Aristotle's discussions of how friendship leads the virtuous to the pleasures of self-realization are highly condensed and cryptic (1170a15-b20). In interpreting them, we unavoidably interpret into them.

For a human being, Aristotle says, to live well is to perceive well and to think well. These are natural *energeiai*: their exercise is paradigmatically pleasurable (1170a16-20). To perceive is to be aware that one is perceiving. We are aware of being active in our activities and are therefore implicitly aware of ourselves as existing.[14] But we are not yet on that account aware that (properly seen) we are substances, and so we are not aware of ourselves as possible objects of contemplation. Of course we recognize ourselves to be members of the human species. But this does not give us the reflective awareness of our substantial identity as Humanity. Friendship provides that sense of our lives as one whole *energeia*, pleasurable when properly lived and contemplatable when properly understood.

What is involved in friends' sharing virtuous activities? In sharing their lives, living together and not merely feeding at the same trough, friends order the day, giving each of their activities the proper weight and measure (1157b16-25; 1170b10-14). They decide when to take walks, when to carouse, when to do philosophy; they hear poetry and go to plays; they mutually determine their attitudes toward their parents and their children. This is presumably not just a matter of engaging in the sorts of activities that only several people can do together, such as discussing political issues and playing competitive games; nor is it merely a matter of using one another to revive flagging energies. Presumably friends also share activities that each does on his own: thinking, and gazing at the wine-dark sea.

Because we are better able to observe (theorein) our friends than ourselves, our friends model the virtues for us, enabling us to see our own reflected in their. In sharing activities, we determine our priorities together. The virtuous do not form a system of priorities by estimating the strengths of their desires; rather the strengths of their desires are determined by their evaluations of the place of various activities and satisfactions in a eudaimon life. But ranking desires and motivations—forming a system of priorities—requires seeing one's life as a whole, with its constituent activities properly defined in the light of that whole. And this is just what virtuous friends sharing and observing one another's lives come to have: we come to be aware of our friends' lives as forming a unity, itself one complex energeia. Since we wish our friends well for their own sakes, we come to reflect what their well-being really consists in. By such reflection, we take pleasure in their *existence*, in their life as the unimpeded exercise of an activity. But as they are another self, we come to a pleasurable awareness of our own lives as a unified existence, constituted by appropriately ordered activities.

It is because sharing activities leads us—indeed, requires us—to see our friends' lives as forming a unity and not merely as a sequence of activities, and because in wishing one another well the virtuous take pleasure in one another's existence, that we are able to move from the sorts of pleasures discussed in Book 7—the pleasures in the exercise of basic energeiai—to seeing these activities as part of a single self-contained whole, with pleasure as an accompanying "perfection" (1174b32-1175a). A virtuous friend is another self because the truly virtuous are Humanity: in them the perfections of the species are realized. Whatever differentiates such friends is not essential to either of them. It is for this reason that it is not inappropriate for Aristotle to say that we *contemplate* rather than merely *see* our friends (1169b33; 1170a3). Through virtuous friendship we move from paradigmatic pleasures to the pleasure of human life as one energeia, the pleasure of our existence as Humanity. This a condition for our coming to be aware of ourselves as objects of contemplation. Of course we knew all along that we were human, but we did not recognize that all our activities form one complex energeia, pleasurable when properly performed.

(In later terminology, every act of perceiving is an act of apperception, but not every act of apperceptive perception makes the transcendental unity of apperception explicit. Friendship conduces to the realization of this transcendental unity. For Aristotle this has non-Kantian metaphysical consequences: one experiences that substantial unity.)

IV

One might think that if this has shown anything at all, it has shown too much. After all, the virtuous person need not be a sage, much less a contemplator of himself as Humanity; and even the most articulate sage and contemplator may be a bumbler among the virtuous. Contemplating the species is not a sufficient condition for virtue; it seems not even to be a necessary condition (1106b36-1107a3).[15] A person may by grace and good fortune have been so brought up that in the very rightness of his actions, and in their balancing, the fruits of contemplation are plucked without his ever having contemplated human perfection. If thinking nobly makes the mind noble, it does not thereby make us act nobly.

And the contemplator has certain problems too: even if he is assured that he can contemplate while eating a peach, and contemplate eating a peach as the activity of nourishing, a basic energeia, there will be times when forwarding the leisure necessary to contemplation will retard political participation, and vice versa. It is of course as a political problem that this emerges most sharply, and it is for this reason that the discussion of politics follows the discussion of contemplation in Book 10. Aristotle is quite clear that there are few contemplators among us; but he is also committed to the view that they are the best among us, their existence being the perfection of the species.

What place shall be given to those whose lives are not those of thinkers or contemplators? Their lives will either become unimportant (like pots a master potter might discard in his work of producing excellent pots) or be thought best organized, for their own sakes so as to develop their limited potentialities by following the model set by the life of the contemplator. I think that Aristotle genuinely does waver; he hopes that the two courses will coincide, that as decisions to promote peak exercises of human faculties are those that will also promote their continuous best exercise in the course of a whole life, so also political decisions to promote the best development of contemplators are also those that promote the flourishing of virtuous noncontemplators.[16] But there is no argument that establishes either claim.

But sometimes, of course, the contemplative and the practical lives diverge, and the political system that supports one seems at odds with the other. Such conflict is a symptom of practical and perhaps also of scientific failure: the real nature and the proper definitions of human energeiai are misunderstood by common opinion and common practice. It is, after all, crucial to virtue that the basic human energeiai should be properly performed, that their ends should be seen in the right light, and that philosophy, friendship, and political activity should be understood for what they really are. The political and moral philosopher who determines the priorities of various activities begins with common opinion, with the lives of those who are taken to be virtuous, with the intentions that define and guide their actions. Even if the minimalist definition of the species is well understood, the expansionist account that links essential potentialities to their standard exercise is, in a bad polity, likely to be awry. Even with the support of wisdom the philosophic sage cannot completely transcend his origins. The most astute contemplator of the stars and triangles begins as a child of his time, begins with common moral opinion. The contemplator of humanity inherits dialectical accounts of the basic political and practical energeiai.

It is one of the signs as well as one of the aims of a good polity that the activities of contemplation and the comprehensive practical life support each other. When they conflict, the palms are given to the contemplative life, because the independence of the intellectual from the moral virtues allows contemplation to continue in the midst of political disaster and practical blindness. Because many of the moral virtues are interdependent and because their exercise often involves social and political activity, it is difficult to lead an excellent practical life when basic energeiai are misconceived. The stars and the divine remain unaffected by the absence of phronesis; that we can contemplate them no matter what else is happening is, however, only an incidental benefit of contemplation. This wry and derivative sense of the independence of contemplation does not reveal its true power and superiority. The benefits assured by contemplation in the worst of times give only a confused understanding of its excellence in the best of times.[17]

NOTES

1. Cf., e.g., Thomas Nagel, "Aristotle on *Eudaimonia*," *Phronesis* 17 (1972), 252-259 (chap. 1 of this anthology); W. Jaeger, *Aristotle* (Oxford, 1948), p. 334; Anthony Kenny, "Happiness," *Proceedings of the Aristotelian Society*, n.s. 66 (1965-66), 93-102; J. L. Ackrill, "Aristotle on *Eudaimonia*," *Proceedings of the British Academy* 60 (1974), 339-359 (chap. 2 of this anthology); A. W. H. Adkins, "*Theoria* versus *Praxis* in the *Nicomachean Ethics*" (unpublished paper); and John M. Cooper, *Reason and the Human Good in Aristotle* (Cambridge, Mass., 1975), pp. 156-177, chap. 3, esp. nn. 6-25.

2. The fullest defense of this is given by Léon Ollé-Laprune, *Essai sur la morale d'Aristote* (Paris, 1881), chap. 5.

3. Cf. David Balme, "Form and Species in Aristotle's Biology," presented at a colloquium on Aristotle's biology, Princeton, 1976. See also idem, ed. and trans., *Aristotle's "De partibus animalium" I and "De generatione animalium" I* (Oxford, 1972), esp. pp. 75-76, 93-101.

4. Cf. Nicholas White, "Origins of Aristotle's Essentialism," *The Review of Metaphysics* 26 (1972-73), 57-85.

5. Cf. G. E. M. Anscombe, "Thought and Action in Aristotle," in *New Essays on Plato and Aristotle*, ed. R. Bambrough (London and New York, 1965); R. A. Gauthier and J. Y. Jolif, *L'Éthique à Nicomaque* (Louvain and Paris, 1958-59), 2: 446-449, commentary on 1139a21-31; and W. F. R. Hardie, *Aristotle's Ethical Theory* (Oxford, 1968), chap. 9, esp. pp. 231-234.

6. *Contra* the suggestion of R. A. Gauthier, *La morale d'Aristote* (Paris, 1958), pp. 79 ff.

7. Cf. Amélie O. Rorty, "The Place of Pleasure in Aristotle's Ethics," *Mind* 83 (1974), 481-497, esp. 485-489, and J. L. Ackrill, "Aristotle's Distinction Between *Energeia* and *Kinesis*," in *New Essays on Plato and Aristotle*, ed. R. Bambrough (London and New York, 1965).

8. Cf. Richard Sorabji, "Aristotle on the Role of Intellect in Virtue," *Proceedings of the Aristotelian Society*, n.s. 74 (1973-74), 107-129 (chap. 12 of this anthology), esp. p. 113: "Practical wisdom . . . enables a man, in the light of his conception of the good life in general, to perceive . . . what virtue and *to kalon* require of him, in the particular case, and it instructs him to act accordingly."

9. Cf., e.g., J. D. Monan, *Moral Knowledge and its Methodology in Aristotle* (Oxford, 1968), pp. 76-81.

10. Ibid., p. 156.

11. Cf. Richard Sorabji, "Body and Soul in Aristotle," *Philosophy* 49 (1974), 63-89.

12. Cf. Joseph Owens, "Aristotle—Cognition a Way of Being," *Canadian Journal of Philosophy* 6 (1976), 1-11.

13. Cf. John M. Cooper, "Aristotle on Friendship" (chap. 17 of this anthology).

14. Cf. L. A. Kosman, "Perceiving That We Perceive: *On the Soul* III, 2," *The Philosophical Review* 84 (1975), 499-519, and idem, "On Aristotle's Views of Friendship and Consciousness" (unpublished paper). Cf. also David Hamlyn, ed. and trans., *"De anima" Books II and III* (Oxford, 1968), pp. 121-123, and two

classical papers summarizing Aristotle's views on *aesthesis:* Charles H. Kahn, "Sensation and Consciousness in Aristotle's Psychology," *Archiv für Geschichte der Philosophie* 48 (1966), 43-81, and W. F. R. Hardie, "Concepts of Consciousness in Aristotle," *Mind* 85 (1976), 388-411.

15. Cf. Ackrill, "Aristotle on *Eudaimonia,*" who attempts to defend the inclusivist over the dominant view of ends constituting eudaimonia. He shows in sec. VII of that essay that stressing the priority of rationality in the ergon argument still allows practical reason to be among the forms of thought that distinguishes humans from other species.

16. Cf. the debate between Rodier, *Études de philosophie grecque* (Paris, 1926), pp. 133-134, and Gauthier-Jolif, 2:904. Gauthier-Jolif argue that the end is "la perfection morale de l'individu meme" and even go so far as to flout the text: "les fins politiques . . . sont délibérément soumises aux fins éthiques."

17. For their discussions of the issues in this paper, I am grateful to M. F. Burnyeat, James Dybikowski, Barrington Jones, L. A. Kosman, Richard Kraut, and Joseph Owens, S. J. This essay is a revised version of an article that appeared in *Mind* 87 (1978), 343-358 and was originally delivered at a meeting of the Canadian Philosophical Association at Quebec, 1976.

21

Shame, Separateness, and Political Unity: Aristotle's Criticism of Plato

Martha Craven Nussbaum

> There's something I feel with nobody else but Socrates—
> something you would not have thought was in me—and that
> is a sense of shame. He is the only person who makes me feel
> shame. . . . There are times when I'd gladly see him dead. But
> if that happened, you understand, I'd be worse off than ever.
> —Alcibiades, in Plato *Symposium* 216ab

In the *Symposium*'s first speech in praise of love, eager Phaedrus tells his friends that love can help men have "something that should lead each man all his life long, if he is going to live well." This is "a sense of shame about shameful things and a striving towards fine things;[1] for without these no city or private individual can do anything great and fine" (178cd). Phaedrus expresses here a belief both deep and pervasive in Greek political thought: that there is an important good in human life which we (giving to his "something" a name no less dark and more controversial) shall call self-respect.[2] Without this good no human being can live well; nor can a city achieve anything fine unless it is successfully secured to the citizen body. But Phaedrus suggests more. He implies that although self-respect—this complex combination of shame before bad actions and striving toward good ones—is fostered by relationships with others, particularly loved others, it is, nonetheless, the sort of thing that properly belongs to *each* "man who is going to live well":[3] not to *all* in some collective way but to men one by one as separate choosers of their own activities. For he goes on to say that a city or an army of lovers would surpass all others with respect to this good. If we now ask ourselves how such an army would differ from a faceless hoplite band, one salient fact is surely that each of its members engages himself in the common cause as a separate individual and is aware of himself as choosing, himself, to display certain human excellences. (The influence of the loved one's presence is to make him more keenly sensitive to any deficiency or failure.) He is respected and respects himself not simply as a part of something larger, or as some leader's delegate, but as this discrete seat of excellences and maker of choices. What matters to him is not just a general outcome but what in it he does and is.[4] Phaedrus's implicit claim is that it is out of such self-aware and independent individuals that strong cities grow.

His remarks thus suggest a close connection between the good of self-respect and genuine political unity, and between both of these and personal separateness. The important good, to be effectively distributed in a city, must be distributed not to the citizen body taken as a whole but to each man seen as a separate controller of goods. But this political idea, unlike the more general claim about self-respect, would, for Phaedrus's contemporaries, be highly controversial. We see it debated, for example, in Thucydides' contrast between Sparta and Athens. Both cities agree that self-respect and the sense of shame are essential ingredients of human good living; but while one tries to secure it to citizens by teaching them to regard themselves as totally subservient to law, their minds as "not their own,"[5] the other insists on the importance of autonomous judgment, freedom from constraint. This difference is also, I want to argue here, central to the debate between Plato and Aristotle about the nature of political unity, a debate that raises issues of lasting importance for any attempt to describe the relationship between political institutions and the human good.

Aristotle's attacks on Plato in Book 2 of the *Politics* are complicated; they address themselves to various different aspects of Plato's political program. But the argument both begins with and returns repeatedly to a central criticism: the kind of unity that Plato wished to establish in his ideal *polis*, and to promote which he designed his communistic system, is neither feasible nor desirable. It is not the sort of unity proper to a truly *political* community. Addressing himself to Plato's claim, "the greater the unity of the polis, the better," Aristotle writes:

It is obvious that as a polis goes on and becomes more of a unity (*hen*),[6] it will not be a polis any longer. For a polis is by nature some sort of plurality (*plēthos*); but as it becomes more of a unity (*hen*), it will become first like a household instead of a polis, then like a man instead of a household. For we should call a household more of a unity than the polis, and a single man (*hen*) more than a household. So that even if we could attain this unity we should not do it. For it would be the destruction of the polis. [1261a16-22]

Aristotle returns several times in the succeeding arguments to his attack on Plato's conception of unity. He charges, "Socrates' error must be attributed to the incorrect assumption from which he starts: for both a household and a polis must be one in some respects, but not in all" (1263-b29; cf. also 1261b16 ff.; 1262b15 ff.; 1263b7-8). Clearly an interpretation of Aristotle's criticism must be able to explain these cryptic remarks. To explain them we must first, however, understand Plato's radical proposals about goods. I shall argue that although Plato and Aristotle agree about the importance of self-respect as a basic good in human lives and agree further that any good city must guarantee its distribution to all citizens, they differ sharply on the controversial issue of whether separateness and autonomy of choice are, in turn, necessary for self-respect. I shall begin by examining a contemporary account of self-respect which brings out clearly some issues dividing contemporary moral theory from both of these Greek views. I shall argue that the Greek texts capture some aspects of our ordinary conception which are not present in this account, and go on to sketch an alternative account that is designed to capture both these "appearances" and the common ground of the Platonic and Aristotelian positions. Turning then to the texts, I shall study Plato's argument in defense of paternalistic coercion as a necessary condition of self-respecting life for most men and try to understand the force of Aristotle's response.

SHAME AND SELF-RESPECT[7]

The most detailed examination of shame and self-respect in recent moral philosophy is in John Rawls's *A Theory of Justice*.[8] Like Phaedrus, Rawls holds that self-respect is a "primary good"—that is, something that each man must have "if he is going to live well." Like Plato and Aristotle, he makes the distribution of its social conditions an important part of his political program.[9] But his account differs substantially from theirs; the contrast reveals some interesting problems that must be faced in any account of these phenomena.

Rawls defines self-respect as having two aspects. First, the "person's sense of his own value, his secure conviction that his conception of the good, his plan of life, is worth carrying out" (440). Second, his "confidence" in his ability to carry out this plan "so far as it is within [his] power." Shame is characterized as "the feeling that someone has when he experiences an injury to his self-respect or suffers a blow to his self-esteem" (442) owing to his failure to have or to exercise valued excellences.

What strikes us immediately about this account, especially if we have comparable Greek views in mind,[10] is its insistence on the subjectivity of these phenomena. Shame is a feeling or emotion, self-respect a *sense* of worth, a *feeling* of capacity, an inner *conviction*. According to this account, apparently, a position that is not felt as shameful is not so. And if you *feel* your life plan to be a worthy one and *feel* confident that you can carry it out, that appears sufficient to make you a person of self-respect. Rawls thus implicitly denies that the objective (or intersubjective) value of my pursuits and the truth of my beliefs about them are at all relevant to the issue of self-respect and shame. He later makes the denial explicit:

> To be sure, men have varying capacities and abilities, and what seems interesting and challenging to some will not seem so to others. . . . Judged by the doctrine of perfectionism, the activities of many groups may not display a high degree of excellence. But no matter. What counts is that the internal life of these associations is suitably adjusted to the abilities and wants of those belonging to them, and provides a secure basis for the sense of worth of their members. The absolute level of achievement, even if it could be defined, is irrelevant. But in any case, as citizens we are to reject the standard of perfection as a political principle, and for the purposes of justice avoid any assessment of the relative value of one another's way of life. [441-442]

The insistent subjectivity of Rawls's account fits uneasily, as I shall argue, with his own defense of the principles of justice—though it would be perfectly at home in the hedonistic utilitarian views he attacks. But what is evident to us right away is that the account leaves some of our intuitions about shame unanswered—intuitions that we do not have to be Greeks to value. I shall sketch four cases, each of which seems to pose a problem for Rawls, even in terms of his own account—and also for us, if we are inclined to accept his view of self-respect.

(1) I am dissatisfied with my life. I feel that I am not reliably exercising excellences that are valuable to me. (My aims are not unrealistic, or even disproportionate to my capabilities; but circumstances are, in various ways, frustrating their fulfillment.) I join a religious group or go in for some fashionable kind of therapy, with the result that I emerge feeling quite at peace and contented with my state, although my objective situation has not improved. Has the treatment given me self-respect?

(2) X works for General Motors. All day long he performs a single repetitive task. The things he helps to make are not under his control. And yet he feels good. He is proud to be part of the bustling capitalist

economy; he may even be convinced that the capability to perform simple repetitive tasks is the only capability he possesses, that he could not handle a larger demand. Does his inner sense of worth count as genuine self-respect, and is GM therefore a successful distributor, in his case, of that primary good?

(3) Y worked for Nixon's reelection campaign. Her enthusiasm for Nixon and the value she accorded to this activity were based on objectively false beliefs about Nixon's character, plans, and actions. If she had not had these (demonstrably) false beliefs, she would not have chosen these pursuits or felt a sense of self-respect concerning her role in them. Should we call her positive self-feelings feelings of genuine self-respect and her life a life free from shame?

(4) Herpyllis is a happy slave. After all, she is the housekeeper and mistress of Aristotle. When she obeys his sober commands, dusts the books in his library, or keeps students from disturbing him while he writes about substance, she thinks she is realizing to the limit the excellences open to her as a woman and a slave. She never does her own practical reasoning, but she doesn't want to. She will probably be terrified rather than happy when she hears Aristotle's will read. If we reject objective value-judgments in deciding questions of self-respect, can we deny that her life is a self-respecting life?

Each of these cases asks us whether we do not need to make some distinction between felt and genuine self-respect, acknowledging that a situation may be shameful for an agent although he feels no shame. It certainly seems to be part of our ordinary conception of shame and self-respect (as it is of the Greek conception) to make such a distinction. Like the Greeks, we recognize a vice of "shamelessness."[11] We criticize a person or his behavior as "shameless" when he evinces good or confident feelings where we think a good man ought to feel shame. Again, like the Greeks, we value and try to teach the sense of shame—the disposition to have feelings of shame in certain situations or in connection with certain actions agreed in general to be base.[12] "You should be ashamed of yourself" is not just a cliché but a central part of our practice of moral education.[13] Rawls's apparent suggestion that we consider self-respect and shame only subjectively would, if adopted, require the removal of these notions from our vocabulary of appraisal. The agent who feels good about what he does just *is* self-respecting; the agent formerly called shameless becomes a man of genuine self-respect. A political design aimed at distributing the social conditions of self-respect could accomplish a lot simply by erasing, or failing to cultivate, the sense of shame, and/or the aspirations with which shame is connected. If we teach men to value only excellences that are easily cultivated and not to be upset about reversals or failures, we could get rid of many of the painful problems of shame which preoccupied the Greeks. (The cheerful inhabitants of Gershwin's Catfish Row greet the "happy dust" pusher Sportin' Life with the rousing chorus, "I ain't got no shame / Doin' what I like to do.")

But if we look at our four cases, we find, I think, that we do not ordinarily think of self-respect this way. In the first case, we do not think that my reducing my expectations and/or becoming more placid about failures to achieve my aims will necessarily be a route to real self-respect. We certainly want agents to have plans that lie roughly within the sphere of their capabilities; and a shame occasioned by failure to fulfill some remote or exaggerated wish could be regarded as irrational. But we do not think that the solution to *all* problems of shame lies in the effacement of the uncomfortable feelings; we think that it makes a difference pertinent to judgments of self-respect whether I solve my problem by removing the obstacles that block my productivity or by simply learning not to care. In the second case, again, I think we feel that there are certain sorts of activities that are unworthy of the diverse capabilities with which most human beings are endowed. Even if X likes his work, *we* can still call it degrading and subhuman, his position a shameful one. Nor is it clear that this judgment must be based on empirical evidence that most men do not like work of this kind or that most, at least, could be enlightened by political argument.[14] This is likely to be false; yet we do not feel that we should abandon our criticism. Nietzsche's portrait of the "last men" describes an entire society that has successfully rid itself of the distinctions of value, and the associated problems of self-respect, involved in X's case: all complex aspirations have been forgotten, and small pleasures, easily procured, bring satiety. These men, who proudly proclaim, "We have invented happiness,"[15] are full of the *sense* of worth and the *sense* of capacity. But should the evident (and not entirely fictional) success of this society persuade us to call them men of self-respect?

The third case is different: for here the false beliefs on which shameful action is based are matters of fact, demonstrable to Y herself. We can expect her to be ashamed of herself and regret her actions when the truth is made clear. How much she has to be ashamed of will depend, to a great extent, on the reasonableness of her false beliefs and on the efforts she has made to ascertain the truth. There was a time when support for Nixon might not have been at all shameful; but after a certain point even the most sincere believer was in a shameful position.

The fourth case is the one that will occupy us for the rest of this paper. I shall not prejudge it.

Rawls, unlike the satisfaction-utilitarians he criticizes, does find each of these cases cause for concern; and he has ways of handling them. The first two are handled, in effect, by denying that they happen—or at least happen often enough to trouble us:

> I assume then that someone's plan of life will lack a certain attraction for him if it fails to call upon his natural capacities in an interesting fashion. When activities fail to satisfy the Aristotelian Principle, they are likely to seem dull and flat, and to give us no feeling of competence or a sense that they are worth doing. A person tends to be more confident of his value when his abilities are both fully realized and organized in ways of suitable complexity and refinement. [440]

Rawls could, presumably, say that x cannot *really* be content with his dull task. But if this is still a claim about subjective feeling, it is not at all clear that it is true. Rawls has an optimistic view of man; he may seriously underrate our capacity for low contentment. (Aristotle, by contrast, says that most men will "choose" the lives of cattle—lives, that is, that do *not* call on their distinctive and complex capacities. At the risk of sounding cynical I must say that this has, for me, the ring of truth.) But if the hypothetical point is not about X's own subjective experience, what could this "real" mean? So far, we have no way of telling.

In our third case, Rawls would again admit the relevance of the question of truth. The theory of the good explicitly requires that a plan of life be chosen with full awareness of all relevant facts (408). And principles must be "consented to in the light of true general beliefs about men and their place in society" (454). Rawls does not allow that a society deceived by a Platonic "noble lie" could be a self-respecting one. But is it possible to show this on the basis of subjective psychology alone? "Noble lies" of various kinds—religious, racial, social, sexual—are constantly used, with success, to enhance feelings of self-worth in a group or a population. Rawls wishes to claim that only institutions meeting the condition of publicity can express men's respect for one another.[16] But this cannot be equivalent to a claim that only such institutions make men *feel* confident of their worth; or if it is, it is probably false.

Finally, our fourth case is one that Rawls clearly must deny to be a real case of self-respect. But again, it is not clear how or where he argues that slaves cannot feel the same feelings about their lives as free people do about theirs. Rawls includes the mention of a life plan in his definition of self-respect (440); but he does not stipulate there that this must be a plan made by the agent for himself. And even if he did, this would seem to be solving a problem by fiat.

Rawls rests the case for the principles of justice on his account of the primary goods and their value in any human life.[17] Self-respect is called the most important of these goods.[18] His case for the value of liberty seems to depend on the claim that it is necessary for the basic good of self-respect.[19] But this claim, in turn, rests on a psychological assertion of dubious plausibility: that a Herpyllis could not feel pleased with or proud of her lot.[20] The Greeks, being greater pessimists, did not want to rest the case for justice on observation of what most men can learn to like. Nor, perhaps, should we.

Rawls himself elsewhere insists that we cannot, as utilitarianism does, put justice "at the mercy of existing wants and interests" (261):

> As we have seen, a certain ideal is embedded in the principles of justice, and the fulfillment of desires incompatible with these principles has no value at all. . . . Thus the contract doctrine is similar to perfectionism in that it takes into account other things than the net balance of satisfaction and how it is shared. [326-327]

He claims that justice as fairness has found an "Archimedean point" (261), without invoking a priori considerations, in an ideal of the person as a rational chooser. But the trouble is that this firm basis comes too high up. Like Nietzsche's "complex dome of ideas pil[ed] up . . . on running water," it must itself rest on the psychological theory of self-respect and the other primary goods.[21] This may not be a very stable place from which to "move the earth." Perhaps an ideal of rationality or of the rational judge may need to be built into the initial specification of the primary good of self-respect.[22] We shall return to this possibility later.

Rawls's announced aim in keeping the account of self-respect subjective was the avoidance of perfectionism. But perhaps perfectionism and subjectivism are not our only alternatives here. If perfectionism is interpreted broadly as the view that some activities are worth more than others and that some satisfactions are without value, then Rawls himself is a perfectionist, at least on the issues raised in our third and fourth examples. If it is interpreted narrowly, as it is in Rawls's text,[23] as a doctrine that directs us to arrange institutions so as to maximize the achievements of human excellence, giving a shameful or slavish life to some in order to foster high levels of achievement in others, then probably neither Plato nor Aristotle is a perfectionist. Both seem to see the job of social organization as one of distributing the conditions of happiness to *all* citizens, not of fostering the development of a single privileged group. In between what we might call Rawls's deliberative perfectionism and the perfectionist theory he opposes are a number of other theories concerning the value of human pursuits, each with its associated accounts of self-respect. Each such theory must be assessed individually and not assimilated to the perfectionism that denies the claim of all citizens to the social conditions of self-respect. But it appears that only a simple egoistic satisfaction-hedonism, resolutely set against even Rawls's value-distinctions, can actually afford to treat self-respect simply as a matter of feeling, reducing the question "What social arrangement will give men the conditions of a really good human life?" to the question—a different one for Rawls as well as for Aristotle and Plato—"What social arrangement will make men *feel* good about themselves and their lives?" (The accomplishment of the former goal might even require cultivating dissatisfaction and the sense of shame.)

I would like now to sketch, in a rough and preliminary way, an alternative account that will both articulate the common ground of the Greek views we shall examine and also capture some of these intuitions about the objective (or intersubjective) components of self-respect. It is easier to begin with the negative pole.[24] Let us say that a shameful condition is one in which a man is failing to exercise what we agree to be valued human excellences—whatever these are in our theory of value—and/or pursuing activities that we regard as degrading or unworthy for a human being. (Either of these is probably sufficient. Base pursuits are shameful even in combination with good ones, and a complete absence of good ones is shameful even without active self-degradation.) *Feelings* of shame will accompany this condition if the agent has a certain degree of awareness both of the conception of value relative to which they are shameful and of the nature of his own pursuits.[25]

The man of self-respect, by contrast, must be one who reliably pursues activities that we agree are worthy ones for a human being to pursue.[26] These activities will have to be selected not just by accident, or on the basis of misinformation, but consistently, in the right way, for good reasons; self-respect thus appears to be closely bound up with character and with the excellences of both character and intellect.[27] Nor would the mere disposition to pursue the activities, without any actual exercise, be sufficient for self-respect.[28] A man who was always asleep or was consistently prevented from putting his plans into execution could not be judged to avoid the shame of failure in excellence.[29] A necessary condition of self-respect would thus be some degree of control both over one's environment and over oneself. Both external and internal forces can prevent a good plan from becoming effective.

These are the objective components of self-respect. But unlike shame, it seems to have a necessary subjective side as well. A person who chose good actions without feeling or being aware that they were good or who acted effectively while feeling himself helpless would be a rarer and stranger character than the man unaware of his own shame. But if we did encounter him, we would not be likely to call him self-respecting. The activities of the self-respecting man, to be worthy rather than merely lucky, must be chosen for good reasons, in awareness of their value. Our objective valuation of an agent's activities thus itself makes reference to his subjective awareness. We will not call his actions fully good if he did not subjectively see them as such.[30] Similarly, when this agent diverges from good activity, he will be disposed to feel shame. Self-respect not only is not incompatible with shame-feelings but actually requires them in various circumstances of reversal or failure. (We would not, however, call the person genuinely self-respecting if these failures are too serious or too frequent.)

Self-respect seems, then, less like a feeling identified subjectively than like a disposition to both act and feel in certain appropriate ways.[31] (The best account of respect for others would, I think, be symmetrical: it is not simply a way of feeling about them, but a disposition to treat them in certain ways *and* to do this with appropriate feeling.) Each of these points needs much more discussion; and a number of politically important points have not even been raised. (Can one be self-respecting in some parts of one's life but not in others? How far do the objective and the subjective aspects of self-respect require confirming associations with others?) But the question that preoccupies Aristotle, and to which we must now turn, is the one we raised at the beginning, and in our fourth example: what is the relationship between self-respect and autonomous choice? Is it important that the valuable activities be planned and selected by me, as a part of the active exercise of my own practical reason? (As a lover rather than as a hoplite?)

PLATO: SLAVERY, UNITY, AND FREEDOM[32]

Plato sees several obstacles in the way of human self-respect. There is our dependence on the natural world, which puts our capacity and our sense of capacity constantly in jeopardy. There are the contingent conflicts that arise between self-interest and friendship, between family and city, between the claims of one virtue and those of another. All these, again, seem to threaten our capacity to do justice to all of our concerns, forcing us to act shamefully in one respect even while behaving honorably in another.[33] But most serious of all, in his view, is the threat posed to our worth and capacity by the strength of our appetites. When the appetitive part of the soul is in control, a man is not truly a man but a beast. Though he may have a high opinion of himself, he and his activities, not selected by the valuations of reason, will be of little worth in the eyes of more fully human associates. And even if he does manage to form rational aspirations, the interference of the lower part is likely to impair his capacity to carry them out, leading him aside to baser activities and their shame. Appetites thus threaten self-respect in two different ways.

They can infect the agent's plans themselves, distorting his view of what matters. Or, if he has a good plan, they can produce *akrasia*. For a man to be truly self-respecting, reason must rule both as a legislator, choosing and ranking activities, and as an administrator, ensuring that the rationally chosen plan is effective.[34]

The *Republic* opens with a portrait of such a self-respecting man, a man who has, at last, achieved rational freedom. Cephalus, approaching death, is secure in his sense of worth and in his feeling of control over his passions; the respect accorded him by the other characters, and by Plato in the dialogue's description, indicates to us that this subjective conviction is not based on delusion. This man lives in a democracy; it seems, then, at least possible for a man in an actual city to achieve this good.

But how has Cephalus come by his freedom from the power of desire? By chance merely—by the contingency of becoming old. Many, he tells us, resent old age as bringing a decline in capacity. He and the poet Sophocles, by contrast, feel it as a release from the harsh tyranny of passion (*agrian despotēn*, 329c4), a source of *eleutheria* (329c7) rather than of slavery. It is like being let loose (*apēllachthai*, d1) from the rule of many mad masters (*despotōn*). Now Cephalus was surely more orderly than most men even when young (cf. d4); he insists that he is not one of the ones whose valuations passion has so corrupted that they regret the onset of old age. His plan was always worthy; but not so, formerly, his capacity to carry it out reliably. It took age and infirmity to free him from the threat of akrasia. Most men, who think of old age as a curse, are worse off still.

Plato endorses Cephalus's judgment. Most of us cannot, even to his extent, take control of ourselves by ourselves. In most actual political arrangements, however, we are allowed and even, *faute de mieux*, forced to do this. Most societies do not, then, secure to us the necessary conditions of a self-respecting life. Take, for example, the average citizen in a democracy—a regime that many think conducive to the personal self-respect of each citizen. Take a regime, then, where "men are, first of all, free (*eleutheroi*, 557b4), and the city is stuffed full of freedom (*eleutheria*) and free speech (*parrhēsia*), and there is license for each man to act as he pleases"; a regime, above all, where "each man can structure an arrangement for his own life, the one that pleases him" (557b8-10). Such men, Plato argues, are far from having the goods of rational order, worthy activity, true belief, and executive capacity that are necessary for self-respect. They are actually prisoners of the unbridled force of their own swelling appetites. The democratic man's soul is like a citadel that, because it is "empty of learning and fine practices and true beliefs," is easily seized by the baser appetitive urges, accompanied by "false and braggart words and opinions" (560bc). Filled with delusion, slave to the appetite of the moment, he cannot allow the truth about the worth of reason and rational planning to hold a place in his soul (561b7-8). Instead he leads what, although he does not recognize it as such, is a shameful and slavish life:

> Does he not . . . also live out his life in this fashion, day by day indulging the appetite of the day, now getting drunk and abandoning himself to the pleasure of the flute, now drinking only water and dieting; now exercising, now taking it easy and neglecting all that, now giving the appearance of doing philosophy? And frequently he goes in for politics, and bounces up and says and does whatever enters his head. . . . And there is no order (*taxin*) and no compulsion (*anankēn*) in his existence, but he calls this a pleasant life, and free (*eleutherion*) and happy, and clings to it till the end. [561de]

This man *feels* that his life is worthwhile and that he is in control of it all. But, Plato argues, once we see how thoroughly it is based on false belief, how devoid of rational ordering and of worthy activities worthily pursued, we will not agree. *He* may "call anarchy freedom and outrageousness good character" (560e-561a), but *we* do not have to be so blind.

Take, again, the successful tyrant. In keeping with the high value we accord to autonomous planning, we might think that such a man, being of all men the most untrammeled, the most at liberty to plan a life and live it out as he plans it, would be the least slavish and most self-respecting among us. Instead, Plato urges us to see, his inner state is such that he is the most shameful slave among us. Intense desires that in many men are restrained by law and the sense of shame are, in this "free" man, set free (*apēllagmenon aischunēs kai phronēseōs*, 571c8-9—an ironic reversal of Cephalus's development). And when the beast in him is set free, he himself (i.e., the man in him, the rational part of his soul) is enslaved: he is tyrannized by passion (574e), unable to control himself (579c). Far from being the most self-respecting, he is among the most shameful of men. The genuine tyrant (*tōi onti turannos*) is, in reality, the genuine slave (*tōi onti doulos*, 579d9-10).

Plato's image of the soul at the end of the *Republic*'s ninth book makes it clear that he believes every man to be in imminent danger of the enslavement to desire that deprives these two "free" men of self-respect. Every creature that looks like a man is, we are told, really a composite of three creatures. The unity of the biological person is only a deceptive envelope (588d), a specious appearance (*hen zōion phainesthai*, 588e); the man-shaped body deceives us concerning the real nature of the contents. Within is a tiny man—the honorable, rational soul, source of human worth. With him live a lion (the *thumos*), and a wild, many-headed beast (the appetitive part). The noble (*kalon*) is whatever sub-ordinates the bestial parts to the man; the shameful (*aischron*) is what-ever enslaves this element to the beasts (589cd; cf. *douloutai*, 589e; *ane-leutheria*, 590b). It is evident from Plato's account of appetition that the dominance of the little man is not possible in most creatures we call men. Indeed, it turns out that only the philosophers, who have both the best natures and the best education, are, on their own, reliably in control of their appetites and plans (431c). Any other condition is unstable and tends, because of the insatiability of appetite, to degenerate into anar-chy.[35] Appetite is "the largest part in any man's soul and is insatiable for possessions"; without constant supervision it increases, takes control, and "upsets everybody's whole life" (442ab). But according to what Plato has said about shame and slavery, a life so upset cannot be self-respect-ing. The city is needed, if the conditions of self-respect are to be secured to all.

In the hypothetical first city of Book 2, men's appetites are not very strong. A simple division of labor, in such a city, is all that is required to guarantee citizens the conflict-free activity and the self-confirming asso-ciations that maintain and constitute self-respect. They "lead their lives in peace with health . . . having pleasurable associations with one another" (372d; b); in their old age they bequeath another such life to their children. This effective distribution of primary goods and the social unity that results make this first city a "true city" (372e), even "the true city." But Glaucon calls it a "city of pigs" (372d), objecting that it does not provide for the satisfaction of the larger appetites of actual men. If the bestial parts are as strong in us, and reason as naturally weak, as Plato thinks they are, the simple arrangement that preserved the separate-ness of individual "envelopes," the freedom of each to make his own plan, will be insufficient. Slavery's shame cannot be avoided unless more radical measures are devised.

The *Republic* proposes a simple and startling solution. It has been established prior to Book 9 that only a few people in the city are by nature equipped to receive the education—moral, mathematical, and dialectical—that is necessary if reason is reliably to dominate in their souls. In each member of the largest class "the best part is naturally weak (*asthenes phusei*), so that it is unable to rule over the beasts within him, but can only serve them, and is able to learn nothing but the ways of flat-tering them" (590c). Such appetitive men, unrestrained, will indeed lead shamefully bestial lives:

With eyes ever bent upon the earth and heads bowed down over their tables, they feast like cattle, grazing and mounting one another, ever greedy for more of these delights, and, in their greed kicking and butting one another with horns and hoofs of iron, they slay one another in sateless avidity, because they are trying to fill with things that are not the part that is not, the incontinent part, of themselves. [586ab][36]

But in a well-ordered city there is hope of something better for these men, if only reason—a stronger and more efficacious "man"—is given them from another source. The distribution of self-respect cannot be accomplished merely by allowing them "negative freedom,"[37] by giving them access to resources or powers, or by offering them appropriate and attractive labor. Appetite, insatiable, will still overwhelm the weak "human" part, shaming the man inside. Nor will education be sufficient. Appetites are, as we have seen, inherently ineducable; they need constant watching and suppression and can never become subservient to the will of a naturally weak reason. The only solution, then, is to distribute to them the strength of another's reason:

Therefore, in order that such a man may be ruled by a principle similar to that which rules the best man, we say he must be a slave to the best man, who has a divine ruler within himself. It is not to harm the slave that we believe he must be ruled . . . but because it is better for everyone to be ruled by divine intelligence. It is best that he should have this within himself; but if he has not, then it must be imposed from outside, so that, as far as possible, we should all be alike and friends and governed by the same principle. [590c]

To the man who can cultivate reason within himself, the state gives a philosophical education. To the rest of its citizens it distributes rational control in the form of external command. Only this slavery can bring *eleutheria* and escape from shame.

What does Platonic "slavery" amount to? And to what extent does the Platonic slave continue to reason for himself? The final result, Plato claims, is that the slave, in virtue of his relation to the good man (like the philosopher in virtue of his relation to himself), will "take only those pleasures that the reasoning part (*to phronimon*) approves" (586d7), his lower desires being "subservient to knowledge and reason" (d5). In the slave's case, however, the phronimon that does the approving will be not his own but somebody else's. The outside reasoner will, presumably, not use the slave bodily like an inanimate tool, pushing him around into the postures that reason dictates. A slave is "a kind of *living* possession" (Ar. *Pol.* 1253b32). He moves and acts himself and does not function simply as a *bodily* extension of the master. Nor is he exactly like a philosopher's tame animal, since he does not live merely by impulse and habit but has a little rational part of his own. (This was what gave him a claim to political consideration in the first place.) He must be capable, at least, of listening to a command and obeying it. The rule of the philosopher's external reason is supposed to have a significant internal effect on him, "training the cultivated plants [the thumos] and cutting back the growth of the wild [the appetites]" (589b2-3), so that his reason is able, finally, to attend to and execute the commands of external reason. It is rather unclear what form these commands will take in the *Republic*. Will they be in the form of general rules, so that the application of command to particular case will still be the work of the slave's own reason? Surely there will be some parts of his everyday existence which will not be subject to direct particular command, some actions he will engage in on his own, albeit according to a general plan of the master's and subject to the master's reproof and correction.

But if we take the analogy to slavery seriously, as we should, we can be sure of three things at least. (1) The slave's plan of life is not his own. He has no opportunity to specify for himself a concept of the good and to work at executing it. In contrast with the democratic city, in which "each man can structure an arrangement for his own life, the one that pleases him," the ideal city is a place where the good is specified through and through by the philosophers who know it; everyone else acquiesces in and helps to execute their plan. A household slave is not given a separate command every time he dusts a piece of furniture; he may in a limited way use his discretionary powers. But what he cannot do is to decide on the *plan* and the *values* according to which the house will be run, the work performed. He is not exactly like a tool, since he moves himself, and even calculates in a limited way. But it is still appropriate to think of him as a tool of his master's reason. In the best city "the appetites of the inferior many are controlled and kept down (*kratoumenas*) by the appetites and the practical wisdom of the fewer and better" (431cd)—*not* by their own practical wisdom, at any point.

(2) It follows from this, and it is evident in the design of the ideal city, that nonphilosophers will have, in particular, no voice in any *political* planning that touches on their lives. The laws and institutions governing them will be the work of the rulers alone. (Indeed, it is inappropriate even to distinguish these two points, so thoroughly has this city erased the public-private distinction.)

(3) In some states a great deal of constraint might be evident in the education of young citizens, but these same citizens, on reaching years of adulthood, might be allowed a share in both public and private planning. In any state there is some imposition of external reason on children; and arguments like Plato's are commonly used (are used even in Aristotle) in support of authoritarian family practices and educational institutions. But it is crucial to see that Plato's ideal city envisages no time of transi-

tion from this dependence to adult autonomy. The rational parts of the laborers are *naturally* weak (590c) and that is the way they will remain. There seems to be no attempt to give nonrulers the sort of education that leads, in the rulers' case, to adult autonomy.[38] The externality of rational control is a permanent fact of adult life.

This Platonic scheme of distribution ignores or denies the importance traditionally attached to personal separateness, attacking the common democratic notion that a person's self-respect must come to him in virtue of his own activity as a planner of a life. All the happy citizens are called "more or less alike"—even though a ruler has his reason "within himself" and the others must have rational control imposed "from without." Their value resides in the bond that joins them to the best; it is as a part of somebody else that they get what is their own. By using the words *within* and *without*, Plato acknowledges that there are these two different ways in which the distribution of reason has been carried out; but the force of his remarks is to deny that this difference is a salient one or has consequences for goodness of life. Later we shall ask whether this denial is legitimate and whether Aristotle has good reasons for opposing it. But first I want to digress in order to try to arrive at a deeper understanding of Plato's reasons for this rather brisk dismissal of what was, after all, an important distinction for almost everyone who would have read him.

SEPARATENESS, SOUL, AND BODY

Our ordinary distinction between "without" and "within" is based on a commonsense conception of the person as a living body. A rational command imposed "from without" is one given from outside this envelope of flesh; a command given "from within" is one issued from somewhere inside it. But this distinction, which would have been basic to most Greeks as well, is one whose relevance Plato has already challenged. He has argued for a dualistic account of soul and body, a soul-based theory of personal identity. The bodily envelope is a mere appearance; within is the real man, trying to fight against the beasts. If we accept this picture, we might agree that giving the "man" some external assistance in this fight is no violation of his own real personal integrity. If a lion tamer has by accident been locked in a cage with some unfed animals, we will think it no violation to break down the door and help him subdue the creatures that are threatening his life. So Plato invokes the aid of good masters to keep down the "many mad masters" that threaten the life of each reason. And if, by some misfortune difficult to imagine, the tamer is trapped in a cage with these animals for life, we will feel that the helper must keep charging in and helping him all his life, if he is to live at all and go about his business. This seems to violate his freedom no more than the existence of a strong national defense force violates ours. Plato's denial of hylomorphism thus appears to be an important step in the direction of his denial of our common views about separateness.

The connection Plato wishes to make between his denial of the moral relevance of the body and his program of slavery emerges plainly when he discusses the reason for introducing communism into the ideal polis. Most men, he realizes, do not want to be slaves in a well-ordered city, their appetites kept down by force of mastership. They think of themselves as units kept apart by a body. They value ties of affection, obligation, and ownership that are clearly bound up with their bodily natures. They love that body's offspring, its sexual partners, the land and the objects that surround, nourish, and delight it. Their misguided identification with their bodies, and the evident separateness of each body from other bodies, constitute an important psychological impediment to their acceptance of the plan that will unify the city under the direction of the best. Plato's scheme of communism promises to secure unity, and, through unity, rational rule, by obliterating from the city all body-based distinctions between what is "mine" and what is "not-mine." Along with these he will, he feels, abolish most of the motivation to try to plan for oneself, apart from others. In most cities

one man would drag into his own house whatever he could get hold of away from the others; another would drag things into his different house to another wife and children. This would make for private pleasures and pains among private individuals. . . . Our people, on the other hand, will think of the same thing as their own, aim at the same goal, and, as far as possible, feel pleasure and pain together. [464cd]

The *Laws* even more explicitly tells us that communistic institutions aim at ridding men of body-based feelings of separateness:

The notion of the private will have been by hook or by crook completely eliminated from life. Everything possible will have been done to make common in some way even what is by nature private, like eyes and hands, in the sense that they seem to see and hear and act in common. [739cd]

If men stop seeing themselves as closely tied to one particular body, they will, Plato argues, be less likely to resist the rational rule that involves outside interference with bodily appetites. And only when the demand for separateness is defeated can the city be fully harmonious and unitary, each *man* unitary and free.[39] There is no greater evil in a city than plurality, no greater good than unity.[40]

Plato has claimed that the separateness of bodies is a psychological
impediment to the acceptance of rational rule. His theory of the person,
according to which the body is not the real me, explains why he feels he
can attack without cost *this* distinction between "without" and "within."
But there remains, we feel, another analogous distinction that ought still
to be important to him. If a man really is a rational soul, and if this soul
is some sort of unitary individual that preserves my identity inside or
outside the bodily envelope, then it ought to be important to ask whether
rational control comes to a man from "within" this immortal unit or from
outside it. Psychologically it may be true that men's *feelings* of separateness from other men are tied up with the body and tend to fall away
when its political relevance is denied. But a believer in Plato's theory of
soul ought to feel and think differently: the rational soul, independently
of the body, is the truly separate individual. It then becomes important
to know how separate, in Plato's political scheme, this "little man" really
is. Do the philosophers really work like a defense force, beating back
alien attackers so that the reason can go about its own daily business? Or
are they more deeply involved in the choices and plans of the rational
soul itself? Plato's analogy to gardening, in which the philosopher cuts
back the weeds so that the good plants can grow, suggests the former,
more innocuous picture (589b2-3). But we have had reason to suppose
that the latter is a better description of the way things are really going to
work. The rulers have no direct access to the bestial parts of the ruled;
they cannot just go charging into the body and fight its appetites without
interfering in the man's rational life and plans. They have no prospect,
for example, of performing some delicate brain surgery that would
accomplish an appetitectomy. The only way they can rule appetites is by
giving orders about behavior to the naturally weak reason. That is why
Plato says that the *man*, and not just his envelope, must be and remain
a slave.

Another image occurs to us here. Suppose we have this same lion
tamer locked in with the unfed animals; suppose he is too badly mauled
for us just to beat back the beasts and let him walk out of the cage. Then
we might feel it right to go and drag him out by force. Again, suppose we
see that he is in mortal danger; but, in the heat of the moment, still barely
conscious, he says he does not want our help—or consents in a way that
we are sure represents no genuine rational decision on his part. Can we
drag him out?[41] To begin to answer these questions we would have to ask
the following as well: (1) Will he recover the autonomous use of his
powers? Will our intervention promote his continued separate life, so
that we will not go on dragging or ordering him around indefinitely?
(2) Is it a case where he can be expected, when he gets out of the immedi-

ate situation and reflects, to endorse our intervention, saying it was lucky for him, and a good thing for his own ongoing life, that we did not wait for his decision?[42] There is a genuine moral problem, even if we have affirmative answers to these questions. In this case it seems clear that we should help; and yet some closely related cases of paternalistic medical treatment seem very unclear. But the Platonic ruler, who never intends to allow the slave a plan, must answer both questons in the negative. The slave may cheerfully acquiesce in command; but he can never endorse it as good from the point of view of a plan of life that is his own.

Plato seems, nonetheless, to ignore this psychic "without/within" distinction as well as the bodily one. All are "more or less alike," rulers and ruled, because all are ruled by the rational part. Doesn't it matter whose? And why, even after the bodily distinction has been attacked, should Plato feel free to avoid this problem? In the *Republic* nothing more is said. In the *Laws* the problem is confronted, and resolved in a most peculiar way. Book 5 begins by asking how I should "honor my own soul." There is, the legislator tells us in answer, a vulgar sense of the expression "one's own" according to which what is most my own is what I control. There is also another, and higher, sense according to which what is most my own and most peculiar to me (*oikeion*) is what is the better and what controls me (726a). I can best "honor my own soul" by regarding myself as one with the rational soul that rules my life. In the case of most men this will mean honoring the ruler's reason as what is most fully me and mine. The vulgar sort of self-love that considers each person as a separate unit (of any sort, bodily or psychic) is attacked as "the greatest of all evils for men" (731de). What is truly shameful is not, as most men suppose, to put one's person (vulgar sense) into the keeping of another, but *not* to do so, when that other's soul is what is in the higher sense most truly one's own self. A man should pursue this rule of the better, "letting no shame deter him" (732b). The claim seems to be not only that my good can and must come from without but that what we ordinarily regard as "without" is actually, if it governs "me," the highest and the most personal or private (oikeion) part of me.[43]

This is a strange picture of the person. Plato seems to be willing here to fuse what we think of as separate persons; he does not even insist on the separateness of unitary rational souls. But, though strange, the picture can perhaps be explained by pointing to some developments in Plato's later metaphysics of the soul. By the time of the *Laws* Plato has ceased to treat the rational soul as an indivisible Cartesian unit that preserves identity outside the body. There is, as is well known, another Platonic view, already in tension with the unit view in the *Phaedo* and the *Republic*, which decisively wins out in several late dialogues. This is the view that my soul is not a unit, but a quantity of soul-stuff. Soul is a mass-term. The *Phaedrus* proves the immortality, not of *each* soul, but of *all* soul. It is often observed that nothing in this proof establishes individual immortality; and there are strong reasons for doubting whether there is a theory of individual immortality in that dialogue or in the *Symposium*. In the *Laws* and *Epinomis* we see a more developed version of this view. Soul, existing en masse long before the advent of body, is subsequently cut up into parcels that are separate only in virtue of being enclosed by some body.[44] These dialogues entirely abandon the eschatology of the middle dialogues except as the content of stories which it will be useful for the average citizen to believe (*Laws* 870de; 872de; 927a; 959bc; *Epin.* 942b).

This view of soul is not explicit in the *Republic*; but it seems to be in the background, waiting to emerge. (It is suggested, for example, by the theory of transmigration: a soul is "the same soul" not in virtue of its capacities or its memories, for these come with the body and are lost with it; it can be "the same," we might think, only in virtue of its spatiotemporal continuity as a quantity of soul.) The mass-view of soul was the most common one in pre-Platonic Greek philosophy; no Greek thinker ever articulated a Cartesian view, and Plato never fully did either.[45] Though a bodily criterion of personal identity may not be necessary to secure my status as a separate individual, its abandonment seems to leave Plato with no well-articulated version of a distinction between "without" and "within," no clear alternative to a view that radically weakens my claim to be considered as separate. Thus, although it is not until late in his life that Plato announces his paradoxical answer to the psychic "without/within" question by suggesting a fusion of rational souls, his silence on this important issue in the *Republic* becomes easier to understand if we see him being drawn, already, in that direction. Such considerations do not provide support for Plato's claim that the distinction is irrelevant —unless we accept his metaphysics. At best they begin to explain why he argues for the irrelevance as little as he does.

At this point in Plato's theory, however, we begin to feel that we have lost our grip on the distributive problem with which we began. We thought that we were talking about giving goods to person, where "persons" were the separate bodies we are accustomed to think them. We were a bit surprised to be told that they were not the living bodies but only one element inside each living body. Still, we could still identify and trace them via their bodies, one to each; ordinary practices of counting and distributing were not seriously upset. But now we are told that the best part of "me" is a rational element located within another body; distributing a good to *me* means getting that element to be in control of "my" (vulgar sense) bodily and psychic nature. The aim really seems to be the achievement of the best overall ordering of Soul in relation to Body, the general dominance of Reason over Appetite. It is hard to see it as anything more like distribution than that. And the wish to effect this order, making one great big person with reason on top, does seem, as Aristotle says, to be a wish for the elimination of the city. The city is a way of distributing goods to persons. It originated, Plato told us in *Republic* 2, because we are each individuals but not fully self-sufficient individuals (369b). The job of a city is supposed to be to secure to us what will satisfy these needs. The whole idea of the polis presupposes as fundamental the separateness (if not necessarily the autonomy) of separate persons and their needs. Plato's strategies for securing political unity did not, in the first place, question this, or set up unity as an end in itself; they were strategies for making the sort of state that would give individuals what they need for living good lives and being happy. Communistic institutions that diminished separateness and promoted unity were introduced as necessary in order to secure to each person the harmony and rational control that make self-respect possible. But now, when we cease to treat individuals as units, either bodily or psychic, we seem to have changed the subject. What, now, is a city, and what is its *raison d'être*?

ARISTOTLE: SEPARATENESS, SLAVERY, AND THE POLITICAL PLĒTHOS

Plato has argued that in order to give men the conditions of self-respecting activity it is necessary to remove their autonomy, making them slaves of the better. To this end he has introduced institutions that should weaken men's psychological demand for separateness. Aristotle directs several different kinds of objections at these parts of Plato's program. Some are based on issues of psychological plausibility. He asks, for example, whether men, in the absence of family ties, will actually be motivated to love all citizens strongly, as brothers, or instead have only a remote and lukewarm feeling about everyone and become indifferent to the public good (1262b33 ff.).

Another group of criticisms is directed against Plato's view of the person. Aristotle insists, throughout his ethical and psychological works, on the moral relevance of the body and the desires associated with it, denying that it makes sense to assimilate these to forces of external constraint. There is, he argues, no good argument for separating off a part of the human creature we ordinarily encounter and calling this bit the "real man," the bodily parts a synthetic envelope. The soul is just the form or functional organization of the entire living body; and there is no good reason not to make the development and flourishing of all our bodily human nature a part of our conception of the human good. "The irrational passions seem to be no less a part of the human being (*anthropika*) [sc. than reason is]; and the same is true of the activities that human beings do from passion and appetite. So it is weird to treat these as involuntary" (111b1-3). This sort of objection would, if successful, considerably change the nature of the philosopher-ruler's aims; but it would not settle decisively the question of separateness and autonomy. If the flourishing of all three "parts" of a man is to be included in our conception of good living, this may make it less obvious that philosophers are the best rulers and that the people who were seen "grazing and mounting" like cattle are, for this reason alone, in a bad way. And it will mean that whoever the rulers are, they will have to modify their aims in the training and planning of human lives.[46] But even in an Aristotelian moral universe the appetites remain dangerous sources of constraint and unfreedom. The threats of wanton pleasure-seeking and akrasia are still major obstacles to self-respect; the many who allow their rational faculties to be overtaken by pleasure are still said to have the shameful lives of mere animals; and men of consistent rational control remain a small minority among us. Hylomorphism tells us we cannot make the problem of the passions disappear simply by telling ourselves that the passions are external enemies, no part of what *I* can be praised or blamed for. It argues, too, that the Platonist is playing a dishonest game—both assimilating akrasia to behavior produced by external compulsion and then, at the same time, treating the akratic as a blameworthy individual liable to punishment and coercion. Finally, it tells us that the psychological strategies of communism used by Plato to undercut the demand for autonomy neglect relationships that should be of permanent moral relevance. What it does not do is to make Plato's original problem go away. Hylomorphism may not even be necessary for a defense of autonomy—for we may, even if Plato did not, find a coherent way of individuating souls without the body.[47] But it certainly does not seem to be sufficient—since the problem of passion remains a problem for Aristotle and for us, and coercion from without is still one of the promising candidates for solution. We must see, then, whether Aristotle has further objections to Plato's program, objections that will clarify the place of autonomy within his own political view.

Aristotle has charged Plato with misconceiving the nature of truly political unity, making the state more like a single man than like a city, which is, of necessity, a plurality. He has also charged Plato with failure to make important distinctions among various types of human associations: "Some people think that mastership is a kind of knowledge and that household management and mastership and political rule and kingly rule are all the same thing" (1253b18-20). We are now in a position to appreciate the point of these claims—and Aristotle's view of the connection between plurality and political association. A passage from the *Magna Moralia*[48] will help us. Discussing the basis of political justice, Aristotle claims that this justice cannot exist in the relationships between master and slave, father and son:

> for this [sc. political] justice consists chiefly in equality; for the citizens are associates of a sort, and tend to be peers by nature, though they differ in their habits. But there does not seem to be any justice between a son and his father, or a servant and his master—any more than one can speak of justice between my foot and me, or my hand, and so on for each of my limbs. For a son is, as it were, a part (*meros*) of his father, until he attains the rank (*taxin*) of manhood and is separated from him. Then he is in a relationship of equality and parity with the father. This is what citizens are like. In the same way and for the same reason there is no justice between master and servant. For a servant is something of his master's. . . . Political justice seems to consist in equality and parity. [1194b5-23]

Aristotle frequently repeats the claim that political association, unlike slave ownership, is an association of peers and equals, that political rule is the rule of free and equal men over each other by turns.[49] This means, he tells us, that each citizen, as a unit, must have a share in controlling the government.[50] The *Magna Moralia* passage (and cf. *NE* 1134b9 ff.) makes it clear what Aristotle believes to be the necessary basis for rational, self-respecting political adulthood. One must be separate, a self-standing, autonomous unit. And it is to separate units, in full recognition of their separateness, that political goods must be distributed. The relationship between a conception of justice that treats individuals as limbs or tools of other individuals, and true political justice, is one of mere homonymy (*MM* 1194b6-7): the political art must treat men not like slaves or children but as adults who take their stand as separate beings.[51] The word *taxis*, used for the "rank" of adulthood, is a revealing one, with its military implications. Manhood is like being lined up side by side with other soldiers (as in Phaedrus's army of lovers)—not becoming somebody else's arm, leg, or even eye.

It is this adult separateness that Plato, Aristotle argues, overrides in his efforts to secure rational control to all. In a revealing passage (*Pol.* 1261-b16 ff.) he remarks that there are two senses of the word *all* (*pas*): a collective and a distributive sense. Plato claims that *all* citizens in his state will say "mine" and "not-mine" of the same things, as a result of philosophical rule and communistic institutions. But, Aristotle insists, they will "all" say it (if they will) in a way that does not imply that "each," taken as a separate person, chooses to say it (1261b25-26). The "each" kind of harmony, in which separate individuals, choosing as such, reach unanimity, Aristotle finds attractive, though impossible (1261b31-32). The "all" kind he finds both impossible and objectionable; it is this collectivity, obliterating autonomy, that destroys the city. In *Politics* 7, he makes the point again: "Even if it *is* possible for all (*pantas*) to be good, but not each citizen taken individually (*kath' hekaston*), we should choose the latter way" (1332a36-37).[52]

Is Aristotle making a merely terminological point in these pages, saying that Plato has called by the name *polis* what would be better called by another name? Perhaps his claim that excessive unity destroys the polis is just the claim that it replaces one sort of institution with another one that will do as well in human life. This seems prima facie unlikely, given the connection Aristotle repeatedly makes between the polis and basic human needs. Man is a political animal; by nature he needs (not merely desires) associations of the *political* type (*Pol.* 1253a7 ff.). But then the question is why man is thought to need, by nature, associations that respect his separateness and grant him political rights, rather than master-slave or parent-child associations of the Platonic kind. What is the morally relevant difference? What do human creatures naturally need that they cannot get by being arms or legs?

A slave is a human being who does not "live as he wishes" (*Pol.* 1317b-13). He does not live according to his own practical choices (*kata prohairesin*, 1280a32-34). "Though he is a human being, he is someone else's, not his own" (1254a14-15). For this reason he cannot share in eudaimonia, in the good life for a human being (1280a33)—a necessary condition of which is the active exercise of practical reason.[53] Nor can he even share in friendship—at least not in the full friendship of character, based on respect for *prohairesis*.[54] Aristotle grants that there may be some beings technically human who do not have the capacity for practical reason: a so-called "natural slave" would be a being who "does not have the deliberative faculty at all" (1260a12)—who, though he may to some extent be able to listen to reason, does not possess it himself (1254-b20; cf. 1259b22 ff.). But it is crucial that a person not naturally suited for mere slavery should not be turned into a slave (1255a25); if a creature is able to make himself a life plan—if, at the minimum, he has the capacity "to foresee things with his reason" (1232a32)—that is sufficient, Aristotle argues, to give him a claim to be an active shaper of his own life. By nature we, or most of us, are endowed with the ability to use reason to organize our lives and plan for our futures. Aristotle argues that the active exercise of practical reason in planning a life is a deep need of each being endowed with reason and that to subdue him to the wishes of another is to deny him the conditions of a good and self-respecting life.

Truly political associations—the ones that respect autonomy—are not just peripheral but necessary to human good living. Each man does, as Plato claimed in *Laws* 5, identify himself with, and respect, the practical reason that rules his life; but because he is this man and not another, he will not have *self*-respect if, as in Plato's state, it is another man's practical reason that rules him.

What does this come to in concrete political terms? Aristotle's views on the question of the best regime are too complex an interpretative problem for a full analysis to be attempted here. But two general points seem clear. First, the mere absence of slavelike coercion is not sufficient, in his view, for a self-respecting political life. In a passage whose autobiographical implications give it added force, he speaks of the life of the *metoikos* —the resident alien in a Greek city, who, while no master's slave, was barred from active political participation and also from holding property. Such a man, because he "does not have a share in political offices" (the word *timē*, "office," also means "honor" or "respect"), is, Aristotle says, like the wanderer described by Homer, "Some alien without honor (*atimēton*)" (1278a34-38). Second, actual *holding* of political office is not itself necessary for political self-respect. A good man, he tells us (*MM* 1212a34-b9), will readily yield both money and officeholding to another who might make better use of them. He will be free of self-conceit and undue ambition.[55] But it is clear here that Aristotle imagines this man as having a *claim* to office (1212a38) and an opportunity either to take the position or to refuse. He is not barred from office/honor, like Aristotle in his rented Athenian gymnasium. He is a ruler in the sense that it is partly up to him what government he has.

We might at this point wish to question Aristotle's claim that *political* rights are necessary for full self-respect. Granted (for the moment) that a self-respecting man must be a maker of his own life plan, why is political deprivation by itself such a terrible thing? Doesn't the case of Aristotle show that a man can lead a good active moral and intellectual life without actual political exercise, his private autonomy not infringed by the state, though he himself is no part of it? To a citizen of a modern democracy, who feels at a great remove from the government that plans his life, it might well seem that voting makes little difference, that the private is the only sphere in which we can act with any hope of control. We surely do not think that a colleague of ours who leads a life similar to ours but happens to be a "resident alien," unable to vote in this country, is *ipso facto* a person of diminished self-respect, deprived of the right to plan his life's course. But this judgment comes, I suspect, very much from a feeling that we are just about as cut off as he is. If we think of the Greek polis, an institution whose distinction, when it functioned well, was that each citizen had a real share in shaping a public conception of the good, nobody was alienated except by his own choice, and civic friendship was not attenuated by enormous numbers and remote distances, then Aristotle's distinction between the citizen and the free alien becomes more meaningful. This difference makes us doubt that Aristotle would consider modern democracies successful distributors of the social conditions of self-respect. In our alienation from active governing we are, perhaps, more like him than like those whose situation he praises.[56]

We now face several objections—for it may be claimed that this analysis has exaggerated the differences between Aristotle and Plato. There are three problems that might seem to provide a basis for such a claim. Here I shall be able only to give a brief account of these problems and sketch a reply to each objection.

(1) *The theory of slavery.* As we have seen, Aristotle does hold that there are people whose natural capacities are significantly below the human norm, and argues in quasi-Platonic fashion that for these, as for tame animals (1254b10 ff.), slavery to the better men is indeed the best life and in their own interests. It might be claimed, because of this, that his theory is very much like Plato's, differing only verbally, that is, concerning the classes to which the name *citizen* should be applied. But what is crucial here is that Aristotle insists, as we have already seen, that the natural slaves must be men so deeply deprived by nature that we can be sure they are altogether incapable of planning a life for themselves. The force of his argument is to indicate how few of the people actually held as slaves really belong in that condition; and the life of the real natural slaves is seen to be a shameful and subhuman one, cut off from eudaimonia, the good life proper to man.[57]

(2) *The manual laborers.* In any city there is labor to be done, and not all of it can be done by animals or natural slaves. But the men who perform this labor will necessarily lack the leisure required, in Aristotle's view, for full intellectual and moral development (cf. 1278a20-21; 1328-b39 ff.; 1329a20-21). They cannot, therefore, despite their natural capacities, be included in the citizen body (3.5; 7.9). We are making some men who are capable of virtue and self-respect do this work so that other naturally similar men may have a good life. This is a dark spot in Aristotle's political theory—a point concerning which he himself is evidently insecure and unhappy. It is a mark of the depth and honesty of his perceptions as a political thinker that he is willing to acknowledge that there may be certain kinds and conditions of labor that are both necessary for life and incompatible with the flourishing of the laborers. Some liberal theorists tend to skate rapidly over this problem, assuming that to give men political rights and opportunities is to give them all they need to

exercise them well, that the man on the assembly line can have as rich and satisfying a moral/political life as the executive, the professor, or the writer. Aristotle, like Plato, acknowledges that conditions of employment make a serious difference in the individual's moral development, a difference pertinent to questions of goodness and happiness. But what makes Aristotle's position entirely different from Plato's on this issue is that Aristotle concedes that injustice is being done to these laborers and that the aims of the distributor are being frustrated. He never claims that he is giving the *banausoi* a good or self-respecting life when he deprives them of political rights; nor does he, like Plato, justify the subordination of craftsmen with reference to their human nature and needs. They, too, will be "aliens without honor"; their practical needs will not be met. Contingent limitations make Aristotle's scheme look something like Plato's in practice; the profound philosophical difference is that what Plato sees as the success of distribution, Aristotle sees as its failure.

(3) *The virtuous ruler.* Several passages in the *Politics*[58] seem to indicate that Aristotle agrees with Plato about the desirability of subjecting all citizens to someone divinely good and wise, disagreeing only about the possibility of setting up a polity that could deliberately cultivate such men to be its rulers. These passages are at the center of the tangled interpretative question of the regime; they are notoriously hard to interpret in a way that renders them consistent with his insistence on shared rule. But there are three reasons why they do not seem to pose a serious problem for our interpretation of the criticisms of Plato.

(a) First there is the question of the *degree of difference.* Aristotle repeatedly says that subjection of citizens to a single man would be justified only if he were as far above them all in excellence (of both body and soul) as they are above animals—a "god among men," a being *generically* different (cf. 1254b16-17); 1284a3 ff.; 1284b31; 1332b16). He mentions no historical example of such a creature, though he knew one of the obvious candidates very well; he does not even tell us whether such a man has ever existed. The passages seem to criticize actual monarchy in much the way that Book 1 criticized the actual practice of slavery: by showing what a change would have to occur in human life in order for such practices to be justified. Others might rank his pupil with the gods; the professor's silence is eloquent. In fact, in Book 7's sketch of the ideal city Aristotle concludes that in real life we do *not* find godlike men; and so we must arrange things so that all may share in ruling and being ruled (1332-b23 ff.). If we did live in a world with beings so far above us in ability that we looked to them as our dogs look to us, we would not be the creatures we now are; human ways of life and our human view of man would be so altered that it is hard even to imagine how political questions would look to us. Perhaps we would have different needs and different conditions of self-respect. As things are, however, and as *we* are, we need a share in ruling.

(b) This points to another deep difference between the two philosophers on this point. For Plato, sure moral knowledge is there to be had by (some) human beings. It is in the having of such knowledge that the superiority of the rulers consists. Aristotle insists repeatedly that the "matter of the practical," as he calls it, is, by its very nature, indefinite—there is no science of it.[59] If this is so, it seems that there never could be a human being thinking about human problems who had the requisite degree of superiority. And Aristotle's entire procedure in the *Ethics* bears this out. For he is evidently searching not for the vision of a single expert but for a reflective consensus of the "many" and the "wise."

(c) Finally, if Aristotle were as close to Plato as the objection suggests, we would expect him to endorse Plato's program as an ideal, objecting only that it is impossible. But as we have seen, he says clearly that it is neither possible nor desirable; even if one could achieve such unity, one should not do it.

CONCLUSION: SHAME AND SELF-KNOWLEDGE

We have seen in Plato and Aristotle two very different views of personal self-respect and its social conditions. One stresses the need for control and order; the other is willing to tolerate a certain amount of disorder for the sake of autonomy. The dispute starts from two different analyses of human nature and needs. Aristotle insists that all human beings who are naturally endowed with the capacity for practical reason have a need to exercise that capacity; social circumstances that do not permit its development and, with adulthood, its separate exercise do not permit real human flourishing. You may not need to be an actual officeholder; the good man may turn down office to pursue his intellectual activities. But he must have a deliberative share in his city; he cannot have the shame of having its laws chosen for him. Plato, by contrast, claims that the need we have is to have our lives ruled by reason and to get our souls into the state of harmony that results from this rule. It does not matter—at least not crucially—how this rule is secured and by whom the planning is done.

It should be stressed here that the issue between the two is not the issue of individualism—that is, the clash between a view that supports diversity in the choice of goods and a view holding that the good is the same for everyone.[60] Aristotle probably believes, as much as Plato, that the good life is the same for us all—or at least that all rational agents, after sufficient reflection and consideration of the alternatives, could agree about the plan of the best life.[61] But he will insist that although the good may be objective—or, as seems more correct, intersubjective—the *choice* of the good must come from within and not by dictation from without. All reflective men might choose the same good life; but what makes each of them a *good man* is that he is the one who chooses it. And what is more, it will not count as a *good life* for him unless it is a life chosen by his own active practical reason: prohairesis enters centrally into the specification of the good life itself.

Plato says we do not need deliberative autonomy. Aristotle says we do. Is this an argument, or merely assertion and counterassertion? We feel we need some way to get behind the conflicting claims, to get some perspective from which to assess them. But how? We cannot find support for Plato simply by pointing to the existence of contented slaves, who live without autonomy and yet *feel* no loss of self-respect and no need for practical reason. I have tried to argue that claims about basic needs cannot be settled empirically in this way, by getting the allegedly deprived person to tell us whether he feels a lack.[62] One of the worst features of slavery is that it makes slaves like it—the reason why Uncle Tom has long been a paradigm of the shameful. But how, then, are we to go about finding the true needs of human agents, if not by asking men what they feel they need? If we are rejecting appeals to a priori knowledge or divinely given norms, it appears that we must *somehow* ask *some* men what they think and feel. We could, of course, simply amass statistics showing that the majority of human beings say they need X and Y and Z —and call the winners in this poll the true needs. The trouble with this is that it is evident that the majority vote would go against Aristotle: most of the world's people probably do not *feel* a need for autonomous exercise of practical reason in political life and cannot, perhaps, even imagine for themselves a life in which this exercise is allowed them. Even in our time and place the case of the Equal Rights Amendment shows us how ready deprived people are to vote against rights for the sake of some real or imagined comfort. And yet we are not convinced that this settles the question of justice, or of needs.

If we must rely on *some* practical intuitions and are reluctant to rely on sheer weight of numbers because we have little confidence in the lucidity, the rationality, and the imagination of the majority, a promising alternative seems to be Aristotle's: that we rely on the intuitions of people who have somehow earned the right to be regarded as competent practical judges—who have displayed the requisite strengths of character, intellect, and imagination and have done enough of the practical work of considering and working through alternative moral conceptions to find themselves in a good position to make sound judgments.[63] The procedure of this paper so far has been based on the Aristotelian assumption that what should be done in thinking about these questions is to describe the alternative conceptions in detail, presenting them as perspicuously as possible to the moral intuitions of the interlocutor. This does not really take us outside of the problem, since our ideal of the practical judge is a part of standards of human rationality which are probably themselves subject to change and revision. If Aquinas was probably wrong to feel that Aristotle's appeal to the *phronimos* as arbiter of virtue was patently circular, still we seem unable to characterize the phronimos in a way that takes us outside of mutable human ways of thinking about practical thought; and insofar as Aquinas demanded a firmer grounding for moral judgments, he was right to revise Aristotle, appealing beyond the phronimos to divine law. We have denied ourselves this solution. Nonetheless, if we really make ourselves think through and feel in some detail what the alternatives are like and what a life based on them would be for us, we can hope to emerge with at least a better understanding of why autonomy is important to us and just how important it is. It is not clear that moral argument can accomplish more than this.

But there is more work to be done at this point if we are really to see and feel the issue in all its complexity. Plato's ideal state and Aristotle's abstract criticisms may seem, so far, too remote to engage us on the intuitive level. If we can look at a complex particular case of Platonic slavery, we may be able to uncover more fully the nature of our emotional and intuitive responses to Plato's plan. It is difficult to find in literature[64] a positive and persuasive example of Platonic slavery in the service of true freedom—one, that is, that is not bound up with religious doctrines in a way that prejudices the outcome. The example I have chosen—from Henry James's *The Golden Bowl*—has two difficulties: first, that the novel is far too complex to be adequately interpreted in less than a book; second, that it is clear from the beginning that the quasi-Platonic program is being subjected to penetrating criticism by the author. But I shall try to describe impartially the Platonic aims involved.

The Prince is a passive and morally weak man, lacking both money and intellectual energy, apparently incapable, on his own, of coherently planning a life. He does not, on his own, *feel* shamed or debased; he is, perhaps, too passive even for that. He accepts amiably whatever comes his way. But neither in the eyes of others nor in his own does he have a dignity other than that attaching to his great name and his gentlemanly bearing. The two Americans, Maggie Verver and her father, "collect" him as a beautiful objet d'art—a European prince to crown a collection of fine things which has been amassed with the most discerning taste. They make him (as Maggie's husband) an object in their valuable collection, giving him, in return, a sense of place and purpose, for which he is deeply grateful. They care for his moral life, infusing him—though always, Platonically, "from outside"—with their indefatigable American purposefulness and their moral energy. The Prince recognizes that he is being treated like an object, albeit a fine one—an object that is expected to fit into other lives (to be "round," not "square," as they say) in a way dictated solely by those others. He is, in some significant sense, their Platonic slave: from them he receives the reason and direction he lacks, but only in return for cheerfully surrendering his autonomy. It is easy to imagine a political generalization of the Ververs' practice which makes no appeal to Platonic metaphysics—one based, as so many such attempts have been based, on the conviction of one civilization (and not infrequently, as James saw, of our own) that it has the responsibility to guide and control its weaker and more backward fellows. But the simpler private case will generate all the questions we want to ask.

The Platonist would claim that only under the Ververs' tutelage (and let us suppose them to be as superior in morality and consistency as they believe themselves to be) can the weak, though amiable, Prince achieve anything like the stability and control necessary for respecting himself and being respected. Without them his projects will be the whims of a moment; he will have no stable character; his life will not be ruled by reason. With them he will be part of a grand and beautiful plan, securely led toward the good. The Aristotelian will answer that, nonetheless, it is no good treating a rational human being like a possession, however precious; that nothing like self-respect can come from that, only a different sort of self-abasement. To be a free man the Prince must be respected and respect himself not simply as a part of somebody else's plan but (as actually happens at the novel's end) as an autonomous being whose worth cannot be calculated relatively to something else and who is seen as the source of his own projects and actions.[65]

In choosing between the two views we will tend, at first, to pose a lot of empirical questions. Are the Ververs really, in fact, superior? Does the Prince actually *want* anything more than comfortable enslavement? Is he in any way capable of achieving self-control on his own? But the force of the Aristotelian answer does not depend, I think, on our receiving any particular answer to these questions. We have already insisted that questions about respect are not decisively answered by discovering the "slave's" own actual desires. Aristotle would insist that once we have decided that a creature is a full member of our human species, not so blighted in capacity that we had better regard him as more like a beast or some other type of thing, we must grant that he has *needs*, paramount among which is the need to exercise practical reason in making his own choices—whether or not he actually wants to. The Prince comes to feel what he has lacked; but if he had not, *we* would still be entitled to think of him as deprived. And I think that our considered intuitions support this judgment.

But Plato has made us look skeptically at what we call deliberative autonomy, asking whether, once we examine the role played in our practical reasoning by the appetites and passions, we can really call ourselves free. Aristotle's argument relies on an assumption that most men can become really autonomous planners if we give them access to political rights and some kind of good initial moral training. But is this right? Look, Plato tells us, at the life of this "free" democratic man. He does a little philosophy, then he goes out and gets a sandwich. (He even likes it, attaching value to the satisfaction of those needs—distortion, as well as distraction.) He does a little more philosophy, then he goes swimming. Then maybe he falls in love with somebody; he forgets all about work now—he cannot conceive of his good except in relation to that person's feelings and body. Is all that really supposed to be *freedom*, and choosing your own rational plan? There seems to be no plan, no order at all in such a life (cf. *Rep.* 561de, quoted above). Wouldn't it be better, if this man is going to be constrained anyway and is going to find his good relatively to contingencies of circumstance and relationship, for him to be constrained by and related to the best man, who is truly free and can reliably plan for his good?

There are many questionable points in the Platonic argument, most having to do with Plato's view of the appetites and their objects.[66] But even if we think, with Aristotle, that the appropriate exercise of appetites and passions is constitutive of the good in a rational human life, we must also admit, as Aristotle does, that they are often also sources of constraint and self-deception. This, of course, does not help salvage Plato's claim to have distributed a *good* to the slaves in the ideal city. If we continue to believe that separateness is a necessary prerequisite of self-respect, we could allow Plato to claim that in his state *some* men are self-respecting, while in a democracy *none* would be. We could even allow him to claim that in the ideal city reason as a whole is dominant over appetite as a whole and that this is not so in actual cities. But neither of these results is the result Plato originally claims to be after—that of securing the conditions of a self-respecting life to *all* citizens of the city. And if we view the end of the polis as the distribution of goods to persons— rather than the promotion of the highest type of good life or the achievement of the most desirable overall arangement—then we shall have to doubt that he has achieved it. But he has nonetheless raised serious problems for the Aristotelian idea that rational freedom is available to most of us, given the right social circumstances.

Well, then; suppose Aristotle is right that only a maker of his own choices and plans is a free, self-respecting man. Suppose Plato is also right that there are inner obstacles to this freedom at least as dangerous as the threat of external constraint and that most of us are shut up for life with such obstacles. Then something bad seems to follow. It is a possibility worth taking seriously. In fact it may be that taking it seriously, in thought and feeling, is about the most, in some cases, that we can do in the direction of self-respect. In *The Wings of the Dove*, James describes another unfree man—bound, in this case, by passion and his loved one's plans for him. But unlike the Prince, Densher has the strength of imagination to become aware of his shame:

The proof of a decent reaction in him against so much passivity was, with no great richness, that he at least knew—knew, that is, how he was, and how little he liked it as a thing accepted in mere helplessness.... His question connected itself, even while he stood, with his special smothered soreness, his sense almost of shame; and the soreness and the shame were less as he let himself, with the help of the conditions about him, regard it as serious.[67]

Densher finds a remnant of dignity in the awareness of his passivity. His shame is mitigated by consciousness of its depth. So, too, others of James's characters, trapped in various ways by circumstance or by passion, achieve moral stature through this sort of finely tuned imaginative awareness of the constraints that diminish them. They would have had more subjective self-respect without this awareness; but James suggests, and I think we feel, that they have, because of it, more of the important kind. How much of this self-awareness, self-criticism, and longing would be available to the slaves in Plato's ideal state, who are not permitted to imagine the good for themselves? (If we think of this as a democratic criticism of Plato, we should remember that it was also Nietzsche's criticism of utilitarian-hedonist democracy.) A great merit of the Aristotelian polis is, by contrast, the centrality in it of character-friendship, with its capacity for refining self-criticism through emulation and the sense of shame.[68] But perhaps it is important to remember that Plato's *Republic* is, after all, a story told to democratic men who, like us, have no prospect of leaving Athens or of putting their lives under a wise ruler's control. Perhaps it is less a blueprint for social change than a myth in the service of self-knowledge, whose effect should be to refine our awareness of unfreedom, changing us from happy slaves to slaves with a "decent reaction against so much passivity." That, according to Phaedrus, would be the work of a lover.[69]

NOTES

1. *Tēn epi tois aischrois aischunēn, epi de tois kalois philotimian.* But Phaedrus three times refers to the combination as a single "something" (178c5; c6; d2). (On Aristotle's distinction between *aidōs* and *aischunē* see nn. 24 and 26 below.) I begin with Phaedrus in order to have a typical example of the traditional Greek view that Plato will be attacking.

2. When I speak of self-respect in connection with Greek texts, I am aware that Greek has no single term that precisely corresponds to the English word. This is understandable, since our notion of self-respect is both complex and a subject of disagreement. I shall go on to argue for an account of our ordinary notion which makes it very close to the complex expressed in Phaedrus's phrase. But as a starting place, a "nominal definition" of what we are talking about, I mean by a self-respecting person one who avoids shame. I leave it open, for now, whether shame and self-respect are best understood as feelings or as something else; and I do not yet try to describe their social and circumstantial necessary conditions. (This locates the common ground between Rawls's view and the Greek views I shall discuss.) And a society or a thinker will be said to display an interest in the good of self-respect if that society or thinker displays concern with the conditions that enable human beings to avoid shame. The negative pole, shame, is thus my starting point. No serious writer on Greek culture would argue that shame and its avoidance are not central in Greek moral and political thought. Indeed, the idea that Greek culture is a "shame culture" has often been pushed too far, especially when it is argued that this means the Greeks had no idea of internalized moral norms. It is clear that a reason for shame is, in many cases, some failure to achieve the *kalon;* this norm is logically prior to shame and gives it its rationale. On this point see M. Dickie, "*Dike* as a Moral Term in Homer and Hesiod," *Classical Philology* 73 (1978), 91-101.

Verbally, the negative pole, shame, is easier to pick out in Greek (*aischron* and related words); the *sense* of shame is usually expressed by *aischunē*. *Aidōs* sometimes means the sense of shame, sometimes a more complex dispositional trait that comes very close to (our account of) self-respect (see esp. Arist. *Magna Moralia* 1193a7, discussed in n. 26 below). On all these words see the fine study by C. E. Freiherr von Erffa, Αἰδώς *und verwandte Begriffe in ihrer Entwicklung von Homer bis Demokrit, Philologus* Supplementband 30, 2 (Leipzig, 1937). The positive side is often also picked out by periphrases, such as Phaedrus's, by locutions involving *timē* ("honor"—e.g., the expression "honoring one's own soul" in Plato's *Laws* 5), and, especially in the fifth century and later, by talk of freedom (*eleutheria*) and what it is to be a free man. Words connected with slavery (*doulos, douleia*) came to be used more generally to designate any shameful condition, as we shall see. On freedom, slavery, and self-respect, see also K. J. Dover, *Greek Popular Morality* (Oxford, 1974), pp. 114-116, 236-242, and G. Vlastos, "Slavery in Plato's Thought," in his *Platonic Studies* (Princeton, 1973), pp. 147-163.

3. The Greek uses a simple plural: "men, if they are going to live well"; but the emphasis is clearly distributive, and there is stress throughout the passage on the

engagement of the agent as a choosing individual (cf. the singular at 178d) and on his self-critical awareness of himself as responsible for his own choices.

4. Two separate issues might be involved here: autonomy and individualism (see n. 60 below and corresponding text). Although in a discussion of love we might expect stress to be on the individual differences, Phaedrus actually emphasizes instead the agent's own personal choice to display virtues that he believes everyone will want to possess.

5. This is the implicit other side of the Athenians' boast that they are taught to regard their bodies as at their city's disposal, their minds as most fully their own. Compare Thuc. 1.84.3 with 2.43.4; see also 1.70.6-7; 2.37.2-3; 2.41.1; 2.41.5. And see the valuable discussion in A. Lowell Edmunds, *Chance and Intelligence in Thucydides* (Cambridge, Mass., 1975). For the two types of distribution see also Pl. *Protagoras* 322a-d; and Ar. *Politics* 1261b20 ff.; 1332a36-37 (discussed below).

6. I have put all forms of *hen* in the neuter, neglecting gender, to indicate the verbal similarities.

7. This discussion in its present form owes much to a conversation with Bruce Vermazen at Berkeley in February 1977, which made me rethink an earlier account.

8. John Rawls, *A Theory of Justice* (Cambridge, Mass., 1971), esp. §§ 29, 67; all page references in parentheses are to this edition. See also the psychological analyses on which Rawls draws: R. W. White, *Ego and Reality in Psychoanalytic Theory* (New York, 1963), chap. 7; and G. Piers and M. B. Singer, *Shame and Guilt* (Springfield, Ill., 1953). For an interesting and related criticism of Rawls's theory of the good, see Mary Gibson, "Rationality," *Philosophy and Public Affairs* 6 (1977), 193-225.

9. It is sometimes claimed that ancient political theory is not concerned with the modern issue of distributing goods to persons. This seems wrong. For Plato's position see n. 32 below; Aristotle's concerns will speak for themselves.

10. By this I mean not only Plato and Aristotle but also the bulk of Greek literature, which ascribes great importance to the sense of shame, attacks the vice of shamelessness, and connects the avoidance of shame with excellence of character and action in accordance with shared norms. For some examples see von Erffa (n. 2 above), and A. A. Long, "Morals and Values in Homer," *Journal of Hellenic Studies* 90 (1970), 121-139; one important case is analyzed in my "Consequences and Character in Sophocles' *Philoctetes*," *Philosophy and Literature* 1 (1976-77), 26-53.

11. See, e.g., Ar. *MM* 1193a3 on *anaischuntos; Eudemian Ethics* 1221a1; 1233-b23-28; *Rhetoric* 1383b14-15. Literary examples are too numerous to cite.

12. Cf. Ar. *Rhet.* 1383b16: "It is necessary for a man to be ashamed of those evils that seem shameful either to him or to those whose opinion matters to him. Things of this kind are all the actions connected with the vices, like throwing away your shield and fleeing" (N.B.: the same example used by Phaedrus at 177a). Aristotle observes that it is also a defect to feel shame all over the place, even where it is not appropriate: *MM* 1193a4-7 remarks that such a man will never do anything. Cf. also *EE* 1221a1; 1233b28-29.

13. For the distinction between shame and guilt cf. Rawls, p. 67, and Piers & Singer, passim.

14. See further below in this section and in my concluding section.

15. F. Nietzsche, *Thus Spoke Zarathustra*, I, Prologue, in *The Portable Nietzsche*, ed. and trans. W. Kaufmann (New York, 1954).

16. See esp. pp. 178, 454, 544-545. Plato's "noble lie" and the advocacy of religion (when not believed) are explicitly ruled out (454, n. 1) on the ground that "conceptions of justice must be justified by the conditions of our life as we know it." The connection between this claim and the argument for publicity as expressive of mutual respect is not fully clear to me.

17. See, for example, pp. 62-65, 260-265, 396-397, 440 ff.

18. See pp. 62, 396, 440 ff.

19. See pp. 178 ff., 260-265, 544-546.

20. See esp. p. 260: "To be sure, the theory of these [sc. the primary] goods depends on psychological premises and these may prove incorrect."

21. See p. 263: the Archimedean point is found "by assuming certain general desires, such as the desire for primary social goods." The Nietzsche reference is from the essay "On Truth and Lie in the Extra-Moral Sense," in *The Portable Nietzsche*.

22. For a different criticism of the theory of primary goods see T. Nagel, "Rawls on Justice," *Philosophical Review* 82 (1973), 220-234.

23. Pp. 325 ff.

24. An account very close to this is Aristotle on aidōs in the *MM*. (Elsewhere, Aristotle concentrates on aischunē, the sense of shame.) Also highly pertinent is the account of *megalopsuchia* in *EN* 4.3; the *megalopsuchos* must have great deserts *and* a correct subjective estimate of them. See W. F. R. Hardie, " 'Magnanimity' in Aristotle's Ethics," *Phronesis* 23 (1978), 63-79.

25. Note that the theory of value could, for our purposes, be as "thin" as Rawls's view, which insists only on distinguishing the chosen from the non-chosen. On shame and its bodily reflexes see further Ar. *Rhet.* 2.6, esp. 1384a33 ff.; Rawls, §§ 29, 67; Stanley Cavell, "The Avoidance of Love: A Reading of King Lear," in his *Must We Mean What We Say?* (New York, 1969), pp. 278, 286 ff.

26. Cf. *MM* 1193a7-11; the man of aidōs "will not, like the shameless man, say and do anything and in any way; nor, like the reticent man, will he hold back in everything and in every way; but he will do and say what is appropriate, at the appropriate time, in appropriate circumstances."

27. Cf. *Rhet.* 2.6 on the intimate connection between the sense of shame and the virtues. (I am, however, constrained in this sketch by a desire not to prejudice the question in favor of an Aristotelian requirement of autonomous personal choice. It should not be assumed here that the good actions are part of a plan made by the agent for himself and have been chosen freely from among alternatives open to him.) In understanding some of these connections I have been helped by reading an unpublished paper by Marcia Homiak.

28. This point is stressed by Aristotle in the account of *eudaimonia*—e.g., *Nicomachean Ethics* 1095b31 ff.; 1178b18 ff.; 1098b33 ff.; 1176a33 ff.

29. Cf. Rawls, p. 440.

30. Here I come close to introducing autonomy into the definition of self-respect; but actually I presuppose here only that the agent has some awareness of the goodness of what he does, and feels proud as a result. This does not mean that the plan must be made, or even comprehended as such, by him. He might think it good and feel proud about it just because a good ruler told him to do it. This is the way Plato's citizens will, he claims, respond; so far, they fit my conditions for self-respect.

31. Kant's account of the duty to respect one's own humanity and the humanity of others (in the *Doctrine of Virtue*) seems to be of this form. The duty of self-respect is summarized in a series of imperatives to appropriate action: "Be no man's lackey.—Do not let others tread with impunity on your right.—Contract no debt for which you cannot give full security.... Complaining and whining—even a mere cry in bodily pain—is unworthy of you...." And so on. And this self-respecting action, Kant claims, will be accompanied by "the feeling of our inner worth," a feeling which, though it is closely associated with self-respect, is not identical with it (secs. 11-12, trans. M. J. Gregor [Philadelphia, 1964]).

32. Two general points need to be made at the opening of this section. First: in speaking of self-respect here, I shall, for my verbal basis in the text, be starting from references to shame and its avoidance; I shall also rely on the connections between slavery and shame, freedom and self-respect, discussed in n. 2 above. Second, I shall be assuming from now on that Plato's initial aim in constructing the ideal city is to distribute the primary good of rational control to all citizens and not simply to create a harmonious organic whole or to promote the development of the highest individuals. There are strong textual reasons for this:

(1) The *Republic* begins with a question about Cephalus's rational control and with a contrast between him and other men. Glaucon's original question is about justice in an individual human life, and the city is introduced as a part of the answer to this question, to help us see certain things about the individual soul. In Book 9 it is claimed that the original question has been answered.

(2) In Book 2 Socrates tells us that the only reason for founding cities is that "each of us (*hekastos hēmōn*) is not self-sufficient but needs many things" (369b). Satisfying the needs of *each* individual is thus the city's point; and the first city, though it does not have very much organic unity or even much government—and though it breeds no outstanding philosophical types—is said to be "the true city" (372a) because it so successfully accomplishes the task of satisfying the needs of each.

(3) The discussion of the individual soul and its parts is intertwined, in Book 4, with the city-soul analogy; but the argument establishing that each of us needs rational control is formally independent of the political analogy.

(4) In speaking of the happiness of the rulers Plato tells us that the aim of law is not "to make some one group in the city outstandingly happy but to contrive to spread happiness through the city, bringing the citizens into harmony with each other by persuasion and compulsion" (519e-520a). Civic harmony is neither an end in itself nor a means to the happiness of the highest but a means to, or a component of, the happiness of all.

(5) In the parallel material in *Laws* 5, communistic institutions are introduced in answer to an individual question about self-respect; how can I best honor my own soul?

(6) In *Rep.* 5, the rule of the philosophers is introduced as a necessary condition for the happiness, "private" and "public," of the human race as a whole (473d).

(7) The discussions of degenerate regimes in *Rep.* 8-9 always focus on the effects of the different social arrangements on the souls of individual inhabitants, criticizing those that fail to secure to each the good of rational order. The nonideal regimes are attacked not as organisms but as breeders of men.

33. The concern of the early dialogues with the unity of the virtues and with finding a measure of value seems aimed, in part at least, at preventing conflicts between important values; the *Republic* admits a plurality of values and relies on political engineering instead for the elimination of conflict.

34. These two different sorts of rational rule are discussed by R. Kraut, "Reason and Justice in Plato's *Republic*," in *Exegesis and Argument*, ed. E. N. Lee, A. P. D. Mourelatos, and R. Rorty (Assen, 1973), pp. 207-234, and, in a different way, by Gary Watson, "Free Agency," *Journal of Philosophy* 72 (1975), 205-220.

35. There is a good discussion of Plato's conception of appetite in J. C. B. Gosling, *Plato* (London, 1973), esp. pp. 17-25.

36. Trans. Shorey, revised (primarily by removing the uses of "unreal" for forms of "to be"). Note that "grazing" (*chortazomenoi*) and "mounting" (*ocheuontes*) are words used elsewhere in Greek just about exclusively of nonhuman animals. (Grube's "fornicate" is exactly wrong.) Plato's description of the appetitive men seems to presuppose that appetite is not a genuine part of our *human* nature.

37. Cf. I. Berlin, "Two Concepts of Liberty," in *Political Philosophy*, ed. A. Quinton (Oxford, 1967), pp. 141-152.

38. See the convincing discussion in G. F. Hourani, "The Education of the Third Class in Plato's *Republic*," *Classical Quarterly* 43 (1949), 58-60. Guardians only are mentioned at 376c5; 378c2; 383a3-5; 387c4-6; 395b8-c3; 398a8-b4; 398e6; 399a1-6; 401c1; 402c2; 403e4-9; 404a9-b8; 410b5-8. References to "the young" which do not specify guardians are interspersed among these passages and should be understood accordingly. Hourani cites other positive arguments for a different upbringing, without *paideia*, for nonguardian children. It should by now be clear that I side with those critics who have denied that the subjectclass has the full virtue that requires rational control, against those who claim, often in the face of the evidence, that the rational development of the subject's *own* reason is sufficient to render them good "from within." And yet these men are said by Plato to be happy, to live well; this must also be stressed. They live well because they live as knowledge orders, doing the actions that the knowers select for them. For a sensible review of other textual evidence on this point see T. H. Irwin, *Plato's Moral Theory* (Oxford, 1977), pp. 329-331; also R. G. Hoerber, *Phronesis* 5 (1960), 32-34, and R. G. Mulgan, *Phronesis* 13 (1968), 84-87, against R. W. Hall, *Phronesis* 4 (1954), 149-158, and J. B. Skemp, *Phronesis* 5 (1960), 35-38, and ibid. 19 (1969), 107-110.

39. On the relation between the unity of the individual and that of the city cf. *Rep.* 423cd; 432a; 433d; 435e; 443c-e; 577c-e; et al.

40. Cf. esp. *Rep.* 422e-423c; 421b; 462ab; also 428c11-d1; 519e-520a; 545cd; 547a; 551d-e; 554d; 557c-d; 558c; 559de; 561c; *Laws* 739b-e; 741ab; 743b-d; 744d; et al. For drawing my attention to several of the passages mentioned in this and the preceding note I am indebted to N. P. White.

41. Cf. Plato *Politicus* 263a; 296b-297b.

42. Compare Rawls's discussion of paternalism, pp. 249-250.

43. Though such a view may seem strange, it is central to several religious views of the person, including the Christian view. Compare, for example, John 15:1: "Abide in me, and I in you. As the branch cannot bear fruit of itself, except it abide in the vine, no more can ye, except ye abide in me.... He that abideth in me, and I in him, the same bringeth forth much fruit: for without me ye can do nothing. If a man abide not in me, he is cast forth as a branch, and is withered."

44. On this question see esp. R. Hackforth, *Plato's Phaedrus* (Cambridge, 1952), pp. 64-68, 71-77. The translation of *Phdr.* 245c5 is disputed (see Hackforth for a critical summary); but the collective sense is plain at 246b6, and Hackforth correctly points out that nothing in the earlier discussion implies the immortality of individual souls. At 246bc Plato moves from speaking of the collectivity of soul to a distributive picture (c2), suggesting that an individual soul is a piece of "all soul" which gets separated off and then joined to a body. *Epinomis* 980d-982a describes in detail the individuation and differentiation of souls by the association of soul with different types of matter. Though the authenticity of this work is sometimes disputed, the passage is a consistent extrapolation of *Laws* 10. 895e ff. A valuable discussion of the alternation between mass- and unit-talk in middle-period texts is in David Gallop's *Plato's Phaedo*, Clarendon Plato Series (Oxford, 1975), pp. 85-90.

45. On some pre-Socratic views see my "*Psuchē* in Heraclitus, I and II," *Phronesis* 17 (1972), 1-17, 153-170. Even in the Atomist view, in which individual soul-*atoms* are indivisible units, the whole soul of a living creature is just some collection of bodies of this kind; and not much is said about arrangement.

46. Earlier I implied that if the rulers had a way to liberate the reason of the ruled by performing an "appetitectomy," this might be an acceptable move; hylomorphism, of course, denies this, making us see how thoroughly personality, and even rationality are embodied and asking us not to draw the distinction between rational and bodily natures, reason and desire, in an arbitrary way.

47. This is probably not possible, however, For further reflections on the connection between a biological theory of personal identity and a social theory see D. Wiggins, "Locke, Butler and the Stream of Consciousness: And Men as a Natural Kind," *Philosophy* 51 (1976), 131-158 (chap. 6 of *The Identities of Persons*, ed. A. O. Rorty [Berkeley, Los Angeles, London, 1976], pp. 139-173).

48. On the authenticity of this treatise see John M. Cooper, "The *Magna Moralia* and Aristotle's Moral Philosophy," *American Journal of Philology* 94 (1973), 327-349.

49. *Pol.* 1255b20; 1261a39; 1277b7 ff.; 1279a20; 1288a12; *EN* 1134b15.

50. *Pol.* 1274a22 ff.; 1275b18; 1276b38 ff.; 1277b7 ff.; 1317b2-3; 1332b32 ff.

51. For similar observations about the connection between self-respect and separation from the parent see Piers (n. 8 above), pp. 30-31.

52. At 1332a32-33 Aristotle insists: "A city is good (*spoudaia*) in virtue of the goodness of the citizens who partake in the regime; and all our citizens partake in the regime." He remarks that if *each* is good, then *all* will be good; but the implication does not go the other way.

53. See the denial of eudaimonia to animals at *EE* 1217a24 and *NE* 1178b23-28 (where, however, the emphasis is on theoretical reasoning). "The good for man is activity of soul in accordance with complete excellence" (*NE* 1098a16), and this excellence has been said to be the practical excellence of the rational part (1098-a3). Book 6 argues at length that full excellence is impossible without practical wisdom.

54. Cf. *MM* 1242a28; *NE* 1161a34; *EE* 1242a28. *Pol.* 1255a12 ff. allows a friendship of utility between slave and master (cf. *EE* 1242a32-33 on husband and wife). *NE* 1161b3 ff. goes on to say that while there is no friendship with a slave qua slave, there can be justice and friendship with him qua man, in virtue of his capacity for "partaking in law and treaty." This is probably a reference to the conventional slave, for he is assumed to have capacities that Aristotle denies to the natural slave. *Pol.* 1255b15-16, however, observes that conventional slaves, who are under a constraint unsuited to their natures, will not easily feel friendly towards the master.

55. For drawing my attention to this passage I am indebted to Janet Hook, whose "Friendship and Politics in Aristotle's Ethical and Political Thought" (B.A. thesis *summa cum laude* in Philosophy and Government, Harvard University, 1977) is illuminating on many of these questions. Aristotle is probably thinking of selection by lot; the situation envisaged is one in which a man is in the pool but waives the office when his name turns up. On lot and voting in Aristotle's political thought see K. von Fritz and E. Kapp, chap. 3 of the Introduction to *Aristotle's Constitution of the Athenians and Related Texts* (New York, 1950), reprinted in *Articles on Aristotle*, ed. J. Barnes, M. Schofield, and R. Sorabji, vol. 2 (London, 1977; New York, 1978), pp. 123-134.

56. Aristotle has a number of related arguments about the importance of the family and of property in the scheme of political justice. The property argument plays a role in his complaint about the metoikos; in this respect he would find the situation of aliens living in our country more promising.

57. His view of women shows, however, that he did in particular cases consider what seems to us to be very weak scientific evidence, based on false biological theory, to be sufficient to establish the natural inability of a group to achieve adult virtue. See W. W. Fortenbaugh, "Aristotle on Slaves and Women," in Barnes (n. 55 above), pp. 135-139.

58. See *Pol.* 3.13; 3.17-18; 7.14.

59. These points are further developed in Essay 4 of my *Aristotle's De motu animalium* (Princeton, 1978).

60. Autonomy, as we see here, does not imply individualism. But neither does individualism imply autonomy—for an authoritarian view might, nonetheless, prescribe the good differently for different individuals and even aim at diversity as a good.

61. The agreement, however, probably occurs at a high level of generality: a life organized by practical reason, including the exercise of such and such excellences of character and intellect. As for specifics like the choice of professions and daily activities, Aristotle both allows and encourages diversity: cf. esp. *Pol.* 1261a22 ff.; *MM* 1194b5 ff. (cited above); *NE* 1172a1 ff. The centrality of *theoria* in *NE* 10 raises problems for this point, as for so many others.

62. Compare B. A. O. Williams, "The Idea of Equality," in *Problems of the Self* (Cambridge, 1975), pp. 230-249, at 233.

63. See the description of such a judge in Rawls, "Outline of a Decision Procedure for Ethics," *Philosophical Review* 60 (1951), 177-197. If we return to our discussion of Rawls and ask whether Rawls could accept such a suggestion, we will first need to decide whether such a judge would need to have a concept of the good. Aristotle would surely argue that he must; the refined practical intuition (*nous*) that is his hallmark must be the outgrowth of long education within *some* such conception. Of course he cannot say that there is any particular conception that the *phronimos* must have, or the argument would indeed be circular.

64. I am defending and explicating further the role of literature in moral inquiry in a manuscript in progress. For some preliminary remarks on this subject see my "Consequences and Character" (n. 10 above), and a discussion of Hazel Barnes's *The Meddling Gods*, in *Philosophy and Literature* 1 (1976-77), 342-353; also Jesse Kalin, "John Barth and Moral Nihilism: Why Philosophy Needs Literature," ibid., pp. 170-182.

65. Notice especially the point at which the language of financial value, commonly used in the Ververs' assessments of persons throughout the novel, is abandoned: "even before he had spoken she had begun to be paid in full. With that consciousness, in fact, an extraordinary thing occurred; the assurance of her safety so making her terror drop that already, within the minute, it had been changed to concern for his own anxiety, for everything that was deep in his being and everything that was fair in his face. So far as seeing that she was 'paid' went, he might have been holding out the money-bag for her to come and take it. But what instantly rose, for her, between the act and her acceptance was the sense that she must strike him as waiting for a confession. This, in turn, charged her with a new horror: if *that* was her proper payment she would go without money" (Penguin edition, 1973, p. 547).

66. Some of these are well discussed by Gosling (n. 35 above).

67. H. James, *The Wings of the Dove*, Signet Classics edition (New York, 1964), p. 340.

68. For an illuminating discussion of the passages pertinent to this question I am indebted to Nancy Sherman.

69. A preparatory study for this paper was read to the Society for Ancient Greek Philosophy at the December meeting of the American Philosophical Association, 1976, and at the University of California, Berkeley, in February 1977. I am grateful to both of these audiences for their suggestions and criticisms. I would also particularly like to thank Julia Annas, Joshua Cohen, Janet Hook, Julius Moravcsik, Thomas Nagel, Amélie O. Rorty, Bruce Vermazen, and Gregory Vlastos for their helpful criticisms of earlier drafts.

Contributors

Thomas Nagel is Professor of Philosophy at New York University.

J. L. Ackrill is Fellow of Brasenose College, Oxford, and Professor of Philosophy at Oxford University.

T. H. Irwin is Associate Professor of Philosophy at Cornell University.

David J. Furley is Charles Ewing Professor of Greek Language and Literature at Princeton University.

M. F. Burnyeat is Lecturer in Classics at Cambridge University, and Fellow and Lecturer in Philosophy at Robinson College, Cambridge.

L. A. Kosman is Professor of Philosophy at Haverford College.

J. O. Urmson is Henry Waldgrave Stuart Professor of Philosophy at Stanford University.

David Pears is a student of Christ Church, Oxford.

Bernard Williams is Provost of King's College, Cambridge.

David Wiggins is Professor of Philosophy at Bedford College, London University

Richard Sorabji is Reader in Ancient Philosophy at King's College, London University.

Amélie Oksenberg Rorty is Professor of Philosophy at Livingston College, Rutgers University.

Julia Annas is Fellow and Tutor in Philosophy at St. Hugh's College, Oxford, and Lecturer in Philosophy at Christ Church, Oxford.

John M. Cooper is Professor of Philosophy at the University of Pittsburgh and Visiting Professor of Philosophy at Princeton University.

Kathleen V. Wilkes is Fellow and Tutor in Philosophy at St. Hilda's College, Oxford.

John McDowell is Fellow of University College, Oxford.

Martha Craven Nussbaum is Associate Professor of Philosophy and the Classics at Harvard University.